CONSTANTINE'S SWORD

JAMES CARROLL

CONSTANTINE'S SWORD

The Church and the Jews

A History

HOUGHTON MIFFLIN COMPANY

BOSTON · NEW YORK

2001

For information about permission to reproduce selections from
this book, write to Permissions, Houghton Mifflin Company,
215 Park Avenue South, New York, New York 10003.

Visit our Web site: www.houghtonmifflinbooks.com.

Library of Congress Cataloging-in-Publication Data
Carroll, James, date.
Constantine's sword : the church and the Jews : a
history / James Carroll.
p.   cm.
Includes bibliographical references and index.
ISBN 0-395-77927-8
1. Christianity and antisemitism — History. 2. Catholic
Church — Relations — Judaism. 3. Judaism — Relations —
Catholic Church. I. Title.
BM535.C37 2001
261.0'6'09—dc21   00-061329

Printed in the United States of America

Book design by Robert Overholtzer

QUM 10 9 8 7 6 5 4 3 2 1

Portions of this book appeared, in different form, in *The New Yorker* and *The Atlantic Monthly*.

Grateful acknowledgment is made to the following authors and publishers for kind permission to reproduce material in this book: *The Confessions* by Saint Augustine. Translated by R. S. Pine-Coffin. Copyright © 1961 by R. S. Pine-Coffin. Reprinted by permission of Penguin Books Ltd. *The City of God* by Saint Augustine. Translated by Henry Bettenson. Copyright © 1972 by Henry Bettenson. Reprinted by permission of Penguin Books Ltd. *Heavenly Powers* by Neil Asher Silberman. Copyright © 1998 by Neil Asher Silberman. Reprinted by permission of Grosset and Dunlap (Putnam). *Inquisition and Society in Spain* by Henry Kamen. Reprinted by permission of Weidenfeld & Nicolson. *Marpingen* by David Blackbourn. Reprinted by permission of the author. *Toward a New Council of Florence* by Nicolaus of Cusa. Translated by William F. Wertz, Jr. Reprinted by permission of the Schiller Institute, Inc. *Helena Augusta* by Jan Willem Drijvers. Reprinted with the kind permission of © Koninklijke Brill N.V., Leiden, The Netherlands. *The Jews and the Crusades* by Shlomo Eidelberg. Reprinted by permission of the author and the University of Wisconsin Press. *Ideology and Experience* by Stephen Wilson. Reprinted by permission of the Littman Library of Jewish Civilization, Oxford, U.K. *A Social and Religious History of the Jews* by Salo Wittmayer Baron. Copyright © 1969 Columbia University Press. Reprinted by permission of the publisher. *European Jewry and the First Crusade* by Robert Chazen. Copyright © 1987 The Regents of the University of California. Reprinted by permission of the publisher. *Dreyfus: A Family Affair* by Michael Burns. Reprinted by permission of the author. *Héloïse and Abelard* by Étienne Gilson. Copyright 1950, © 1978 by the Pontifical Institute of Mediaeval Studies, Toronto. Reprinted by permission of the copyright owner. *Vatican Diplomacy and the Jews During the Holocaust, 1939–1943* by John F. Morley. Reprinted by permission of Ktav Publishing House, Inc.

FOR BILL AND MARGARET
AND FOR DON

For it is the bitter grief of theology and its blessed task, too, always to have to seek (because it does not clearly have present to it at the time) what in a true sense — in its historical memory — it has always known . . . always providing that one has the courage to ask questions, to be dissatisfied, to think with the mind and heart one actually has, and not with the mind and heart one is supposed to have.

— Karl Rahner, S.J.

CONTENTS

PART SIX

Emancipation, Revolution, and a New Fear of Jews

PART SEVEN

The Church and Hitler

PART ONE

THE CROSS AT AUSCHWITZ

Sign of Folly

THE CROSS IS MADE of stout beams, an intersection of railroad ties. It stands in a field of weeds that slopes down from the road. The field is abutted on one side by the old theater, where gas canisters were stored, also looted gold; where, much later, Carmelite nuns accomplished cloistered works of expiation, sparking fury; and where, now, a municipal archive is housed. On another side, the field runs up against the brick wall, the eastern limit of the main camp.

At more than twenty feet, the cross nearly matches the height of the wall, although not the wall's rusted thistle of barbed wire. Immediately beyond are the camp barracks, the peaked roofs visible against the gray morning sky. The nearest building, close enough to hit with a stone thrown from the foot of the cross, is Barracks 13, also known as the death bunker or the starvation bunker. In one of its cells the Franciscan priest Maximilian Kolbe was martyred. He is now a saint of the Roman Catholic Church. Kolbe is the reason for this cross.

In 1979, Karol Wojtyla came home to nearby Kraków as Pope John Paul II. He celebrated Mass in an open field for a million of his countrymen, and on the makeshift altar this same cross had been mounted — hence its size, large enough to prompt obeisance from the farthest member of the throng. Visiting the death camp, the pope prayed for and to Father Kolbe, who had voluntarily taken the place of a fellow inmate in the death bunker. The pope prayed for and to Edith Stein, the convert who had also died in the camp, and whom he would declare a Catholic saint in 1998. She was a Carmelite nun known as Sister Teresa Benedicta of the Cross, but the Nazis murdered her for being a Jew. In his sermon that day, the pope called Auschwitz the "Golgotha of the modern world."[1] As he had at other times, John Paul II expressed the wish that a place of prayer and penance could be built at the site of the death camp to honor the Catholic martyrs and to atone for the murders: at Auschwitz and its subcamp, Birkenau, the Nazis killed perhaps as many as a quarter of a million non-Jewish Poles and something like a million and a half Jews. Fulfilling the pontiff's hope, a group of Carmelite nuns moved into the old theater in the autumn of 1984. They intended especially to offer prayers in memory of their sister Teresa Benedicta. The mother superior of this group was herself named Teresa.[2]

The Carmelite presence at the gate of Auschwitz was immediately protested by leaders of Jewish groups throughout Europe and in the United States and Israel. "Stop praying for the Jews who were killed in the *Shoah*," one group pleaded. "Let them rest in peace as Jews."[3] Jewish protesters invaded the grounds of the convent, carrying banners that said, "Leave Our Dead Alone!" and "Do Not Christianize Auschwitz and *Shoah!*"[4] The protesters registered complaints about Father Kolbe, who before his arrest had been the publisher of a journal that had printed antisemitic articles, and about Edith Stein, whose conversion could only look to Jews like apostasy.

Polish Catholics from the nearby towns of Oświęcim and Birkenau rallied to the nuns' defense. Fights broke out. "One More Horror at Auschwitz," read a headline in a British paper. "They crucified our God," a boy screamed during one demonstration. "They killed Jesus."[5] At one point the nuns' supporters arrived carrying the stout wooden cross from the papal altar in Kraków. They planted the cross in the field next to the old theater. However piously intended, it could seem a stark act of Christian sovereignty, a sacrilege. Eventually John Paul II intervened in the dispute, offering to fund a new convent building for the Carmelites a few hundred yards away. He prevailed on the nuns to move. The sisters did so in 1994. In the compromise that was worked out, Jewish leaders in turn accepted that the cross would remain in the field near the wall, but only temporarily.

In early 1998, the Polish government, perhaps responding to pressure from American senators friendly to Jews — pressure exerted just prior to the U.S. Senate's vote on Poland's admission to NATO — announced that the cross, like the convent before it, would be removed. "The cross overlooks the camp, which is unacceptable for Orthodox Jews," a Polish official said, "because it imposes Christian symbols." But a month later, before the removal had occurred, Poland's Roman Catholic primate, Cardinal Jozef Glemp, insisted that the cross should remain where it was. Jewish leaders again protested, prompting an expression of concern from the Vatican. At Auschwitz itself, Polish Catholics began to plant new crosses, appropriate to a cemetery, making the point that Catholics, too, died at the camp. The dispute raged throughout 1998, with escalations even to the point of homemade explosive devices being planted in the field by radical Catholics. More than one hundred small crosses were put in the ground. Finally, in 1999, in an odd "compromise," the Polish parliament passed a law requiring the removal of the smaller crosses but making the papal cross permanent. The small crosses were taken away by Polish officials, but the large cross remains at Auschwitz to this day.

What does the cross of Jesus Christ mean at such a place? What does it mean to Jews? What does it mean to Christians? Or to Polish Catholics? Or to those for whom religious symbols are empty? What does the cross there signal about our understanding of the past? And what of the future? If Auschwitz has become a sacred center of Jewish identity, what does the cross there imply about the relations between Jews and Christians, and between Judaism and Christianity? These questions were in my mind one November morning as I stood alone before that cross.

I thought of the pope's designation of this place as Golgotha, and I recognized the ancient Christian impulse to associate extreme evil with the fate of Jesus, precisely as a way of refusing to be defeated by that evil. At the Golgotha of the crucifixion, death became the necessary mode of transcendence, first for Jesus and then, as Christians believe, for all. But I also thought of that banner, "Do Not Christianize Auschwitz and *Shoah!*" Can mechanized mass murder be a mode of transcendence? I could imagine the narrowed eyes of a Jewish protester as he detected in prayers offered before the cross at Auschwitz echoes of the old refrain "Jews out!" — only now was it Jewish anguish that was expected to yield before Christian hope? If Auschwitz must stand for Jews as the abyss in which meaning itself died, what happens when Auschwitz becomes the sanctuary of someone else's recovered piety?

Christians are not the only ones who have shown themselves ready to use the memory of the six million to advance an ideology: Orthodox Jews can see a punishment for secularism; Zionists can see an organizing rationale for the state of Israel; opponents of "land for peace" can see a justification for a permanent garrison mentality.[6] The "memorialists," who have raised the new temples of Holocaust museums and memorials in the cities of the West, have anointed memory itself as the deepest source of meaning. The legend engraved at Yad Vashem in Jerusalem, the first Holocaust memorial, reads, "Forgetfulness is the way to exile. Remembrance is the way to redemption."

The God who led a people out of Egypt is, of course, a redeeming God, but at Auschwitz the question must have become, Are God's saving acts only in the past? Some formerly religious Jews saw in the Holocaust only the absence of God, and moved on without faith. Other Jews went from atheism to the faith of Job, an affirmation devoid of piety. There are the Jewish voices, from Elie Wiesel to Richard Rubenstein to Emil Fackenheim, who reject the idea that suffering such as Jews underwent in the death camps — a million children murdered — can be meaningful. To value those deaths in such a way is to diminish their horror. And there are the voices of Emmanuel Levinas,[7] who speaks of the Holocaust as a "tumor in the memory,"[8] and Theodor Adorno, who, in a famous essay, argued that the entire enterprise of education must change after the Holocaust.[9] "Auschwitz negates all systems, opposes all doctrines," Wiesel argues. "They cannot but diminish the experience which lies beyond our reach."[10] These and other figures insist that the Holocaust shatters all previous categories of meaning, certainly including Christian categories. But isn't the state of being shattered, once reflected upon and articulated, itself a category? Does the very act of thinking about the Holocaust, in other words, diminish its horror by refusing to treat it as unthinkable? The more directly one faces the mystery of the Holocaust, the more elusive it becomes.

Perhaps the voice a troubled Christian most needs to hear is that of the Jew who says the Holocaust must be made to teach nothing. "What consequences, then, are to be drawn from the Holocaust?" asks the theologian Jacob Neusner. "I argue that none are to be drawn, none for Jewish theology and none for the life of Jews with one another, which were not there before 1933. Jewish theologians do no good service to believers when they claim that 'Auschwitz' denotes a turning point."[11] That voice is useful because if Jewish responses to the Holocaust, which range from piety to nihilism, are complex and multifaceted, Christian interpretations of the near elimination of Jews from Europe, however respectfully put forth, must inevitably be even more problematic. The cross signifies the problem: When suffering is seen to serve a universal plan of salvation, its particular character as tragic and evil is always diminished.[12] The meaningless can be made to shimmer with an eschatological hope, and at Auschwitz this can seem like blasphemy.

But what about an effort less ambitious than the search for meaning or the imposition of theology? What if the cross at Auschwitz is an object before which Christians only want to kneel and pray? And, fully aware of what happened there, what if we Christians want to pray for Jews? Why does that offend? How can prayers for the dead be a bad thing? But what if such prayers, offered with good intentions, effectively evangelize the dead? What if they imply that the Jews who died at Auschwitz are to be ushered into the presence of God by the Jesus whom they rejected? Are Jews then expected to see at last the truth to which, all their lives, they had been blind? Seeing that truth in the beatific vision, are they then to bow down before Jesus as Messiah in an act of postmortem conversion? Shall the afterlife thus be *judenrein* too? Elie Wiesel tells "a joke which is not funny." It concerns an SS officer whose torment of a Jew consisted in his pretending to shoot the Jew dead, firing a blank, while simultaneously knocking him unconscious. When the Jew regained consciousness, the Nazi told him, "You are dead, but you don't know it. You think that you escaped us? We are your masters, even in the other world." Wiesel comments, "What the Germans wanted to do to the Jewish people was to substitute themselves for the Jewish God."[13] Here is the question a Christian must ask: Does our assumption about the redemptive meaning of suffering, tied to the triumph of Jesus Christ and applied to the Shoah, inevitably turn every effort to atone for the crimes of the Holocaust into a claim to be the masters of Jews in the other world?

Once, for Christians to speak among ourselves about the murder of the six million as a kind of crucifixion would have seemed an epiphany of compassion, paying the Jews the highest tribute, as if the remnant of Israel had at last become, in this way, the Body of Christ. Yet such spiritualizing can appear to do what should have been impossible, which is to make the evil worse: the elimination of Jewishness from the place where Jews were eliminated. The Body of Christ? If Jesus had been bodily at Auschwitz, as protesting Jews insisted, he would have died an anonymous victim with a number on his arm, that's all. And he'd have done so not as the Son of God, not as the redeemer of humankind, not as the Jewish Messiah, but simply as a Jew. And in a twist of history folding back on itself, his crime would have been tied to the cross — "He killed our God!" That indictment, first brought as an explicit charge of deicide as early as the second century by a bishop, Melito of Sardis,[14] was officially quashed by the bishops of the Second Vatican Council in 1965,[15] yet it remains the ground of all Jew hatred. That, at bottom, is why it is inconceivable that any Jew should look with equanimity on a cross at Auschwitz, and why no Christian should be able to behold it there as anything but a blow to conscience. "Though there were other social and economic conditions which were necessary before the theological antecedents of antisemitism could be turned into the death camps of our times," the Jewish theologian Richard Rubenstein has written, "only the terrible accusation, known and taught to every Christian in earliest childhood, that the Jews are the killers of the Christ can account for the depth and persistence of this supreme hatred."[16]

I am certain that the first time I would have heard the word "Jew" was from the pulpit of St. Mary's Church in Alexandria, Virginia, where I lived as a child. My father was an Air Force general working at the Pentagon, but we made our family life in the Old South river port down the Potomac, where the Catholic parish was the oldest in Virginia. It would have surely been one Holy Week when I was six or seven that I heard the mythic words proclaimed: "The Jews cried out with one voice, 'Crucify him!'" But the first remembered time I heard the word "Jew" was from a boy who lived next door. Let's call him Peter Seligman. The hint of something in his last name had registered with me not at all.

Peter and I were probably about ten years old. Though he went to the local public school — the Protestant school, to me — Peter was then my best friend. I loved running with him through the woods just south of Alexandria, slapping our thighs as if we rode in the cavalry — a word I was already confusing with Calvary — dodging branches, leaping the narrow creek that was our constant point of reference. I remember one summer day coming upon an overgrown stone wall surrounded by tall trees and choked by briars, the vestige of a former pasture or farmer's field. The aura of a lost past drew us, and when Peter announced solemnly, "I bet this was built by slaves," I stepped back. A door in my brain snapped open, and whenever I think of slavery, I think of that wall.

Perhaps it was the same wall that inspired a game we used to play, the two of us betraying our northern origins — I was born in Chicago; the Seligmans seemed, perhaps in stereotype, to be New Yorkers — by pretending to be Mosby's Rangers. We called ourselves Jeb Stuart and Stonewall Jackson. I see now the shared loneliness in our romping fantasy, because the other boys with whom we might have played were native Virginians, defensive heirs of a rural culture that was being turned into suburb before their eyes, not only by outsiders, but by the ancient enemy — us. The other boys had shunned me and Peter as Yankees, which perhaps accounts for our rather desperate play at being not just Johnny Rebs but true Confederate heroes.

Sometimes our hard rides through the woods took us to Gum Springs, a shantytown with dusty, unpaved streets where Negroes lived, the hired laborers and croppers whom we often saw doing menial chores for the white contractors of the new subdivisions. In Gum Springs we saw black people with each other. Once — it must have been a Sunday — Peter and I crept up a deserted street to a small white-steepled church. We listened to the congregation singing hymns, glimpsing the men's dark suits and ties, the ladies' hats, the uplifted brown faces. When a deacon looked our way, we turned and ran.

After that, reciting the Lord's Prayer with its confession of the sin of "trespass," I thought of Gum Springs. Even now, the image of its shacks and dirt streets stabs me with guilt. Gum Springs, teaching me that I am white, laid bare another meaning of Mosby's raids. I associate this first felt recognition of anti-black racism with Peter, my fellow would-be Reb, my fellow crypto-Yankee, my fellow white, my friend. Rarely would I share a sense of so many levels of complexity with another. But then Peter forced a next recognition, and it changed everything.

Within a year or two of our move to Alexandria, my father, an avid golfer, was elected to membership in the Belle Haven Country Club, an old Virginia enclave a mile or two up Fort Hunt Road from where we lived. As an Irish Catholic carpetbagger, Dad would have been decidedly unclubbable, but this was Red Scare time, and as head of Air Force counterintelligence, he was a spymaster with profile. I took the "privilege" entirely for granted, but at Belle Haven, too, I sensed the difference between me and the sons and daughters of the first families of Virginia. So one day I asked Peter why he and his parents never came to the swimming pool at Belle Haven.

"We don't go there," he said simply.

"Why not?"

"Because it's a club, and we're Jews."

I do not recall what, if anything, the word "Jews" meant to me, but "club" — Peter and I were a club of two — seemed only friendly. I pushed, saying that Belle Haven was fun, that we could go there on our bikes.

Peter explained calmly what he knew, and what I had yet to admit: "Jewish" was a synonym for unwelcome. "Unwelcome," he could have said, "in this case by you." I was a notorious blusher, and I blushed then, I am sure.

"No big deal," he said, but I saw for the first time that Peter and I were on opposite sides of a kind of color line. I took for granted that Negroes were unwelcome at Belle Haven, except as caddies. But Jews?

"No big deal" meant, We're not discussing this further. Which was fine with me.

Later, I asked my mother, and she explained that the Seligmans' being Jewish meant they did not believe what we believed. About Jesus, I knew at once. And those Holy Week readings from the pulpit at St. Mary's must have come back to me: This has to do with Jesus and what they did to him. That easily, I was brought into the sanctuary of the Church's core idea, even without removing my hat.

My mother added a phrase that served her as standard punctuation. "Live and let live," she said with a shrug. "The Seligmans are good people." Much later, I would understand the slogan and my mother's coda as her own private rejection of the then reigning Catholic ethos of "Outside the Church there is no salvation," but to me that day her reaction seemed dismissive. She had efficiently sidestepped the fear I had that my one friendship in that alien territory had somehow been put at risk. Indeed, my belated recognition of the Seligmans' Jewishness in the context of their exclusion — Jewish means unwelcome — accounted for why my and Peter's parents had extended to each other nothing beyond a minimal neighborliness. If the Seligmans were unwelcome at Belle Haven, they were just as unwelcome in our house. It would take many years before I began to understand the deadly effect that this introduction to Jewishness had on me. Even as I set myself against antisemitism,[17] this essentially negative framing would condemn me to think of Jews as candidates for rejection. Although I self-consciously refused to reject Jews, I was still defining them by my refusal. Whether I am capable of allowing Jews to define themselves in purely positive terms, with no reference to a dominant Christian culture, whether anti- or philosemitic, remains an open question. That, in turn, underscores "the depth and persistence," in Rubenstein's phrase, "of this supreme hatred." How could hatred have stood in any way between Peter and me? Yet now I see that it did.

Even when the cross of Jesus Christ is planted at Auschwitz as a sign of Christian atonement for that hatred, and not of anti-Jewish accusation, the problem remains. By associating the Jewish dead with a Christian notion of redemption, are the desperate and despised victims of the Nazis thus transformed into martyrs whose fate could seem not only meaningful but privileged? What Jew would not be suspicious of a Christian impulse to introduce that category, martyrdom, into the story of the genocide? Jews as figures of suffering — negation, denial, hatred, guilt — are at the center of this long history, although always, until now, their suffering was proof of God's rejection of them. Is Jewish suffering now to be taken as a sign of God's approval? Golgotha of the modern world[18] — does that mean real Jews have replaced Jesus as the sacrificial offering, their deaths as the source of universal salvation? Does this Jew-friendly soteriology turn full circle into a new rationale for a Final Solution?

Uneasiness with such associations has prompted some Jews to reject the very word "holocaust" as applied to the genocide, since in Greek it means "burnt offering." The notion that God would accept such an offering is deeply troubling.[19] When the genocide is instead referred to as the Shoah, a Hebrew word meaning "catastrophe," a wall is being erected against the consolations and insults of a redemptive, sacrificial theology of salvation. *Shoah*, in its biblical usage, points to the absence of God's creative hovering, the opposite of which is rendered as *"ruach." Ruach* is the breath of God, which in Genesis drew order out of chaos. *Shoah* is its undoing.[20]

Such subtleties of terminology were not on my mind when I went to Auschwitz as a writer working on a magazine article. I am a novelist and an essayist, and in presuming to relate a history that culminates at the cross at Auschwitz, I do so with an eye to details and connections that a historian might omit or that a scholar might dismiss. I am looking for turns in the story in which one impulse overrode another, one character reversed the action of another, all with unanticipated, ever-graver consequences. And if I am a professional writer, it is not irrelevant to my purpose that I am an amateur Catholic — a Catholic, that is, holding to faith out of *love*. Yet love for the Church can look like grief, even anger. Nevertheless, my intensity of feeling is itself what has brought me here. So my life as a storyteller and my faith as a Catholic qualify me to detect essential matters in this history that a more detached, academic examination, whatever its virtues, might miss.

Yet in coming to Auschwitz, I knew enough to be suspicious of emotional intensity, as if what mattered here were the reactions of a visitor. So I had summoned detachment of another kind. In coming to the death camp, I had resolved to guard against conditioned responses, even as I felt them: the numbness, the choked-back grief, the supreme sentimentality of a self-justifying Catholic guilt. I had visited the barracks, the ovens, the naked railway platform, the stark field of chimneys, more or less in control of my reactions. But before the cross something else took over. Even as I knew to guard against the impulse to "Christianize the Holocaust,"

I was doing it — by looking into this abyss through the lens of a faith that has the cross embedded in it like a sighting device. Perhaps I was Christianizing the Holocaust by instinctively turning it into an occasion of Christian repentance. The Shoah throws many things into relief — the human capacity for depravity, the cost of ethnic absolutism, the final inadequacy both of religious language and of silence. But it also highlights the imprisonment of even well-meaning Christians inside the categories with which we approach death and sin. Christian faith can seem to triumph over every evil except Christian triumphalism. When I found myself standing at the foot of that cross, on the transforming edge of a contemporary Golgotha, I knew just what the pope meant when he evoked that image. Yet I reacted as I imagine a Jew might have. The cross here was simply wrong.

Even so, perhaps I was just another Christian presuming to supply a Jewish reaction. But perhaps not. Because of the insistence of Jewish voices — protesters at the cross at Auschwitz and Jewish thinkers who have claimed a preemptive right to interpret the Holocaust in terms consistent with Jewish tradition — the old Christian habit of seeing "the jews"[21] as a scrim on which to project Christian meanings no longer goes unchallenged. I love the cross, the sign of my faith, yet finally the sight of it here made me, in the words of the spiritual, tremble, tremble, tremble. Because of a resounding Jewish response, I saw the holy object as if it were a chimney. But also, Christian that I am, I saw it through the eyes of the man I have always been. The primordial evil of Auschwitz has now been compounded by the camp's new character as a flashpoint between Catholics and Jews. So the ancient Christian symbol here, despite my knowledge that it was wrong, was a revelation. I was seeing the cross in its full and awful truth for the first time.

→ 2 ←

Stumbling Block to Jews

W
HEN I WAS A college freshman at Georgetown University, I attended a weekend retreat that was mandatory for undergraduates at that Jesuit school. I remember the stark corridors and monkish cells of some novitiate or minor seminary to which we crew-necked college Joes had been bused deep in the Virginia countryside. Our first day was spent in the chapel, listening to the stern warnings of a crucifix-wielding Jesuit out of James Joyce. The long axis of the missionary cross he held up, as if warding off the evil eye of our indifference, was the length of a slide rule. With just that mathematical infallibility, it worked. By the end of the day, damnation had never seemed so near. Ignatius Loyola was the poet laureate of the crucifixion, and in our rooms, Gideons Bible style, were copies of his *Spiritual Exercises*. They were verbal versions of the El Greco imitations on the chapel walls, with Jesus crying out from the cross — not to God, but to us. The call of Jesus — it was coming to me. No wonder I welcomed it when they banged on the door to say lights out.

That night I slept fitfully. At one point, I snapped awake in the middle of an ominous foretaste of eternity. My eyes opened to the glowing figure of Jesus on the cross, hovering in the air a few feet above the end of my cot. Conditioned, no doubt, by that day's apparition-laden tales of Saints Paul, Francis Xavier, and Ignatius Loyola, I froze. Suspended in that moment, I felt visited.

Visited by the broken Lord to whom, in fact, I had long before commended myself. But, so it seemed, I'd been in flight from him until now. Not just from him — from his suffering. As a child, kneeling beside my mother at the foot of the cross in St. Mary's Church in Alexandria, always in the very early morning — Monsignor's Mass — I had learned that the suffering of Jesus was for the purpose of mitigating my mother's own. My brother Joe had contracted polio when he was four and I was two. My first experience of the disease was of my mother's agony more than his. But then it became everyone's. The disease attacked Joe's legs, as did a succession of surgeons. I used to see his bandaged shins in my sleep, then wake up certain that I was the one who could not walk. Certain, then oddly relieved. My brother's wounded legs were what taught me about suffering. My own whole legs began to seem like contraband, as if I had stolen them from him. Sometimes at night — say, after yet another set of his casts had been removed — I would lean down from the top bunk to pull his blanket back and stare at his bones. When I saw my first pictures of liberated inmates of the concentration camps — this would have been in 1947 or 1948 — I thought they had legs like Joe's. And not surprisingly, I grew up recognizing those selfsame battered legs on every crucifix. Joe's suffering, my mother's, and therefore mine — and the suffering of those photo-ghosts behind barbed wire — were made bearable by knowing that God too, in Jesus, had suffered like this. The nails in Jesus' feet were his polio.

The cross in the night helped me decide to become a Catholic priest. I chose not the Jesuits but the Paulists, yet still a preaching order, convert-makers, holy men who wore the mission cross in their cinctures, where it looked less like a slide rule than a dagger. I spent most of the 1960s in the Paulist seminary at Catholic University in Washington, D.C., was ordained to the priesthood in 1969, and left the priesthood five years later. Despite publishing ten books in the twenty-five years since, and numerous articles and columns for the *Boston Globe* and various journals, my brief time as a priest marks me more indelibly than anything else.

Such was the power of that nighttime vision of the cross that when I leaped from the cot to turn on the light, to find hanging on the crowding wall a pale green plastic Day-Glo corpus, the aura did not quite dissipate. I went to sleep smiling at the joke, but also feeling sure that Jesus on the cross had truly come. It was a feeling — crazy, I know, but sure — that remained a sacred, if secret, aspect of my identity for a long time.

I left Georgetown in 1961, but I have always followed the basketball team, and I regularly note the university's bullpen function — Kissinger to Kirkpatrick to Albright — for the aces of foreign affairs. But lately Georgetown has found itself in the news, and it is because of the crucifix. "Georgetown to Go Way of the Cross," a 1998 *Boston Globe* headline read. "Amid Widespread Debate, a Decision to Be Catholic."[1] Decades after the abandonment of mandatory religious retreats for students, a heated argument broke out at my alma mater over the absence of the crucifix from the walls of newer classrooms. A vocal circle of young Georgetown Catholics, supported by elder traditionalists, accused the university of abandoning its core identity. At first the Jesuit president tried explaining the absence of the crucifix with an ecumenical rationale: Georgetown students and faculty have come to include many non-Catholics. Classrooms, even at Jesuit universities, are not sanctuaries. But the older classrooms have crucifixes, the critics insisted; crucifixes sanctify the daily work of study and learning. Crucifixes root the college in Catholicism, a point that was made by Washington's Roman Catholic archbishop when he joined the argument. "The crucifix," Cardinal James Hickey wrote, "is a basic, identifying Catholic symbol. It coerces no one. It offends only those who are intolerant of the Catholic faith."[2]

But by then many outside the university, thinking perhaps of all the Kissingers who'd stood at the front of those classrooms, had begun to take offense. The discovery in the same season of former Georgetown professor Madeleine Albright's secret Jewish background — she is an Episcopalian but was raised a Roman Catholic[3] — seemed an eerie counterpoint. What is coercion anyway? To an editorial writer of *Washington Jewish Week,* "Jesus on the cross is a repugnant symbol . . . represent[ing] two millennia of bloody crusades and pogroms that directly led to the Holocaust."[4]

The editorialist did not speak for all Jews. Leon Wieseltier, referring to a controversy over how Christian history is tied to the Holocaust, wrote in *The New Republic:* "No, 'Jesus on the cross' is not a repugnant symbol to me. But the sight of it does not warm my heart, either. It is the symbol of a great faith and a great culture whose affiliation with power almost destroyed my family and my people."[5]

Power, not the cross. Affiliation, not identity. Perhaps such distinctions can be maintained when the point of controversy is the wall of a classroom. But what about the wall of Auschwitz? The cross there continues to spark fire between Catholics and Jews. Its shadow is pointed, piercing through the hard-won civility of "Christian-Jewish dialogue" to the question of violence — the violence of the Polish Catholics who dared to bring explosives into that field, and then be rewarded for it; the violence of the genocide, which to Jews can never be explained, understood, or redeemed; and ultimately the violence of the cross itself, that sadistic Roman execution device. Lenny Bruce, the Jewish shockmeister, used to send a naughty thrill up the spines of his audiences by professing relief that Jesus wasn't born in twentieth-century America, because then, Bruce would blithely aver, pious Christians would have to wear tiny electric chairs around their necks. In fact, the cross did not serve as a Christian icon until it ceased being a Roman execution device in the fourth century.

Despite these associations, it is blasphemy of another kind than Bruce's to lay responsibility for the Holocaust at the foot of the cross. The genocide of Jews was the work of Nazism, not Christianity. The individual and particular character of the killers — as opposed, say, to a faceless bureaucracy or an impersonal antisemitism — must always be insisted upon. But it is also important to emphasize that the perpetrators of the genocide were not a group apart from the broad population of Germans. It is true, as we shall see, that German Christians remained attached to their religion during the Nazi years and that Nazi ideology borrowed heavily from Christian eschatology — the subordination of the present to the expectation of a glorious End Time. But the Final Solution was a contradiction of everything Christianity stands for. If I did not believe that, I would not be bothering with any of this, and I certainly would not be a Christian.

It may seem a Christian's defensiveness to say so, but everything we know of Hitler suggests that, once finished with the Jews, he would have targeted for elimination, one way or another, those whose loyalty to Jesus competed with loyalty to the Third Reich. But the absolute priority given to Jews in Hitler's scheme; their place as the extreme negative in *volk* mythology, standing against everything the Third Reich was meant to be; their place, therefore, as the embodiment of an evil to be eliminated at all costs — all of this built upon the Jew hatred that, as the *Washington Jewish Week* editorial so baldly asserts, has been an unbroken thread of Christian history, not just since the Crusades, but beyond Constantine, almost back to the time of the crucifixion itself. One need not believe, with the editorialist, that such history "directly led" to the Holocaust in order to sense a connection that has not been fully faced.

What is the relationship of ancient Christian hatred of Jews to the twentieth century's murderous hatred that produced the death camps? The cross need not be labeled as the cause of the Holocaust for the link to be felt. When can that link be seen for what it is? What does it mean when Christians as well as Jews are jolted by the imposition, across two thousand years, of the name "Golgotha" on the place called Auschwitz? What is going on here? I asked myself that November day, standing before the cross. And I ask it still.

The questions force one into a reconsideration of a familiar history, an exploration of how, if not "directly," one thing led to another, a meditation on what else might have unfolded if certain key events had gone another way. In order to face as squarely as I could the questions posed by the cross at Auschwitz, I have undertaken this work of history. As is already evident, this is history refracted through one man's own experience, because antisemitism is never abstract. The objective record requires, of this writer at least, if not of every reader, an intensely subjective examination of conscience.

I found it necessary to return to the original cross of Jesus of Nazareth, tracing through the generations of his followers who interpreted that cross as a sign of God's favor, who put it on their martial banners and at the center of their creed, who wore it on their breasts, attacking Jews. I have traced the story through the advent of conversionism, to the Inquisition, to the Enlightenment, when the organized hatred of Jews served the Church's purpose in new ways. In the journey through time that ended at the platform at Birkenau, "whose flames touched, must have touched," in Elie Wiesel's words, "the celestial throne,"[6] what were the roads not taken?[7] And where were the chapels of sanctuary in which the hatred of Jews was forbidden entrance? Only by imagining what else might have happened than those "two millennia of bloody crusades and pogroms" can we fully take the measure of what did happen. The study of history always implies a study of its alternative. To ask what was the alternative to European Christianity's hatred of Jews in the past is to assert that such hatred is not necessary in the future.

Because I am a Catholic, I approach this history with a focus on the Roman Catholic Church. The story unfolds over the course of two millennia, but decisive turns come in the eleventh century with the East-West schism and in the sixteenth century with the Protestant Reformation. Because the twentieth-century climax occurs in Germany, with its connection to the Reformation — occurs, that is, in the rise of Nazi antisemitism, with its taproot planted, perhaps, in a particularly Lutheran hatred of Jews — an exclusive focus on the history of Jewish-Catholic conflict would be misleading, and might seem to overemphasize Roman Catholic antecedents of Nazism.

Therefore, at appropriate points in the history that follows, the relationship of German Protestantism to lethal antisemitism will be explored, as will the secular ideologies of the Enlightenment and the racism of colonial imperialism. This will be done not only to show that the Holocaust had its origins in more than Catholic anti-Judaism, but to assert that the

Holocaust resulted not from some abstract Christian ideology (as the editorialist in *Washington Jewish Week* implies) but from a complicated convergence of particular ideas and choices. Hannah Arendt warned of the danger of seeing the Holocaust as the inevitable outcome of what she called "eternal antisemitism,"[8] a force operating outside normal causality. Removed from history, the Holocaust becomes a kind of universal manifestation, the mass murder of Jews a mere instance of an already written script. Only by emphasizing the broad but always specific historical context, continually shaped by political forces, religious ideas, economic necessity, and human freedom, only by proclaiming the connection between Europe's fantasy of "the jews" and the true condition of real Jews, can one emerge with the sense that the Holocaust did not have to happen. Jews did not have to be defined by Christian culture as the demonic other, nor did their status as such have to be transformed in Nazi Germany into the cause for elimination.

Having said that, it is important to acknowledge that my concentration on the Roman Catholic Church as a locus of anti-Judaism — inevitably so before the Reformation, and, to a large extent, since then — is a consequence not only of my personal preoccupation. Eastern Christianity has its own history of religion-based Jew hatred, and the Russian Orthodox Church, in particular, has been implicated in the sad history of the pogroms, but it is in the West that antisemitism became genocidal. Roman Catholicism remains the central institution of Christianity, not only because of the vast numbers of people — more than a billion — who identify themselves as Catholics, but because its dominant institutions — universal governance, uniform cult — give it an influence, especially in the West, that no other form of Christianity can approach. Therefore, an inquiry into the origins of the Holocaust in the tortured past of Western civilization is necessarily an inquiry into the history of Catholicism. In addition, the absolute character of Catholic universalism has meant that Catholicism has stood as the counterpoint to a Judaism that understands itself as a people apart. It is as if the Jewish people and the Roman Catholic Church are knotted together in the same snarl of history. The Catholic Church and the Jews are tied together, in effect, by what separates them.

⇥ 3 ⇤

The Journey

T HE SURPRISE IN THE tangle of feelings and questions, when I was first snagged by it at the foot of the papal cross in sight of the starvation bunker, was that it mattered so much to me. I had arrived at Auschwitz as anyone of my age, background, and temperament would — braced for ovens, mounds of shoes and human hair, railroad tracks, chimneys. But I'd thought of the place as "theirs." No one had told me about the cross at the wall, or warned me about memories of my brother's legs, or reminded me to leave behind the old longing for the consolation of knowing that Jesus died for me. The cross. A pole planted in the fracture at the heart not only of the West, or of the Church, or of "Jewish-Catholic relations," but — here was the surprise — of myself.

So first, this must be a journey across the geography of conscience. For that reason, I presume to measure the sweep of history against the scope of my own memory. By definition, therefore, the boundaries here are narrow, and my vision is limited. The permanent question is whether I can escape the constraints of my own experience and of the way people like me have addressed these questions in the past. For example, it must be acknowledged at the outset that the Catholic anti-Judaism that is my subject carried down the centuries a double insult, for it was largely a response to an imagined Judaism. There was little authentic interaction between Jewish communities and the Church. From early on, as we shall see, "the jews" were defined by Christians far more in terms of the anachronistic categories of the Old Testament than of the living and changing traditions of Jewish culture, understood as more than religion, as it developed in the Mediterranean, in Iberia, in eastern Europe, and later in the cities of modern Europe.

Nevertheless, the history of Jewish-Catholic conflict did involve a dynamic interaction of two parties, whether they knew each other well or not, and as I set out to render that history, I must acknowledge my limited ability to represent the Jewish side of it. Before any Roman Catholic attempting to tell the long story of mutual miscomprehension between Judaism and Christianity lies the danger that once again the Judaism discussed will be constructed more out of fantasy than reality. Therefore, at decisive moments in the history of this interaction — for example, in Iberia when Jewish translators helped prepare the ground for medieval rationalism, or during the Italian Renaissance when Kabbalah helped spark the new humanism, or when Spinoza proposed the idea of religious tolerance — I will lift up the thread of Judaism's independent evolution. Yet mostly that thread will weave below the surface of the story I am telling.

A reader might be wary of the work of a Catholic, because my kind have often gotten it wrong. Either the Jews are the absolute other in relation to whom we Christians define ourselves by opposition and rejection, or they are "anonymous Christians"[1] whose faithful expectation of the Messiah is an implicit harbinger of the Second Coming of Jesus; or they are the faceless victims of a terrible history that belongs less to them than to a haunted Christendom. When Jews are defined as crypto-Christians, Christianity is understood as a branch of Judaism, and when Jews are assigned the victim's role in the Church's own Passion play, "repentance" becomes denial. Jewish-Christian reconciliation then becomes a matter not of honoring differences but of assuming that differences are illusory. Whether we come at the question as antagonists or as would-be healers, in other words, we Christians have difficulty recognizing Jews as truly distinct without turning them into our polar opposites. Obviously, these dense questions out of the past boil down to the ever more urgent question of the Church's relationship to Judaism, and nothing focuses it more dramatically, for the past and the future both, than the cross at Auschwitz.

I referred to the cross earlier as a kind of sighting device, like the crosshairs of a rifle scope. If one were to look back in history through the juncture of the cross at Auschwitz, what would one see? As I said, the narrative form is my métier, and it offers me a structure. The story unfolds with a beginning, a middle, and an end. The end is the cross at Auschwitz. As is so with every story, once the end reveals itself, the beginning and the middle can be understood anew.

In the story of Oedipus, for example, the moment of revelation comes when the king blinds himself, an act that redresses the moral imbalance that had caused the plague in Thebes and that lays bare the meaning of everything that went before. In the climax of the narrative, the moral links that join the elements of the story are revealed. At last we see how the beginning led to the middle, which led to the end. In laying out the history of conflict between the Church and the Jews, I am less concerned with the episodes themselves — from Constantine's conversion to Augustine's, from the Inquisition to the Dreyfus case — than I am with the underlying narrative arc that joins them in a coherent whole.

"The king died, and then the queen died" is a story summed up as an episodic sequence, a famous one given by E. M. Forster to make a point about the underlying unity of narrative structure.[2] The two deaths have nothing to do with each other, and if the story consists only of the coincidence of their chronology, it illuminates nothing. But what if the story is "The king died, and then the queen died of grief"? There is an action here, and that action, grief, is what we care about. Our question has moved from "What happened?" to "Why?" And our concern has moved from an alien figure, the queen, to ourselves, because we too know what it is to grieve. This movement is at the heart of the distinction, made by Aristotle, between pity and fear. When we experience the action of the tragedy as involving the character whose story we see unfolding, we feel pity for that character. But when we recognize the tragic action as involving us, we feel fear. Detachment evaporates, and we forget that the story is not ours.

It is only such a frame of reference that enables us respectfully, and without presumption, to embark on a journey of moral reckoning through a history that culminates in the Shoah. And it seems an odd but compelling concidence that Aristotle's word for such a climax is "catastrophe,"[3] the word that also translates "Shoah," suggesting not only calamity but connection. If one end of the narrative arc is tied to the mass murder of Jews, the other end cries out to be uncovered, and the underlying action, a source of tragic unity through historical complexity, demands to be identified. What happened forces us to ask why. And a genuine concern for unspeakable Jewish loss forces us to acknowledge the moral loss — a loss that always pales by comparison — that belongs to those of us whose hatred of Jews carved the arc of this story.

Ethical coherence depends, in other words, on a grasp of the causal relationship between events. But that does not imply their flowing one from the other in a train of inevitability, as if driven by fate or an impersonal force like Arendt's "eternal antisemitism." Instead, we are asking how freely made human choices led to consequences, which led to new choices and graver consequences. But always we are conscious of that human freedom, which means we are conscious at every turn that events could have gone another way. Yet it is also always true that we know how the story ends, and where. That is why the cross at Auschwitz is the epiphany. As a sighting device through which to view the past, it illuminates the real, showing us what is at stake in this story from the beginning, through the middle, to the end. What makes the cross at Auschwitz "a stumbling block to Jews" — in Saint Paul's phrase, "folly to Gentiles"[4] — is that the story did not have to end that way at all.

Obviously, readers come to this history from varying places and take its weight in different ways. Catholics may recognize their Church's record, both its glories and its ignominies, as the narrative thread to which the advances and reversals of Jewish-Christian interaction adhere. The overwhelmingly negative aspect of that interaction may prompt in Catholic readers a spirit of repentance. Protestant Christians may have old anti-Catholic prejudices confirmed by the story told here. But since the dreaded climax of this narrative occurs in a densely Protestant culture, with essential elements of Protestant collaboration with the Nazi project, rooted perhaps in a legacy of Martin Luther, the revelations of deep-seated Jew hatred that wind through time can hardly be read as exonerating any Christian. We are concerned here with Western civilization itself.

Auschwitz is the climax of the story that begins at Golgotha. Just as the climax of *Oedipus Rex* — the king sees that he is the killer — reveals that the hubris that drove the play's action was itself the flaw that shaped the king's character, so we can already say that Auschwitz, when seen in the links of causality, reveals that the hatred of Jews has been no incidental anomaly but a central action of Christian history, reaching to the core of Christian character. Jew hatred's perversion of the Gospel message launched a history, in other words, that achieved its climax in the Holocaust, an epiphany presented so starkly it can no longer be denied. We shall see how defenders of the Church take pains to distinguish between "anti-Judaism" and "antisemitism"; between Christian Jew-hatred as a "necessary but insufficient" cause of the Holocaust; between the "sins of the children" and the sinlessness of the Church as such.[5] These distinctions become meaningless before the core truth of this history: Because the hatred of Jews had been made holy, it became lethal. The most sacred "thinking and acting" of the Church as such must at last be called into question.

The work of Sophocles is instructive in this awful history because the cumulative effect of *Oedipus Rex* is not depressing but ennobling. What mitigates the unrelenting ugliness of that tale of incest and parricide is not a counternarrative in which positive elements are emphasized, but the fully realized narrative of tragedy itself. The revelation of moral causality, that one choice leads to a consequence, which leads to a new, more fateful choice, is a revelation of moral coherence. Oedipus, in the moment of his self-blinding, *sees*. The catharsis of tragedy leaves an audience more human than before because the unity of the drama denies the meaninglessness of life conceived as a series of unconnected episodes. And the action of the drama, driven by choice, leads to a consequence that did not have to be. Likewise, even this history opens to possibilities of a new future, and even this reckoning can be offered in hope.

As a Catholic, it is a matter of urgent importance to me that my Church is attempting, however fitfully, to face this history and imagine a different kind of future. We know that the Catholic Church has solemnly repudiated the ancient charge that Jews are guilty of the violent murder of God. We know that Pope John Paul II has done more to heal the breach between Christians and Jews than any previous pope. We know that the Church, in all its educational efforts and liturgical practices, is painfully extracting vestiges of explicit antisemitism.[6] But the cross at Auschwitz, with its origin in Wojtyla's own good will, with its origin in the ambiguities of two Roman Catholic saints, with its assertion of a particularly Catholic cult of martyrdom before a people who resent it — the cross at Auschwitz raises, in addition to everything else, a question that can only seem like blasphemy: Thinking of the Holocaust and all that led to it, what kind of God presides over such a history? But is that history's version of a more ancient question? What kind of God shows favor to a beloved Son by requiring him to be nailed to a cross in the first place?

→ 4 ←

My Mother's Clock

WHEN I WAS A BOY — after my brother contracted polio but before I went off to Georgetown — we lived in Germany, where my father was transferred by the Air Force. It was the 1950s, and the postwar continent was up from its knees but not quite on its feet. To America's everlasting credit, as I saw it then, we conquerors had not looted the vanquished but were helping them recover. There was under way, nevertheless, a genteel form of plundering, as we relatively affluent Americans bought up the treasures of impoverished Europe on the cheap.

My mother had a passion for old things, and as an officer's wife she could indulge it. She was a good-looking redhead with a sense of style. Not even the language barrier dampened her innate love of the friendly greetings exchanged with shopkeepers. Nothing sparked her adventurous spirit like the search for quality at bargain prices. I loved to wander with her through patched-together shops and Quonset arcades in which the worldly goods of what we thought of only as a lost aristocracy were for sale. Bavarian crystal, Dresden platters, Meissen dishes, Belgian lace, Delft figurines — I first heard such names not knowing they referred to places. I remember the somber mood into which my mother would fall, moving past the makeshift shelves. Perhaps she was thinking of the tables laid with these beautiful things. Carefully selecting, piece by piece, the settings of family banquets, was she somehow trying to rescue the dreams of lost women with whom she secretly identified? Decades later, as I set the table for my parents' fiftieth wedding anniversary dinner, I opened the corner cupboard for those Bavarian crystal goblets. My mother protested. The glasses had not been used since she'd purchased them in Germany. "What are you saving them for if not your golden anniversary?" I asked. A wounded look blew into her eyes — because of me, I thought then, wrongly. I know better now.

Mom was the daughter and granddaughter of Irish immigrants who'd arrived in America destitute. In Germany, was she unconsciously trying to accumulate her own legacy, the heirlooms that history, and a British over-lord, had denied her? Then the point was never actually to use what she bought, but only to have it, and then to hand it on. If she had such a stripped-bare motive, she never spoke of it. If I had asked, she'd have only teased herself as a woman born to shop — a mall maven ahead of her time. She never threw the lavish dinner parties that would have justified such possessions. Most of what she bought in Germany sat in crates in the basement, forever unopened. Yes, the antidote to dispossession was pos-sessions, and the point of such beautiful things was to pass them on, offer-ing her progeny tangible connections to a past, even if it was a dream past unconnected to our reality and the unknown reality of the things themselves.

In a rough warehouse in Wiesbaden, not far from the Rhine, my mother had bought a beautiful grandfather clock, a seven-foot Bavarian masterpiece. The case was made of oak. A pair of carved cornucopias en-circled the face, time itself as the giver of all the earth's bounty. When Mom died a few years ago, I inherited that clock; my brothers and I drew straws for it, and I won.

A full year passed before I could reassemble its weights and chains and chimes in my own living room. The silence of the clock had been a mea-sure of my grief, and setting it in motion again meant I had begun to re-cover from her death. The music of the clock, Westminster chimes, began to waft through our house every fifteen minutes. While it evoked my mother's absence, it did so consolingly, a kind of presence after all.

But then the clock began to mean something else as well. Recent news stories have revealed how the possessions of Europe's annihilated Jews ended up in the homes of respectable people; their savings accounts in the general funds of respected Swiss banks; their gold and jewels in the vaults of prestigious institutions from Spain to Argentina; their art on the walls of great museums — all without compensation to anyone.[1] And what about the slave labor that built profits for Volkswagen and subsidiaries of Ford, for Krupp and Bayer? We have just begun to ask.[2] The willed naiveté, the denial, the moral obtuseness — whatever one chooses to call it — with which the vast majority responded to the Holocaust for so long has evaporated, leaving the telltale salt of truth on every surface. My mother's lost aristocrats surely included Jews, of whom genteel postwar looters like us never thought, as we never doubted our German servants' unprompted assertions that they had always hated Hitler. Now I find myself staring at my mother's clock, half hypnotized by the swinging pendulum, the metronome click of which seems to ask: And you? Who are you to assume your innocence?

I was born in 1943, the year before the jurist Raphael Lemkin coined the word "genocide."[3] By then, most of the murders of Jews had been carried out. People of my generation, especially Christians, have viewed the Holocaust from the moral high ground, as a crime for which we bear no responsibility. Yet the Holocaust was not simply what happened to Jews between 1933 and 1945. It involved not only the six million, but the tens of millions of their lost progeny. It is the absence of that Jewish legion — the heirs of those paintings and clocks — that the world has come increasingly to feel as a real presence. Jews accounted for 10 percent of the total population of the Roman Empire. By that ratio, if other factors had not intervened, there would be 200 million Jews in the world today, instead of something like 13 million.[4]

With that as a background, and aware of those "other factors," one may ask why. And with the explosion of news about Jews and the Shoah — in 1945, the year of "revelation," about 250 Holocaust-related news stories appeared in the *New York Times;* in 1997, there were nearly double that[5] — one must ask why. Is it safe to remember the lost legion of Jews because finally it is clear that Jews as a key presence in Europe have at last been gotten rid of? Or because, as a factor in American life, inexorably pushed by demographics, intermarriage, and secularization, Jews as a group are growing less significant?[6]

History must name forever the perpetrators of the Final Solution, and the particular crime of the Nazis must never be universalized. Western civilization did not operate the crematoria; men did. The theory of corporate guilt is properly derided, because it is true that if all are guilty, no one is. Nevertheless, the prosecutor's method applies: Once one asks why, one must also ask who benefited.

Who benefits still? What about the unclaimed money in Switzerland, not in 1945 but now? What about Picasso's *Head of a Woman,* known to have been in the private collection of one Alphonse Kann, but now, as of this writing, in the Pompidou Center in Paris? What about the unprobated moral legacies of universities, churches, and nations? And yes, what about my mother's clock? Unlike meticulously recorded bank accounts, famous artworks, or real estate, the provenance of this lovely but ordinary timepiece can never be established. That means I will never know whether it was stolen from a Jewish family, or whether it wasn't. In that way, my mother's clock has taken on a new character as a chiming icon of the twentieth century's most difficult question. Who benefits? Who benefits, that is, from the perhaps coming disappearance of Jews from everywhere but Israel, their garrison outpost? The vanishing of Jewish culture through assimilation is not, of course, the urgent moral problem that the attempted elimination of Jewish culture through mass murder is, but it should be acknowledged that the potential demographic crisis facing the Jewish people is defined by the loss of the murdered millions, not only in the twentieth century, but in all the others.

The material consequences of *judenrein* — the gold, the apartments, the clocks — are only emblems of the spiritual consequences. Why should Europe — the Nazis with their active and passive collaborators — have turned so violently on the Jews? Despite an apparently broad cultural preoccupation with the Holocaust over the last generation, this is a question non-Jews have barely begun to ask. The prosecutor's question must be put not materially but spiritually. Who benefits when certain ancient observances, certain ways of asking questions, certain ways of thinking about God, and certain ways of asserting peoplehood disappear from Western consciousness?

As a Catholic, I have been summoned by the pope himself to ask such questions. John Paul II warned Catholics not to cross the threshold of the new millennium without having fully reckoned with our particular failure in relation to Jews. "How can we not lament the lack of discernment," he asked in 1994, "which at times became even acquiescence?"[7] John Paul II, perhaps more eloquently than any non-Jew, pointed to the Holocaust as a challenge to the Christian conscience.

Yet much of what one hears lately from the Vatican about the role of the Catholic Church during the Hitler years, including the long awaited 1998 statement "We Remember: A Reflection on the Shoah" and the 2000 statement "Memory and Reconciliation: The Church and the Faults of the Past,"[8] is defensive and self-exonerating. The behavior of a relatively few heroes is highlighted, and the hierarchy's choice of pragmatic, behind-the-scenes diplomacy over moral confrontation is presented in the most favorable way. For example, in both documents "many" Christians are credited with assisting persecuted Jews, while some "others" are faulted for not doing so. The truth requires a reversal of that construction: "many" did nothing, while "others," a few, gave assistance.[9] In "We Remember," the pagan quality of Nazi ideology — its hatred of all things reli-

gious, including Christian, and perhaps especially Catholic — is emphasized rather than the way Protestant and Catholic attitudes toward Jews
were so well exploited by the Nazis. Pius XII is praised as a hero of resistance.

I will take another view in this book, aware that the final verdict on
these questions will be rendered by future generations.[10] But I should acknowledge that I am considered by some of my fellow Catholics as an unreliable witness. In the *New York Times,* I have been identified as a papal
critic whose complaints against the pope "enraged Catholics less liberal"
than I.[11] Despite my criticism, I was invited in 1999 to participate, as one
of fifteen Catholic scholars, together with fifteen Jewish scholars, in a
consultation with Cardinal Edward Cassidy, the head of the Vatican's
Commission for Religious Relations with the Jews and the chief author of
"We Remember." The subject of that consultation was the document's
shortcomings and the Vatican's remaining responsibility for resolving
them. We will return to those shortcomings and that responsibility later
in the book.

The questions remain. Who benefits? What does history teach about
the Church's relationship to anti-Judaism, about anti-Judaism's relationship to antisemitism, about antisemitism's relationship to the near elimination of European Jews? Can the Roman Catholic memory, in the words
of John Paul II, "play its necessary part in the process of shaping a future
in which the unspeakable iniquity of the Shoah will never again be possible"?[12] But memory is less a neutral accident of the mind than a conscious
work of interpretation, marked as much by deletion as by selection. How
a community remembers its past is the single most important element
in determining its future. But a community as large and complex as the
Roman Catholic Church can accomplish such reckoning only in fits and
starts.

Yes, a work of memory, but far more is at stake than assessments of the
behavior of Pius XII. It is not sufficient to emphasize that Hitler, though
technically and officially a Catholic until the day he died, was in spirit a
pagan. Hitler's genocidal assault on the Jews became the work of an entire
people, and an entire civilization was prepared to let it happen. How, a
civilization Christian to its core? How, the German citizens, 95 percent of
whom in 1940, seven years after Nazism took hold, were still affiliated with
a church?[13] If pagan ideology accounts for the brutality of Nazism, why
did the "religiousness" of German Christians grow throughout the period
of the Third Reich? Attendance at Catholic services, for example, in-

creased as the war progressed. It is true that the Reich's leaders encouraged Germans to observe their rites of passage with pagan-style Nazi ceremonies instead of church baptisms, marriages, and funerals, but statistics were kept: In the first half of 1943, in Thuringia, a region in central Germany, 1,427 of the concocted rituals were conducted by the Nazi Party, while 35,853 were conducted traditionally, in churches. According to the Third Reich's own survey, a mere 3.5 percent of the German population described themselves as *Gottgläubige* (neo-pagan) as late as 1944.[14] When the Nazis tried to remove crucifixes from the schools of Bavaria, Catholics protested, and the Nazis backed down. In other words, the German people, whatever else they did, maintained their ostensible Christian identity — which is why the question about, at the very least, acquiescence in genocidal crimes is a question about the content of that identity.

How, the clergy? One hears quite a lot about Dietrich Bonhoeffer, the Protestant theologian, and Bernhard Lichtenberg, dean of the Catholic Cathedral in Berlin, both martyred. They were true heroes for all. More than three thousand Catholic priests and nuns perished in the camps, although most of those were Poles put to death more for being Slavic than Catholic. German clergy were killed at the front as chaplains in the German army at a rate greater than priests and ministers were ever sent to the camps. As the historian William Sheridan Allen wrote about the German clergy, "From an actuarial point of view it was safer to oppose Hitler than to support him."[15]

Nevertheless, it is a slander to say that the Catholic Church did not resist Hitler. It fails "moral memory" not to emphasize that an expressly Catholic resistance, boldly led by the hierarchy, did in fact succeed in deterring the Führer from one of his most evil plans. Seventy thousand "undesirable" people under German authority were put to death in a Nazi euthanasia program. It was slated to kill hundreds of thousands, if not millions, more. But the open pursuit of this policy was stopped by the protests of churches, with a key role played by Bishop Clement August von Galen of Münster. He applied the word "murder" to the program. In a sermon preached on August 3, 1941, he said, "If they start out by killing the insane, it can well be extended to the old, the infirm, sick, seriously crippled soldiers. What do you do to a machine which no longer runs, to an old horse which is incurably lame, a cow which does not give milk? They now want to treat humans the same way."[16] As von Galen's resistance drew support from other bishops and the Vatican, the Nazis wanted to retaliate against him. But they were afraid to because, as Joseph Goebbels himself said, "The population of Münster could be regarded as lost during the war if anything were done against the Bishop . . . [indeed] the whole of Westphalia" would be lost to the cause.[17] Exactly three weeks after von Galen's sermon, Hitler ordered a halt to the euthanasia program.[18]

Why was the fate of the Jews so different from the fate of the planned victims of the euthanasia program? Why did one rouse Church leaders to an effective and courageous open protest, while the other — with few exceptions — roused nothing? Was it because the seventy thousand euthanasia victims and their likely successors had Christian brothers and sisters and mothers and fathers who could conscript pastors and bishops into the struggle? Was it because euthanasia, then as now, is an issue close to the center of Roman Catholic moral preoccupation? Explicitly and uneuphemistically, Church protests against Hitler, including Pius XI's 1937 encyclical *Mit Brennender Sorge* ("With Burning Sadness"), always concerned matters of Church prerogatives, power, and doctrine. Euthanasia, like crucifixes on schoolroom walls, qualified. Jews did not. The contrast speaks for itself. "Had the Nazi hierarchy encountered unambiguous and sustained revulsion by non-Jewish Germans at their antisemitic policies," the historian Deborah E. Lipstadt concluded, "there probably would have been no Final Solution."[19]

The monstrous question to Europe, to Western Christianity, and to Catholicism is not How could you have murdered the Jews? Because again, it was the Nazis, not "Europe," who murdered the Jews. Even discounting the Church-affiliated Germans who were among the perpetrators of the crime, the monstrous question is How could you have not cared that the Nazis prepared to murder, and then did murder, the Jews in front of you? How could that murder not have been experienced as directly involving you? And finally, when the roundups and deportations and transports began to be conducted openly in 1942 and 1943, when the killing of Jews replaced the war effort as Hitler's main purpose, why did you not see that your passivity had effectively become collaboration? "How is it," Cynthia Ozick asks, "that indifference, which on its own does no apparent or immediate positive harm, ends by washing itself in the very horrors it means to have nothing to do with? Hoping to confer no hurt, indifference finally grows lethal; why is that?"[20]

⇥ 5 ⇤

Passion Play

IN GERMANY, beginning when I was fifteen or so, in addition to the treasure hunts on which I had watched my mother buy, among other things, that clock, I had made Holy Week pilgrimages with her. We went to Rhineland shrines not far downriver from our home in Wiesbaden. My father had been named chief of staff of the Air Force in Europe in 1957, and I lived there until 1960, the year of my enrollment in Georgetown. Our time in Germany coincided with the end of the occupation era, when American virtue was defined by the utter absence of the evil enemy whom we had vanquished. The Germany we knew, our stalwart ally in the cosmic struggle against Communism, had nothing to do with Hitler's Germany. And nothing demonstrated that more than the outpourings of fervent piety we witnessed whenever German Catholics gathered in market squares for church festivals.

Germany is famously Lutheran, but most of the area historically dominated by Protestants had fallen behind the Iron Curtain, and the Federal Republic, with its capital in traditionally Catholic Bonn, seemed a mainly Catholic nation to us. In its flamboyant, if not altogether authentic, program of denazification, it had served West Germany's purposes to elevate Catholic leaders like Konrad Adenauer, who was born near Bonn. As we shall see, his record as an anti-Hitler resister served as an exonerating blanket not only for the German nation but for much of German Catholicism. In the Rhineland, where we lived, Catholicism was strong, and in the postwar years its public assertion was a way not only to forget Hitler but, implicitly, to deny that he had ever had much of a following there. At times, in the religious pageants that often spilled into the streets of river towns and cities, I might have thought otherwise — except that the venomous portrayals of Jews that informed New Testament dramatizations must have seemed normal to me, too.

My mother's piety always came into its own on Holy Thursday and Good Friday, and in those years the Passion of Jesus stirred us as never before. Passion plays in Germany dated to the late Middle Ages, when they were offered in thanksgiving for deliverance from the Black Death. The Passion play tradition, which took root in Germany as nowhere else, was already a signal of the explosive power that would be unleashed when certain strains of Teutonic culture meshed with the "normal" anti-Judaism of European Christianity. For, even more than the Gospels from which it derives, the Passion play enacts a drama that is as much about the Jews as it is about Jesus. It is the perfect distillation of the stark polarity by which the Church defines itself entirely by its enemy. For a long time I carried vivid images of Passion plays I associated with Germany, and I took them for renditions of a sacred truth. They were not the full-blown productions of, say, an Oberammergau, but the story of the death of Jesus, enacted as a pageant, with tableaux, choruses, and costumed actors, had stamped my adolescent imagination. I remembered the action spilling into the crowd of pilgrims as we thronged enclosures between the ancient walls of towering churches and monastic arcades. I thought of my mother and me standing together on planks, her clutching the rosary. When the white-robed figure of Jesus appeared — the wreath of thorns was more striking than the cross, which seemed small for what it had to do — she blessed herself. I remembered wanting to tell her once that it was only a play.

Other characters appeared before us like figures from a Bavarian woodcut. I remembered Pontius Pilate with his toga, laurel crown, and white enamel pan of water. I remembered Simon of Cyrene, leather bracelets on his naked biceps, sandal thongs laced above his ankles, the ease with which he handled the cross. Jesus trailed behind, his hands bound, his hair matted with blood from thorns that seemed real. I remembered the weeping Veronica, how she clutched her towel, with its imprint of the face of Our Lord. And I remembered the mother of Jesus, on whom, alone of all the figures, my eyes found it possible to rest. She was a pretty girl whose stoic passivity — her head unmoving, held at that famous angle, even as she strode through the press of that Via Dolorosa — seemed very sensual to me. Subliminally, as with the Virgin of Michelangelo's *Pietà*, she was less a mother than a figure of thwarted desire, which was why, throughout my youth, her virginity underwrote my own. In the Mary of the sorrowful mysteries, spirituality and sensuality were not at war. In her, the word "passion" could slyly open to its other meaning. And I could turn to her when devotion to my own mother had become taboo.

Mary's enemies would be forever mine. As much as I remembered the Pharisees and the Sadducees who trailed along behind, the High Priest with his turban, and the Rabbis with their robes and hooked noses, I remembered the Jews with their conical hats and unsubtle horns, which made them like devils. Michelangelo had put horns on his great *Moses* because he was influenced by a mistranslation, I would later learn, of the Hebrew word for "rays."[1] The rays of mystical light streaming from Moses' forehead after seeing God thus became diabolical protrusions. These were the only "Jews" I ever knew of in Germany, a classic instance of the Christian's negative fantasy. Those hooked noses, like the blood on the brow of Jesus, must have been false, but that did not occur to me.

I remembered those "Jews" waving their knotted leather cords above their heads, to whip down on Jesus. As the tableaux passed before us, in my memory, the Passion was being read over loudspeakers. But why in English? I would wonder later. When the chorus of "Jews" cried out their "Crucify him!" I understood. Jews. Jews all. Jews forever with blood upon them and upon their children. The facts of the story were clear, and the evidence was irrefutable. "He came to his own home, and his own people received him not."[2] The whole meaning of the story of Jesus depended on his being rejected in the deepest and most hurtful way — a way to which Romans would forever be irrelevant. In the tableau featuring the apostles at supper, the image seared into every Christian imagination, and therefore mine — whether from Leonardo or just an illustrated children's Bible — there was only one Jew, as we knew by the purse at his belt, which tied him to Fagin, Shylock, and the shylock mobsters hired to do their tax evasion. And wasn't his name Judas, which itself said Jew?

A paradigmatic Holy Week pageant had scorched my teenage mind. I accepted its assumptions entirely. Surely the intensity of my reaction had to do with associating the Passion of Mary's son with my own sorrowful Catholic mother. The dramatically posed Mary of every *Pietà*, an avatar of static stoicism, was a figure of my own Mary, which was my mother's name. She had identified herself to me, from my earliest memory, as "the Blessed Mother's representative here on earth," a phrase she could utter without pompousness or irony, and which I accepted without question as the overlapping definition of both her authority and her virtue. If I could see Mary the mother of Jesus as my mother, it never occurred to me to complete the identification, despite my father's name of Joseph and my own initials, by embracing Jesus as my personal ideal. His victimhood was too extreme for that, and so was the venom of those who had hated him.

My deeply felt ambition already ran in the opposite direction, which was at all costs to be well liked.

By this point in Germany, I knew no one who was Jewish, and so "jews" could begin to loom as fantasy figures, and did. This *was* Germany, and I knew to think of them as the doomed, as our new measure of victimhood, as the unredeemed. If I dared entertain a conscious thought of the Holocaust — while, of course, "deploring" what I had learned to call genocide — it would have nevertheless been to understand exactly how and why it happened.

But in truth, "jews" impinged on my awareness less than my mother did. As I came to the threshold of manhood in Germany, I faced the long-deflected truth of my situation, that having been put on earth to please her — being well liked by Mom was the point — I would have no choice but to join the company of those apostles whose unworthiness — in contrast to the Jews' — had been transformed by the miracle of Jesus' misery into holiness itself. The foundation of what remains my piety was poured here: the unwilled conviction that suffering precedes any hope of happiness; no, that suffering *promises* happiness; or, no again, that suffering *is* happiness. This was the meaning of the bloodied body of Jesus and of the downcast eyes of Mary. And it was the meaning of the odd, horrible, irresistible thrill it was to behold them both at the deicide pageants, especially with my elbow pressed against my mother's.

Though I would have an equivalent and independent epiphany with my father — one tied to the imminence of nuclear Armageddon during the Berlin crisis of 1960, with the role of the horned Jews being played by the Soviets — the Rhineland pilgrimages of Holy Week awakened in me a vocational recognition to which my mother's presence was crucial — "crucial in the literal sense of *crucialis,* as pertaining to the *crux Christi.*"[3] Both experiences would blossom in my Georgetown "vision" of the crucifix. But my mother provided the primordial flare of intimacy, my first felt sense of the living other whom I could recognize on the cross. The suffering and death of Jesus, which I learned firmly to believe he would have undergone for me alone, became proof of a trustworthy God.

Unknowingly I was treading a well-worn path — mother as sponsor of faith — along which not only Jesus had walked, but figures as varied, and as important to this story, as Constantine and Augustine, and much later, Captain Alfred Dreyfus. The point isn't to put myself in such exalted company, but to acknowledge the way a certain kind of boy is at the mercy of a certain kind of woman. As I came of age, even as an Elvis worshiper, a soldier's son, a cheerleader's boyfriend, my mother remained the measure of my imagination — religious, but also somehow erotic.

She was a former telephone girl. "Number, please," she'd say, instead of "What?" She smoked Chesterfields, leaving a crown of lipstick on the butts, which I would secretly put to my own lips. She sat with her legs crossed to swing her right foot to the Glenn Miller music in her head. I could watch that bouncing ankle as if it wore bobby sox. It would be my mother's ankle I thought of when I later read Freud, as the expression on the face of Bernini's Saint Teresa in the throes of Passion mysticism would remind me of the lipstick on those Chesterfields. Sexual longing, the desire for an infinite intimacy, a physically religious faith, and vice versa: the Word made flesh, the Body of Christ, the secret pleasure of pain — all this, consciously and unconsciously, I had from her. But my competition included my polio-stricken brother, whose bones were like those of the crucified. And so I could not be her *cushlamochree,* a favorite Gaelic endearment of hers. The "vein of her heart" was the sword through it, which was always Joe.

Yet I was the one to whom she showed her suffering. I was the one who went with her in Holy Week. Of all her men — in addition to Joe and Dad, there were my three younger brothers — I alone could look upon the streaked face of Jesus, could hear the throaty cries of Jews, could register the weight of the joined wooden beams. I alone, that is, could feel not what Jesus felt but what his stunned mother felt, and therefore what mine did. My mother's fingers in tan kid gloves, one hand clutching a rosary, the other pressing into the bone at my elbow. I too have bones. We had come to watch the murder of our God, which made me want to protect her. Later, as we shall see, the Church, at Vatican II, would tell the world this murder had not happened. Or rather, that the murderers had been not the Jews but — what, a generic human weakness? the sin of the world? an abstract evil to which all could be attached? The power of this story, the truth of it, was to be found in the particularity of its conflict. What would be left of that if the Jews were set aside? And what would be left of my own first religious intuition — that to stand *for* was necessarily to stand *against?* The drama of the Passion play made the thing clear, required a choice, and implied the eternal conscription that could prepare a boy to surrender his life. Only one future could be worthy of such emotion. Only one future could keep me where I knew absolutely I belonged — at our forsaken Lord's side, which was how to be at hers. Not for nothing do they call it Holy Mother Church.

"Then we went in and told my mother," Augustine writes of his conversion, "who was overjoyed. And when we went on to describe how it had all happened, she was jubilant with triumph and glorified You, who are powerful enough, and more than powerful enough, to carry out your purpose beyond all our hopes and dreams . . . You converted me to yourself so that I no longer desired a wife or placed any hope in this world, but stood firmly upon the rule of faith, where you had shown me to her in a dream so many years before." And here was the payoff for mothers' sons like Augustine and me: "And you turned her sadness into rejoicing, into joy far fuller than her dearest wish, far sweeter and more chaste than any she had hoped to find in children begotten of my flesh."[4]

As was true of Augustine's, mine was a commissioning into an army — not for nothing is its elite called the Legion of Mary — whose permanent enemy was the Jews.

"Truth? What is truth?" an exonerated Pilate asks. But Holy Week renditions of the Passion made my truth clear. The Jews of Matthew, Mark, Luke, and John, with their pointy hats, soiled robes, and odd phylacteries, were doing for me by now what they had done for Augustine and all Christians since: telling me who I was by who I wasn't.

Peter Seligman, my first chum, was gone, replaced in this way by the Western figments of Christ's Passion, the only Jews I would know for a decade. Chief among them was not the wicked High Priest but Judas Iscariot, whom we knew as the only Jew among the Twelve. His Jewishness was evident not only in his greed but in his choice of suicide rather than forgiveness. I learned soon enough to think that if I abandoned my vocation to the priesthood, or turned against Holy Mother Church as a critic, I would be Judas too, which implied, No better than a Jew. When it came to that, in my much later association with Catholic dissenters, I would recognize dissent as the primordial Jewish crime, long before it was mine. The death of Judas proved that the savage hatred of this stiff-necked people — "His blood be upon us and upon our children!" — extended even to themselves.

⇥ 6 ⇤

My Rabbi

THE EVENTS OF 1933 to 1945 are the necessary background for understanding both why the Christian Church needed to change and then why it did. The key to that change among Catholics was John XXIII, the roly-poly peasant pope who replaced Pius XII in 1958. An elderly compromise candidate who was expected only to keep the Chair of Peter warm, he startled the Church by promptly announcing his intention to convene an Ecumenical Council for the purpose of *aggiornamento*, or updating. Pope John's immediate impact on the Church was the result of his magnanimous personality. His great heart was the perfect antidote to the wounded spirit of the age. I had my own moment in the presence of that large heart when Pope John received my family in a private audience at his residence, the Apostolic Palace — an honor paid my father because of his status as a senior Catholic in the American military. When the pope embraced me, I let myself fall for the first time into a sure trust in God's love, an experience that led to my entering a seminary less than two years later.[1]

I knew nothing of this at the time, but for John XXIII, the definitive demonstration that the Church needed to change was its record in relation to the Jews. He had come to this not through an imagined projection of Jewish experience but by paying close attention to a Jew speaking for himself. As a papal legate in Turkey during World War II, when, still known as Angelo Giuseppe Roncalli, he had provided counterfeit baptismal documents to Jews in flight from the Nazi onslaught, the future pope had firsthand experience of the Holocaust as it was happening. After the war, as the scope of the genocide came to light, Roncalli would have been like many Christians in deploring Nazi antisemitism. But he soon realized that a deeper encounter with the history that preceded it was necessary.

In 1948, the Jewish historian Jules Isaac published *Jesus and Israel*, a

study of the connection between fundamental Christian belief, as enshrined especially in the New Testament, and Europe's endemic contempt for Judaism, which had reached critical mass with Hitler's program.
Isaac's book challenged basic Christian assumptions and repudiated the
caricature of Judaism found in the Gospels and elsewhere. Many Catholics reviled Isaac's work, but instead of shunning it, John XXIII took it in.
He invited Isaac to meet with him in the Vatican, and the encounter took
place in 1960. Isaac presented the pope with a copy of his book and proposed that the pontiff undertake to correct the anti-Jewish teachings of
the Church. In his diary, Isaac describes the pope's reaction as positive,
even warm.[2] Their highly publicized encounter was a first signal that fundamental shifts in Catholic attitudes were under way.

The greatest shift took place when, in 1962, Pope John convened the
Vatican Council, a meeting of the world's 2,600 Catholic bishops, gathered in the nave of St. Peter's Basilica. There is reason to believe that the
visit of Jules Isaac led Pope John to call on those bishops to take up as a
priority the Church's relationship with the Jews.[3] This led to the milestone
declaration *Nostra Aetate* ("In Our Time"), which includes these words:
"Since the spiritual patrimony common to Christians and Jews is thus so
great, this sacred Synod wishes to foster and recommend that mutual understanding and respect which is the fruit above all of biblical and theological studies, and of brotherly dialogues." It is noteworthy that the whole
project of the Church's reconsideration of "biblical and theological" assumptions, which has led to the most basic questioning of the Church's
anti-Judaism, was undertaken at least partly in response, at the highest
level, to a Jewish challenge offered in "brotherly dialogue."

Against nearly two thousand years of common Church teaching, *Nostra
Aetate* affirms that the covenant God made with the Jewish people has not
been broken and that the ongoing vitality of the Jewish religion is part of
God's plan. The council declared, "Although the Church is the new people
of God, the Jews should not be presented as repudiated or cursed by God,
as if such views followed from the Holy Scriptures."[4] In Part Two, we will
address the unfinished business implied by this statement — namely, that
such repudiation does indeed seem to follow from Christian Scripture —
but here it is enough to say that the Vatican Council, responding to a vivid
sense of the effect of the teaching of religious contempt, initiated a major
move away from it.

Nostra Aetate zeroed in on the central pillar, in Richard Rubenstein's
phrase, of "supreme hatred," the old charge of deicide. "True, authorities

of the Jews and those who followed their lead pressed for the death of Christ . . . still, what happened in His passion cannot be blamed upon all the Jews then living, without distinction, nor against the Jews of today."[5]

When this declaration was mistakenly summarized in news accounts as a Catholic act of absolution for an ancient Jewish sin, some Jews, not surprisingly, took offense. Christians and Jews alike who had been sensitive to the disastrous consequences of the deicide accusation welcomed the council's declaration, but a broader public was simply confused. It was into that group that I fell. The gentle pope had removed the cruel words *perfidis judaeis* ("perfidious Jews") from the Good Friday liturgy, and I understood, at that dawn of the ecumenical age, the necessity for civility.[6] Yes, *perfidis* is an insult and doesn't belong in church. I saw that.

Years later, scholars would add nuance to my grasp of the origins of the anti-Jewish polemic of the New Testament, but my seminary Scripture courses did no such thing. The historical-critical method, yes. The concordance of the Gospels, yes. Textual and contextual analysis, yes. I learned that in the earliest Gospel, Mark, it is "the crowd" that sets itself against Jesus; then, in Matthew, the antagonist is identified as "all the people"; but those categories I saw through the lens of John, who identified the enemy of Jesus as "the Jews." In John the record is crystal clear, and his account of the crucial events shapes the Christian imagination still:

> Pilate said to them [the chief priests and the officers], "Take him yourselves and crucify him, for I find no crime in him."
> The Jews answered him, "We have a law, and by that law he ought to die, because he has made himself the Son of God . . ."
> He said to the Jews, "Here is your king!"
> They cried out, "Away with him, away with him, crucify him!"[7]

After *Nostra Aetate,* scholars and preachers would try to shift the blame for the death of Jesus to the Romans, who after all invented crucifixion. Jesus would be presented as a peasant revolutionary whose crime was merely political. Or his death would be spiritualized, indicting the generic fault of a sinful human race. In this case, the long-running subtext of Christian piety — Jesus died for *my* sins — would be brought forward as paramount. I would learn these lessons. My question remained, however. What about the Gospels? The enemies of Jesus were Jews, not Romans: "his own people received him not."[8] The very structure of the Jesus story required his rejection by the people with whom he first identified. If that wasn't true, what was? If the Jews had not rejected him, even to sponsoring his murder, then Christian religion was based on fiction, and worse. If "the Jews" were innocent of the death of Jesus, then the Gospel writers were guilty of a vicious slander. And not just the Gospels. The Acts of the Apostles tells the story to highlight conflict with the Jewish Temple guard, Jewish high priests, Pharisees, scribes, and Sadducees — an undefined litany that boils down to "the Jews." The Romans? Wasn't Saint Paul's claim to Roman citizenship what rescued him from the Jews? "[The Jews] are enemies of God," he says in Romans, an indictment that hardly seems tempered by the following clause: "but . . . they are beloved for the sake of their forefathers."[9]

To say that the Jews were not in some way the enemy, it seemed to me at the time, undermined the Catholic reading of the New Testament, its composition, divine inspiration, and, as I had recently learned to call it, "indefectibility." I was as yet incapable of asking the basic question: Is hatred of "the Jews" in the Christian Scripture a signal that followers of Jesus, even as mostly Jews themselves, proved all too human not only in their initial response to him — all those Good Friday desertions — but in their subsequent "inspired" interpretations of his message? The idea of the essential reliability of the New Testament witness is so central to Christian faith that even radical contemporary Scripture scholars suggest not that evangelists were wrong in the way they constructed the narrative, but that we are wrong in the way we understand it. Such convoluted thinking only serves to put the question more directly: Are the New Testament writings, twisted by a hatred of Jews that a Church council would later renounce, a betrayal of the message of Jesus? If so, where does that leave us?

There was no escaping the source of conflict: Jesus was the Messiah, and Jews *as Jews* rejected him. That happened in the beginning, and it was still happening. I knew, by the time I was a seminarian, to say no in principle to antisemitism, with its crude sweeping racism, but Christian religious opposition to Jews was something else. In Scripture class we were taught to distinguish between antisemitism and anti-Judaism, with the clear meaning that the latter was an appropriate part of the defense of the faith. Love the sinner but hate the sin — hate the sin, that is, of the Jews' rejection of the Lord. The exonerated Pilate, washing his hands of the crucifixion, carried more dramatic weight in the Passion narrative than did Jesus washing the feet of his disciples. That Pilate, not the Jews, was charged with the death of Jesus by the creed we daily recited at Mass — "For our sake, He was crucified under Pontius Pilate" — carried weight, but the creed was composed at Nicaea three centuries later, and it did not cancel the Gospels' assertions. I remember how the question was finally put to our professor one day: Either the Jews are guilty or the Gospels falsify history — which is it? Our professor could not answer us.

Nostra Aetate, in other words, raised more questions than it answered. "Although the Church is the new People of God, the Jews should not be presented as rejected or accursed by God . . . Furthermore, in her rejection of every persecution against any man, the Church . . . decries hatred, persecution, displays of anti-Semitism directed against Jews at any time and by anyone." Contradictions notwithstanding, the meaning of the Vatican Council declaration was clear. It was considered antisemitism now to say that the Jews killed Jesus. The date of this pronouncement was October 28, 1965 — well away, fortunately, from the springtime liturgical cycle in which, to the ears of those in pews, the Church's solemn Holy Week lectionary would simply defy it. The questions raised by *Nostra Aetate* — from the meaning of corporate guilt, to the interplay of Old Testament prophecy and Christian revelation, to the "inerrancy" of the Church — gave shape not only to our classroom discussions but to those of our dinner table and common room as well.

I, for one, had to face the way in which a fiercely negative image of the Jew served as a girder of my religious imagination. What could move it, much less remove it? I could not have directed you to a synagogue in Washington, my native city. I knew no Jews by then, and I knew nothing of Jewish piety as it had developed over the nearly two thousand years since Caiaphas. Even Peter Seligman was a distant memory.

The year 1965 was the twentieth anniversary of the liberation of the camps in Europe. While the council fathers had debated their text, the cult of Anne Frank had swept the West and the trial of Adolf Eichmann had reached a climax. The news in Europe had been dominated by jurists' efforts to extend the statute of limitations on war crimes, as the broad society finally acknowledged that some key figures of the Third Reich had yet to be brought to justice. In other words, the first phase of a culture-wide Holocaust denial was coming to an end. No one in Rome described *Nostra Aetate* as an effort to reckon with the Church's relationship to these events, but what else accounts for the jubilation with which it was promulgated?

My beloved John XXIII had died in 1963, but his successor, Paul VI, seemed as committed to this transformation as Roncalli had been. Pope Paul's speech is still vividly in my mind. I remember staring up at the common room Philco, one of a hushed group of robust American men in their twenties, how we stretched to understand the Latin, falling back gratefully on the *sotto voce* of the papal translator. The pope declared, "The Church is alive! Well, then, here is the proof!" For us Catholics, there was always proof. His Holiness held up the pages of the declaration. "Here is the breath, the voice, the song . . ."

Nostra Aetate was being taken as an absolution of the Jews, yes, but did this exuberance hint that it was, at a deeper level, an absolution of the Church? There was the necessary rejection of the deicide charge, that Jews as a group could not be indicted for the murder of Jesus, but there was also the unexplained assertion that the charge was not grounded in Christian Scripture. Wasn't this a moving away from accountability instead of toward it? And precisely what did it mean to say that the Jewish religion continued to have validity if, in fact, Christian claims about Jesus as the Jewish Messiah were true? *Nostra Aetate* read, in other words, like a post-Shoah attempt to disassociate the Church from the diabolical effects of its own teaching without really addressing the problem of that teaching.

Instead of reexamining the oppositional habit of mind according to which Jews were defined as the Church's negative other, the council fathers seemed to think it was enough to say of Jesus that he was from the Jews. Wasn't he "the son of the Virgin Mary,"[10] who with the apostles and most of the disciples "sprang from the Jewish people"? Was this more than saying, "Some of our best friends are Jewish"? Jesus, Mary, Peter, John, even the "convert" Paul — Jews all! How could that pronouncement seem an illumination? Yet it was. Basic questions about Christian assumptions of superiority were sidestepped, perhaps, and a definition of Jewishness keyed to suffering was left intact, but the council document still blasted the lid off Christian prejudice. It was far from nothing that the most savage antisemitic stereotypes, which were also the most ingrained, were roundly repudiated by the Church. For example, imagine Mary in a conical hat. Imagine Mary as guilty of the murder of her son. Roman Catholicism's absolute reverence for the mother of Jesus, once she was seen to be a Jew, could open the way to a new realm of religious imagination. Thus Paul VI saluted "especially the Jews, of whom we ought never to disapprove and whom we ought never to mistrust, but to whom we must show reverence and love, and in whom we must place our hope."[11]

What could such words have meant to that focused yet confused twenty-two-year-old man, with the freckles and big ears, whom I see in the photographs taken of me then? *Nostra Aetate* still proclaimed "the burden of the Church's preaching to proclaim the cross of Christ," so the spine of my vocation was intact, if not stiffened. It was the cross, the document said, that "reconciled Jews and gentiles, making both one in Himself." "No salvation outside the Church" was entirely passé by then, but there would still be no salvation outside the cross. So whether Jews knew it or not — liked it or not — the cross itself, whoever hammered its nails, would one day be revealed to them, too, as "the fountain from which every grace flows." Jews, I told myself, would one day know what I already knew. We Christians would never again kill them for it, and in the new spirit of ecumenism we might not refer to it, but eventually Jews would know that they were wrong. If one pope could speak of Jews as our hope, why should not another speak of Auschwitz as a contemporary Golgotha?

A few days after watching the pope's *Nostra Aetate* speech on television, we saw news coverage of a young Quaker named Norman Morrison protesting the war in Vietnam by immolating himself on the pavement outside the Pentagon. "A column of orange flame leapt twelve feet high as the clothes and flesh burned," Robert McNamara's biographer would later write.[12] Compared to the eruption of the Vietnam War as a source of my personal turmoil, the reshaping of Catholic attitudes toward Jews, *Nostra Aetate* notwithstanding, should have induced a subtler shift, but something else cracked the bedrock of Roman Catholic certainty around that time. In 1965, a play by Rolf Hochhuth, a German Protestant, was charging Pope Pius XII with a primary responsibility for the Holocaust. Known as *The Deputy* in the United States and *The Representative* in Britain — both titles rendered a word usually given in English as "Vicar," as in "the Vicar of Christ" — the play accounted for the pope's refusal to condemn openly the Nazi anti-Jewish genocide by implying that he cynically played a game of realpolitik, sympathizing with Germany and narrowly seeking only the Vatican's welfare.[13]

Pius XII was my first pope. When they had told me at St. Mary's School in Alexandria that His Holiness could not make a mistake, I had no trouble believing it. His bespectacled profile adorned the covers of *The Pope Speaks*, the periodical pamphlet that was often in our house. The same profile was etched within a wooden frame inside our front door, and a larger, more colorful photograph of the same face hung above the blackboards at our school. That face functioned as a Catholic icon, and loyalty to the pope was the way we measured our religious faith. The doctrine of papal infallibility was always hedged by the restriction that it was limited to "matters of faith and morals," but I grew up taking the broad perfection of Pius XII for granted. He was our living saint.

And then *The Deputy*. "Whoever wants to help must not provoke Hitler," Hochhuth's pope says. "Secretly . . . silently, cunning as serpents — that is how the SS must be met."[14] But an old Jesuit advisor, Fontana, says, "Your Holiness, may I ask in all humility: Warn Hitler that you will *compel* five hundred million Catholics to make Christian protest if he goes on with these mass killings!" To which the pope replies, "Fontana! An advisor of your insight! How bitter that you too misunderstand Us. Do you not see that disaster looms for Christian Europe unless God makes Us, the Holy See, the *mediator?*"[15]

To Hochhuth's pope, Communism is the real evil to be resisted. "Hitler alone, dear Count, is now defending Europe. And he will fight until he dies because no pardon awaits the murderer. Nevertheless, the West *should* grant him pardon as long as he is useful in the East."[16] This portrait of Pius XII has been discredited — "at best, a very dubious sort of armchair psychologizing," as one critic put it.[17] *The Deputy* sought to scapegoat the Vatican at a time when other major institutions of the West — Swiss banks, the Red Cross, French governmental offices, the U.S. State Department, Volkswagen, Bayer, and others — were still in rank denial of their share in responsibility for the near success of the Nazi project. Pius XII's defenders mocked the idea that a word from him could have deterred, or even slowed down, the Final Solution. Nevertheless, there was a ring of truth in the denunciation of the pope's World War II "silence," and no one heard it more clearly than we seminarians.

We knew enough to contrast Pius XII's silence in relation to Nazism with his forthright condemnations of Communism, including his 1949 excommunication, "at a stroke," of Communist Party members everywhere in the world.[18] Yet not even Hitler was ever excommunicated, and it shamed us to realize only now that the German dictator died still on the rolls of the Roman Catholic Church into which he had been baptized as an infant.[19] So we passed contraband copies of *The Deputy* from hand to hand as if it were pornography, and for a time the debate among us was endless. In one heated session I remember, we read passages from the play's climax to each other. It concerns the harsh fact of the Gestapo roundup of Jews in Rome, "as it were, under the pope's window."

We learned that it was true. On October 16, 1943, more than twelve hundred Jews were arrested practically within sight of the Apostolic Palace. They were held for a time in a building a stone's throw from the Vatican, then taken away, most to die in Auschwitz. There is no record of a public Church protest. "He who knows evil is being done, and does nothing to stop it, is guilty with the evildoer" — the aphorism is attributed to Saint Ambrose of Milan.[20] Years later, Pius XII's defenders would insist that he worked behind the scenes to help Jews, and, in particular, that he quickly, if quietly, brought the Roman deportations to a halt. We will see more of the question later, but for now, suffice to say that such assertions remain in dispute.

In the 1960s any suggestion of papal failure landed with a jolt. Hochhuth's contempt for the pope offended us — Hochhuth was a German Protestant, after all — but his central thesis, pointing to the absence of any open resistance, seemed finally irrefutable: If Christ's "deputy" would say nothing even as Jews were hauled away at the foot of Vatican Hill, Hitler could reasonably count on Church silence everywhere. And Church silence licensed the silence of others. At the very least, Pius XII was guilty of a serious strategic mistake. Within a couple of years, we seminarians could pass among ourselves the report of Hannah Arendt, recounted in her essay "Angelo Giuseppe Roncalli: A Christian on St. Peter's Chair, from 1958 to 1963," that not long before his death, Pope John XXIII had read *The Deputy*. "[He] was asked what one could do against it," Arendt wrote. "Whereupon he allegedly replied: 'Do against it? What can you do against the truth?'"[21] The story made John XXIII's memory even more precious to us, but his simple authenticity was coming to seem like an exception, as much in relation to ourselves as to Pius XII.

In the same period, fueling our debate along with our anxiety, there appeared a book by a Catholic sociologist named Gordon Zahn entitled *German Catholics and Hitler's Wars*. It was a frontal assault on our proudly held assumption that German Catholicism — typified by Konrad Adenauer, a concentration camp survivor and the postwar architect of the democratic West Germany I had seen for myself — had been a bastion of anti-Nazi resistance. As a teenager in Germany, I had had no knowledge of the uses to which such a myth was being put — enabling the Catholic-dominated Christian Democratic Party to serve as the spine of Allied containment of the Soviet Union. With Zahn's work, the myth of German Catholic heroism collapsed. He applied Saint Thomas's principle of the just war to the German situation in the 1930s and 1940s, showed how Hitler's war was in obvious violation, and how, nevertheless, Catholics enthusiastically supported it. The German Catholic hierarchy and clergy, in particular, were guilty of a grievous moral failure, and we saw it. "In World

War II," Zahn wrote, "the leading spokesmen of the Catholic Church in Germany did become channels of Nazi control over their followers, whether by their exhortations to loyal obedience to legitimate authority, or by their even more direct efforts to rally those followers to the defense of *Volk, Vaterland,* and *Heimat* as a Christian duty."[22] Support of Hitler was not only allowed to Catholics, but was required of them.

But just as I turned away from devotion to my mother toward conflict with my father, away from Europe's past agony toward the brutal war in Vietnam, away from the nightmare question of Jew hatred in the name of Jesus toward white people's hatred of yellow people — just then, a Jew came as powerfully and unexpectedly into the story as, in a different way, years before, Peter Seligman had. "To speak about God," Abraham Joshua Heschel said in 1965, "and remain silent on Vietnam is blasphemous."[23] In that year of *Nostra Aetate, The Deputy,* and Operation Rolling Thunder, the year of Norman Morrison, Rabbi Heschel joined with Daniel Berrigan, William Sloane Coffin, and others in founding Clergy Concerned about Vietnam, which quickly evolved, in that anticlerical time, into Clergy and Laity Concerned.[24] At my seminary, St. Paul's College, we formed a chapter, which, in my weak-kneed case, would provide the support I needed not just to break with the war but with my father. And that conflict was what drew me to Heschel, who seemed like nothing if not a father one could trust.

Abraham Joshua Heschel was a longtime professor at the Jewish Theological Seminary of America in New York. He was, in his daughter Susannah's phrase, "an Orthodox Jew with a white beard and yarmulke."[25] Yet he was something for me, too. He was born in Warsaw in 1907, but he went to Berlin for university and rabbinical studies. His early work on the prophets of Israel established his reputation, but it also forged a moral vision that joined piety and hunger for social justice — always a dangerous combination. One night in 1938, the Gestapo rousted him from his apartment, expelling him from Germany back to Poland, which he then fled just ahead of the Nazi invasion. His mother and two sisters died in the Shoah. (A third sister was killed during the invasion.) Heschel made his way to New York, describing himself later as a "brand plucked from the fire of Europe."[26]

His daughter, Susannah Heschel, is a professor of Jewish studies at Dartmouth. She writes of her father, "His survival was a gift, because he became a unique religious voice in an era in which religion was in grave danger."[27] In the early and mid 1950s, he published two works that remain classics of American theology: *Man Is Not Alone* and *God in Search of Man*. He was at the peak of his intellectual influence when I entered the seminary. As was true for many Christians, my reading of Heschel, sparked by his resolute rejection of my father's war, was my first direct experience of postbiblical Jewish thought. To read Heschel was to step aboard the endangered but still seaworthy idea that the most transforming adventure of all can be intellectual. Heschel changed my notions not only of Judaism but of religion itself, and of God.

As is obvious by now, I had been raised with an anachronistic idea of Judaism: the Scribes and the Pharisees, worship at the Temple, the stereotype of the vengeful Old Testament God. Catholics like me knew nothing of the living tradition of Jewish thought and observance, ignorance that reflected the Christian assertion that after Jesus, Israel had been superseded by the "new Israel," the Church. Heschel's vital theology, rooted in a biblical vision but informed by two millennia of rabbinical wisdom, was a stark rebuttal of all this. "The central thought of Judaism is *the living God*," he wrote. "The craving for God has never subsided in the Jewish soul."[28] Heschel put words on that craving as I experienced it, requiring me to revise entirely what I thought of Judaism. He did something similar for many Catholics. Indeed, he was present as a consultant at the Second Vatican Council, helping to shape *Nostra Aetate*.

Heschel was a loving critic of religion, his own included. He had seen with his own eyes the failure of religion to resist Nazism, and his testimony forced a generation of Christians as well as Jews to see through "parochial saintliness," how easily it can amount to "an evasion of duty." It was worth volumes of theology to see his white beard and yarmulke in the front ranks of the march in Selma, Alabama, arms linked with Martin Luther King, Jr. A photograph of the pair gave me my first image of Heschel. I never met him, although I heard him preach at a service on the eve of an antiwar demonstration in Washington, D.C. I don't recall what he said, but I felt his gentle authority as an antidote to the self-righteous judgmentalism of the radicals who never failed to make me nervous on the streets.

But politics paled: The deepest change I trace to this rabbi is in my notion of God. I remember thinking at first that the title of his masterwork, *God in Search of Man,* was backwards. Aren't we the ones who do the searching? Hadn't that been my own frenzied experience dating back to those pilgrimages with Mom, or to the cross-bearing cell in a Georgetown retreat house? "My heart is restless, Lord," I'd learned to say with Saint Augustine, "until it rests in Thee." But what if the restlessness is God's? In Heschel's view, God was not the aloof, detached figure of the scholastics, whom I was studying in the classroom — the "Unmoved Mover" — but a lover who creates human beings out of a passionate longing. Our craving is met by God's own. "To be is to stand for," he wrote, "and what human beings stand for is the great mystery of being God's partner. God is in need of human beings."²⁹ Susannah Heschel says that the idea of God's need for us is "the central pillar" of her father's theology.³⁰ God needs partners in gathering up the precious fragments of the earth into a new whole of peace and justice. Impossible? "The grand premise of religion," the rabbi wrote, "is that man is able to surpass himself."³¹

By the time Rabbi Heschel died, on December 23, 1972, I was a priest, the Roman Catholic chaplain at Boston University. When I had received that assignment upon ordination in 1969, a senior priest of the order had poked me, intending a show of sympathy. "B-Jew," he said, implying, for that reason, I would hate the place. He was right about Jews at BU — they made up perhaps a third of the student body — but wrong that I would hate it. Jewish students dominated the peace and civil rights groups that drew me in, much as Catholic students dominated ROTC. As a chaplain, I had ties to both groups, but as the war dragged on, I stopped pretending to be neutral. When I joined a picket line at the entrance to the university placement office, to keep a Marine recruiter out, I realized that the defiant kids who sprawled on the floor to block the doorway were mostly Jews; the kids waiting nervously to be interviewed by the Marine were Catholics. They looked at me with hurt eyes.

A few of us mounted a BU production of *The Trial of the Catonsville Nine,* Daniel Berrigan's antiwar play. "Our apologies, our apologies, Good Friends . . . ," Berrigan the defendant says, "for the fracture of good order . . . for the burning of paper instead of children." The play has a Catholic cast of characters, but we knew to put it on at Hillel House instead of Newman House, the Catholic Center, and not only because of the enviable theater space. Berrigan was a fugitive at the time, and I would later learn that the BU professors helping to hide him, including Howard Zinn and David Rubin, were Jews. Was it that dissent came more naturally to Jews? What was Jewishness in the Christian West, I began to ask, *except* dissent? B-Jew? I too was beginning to think like a Jew. I didn't know yet to wonder if even here, in defining dissent as somehow essentially Jewish, I was assuming the dominance of Christianity and accepting as inevitable a certain pariah status for Jews.

Still, the structure of my inner life had been upended. Had I, in Heschel's phrase, surpassed myself? I wanted very much to think that I had left behind my anti-Jewish triumphalism. That fall, with many others, I had experienced in a flash of recognition something of what the Holocaust must have meant when eleven Israeli Olympic athletes were murdered in Munich by the terrorist group Black September. It was the first time I had any idea of what the explicit and exclusive targeting of Jews *as Jews* meant. By then we had been through the assassinations and riots of the sixties, had thought ourselves hardened, but Munich revealed a horror we had heard of but never felt. "Munich," to our parents, meant Chamberlain's appeasement of Hitler, but to us it spoke of the anti-Jewish genocide.

Out of that recognition, and, as I thought, out of my complete identification, I proposed to the BU rabbi a joint Jewish-Christian memorial service so that the whole community could express its grief and rage at that crime. I sensed the rabbi's reluctance. For him, I think, the events at Munich had reinforced an old feeling of isolation and rejection, and it seemed a time for an expressly Jewish solidarity. But I pressed, assuring him that we had all experienced the murders as Jews had. Finally, he agreed. And then I proposed as the place to hold the service the monumental Marsh Chapel in the center of the campus. It is a kitsch-Gothic church, a vestige of Boston University's origins as a Methodist school. It seemed an entirely ecumenical venue to me: We Catholics had only recently been permitted to use it for Mass. It was a function of my "parochial saintliness" to assume that that inter-Christian denominational breakthrough had made Marsh Chapel everyone's. The rabbi, though, could not keep the surprise from his face. Marsh Chapel? That vaulted hall with the cross suspended above an altar? "No way," he said to me, but bitterly. You still don't get it, do you?

I could have told him, Some of my best friends are Jews. That spring, determined to defuse the anti-Jewish powder keg of Holy Week, I invited some Jewish friends to join us at Newman House for a Passover Seder. The Jews present were not, to my knowledge, religious, and it did not occur to me not to preside. As I went through the Haggadah, having carefully rehearsed, I felt personally responsible to undo centuries' worth of Christian Holy Week Jew hatred. I was celebrating the Jewishness of Jesus, having come to the belief, I suppose, that nothing significant really separated our two religions. Implicitly I assumed that once Jesus was proclaimed in his Jewishness, Jews would finally accept him. When I lifted the matzo, I cited his act at the Last Supper, *his* Seder. "This is my body," I said, "broken for you." Moved, I sought the eyes of my Jewish friends, but did not find them. Religious or not, they knew better than to join me in my presumptuous gesture. I would not recognize it for what it was until years later.

When the priest at the consecration says, "This is the cup of the New Covenant," he is pronouncing the Old Covenant superfluous. Its job, after Jesus, is to leave the sanctuary. The Jew's job is to disappear. From a Christian point of view, just by continuing to exist, Jews dissent. Because of the threat it poses to the faith of the Church, that dissent can be defined by Christians as the core of Jewish belief, which of course continues the insult. These were the currents running below the surface of that liturgy. By refusing to meet my eyes, my Jewish friends were withholding assent from my Seder-turned-Eucharist. Even as I wished to root out the ancient assumptions, in other words, I was reiterating them. Old Testament promise leads to New Testament fulfillment. Real prayer involves Jesus. The "chosenness" of Israel extends to all human beings. I felt deputized — a "deputy" myself — to declare for Jews the universal extension of their covenant with God, whose name I felt free to pronounce aloud. The New Covenant was my watchword as I claimed a kind of Jewishness myself, not knowing yet to call it "Judaizing." Christian Jewishness was only the awareness of having been adopted into God's chosen people, as my patron Paul had put it. But if, through Jesus, God "chooses" everybody, why are the once chosen Jews still here? I'd been taught to think of that as Paul's question, as if he were the first Christian universalist.[32]

And always, like a stake in the heart of such considerations, there stood the cross. Before the cross, in my most solemn moments, I bowed. I had long since left behind my personal share of the anguish of my brother's polio — he had grown by then into a confident young scholar — but the anguish of my own unhappiness as a young American at the mercy of that conflicted age was pointed. I lay the bundle of my feelings before the cross each day, and in truth the burden lifted as the cross carried some of its weight away. In particular, my noontime routine of saying the Mass — the *sacrifice* of the Mass — was deeply consoling. What I prayed for mostly was peace.

The war had become my personal obsession. Indeed, the silence of American bishops on Vietnam — what Rabbi Heschel had called "blasphemy" — had become, to my mind, a replay of the silence of German bishops. That was the occasion of a life-changing epiphany: If American B-52s had been dropping condoms on Vietnam, as wags noted, the Roman Catholic hierarchy would have vigorously and unambiguously condemned the war as intrinsically immoral. But they had no moral competence to make such a judgment, they said in effect, because the B-52s were only dropping napalm. On that Good Friday, I joined a protest demonstration outside the residence of Boston's cardinal archbishop. Standing on the sidewalk before passing traffic, I held up a sign that I had lettered myself: "Another Crucifixion in Indochina." Yet it had not occurred to me that it was mostly Christians who were dropping gelatinous fire on the heads of mostly Buddhists. Would Buddhists have been consoled to be told they were Jesus Christ?

This was the time of my self-surpassing, in Heschel's word, yet I heard nothing discordant in a line I often quoted from our hero Thomas Merton, that war in the nuclear age is an evil "second only to the crucifixion."[33] Long the touchstone of my religious imagination, the crucifixion had become my political touchstone as well. *The Non-Violent Cross* was the title of a book by James Douglass that caught the spirit of our engaged theology. "One finds real revolution . . . ," Douglass wrote, "by immersing oneself in the dark beauty of space and time where the crucifixion of man is felt most deeply."[34]

"I will give you the treasures of darkness," the Lord told Isaiah, "and the hoards in secret places that you may know that it is I, the Lord."[35] Eventually, there was nothing beautiful in my darkness, and the sum of my twenties seemed the farthest thing from treasure. In January 1973, the American phase of the Vietnam War ended. The American-supplied South Vietnamese army would fight on for two more years, but GIs fired their last shots on January 22. It was the day Lyndon Johnson died of heart failure in Texas, the day the Supreme Court handed down its *Roe v. Wade* decision concerning abortion, and the day I turned thirty. By then, everything I believed in had been upended. There seemed only one place for me to go, given the shape of those beliefs, to try to set them right.

The next turn in my story took me to Jerusalem. Only in hindsight does it seem inevitable that I should have gone there in the summer of 1973, following the war's end and my coming to maturity. "It had something to do with God," I wrote, the first sentence of a journal I kept during that sojourn. "At the Holy Sepulcher, I tried to imagine the death of Jesus. But all I could see were the warring monks, the bad art, the dollar candles and the tourists." Treasures of darkness? By coming to Jerusalem at this point in my life, I learned that I did not even know what my question was. The calcified geography was no help. I looked for the place where they had crucified my Lord, and I could not find it.

It was the summer before the Yom Kippur War. One day in August, on the Jewish fast of Tisha b'Av, I joined the thousands of Jews hurrying into the Old City, passing closed stalls and shops, going through alleys, gates, and checkpoints, down into the vast open space before the Western Wall. I covered my head and watched as the devout approached the wall, waiting their turn to touch it, to squeeze jotted prayers into its crevices, to kiss the stones. On Tisha b'Av, the ninth day of the month of Av, Jews mourn the destruction of the Temple. A story in the tradition says that when the Romans set fire to the Temple, six angels came down from heaven, lighting on top of the Western Wall. As the violence mounted and the fire intensified, the angels wept. Their tears kept the flames away from that one part of the Temple, which is why the wall survives to this day. Those angels are still there, tradition says, and they are still weeping.

Another tradition says that on Tisha b'Av, each of the children of Israel who had left Egypt dug his grave, and that night he slept in it. In the morning, fifteen thousand of the people did not wake up. Their graves were filled in, and the rest of the people continued to wander. Each year for the forty years that Israel wandered in the wilderness, the same thing happened — everyone sleeping in his grave on that day, and all but fifteen thousand waking up. This is how it came to pass that, by the time the children of Israel entered the Promised Land, all of the generation that came from Egypt were dead. And for this reason, to this day, on Tisha b'Av a Jew sleeps with a stone beneath his pillow, a symbol of his grave.[36]

On Tisha b'Av I stood before the surviving wall of the Temple, ignorant of the Arab houses that had been leveled in 1967 to make room for such gatherings. The Palestinian complaint had not registered with me. My theology had been recast by the Holocaust, and central to it now was not the innocence of Jesus but of Jews. I had come to depend as much on a notion of Jewish victimhood as my forebears depended on an idea of Jewish villainy. The symmetry of my theological assumptions required, in effect, that Jews replace Jesus on the cross. And just as it was once forbidden to ask if Jesus could have sinned, so, by the time of my arrival in Jerusalem, was it forbidden to ask if the state of Israel could commit acts of injustice. The symmetry of a supersessionist imagination still required that Jews fulfill a set of Christian expectations. Jewish victimhood and innocence had trumped the charge of deicide.

The Yom Kippur War, only months away, would begin to change all this, as the illusion of Israel's exemption from the rules of real-world politics would be harder to sustain. The "creation of facts" on the West Bank, with Jewish settlers usurping Palestinian land; the ruthless Israeli invasion of Lebanon in 1982; the Intifada and the Israeli war against Arab teenagers; the push-pull of Likud and Labor; the political rise of messianic Orthodoxy — through it all, Israel refused to enact a script written by the West, which is to say, by Christians. It seemed an old story. Christian disappointment in the harsh policies of Israel would fuel a new current of mutual suspicion. Israel, a nation like other nations, with a hard-line pursuit of narrowly defined self-interest? But wasn't Israel, born of the ashes of Auschwitz, required thereby to be different? Why else had the children of Israel slept in graves, if not to be resurrected as more than others? These were questions of which, in 1973, I was entirely innocent. And I was ignorant of the painful history that would eventually demand an accounting — this accounting.

In truth, my first journey to Jerusalem was a journey more into myself than into history, ancient or recent. I was less a pilgrim than a refugee, yet Jerusalem opened itself to me. Jews refuse to refer to the Western Wall as the Wailing Wall anymore — it is referred to by many as the Kotel — yet it was grief that seized me. I felt no presence of weeping angels, and when I raised my eyes to the Temple, it was no longer there. In Jerusalem — "Jerusalem my mother," Augustine wrote[37] — my own consoling faith revealed itself as having been destroyed. In Jerusalem I could admit that the time had come for me to leave the priesthood. Augustine, too, would be displeased.

A few months later, perhaps as the Yom Kippur War raged and as another annihilation of Jews seemed possible, I began the formal process of "laicization." Oddly, I now understand that I left the Catholic priesthood as a way of preserving my Catholic faith, for by then I could only have a doubter's faith. A dissenting priest is a figure of the absurd; I already knew that. I had become a priest because of the cross, and I stopped being a priest because . . . Was it the Vietnam War? Was it the German bishops and the American echo of their silence? Was it the hatred I sensed at the cold heart of my own Church? Silence, I would learn, was the least of it.

Rabbi Heschel taught me not only that silence can be blasphemy, but that the breach between his kind and mine can be a form of blasphemy too. Indeed, didn't the one lead to the other? In Heschel's God I saw mine, which taught me that Catholics and Jews did not have to be enemies — in fact, should not have been. Heschel, "the brand plucked from the fire of

Europe," was a living demonstration of the permanent relevance of the Holocaust, not just to Zionists or other Jews, but for anyone longing to believe in God today, including, and perhaps especially, the Catholics who recognized themselves in that white-bearded rabbi. "Religion," Heschel wrote, "is the source of dissatisfaction with the self."[38] What befell the Jews of Europe in the twentieth century is the source of the Church's dissatis-faction, whether the Church knows it yet or not. It is surely the source of mine. That it took the Holocaust to open an honorable and reciprocal di-alogue between Jews and Christians is an outrage. But that the Holocaust requires us, personally as well as institutionally, to understand how such events were prepared for by other events is an absolute moral legacy. The question posed itself not to me but to history: How did the cross of Jesus Christ become the cross at Auschwitz?

But the cross at Auschwitz raises its first question about the cross in Je-rusalem. When the crucifixion of a particular man at a particular place and time is removed from the realm of the vividly real — the abject failure it could only have been to Jesus and those who loved him — and made a universal emblem of victory over death, does it become something false? We will see how, once the crucifixion was made central to Christian piety, the Jews came to the forefront of Christian consciousness as the enacters of that crucifixion, and how their being tagged as such amounts to slan-der. But here I am asking something more basic, a question prior to the question implied by *Nostra Aetate:* Who killed Jesus?[39]

Or perhaps that is just the question after all. We will see how Saint Paul domesticated the meaning of the cross in such a way that, ultimately, con-solation-seeking Christians could erect it at a death camp. But what a strange consolation. Those coming after Paul, especially, as we will see, Saint Anselm, would regard the crucifixion as God's saving will, would conclude, that is, that the killer of Jesus was God. And since God, despite everything, was to be trusted, death was deprived of its sting. Even the death of Jesus. In this way, Paul turned the Roman execution device back on the Romans, as the first generations of Christian martyrs, going to deaths equally willed by God, would turn their violent deaths into the fer-tile ground of a burgeoning Christian faith.

The crucifixion of Jesus Christ, as interpreted by Paul and later incor-porated in the Passion narratives of the Gospels, became an image of hope precisely because it gave such complete expression to despair. The brutal death of one taken to be the Messiah, a defeat that included his being abandoned by his most cherished and committed followers, would not have been enough to brace the religious imaginations of believers through their own brutal deaths. The awful fate of Jesus on the cross had to be the fate chosen for him by God. Only then could abject failure itself be transformed. Among followers of Jesus, remembering his last words as "My God, my God, why have you abandoned me?" — the felt experience of God's murderous absence, which reaches to the religious heart of human mortality — would not undercut faith but prompt it. By sacralizing the profane cross in this way, Paul gave Rome an unprecedented problem: How do you defeat a movement that defines defeat as victory?[40]

But when the Christian movement, so ingeniously braced, became the victorious Church, this structure of meaning reversed itself, a development that, beginning with Constantine, we will track in this book. The triumphalism of an empowered Christianity led to a betrayal of faith that all of pagan Rome's legions had failed to bring about. And what reveals that betrayal so clearly, of course, is the Church's relations with the Jews. It was at Nicaea — the city named for Nike, the goddess of victory — at the council enshrining the Christian victory, that Constantine, forbidding the observance of Easter at Passover time, declared, "It is unbecoming that on the holiest of festivals we should follow the customs of the Jews; henceforth let us have nothing in common with this odious people."[41] But in this victory — here is the other side of Saint Paul's magnificent irony — lay the seeds of the defeat implied in that "henceforth," and which we must now chronicle.

In what follows we will see that the Church, precisely when it claims to be above the human condition, embodies the human condition. This is no revelation to Jews, who have stood as witnesses against Christian self-aggrandizement from the beginning. From the beginning theirs has been, in a phrase of Rosemary Radford Ruether's, a "prophetic critique refused."[42]

This refusal extends to central Christian affirmations about the Messiahship of Jesus Christ, because a Messiahship defined by an idea of redemption that occurs outside history could seem to Jews like Messiahship cut loose from biblical hope. Jews awaited a Messiah whose redemptive act would heal not another world — "My kingdom," Jesus said, "is not of this world" — but *this* one. We will see in Part Two how the rejection of messianic claims for Jesus, far from heretical, was required of a religious Jew by everything he'd been taught to value and defend as a faithful son of Abraham, Isaac, and Jacob. Thus, to the rabbis, Jesus came to exemplify the "false Messiah," and the rejection of Jesus came to be a measure of Jewish devotion. Rabbi Irving Greenberg, a New York–based veteran of Jewish-Christian dialogue and chair of the U.S. Holocaust Memorial Museum, suggests that in this the rabbis made a mistake. "Out of defensiveness," he writes, "the rabbis confused a 'failed' messiah (which is what Jesus was) and a false messiah. A false messiah is one who has the wrong values . . . A failed messiah is one who has the right values, upholds the covenant, but who did not attain the final goal."[43] Rabbi Greenberg demonstrates how a Jew can retrieve some measure of reverence for Jesus by seeing him in the context of other failed Messiahs, like Bar Kochba, who led the unsuccessful revolt against Rome in 130 c.e. Greenberg goes so far as to compare the failure of Jesus with the "failures" of Abraham, Moses, and Jeremiah, each of whom died without attaining the final goal.

But the notion of Jesus as a failed Messiah can take the faith of a Christian even further. Instead of blithely assuming that the plan of God was fulfilled in the disaster of the crucifixion, we might consider that, in the mystery of God's submission to human freedom, God's plan for creation was profoundly thwarted. It is important to know, as the third part of this book will show, that the idea of the Father of Jesus callously presiding over his son's death, willed by the Father as a means of salvation, takes root in the Christian imagination only with the emperor Constantine, at a time when he had compelling political and personal reasons for embracing such an ideology. It is equally important to know, as Part Four describes, that this idea takes lasting root in Christian theology only with Saint Anselm, who saw in the mortal obedience of the Son of God a courtly adjudication proper to the violent eleventh century. God is the offended Lord who must be appeased by an offering commensurate with the offense, and the only such offering the Son of God could make was his death. What if Constantine and Anselm and all those who, following them, have gilded the cross, turning it into a symbol of triumphalism, are in understandable but mistaken flight from the more evident meaning of the cross — that the world remains unredeemed?

The cross at Auschwitz puts the question baldly: Who is this God who requires human suffering and death as a proof of human subservience? What does it mean that the death and suffering of Jesus have been made the source of salvation? Does it mean that the deaths and sufferings of all other human beings are fit, in my mother's phrase, to be "offered up," like so many turtledoves, so many goats? It is the rejection of even the hint of such sacrificial thinking that prompts some Jews to refuse to refer to the events of the Shoah as a "holocaust," the burnt offering with smoke wafting up to heaven.

But what does this do to our understanding of God? "The worst day of my life was Tuesday, January 11, 1983." This is the Reverend William Sloane Coffin, the distinguished former chaplain of Yale who, with Rabbi Heschel and Daniel Berrigan, founded Clergy and Laity Concerned about Vietnam. Coffin is an eloquent preacher, and it seems fitting that his words should make the dark meaning of this theology clear. Coffin is referring to the day that his twenty-four-year-old son, Alex, died. The eulogy he preached at Riverside Church in New York includes these lines:

> When a person dies there are many things that can be said, and there is at least one thing that should never be said . . . The night after Alex died, a kind woman came into the house carrying about 18 quiches, saying sadly, "I just don't understand the will of God."
>
> I exploded. "I'll say you don't, lady. Do you think it was the will of God that Alex never fixed that lousy windshield wiper, that he was probably driving too fast in such a storm, that he probably had had a couple of beers too many? Do you think it is God's will that there are no streetlights on that road and no guardrail separating that right-angle turn from Boston Harbor?"
>
> For some reason, nothing so infuriates me as the incapacity of seemingly intelligent people to get it through their heads that God doesn't go around this world with his finger on triggers, his fist on knives, his hands on steering wheels. Deaths that are untimely and slow and pain-ridden raise unanswerable questions . . . Never do we know enough to say that a death was the will of God . . . My own consolation lies in knowing that it was not the will of God that Alex die; that when the waves closed over the sinking car, God's heart was the first of all our hearts to break.[44]

The alternative to thinking of God as a "cosmic sadist . . . an eternal vivisector," in Coffin's phrases, is to stand before the unfathomable mystery of death — the death of Jesus, the death of one's own son, the deaths of the six million — without attempting to understand it, and also without attempting to deny its character as a terrible outbreak of evil. It is here that these questions break out of any narrow reference to religion, Christian or Jewish, to press against the awful anxiety that every human must feel in the face of death. For all of the questions entangled in the cross at Auschwitz are put to every person, even if here they seem cast in the categories of theology and history. How do we live on earth with failure and evil? Not only the evil done to us, but the evil we do? How do we come in contact with the transcendent for which every human spirit longs? Or is it possible to hope, as Heschel does, that the transcendent longs for us?

→ 7 ←

Between Past and Future

I N ADDITION TO signifying the problem that death puts to God, whether a Jew's God or a Christian's, the cross at Auschwitz evokes with rare immediacy everything that has separated Jew and Christian during the two-thousand-year-old conflict between the two religions. The technical term for that conflict is supersessionism, a word I have already used. It comes from the Latin *supersedere,* meaning "to sit upon."[1] The idea is that the Jesus movement, as it evolved into the Church, effectively replaced the Jews as the chosen people of God. Replacement became the motif, even in trivial ways, and even in relation to the emerging symbol of the cross: Before any follower of Jesus had touched a hand to forehead, heart, and shoulders, making the "sign of the cross," some Jews had used a similar manual rubric to symbolize the Hebrew letter with which the word "Torah" begins.[2] When the Jesus movement took up the sign — it is referred to in Tertullian (c. 160–225)[3] — rabbinic Judaism dropped it.

As we shall see in Part Two, Christianity "sat upon" Judaism by claiming to be the "true Israel." Saint Paul is commonly regarded as the initiator of this claim, indeed its poet laureate, especially in Romans 9–11: "Brethren, my heart's desire and prayer to God for [the Jews] is that they may be saved . . . [but] they did not submit to God's righteousness. For Christ is the end of the law, that every one who has faith may be justified."[4] Paul's attitudes toward "the Jews" were, in fact, far more complex than such citations indicate, and we will see more of that, too. Suffice to note here that, from a very early time, Jews were dismissed by Christians as custodians of a false Israel. The New Testament "sat upon" the Old Testament, the New Covenant upon the Old, and so on.

This dynamic is classically enacted by younger siblings usurping the place of older siblings, and the pattern is even played out repeatedly in

Jewish religious mythology. One need think only of Cain and Abel, Ishmael and Isaac, Reuben and Judah, Menassah and Ephraim, Jacob and Esau, Joseph and his older brothers. In each case, the younger sees his brother as hoarding the family blessing, which amounts, of course, to the love of the parent. Sibling rivalry, a struggle for the most precious thing there is, presumes its scarcity. A parent has only so much love, and what one sibling gets, or so the feeling runs, comes at the expense of the other — a dread echoed, for example, in the "bitter cry" of the supplanted Esau: "Bless me, even me also, O my father! . . . Have you not reserved a blessing for me? . . . Have you but one blessing, my father? Bless me, even me also, O my father." And Esau, the Scripture says, "lifted up his voice and wept."[5]

That this pattern provides the structure of Jewish-Christian conflict only proves how deeply rooted in Judaism the Church is.[6] But something new began to happen when the energy of such a conflict was generated by Christian claims over the Jews. On the one hand, there was a mortal aspect to this competition, with the Christian assumption that the no longer chosen people had forfeited their right to continue in existence, especially once the power relationship between the two groups had shifted. Replacement implied the elimination of the replaced. This strain would lead to conversionism and expulsions, and ultimately it would be reduced to its perverted essence by the attempted genocide. On the other hand, Christianity's self-awareness depended on the continuing existence of the Jewish people as the negative other against which positive Christian claims were made. "Christianity could have had no other religion as precursor," Søren Kierkegaard wrote, "for no other but Judaism could establish, by means of negation, so definitely, so decisively what Christianity is."[7] This is what has always set Jews apart from every other religious entity with which Christianity has found itself in conflict, whether it be the "pagans" of the ancient world or, say, the Buddhists of today. Only Jews, because of what they deny, tell us Christians who we are — which is why, as an enemy, Jews have always been the enemy inside. This dynamic would play itself out in various ways through the centuries, from Augustine to the rationalist theologians of the Middle Ages, to the Catholic anti-Semites of post-Enlightenment France.

What emerges here is a Christian response to Jews that is defined by its ambivalence. In the long course of Christian Europe's history with the Jews, there were many times when the positive side of that ambivalence held sway, to good effect. We will see that, for example, in Iberia, in Renaissance Italy, and during the Enlightenment. But when the negative en-

ergy of this conflict outweighed the positive, the result was so dispropor-
tionately lethal as to raise the question of whether Christians had kept
Jews "inside" for any other purpose than mortal betrayal. What kind of
ambivalence is it when even the positive aspect is finally revealed as serving a negative end that reveals itself as absolute? Such is the ambivalence
uncovered by the cross at Auschwitz: The mass graves are the ultimate
evil, but they are also a source of ultimate redemption. Those who squirm
in the presence of the cross at that place do so out of a sense that honoring such ambivalence there only enshrines supersessionism more grotesquely than ever. If the sight of that cross forces us into an exploration of
the past, it is not for "so-called lessons of history,"[8] but to understand
where that ambivalence comes from, and to ask if there can be a future
without it.

So here I am, at the foot of the cross at Auschwitz. I will remain here, in
effect, throughout the telling of this story. Here the sibling rivalry between
Judaism and Christianity has been twisted into a contest not over who
is the "true Israel" but over who can lay claim to the mantle of "suffering servant," an image that the Church applies to Jesus but that originates in the prophecy of Isaiah. Here suffering has been defined as the
source of identity, and ironically, on the Christian side, as the source of superiority. That is what it means when Polish Catholics from towns around
Auschwitz complain that their victimhood is being slighted by a Jewish
monopoly on the Holocaust.

It is no small complaint. Polish Catholicism particularly is inclined to
define itself around the idea of its victimhood. Since the nineteenth century and through most of the twentieth, Poland was a self-styled "Christ
among the nations," an epithet associated with the nineteenth-century
Romantic poet Adam Mickiewicz.[9] Poland's passion and death, repeatedly
enacted at the hands of imperialist neighbors from the early 1800s to 1939,
engendered a stoic hope. Poland's suffering would redeem the godlessness
of modern Europe and would at last restore Christendom. This ideology
braces Karol Wojtyla, and, as the Polish pope, especially in his years of decline, John Paul II has become an embodiment of suffering. In March
2000, he made a pilgrimage to Israel and Jerusalem which, despite the
thicket of political and religious problems that awaited him, was taken to
be, in the words of Israeli Prime Minister Ehud Barak, a "historic journey
of healing."[10] The pope's ability to overcome Jewish misgivings, even those
based on criticisms of what many regarded as the Church's unfinished
self-examination, seemed mainly to be a matter of the patent anguish

with which the ailing pontiff carried himself. As he bent to kiss the bowl of Israeli soil, held to his lips by children, observers could feel the tremor of his pain. As he greeted a Polish woman, a camp survivor who credited him with saving her life near Kraków in 1945, he touched her arm softly, then said of the horror, "It makes us cry out!"[11] The woman wept before him.

To those who saw John Paul II in Jerusalem, he seemed a man prepared to spend the last energy of his life on what had brought him there. As he pressed into a crevice of the Western Wall a piece of paper that included as a prayer the words "We are deeply saddened by the behavior of those who in the course of history caused these children of yours to suffer,"[12] both the sadness and the suffering seemed very real. And when John Paul stood in the shadows of the hall at Yad Vashem, even those who had hoped to hear a more explicit acknowledgment of the failures of the Church to oppose the Holocaust saw something they could never have expected. "The sight of this pope expressing his sorrow," as the historian Karen Armstrong summed up the event, "surrounded by the symbols of Jewish suffering and in the full knowledge that he was being watched closely by millions of people all over the world, was a far more eloquent apology than any sermon or papal document."[13] We will return to the matter of apology later, when the full shape of what requires it has become evident, and when the question of whether the category of apology is adequate can be answered, but here we can recognize the depth of John Paul II's witness, from the dawn of his papacy, to Auschwitz, to its twilight in Jerusalem. He has put the question of Jewish-Christian reconciliation at the center of Catholic concern, and therefore mine.

John Paul II has begun something, not completed it. Difficult questions remain, and the pope's own cross, still at the death camp wall, embodies perhaps the hardest of them, beginning with the question Jews put to Christians at Auschwitz: Where in your theology of redemption is there any room for the bottomless evil that the death camp had to have been for those who died here? Every question I ask in this book will be a way of asking, How did this happen? But I will do so as a way of asking, How might this not have happened? I will be asking, What choices led to this, and who made them? But I will do so as a way of asking, What choices could have led to something else? In pursuing this inquiry, I mark as a kind of mantra the words of John Paul II, spoken in 1999 and repeated in "Memory and Reconciliation" only a week before his journey of healing. The Catholic Church, he said, is "not afraid of the truth that emerges from history and is ready to acknowledge mistakes wherever they have been identified."[14]

I am fifty-seven years old, a quarter of a century out of the Catholic priesthood, which nevertheless defines me still. When I left the priesthood, I was distraught and self-obsessed, yet I knew where to begin such work. What I did not know yet was how. And so once again — but this time with the question clear — I carry it back to Jerusalem, where the story begins, and where, during John Paul II's pilgrimage, its urgency became apparent to the world. This is a story about the cross — as I remember it, as the Church remembers it, and as Jews remember it. Christians and Jews have an obvious stake in such an inquiry, but so does everyone who carries the weight of this history. And who, in our culture, does not?

Hannah Arendt entitled a collection of essays *Between Past and Future*, which evokes the way she pursued the work of history. For Arendt, the present hovers between the remembrance of tragedy past and the desire for a more humane future. But in contrast to the way the past and future are traditionally conceived, for her it is their impact on the present that matters. She quotes Faulkner: "The past is never dead, it is not even past."[15] It is the act of memory, cultivated in the present, in which past and future meet. Memory — as opposed to a mere cataloguing of bygone episodes and doctrines — presumes a personal commitment, a sense of urgency, an implicit hope. Doing history as an act of personal and institutional memory, and not merely as the repetition of records or the reassertion of conventional interpretations, is thus an act of responsibility to the future. History differs from memory, of course, because, to use a distinction of the scholar Paula Fredriksen, public knowledge differs from personal recollection. But both presume an active work of imagination, in resistance to the forces of forgetting that block the way. The past must, in effect, be reinvented, albeit in faithful adherence to the facts of the past as they are able to be known, for "history is in some sense testable," as Fredriksen puts it. "It is in its obligations to both evidence and testability that history as a discipline is scientific."[16]

To expose the biases of the past, however, does not mean one does so free of the biases of the present. It is the nature of bias that the one inflicted with it is the last to know. The study I am undertaking may be no less conditioned than previous perceptions have been. But Arendt's insight is that present experience demands a constant turning to the past, not for the sake of an absolute knowledge, but because the perennially contingent nature of our knowing leaves us no choice but to try to refine it. And in that process, present experience is a constant revelation that reveals the past as never before; equally, the past illuminates the present. "Looking backward," the historian David Landes writes, "we think we know what happened. Looking forward, we have to contemplate diverse outcomes. Such questions focus attention on cause and effect, help us distinguish between major and minor, direct and indirect influences, suggest possibilities otherwise overlooked."[17] The discovery that the past might have gone another way is simultaneously the discovery that the future can be different. The present is revealed as far more open to new meanings than official dogma ever has it, and the future takes on added weight as the source of the questions that must be faced. Still the goal is relatively modest — not to offer ultimate answers to what are, at times, impossible perplexities, but, as Arendt said, "to live with them without becoming, as Sartre once put it, a *salaud*, a hypocrite."[18]

I presume to undertake precisely such a work, and I welcome the participation of fellow Catholics, all Christians, Jewish readers, and everyone who recognizes in the Holocaust the dark heart of our civilization. For all of our sakes, may this be a work, in John Paul II's phrase, of moral memory. "May it enable memory to play its necessary part" — his words bear repeating as a kind of anthem — "in which the unspeakable iniquity of the Shoah will never again be possible."[19]

PART TWO

NEW TESTAMENT ORIGINS
OF JEW HATRED

⤛ 8 ⤜

My Great-Uncle

I T WAS THE YEAR of the Rising against the British, and he died an Irish hero." So my mother was told, as a girl in Chicago, about her father's brother Jim back in Tipperary, and so she told me. She never knew him. Before my mother was born, her father had emigrated from the elegantly named Irish village of Four Mile Water, in the hills above the River Suir. Yet my mother grew up revering the memory of her martyred uncle, one of two Jims for whom I am named. Like her, I grew up attached to the legend. The glow of Jim Morrissey's rebel heroism settled on me, his namesake, as an inherited halo. From an early age, I knew the songs of Irish resistance. Even while fancying myself a Johnny Reb, I carried an image of my uncle linking arms with Michael Collins. The myth would inspire my early novels *Mortal Friends* and *Supply of Heroes*.[1]

When I was ordained to the priesthood in 1969, family and friends gave me envelopes containing checks and money orders — the young priest's trousseau. I took in more than a thousand dollars, a small fortune. As a Paulist, I was bound by a promise of poverty, so there was no question of my actually keeping the money, but — perhaps this was the beginning of my own downfall, my rebellion — instead of turning it over to my religious superior, I bought an airline ticket for Ireland, a first-time trip I would take on my vacation. So it was that I found myself that summer in Four Mile Water, outside Clonmel, Tipperary. I tracked down the house where my grandfather Thomas Morrissey was born most of a century before. I found the family baptismal records in the local church, including Jim's. The priest told me that there had been no Morrisseys in the parish during his time, but one day I struck up a conversation with an old man in the road. He had hitched his horse to the rusted chassis of an engineless truck. When I said "Morrissey," his eyes brightened. He had known Bridgit, he said, the sister Tom left behind. When I asked about their brother Jim, the old gent said, "Sure," and he pointed to a distant hilltop. He explained it was the site of a long-abandoned cemetery. It had not occurred to me that my mother's hero uncle would be buried in Four Mile Water. I had always pictured him at the General Post Office in Dublin, one of the victims of that Easter Week massacre, and of the British punishment of an unmarked grave along the Liffey. But the old man said, "Jim's up on the hill there with the other Morrisseys. You'll find his stone." And I did. I pushed the high grass away to read the inscription: "James Morrissey, RIP." Sure enough, the date of his death was 1916. So the story was true.

What I saw then, while confirming the literal facts of what my mother had been told, turned the myth of my hero uncle on its head. I now made out before his name the letters "Pvt.," and below it was the seal of the British Empire. I read the words "Killed in France." I was confused only for a moment. Private James Morrissey "died an Irish hero in the year of the Rising against the British," but instead of as an Irish Republican Brotherhood rebel, he died as a British soldier, fighting for the king in the Great War.

Nothing I had been told prepared me for that recognition, and a mystery still shrouds it, since the remains of few who died in the trenches were repatriated to Britain, much less Ireland. Yet there it was, that British seal. Only later would I learn that, while 250 Irish rebels took over the Dublin GPO on Easter Monday, there were 250 *thousand* Irishmen in British uniform, most of them Catholics like my great-uncle, and most of them serving in France, where the savage killing in the trenches was at its peak. More than 50,000 Irish soldiers would leap from the trenches only to be cut down. The Irish regiments were often the first to go over the top, and that would be especially true after Easter 1916, when the last thing London wanted was a sizable population of trained veterans returning alive to a restive Ireland. At the Somme, a few months after Easter, the Irish went first into the German maw, and were decimated.[2]

Irish Catholics volunteered for the British Army during the Great War for numerous reasons. Lloyd George had promised that Irish support of the war effort would lead to home rule at war's end, and many Catholics channeled their nationalist aspirations into this hope. Others enlisted for the bonus, which, to an impoverished peasant family, offered the sole chance at a sum of cash. Many Irish girls paid for their passage to America in those years with money their brothers accepted from British recruiters. Some Irish Catholics enlisted because they identified with "wee Belgium," and happily took up the fight against the kaiser. The point is that in the post–Easter Rising mythology of the south of Ireland, these Irishmen were forgotten. The Ulster Brigades in Northern Ireland would be memorialized with poppies every November, but both the Irish Republic and England would wipe out all memory of the Catholic regiments from the south. The martyrdom of Patrick Pearse and James Connolly; the glamour of Michael Collins and the fierce resistance of Eamon de Valera; the diehard extremism of fewer than two thousand members of the Irish Republican Army, when reinforced by the brutality of post-Easter British repression, particularly the marauding Black and Tans — all this took over the entire field of the Irish Catholic memory. For the rest of the century, with disastrous political consequences, the fact that the broad Irish population of 1916, including my mother's uncle Jim, saw London as other than an enemy was simply forgotten. "It was the year of the Rising against the British, and he died an Irish hero." This was true. But in what we had made of it, it was not true. The loss of a full political and social context to an amnesia that was itself shaped by a competing political and social context turned a factual statement into a damaging falsehood.

My subject is not the conflict between the Irish and the English, but rather the conflict between Catholics and Jews. Yet the two illuminate each other, an insight I first encountered in the work of the Catholic scholar John Dominic Crossan, a native Irishman. Discussing what he calls "autobiographical presuppositions," he compares his experience as a postcolonial Irishman with that of the colonized Jews of antiquity.[3] Even if my legacy as the great-nephew of a man in the middle differs from Crossan's, my reflections on my own family's version of the Irish-Jewish analogy are inspired by his.

Is it possible that something similar to the way my family misremembered its past happened in the Christian memory? Is it possible that the dominant memory of Christianity's foundational events, a memory that features Jesus' conflict with the Jews and then his followers' conflict with the Jews, by omitting or distorting the full political and social context within which those events unfolded, has enshrined a falsehood?

Crossan and others note that the New Testament records a polemical dispute — or rather, one side of a polemical dispute — between "Christians" and "Jews" that is traced to disputes between Jesus and "Jews." As with my great-uncle, certain remembered "facts" seem clear: Jesus was put to death on a cross, as the Gospels and also the Jewish historian Flavius Josephus (37–100 c.e.), writing at the end of the first century, testify. The

main extrabiblical source of information about Palestine in the first century, Josephus was an upper-class Jew who served in the Roman army and
wrote about it in *Jewish War*. His patrons included the emperor Vespasian
and the emperor's son Titus. Josephus was friendly to Rome, yet the cal-
lousness of its colonial administration and the brutality of its war machine clearly come through in his writing. His important work about Judaism is *Jewish Antiquities*. He is regarded by most scholars as a more or
less reliable witness,[4] although readers should always keep in mind his
broad purpose of advancing his brand of establishment Judaism at the expense of marginal groups.

"When Pilate," Josephus wrote, "upon hearing him accused by men of
the highest standing amongst us . . . condemned him to be crucified . . ."[5]
Indeed, the death of Jesus, Crossan writes, "by execution under Pontius
Pilate is as sure as anything historical ever can be."[6] Yet our knowledge of
what are taken to be sure facts of history goes beyond that. Thus it is a
"fact" that Jesus proclaimed a God of love over against the Pharisees' God
of legalism and revenge; a "fact" that Jesus attacked the money changers in
the Temple and proposed to destroy it, which is why the Jews accused him;
a "fact" that, in actions and words, Jesus "fulfilled" key prophecies of Jewish Scripture, proving the truth of claims made about him by his followers; a "fact" that those claims (he was the Messiah, he was *Christus,* he was
Son of God) were rejected by Jews; a "fact" that some of those followers
were attacked and killed by Jews (Stephen, James, the brother of Jesus); a
"fact" that Christianity did not thrive as a new religion until it broke free
(in Antioch, Asia Minor, Rome) of a limiting Jewish culture; a "fact" that
the meaning of Christianity, even in a non-Jewish world, would depend
on Jews, far more than on pagans, as the permanent embodiment of what
Christians were not.

But what happens when such foundational "facts" are remembered
without regard for the social and political ground out of which they grew?
As with Jim Morrissey, partially remembered "facts" can turn the truth on
its head. The "longest lie" is what Crossan calls the web of distortions that
are thus woven into the primal Christian narratives.[7] It is a lie about the
Jews — or is it, first, a lie about Jesus? As with my mother's uncle, is there
an overgrown but reliably engraved tombstone in the presence of which
we can finally face the truth?

↣ 9 ↢

Jesus, a Jew?

WHAT RELIGION WAS JESUS? A college professor I know routinely includes this question on a comprehensive quiz he gives to incoming freshmen each year. The pattern of responses is constant. Some students answer "Catholic," most answer "Christian." A distinct minority answers "Jewish." It is easy to condescend to students who do not know that Jesus was a Jew, but in fact there are good reasons to be confused about his religious identity. Some of those reasons have to do with the difficulty of imagining what this extraordinary person's inner life consisted of, and some with whether our compartmentalized idea of religion is relevant to the question. Part of the difficulty has to do with the rampant ambiguities of "Judaism" itself at the time Jesus lived, and part has to do with Christianity's long attempt to purge itself of Semitic content.

The famous "quest for the historical Jesus" that so gripped Protestant scholars in the nineteenth century led both to a new appreciation of Jesus' ties to his native Jewish milieu and to a new emphasis on what separated Jesus from his Jewishness. Jewish scholars at first welcomed Christian explorations into the Jewishness of Jesus, thinking that, as Susannah Heschel puts it, "the more Jewish Jesus could be shown to have been, the more Christians would respect Judaism." But that is not what happened. "Christians had a different agenda," Heschel writes. "For them, the more Jewish Jesus was shown to be, the less original and unique he was. If Jesus had simply preached the ordinary Judaism of his day, the foundation of Christianity as a distinctive and unparalleled religion was shattered . . . As strongly as nineteenth-century Jews tried to show an identity between Jesus and Judaism, Christians tried to demonstrate a difference."[1]

That theological debate was skewed by political developments, especially in Germany, where, ludicrous as it may now seem, the image of the

Aryan Christ emerged as something to be taken seriously. Under Otto von Bismarck (1815–1898), pan-German nationalism jelled, spawning a unifying racial theory, which led to a purified notion of a German *volk*. Similar efforts had marked Christian dogma and practice, going back to the early times of the Church, but nineteenth-century nationalism brought a new edge to such discussions. Ideas of racial purity as a component of social identity influenced religious identity, leading to a notion of Christianity stripped of all Semitic influence. As important a figure as the philosopher Johann Fichte (1762–1814), for example, had posited a Jesus who was not Jewish at all, and throughout the century theologians followed suit.[2] This would be one of the ways that German Protestant scholars tilled the soil for Nazi antisemitism, promulgating an idolatry of Aryan racial identity by defining Jesus over against Jewishness, not only religiously but racially. Eventually German Protestant hymnals would be "de-Judaized" by the removal of words like "amen," "hallelujah," and "hosanna."[3]

In the Christian world, the influence of nineteenth-century German Protestant theology was so dominant that it was felt even within Roman Catholicism, especially in the matter of a historical quest for Jesus that led to his removal from the Jewish milieu. As critics of that "quest" remind me now, the illustrated books used in Catholic schools that I attended as a child had been subtly shaped by visual cues. Jesus, Mary, Joseph, and all their intimates, save one, were portrayed with the racial and sartorial characteristics — blue eyes, light brown flowing hair, graceful robes — of northern Europe, in stark distinction to the pictured Pharisees, Sadducees, and high priests, with their odd headdresses, phylacteries, tasseled prayer shawls, oversized noses, and dark skin. It was as if the residents of the towns of Galilee were of a different racial strain than those of Judea — indeed, in the nineteenth century Jesus commonly came to be referred to as "the Galilean," or "the Nazarene," an implicit distancing from "Judea," the region of the Jews. The only obvious Semite in Jesus' inner circle, of course, was the one named for that region, Judas. The betrayer functioned in this filtered narrative as the one Jew, and the story forever emphasized his motive as greed.

The occupations of the fishermen friends of Jesus, like Jesus' own trade of carpenter — think of those pastel scenes of the boy and his dad in that airy, neatly swept workshop, making cabinets — were emphasized to contrast with the Judas-like moneygrubbers whom Jesus would go to Judea to attack. The nineteenth-century quest for the historical Jesus, in other words, in its effort to get behind the façade of an overly divinized Lord, led to the application of nineteenth-century racial categories and cultural stereotypes to first-century Palestine, a way of making Jesus human without making him Jewish.[4] I have been saying "nineteenth-century," emphasizing the German Protestant origins of this mindset, but this was all still thoroughly in place in the crucifix and stained glass of St. Mary's Roman Catholic Church in Alexandria, Virginia, and in the textbooks and bulletin-board posters of my parochial school, by which, despite myself, I continue to measure God.[5] One would think that six years of Scripture study and theology in a rigorous seminary at the time of the revolutionary Vatican II would have remedied this shallow notion of who Jesus was, but German Protestant theology and scholarship, still largely uncriticized for its implicit anti-Judaism, was in the early 1960s more influential in Catholic circles than ever.

True, the most patently childish notions — that cabinetmaker's workshop, Jesus hand-carving birds, then bringing them to life — had dropped away. But an idea that distanced Jesus even further from Jewishness had taken over my understanding. I learned to think of Jesus as a mystical genius whose direct experience of God the Father, whom he called Abba ("Daddy"), was such that he had no need of any mediating culture. Religion is by definition such a culture. Here is how one of the theologians I learned this from, Bernard Cooke, explains it: "What was distinctive about Jesus' experience [of God] was its intimacy and immediacy. All the textual evidence points to the fact that Jesus' knowledge of his Abba was immediate personal acquaintance."[6]

The word "religion" shares a root with "ligament," meaning "tie." Religion exists to overcome the gulf between creatures and Creator. It is a system of beliefs and rituals that ties the human to God. But Jesus was presented, in this understanding, as the one man who had no need of such a tie. "Believe me that I am in the Father and the Father is in me," the Gospel of John reports him as saying.[7] The theology that develops from that mystical union makes Jesus himself the ligament. So the question of the religious identity of Jesus never arises — not Jewish religion, not Christian religion — because his knowledge of God is immediate. He has no need of the ligament of religion. If he at first participated in Jewish ritual, he did so for the sake of form, not because he needed it. And the Gospels show him distancing himself from Jewish religious observances. As Paula Fredriksen points out, for example, the Gospel of Mark shows Jesus dismissing central religious traditions of Judaism like "Shabbat, food, tithing, Temple offerings, purity — as the 'traditions of men.' To these he opposes what Jesus ostensibly propounds as 'the commandment of God' (7:8). The strong rhetoric masks the fact that these laws are biblical and, as such, the common concern of all religious Jews: It is God in the Torah, not the Pharisees in their interpretations of it, who commanded these observances."[8]

When the disciples of Jesus asked him how to pray — this story became the core of my belief in him — he replied with the Our Father.[9] Christians recite this prayer in rote fashion, as if it were the farthest thing from religiously revolutionary, when in fact it is nothing less than an invitation to call God "Daddy" — that is, to think of the Almighty One, the Ineffable, in the most intimate way. Ironically, this aspect of Jesus' spirituality, which for most Christians has had the effect of distancing him from Judaism, actually shows him participating in its vital and at that time multifaceted manifestation. As the Catholic scholar John Pawlikowski has written, "In particular, Jesus' stress on his intimate link with the Father picks up on a central feature of Pharisaic thought."[10] Indeed, there is evidence that, by the time of Jesus, Jews were regularly praying to God as Father.[11] But that was never explained to us. The intimacy Jesus claimed to have with God the Father was made to seem unique, entirely his. More than anything else, to us, it set him apart from Jews.

Based on what was presented to us, we could only have concluded that, if anything, Jesus' Abba experience put him at odds with Jewish religion, for, as Cooke puts it, "There were fundamental incongruities between the Abba he experienced and the God known and explained by those around him."[12] This spirituality had the simple effect of deleting any reference to Jewish cult in the life of Jesus. It was impossible to picture him in that tasseled prayer shawl, wearing phylacteries, entering the Temple not to protest but to pray. Having learned in parochial school that Jesus was racially not Jewish, I learned in graduate theological school that he was religiously not Jewish either. Susannah Heschel characterizes the Aryanizing of Jesus as an effort "to create a *judenrein* Christianity for a *judenrein* Germany,"[13] but this spiritualizing of Jesus was a *judenrein* of such subtlety that I did not know, until reflecting on Heschel's recent work, that it had completely dominated my religious imagination.[14] What religion was Jesus? I'd have surely answered Jewish, unlike those ill-informed college freshmen — but their answers were more honest than mine.

What is a Jew anyway? At the end of the second millennium, Jews themselves carry on the argument, with the ultra-Orthodox of Mea Shearim, their enclave in Jerusalem, aiming anathemas at the secular children of David Ben Gurion, modern Israel's first prime minister. Hitler said that a Jew was anyone who had at least one Jewish grandparent, and, as if to spite him, many Jews adopted that definition. The rabbis, holding to matrilineal descent, define a Jew as someone having a Jewish mother. In the state of Israel, a Jew can be an atheist, although not a baptized Christian. Part racial, part religious, the meaning of Jewishness today is ambiguous. In his memoir, the drama critic Richard Gilman described a life's journey that had taken him from the Jewish faith into which he was born, into unbelief, then into Roman Catholicism, from which he subsequently "lapsed." And where did that leave him? As "a lapsed Jewish-atheist-Catholic. Fallen from all three, a triple deserter!" But not quite. In the end, he had, without choosing it, resumed his original identity. "The difference is that you stay Jewish in your bones and pores, there's no lapsing from that; changed names or nose bobs won't do."[15]

The contemporary argument among ultra-Orthodox Jews, Reform Jews, and secular Jews over the question Who is a Jew? points to a piece of the social and political context that is mainly missing from the Christian memory of foundational events. To imagine that first Jesus and then his followers were in conflict with "the Jews," a conflict with the sequential climaxes that occurred when "the Jews" killed Jesus and then certain of his followers, is, of course, to ignore the fact that Jesus and his first followers were themselves Jews. But on a more basic level, it is to assume that there was a social-religious entity called "the Jews." Obviously, a period of time had to pass before something called "Christianity" came into being as a distinct community, but emphasis on that evolution ignores the fact that, in the same period, there was no clearly defined "Judaism" either. Indeed, the suffix "ism," suggesting a set of coherent ideological boundaries, a membership definition, a precisely notated theology and cult, is anachronistic. If my great-uncle's story was misremembered by my family, it was because the post-1916 Irish imagination could no longer contain the ambiguous experience of a dual loyalty to London and Dublin. If the story of Jesus is misremembered, with devastating effect on the Jews, however defined, it is first because a later Christianity presumed a univocal — and, not incidentally, flawed — Judaism against which to define its uniqueness and value. But there was no such Judaism.

"When Jesus was born," the Columbia University scholar Alan Segal writes, "the Jewish religion was beginning a new transformation, the rabbinic movement, which would permit the Jewish people to survive the next two millennia. The complex of historical and social forces that molded rabbinic Judaism also affected the teachings of Jesus, helping to form Christianity into a new and separate religion."[16] Segal entitled his book *Rebecca's Children,* reflecting a theme already noted, that it is useful to think of the two religions as siblings, which, like Jacob and Esau, struggled against each other even in their mother's womb. The history of the origins of Jewish-Christian conflict suggests that the metaphor of rivalrous fraternity is more than a metaphor; it actually defines the way these two religions came into being. In Jesus' lifetime and shortly after it, Segal writes, "Dislocation, war, and foreign rule forced every variety of Jewish community to rebuild its ancient national culture into something almost unprecedented, a religion of personal and communal piety. Many avenues were available to Jews for achieving this new sense of personal piety, one of which was Jesus' movement."[17]

When a Christian asks Who is a Jew? he risks falling into the trap of a mythic projection of perennial Christian anxiety, defining Jewishness in a way that serves a Christian purpose. Obviously, Judaism defines itself in its own terms. In trying to understand the origins of Jewish-Christian conflict, perhaps it would be more useful to put the question as those first rivals within the broad Jewish community might have, which would be to ask, in effect, Who is the "true Israel"?[18]

Competing answers were offered by the groups characterized in the New Testament. There were the Pharisees, whose movement evolved into rabbinic Judaism, referred to earlier. Some Pharisees were priests, although most were laymen, and their religious impulse, competing with Temple sacrifice, emphasized the study of Torah in their synagogues and the rigorous keeping of the Law. Josephus says that six thousand Jews were Pharisees.[19] There were Sadducees, whom we might recognize as aristocrats, and some of them were high priests whose religious focus was the sacrificial cult of the Jerusalem Temple. They were inclined to cooperate with the Roman occupiers.[20] It is not clear how large this party was, but according to the distinguished scholar E. P. Sanders, there were many thousands of priests.[21] Josephus argues that the majority of Jews would have inclined toward such cooperation with Rome.[22] The Sadducees, in effect, formed a core of the establishment. There were Essenes, famous now for their caves in Qumran,[23] but in the first century they were a countersect that rejected the corruptions of the cities, and in particular of Herod's Temple, which to them was a Hellenized blasphemy. Herod the Great (c. 73–4 B.C.E.), the half-Jewish Roman puppet, had ruled as king of

Israel, including Judea and Galilee, since 37 B.C.E. He is remembered by Christians for the story of his slaughter of the innocents at the time of Jesus' birth, but his greatest undertaking was the restoration of the Temple in Jerusalem, which for him fulfilled a political purpose as much as a religious one. The Temple was designed to impress his Roman overlords as much as his Jewish subjects. But because of that duality, the Temple was a flashpoint to the Essenes, who wanted to replace the Romans as rulers of Israel with their own leaders. Josephus put their number at more than four thousand.[24]

The numbers offered by Josephus, while not to be taken as precise, indicate that relatively few Jews belonged to the identifiable parties. But the broader population would have had clear sympathies one way or another. At one extreme — in our terms, perhaps, the "liberals" — would have been the Hellenizers, those open to the customs of the Gentiles. By and large, these Jews would have been of the Diaspora — Greek speakers, men and women who had learned to live within and take for granted the pagan culture of Greek and Roman cities. Most famous of these would have been Philo of Alexandria (c. 30 B.C.E.–45 C.E.), who wrote favorably, for example, of the emperor Augustus. But many Palestinian Jews would probably have rejected Hellenization, and that is especially true of the rural people, whose experience of the wider world would have been limited.

At the other extreme from "liberals" would have been "zealots," whether pacifists or violent revolutionaries — pietists or apocalyptic believers who looked for divine intervention as a means of restoring Israel. An example of such a movement, perhaps, would have been that of John the Baptist. He was a radical spiritualist, yet his direct challenge to Herod, for which he was beheaded, demonstrates the impossibility of separating religion from politics in this milieu. In addition to the main parties and the sects, there were powerful regional divisions among those who identified themselves as the "true Israel." Judeans were dominant because the cultic center was in Jerusalem, yet there were Samaritans who, worshiping at their own Mount Gerizim instead of on Mount Zion, were disdained by Judeans.[25] And there were the villagers of Galilee, whom city-dwelling Judeans would have looked down upon as peasants. In turn, Galileans would have regarded the Jewish oligarchs of Jerusalem both as near traitors for accommodating Rome and as idolaters for allowing images of Caesar to be venerated, if only on coins. (Jesus' question about the coin, "Whose likeness and inscription is this?,"[26] is a sly jibe at his challengers' idolatry.)

The true Israel. Centered in the Temple. The Torah. The oneness of God. The idea of election. The covenant. Each of these metaphors had adherents who gave it priority. But it is important to recall the rather obvious fact that such debate, in Fredriksen's phrase, "coexisted with consensus."[27] Indeed, agreement on those elements as essential, however much one or the other was emphasized, would have been the precondition of diversity within the community. Still, it is impossible to detect in the vibrant religious expressions of first-century Palestine an all-encompassing Jewish orthodoxy. The very sectarianism of Israel in the time of Jesus appears to be its defining note. Segal argues that sectarian multiplicity amounted to an efficient channeling of conflict among classes and across ideologies, achieving a remarkable social balance in an era of massive cultural mutation.[28] That is why Jesus was acting exactly like a Jew of his time when, apparently influenced by John the Baptist, he initiated yet another sectarian movement, and like a Jew of his place — Galilee — when he targeted the Herod-compromised Temple in Jerusalem as the site of his defining spiritual-political act.

So the college students who didn't label Jesus as a Jew inadvertently score a point, because Jesus, while taking his membership in the covenant people Israel for granted, would likely have thought of himself not as a Judean (from which our word "Jew" derives, but which to him would have implied geography) but as a Galilean. "The Nazarene" after all. What was it to be a first-century Galilean? In trying to imagine Jesus' experience — and in trying to understand how his became a story told against Judaism instead of within Judaism — there is a key element yet to be considered. It is the most important element, yet it is also one often left aside. To tell the story of Christian origins (or the origins, for that matter, of rabbinic Judaism) without reference to it is equivalent to telling the story of the 1916 Irish Rising without reference to the Great War. And war — war every bit as savage, in relative terms, as World War I — is the missing element.

War was not in any way missing from Palestine when Jesus was born. Nor was war missing from the direct experience of his followers, his followers' children, of their children, and of their great-nephews. The origins of the Jesus movement, and ultimately of Christianity, cannot be understood apart from the century-long Roman war against the Jews, albeit a war punctuated by repeated acts of Jewish rebellion. That is the social and political context that is all too often missing from the memory: Jesus and his movement were born in the shadow of what would stand as the most grievous violence against the Jewish people until Hitler's attempt at a Final Solution.[29] (I would add here that it is equally misguided to consider the late-twentieth-century ferment in Christian theology, symbolized by the Second Vatican Council, apart from the trauma of the Holocaust, including the failure of the Christian churches to resist it.)

Between half a million and a million Jews lived in Palestine at the time of Jesus' birth.[30] Some scholars put the Jewish population there as high as two and a half million, with a few hundred thousand Gentiles. Sanders accepts a figure of "less than a million, possibly only about half that."[31] Later we will see that Josephus posits Jewish casualty figures in the war with Rome that Sanders finds too high. Whatever the totals, the ratio of Jewish dead in Palestine at the hands of Rome may well approximate the twentieth-century record of one in three. Already, when Jesus was born, the inhabitants of his region were a defeated, violated people. The brutally effective Roman general Pompey (106–48 B.C.E.), undertaking a major clampdown on the Asian provinces of the empire, had set his legions loose throughout the area little more than half a century before (63 B.C.E.).[32] He conquered Jerusalem. Thus began a period of oppressive colonial occupation[33] that would climax twice: when Roman garrisons leveled Jerusalem in 70 C.E., and again — once and for all — in 135 C.E.

Largely because we are heirs to a Roman imperial culture that controlled the writing of history, we are inclined to read Rome's story through rose-colored lenses. We tend to see the march of the Roman Empire as a civilizing work of human progress. Every schoolchild knows that the darkness of barbarianism was penetrated by Julius Caesar, who brought order to its chaos. "All Gaul," we learned, "is divided into three parts." But we never asked who was doing the dividing, or how the dividees felt about it.[34] We accepted the idea of a system according to which only citizens had rights, and roles in the story. Saint Paul's story, for example, takes a dramatic turn when, as Acts tells it, he announces his citizenship.[35] Only then are the Romans who arrested him bound by what we call due process. In the story of Rome, all others, especially that invisible mass of slaves, are the forever unnamed — and forever unentitled to any semblance of due process. We mark Rome's progression from a republic to a dictatorship, and while we take note of the madness of a Caligula (12–41 C.E.), who had himself worshiped as a god, or a Nero (37–68 C.E.), who killed himself saying "What an artist I perish," reports of their brutality serve mainly to emphasize the relative worthiness of most rulers. We are conditioned to think of the decline and fall of Rome sentimentally, as tragedy pure and simple. The gradual dissipation of imperial power, leading to vulnerability before the northern hordes, is the condition only of a new darkness.

But what if Roman imperial power itself, not in decline but at the peak, was the real darkness? A British critic and author of several important works on early Christianity, A. N. Wilson, says that Rome "was the first totalitarian state in history," the first to extend absolute control over the lives of a vast population. When compared to other empires of antiquity, Rome comes off well in some ways. The Greeks under Alexander, for example, imposed their language on those they conquered, while the Romans allowed local languages and cultures to remain intact. That is why Greek was the lingua franca of the Hellenized world. In addition, the breadth of religious diversity in Rome itself shows that the caesars tolerated, and even admitted to the pantheon, local gods. But the Roman war machine, once set running, was ruthless beyond what the world had seen. And though local gods were left alone, Rome was perhaps the first empire to require of its subjects an at least outward show of assent to the proposition that the emperor, too, was God.[36]

It is the glories of Roman dominance that are emphasized in the cultural memory of Western civilization — those arrow-straight roads, elegant aqueducts, timeless laws, conjugated language — to the exclusion of what the imposition of those glories cost those on whom they were imposed. What if, when we thought of Caesar, we thought less of Cleopatra's lover or Virgil's patron or Marcus Aurelius's delicate conscience than, say, of a Joseph Stalin or a Pol Pot whose program worked? How would history tell the story of the twentieth century if it were the first century of the thousand-year Reich? It all depends on where you stand. It may be anachronistic to judge the policies of a great empire of antiquity by the standards of the U.N. Declaration of Human Rights, but if being human means anything, it is that a minimal level of decent treatment is required in every culture and era.[37] It is clear that from the point of view of those on the bottom of the Roman pyramid — indeed, under it — that such a minimal standard was not met.

To the peasant peoples of the Roman-dominated world, to the millions of slaves and petty laborers (in Rome itself, fully one million of the population of two million were slaves[38]), to the lepers and beggars, to the troublemakers whose lives could be snuffed out with little notice taken, no characterization of Caesar's evil would have been too extreme. We have looked back at Rome from above — from the point of view, that is, of those who benefited from its systems, traveled its roads, beheld its architectural wonders, learned to think in its language — but what of that vast majority who drew no such benefit? There is no understanding either the Jesus movement itself or the foundational memory of its violent conflict with the Jews if we cannot look back from below, from the vantage of those for whom the Roman systems were an endless, ever-present horror. It was to them, above all, that the message of Jesus came to seem addressed.

Most of the subjugated peoples in the Mediterranean world yielded to the Romans in what Romans regarded as essential, and those who refused to do this found themselves required to yield in everything, surrendering whatever was distinctive in their cultural identities to the dominant occupier. That is why we know so little of the Phoenicians, say, or the Nabataeans. The people in Palestine proved to be especially stubborn, clinging doggedly, and despite efforts at coercion and co-optation, to a self-understanding that permanently set them apart. But Jewish resistance arose from something far deeper than some pseudogenetic stiff-necked stubbornness that would one day inspire an antisemitic stereotype. For the Jews of Palestine, the indignity of an emperor-worshiping colonizer's foot on the throat was compounded by the religious convictions that no such emperor was divine and, more pointedly, that their freedom in this now violated land was a gift from the one true God — their God. Despite everything that set them apart, the rivalrous groups of Jews agreed that the land was a sacred symbol of that God's enduring promise. So for Palestinian Jews of all stripes, the Roman occupation as such was a religious affront as well as a political one. Furthermore, and equally across the board, a Jew's belief in the covenant included the belief that, one way or another, sooner or later, God would fulfill the promise again, as God had done repeatedly in history. God would do this once the purpose of this humiliating defeat — some, like John the Baptist, said its purpose was to bring the people to repentance — was fulfilled. God would do it by vanquishing the foreign invader and restoring to Israel its holy freedom. In other words, Jews *as Jews* had a reason to resist Rome, and a reason to believe, despite Rome's overwhelming military superiority, that the resistance would be effective.

What Jews did not have was anything approaching agreement on the form this resistance should take. And it is here that the other, negative meaning of Jewish sectarianism surfaces. Typically, imperial powers depend on the inability of oppressed local populations to muster a unified resistance, and the most successful occupiers are skilled at exploiting the differences among the occupied. Certainly that was the story of the British Empire's success, and its legacy of nurtured local hatreds can be seen wherever the Union Jack flew, from Muslim-Hindu hatred in Pakistan and India, to Catholic-Protestant hatred in Ireland, to, yes, Jew-Arab hatred in modern Israel.[39] Rome was as good at encouraging internecine resentments among the occupied as Britain ever was. At one level, it is a matter only of exploiting the temperamental differences that perennially divide conservatives, moderates, and radicals from one another. E. P. Sanders says that for Jews confronted with "the great empires of the Mediterranean," the various parties had to decide "when to fight, when to yield; when to be content with partial independence, when to seek more. In terms of internal affairs, the primary issue was who would control the national institutions: the temple, the sacrifices, the tithes and other offerings, and the administration of the law."[40]

Sectarian conflict amounted to more than mere squabbling. There were grave tensions involving the life and death of the nation of Israel, and every aspect of its existence could be disputed because Israel's God had become involved at every level. Today, even believers take for granted the "wall of separation," in Jefferson's phrase, between areas of God's concern and those of government's, but it was not so at the time of Jesus. "There was no simple distinction," Sanders says, "between 'church' and 'state' or 'religion' and 'politics.' God, in the eyes of Jews, cared about all aspects of life; no part of it was outside 'religion.' Thus, in any case in which there was a choice — whether between would-be rulers, competing architectural plans for the temple, or various prohibitions on the sabbath — Jews would attempt to discern and follow *God's* will. Not infrequently they disagreed."[41] In every case, their disagreement served the purposes of Rome.

To the radical revolutionaries who wanted to mount an immediate, violent assault on the occupier, the impulse of aristocrats to cut the best deal with the enemy looked like collaboration or treason; equally, from inside the Temple precincts, the radicals' fanaticism looked like suicide. So the establishment party of Sadducees, associated with the priestly class, participated from their place at the Temple in the administration of Roman power in Jerusalem; the separatist Zealots, like the monastics at Qumran, pursued a rejectionist path; the Pharisees advocated an adherence to Mosaic law as a way of ushering in God's liberating intervention; and the Sicarii launched knife-wielding terrorist attacks against agents of the occupiers. What the Romans could depend on — a classic exercise of divide-and-keep-conquered — was each group's readiness to identify a competing group as the primary enemy, often leaving Rome above the fray. For our purposes, the point is that even in the way events of this era are remembered, the unleashed sectarian impulse continued to keep the Roman overlords at the margin of the story.

Take two examples, one from the beginning and one from the end of the story of Jesus, as his followers told it to each other and the world. First, in the year 4 B.C.E., which also happened to be the year of Jesus' birth,[42] Herod the Great died. His death left a temporary power vacuum, which caused violent outbreaks among forces loyal to various pretenders to succeed Herod as Rome's client king and among the followers of messianic movements who sought to seize an opening against Rome.[43] The Romans smashed every rebellion and, with those legions pouncing from Syria, restored direct imperial rule. As summed up by the scholars Richard Horsley and Neil Asher Silberman: "The Roman armies had swept through many of the towns and villages of the country, raping, killing, and destroying nearly everything in sight. In Galilee, all centers of rebellion were brutally suppressed; the rebel-held town of Sepphoris was burned to the ground, and all its surviving inhabitants were sold into slavery."[44] Thousands of Jews were killed. Villages in Galilee were laid waste. In Jerusalem, where rebels had briefly taken charge, the Romans showed the lengths to which they were prepared to go to maintain control by swiftly executing anyone even suspected of collusion in the rebellion — Josephus puts the number at two thousand.[45] The Roman means of execution, of course, was crucifixion, and Josephus makes the point that indeed the victims were crucified. This means that just outside the wall of the Jewish capital, crosses were erected — not three lonely crosses on a hill, as in the tidy Christian imagination, but perhaps two thousand in close proximity. On each was hung a Jew, and each Jew was left to die over several days the slow death of suffocation, as muscles gave out so that the victim could no longer hold himself erect enough to catch a breath. And once squeezed free of life, the corpses were left on their crosses to be eaten by buzzards. This grotesquery was its own justification. Its power was magnified because for Jews, coming into contact with a corpse made one ritually impure — a priest, for example, could not bury a parent. Such impurity could even be acquired by "overshadowing" a corpse, or being "overshadowed" by one.[46] The shadows of those crucifixes, in other words, were also the point. The Jews who'd been left alive were being reminded whom they were dealing with in Rome, reminded for weeks by the sight and stench of the bodies. The image of those scores of crosses would stamp Jewish consciousness for a generation.[47]

The opening chapters of the Gospel of Matthew evoke the political and social stresses of the world into which Jesus was born, but doesn't it seem odd that the ruthlessness displayed in Matthew's account of the slaughter of the innocents — the murder of every male child under two in the town of Bethlehem, a very few miles from those crosses — belonged not to the Romans but to the Jewish king Herod? This is not to dismiss that crime, if it occurred, nor to deny Herod's brutality, especially in the madness of his last years, but only to note that in the Christian memory — the Gospel of Matthew, usually dated to the decade of the 80s C.E., was written long after these events took place — the Roman crime is forgotten while the Jewish one is highlighted. Similarly with the Gospel of Luke, which was composed about the same time as Matthew. Luke's nativity-narrative reference to Caesar Augustus (63 B.C.E.–14 C.E.) as issuing a decree "that all the world should be enrolled,"[48] which moved the action of the Mary and Joseph story to Bethlehem in the first place, cries out for elaboration. It was the same Caesar Augustus who declared himself "Savior of the world," making him anathema to Jews. When he came to power with the Senate's authority in 27 B.C.E., it was as the head of a republic, but when he died in 14 C.E., it was as the emperor of a dictatorship, one tool of which was that world census. The perfect symbol of Caesar's regime was the gibbet on which those who refused to be part of his all-encompassing blasphemy were hung to die.

Now the second example, from the end of Jesus' life. When that Roman gibbet finally enters his story, by an extraordinary set of narrative machinations it is hardly Roman at all. Certainly the Gospel accounts are explicit in describing the Romans as the executioners of Jesus, but if they are coconspirators with the Jewish high priests and leaders of the Jewish ruling body, the Sanhedrin, they are decidedly *unindicted* coconspirators, which in modern law is a distinction between parties to a crime and perpetrators of it. According to the Christian memory, as conjured again by Matthew, the hand of the hand-washing Pilate (whose term as procurator, or appointed governor, in Judea ran from 26 to 36 C.E.) is forced by the bloodthirstiness of the crowd. "I am innocent of this man's blood," Pilate says.[49] This procurator is remembered somewhat differently by the Jewish philosopher Philo of Alexandria, who lived when Pilate did, and wrote sometime around 41 C.E. that the Roman used "bribes, insults, robberies, outrages, wanton injuries, constantly repeated executions without trial, ceaseless and supremely grievous cruelty."[50] Crossan, having cited these words, nevertheless asserts that Pilate "was neither a saint nor a monster."[51] Fredriksen, however, makes the point that Philo, Josephus, and the Roman historian Tacitus all single out Pilate "as one of the worst provocateurs."[52] Even by the standards of brutal Rome, Pilate seems to have been savage. When, six or so years after the death of Jesus, he wantonly slaughtered Samaritans for gathering to venerate Moses on a sacred mountain they associated with him, Pilate was recalled to Rome.[53]

Given the ways in which his occupying force routinely maintained control over a restless population, the Roman commander's self-exculpation, as recorded in Matthew, in the matter of one particular crucifixion is the moral equivalent of Adolf Eichmann's standing in his glass booth and declaring himself innocent. "And all the people," Matthew says, "answered, 'His blood be on us and on our children!'"[54] Which, of course, it has been.

This start-to-finish pattern in the Gospels of deflecting blame away from Romans and onto Jews is commonly taken now as evidence of a primordial Christian anti-Judaism, or worse: an anti-Judaism at the service of a craven attempt to placate Roman authorities. But this perception fails to take the "Christian" impulse here as one of people who are in fact Jews. So this anti-Judaism is evidence not of Jew hatred but of the sectarian conflict *among* Jews. Yes, there may have been an element of attempted ingratiation with Romans, but Jewishness was not the point of distinction in that attempt.[55] As early as 64 C.E., well before the Gospels were composed, the emperor Nero had singled out the Jewish sect that claimed Jesus as its *Christus,* blaming them for the fire that had just then ravaged Rome.[56] Tacitus writes of the violence that Nero inflicted on them,[57] which is the first recorded mention of the movement. The Christian Jews were labeled as arsonists. They were crucified, burned, and driven out. One of them would flee from Rome to the Aegean island of Patmos to compose the fire-ridden Apocalypse, which labels Rome the beast.[58] The Christian Jews were punished not for what they believed or refused to believe, or for any political threat they posed, but because, as a readily identifiable and vulnerable group, consisting in all likelihood mainly of slaves and lower-class workers with whom other Jews seemed not to identify, they were useful to Nero in providing the angry citizens of Rome with another target for their hatred besides him.

A. N. Wilson makes the point that Nero's savage scapegoating of the Christian Jews was for them an organizational boon, giving the until then inconsequential movement a reputation in the empire and numerous martyrs around whom to rally.[59] Two of these, apparently, were Peter and Paul. Long-run organizational boon or not, in the short run Nero's persecution traumatized the Christian Jews, who knew they had been falsely punished. They knew themselves not to be the violent threat to Roman order that Nero accused them of being. If the Gospels, just then starting to jell in their final forms, emphasized a relative friendliness to Rome, there was a reason for it. The followers of Jesus had just been slandered, defined not merely as Rome's mortal enemy but as violent insurrectionists. It was not true, and the Gospels were slanted, in effect, to emphasize that followers of Jesus fully intended to render unto Caesar what was Caesar's. Sectarian tensions between Christians and what Wilson calls the "generality" of Jews may have been exacerbated by the narrow scapegoating, but again, those tensions were multilayered, still decidedly intra-Jewish. But soon enough, after the Gospels had jelled, Rome's murderous assault on the Jews of Judea would make Nero's violence seem benign, and explode the boundaries against which Christian-Jewish stresses had begun to press. The trauma of bloodshed on an imperial scale, unprecedented for the Jews, is the necessary context for understanding what was happening in those years among the Jews. Christian anti-Judaism, in others words, is not the first cause here; the Roman war against Judaism is.

By the Irish analogy, think of the ultimate effect of British imperial power among the Irish themselves. The Irish war with England, begun in 1916, was extremely violent, including as it did the twentieth century's first indiscriminate shelling of an urban center, Dublin. Part of England's "draconian reaction"[60] was the unleashing on an unarmed populace of the criminal-terrorist Black and Tans and the post-1918 deployment of trench-veteran tommies, who viewed the Irish war as an extension of the no-holds-barred war against the Hun and fought accordingly. And the first result of all this violence? The Irish population, which in 1916 had been overwhelmingly inclined to favor London — as my great-uncle probably would have — over the self-appointed, self-aggrandizing liberators of the Irish Republican Brotherhood,[61] by 1920 thought of London as the devil's own. The fierce, universal Irish hatred of England, a twentieth-century cliché, was in fact born in the twentieth century — just then. Thus even a diehard like Winston Churchill came to recognize that an English victory over this despicable people, short of the outright elimination of the native population, was impossible. Empowered to do so by Eamon de Valera, Michael Collins negotiated the Anglo-Irish Treaty of 1921. There would not be another until 1986.

There was a second result of the violence of that war. In addition to a unifying Irish hatred of the English, there would be a terribly disunifying Irish hatred of the self. "I tell you this — early this morning I signed my death warrant," Collins wrote to a friend after agreeing to the treaty, instinctively grasping what awaited him at home.[62] No sooner had the Anglo-Irish war ended than the even more dispiriting Irish civil war began. Forces loyal to de Valera would eventually murder Collins, proving him a prophet. De Valera rejected the central terms of the treaty — an oath of allegiance to the Crown, British hegemony over the six counties in the north — but would later accept them once the paroxysm of Irish self-hatred had run its course. The Irish civil war — unlike, say, the American one — accomplished nothing, except to enable one Irish faction to vent its rage on another. Irish sectarian hatred served the overlord's purpose well, resulting in an Irish impotence the English could depend on for most of a century. Indeed, Irish sectarian violence was efficiently, if slyly, stoked by London all that time, from Lloyd George's government to Margaret Thatcher's.

Intra-Jewish conflict served Rome's purposes in just such a way. There is perhaps something craven in the Gospels' emphasis on "Jews" as a threat to order in the empire, as opposed to "Christians," and it does not mitigate the Gospel writers' responsibility for driving this wedge to note that they were responding to Roman oppression. But the more fundamental point is that in doing this, the followers of the murdered Jesus were only demonstrating how effective the imperial overlord had been in infecting the dominated population with its own cynicism and contempt. This dynamic becomes even clearer in the context that has provided us our starting point: One measure of the diabolical efficacy of Nazi torment in Auschwitz, besides the way Jews were victims of SS guards, was the way Jews were victims of fellow Jews, the capos who served as SS surrogates. The collapse of the moral universe that led Jews to participate in their own destruction in the death camps, or to take upon themselves a feeling of guilty responsibility for the evil around them, only emphasizes the abject evil of an absolutely oppressive system. That evil lies in the system's capacity to destroy the innocence of everyone it touches.[63] When Jewish factions turned Rome's venom against each other, Rome won yet another victory. There is no question here of "Christian innocence," because among human beings there is no innocence when the question becomes survival. Extreme violence and extreme measures to survive it form the ground on which this entire story stands.

It is nevertheless important to emphasize that, well after the life of Jesus, those who remembered the conflicts surrounding both its beginning and its end mainly as conflicts among Jews — Herod's villainy, not Caesar's; the high priest's, not Pilate's — were being true to the ways these events had come to be understood in the period of heightened Jewish sectarianism that followed Jesus' death.[64] Not "innocent," yet they were not liars either. The Gospel of Matthew was not composed by someone who had been there, not composed by someone who knew well that Pilate was a sadist who'd have thought nothing of dispatching an unknown Galilean troublemaker, and, knowing this, still consciously and falsely portrayed the Romans as innocent and "the Jews" as guilty. It would be a slander to say such a thing of Matthew (or the writers of that Gospel), just as it would slander my mother to say she lied to me when she led me to think her uncle was a hero of the Easter Rising.

Earlier, I cited John Dominic Crossan's 1995 characterization of the claim that the Jews murdered Jesus as "the longest lie," but in a subsequent work, in 1998, he amended that judgment. The authors of the foundational Christian documents, writing years after the event,[65] "did not say this: I know that the Roman authorities crucified Jesus, but I will blame the Jewish authorities; I will play the Roman card; I will write propaganda that I know is inaccurate. If they *had* done that, the resulting text would have been a lie."[66] Crossan does not attribute such venality to the Gospels, because to do so would impose a post-Enlightenment notion of history on a far more complex phenomenon. Rigid concern for "how it happened" is a contemporary preoccupation of ours, but no such emphasis informed the way the ancients wrote history. Reports of the words and deeds of the late Jesus evolved as his movement grew, and so did the understanding of who his friends and enemies were, depending on the experience through time of who the friends and enemies of the movement were. "As Christian Jewish communities are steadily more alienated from their fellow Jews, so the 'enemies' of Jesus expand to fit those new situations. By the time of 'John' in the 90s, those enemies are 'the Jews' — that is, all those other Jews except us few right ones. If we had understood (the literary genre) gospel, we would have understood that. If we had understood gospel, we would have expected that. It is, unfortunately, tragically late to be learning it."[67]

Just as the original fate of Jesus was shaped in part by intra-Jewish disputes, the communal memory of how that fate unfolded was itself shaped by those disputes, especially when Roman domination of Jews started to unravel. Writing fifty or seventy years after the death of Jesus, the Gospel authors continued to be influenced by the climate of crisis and dispute, Roman terror and Jewish polemic. But around the time of their writing, something new, and for this story something deadly, began to happen.

10

The Threshold Stone

A NOTHER THING WRONG with blaming the anti-Jewish texts of
the New Testament on a primitive and essential "Christian" hatred of Jews is that doing so continues the victim's habit of exonerating the true villain in the story, which was and remains
Rome. I acknowledge the apparent absurdity of this attempt, two thousand years after the event, to reconstruct its shape and meaning with more
accuracy than the people who lived only a generation or two later. But in
this one regard at least — the crucial influence of a dominant overlord —
we have a distinct advantage over those first Christians and rabbinic Jews.
For us, the grip of the overlord has long since been released, and the myth
of hierarchy has been broken. The blanketing fog of an imperialist occupation blinded those who lived through it to the all-encompassing nature
of Roman oppression. Similarly, the Romans, by controlling the future,
controlled the way even their extreme savagery would be remembered by
Jew and non-Jew alike. Yet neither of these facts excuses us from emphasizing that the story of Jesus, at a fundamental level, is one part of the
story of Israel's refusal to yield to Rome. And this can be perceived more
clearly now than it was then.

The empire's contest with Israel was one that, even if it took centuries,
Rome was fated to lose. Worship a man in a toga because he wears a laurel
wreath? Does not worship belong alone to the one God? Honor that man's
face on coins or battle standards, much less on altars, when God has forbidden the honoring of images? Acknowledge the sovereignty of the invader over land that is itself the seal of God's covenant with God's people?
Depend on Rome when God has long since proven to be absolutely
dependable? Beginning with the violent arrival of Pompey's legions in
63 B.C.E., most Jews may have decided against open defiance of the occupiers, but there was never any question of the people's being folded into

the empire with all the others. Even the Roman-friendly Josephus wrote proudly, as a Jew, "[We face] death on behalf of our laws with a courage which no other nation can equal."[1] Nor should we fail to emphasize that Rome's brutal response to that refusal, especially in the climactic war of 66–73 C.E. when Jerusalem was laid waste and hundreds of thousands of Jews were killed (Josephus and Tacitus put the number of Jewish dead in this first war at around 600,000; in the second "Jewish War" sixty years later, the tally for Jewish victims is put at 850,000[2]), traumatized all Jews, including the followers of Jesus. Whatever the actual totals (and the size of these reported figures alone indicates the shock Jews must have felt), the vast number of victims were killed without the mechanized methods that make modern wars so lethal, which is why analogies between Rome and the worst of twentieth-century dictators may not be misplaced here. Rome had no apparent "racial motive" in its crackdown on provincial rebels,[3] but if the legions had had machine guns, bombs, railroads, and gas at their disposal, who is to say any Jew would have survived the second century?

So of course that war affected how the story of Jesus was remembered, and then how it was told, especially to the non-Jews of the Mediterranean world. In this era there were Jewish risings against Rome not just in Judea but in Mesopotamia, Egypt, Cyrenaica (near present-day Tunisia), and Cyprus.[4] The war had such significance to Rome that in 70 C.E. Trajan built a triumphal arch at the Colosseum to honor the hard-won victory, and Roman coins were inscribed *Judea Capta*.[5] In the second war (132–135 C.E.) Judea was stripped of its Jews and renamed Syria Palaestina.[6] It cannot be overemphasized that the texts of the New Testament were being written at one of the most violent epochs in history, with the twin assaults on Jerusalem, in 70 and 135, serving as rough brackets within which the composition occurred. The events of those years, and in particular the destruction of the Temple in 70, mark such a watershed that Paula Fredriksen can say that "the evangelists' position as regards the Temple . . . is closer to ours, despite the nineteen centuries that intervene between us, than to that of those generations who immediately precede them."[7]

To read the New Testament apart from the context of the Roman war against the Jews — as it almost always is — amounts to reading *The Diary of a Young Girl* without reference to the Holocaust. For one thing, the non-Jewish citizens of Galatia, Macedonia, Antioch, Armenia, and the slaves of Rome, would have been far readier to practice a religion — or better, adopt a way of life — that, while offering an implicit alternative to the degrading Roman worldview, explicitly defined its enemy as the Jews, who were such a flashpoint, than they would have been to practice one that explicitly defined the enemy as that same ruthless overlord whose foot was on their throats too. It was the *implicitness* of the challenge to Rome that would eventually lead to the Christian victory, and so in that way the explicit definition of Jews as the Christian enemy par excellence proved, as a kind of feint, to be quite useful. The difference from then on, in all those Gentile cities — and, with the one large Jewish city gone, the tragic difference that would set in motion the razor-edged arc of this narrative — was that they who now heard this story, and who now retold it, were not Jews. Therefore, they could only experience the disheartening, self-hating, imperium-inspired polemic of the Jesus movement from outside. And from outside there could be no loving assumption that the ultimate aim of this struggle, whatever else it accomplished, was a renewal of Israel. The hateful polemical language used by those outside the initiating, faction-torn community would begin to fall differently on the ear, the way it falls on modern ears.

When an ultra-Orthodox Jew of Mea Shearim in frock coat and leggings uses extreme language to vilify his opponent — say, the secular American Jews to whom he is only an oddity — almost no one hears that language, however contemptuous, as antisemitic. But the same language in the mouth of an Irish kid in Dorchester, Massachusetts, will reek of Jew hatred. Accusations heard in one context as vicious but simple polemic can in another take on the tone of racist slander. Once Christian became "Christian," once the embattled Jewish sect became the mostly Gentile "Church," the structure of the foundational story was set, the ground of Christian memory, the longest lie. "The Jews" would be the archenemy of Jesus, and of his people, from then on.

If I seem to be going to some length here to dilute, if not refute, the Jew hatred we so easily detect in the New Testament, and that would flower in anti-Jewish violence, it is to make the case that the Jew hatred that stamps the beginning of Christianity is not essential to this religion. If I believed it were, either to Christianity's origins or to its development, I could, I repeat, have nothing to do with this religion. That is the point of distinguishing between the impulses and beliefs of a faithfully Jewish Jesus and his faithfully Jewish first followers and those of their traumatized successors. Earlier in this book, when writing of the Vatican Council's denial of Jewish culpability for the death of Jesus, I derided efforts to place the blame at the feet of the Romans, in obvious contradiction to the record of the New Testament. I am attempting something different here. While certainly blaming the Romans, I am also trying to show that the New Testament impulse to blame Jews took root in soil that, yes, the Romans had contaminated — not Jesus. And if Christian Jew-hatred did not originate with the Jew Jesus, no matter how it developed, then it is not essential to Christian faith.

In other words, I am a Christian at work here, and everywhere in this book, on the project of clinging to that faith. But this is not enough. A generous understanding of intra-Jewish polemic is not enough. "Christians," in addition to slandering "Jews" about their role in the crucifixion of Jesus, began eventually — over the decisive years of the Roman war against the Jews — to define them as not just their enemy, or Jesus', but as God's. And that, when later, mainly Gentile Christians misread the story, is what made it lethal.

Elaine Pagels, in her groundbreaking study *The Origin of Satan,* showed how the antagonism between a Jewish establishment and the followers of Jesus evolved, in the experience of those followers, into a cosmic struggle between evil and good, with "the Jews" defined as evil. In the earliest Gospel, Mark, dating to around 68, Jesus is locked in conflict with an embodied Satan who has possessed a man,[8] who energizes the antagonism of the Scribes[9] and that of his own family,[10] and who even tempts Jesus through the mouth of his favorite, Peter.[11] By the time Luke is written, a decade or more later, the enemy of Jesus is still the "evil one," but now he is identified with the leaders, "the chief priests and captains of the temple and elders."[12] Pagels shows how, with the last Gospel, John, dating to around 100 and clearly reflecting the intensification of intra-Jewish sectarian conflict that followed the destruction of the Temple, the identification of "the Jews" and Satan himself has become complete. This movement is reflected in the fact that the loaded phrase "the Jews" (in Greek, *hoi Ioudaioi*) appears a total of 16 times in the Gospels of Mark, Matthew, and Luke, while in John it appears 71 times.[13] As Pagels says, "John chooses to tell the story of Jesus as a story of cosmic conflict — conflict between divine light and primordial darkness, between the close-knit group of Jesus' followers and the implacable, sinful opposition they encountered from 'the world.'"[14] But in John, Jesus himself identifies the evil one with the people. The "temptation scenes," which are played out in other Gospels between Jesus and Satan, are played out in John between Jesus and the people. This is why the phrase "the Jews" appears so frequently. The climax of this movement comes in chapter 8 of John when Jesus is portrayed as denouncing "the Jews" as the offspring of Satan. "You are of your father the devil, and your will is to do your father's desires. He was a murderer from the beginning."[15] Thus Jews have become not just the historical enemy but the ontological enemy — the negative against which every positive aspect of Christianity is defined. This Manichaean demonizing of Jews by the first-century followers of Jesus — themselves mostly Jews — and the sanctioning of that demonizing in the canonizing of the Scriptures are what made this story murderous down the centuries. Pagels concludes, "John's decision to make an actual, identifiable group — among Jesus's contemporaries and his own — into a symbol of 'all evil' obviously bears religious, social, and political implications. Would anyone doubt this if an influential author today made women, or for that matter Muslims or homosexuals, the 'symbol of all evil'? Having cast 'the Jews' in that role, John's gospel can arouse and even legitimate hostility toward Judaism, a potential that New Testament scholar Reginald Fuller says 'has been abundantly and tragically actualized in the course of Christian history.'"[16]

Despite all that we have seen of context and milieu, the question remains: How did this happen? In attempting to retrace the arc of this lethal narrative, I have, inevitably perhaps, pushed farther and farther into its past. Yet scholars emphasize that when it comes to Jesus, there is a limit to how far back we can go. Only a few lines ago, I asserted that Jew hatred could not have begun with Jesus. By what authority can I make that claim? Can we gain access to the actual history of Jesus, or to that period immediately after his death, decades before the Gospel accounts were written? Was it then that the hidden wound was inflicted on the minds of "Christians" toward "Jews"? As a seminarian many years ago, I had read my Rudolf Bultmann, the German scholar who held that it is impossible to get behind the mythmaking of the New Testament to that chimera "the historical Jesus."[17] Like Albert Schweitzer before him, Bultmann debunked the quest, insisting that what searchers invariably found was less a real Jesus than projections of their own cultural and theological assumptions. The perfect example of that is the so-called Aryan Jesus that pre-Nazi German Protestantism embraced, a legacy that no doubt seeded Bultmann's own skepticism of the entire project. Bultmann affirmed, instead, "the Christ of faith," the figure whom the Church from the first generation holds up to us. Thus faith need not be tied to the real or the historical. What "happened" to spark this community's vision is less important than the vision itself. Our faith, in other words, is less in Jesus than in the community, in the community's memory, which is what we mean by the Church, alive with the Holy Spirit.

Without knowing why, I did not assent to this view even in my youth. My first trip to Jerusalem, that summer of 1973, was decidedly my version of the quest for Jesus. The Christ of faith had become an ephemeral figure to me, an icon of triumphalism. And his Church — alas, the lens through which I saw it then was the distorting one of Vietnam. The late Cardinal Spellman's role as an instigator of the war, Ngo Dinh Diem's role as its Torquemada, my own bishop's role as yet another silent bystander, all compounded my starkly Oedipal struggle with my Air Force general father and my stalwart mother. This combined weight fell on the fragile structure of my own priesthood, but was it fragile because I knew so little of Jesus, who should have been my strength? So of course, in the midst of such a crisis, I had to go in search of him.

I tracked through the Gospels, commentaries, sources, epistles, and traditions; the rumors, gossip, and wishes — all that had once been bolted together as the scaffolding of faith. But the scaffold was tottering. American violence against an Asian people — what was that to me? European violence against the Jewish people — if it were somehow Catholic, why hadn't anybody said so? Unspeakable violence of the past and present, committed in the name of the Father and of the Son — why shouldn't the soul of this failed young American priest have been troubled?

It is hard to explain now, but all of these questions — Vietnam, Auschwitz, Spellman, a devoted mother, an Air Force father, Pius XII, the bystanding U.S. bishops, the Body of Christ which I would place into the cupped hands of the shaken young — were tied in the same knot. The texts had not undone it, because the knot was in my chest. It took me to Jerusalem, where I saw something new about Jesus, and was saved by it. Never mind, yet, that it was wrong.

"Jerusalem is builded as a city, strongly compact." Psalm 122 was one I had often recited as part of my daily priestly office, and the lines were in my mind. "I was glad when they said unto me, 'Let us go into the House of the Lord. Our feet shall stand within thy gates, O Jerusalem.'"

The gates were still there. Josephus had described a city of marble walls and gilded palaces that dazzled from whatever direction it was approached. Because I was staying that summer in a religious house on the edge of the Judean Desert, near Bethlehem, I approached from the south. Along that road was a ledge that looked across the Kidron Valley, which displayed the hilltop city as on a pedestal. Though the marble was gone, the white Jerusalem stone of the city walls still gleamed in the baking sun, and the gold of the Dome of the Rock dazzled as much as any ancient sanctuary ever could have. The sight of the great Muslim shrine on the Temple Mount, together with the sight to the west of the dull gray but striking dome of the Church of the Holy Sepulcher — the juxtaposition of the three sources of conflict brought to mind other lines from the same psalm: "Pray for the peace of Jerusalem: they shall prosper that love thee. Peace be within thy walls, and prosperity within thy palaces."

I tried to imagine Jesus taking in this view as he so fatefully approached the holy city. The synoptic Gospels say he came here once, to die; John says he was here perhaps three times.[18] But Jesus the Galilean would have come from the north, either down the Jordan River Valley and up the Judean Hills from the east, or descending the Mount Bezetha ridge, so the city would not have appeared to be on a hill to him. Nothing about Jesus seemed available to me, not even a glimpse of his last vista.

Instead of a sharp image from Scripture, I carried in my mind something from T. S. Eliot, Jesus as the ghost he had become to his grief-stricken followers along a road — was it the road to Emmaus? "But when I look ahead up the white road / There is always another one walking beside you / Gliding wrapt in a brown mantle, hooded / I do not know whether a man or a woman / — But who is that on the other side of you?"[19] I followed the hooded figure, as it were, into the city and past its holy sites: the pit of Siloam Pool where the blind man was healed, the shrine of the Virgin above the beautiful gate, the olive grove at Gethsemane, and the Church of Mount Zion where the upper room is revered. I shouldered among the credulous tourists and pious pilgrims, a self-anointed refugee. I saw myself as above the commercial phoniness of the Via Dolorosa, and deplored the vise grip of Byzantine-crusader competition, still, for the filthy places — all in the same crumbling church — where Jesus died, was wrapped in oil, and laid to rest. I went from Judgment Gate to the Gates of Sorrow, increasingly blind myself, seeing no more of Jesus there than I could in the blessed carnage of Ngo Dinh Diem or in the holy war against the Jews. When I entered the dark cell that claims to be the tomb of Jesus, alas, it was not empty. A toothless Greek monk ambushed me with his last candle, demanding a dollar for it.

It was only when a skeptical old Frenchman, a biblical archaeologist, took me into the bowels of a Russian convent in the Old City, not far from the embattled Holy Sepulcher, that I sensed — literally sensed, in that dank air — what I had come for. He showed me an excavation beneath a string of naked light bulbs and pointed to a large stone slab at our feet. "This was the threshold stone of the city gate at the time of Jesus," he said. "It was buried in the rubble of the Roman destruction and is only now being uncovered. It is certain" — the Frenchman had used this expression of nothing else he had shown me — "that Jesus of Nazareth would have stepped on this stone as he left the city for Golgotha."

I knelt — a simple, automatic gesture — as if I were an altar boy again, with the Host passing before me. Equally automatically, I bent to kiss the stone. My quest, such as it was, seemed concluded. If Jerusalem gave me nothing else, this would be enough. Enough for me that behind the Christ there was a man, that I could touch what he had touched, that the stark simplicity of his life on earth — no gilded raiment now, no triumphalism — could be as clear and incorruptible as the sensation of cold stone against dry lips.[20] I was thirty years old. I understand now that what I saw in the shadow of the man who'd crossed that stone on the way to a rebel's death was, as Schweitzer and Bultmann and all agnostic therapists said it would be, a rank projection of myself. Thirty years old, as Jesus was, was the first point. As old as Jesus was when he began to be in trouble was the second. The aspect of Jesus' character that became real to me, that summer of my first visit to Jerusalem, was his having been a troubled man who made trouble. Which is how, with the help of several judges at antiwar trials, my father's open anger, and my bishop's increasingly unmuted displeasure, I had come to think of myself.

As I disapproved of the vanities of Holy Land religiosity, it was so easy to imagine Jesus doing the same. As I found myself at the mercy of a lusty restlessness with my vow of celibacy, I cherished the scandal of his friendliness toward prostitutes. I clung to the idea of Jesus as a "marginal Jew," as one scholar would dub him much later,[21] a misfit who, while opposed to the religious and political establishment of his day, had no fixed attachments among the Essenes or Zealots or even the movement of John the Baptist. He had nowhere to lay his head; I blanketed my loneliness with his. But mostly, his contempt for his "religious superiors" — the high priests, the Pharisees, the scribes — made mine for Cardinal Spellman's jingoism and Pius XII's apparent complacency seem legitimate.

So of course I knew why Jesus did what he did, though doing it got him killed. Jesus was radically with the poor, as I thought I should have been. A relatively privileged man — that carpentry shop, that learned eloquence — still he was the avatar of liberation theology. "And Jesus entered the temple of God and drove out all who sold and bought in the temple, and he

overturned the tables of the money-changers and the seats of those who
sold pigeons. He said to them, 'It is written, My house shall be called a
house of prayer; but you make it a den of robbers.'"²² In the Gospel of
John version, the narrative continues, "His disciples remembered that it
was written, 'Zeal for thy house will consume me.' The Jews then said to
him, 'What sign have you to show us for doing this?'"²³

The Jews. In this scene of upended cash boxes, scattered coins, scales,
and counting tables, it was easy to picture them as Fagins and Shylocks,
userers and pawnbrokers, crafty shopkeepers of the inner city, and master
financiers who kept the Third World poor. Jesus was attacking "Jews" we
knew so well. "What sign . . . ?" they asked, and the text goes on: "Jesus answered them, 'Destroy this temple, and in three days I will raise it up.' The
Jews then said, 'It has taken forty-six years to build this temple. And you
will raise it up in three days?' But he spoke of the temple of his body.
When therefore he was raised from the dead, his disciples remembered
that he had said this; and they believed the scripture and the word which
Jesus had spoken."²⁴

In Mark, there is this coda to the story: "And as he came out of the temple, one of his disciples said to him, 'Look, Teacher, what wonderful stones
and what wonderful buildings!'"²⁵

It was true. Josephus said that the whole façade of the Temple, 150 feet
square, was covered with gold plates, as were the entrances and the portico. Titus would bring a huge solid-gold menorah to Rome as his greatest
piece of war booty; its image can still be seen on the Arch of Titus near the
Colosseum. In the Holy of Holies, every inch of wall surface was overlaid
with gold. Josephus says that after the sack of Jerusalem in 70 C.E., gold
from the Temple flooded the market, so much so that "the standard of
gold was depreciated to half its former value."²⁶ But to Jesus, wealth was
the enemy. He replied to his awestruck disciple in Mark, "You see these
great buildings? Not one stone will be left upon another; all will be
thrown down."

And I knew that Jesus attacked the Temple for another reason. I had
learned in seminary that the Temple cult had violated the Mosaic command to keep the Ark of the Covenant enshrined in a simple tent, a symbol of Israel's perennial readiness to pull up stakes in response to the
command of Yahweh. The Temple cult — I had preached on this! — owed
more to Canaanite traditions than to the Torah. The Temple's rigid clerical hierarchy ran against the egalitarian spirit proper to the people of God.
With its narrow identification of God's presence in one place, the Temple

was wrongly exclusive. The compulsively observed rituals were effectively a denial of grace, as if God's love could be purchased by the coin of form over substance, another way to turn the Father's house into a thieves' den. In all of this I was exercising, without knowing it, the age-old Christian prerogative of defining the meaning of Israel's religion, so that the meaning of Jesus' rejection of that religion would be unmistakable. Jon Levenson of Harvard Divinity School shows how "members of the senior generation of [Christian] Old Testament scholars in America find in the Temple of Solomon a notorious lapse on the part of Israel into the culture that surrounds it . . . The Temple is a negative model, the pole to be rejected or subordinated if authenticity is to endure."[27] Having gotten my theology from such scholars, I was convinced that I knew what the Temple meant not only to Jesus but to Jews. Of course he would attack it.

If you had told me that my characterization of the Temple culture — the greed of the moneychangers, the exclusivity of the priests, the near idolatry of the edifice as such — partook of antisemitic stereotyping, I would not have known what you were talking about, especially since I extended such critiques to my own Roman Catholic Church. But in that, was I perhaps indulging the mental habit of supersessionism, setting myself above my own tradition, just as my tradition had set itself above Israel?

My perceptions in 1973 may thus have been shaped by an unknowing projection of my own prejudices, needs, and wishes onto a figment scrim named Jesus. My perceptions may have unconsciously banalized the beliefs of Jews. My perceptions may have assumed the ancient supersessionism by which the Old Covenant was replaced by the New. Nevertheless, these perceptions rescued my tottering faith. Indeed, the idea of Jesus as disapproved by the powerful, attached to the powerless, still serves as the spine of my religious conviction. But now, looking back, I see the limits of those perceptions, particularly in relation to the question that drives this book. I saw Jesus as marginal — but marginal to his own religious tradition. I saw him as rebellious — but in rebellion against the piety of the Pharisees and the scribes, whom I thought of as Spellman and Pius XII. My hero Daniel Berrigan was in jail, which was where I'd have been if I weren't a coward. (As I write this, twenty-five years later, his brother Philip is in jail again, a felon in his seventies whose crime this time was a symbolic attack on American nuclear weapons.) I cherished the thought of Jesus as a breaker of the law. The "brown mantle hood," in T. S. Eliot's phrase, had fallen from his face, and I knew he was a man, not a woman. He was of the earth, of the stone I had kissed. He was closer to me than ever.

Like those naive college kids confused about his religion, I saw Jesus as anything but what he was. With the Vatican, I may no longer have been capable of indicting the Jews for deicide, but I saw Jesus so clearly then, because in my eyes he stood in such sharp contrast to his own people. "The Jews" still embodied everything he was against, and therefore so was I. "O Jerusalem, Jerusalem, city that murders the prophets, and stones the messengers sent to her!" None of this made Jesus — or me — antisemitic because, as is clear from his heartbroken lament in Matthew, Jewish recalcitrance made him not vengeful but sad. In any case, his rebuke of Jerusalem here is mild compared, say, to that of Israel's prophet Amos.[28] Jesus laments, "O Jerusalem, Jerusalem, killing the prophets and stoning those who are sent to you! How often would I have gathered your children together as a hen gathers her brood under her wings, and you would not! Behold, your house [the Temple] is forsaken and desolate. For I tell you, you will not see me again, until you say, 'Blessed be he who comes in the name of the Lord.'"[29]

11

Destroy This Temple

WE ARE TRACKING here the shifting perceptions of a mind deeply, if unconsciously, rooted in traditions of anti-Jewish contempt. The modern history of Israel has taught one set of lessons: for example, that the Jewish state is not to be judged by standards different from those used in judging other states, or that Jews themselves, struggling to survive after the Yom Kippur War and the Intifada, do so with "pain, introspection, and grim self-criticism."[1] But among Christians another set of lessons has been taught, as part of a remarkable renewal among scholars who have studied the life of Jesus, some of the most important of whom I have already cited. No doubt these scholars, coming of age in the post-Holocaust era, have been influenced by the profound, if implicit, challenge to Christians represented by Holocaust studies conducted mainly by Jews. "How can we pretend to take history with theological seriousness," the Catholic theologian David Tracy asks, "and then ignore the Holocaust?" That catastrophe is, in Tracy's words, a fundamental interruption in the flow of history, changing everything.[2]

For Christians the change must involve Jesus Christ, and that is fully reflected in the work of the new scholars. A "Third Quest" for the historical Jesus, as scholars refer to it,[3] has been under way since the late twentieth century, with special urgency since 1980. Qumran discoveries, further studies of the Dead Sea Scrolls, archaeological explorations, and the application of modern anthropological analysis to first-century Galilee and Judea have led to major revisions of assumptions about Jesus and the movement he inspired. The Jesus Seminar, led by John Dominic Crossan and Robert Funk, involving a score or more of scholars meeting regularly since 1985, has questioned the historicity of much of the information provided about Jesus in the Gospels. Not only are his miracles questioned, but so are his claim to be the Messiah and much of what he is reported to have said. The litmus test of assertions about Jesus has become their relationship to the overriding issue of the hatred of Jews.

Some scholars find reasons to imagine Jesus as a peasant revolutionary, as a prophet come to obliterate male dominance, as a wandering sage who preached a universal and subversive equality, as a divine agent announcing the imminent End of Days.[4] Much of recent Jesus research is greeted skeptically by more traditional scholars. Raymond Brown, for example, who among Roman Catholics was perhaps the most widely respected New Testament expert of the late twentieth century, responded sharply. "Those who advance such views of Jesus often claim they are trying to reshape Christian belief and proclamation. More bluntly, however, their views of Jesus would make traditional Christian belief illusory and traditional proclamation irresponsible."[5] But isn't "traditional proclamation" the issue here? The scholars have their arguments, Crossan and Brown in particular. A key question divides them, and we will return to it. The Jesus Seminar is mocked by its critics because of a penchant for calling news conferences, peddling its radical critiques in the popular media. Scholars wince, but the popular media are what the rest of us read and see. We are the ones whose attitudes about Jesus, and therefore about "the Jews," have done so much to shape (and misshape) history. Are ordinary believers worthy of the insights of scholarship? Will we be scandalized, for example, by the suspicion that Jesus — in his interior life and in his observances; in his preaching, even, and in his death — really was a Jew?[6] Can the Christian imagination envisage Jesus as the Jewish artist Marc Chagall did in his *White Crucifixion*, as a crucified figure saved from the indignity of nakedness not by a loincloth but by a *tallit*, the fringed shawl worn by a Jew while praying?[7] If Jesus were alive today, would he be one of those fervent black-hatted figures davening at the Western Wall?[8]

In other words, what if Jesus was really a Jew from beginning to end? What if that was the single large conclusion of all the work of history, archaeology, anthropology, and cultural analysis? To repeat Susannah Heschel's question, Would "the foundation of Christianity as a distinctive and unparalleled religion [be] shattered?" Heschel was writing of the nineteenth-century Christian urge to "demonstrate a difference," but don't the origins of this problem rest with those first-century "Christians" acting on the same impulse?[9]

The most radical and precedent-setting critique of that first-century impulse, at least as written by a Christian, was offered in 1974 in *Faith and*

Fratricide: The Theological Roots of Anti-Semitism, by the Catholic feminist theologian Rosemary Radford Ruether. That Jesus was proclaimed
early on as the Messiah of Israel, opposed by the forces of evil yet victorious over those forces, required a reading of the Torah that not all agreed
with. For example, some groups of Jews, like the Pharisees, gave little or
no emphasis to messianic expectation, so that when Jesus was proclaimed
as a Messiah, instead of as, say, a teacher, such groups were inevitably
alienated. Those who declined to assent to a messianic reading of the tradition were quickly placed in the story as embodiments of the evil forces,
and in the story they were designated as "the Jews." Thus a later dispute
involving a telling of the original Jesus story led to a recasting of that story.
The religious claims made for Jesus required a set of villains to reject those
claims, and this was a role for which the religiously detached Romans
were unsuited. A religious rejection of Jesus by his own people — "his
own people received him not"[10] — became an essential note of the theology, or Christology, implied in the messianic proclamation. So for
Ruether, "the left hand of Christology"[11] is a rejection of Judaism, particularly its way of reading the Scriptures. That rejection amounts to an act of
revenge for "Judaism's" prior rejection — not of Jesus but of the story told
about him. Christology itself is a source of Christian contempt for Jews.

Ruether's critics have dismissed her work for what they took to be an
implication that the hatred of Jews is ontologically tied to Christian faith.
One Catholic official ranked Ruether's book with Hochhuth's *The Deputy*
for having "skewed" the debate about Catholic responsibility for the
Holocaust. This official defined Ruether's assertion that antisemitism is
rooted in Christology as "the 'straight-line method' of going immediately
from the Gospels to the death camps," and accused her of "conveniently
ignoring that, in fact, it took almost two millennia to move from the one
to the other, a rather long period of time to fail to account for. Ruether's
thesis is seriously flawed. It leaves Christians with the stark choice of
abandoning our faith in Christ or learning to live with being endemically
antisemitic."[12]

Critics of Ruether's sweeping indictment of Christology are right to insist, as Krister Stendahl put it to me in conversation, "that it all depends
on what Christology you have." But it is not true that Ruether's position regarding the Christology that has dominated Christian thinking for
centuries is "seriously flawed." The criticism just cited is wrong on two
counts. First, the matter of time. If the death camps are causally linked
through two millennia to mistakes made by the first generation of Chris-

tians — and I believe they are — can they still not be acknowledged as mistakes? What difference does it make whether two years have passed or two thousand if the causal link can be made? And second, we Christians have another choice besides rejection of Jesus or living with an antisemitism supposedly intrinsic to Christianity. In the light of what those first-generation mistakes led to, we can revise even now what we believe about Jesus. I make the assertion as a *Catholic* Christian, for what has been distinctive about the Catholic tradition ever since Martin Luther raised the banner of *sola scriptura,* or "Scripture alone," as the measure of truth has been its emphasis on the claim that the normative literature of our community was produced by that community, and not the other way around. The New Testament, that is, was made by the Church; the Church was not made by the New Testament. That is why, speaking generally, Catholics differ from Protestants in the importance given to the authority of the Bible on the one hand, and to the authority of the Church on the other. Therefore, Catholics more than Protestants would tend to say that the community has authority over its normative literature. How that authority is to be exercised and how that literature — if shown, for example, to be in some part antisemitic — should be reinterpreted are questions that arise only after the basic confrontation with this truth occurs. The assumption of this book is that a revision in what we believe about Jesus and what we say about him is necessary.

But is it possible? No less a figure than Karl Rahner, widely acknowledged to have been the greatest Catholic theologian of the twentieth century, declared, "Let no one say that nothing more is really possible in this field [Christology] any longer. Something is possible, because something *must* be possible, if it is a matter of the inexhaustible riches of God's presence with us."[13] And Rosemary Radford Ruether helps. She too believes that change at the level of faith, even a once fratricidal faith, is possible. The key is Jewishness, the Jewishness of Jesus, but not only his. "The Christian anti-Judaic myth," she writes, "can never be held in check, much less overcome, until Christianity submits itself to that therapy of Jewish consciousness that allows the 'return of the repressed.' This means establishing a new education for a new consciousness."[14] Or, as Paul van Buren, a pioneer of the Jewish-Christian dialogue, put it, "Israel's story is the primary context that makes the Church's language about Christ intelligible." Jesus, van Buren said, must be "set within Israel's story, and Israel's story is still unfolding . . . By the way in which it speaks of Jesus Christ, the Church is always defining itself before God."[15] Which is why the Church must learn to speak of Jesus Christ in a way that honors his Jewishness not only as something past but as something permanent.

In the course of writing this book, I went twice to Jerusalem. I returned there with a revised sense, shaped by personal as well as political history, of what religion is. I stood on the ramp above the Western Wall that leads to the Temple Mount, looking down. From that spot, or one near it, Josephus had looked down. "For while the depth of the ravine was great," he wrote, "and no one who bent over to look into it from above could bear to look down to the bottom, the height of the portico standing over it was so very great that anyone looking down . . . would become dizzy and his vision would be unable to reach to the end of so measureless a depth."[16] For me, to paraphrase Nietzsche, the depth stared back. I saw the difference between now and 1973. As a mature man, I looked down at the Jewish worshipers below me, the black-hatted figures in the ravine before the wall. Instead of seeing strangers, I saw a group that included that shrouded figure who, despite everything, remained my dear companion. This was what the Third Quest for the historical Jesus had boiled down to for me. "Before it was anything else," Ruether wrote, and certainly before it was a species of Jew hatred, "the Christian messianic experience in Jesus was a Jewish experience, created out of Jewish hope."[17]

The wall of the Temple is the last remnant of the world in which ours was born. Here is what I saw from my perch above it early in the twenty-first century: Everything we know and believe about Jesus began when he walked the same ramp, or one near it. He crossed into the sacred precincts of the Temple Mount, there. Twenty-five years before, I had thought the decisive threshold was one leading to Golgotha, but now I saw it was one leading to the Temple, for we are talking about Jesus here, not me. The witness of the davening Jews below underscored what the Temple must have been to him, and at last I saw it. Jesus and I were drawn to Jerusalem by like yearnings, but with this difference: What Jesus is to me — "the sacrament," in the great phrase of the Catholic theologian Edward Schillebeeckx, "of the encounter with God"[18] — the Temple would very likely have been to him.

Here was the *place* that would have most revealed Jesus to himself and others as a Jew to his core. We saw earlier the ways in which such an identity in his time was problematic, and we saw that, whether Jesus was one of them or not, some Jews would have been appalled by the contamination of the Temple by a collaborating priesthood. But that only underscores the basic fact that the Temple could only have been sacred to one identified with Israel. The assumption that Jesus came to the Temple to oppose it — to destroy it — not to worship at it or to defend it, is the first mistake that second-generation non-Jewish followers of Jesus would have made — because as non-Jews they would not have known what the Jews who preceded them knew: God had touched the earth in this place, and still did.

Instead of Christian disparagement of the Temple, here, from the Midrash, the collection of Jewish commentaries on the Scripture, is a Jew's assessment of the Temple's meaning: "Just as the navel is positioned in the center of a man, thus is the Land of Israel positioned in the center of the world, as the Bible says, 'dwelling at the very navel of the earth' (Ezekiel 38:12), and from it the foundation of the world proceeds . . . And the Temple is in the center of Jerusalem, and the Great Hall is in the center of the Temple, and the Ark is in the center of the Great Hall, and the Foundation Stone is in front of the Ark, and beginning with it the world was put on its foundations."[19]

Even the worldly Josephus attributes a transcendent significance to the Temple.[20] That attitude was central to his being Jewish.[21] Indeed, judging from the fact that the mountaintop site marked by the "Foundation Stone" shows signs of having been revered since the Middle Bronze Age (2800–2200 B.C.E.),[22] one could say that attitude was central to his being human. That such numinous sites are universally recognized as places where the divinity can be contacted only emphasizes the importance of this one since King Solomon, fulfilling the hope of his father, David, constructed his Temple here in the tenth century B.C.E. In the fifth century B.C.E., after the Babylonian conquest of Jerusalem, the Temple was rebuilt, and then enlarged by the two Herods just before and during Jesus' lifetime. Throughout its history, the Temple's function as a gathering place for worship — actually, the gathering occurred in the courtyards and porticos of the complex — was always secondary to its character as God's dwelling place on earth. That was the Holy of Holies, to which only the High Priest had access, and then only once a year, on Yom Kippur.[23]

The "Foundation Stone" on the site of that forbidden inner sanctum is regarded by many scholars to be the dramatic stone over which the Dome of the Rock stands. The rough outcropping, about the size of the bed of a truck, is surrounded now by a spread of Persian carpets and enclosed by an elaborately carved eye-level screen. Above this sanctum is the fantastic mosaic elaboration of Islamic geniuses. The stone revered by Jews as the site of the binding of Isaac in Genesis[24] — the story of a father's readiness to kill his beloved son, which has such resonance in the story of Jesus — is the stone revered by some Muslims as the site from which Muhammad ascended to heaven. When Muslims took control of Jerusalem from the Christians in the seventh century, the ban on Jewish settlement in the city, in force throughout the Roman and Byzantine periods, was revoked, and Jews returned.[25] When the Temple Mount was consecrated as a place of prayer for Muslims, Jews were allowed to serve as the caretakers of the Dome of the Rock. They swept it lovingly.[26]

Today one enters the Dome of the Rock in stockinged feet. Hanging oil lamps flicker, making the golden chips in the mosaic dome sparkle. Columns and hexagonal portals ring the broad open space in which the stone lies. There is a hole into which a pilgrim can slip a hand to touch the spot revered as one the Prophet touched. Exotic as it is, the place seems vaguely familiar, because it inspired the design of some of the great churches in Europe. Oddly, it conveys more than a hint of St. Peter's dome, above that other "rock." But this rock, one sees soon enough, is no metaphor. One moves slowly around it, eyeing the rough surface, an uneven igneous slope of the kind boys slide on everywhere. Isaac, David, Solomon, Muhammad, God. Pilgrims sink to their knees on the soft carpet to pray, to sit in silence before the impulse that has brought humans here for four thousand years. Lingering pilgrims, poked by stern ushers with sticks, then stand to resume the slow-motion pedestrian circuit that can also be an act of contemplation.

The biblical tradition emphasizes that while the Temple cannot contain God,[27] any more than heaven can, still God has chosen the Temple as an earthly dwelling place. The Holy of Holies is the particular in which the universal resides — which is the Greek way of putting an idea that is also expressed by the Christian notion of Incarnation. How is God present to the world, not in the abstract but in the concrete, which is the only meaning "present" can have? As a Christian believer answers "in Jesus," and a Muslim "in the Koran" (not Muhammad), so a Jewish believer today might answer, "through Torah." But all three — Christ, Koran, Torah — effectively replace the Temple. Following a tradition that begins with the Temple, all three religious impulses are incarnational. In Krister Stendahl's image, the Temple served as the magnet that organized the filings, but that role is now played by Christ, Koran, Torah. Yet among Jews, the idea of the Temple continues to have vibrancy and relevance.

Rabbi Heschel wrote that the Sabbath is like a temple in time. Levenson elaborates the idea: "The Temple is to space what the Sabbath is to time."[28]

As observant Jews take a weekly break from the mundane as a way of entering the realm of holy time — not only the time when the Creator rested, but the time when the Creation was, as Genesis puts it so simply, "very good" — so do such Jews approach the Temple of Jerusalem. This is true even in the aftermath of the Temple's destruction, for the banished Jews created an imagined Temple in the Mishnah, the first great work of rabbinic Judaism, a collection of oral traditions compiled at the end of the second century. As Jacob Neusner points out, the Mishnah is a response to the catastrophe of the destruction, a stunning act of imagination, a continuation of the idea that the center of an ordered cosmos is in a place and a ritual. But the place and the ritual must be temporarily made of words — here is the Jewish hope that, apparently, survives everything — until the physical Temple is restored.[29] "The world which the Temple incarnates in a tangible way is not the world of history," Levenson writes, "but the world of creation, the world not as it is but as . . . it was on the first Sabbath . . . The Temple offers the person who enters it to worship an opportunity to rise from a fallen world."[30]

This is the Temple held in the imaginations of davening Jews at the Western Wall. Christians behold such Jews in their relentless bobbing and assume that the motivating impulse is grief for the loss of a great church, as if the Temple were a St. Peter's Basilica. Levenson points out that such a comparison inevitably confuses the matter, for as St. Peter's became an emblem for Protestants of the excesses of Renaissance Catholicism, so it is easy for Christians to think of Jesus storming the Temple as a kind of Luther, as if the gilded marble were the scandal, as if the corruptions of high religious office were the issue, as if money were.

On this point the religious imaginations of Jews and Christians are mismatched. The Temple was never a St. Peter's Basilica enshrining the bishop's seat, not even the greatest bishop of them all. The Temple was from the first the flashpoint between "Christians" and "Jews" — a navel, but also the core of conflict around which so much is twisted. Having affirmed that Jesus, a Jew, could have come into the Temple only in devotion, it is necessary also to say he may well have been one of those whose very devotion led to opposition to the collaborationist priesthood. Scholars are divided on the question, but most agree that the Temple was in fact the scene of whatever act got him into trouble.[31] As the Gospels recount it, the crime of Jesus was against the Temple; then, upon his death, as Mark relates it, the curtain of the Temple was torn in two, a symbolic — vengeful? — destruction.[32]

The story involves not only Jesus. Paul may have been a member of the Temple guard on the day that guard arrested Jesus.[33] Acts of the Apostles places Paul as an antagonist at the stoning of Stephen, the first Christian martyr, whose crime was a violation of the Temple.[34] James, the brother of Jesus and leader of the Jerusalem Christians, was executed by being thrown from the Temple parapet, and Paul himself was probably put to death for violating the sacred Temple.[35] To first- and second-century Christians, the destruction of the Temple by the Romans was "proof" that God had sided with them against "the Jews," and Christians promptly appropriated the savage Roman war crime for their own theological purposes. Even at the dawn of the twenty-first century, Christians take the ongoing Jewish attachment to the ideal of the Temple as a kind of retrograde idolatry, and, by extension, many Christians take modern Israeli attachment to the land around the Temple as rank imperialism, pure and simple. As the destruction of the Temple once proved the Jews' unworthiness, so the intractable conflict with Palestinians today does too.[36]

But all of this shows a Christian misreading of Jewish belief, past and present. With the destruction of the Temple and the exile from Israel, Jewish belief and practice coalesced under the leadership of the educators known as Pharisees, around the study of Torah in the synagogues, and around the observance of the Law. The family table became the center of cult. The Pharisees became the rabbis. But the Temple continues even now — if only in the idea of it — as the solitary site of Jewish worship.[37] While the idea thus remains central, the Jewish hope is rooted not in a mythic never-never land but in a place on earth. Its specificity is the point. The Temple and, by extension, the land are tied to the unbreakable covenant God has made with this people. There will be no understanding of Jewish religion, or, for that matter, of modern Israeli politics, until the significance of that tie is grasped.[38]

The Christian imagination must shift. The Temple, as the house not of a pope but of God, must be compared not to St. Peter's Basilica but to Jesus himself. The very first Christians, because they were Jews, knew this. The comparison of the Temple to Jesus was made early — but, alas, vindictively so. As we saw, already in the Gospel of John, Jesus is remembered as defining his body as the Temple: "But he spoke of the Temple of his body. When therefore he was raised from the dead, his disciples remembered that he had said this, and they believed the scripture and the words which Jesus had spoken."[39]

In some ways this anecdote epitomizes the Jewish-Catholic problem, and in some ways this anecdote causes it. Worship of Jesus makes worship in the Temple obsolete. This idea was the perfect solution to the overriding religious trauma that took place as the anecdote was being written down, which was the Roman obliteration of the Temple. Not only was the Temple destroyed, so were the sects that defined themselves by it — the Sadducees and priests, who did so positively, and the Zealots, who did so negatively. In Alan Segal's image, only "Rebecca's children" survived the destruction — the Judaism of the Jesus movement, which evolved into the Church, and the Judaism of the Pharisees, which evolved into rabbinic Judaism. Segal explains, "Both Judaism and Christianity consider themselves to be the heirs to the promises given to Abraham and Isaac and they are indeed fraternal twins . . . As brothers often do, they picked different, even opposing ways to preserve their family's heritage. Their differences became so important that for two millennia few people have been able to appreciate their underlying commonalities and, hence, the reasons for their differences."[40]

Human memory is inevitably imprecise, and it is not uncommon for the past to be retrieved in ways that serve present purposes. How convenient for the purposes of the post-destruction competition with the surviving sibling for Christians to have creatively retrieved "memories" both that Jesus predicted that destruction and that it was caused — again, not by Rome — by the "Jewish" destruction of the Temple that was Jesus' own body. We shall soon see how this opposition between the Temple and Jesus combined with a Christian theology that made something positive of the destruction of Jerusalem and the banishment of the Jews, but the point to make here is that the necessary shift in modern Christian attitudes toward Judaism must be tied to this basic question. And, not incidentally, it is precisely here that the pilgrimage of John Paul II to Jerusalem in 2000 was so significant.

Even though the pope's visit to Yad Vashem was the emotional high point of that week, his subsequent stop at the Western Wall was more important. For the pope to stand in devotion before that remnant of the Temple, for him to offer a prayer that did not invoke the name of Jesus, for him to leave a sorrowful *kvitel,* a written prayer, in a crevice of the wall, in Jewish custom, was the single most momentous act of his papacy. It was a culmination of the slow reversal of ancient Christian denigration not only of the Temple but of the Jews who had, as the scholar Sidra DeKoven Ezrahi writes, constructed "memory temples . . . out of the ruins of their material existence."[41] That denigration has been the essence of supersessionism, and the source of antisemitism. The pope's unprecedented presence in Jerusalem had said, in effect, that the Catholic Church honors Jews at home in Israel — a rejection of the ancient Christian attachment to the myth of Jewish wandering, even if Catholic ambivalence about the Jewish state seems less than fully resolved. But whatever political problems remain,[42] a religious threshold has been crossed. The pope's religious devotion at the Western Wall was an unmistakable act of affirmation of the Temple, and of God's unbroken covenant with the Jewish people today.

In Matthew, Mark, and Luke, Jesus' assault on the money changers and pigeon sellers in the Temple is the immediate cause of his death, although in their accounts, it is Jesus' symbolic destruction of the Temple that is emphasized. By contrast, in John, the Temple authorities are imagined as destroying Jesus,[43] a process that begins with the disturbance but unfolds more gradually. The point is that all accounts tie the fate of Jesus to this Temple event.

In the Gospel re-creations of the conflict, especially in Matthew,[44] the main antagonists confronting Jesus throughout his public life are not the Sadducees of the Temple establishment, much less the Romans, but the Pharisees. That alone suggests that Jesus was not generally motivated, like a Zealot, by a hatred of the priestly caste, which had found it prudent to cooperate with Rome. On the other hand, the Pharisees are absent as antagonists in the Passion narratives, where the enemies of Jesus are very much the priests. In fact, Jesus' movement had more in common with that of the Pharisees than perhaps any other Jewish sect. Ironically, this closeness no doubt intensified the competition, especially as time wore on, which may be what accounts for the Pharisees' role as preeminent villains, as later recalled in the pre-Passion life of Jesus. As a result, the name Pharisee, in a Christian mouth, is pejorative.[45]

Of all the characters in the Jesus story, none are more vilified by the Christian imagination than the Pharisees, and not because they would have so opposed what Jesus represented, or because they actually challenged him during his lifetime. While Jesus lived, the Pharisees would have been relatively powerless missionaries, teachers, and low-level administrators. It is only with the elimination of the Temple and its priesthood that the Pharisees emerge as rivals — not of Jesus, but of his movement a full generation removed. That is why they are cast as enemies in the Gospels, which is why, in turn, almost nothing said by Christians about these particular Jews is true. Even Paul, who was one of them, misrepresents what the Pharisees believed for his own polemical purposes.

As for the initial disturbance caused by Jesus in the Temple, even the most skeptical scholars see a reason to believe that a "historical" occurrence of some kind took place. Jesus committed a violation in one of the courtyards or colonnaded porticoes where the changing of money, the paying of Temple taxes, and the selling of animals for sacrifice took place. He caused the disturbance during the volatile Passover festival that year, and — consistent with all that is known of Roman methods — he was quickly taken out and summarily executed.[46]

The details of the account of his crime given in the Gospels raise more questions than they answer, for, as commonly read by Christians, the Gospels have him challenging the Temple as if he were not a Jew. The usual Christian understanding is tied to the notion of his "Abba intimacy" with God, referred to earlier. If God was present to him *immediately*, not religiously, then he had every right to enter his "Father's house" not as a Jew, not even as a new version of the ancient Jewish prophets who criticized Temple abuses. Rather, he issued his challenge with a unique claim to authority. "The priestly reaction to his 'cleansing' of the Temple," the Catholic theologian Bernard Cooke writes, "makes it clear that he was considered by the official establishment as an outsider who was unjustifiably interfering in what was not his business. That he himself obviously did think it was his business appears to have stemmed from his Abba experience: the Temple was his 'Father's house' and Jesus' devotion to the Temple was but a reflection of his devotion to his Abba." Cooke is like most Christian interpreters in seeing the Temple event, whatever it was, as a definitive break between Jesus and his Jewishness. "In conflict were Jesus' experience of God and his experience of religious institutions; Jesus remained faithful to his Abba, though this meant death amid alienation from all he had most cherished as a Jew."[47]

Is that true? We saw earlier the difficulty of ascribing a univocal set of beliefs or practices to "Judaism." The attitudes of Jews toward the Temple were complex, as the prophetic tradition with its criticisms of "empty worship" indicates. Even while the post-destruction Mishnah idealized the Temple, some rabbinic sources criticized its corruptions.[48] The architect of the Temple of which we are speaking, after all, was the wicked Herod, and every devout Jew would have been sensitive to the contradictions implied in that.

But the point must be made again: This building's transcendent meaning would have trumped all such paradoxes. And whatever Jesus' experience of God, it makes nonsense of his whole life to think that experience would set him fundamentally against the God of Abraham, Isaac, and Ja-

cob, who was the God worshiped in the Temple. Scholars agree that Jesus'
use of "Abba" to address God was unusual, but did that mean alienation
from the Jewish idea of God? Can't the Abba experience be understood
within the Jewish context? Schillebeeckx emphasizes that the Abba experience of Jesus was "fostered in the religious life of the Jewish followers of
Yahweh . . . The core of what was enunciated in Israel's best moments of
its experience of God is somehow in Jesus condensed in an original and
personal way."[49] Thus the originality of Jesus' intimacy with God, instead
of alienating him from his Jewishness, can qualify him as a Jew.

And *how* that God was worshiped could almost certainly not have been
the issue either. However Herod's collaborationist hegemony shadowed
the Holy of Holies, it is highly unlikely that a Jew of Jesus' time and background would have taken offense at money changing or pigeon selling in
the Temple portico. As Sanders and others point out, those activities were
essential to the Temple cult: Jews traveled here from all over the Mediterranean to offer sacrifices, the single holiest act of Jewish piety. At Passover,
tens of thousands of Jews from throughout Palestine and beyond would
have come to Jerusalem for just that purpose. They had to purchase animals and they had to pay the Temple tax, and they needed local currency
for both. Money changers, like those ubiquitous *bureaux de change* in the
cities of pre-euro Europe, enabled them to do so. Likewise, the pigeon sellers provided only what a devout pilgrim needed. There is no question of a
Jew like Jesus taking offense in this way, as if usury were the issue, or as if
Temple functionaries presided over a system, as bigoted Christian memory might put it, of "Jewing" people down.

What then? Some theorize that Jesus would have been appalled by the
blood running in the gutters of the Temple, spilloff from the slaughter of
thousands of animals, as if the very practice of animal sacrifice were at issue. But would a religious figure so motivated *then* be memorialized in a
cult based on violence of what was, after all, the *human* sacrifice of his
own death? No, Jesus would have understood animal sacrifice, given its
root in the story of the binding of Isaac, as the religious observance that
put an end to human sacrifice. It seems anachronistic in the extreme to attribute the blood squeamishness to him of a people who prefer to pretend
that the meat we eat comes to us without slaughter.

It is better to acknowledge the impossibility of our knowing for sure or
in detail what the disturbance caused by Jesus in the Temple at Passover in
30 C.E. amounted to. It is clear only that Jesus did something, and that it
was taken by the authorities to be a subversive act. Whether his act would

have been widely noted, given the holiday throng, is unclear — Fredriksen, for one, argues that Roman soldiers would not have been in a position to notice such an incident.[50] The Gospel accounts suggest an element of violence — those overturned tables, the whips — that has always troubled the devotees of a sweet, cheek-turning pacifist. Was Jesus then a revolutionary after all?

Around the year 68, according to Josephus, a group of Zealots took control of Jerusalem, an act that would spark the vengeful rage of the Roman general Vespasian.[51] In their siege of the ruined Temple, the Zealots violently targeted in particular their fellow Jews, the priests and other Temple officers who probably appeared to the radicals as craven collaborators, according to the sectarian-political divisions we have been tracking. This slaughter by Jewish Zealots of Jewish Temple authorities establishes the possibility that a peasant revolutionary from Galilee could have targeted Jews as such in enacting a demonstration in the name of a purified Temple. Such an act would have had elements of anticolonial resistance and class warfare both — and for that reason, this kind of reading of Jesus' Temple disturbance had great appeal in the turbulent 1960s, when I first studied these texts. Crossan's view is more sophisticated than that, yet he finds it illuminating to compare Jesus' demonstration in the Temple to the draft board raids of Vietnam War protesters.[52] The analogy can be misleading, since the Temple was not a Roman war engine. Crossan sees Jesus' attack on peripheral, and in themselves legitimate, Temple activities as a peasant revolutionary's symbolic attack on the entire Temple enterprise. But why? Not only was the Temple not a Selective Service office — that is, not an arm of violent Roman oppression — it was, despite the paradox of its place in the power structure of the occupation, the only institution that allowed Jews to stand against Rome and its identity-smashing totalitarianism. Just as, for centuries, the dominated Irish were able to resist the overlord English by aggressively practicing their Catholic faith — religion as a political force, as the only political force — so every Jew who entered the Temple to participate in God's cult of sacrifice was defying Rome.

Scholars like Richard Horsley and Neil Asher Silberman emphasize that Jesus' attack should be seen not in the light of later Christian denigration of the Temple, which opens into antisemitic stereotyping, but in light of the earlier prophetic tradition: "'What to me is the multitude of your sacrifices?' says the Lord."[53] In this view, the Temple offends Jesus because of the lavish, Hellenized style of Herod's construction.[54] Jesus' protest is for the sake of a purified Temple, true to an unpolluted Israel, what the prophets always wanted. Objecting to the distance between the realities of the Temple and the ideals of the Covenant was nothing new. But the Christian emphasis on the prophets' contempt for the institutions of Israel has itself become problematic, a way of judging, and rejecting, the present against an idealized past. Why is the flawed present such a scandal? Isn't the point of biblical faith that God has chosen to be at home not among angels but among humans? And won't every human community and its every institution be therefore flawed, compromised? Would Jesus set himself against the very humanness — contingency, finitude, and, yes, political paradox — of the Temple when God's making a home in that humanness is the point?

When I first visited the Holy Sepulcher in 1973, I was offended by the filth and disrepair of the ancient church. It smelled of mold. Its corners had accumulated bushels of dirt. Its crumbling walls were supported by makeshift scaffolding. The sacred shrine had been allowed to decline to this degree because Western Christians, represented on the scene by Franciscan friars, were locked in a jurisdictional dispute with Eastern Christians, the Orthodox monks who had sold me a candle in the tomb of Jesus. This ecclesiastical quarrel was a vestige of the brutal crusader wars, and all in all it was enough to make a pilgrim flee the place.

In the late nineteenth century, a group of Protestant pilgrims had seen something similar at the Holy Sepulcher and concluded that it could not possibly be the authentic site of the death and Resurrection of the Lord. They "discovered" an alternative place on the outskirts of the Old City, the so-called Garden Tomb, which still competes for pilgrims, claiming to be the real site of the foundational Christian events. The Garden Tomb, in contrast to the Holy Sepulcher, is tidy and quiet, conducive to pious meditation. Lovely. One can picture the rolled-back boulder, well-trimmed bushes and shrubs. But when I visited it, the place struck me as lifeless and artificial, and I realized that if there was any point to an incarnational faith, it was that God comes to us precisely in our need for God. This is not to say that God's coming to us does not always imply the challenge to change our world, but the evident need for change is no proof of God's absence. When I returned to the conflict-ridden Holy Sepulcher, I saw it differently.

As noted earlier, the image of Jesus as a peasant revolutionary — recall that widely circulated poster of the 1960s, Jesus as Che Guevara — is central to the liberation theology so many of my kind embraced, and which clearly continues to inform much of the scholarship of the historical Jesus. But, as before, one is left asking, Is the face on that wanted poster really the face of a Jew? Is this ongoing Christian denigration of the Jewish Temple cult really necessary? In other words, with the new scholarship, has anything really changed?

Against much of this, E. P. Sanders argues that the Temple hierarchy would not have been seen as immoral.[55] The officials would have made an unlikely target for a man like Jesus. Nothing we know of him suggests the character of a radical purist. The Gospels, contrasting Jesus with the hair-shirted John the Baptist, and placing him with revelers and at dinner tables, take pains to show him as the opposite. Indeed, the idea of the Incarnation itself — human flesh as the locus of the divine — argues against the angelic imagination of the rigid revolutionary who takes offense at the compromises required by life in the real world. It is in this way that the ideas of the Incarnation and of the Temple mesh. In the Roman world, a certain compromise, a knack for living with the enemy, for living with what is as opposed to with what ought to be — all of this would have been the price of survival. In the history-bound religion of Jews — the religion of Jesus — the accommodation necessary to human as opposed to angelic life would not have been a sin. In respectfully differing with what I take to be the views of scholars like Crossan, Horsley, and Silberman, I acknowledge that such a perception may be a matter of temperament and background. I write, after all, as the great-nephew of an Irishman who died in 1916 in a British uniform.

But the Irish story, with its tradition of the informer, is a reminder that accommodation with the overlord can be carried too far. Not all compromises are required, and sometimes survival must take second place to integrity. Sanders, however, doubts that the Jewish authorities of Jesus' time were corrupted in this way.[56] He argues that the Sadducees and priests of the Temple would in all likelihood have been upright Jews, working hard to shield the populace from the worst of Roman abuse, and that populace would have repaid them with respect. Was Jesus an elitist who set himself above the religion of most people?

What about the disparity between the rich and the poor? Was that inequity at the heart of Jesus' protest? The fabulous mansions of the Temple aristocrats are even now being laid bare by archaeologists in the upper-city digs of ancient Jerusalem. By our standards, such wealth, built on the backs of the poor, is a clear injustice, doubly so when linked to religion, but again, are we here seeing Luther rejecting St. Peter's Basilica more than Jesus rejecting the Temple? We shouldn't make too much of Zealot assaults on the Temple aristocrats, Sanders says, because there is evidence that many of these same aristocrats wound up as anti-Roman revolutionaries.[57] In other words, we should beware of the urge, so highly developed among Christians, to define Judaism and its sects in ways that serve mainly to buttress conclusions we already draw.

Just as there is a problem with the idea of Jesus symbolically "destroying" a Temple that would have been sacred and beloved to him as a Jew, there are two problems with the idea of Jesus storming the Temple to rebuke its leadership, even if the debatable characterization of that leadership as greedy, wicked, hated, and collaborationist was true. This denigration of Jewish cult, worship, and society is the primordial idea of Jewish-Christian conflict, and it is still very much with us. The first problem is that this idea epitomizes the structure of antisemitic thinking: Jews as they exist are compared to Jews as they *should* exist, and are found wanting, sometimes to forfeit that existence. Second, this idea conflicts with all that we know of the message that Jesus actually preached.

Jesus may have been an illiterate peasant (Crossan, Horsley, et al.) or a relatively learned member of the middle class (Koester, Brown, et al.); we do not know. He may have been an apocalyptist (Fredriksen) or a magician (Morton Smith), a "wisdom" sage or a self-styled prophet. Scholars disagree on what to emphasize. But the essential message of Jesus — despite all questions of sources, sayings, oral and written traditions, and situations of Gospel composition — comes through every aspect of the communal memory with ringing eloquence. That message is love.

The word is used in so many different ways, and so cheaply; as Krister Stendahl said to me, "When the preacher does not know what to say, he speaks of love." The word has been attached to the name of Jesus with such saccharine domestication that it is almost impossible to use it now with anything like the required bite. Ordinarily, for example, "love" is taken to be an act of relatively private devotion, and the preaching of Jesus is most often understood as having to do with relations among friends, family members, communities, the Church. Jesus reiterates as the greatest commandment the injunction from Leviticus to love thy neighbor.[58] But there are sayings about the loving of enemies and the loving of those who are different. There are demonstrations of love, as Jesus is reported to have gone out of his way to care for the poor, to affirm sinners, even the collaborationist and corrupt tax collectors. There are sayings about loving the Father, and the Father loving. And there are reasons to understand, in what is recorded and in what happened, that for the followers of Jesus, the sayings about love originated in a rare, life-changing experience of a relationship of love. The word, as they said, must have been flesh. That most banalized and inflated word was spoken by this man in an original, authentic, generous way — presumably because of how he was seen to have lived it out. Love informed, shaped, inspired, *drove* the Jesus movement forward into history.[59]

We are not talking about puppy love, nor about an ocean of warm feelings, nor about a network of the merely friendly or the narrowly religious. "This was not mere pacifism or meekness," Horsley and Silberman observe, "but the first step in the reconciliation and renewal of the People of Israel."[60] We began by remembering the larger social-political milieu that was shaped by the culture of a ruthless occupying military force on one side, and by a sorely divided occupied population on the other. The sect-beset Jews, like the Irish and every similarly victimized people, shifted the brutal weight of oppression onto each other. What Jesus spoke of, and in his life embodied, was the opposite of Roman domination. It was also the opposite, not of anything "Jewish," but of an oppressed people's readiness to turn against itself. Thus "love" defies the occupying enemy, not in some sweetly powdered passive aggression — as if Caesar could be shamed by a timidly turned cheek, as if masochism could function as a strategy — but by truly realizing something entirely other than the institutionalized hatred of phalanx, standard, legion, centurion, siege machine, and, yes, crucifix.

For Jesus, "love" changes everything. That is why his reiteration of the command to love the neighbor opens into the command to love the enemy. In the context in which Jesus preached, that exhortation would have been double-edged, applying to the love of Rome, the ultimate enemy, and to the love of one's rival sect. "The dignity of human beings which requires such deeds of love," Koester comments, "cannot be derived from one's membership in a particular social class or religious group (elect people of God), nor from political affiliation or common interest groups."[61] The model for the love of which Jesus speaks is the love of God, who created not just one group but the whole cosmos (and in affirming this all-inclusive creation, Genesis is a mold-shattering myth). This God makes rain to fall and sun to shine on every person, just and unjust alike.[62]

The foundational Christian slander against the Jews is that the "God of the Old Testament" is the heartless God of the Law, of revenge, of punishment, while the "God of the New Testament" is the God of love, mercy, and forgiveness.[63] To emphasize here that the message of Jesus was a message of love is to risk being understood as repeating this canard, which is why equal emphasis must be given, again, to the Jewishness of Jesus. He was never more Jewish than in this proclamation.[64] The liberating and system-shaking message of love was given its *renewal* by Jesus. In Horsley and Silberman's useful formulation, what we have here is a "renewed Covenant" more than a new one.[65]

There is little reason to doubt that Jesus' preaching was heard in the villages of Galilee and the towns of Judea as having a powerful freshness — perhaps because it was tied, as Fredriksen and other scholars suggest, to a message that the End Time of Israel's God was at hand.[66] However this message of love is understood, the thing to emphasize is that it was original in comparison to the situation of a divided, demoralized people imprisoned in their own land, not in comparison to that people's own history. Indeed, one must assume that people responded to Jesus because they recognized in him something of their own.

The phrase "New Covenant," which has come to define Christianity's status as the superseding religion, has its origin, in fact, in Jeremiah, but the Hebrew word that prophet used carried exactly this connotation of renewal, a notion that does not open into the deadly dichotomy between new and old. For Jeremiah,[67] and for Jesus, there was only *one* covenant.[68] So we are not talking here about Judaism's being brought to fulfillment in the discontinuous message of a different movement. The point, again, is that Jesus offers a Jewish renewal, and it is tied to love. Jesus' message was thus rooted not only, say, in the opening chapters of Genesis, but in the piety of Judaism as such. I read it as a Christian, yet the record of the Torah seems clear: before God gave commandments, God gave blessings. Before the Law, there was the rescue from Egypt. Hosea, Isaiah, and other prophets strike the theme repeatedly: If Israel behaves like a faithless wife, sometimes provoking God's rage, God nevertheless takes her back every time. Nothing Israel does can undo this love.

If there is a Jewish hope in an afterlife, it has nothing to do with the "immortality of the soul," a Greek idea foreign to the biblical tradition. Jewish hope has everything to do with the faith that "the God of Abraham, Isaac, and Jacob" does not break the covenant with Jews when they die. Not even human mortality outweighs the love of God. Thus God does not need to be appeased like some puny clay idol, nor does God's grace need to be earned. Despite a two-millennia-long exploitation of the crassest stereotype, the Jewish God is no garment-district bargainer shuffling dress racks, looking among his creatures for the ones who offer wholesale. No. Again I say this is a Christian's reading, but the tradition is clear: The Jewish God's attitude is one of love. Period.

You would not know that if all you had to go on was the Church — not only in its preaching but in customary readings of its foundational documents, the Gospels and the Epistles of Paul. As Sanders writes:

> Discussions of New Testament theology have often contrasted Christian theology, in which "indicative" precedes "imperative," with Jewish theology, which (it is believed) works the other way around. That is, whereas Christianity says "God loves you; therefore love one another," Judaism is believed to say: "love one another and thereby earn God's love." Christianity is a religion of grace, Judaism a religion of merit and works-righteousness, in which people must strive to purchase God's favor, and in which they are always anxious that they have not done enough to earn it. In favor of this distinction, Christians can quote John 1:17: "The law was given through Moses; grace and truth came through Jesus Christ." This proves that Christianity was the first religion of grace. Historically, that is not so.[69]

And historically, Christians have used these definitions to show — as Susannah Heschel says we have always been desperate to[70] — that, yes indeed, with Jesus something new and unprecedented has broken through to the human realm. Never mind that in order to do this Christians have had to redefine Judaism in the narrowest terms and, with grave consequences, in the most negative terms. Judaism was the shadow against which Christianity could be the light. Nowhere has this dynamic been more forceful or more damaging than on the matter of love. Yet the fact remains that nowhere more pointedly than on this matter of love was Jesus a faithful Jew. He was proclaiming the love of the Jewish God.

Moved by such a love, Jesus would simply have refused to embark on any course that would have reintroduced the element of exclusion, especially one that played into the hands of the imperial system of divide-and-keep-conquered. While I presume to differ with Horsley and Silberman on what I take to be their denigration of the Temple cult, on this other point they are eloquent: "During the months preceding his final journey, Jesus initiated his movement of community renewal, dedicated to restoring reciprocity and cooperation in the spirit of the dawning Kingdom of God. Yet his movement of revival of village life could not become just another separatist movement, withdrawing from confrontation and seeking

the shelter of obscurity in the backcountry valleys and remote mountain-
ous areas of Galilee."[71]

Jesus had to take his message to Jerusalem — not *against* Jerusalem, as
the story is so often put in the Christian telling — because as a loyal Jew he
was summoned to preach it in his nation's religious and political capital.
The motive was not a shallow patriotism; it would be anachronistic to associate the national feeling of a first-century Jew for Israel with a twentieth-century attachment to the modern nation-state. Jesus' progress from
Galilee to Jerusalem was not the same as Michael Collins's majestic journey from Cork to Dublin. The Temple was not a Jewish version of the
General Post Office on O'Connell Street. Jesus went to Jerusalem for reasons akin to those that drew me and countless others over the centuries to
the same city — first Jews, then Christians, and, just as powerfully, Muslims. While this city embodies the divisions of the human condition, it
also transcends them. That transcendence was the point.

What Jesus foresaw as a consequence of his arrival in Jerusalem we do not
know, but there would have been no surprise that it meant suffering. Presumably, he had already experienced the conflict between the attitude of
radical openness that he advocated and the mail-fisted defensiveness of
the imperium. He would have known what had happened to his mentor
John the Baptist and to countless others of his generation who, in large
and small ways, had defied Rome. The buzzard-ridden remains of some of
those may well have lined the road into Jerusalem. The cross, which to us
is a ubiquitous symbol of a certain religion, was to Jesus, as a Jew, an
equally ubiquitous symbol of a certain politics — the deadly politics of
Rome.

Scholars credit the religious and imaginative genius of Paul for turning
the crucifix against the Roman enemy.[72] As Helmut Koester points out, he
did so by viewing it in the light of Jewish cultic notions of the expiating
sacrifice.[73] Yet in the Christian memory of the Jewish response to Christian preaching, the fact that Jesus was "hung on a tree" made him "a stumbling block to Jews." This assertion depends on one verse from Deuteronomy,[74] that to be hung on a tree is to be accursed by God, a verse
invoked by the relatively small number of Jews who embraced faith in Jesus as Messiah to explain the rejection by so many Jews of the crucified
one. The cross was thus turned into a polemical tool, with Christians den-
igrating Jews for their legalistic obsession with the Deuteronomic proscription. But this literal reading of an obscure line in the Bible ignores

the fact that for the people under the boot of Rome in that time, death by crucifixion would have already been the fate of some of the noblest and bravest Jews, if not the most prudent.[75] And anyway, the Deuteronomy reference becomes unintelligible in the situation of war with Rome. Political and social context — to repeat the mantra — is of overriding importance. The horrid, ignoble death by crucifixion at the hands of Rome would have become, even before Pilate, a point of Jewish pride. Remember Josephus: "[We face] death on behalf of our laws with a courage which no other nation can equal."[76]

And how was it that Jews mustered such courage? In the case of Jesus we have an answer. His message of love, based in tradition, opened into life — "abundant life," in the phrase John attributes to him.[77] Life that can be expected to overcome death, because life to the full is what "the God of Abraham, Isaac, and Jacob" offers as a measure of God's love. The ongoing life of the people Israel is the proof of this love. Thus love is the farthest thing from an abstraction, is not reduced to feelings or limited to the narrow realm of relationships. Instead, love is the attitude that shows itself in what it brings about — God's attitude, and therefore ours. Such love, bringing life, is doubly relevant in the midst of a martial occupation that uses brutal death-dealing as a form of control. Here is why Rome was the dead opposite of Israel. That a weary, heartsick group could recognize such love in a Galilean of no importance, who had nevertheless grasped this core of the faith and showed it, did not set him against Israel but stood him in its center. The biblical record attests, from the first verse on, to the most basic Jewish belief, which is belief in the power of God to create life. Nothing Rome does, nothing any human does, can take away that power. Life is the fundamental principle of morality undergirding all the commandments, which always ask, What is for life? And so life is the sign of faith, never affirmed more than when death seems imminent. Each human instance of death is a return to the first chaos of Genesis: What God did then, out of love, God does now. So life is the distilled word for hope, as one hears in every Jewish toast, *L'chaim* — To life.

For all this, Jesus of Galilee came to the end, fully aware of what a man like him, with a message like his, in a place like that, was up against. The point is that his courage was Jewish courage, his faith in God was Jewish faith. And, perhaps surprisingly to all observers by now, the last turn in his story, from brutal death to new life, a sign of God's vindicating love, was Jewish before it was anyone's.

⤜ 12 ⤛

The Healing Circle

AND THEN there were those who loved him.

> Who is the third who walks always beside you?
> When I count, there are only you and I together
> But when I look ahead up the white road
> There is always another one walking beside you
> Gliding wrapt in a brown mantle, hooded
> I do not know whether a man or a woman
> — But who is that on the other side of you?

In his notes to *The Waste Land* T. S. Eliot associates these lines with the story of the journey to Emmaus, which in Luke comes immediately after the discovery that Jesus' tomb is empty. "That very day two of them were going to a village named Emmaus, about seven miles from Jerusalem, and talking with each other about all these things that had happened. While they were talking and discussing together, Jesus himself drew near and went with them. But their eyes were kept from recognizing him."[1]

Eliot explains that his lines about the mysterious third companion were "stimulated by the account of one of the Antarctic expeditions . . . : it was related that the party of explorers, at the extremity of their strength, had the constant delusion that there was *one more member* than could actually be counted."[2] We are talking here about the extremity of human experience, yet to Christian piety, the story of the death and Resurrection of Jesus has long since been stripped of anything like extremity. For most worshipers on Easter morn, it is a pageant, a domesticated soap opera, and only by a stretch of the imagination can we put ourselves in the places of those men and women who knew Jesus personally, who loved him, and who, after the horrible events of that Passover in Jerusalem, must have been in a state of what we can only call extremity.

They did with their grief what we do with ours. While I was preparing to write this book, a dear friend was dying of cancer. At her request, a few chosen friends gathered to sit with her for an hour or two each week during the last two months or so of her life. Then she died. For a few weeks more, we continued to come together. This is a not uncommon phenomenon among those of us reared in the era of the T-group, now that we are aging and dying. This coming together for shared grief is sometimes called a healing circle, but it is an experience of raw extremity. There are the pains of loss, loneliness, and fear, but also, oddly, there are the consolations of companionship and hope. In our gatherings before and after our friend's death, we wept. We sat in silence. We paid attention to our breathing. We ate and drank. We tried to express our feelings and found it hard to do so. The sense of time itself changed in that situation, as we drew closer and closer, first to the death of our friend, and then to the abyss that opened under it.

Time seemed to slow down, and the past became freshly present as we spontaneously related the stories of our bonds with the one who had gathered us. But the stories, favorite memories, and anecdotes that elaborated all that we loved about our friend soon opened into the stories and memories of our whole generation. A pre-boomer group of East Coast lefties more or less the same age, we had been through a powerful set of common experiences, beginning long before we'd actually met — from the assassinations of the 1960s and the Vietnam protests to the transformation from rebel children to worried parents, from free love to retirement accounts. We each began bringing to our circle texts to read aloud — bits of poetry, fiction, political rhetoric — that evoked the rare days that had prepared us to be friends. We read from and listened to Mary Oliver, Albert Camus, Bobby Kennedy in South Africa, Allard Lowenstein, Betty Friedan. Above all, such readings reminded us of what we had loved about the one we had lost. And, aging flower children that we were, we sang Peter, Paul, and Mary songs and the Judy Collins version of "Amazing Grace."

Lament. Texts. Silence. Stories. Food. Drink. Songs. More texts. Poems. We wove a web of meanings that joined us. It was "grief-work," as Elisabeth Kübler-Ross had taught us to call it, years before we had a clue what it really was.[3] Our circle was an extended American version of the Irish wake, of Italian keening, of African drumming in honor of ancestors. It was a version of the Jewish custom of "sitting *shiva*," from the Hebrew word for seven, referring to the seven days of mourning after the death of a loved one. It was what we did with the extreme disappointment that death must be to every human being — the extreme loss of hope, the ex-treme loneliness, the foretaste of what awaits us all. The circle was our common act of love for our dead friend, and, because of her — a last and quite typical gift — an act of love for each other and for ourselves.

> Then one of them, named Cleopas, answered him, "Are you the only visi-tor to Jerusalem who does not know the things that have happened there in these days?" And he said to them, "What things?" And they said to him, "Concerning Jesus of Nazareth, who was a prophet mighty in deed and word before God and all the people, and how our chief priests and rulers delivered him up to be condemned to death and crucified him. But we had hoped that he was the one to redeem Israel."[4]

Immediately after Jesus' death, the circle of his friends began to gather. Their love for him, instead of fading in his absence, quickened, opening into a potent love they felt for one another. Their gatherings were like those of a bereft circle,[5] and they were built around lament, the reading of texts, silence, stories, food, drink, songs, more texts, poems — a changed sense of time and a repeated intuition that there was "one more member" than could be counted. That intuition is what we call the Resurrection. That the followers of Jesus thought of him in its terms does not separate them from Jewishness but locates them within it, for resurrection of the dead, as Fredriksen notes, "was one of the redemptive acts anticipated in Jewish traditions about the End of Days,"[6] which Jesus had called his Kingdom. To imagine Jesus as risen was to expect that soon all would be. This theological affirmation that Jesus had been raised from the dead by his faithful Father followed upon the human experience that when they gathered in his memory, he was still with them. In a similar way, the later theological affirmation that Jesus was divine would follow from the com-munity's instinctive impulse to pray not *for* him but *to* him.

To the eyes of faith, Jesus was really present. Whether a video camera could have recorded his "appearances" or not is less important than the fact that for those who loved him, and for those who sensed the full power of the love he'd offered them, the continued presence of Jesus beside them was no mere "delusion," in Eliot's word. His presence, of course, was dif-ferent now. Instead of being immediate and physical, it was mediated. In part, at least, it was mediated as my friend's had been, through the stories told about him and the affirmations made in his name. His presence was real. On this claim rests the entire structure of Christian religion, and I, for one, recognize it as an unwilled claim of my own experience. The writing of this book is a response to the undefined, unseen, continuing presence in my life of Jesus Christ. By now it is clear that my knowledge of Jesus is indirect, incomplete, a matter more of inference than experience, which is why my reflections on his meaning are less than certain. This is not knowledge of Jesus, but faith in him. I am one of those haunted friends who found themselves incapable of believing him simply gone, but I am also one who knows him in the first place only through the story those first friends gathered to tell.[7]

The story of the journey to Emmaus is important for its strong hint of what happened to enable the friends of Jesus both to understand what his coming and going had meant and to experience him as still present in their midst, if indirectly. And what happened was the singing of their songs and the reading of their cherished texts, activities that, over time, gave them a way to put the theretofore inexpressible experience into words. This is how the basic story of Jesus took shape in the first months and years after his death, what scholars call the kerygma.[8] Remember that the New Testament consists solely of words that were written down decades after the year 30. Recall that the earliest materials are the letters of Paul, dating to the 50s.

The healing circle of men and women was, at the beginning, still under the spell of the love of Jesus. Their love for him was surely powerful, but eventually a felt experience of *his love for them* overwhelmed their disappointment. Just as their hope in the continued life of Abraham, Isaac, and Jacob rested in the conviction that God's power to create life was not undone by death, and that God's love for those three and for all God's people outweighed human mortality, the followers of Jesus soon sensed the same thing about Jesus' love for them. His love survived his death — which is what the Resurrection means.

They came to that experience not mystically or magically, but — as this people always had come to faith — through prayerful consideration of their texts and through reflection on a tradition that looked forward to the resurrection of the dead. The songs they sang were the Psalms of David, and the readings they brought to their gatherings were the Jewish Scriptures. The Psalms and Scriptures gave them the story by which they could finally name the one in the hooded shroud beside them. Or, as the mysterious companion on the road to Emmaus himself put it to the bereft pair whose grief had undercut their hope, "'O foolish men, and slow of heart to believe all that the prophets have spoken! Was it not necessary that the Christ should suffer these things and enter into his glory?' And beginning with Moses and all the prophets, he interpreted to them in the scriptures the things concerning himself."[9]

Remember that this anecdote, in Luke, concerning what happened within days of Jesus' death was in fact composed years after the event, a fully theologized reflection on what took place. The point is that Jesus' followers used the materials of the prophets and psalmists — incidents and metaphors and figures of speech — as the raw material out of which to create an elegant and coherent story, indeed a literary masterpiece, of experiences that would, in actuality, have been anything but elegant, coherent, or patently meaningful. Scholars agree that, within a relatively short time, the followers of Jesus had constructed an account of his last days that would become the source of each of the four Gospels' Passion narratives. John Dominic Crossan calls that primordial account the "Cross Gospel."[10] Where scholars differ — and this difference is relevant to our attempt to name the ultimate source of anti-Jewish contempt — is on the question of whether the Passion story thus told is essentially a historical or a literary composition. Most agree on the historicity of the basic elements — that there was a crime, committed by Jesus, probably in the Temple, an arrest, and an execution.

A traditional reading of the elaborated account, typified by Raymond Brown, sees the Gospel story of the Passion as essentially true to what happened, as remembered by the friends of Jesus, who would have been witnesses.[11] If this way of reading the Gospel texts is correct, Christians sensitive to the anti-Jewish elements in the story, and Jews who are offended by them, are stuck with the facts that, as matters of history, Jesus' offense was against Judaism, not Rome, and Jews sponsored Jesus' death, even if Romans carried it out. That so many elements of the Passion narrative echo the themes, language, and events of the Jewish Scriptures may show that the narrative's composition was influenced by exegesis of such texts, but since most of what is reported can be assumed to have actually happened, such echoes more importantly show that Jesus was consciously modeling himself on the prophetic tradition of Israel, and fulfilling it. This is what Crossan calls "history remembered."[12] It has served as the traditional Christian mode of reading the Passion story because all those fulfilled prophecies are the proof that it is true. That is what the stranger of Emmaus demonstrated to the disciples, the Scriptures concerning himself.

"My God! My God! Why hast thou forsaken me?" for example. These last words of Jesus, in Mark and Matthew,[13] were "foretold" in Psalm 22.

His last words in Luke, "Father, into thy hands I commit my spirit,"[14] were "foretold" by Psalm 31. The fact reported in Matthew, Mark, and Luke that "darkness came over the land until three in the afternoon," as Jesus died, was "predicted" by the prophet Amos.[15] That the curtain of the Temple was "torn in two" at the moment of Jesus' death, that "the earth shook, the rocks were split, and the tombs also were opened,"[16] all was "foretold" by the prophets as signs that the Messiah had come.[17]

Moreover, the unexpected arrival of the Messiah as a suffering servant instead of as a victorious king had been anticipated by the image of the king entering the city "on the foal of an ass" in Zechariah[18] and, more elaborately, by certain songs of the prophet Isaiah: "He had no form or comeliness that we should look at him, and no beauty that we should desire him. He was despised and rejected by men; a man of sorrows, and acquainted with grief; and as one from whom men hide their faces he was despised, and we esteemed him not. Surely he has borne our griefs and carried our sorrows . . . he was wounded for our transgressions, he was bruised for our iniquities; upon him was the chastisement that made us whole, and with his stripes we are healed."[19]

That wounding was rendered in the Passion narrative as the piercing through of Jesus' side. The thirst of Jesus on the cross, the vinegar to slake that thirst, the presence of the two thieves beside him, the crown of thorns, the mockery of passersby — these details originate in the Jewish Scriptures. And such details were soon put to a polemical purpose. Here is an anecdote from the Passion according to John, and an indication of the argument that was made from it at the start: "When the soldiers had crucified Jesus, they took his garments and made four parts, one for each soldier. But his tunic was without seam, woven from top to bottom; so they said to one another, 'Let us not tear it, but cast lots for it to see whose it shall be.' This was to fulfill the scripture, 'They parted my garments among them, and for my clothing they cast lots.' So the soldiers did this."[20]

But what if they didn't? Obviously, no scholar in this debate was present for these events, so we can never know for sure that such details in the Passion narratives never happened, and it is possible that at least some of them did. For example, a devout Jew might well have prayed the line from Psalm 22 — "My God, my God, why hast thou forsaken me?" — as Matthew and Mark say Jesus did. That the words originate in Hebrew Scripture does not mean, ipso facto, that Jesus did not repeat them, and internal evidence may suggest he did.[21] And so with some other details. But the broad pattern of the Passion accounts does indicate that the motive is not the recounting of history as we think of it. When John reports that the dying Jesus said, "I thirst," he declares that Jesus did so not because he was in fact thirsty, but "to fulfill the Scriptures."[22] That verse, in other words, has a clear literary purpose, or even a polemical purpose, not a "historical" one.

That Jesus may have indeed cried out in prayer the "My God, my God" line from Psalm 22 might mean that his followers used other details from the same psalm to elaborate the story of his death. Which brings us back to the question of what those soldiers did at the foot of the cross. What if, fifty or sixty years before those verses of the Gospel of John were committed to parchment, a man or a woman who loved the only recently dead Jesus had opened a scroll to Psalm 22, perhaps because Jesus had cited it in his prayer? And what if that disciple read aloud this verse, appearing a bit later in the text: "Yea, dogs are round about me; a company of evildoers encircle me; they have pierced my hands and my feet — I can count all my bones — they stare and gloat over me; they divide my garments among them, and for my raiment they cast lots"?[23]

Perhaps these verses so perfectly captured the dread spirit of what their friend had undergone that the circle got in the habit of reading them, or chanting them, every time they gathered. This would have been in the year 30 or 31. By the year 35 or 40, it is easy to imagine that the fine details of Psalm 22 — the thirst that makes a "tongue cleave to my jaws," the jeer "Let the Lord save him!," those soldiers casting dice for his garment — had begun to form the core of the story. If this is what happened, those who told the story to each other in this way would have known very well that such details were not "historical." They would have known, say, that the "seamless robe" had nothing to do with the robe Jesus wore but was an allusion-rich metaphor, since the only figure who wore such a robe was the High Priest, and only upon entering the Holy of Holies. To that first circle, such details proved nothing. The point was not "proof"; it was expression. The point was lament. The point was grief. The point was drawing order out of chaos, out of the worst thing that could have happened. The point was the story.

In their gatherings around his story, around the Scriptures, and around the table fellowship they had first had with him, the followers once again felt the presence of Jesus, were certain of it, were healed by it. So the story says it was that day in Emmaus. "When he was at table with them, he took the bread and blessed, and broke it, and gave it to them. And their eyes were opened and they recognized him; and he vanished out of their sight. They said to each other, 'Did not our hearts burn within us while he talked to us on the road, while he opened to us the scriptures?'"[24]

Here is the key issue: "opening the scriptures." By the time this story jells as the narrative we know, two decisive things have happened to change everything. First, most of those who knew Jesus, who knew firsthand how the story was composed, have died. Second, the next, hyperviolent phase of the war with Rome has begun; the Temple, and with it the central cult of Jewish religion, has been destroyed. At that point, the followers of Jesus found themselves in fierce and unprecedented competition with the Pharisees for control of the legacy of the "true Israel." Dispersed from a ruined Jerusalem, and increasingly influenced by Gentile members who knew nothing of the Jewish Scriptures, they began to argue that the claims they made for Jesus as Messiah could be "proven" by the "fact" that the very things he said, did, and underwent, according to the story they all knew, had been predicted in what could only seem miraculous detail by those same Jewish Scriptures. Although the late-first-century Christians claimed, and probably believed themselves, to be working from what Crossan calls "history remembered," it is far more likely — I accept Crossan and Koester here against Brown — that they were working from "prophecy historicized."[25]

Gentiles throughout the Mediterranean world were rapidly won over by the kerygma, a story of liberation, of imminent deliverance, of a transcendent love that spoke powerfully to their situation. These Gentiles could recognize themselves in the figure of the Roman centurion who, in the accounts of Matthew and Mark, after witnessing the crucifixion, declared, "Truly this was a Son of God."[26] In Luke's account, there appears a small but significant difference, for there the centurion declares, "Certainly this man was innocent."[27] The Hebrew word rendered here as "innocent" has the sense of "righteous," which is a reference to "the Righteous Man" from the Jewish text known as the Wisdom of Solomon, a detail that brings to the surface a large problem that the missionary preachers of the Good News of Jesus confronted at every turn. Their magnificent proclamation was shaped as a story of the fulfillment of Jewish hopes: Why were Jews so much slower to accept it than Gentiles? The converted centurion served a polemical purpose in the Gospel accounts — reinforcing Roman innocence — but he underwent something decisive, too. Especially after the community of Jewish Christians in Jerusalem was dispersed when the Romans attacked the city in 70, relatively few Jews accepted Jesus as the Messiah. Their rejection threatened the Christian idea far more profoundly than any pagan rejection. Why, of all people, would Jews be unmoved by the logic, so elaborately displayed in the kerygma, of their own Scriptures? The truth of Jesus Christ is *proven* by Jewish Scriptures. This essential structure of the Christian claim must be confronted anew by Christians. Why? Because Jewish denial of that claim *remains* a mortal threat. The entire history of conflict between Judaism and Christianity begins here. And the problem abides.

The point, however, is that this phenomenon of Jewish indifference to the coming of one announced as the Jewish Messiah called that kerygma into question from the start. This was true despite the fact that, in the decades after Jesus, there were various tellings of his story, with some Christians emphasizing the Wisdom literature of Israel over the "suffering servant" tradition, and others seeing Jesus mostly in the context of apocalyptic expectations.[28] But whether Christians were householders or itinerants, city dwellers or rural peasants, Judean Jews or Hellenized Jews, always the impulse involved a justification of Jesus' authority as "the Christ" by an appeal to Jewish Scriptures.

Ultimately, that appeal was made as much by non-Jewish as by Jewish Christians. Indeed, one of the consequences of the centrality of Jewish Scriptures to the story of Jesus was the ready presumption from the beginning — a presumption one still finds today — that even non-Jewish Christians were authorized and qualified to define Jewish traditions. I have learned this by making such a presumption myself. In the course of investigations like mine, Christians commonly ask the question What is a Jew? — and then answer it. For example, in his book *The Partings of the Ways,* the distinguished Christian scholar James Dunn has a chapter entitled "The Four Pillars of Second Temple Judaism." He defines those pillars as monotheism, election, land focused in the Temple, and covenant focused in the Torah. He shows how each one is undercut by an essential Christian affirmation, exemplified by Stephen's challenge to the Temple, Paul's to the Law, John's assertion of the Word's divinity, and Paul's extension of election to Gentiles. This analysis forces the conclusion that the "parting of the ways" between Judaism and Christianity was inevitable.[29]

But what if Judaism is not so neatly defined? In his book *Telling Tales,* the Jewish scholar Jacob Neusner objects to the way in which Christians define Jewish concepts of God in order to claim a greater humaneness or uniqueness for Christian concepts. In a footnote, he comments on Dunn's four pillars, which he calls "excellent proposals." "My problem," Neusner writes, "is only whether these 'pillars' really supported the Judaic systems that will have rested on them; whether they really make much difference in the systemic statements of various Judaisms."[30] To suggest that the "ism" of Judaism was far less clearly defined at that time than subsequent Christian interpretations assert is, at least implicitly, to suggest that the split between "Judaism" and "Christianity" may not have been inevitable at all.

If there was a diversity among the first-century followers of Jesus, there was an even greater diversity among Jewish groups. Dunn's four pillars notwithstanding, the Greek-speaking Jews of the Diaspora probably had more in common with the Hellenized followers of Jesus than with the Pharisaic-rabbinic Jews, or the Qumran factions that emphasized a narrow reading of the tradition. One might say, equivalently, that secular American Jews today have more in common with their secular Gentile fellow citizens than with the ultra-Orthodox of Mea Shearim. To take one example, late-first-century Pharisees would have agreed with Christians, as reflected in Jesus' lament over Jerusalem, that the destruction was the result of Israel's once again turning away from God: "O Jerusalem! Jerusalem, killing the prophets and stoning those who are sent to you!"[31] But the Pharisees took Israel's contemporary lapse, as revealed by the destruction, which was an enactment of the will of God, to mean that a rededication to a strict reading and observance of the Law was required. Just as Christian Jews saw the Temple's destruction as proof of establishment Judaism's failure in rejecting Jesus, Pharisaic-rabbinic Judaism saw that same destruction as proof — proof everywhere! — that overt challenges to Rome, which the story of Jesus could be taken to typify, were self-defeating. The post-destruction rabbis settled in Galilee, centering their piety on the Law and rejecting the Jesus movement more than ever.

Whatever it "proved," the destruction of 70 C.E. served to focus the dispute among surviving Jewish groups, not only by narrowing their number, but by causing a religious identity crisis for all, with the elimination of the cultic center. As we saw earlier, the rabbis and the Christians were now locked in a struggle over the future of Israel. The rabbinic side of the conflict has been sketchily preserved, but one assumes its intensity. The Sanhedrin at Yavneh, where the rabbis had established themselves, for example, issued a condemnation of those who followed Jesus: "May the *minim* [heretics] perish!"[32] When this occurred and whether the judgment applied to all followers of Jesus are uncertain.[33] It is clear, however, that in some synagogues at least, Jesus' followers were early defined as apostates.

The Epistles of Paul and Acts of the Apostles assume a high level of "Jewish" violence against "Christians" (the killing of Stephen and of James, the brother of Jesus; Paul says, "Five times I have received at the hands of the Jews the forty lashes less one"[34]). There are records also of a "Jewish" massacre of "Christians" in the year 132.[35]

On the Christian side, as the drafting of the kerygma with its polemical element went through numerous stages, beginning with those first post-crucifixion sessions of the "healing circle," one can see how the rules of narrative construction were followed. Not only did real-time competition with the rabbis lead to an emphasis on conflict, so did the very form of the story. Every schoolchild knows that a story consists of a beginning, middle, and end, as we saw earlier with Aristotle's masterly reflection on *Oedipus Rex*. In his terms, the structure of dramatic narrative involves conflict, crisis, and resolution. If the story of Jesus were written as straight history, the conflict would be defined as one between the Jewish Jesus movement and the Roman overlords, with some Jewish characters in supporting roles as Roman collaborators. But the conflict of the story as set in the year 30 took shape to reflect the conflict of the storytellers between, say, 35 and 90 — an intensifying conflict ever more with fellow Jews than with Rome. The venality of Rome was a given for all concerned. There was no need to assert it or to make it central, in contrast to the struggle with one's sibling rival. That is why the Gospels prefer the centurion to the rabbi.

The long account in Matthew of Jesus' rebuke of the Pharisees is an example.[36] Here Jesus proclaims his intention to "fulfill" the Law and the Prophets, which means setting a higher moral and religious standard than the "men of old." To them it was said, for instance, "You shall not kill . . . But I say to you that everyone who is angry with his brother shall be liable to judgment . . . You have heard that it was said, 'You shall not commit adultery.' But I say to you that every one who looks at a woman lustfully has already committed adultery with her in his heart."

As if the tradition of the "men of old" were concerned only with form, not meaning; with the exterior, not the interior; with appearances, not reality. No one with the slightest acquaintance with Jewish Scriptures — certainly, from what we know of him as a Jew, not Jesus — could have characterized the "old" morality so crudely. This is the initiating, perhaps the licensing, example of what Neusner derides as the Christian habit of offering derogatory definitions of Judaism for the express purpose of highlighting a more benign Christianity. "For I tell you," Matthew has Jesus say, "unless your righteousness exceeds that of the Scribes and Pharisees, you will never enter the kingdom of heaven."[37] At the risk of overemphasizing the point, but also, familiar as I am with what is still routinely preached in Church pulpits, I repeat: This slander of the Pharisees originates not in Jesus' contest with them but in the conflict of the second generation of his followers with the Pharisees.

Conflict, crisis, resolution. Of course, the crisis in the story, what Aristotle defines as the "catastrophe," or moment of recognition[38] — what James Joyce calls the epiphany[39] — comes in the crucifixion-Resurrection event. Because "the Jews" with whom Christian Jews were in conflict were blind to that epiphany, which even a centurion sees, the resolution of the story — the end — follows from it. The resolution is that the old Israel is superseded by the new Israel. Implicit in supersession is a fact fraught with implication for the future — that the old Israel no longer has any reason to exist. In effect, the old Israel, by rejecting Jesus, has forfeited the right to be part of the new Israel, which defines itself now as the "true Israel."[40]

All of this — from the denigration of the Pharisees, to the delegitimizing of Israel's right to exist, to the implicitly supersessionist division between old and new, false and true — is what is meant by the teaching of contempt, a phrase originating with Jules Isaac, the scholar whom we earlier cited as a decisive influence on Pope John XXIII.[41] All of this is why Rosemary Radford Ruether can regard antisemitism as the left hand of Christology. It is built into the permanent structure of Christian worship, as Old Testament readings lay out "types" and "foreshadowings" and "promises" that in themselves are partial and superficial — mere shadows. And then the New Testament readings follow, reflecting the inherent structure of the kerygma, laying out the ways in which those insufficient promises are "fulfilled" in Jesus. The idea of fulfillment is itself a denigration, a reflection of the deeply embedded structure of conflict between "the Jews" and the followers of Jesus.[42]

At its most basic level, this polemic violates everything Jesus can be presumed to have taught about love, and surely contradicts what we can presume about his program of ending intra-Jewish sectarian dispute. As disheartening as this would have been initially, it became even more so as time passed. Those who carried the polemic forward were increasingly of the Gentile world. What we have here is not restricted to that particular era or movement, but is a manifestation of the inbuilt limits of human thinking about the past — the way people habitually read their own experience back into an earlier, different experience. Each generation can be counted on to misread the full context of its predecessor, which is why historical judgments, including those of this book, must be rendered as self-critically as possible. Human history is by definition contingent, and accidents of history — the Roman war, the loss of the Temple, the dispersal from Jerusalem, the readiness of Gentiles to be recruited — make it more so. Because the Scriptures, however sacred, are the record of human perceptions developed over time, we should not be surprised that they, too, reflect this fact of the human condition. It is when Scriptures are read as if they were exempt from the human condition that their effects can become lethal.

Thus the war and the Gentiles changed everything. Unlike the originators of the story of Jesus, these new Christians, when they used the words "the Jews," were not talking about a group to which they themselves belonged. It is at this point that something unprecedented and truly dangerous began to happen: "Jews" became the embodiment of the other. Because the conflict was cast as one between good and evil, consistent with Jewish apocalyptic tradition within which all of this unfolds, "the Jews" now became identified in the minds of Christians with the devil. An ethos of fulfillment became an ethos of demonization.[43]

⤙ 13 ⤚

Paul, the Martyr of Shalom

HOUGH THE FEROCIOUS conflict between "Christians" and "Jews" developed gradually over the decades of the first century, and then the next, the direction of its unfolding was apparent early. One who is so often faulted for having imposed this structure on the Christian story was also the first to bemoan it. I am thinking, naturally, of Paul, whose role here I take quite personally. I referred in Part One to my vocation to the priesthood, and it is relevant that the religious order to which I belonged through most of my youth was the Paulist Fathers, more formally known as the Missionary Society of Saint Paul the Apostle. Beginning with my taking of "final promises," which is how we referred to our lifelong vows, I was entitled to use the letters CSP after my name, for Congregation of Saint Paul.

Paul never knew Jesus. We learn mainly from Acts of the Apostles that he was a tentmaker by trade, of a family established enough to have inherited the rights of Roman citizenship. He was probably born in Tarsus, a provincial capital located in present-day Turkey, sometime between 1 and 5 C.E., which would have made him five or ten years younger than Jesus. There is reason to think that he was a short man (the Latin word *paulus* means "small"),[1] that he was physically resolute (despite some kind of disability, perhaps epilepsy), and that he was fiercely intelligent. While Jesus was coming to maturity, then moving inexorably from Galilee toward Jerusalem, Paul was being well schooled in Greek and Hebrew. He pursued his vocation as a pious Jew, associated with the Pharisees. He may have been present as an antagonist at the stoning of Stephen, who is remembered as the first Christian martyr. Paul participated not in the "Jewish" persecution of the Church, as it is so often put, but in the intra-Jewish sectarian dispute between those who followed the rabbis and those who followed Jesus. Around the year 35, or about five years after the death of

Jesus, something happened "on the road to Damascus" that drew him to the Jesus movement. He became one of its most energetic proponents. During a ministry that lasted until his death, sometime around 65, Paul preached all over the Mediterranean world, and he wrote letters to those who'd associated themselves with the movement through him. These writings, later canonized (made part of the canon, or list), formed the oldest part of the New Testament, the so-called Epistles of Saint Paul.

I loved being a Paulist, and I grew to love our patron. I thought of him as a manly adventurer whose quick reference to images of sport ("I have run the race") and combat ("fought the good fight") seemed the perfect rebuttal to our great, if unspoken, fear that the celibate vocation was effete. Paul's life of physical struggle — those shipwrecks and jail terms and narrow escapes — gave us privileged white males more courage than we needed. Yet that "thorn in the flesh" of which he famously complained seemed familiar, since I took it as some kind of sexual obsession. Sexual desire was a thorn I knew of. But, above all, I valued the ample evidence of his spiritual struggle, his restless zeal, his longing for God. It was all a model for me, and a consolation. The things I would do, I didn't — to paraphrase him. The things I wouldn't do, I did. I burned to be good.

There was a stone statue of Paul in the grassy circle outside St. Paul's College, the seminary in Washington, D.C., where I lived from 1963 until 1969. It had him crouching, but carrying a sword and a book. (The sword evoked the way he died. As a Roman citizen, he would not have had to suffer the indignity of crucifixion, as Peter did. Paul would have had the honor of being beheaded.) As the son of a soldier, it was the sword that I favored first, but through the 1960s two things happened. First the coming, and the worsening, of the Vietnam War weaned me from the love of swords and swoop-winged warplanes. Once, when I found myself in jail after an antiwar demonstration, I consoled myself with Paul's prison refrain: "You cannot imprison the Word of the Lord." Then, also in those years, I discovered the book — the Scriptures, of course, which the statue's stone book intended to represent, but all other books as well. In the seminary I learned to read, really read, and I began to write. It was the discovery of Paul's eloquence as a poet that finally sealed my bond with him.

Perhaps the most familiar passage from the Christian Scriptures are these lines from the first letter Paul wrote to his friends at the Greek city of Corinth. Nothing displays Paul's literary genius more eloquently.

> If I speak in the tongues of men and of angels, but have not love, I am a
> noisy gong or a clanging cymbal. And if I have prophetic powers, and un-

derstand all mysteries and have all knowledge, and if I have all faith, so as to remove mountains, but have not love, I am nothing. If I give away all I have, and if I deliver my body to be burned, but have not love, I gain nothing. Love is patient and kind; love is not jealous or boastful; it is not arrogant or rude. Love does not insist on its own way; it is not irritable or resentful; it does not rejoice at wrong, but rejoices in the right. Love bears all things, believes all things, hopes all things, endures all things. Love never ends; as for prophecy, it will pass away; as for tongues, they will cease; as for knowledge, it will pass away. For our knowledge is imperfect and our prophecy is imperfect; but when the perfect comes, the imperfect will pass away. When I was a child, I spoke like a child, I thought like a child, I reasoned like a child; when I became a man, I gave up childish ways. For now, we see in a mirror dimly, but then face to face. Now I know in part; then I shall understand fully, even as I have been fully understood. So faith, hope, love abide, these three; but the greatest of these is love.[2]

A. N. Wilson, who wrote a life of Paul, cited this passage, as I have after him, and said that "if he had written nothing else, [it] would have guaranteed that subsequent generations would have revered Paul, seeing him as one of the most stupendous religious poets and visionaries whom the world has ever known."[3] An extravagant assertion, perhaps, but it seems impossible to read this text, and others, without knowing that Paul had somehow penetrated to the heart of Jesus. For Paul, the manifestation of this self-giving love — the epiphany, as Joyce would have it — was the mystery of the cross. A vivid sense of Christ's Passion drew Paul into his circle — that primal healing circle. How Paul acquired that sense we do not know; Wilson theorizes that Paul was a Temple guard who personally witnessed Jesus' torment, in his trial and at Golgotha.[4] The story of the Passion was well developed by the time Paul would have heard it, but it was Paul who gave foundational expression to its meaning, turning the dreaded crucifix against the Romans by declaring it the source of salvation. Why is 1 Corinthians 13 read as often at funerals as at weddings if not because its crystal-clear affirmation of love transforms suffering into its opposite, not something happy — as if a magical Resurrection redeems a horrid crucifixion or, say, an auto wreck — but something hopeful. In this transformation, absurd and violent death is experienced as pointing beyond itself, to God's unbreakable promise. For Paul, this discovery, tied to his experience not of Jesus but of the story the first followers had made available to him, was a confirmation of his Jewish faith, and the Passion, death, and Resurrection of Jesus was a revelation of the faithful love of the God of Israel.

It was during my years under the spell of Paul that I became the man I am — became, that is, haunted by the elusive but trustworthy presence of Jesus Christ, who loves me and, as I first grasped while kneeling beside my mother as a young child, died for me. I never experienced a conversion as such, but I was taught to believe that Paul did. We Paulists emphasized it, celebrating our greatest annual gala on January 25, the solemn feast. That crouching posture of the statue in front of the college was meant to render the very moment of his having been knocked from his horse. The Paulist Church in New York, named for the patron, has a vaulted ceiling under which I was ordained. It is painted with the night sky to show the constellations as they appeared on the night of Paul's conversion. I accepted that moment as the radical demarcation between Paul's life as a Jew, whose name was Saul, and as a Christian, whose name ever after was Paul.

The emphasis in the Christian memory on this distinction between a Jewish and a Christian name — Jewish-Christian conflict reduced to nomenclature — is misplaced. As is clear from Acts, in a scene that occurred long after his supposed conversion, he was "Saul, who is also called Paul." It is the presence in that scene of the Roman proconsul Sergius Paulus that occasions the switch to Paul, the Latinized version of his name.[5] The Christian preference for "Paul" that follows only reflects the growing Christian preference for Romans over Jews. Not only was this Saul-Paul dichotomy unknown to the man himself, but so would have been our idea of the conversion it supposedly symbolized. I did not know it when we Paulists were celebrating the feast, but our patron's awakening to Jesus Christ could not have been such a radical demarcation between separate religions to him. Paul died thinking of himself as a Jew, and this emphasis on conversion as a moment of ontological change amounts to a denigration Paul would not have recognized.

Paul's ferocious interior struggle between the Judaism into which he was born and the Judaism as he then saw it in light of Jesus Christ gave external shape and language to the equivalent struggle of the entire Jesus movement. E. P. Sanders says that, for Paul, "the experience of being 'in Christ' was not the same as the experience of being 'in Israel.'"[6] It is a distinction that can be, and has been, read as supersessionist, implying that the former had completely displaced the latter — which is, of course, how Christians soon began to talk. But what if, instead of being taken as opposites, the two experiences are taken together, not with reference to divergent Judaism and Christianity, but pointing to the covenant of Israel, which remains the one tie to God. In other words, the real meaning of

Paul's struggle is lost when what is essentially a paradox comes to be defined as a contradiction.

As a young man, a literal Paulist, I was bothered to hear Paul characterized as the true founder of Christianity, implicitly charged with a betrayal of Jesus by turning the free-spirited movement into a bureaucratic Church. Later, I heard Paul defined — when, say, he coins the phrase "Old Covenant" — as the initiator of Christian contempt for Jews. Now I understand that Paul's preoccupations, reflected in these charges, were an inevitable expression of the tensions of a Jesus follower who was also a Jew of his time. As such, his every action, wish, hope, and belief was conditioned by the Roman oppression that was soon to explode into violence. But perhaps a stronger determinant of his theological preoccupation was his clear conviction that the End Time, with the return of Christ, was imminent. Paul wrote of hearing the trumpets, and the people he assembled shared his passionate expectation. If he did not urge his Gentile followers to become Jews, that was because the Jewish expectation of the Messiah included the conviction that "the nations . . . [would] walk in his paths," as Isaiah put it.[7] They would do so *as* the nations, not as converts to Judaism. Paula Fredriksen's work clarified for me the importance of understanding Paul's reflections on Jews and Gentiles in the light of his heightened sense that Christ's return was near, and that that return would resolve the ever more apparent conflict arising between Jewish and non-Jewish believers. Here, in her words, "we see most clearly the measure and consequences of Paul's foreshortened perspective on time."[8] Paul's belief in Christ was the belief that he was returning soon — precisely as the Messiah of the Jews, who, as Jews firmly believed, would be the Lord of all.

Thus the emphasis on Paul's theology as innovation entirely misses its point. What we have in Paul is not innovation but a deepening of biblical faith, as it would necessarily appear on what was taken to be the very eve of the End Time. The perhaps inevitably complicated long-run implications of Paul's firm distinction between "in Christ" and "in Israel" were of no concern to him because, as Fredriksen puts it, Paul "did not expect a long run."[9] That there has been one, it turns out, is another of those accidents that has shaped history.

So when it comes to the question of the origin of Christian hatred for Jews, Paul is at the story's center. His letters, as the oldest extant Christian writings, reflect the turmoil and contradictions of the kerygma as it was being composed in the decades after Jesus. The letters also show him at his most flawed. His rage, prejudice, and self-obsession are as evident as his courage, gentleness, and faith. Yet it seems that Paul's appeal, then and now, lay in his being so prodigiously complex. His influence in that period was great, particularly regarding the tectonic shift separating Christians and Jews. Volumes have been written attributing to Paul's habit of mind the opposition between Jewish "works" and Christian "faith," between Jewish "law" and Christian "freedom," between the Temple and Jesus who replaced it, between religiosity and true belief. Martin Luther's dichotomizing in this way, as much against the Roman Church as against the Jews, has skewed, perhaps forever, our ability to read Paul as he himself might have wanted to be read. Paul would acknowledge such faith-law oppositions, of course — he does so often — but he would have insisted on what those who came after him quickly lost sight of: The oppositions occur within one people, Israel. Paul could never forget that, because these same oppositions occurred first within one man — himself.

"We ourselves, who are Jews by birth and not Gentile sinners, yet who know that a man is not justified by works of the law but through faith in Jesus Christ, even we have believed in Christ Jesus . . . Are you so foolish? Having begun with the Spirit, are you now ending with the flesh?"[10] Paul asks versions of this question about "works of the law" often, and his opposition between Law and Christ, between exterior and interior, between flesh and spirit, must have taken on special power to those who knew that, at the same time, the Pharisaic movement — that sibling rival — was giving new emphasis to observance of the Law as Israel's only hope. But Paul had himself been a Pharisee, and he would have known that characterizations of Pharisaic piety as merely outward, as unconcerned with faith, as intrinsically hypocritical, were false.

Krister Stendahl helped me understand this movement in Paul's perceptions of this conflict with "the Jews."[11] In his earliest letter, written to the Thessalonians around the year 51, "he had no hesitation," as Stendahl writes, "about the punishment of Israel for not having faith in Jesus Christ: 'God's wrath has come upon them at last.'"[12] Stendahl notes that that phrase "at last" can also mean "in full," or even more ominously, "forever." But some years later, as the conflict between the Jewish followers of Jesus and the Jewish rejection of Jesus had begun to evolve into a conflict between Christians (many of them Gentiles) and "the Jews," Paul had reason to reconsider. He also had to take into account the passage of time, which in his first flush of apocalyptic fervor years before, he would have been hard put to imagine. That Christ had not returned was already beginning to challenge the movement's first assumptions, and now there were things of which to be truly wary. "In his mature reflection on the 'No' of Israel to Jesus Christ," Stendahl says, "Paul sharply warns his gentile followers against feeling superior to Israel."[13] Indeed, Paul's warning to the Christian community at Rome, sent about ten years after Thessalonians, reads like a warning to all who will ever think of Israel as surpassed or superseded. "Lest you be wise in your own conceits," he writes in Romans, "I want you to understand this mystery, brethren: a hardening has come upon part of Israel, until the full number of the Gentiles come in, and so all Israel will be saved; as it is written, 'The Deliverer will come from Zion, he will banish ungodliness from Jacob; and this will be my covenant with them when I take away their sins.'"[14]

Paul knows from his own painful experience how most Jews have refused to accept Jesus as the Messiah. Yet here he does not make the meaning of that rejection absolute. "As regards the gospel," he goes on, and the clause is restrictive, "they are enemies of God, for your sake; but as regards election they are beloved for the sake of their forefathers. For the gifts and the call of God are irrevocable."[15] If I may presume as a Christian to say so, this felt sense of the permanence of God's promise is the essence of Jewish faith. It is the meaning of the covenant, but it is also the meaning of the Resurrection. God's love conquers everything, including the inherent divisiveness of human beings, including the vicissitudes of time, including death. Paul put this perception into practice as he tried desperately to heal the breach that was opening between Christians who valued the Law and clung to the essential Jewishness of the kerygma, and those who wanted to define Jews as the enemy pure and simple.

"Paul tried to accomplish the impossible," Helmut Koester writes, "namely, to establish a new Israel on a foundation that could include both Jews and Gentiles."[16] That foundation was the quick return of Christ, which was not to be. Paul's whole story, in effect, is a struggle to change the narrative's frame of reference from the conflict whose resolution is achieved by the victory of one side over the other — condemning the loser to historical irrelevance and expendability — to "shalom," which, as Stendahl says, "does not picture peace as a victory, but as a balance, a harmony,"[17] where God's all-encompassing love, rather than excluding human power, is the source of resolution. It was a matter of living as if the End Time had already begun. Because this remained his frame of reference, Paul avoided the temptation to which other key followers of Jesus were then beginning to yield — to define "the Jews" as absolutely evil, especially by laying the full weight of the cross on them. "For all his fulminations against the observance of Jewish Law," Jon Levenson writes, "Paul never blames the Jews for the death of Jesus or ascribes the founding of the Church to God's wrath against the people of the old covenant. Indeed, he does not attribute Jesus' demise to the Jews at all — an extraordinary datum in light of the reports of the trial and execution of Jesus in the canonical Gospels."[18]

In his last years, wherever he went among Gentile churches, Paul took up a collection for the Jerusalem community, those fully Jewish Christians who were still observing the Law and worshiping in the Temple. Paul's great hymn to love, addressed to the Corinthians, was no sentimental abstraction, no mere wedding song, but a response to the worst crisis of his life, as he saw members of his new community define his old community as the enemy. Against that definition he staked his life — he had to. He was trying to live out the message of love he had learned from Jesus, and from the Jewish God.

Eventually Paul returned to Jerusalem, knowing he would be a controversial figure there among both the Jewish authorities and the Jewish Christians. He arrived with the collection, apparently a considerable sum of money, a symbol of "shalom." He made the gift of it to the Jewish Christians, and in deference to their express wish, he then went to the Temple to demonstrate his continuing devotion to the traditional cult of Israel. Paul knew nothing of supersessionism. He remained a Jew.[19] Indeed, his faith in Jesus was, to him, a way of being more Jewish than ever. But something happened in the Temple. We don't know what. The similarity with the defining "crime" of Jesus is eerie. Here is Luke's account in Acts: "When the seven days were almost completed, the Jews from Asia, who had seen him in the temple, stirred up all the crowd, and laid hands on him, crying out, 'Men of Israel, help! This is the man who is teaching men everywhere against the people and the law and this place; moreover he has also brought Greeks into the temple, and he has defiled this holy place . . .' Then all the city was aroused, and the people ran together; they seized Paul and dragged him out of the temple, and at once the gates were shut. And as they were trying to kill him, word came to the tribune of the court that all Jerusalem was in confusion. He at once took soldiers and centurions, and ran down to them; and when they saw the tribune and the soldiers, they stopped beating Paul."[20]

Once again, Jewish villains and Roman rescuers. Once again, an undefined crime in the Temple. Once again, an account written years after the event as an anti-Jewish slander. Luke wants his readers to fault "the Jews," but the Jews who would have felt most passionately about Paul, the Jews most likely to have erupted at the sight of him, were in fact Jewish followers of Jesus — *Christians* — who disagreed with him about the observance of the Law.[21] As John Gager and others point out, there is reason to believe that Paul's fulminations against "the Jews" were aimed at just such Christians.[22] It was his purpose to heal the breach with this very group that got him arrested then. Since disturbances in the Temple could be defined by Rome as a capital crime, that purpose ultimately got him killed. As a Roman citizen, he could not be summarily executed, as Jesus was. Tradition holds that the prisoner Paul, having been brought to Rome, was executed there.

Saint Paul, so often identified as a culprit in the Jewish-Christian conflict, was in fact a victim of it. So many of the later phases of the Christian assault on Jews would be carried out in his name, yet in this first phase, he saw that dynamic taking shape and tried to stop it. Ironically, it is likely that he met a martyr's fate because of a Jewish-Christian conflict *within* the community of those who had accepted Jesus. The words "the Jews," convey none of these complexities. For Paul's insistence on such complexities — and for all of this — I love him still.

Parting of the Ways

THE SO-CALLED "parting of the ways" between Christians and Jews would take place gradually over two or three centuries. All early conflict occurs within the multifaceted world of Judaism, not only in the sense that various sects and subgroups still identify themselves as "Israel," but also in the sense that the nature of the disputes reflects the long tradition of intra-Jewish tensions, especially between prophetic and priestly strains.[1] The New Testament writings come late in reference to the lifetime of Jesus, but they come early in reference to the final split between entities called Christianity and Judaism.

In Judaism, differences between Galilee-based rabbinic modes and Hellenized Diaspora modes would be detected for centuries. To take one example, Greek-speaking Judaism, like that in the lively community of Alexandria — which in the first-century may have had as many Jews as Judea itself[2] — would have developed quite apart from what the rabbis taught in Yavneh in Palestine. In basing itself on the Septuagint, the Greek translation of the Hebrew Bible that dated to the second or third century B.C.E.,[3] the Jewish community of Alexandria would have had much in common with Christianity, which did the same.

Archaeological surveys of gravesites in the ancient Mediterranean world show that it is often impossible, into the second and third centuries, to tell the difference between Jewish and Christian tombs.[4] The remains of churches and synagogues dating even later show traces of mosaic decoration — a sacred vine motif, for example — that are similar.[5] Christians have long been accustomed to thinking of representations of the fish, of bread, and of the cup as expressly Christian symbols, but in the age when such signs were being engraved on the walls of what we think of as Christian catacombs, non-Christian Jews were using the same symbols, so much so that one historian concludes that, while Christians were gathering at the Eucharist, some Jews also were using bread and wine "as vehi-cles of Jewish worship and hope."[6] Among Jews today, Kiddush with chal-lah and wine, like the Passover matzo, is a vestige of this usage. Bread and wine are central to the cult of Christians; that these elements are key to both Jewish and Christian ritual indicates the strength of common sources.

The fluidity of interaction between these groups is reflected in the ways that Church fathers, well into the fourth century, warn against Christian participation in Jewish observances. For centuries, Christians' celebra-tion of Easter coincided exactly with Passover, and their observance of the Sabbath continued to take place on Saturday.[7] It took the order of Constantine, referred to earlier, and decrees of the fourth-century Church councils to draw fast distinctions between Jewish and Christian obser-vances, but the purpose of such decrees was to clarify the minds of Chris-tians, who continued to think of themselves as Jewish. For example, some of the most apparently anti-Jewish sermons of Saint John Chrysostom, preaching in Antioch in the late fourth century, were aimed less at Jews than at Judaizers, those Christians who wanted to adopt or maintain Jew-ish practices.[8]

Ultimately, both Jews and Christians rejected the middle group of be-lievers who sought to honor the organic link between the religion of Jesus and the religion of Jews — what Jesus, his mother, and his first followers, including Paul, all took for granted. Jewish Christians, like those who cele-brated the Eucharist as a Passover meal, and Christian Jews, like those who'd continued worshiping in the Temple until its destruction or rever-ing Jerusalem until its final obliteration, disappeared from this story and from history, if only over a very long time. Their fate is common in history for groups holding the middle ground once a dispute has been polarized. Thinking back to my great-uncle, the Irish Catholic who fought for the British in France in 1916, it is not only that the Irish who stood between London and the radical republican nationalists were lost to memory, but that they were often physically targeted by both sides. Thus the British high command ordered Irish regiments put into the front ranks at the trenches of the Western Front, guaranteeing their slaughter, while the Irish Republican Brotherhood took special aim at the Anglo-Irish gentry, torching their homes and driving many off. Once such a conflict is joined, those who refuse to identify with the polar extremes are in grave danger.

Despite the gradual character of the Jewish-Christian split, it is still possible to detect, early in the second century, a definitive event that in ef-fect set the course. Within a few decades of the composition of John, the last canonical Gospel, and within a few years of the final Roman destruction of Jerusalem, in 135, a Christian preacher named Marcion (85–160) carried the idea of supersessionist "fulfillment" to its logical conclusion, arguing that the Jewish Scriptures no longer had validity as the revealed Word of God. As Jesus replaced the Temple, and as a God of love replaced a God of Law, the foundational writings of the kerygma — Marcion proposed the Gospel of Luke and a de-Judaized version of Paul's letters — replaced the Torah and other books of the Bible.[9] This was a new Bible for a new Israel. A great debate ensued, and a crisis, too. What did Christians believe about Israel and its Scriptures? If the denigrations were true, why not abandon those texts, as God had abandoned those people?

Eventually Marcion's opponents — Clement of Rome, Justin Martyr, Irenaeus, and others — carried the day. The Jewish Scriptures, as the source of the prophecies that Jesus fulfilled, were necessary for Christian faith. The dynamic interaction of foretelling and fulfillment was essential to demonstrating the truth of claims about Jesus, especially in that period when the claim that he was the Messiah was evolving into the claim that he was divine. It was the foretelling-and-fulfillment mode that demonstrated the inadequacy of the Jewish moral code and the superiority of Jesus' morality of love. The Jewish Scriptures, which began as the source — Crossan's "prophecy historicized" — of the fully vivified Passion narrative, had now become the negative background against which Christian truth could shine. Oddly, this backhanded defense of Jewish texts would be replicated more than two centuries later, by Augustine, in defense of the Jewish people themselves. By then, the hysterics of the heresy-hunting fourth century were already slaughtering Arians and other Christian misfits, and they wanted to kill Jews as well. But Jews were the "witness people," whose continued existence as a negative proof was necessary. We shall see more of Augustine's fateful defense of the Jews in Part Three — a defense that was soon perverted, with terrible consequences, but a defense nonetheless that may well have spared the people.[10]

In the second century, Marcion won half the battle, for his idea of a canonical set of Christian Scriptures was accepted. The creation of a New Testament to stand permanently in tension with what now is designated as the Old Testament crystallized the foretell-fulfill structure. The tags "Old" and "New" institutionalized the Christian habit of Jewish denigration. More than that, the creation of a New Testament amounted, in Koester's words, to the creation of "an authoritative instrument . . . that would establish Christianity as a separate religion."[11]

Something similar was happening at the same time among the rabbis in Judea and Galilee, who, as Koester puts it, "codified the tradition that had empowered the reconstitution of Palestinian Judaism, the Mishnah."[12] The Mishnah, as we saw, is a compilation of the oral traditions of the first years of rabbinic Judaism. It consists of civil and religious law, commentaries, and discussion. In contrast to the equivalent foundational texts of Christians, which included as canonical the anti-Jewish polemic, the Mishnah, in the words of the Christian scholar Clemens Thoma, "does not contain a single passage clearly denouncing Jesus or Christianity. At a time when the Church Fathers loudly and aggressively preached and wrote against the Jews, such refraining from polemics is proof of considerable inner strength."[13] It is also an indication that rabbinic Judaism had no need to define itself against what could be dismissed as a minority breakaway sect. In this it was unlike nascent Christianity, which of necessity — here is the legacy of Marcion — defined itself against a Jewish negative. Nevertheless, the gulf between the sibling rivals grew, even if its insurmountability was more openly insisted upon by Christians than by Jews. The Mishnah became an emblem of a new rabbinic identity with which few Christians had any acquaintance. As such, it calcified the Jewish side of the growing break, while the newly canonical Christian writings did as much for those who followed Jesus. In other words, while Christians were devising structures that would separate them from the community once designated "Israel," rabbis were inventing forms of religion in which Christians could not participate, even if they wanted to. The books both symbolized the break and reified it.

In addition to being a Harvard professor and world-renowned Scripture scholar, Helmut Koester is a Lutheran pastor who has devoted his life to the study of, and worship through, the Gospels and the Pauline letters. Yet he quotes with approval a statement by a Harvard colleague that the New Testament is "a tragic historical mistake." With the Mishnah on one side and this new canon of all too human — if still somehow sacred — Scriptures on the other, the "reconciliation of the two heirs of the tradition of Israel was no longer possible."[14]

For one thing, from now on it would be impossible for a believing Jew to accept a Jesus whose meaning, by definition, involved a *de*meaning of the Jewish Scriptures, the Jewish cult, the Jewish covenant with God. The intellectual and moral structure of the kerygma could now be seen as inherently dismissive of Judaism. Matthew had Jesus assert that he had come "not to abolish the Law and the prophets, but to fulfill them."[15] Jews were accustomed to reading their Scriptures with an eye on the patterns of what Stendahl calls "benevolent typology,"[16] appreciating how similarities of event and symbol from one era to another reinforce the continuity of tradition, but "fulfillment" goes beyond typology, using the events of one era to "trump and trounce," in Stendahl's phrase, those of another. Fulfillment like this was abolition itself. For all the talk of wanting Jews to accept Jesus as the Messiah — and as we shall see, there has been a lot of such talk down through the centuries — it was clear early on that a Jew could accept Jesus only by rejecting — betraying — everything Jesus himself believed. Thus the early-second-century rabbis sent the word out from Judea and Galilee to have nothing further to do with Christians, whose attitude, in turn, given the threat posed by such firm Jewish rejection, was necessarily even more antagonistic.[17] The siblings had moved from mere rivalry to open hostility — a fight over the vision that, in such a trying world, could have united them. Instead of realizing the vision of either the prophets or Jesus, it was Rome's vision — divisive, violent, totalitarian — that the relationship of Jews and Christians would embody.

On the Christian side (and I assert this as a Christian), the canonization of this dispute — putting into the mouth of Jesus, say, a sweeping characterization of the Pharisees as a "brood of vipers"[18] — was a profound betrayal of the life and message of that same Jesus. As I declared at the outset, one of my purposes is to mark the decisive turns in this story, points where things might have gone in a different, better way. Surely here is the primordial one. Given all that led to this split between Christians and Jews — Nero's scapegoating of the Jesus movement, the savage Roman war, the consequent dispersal of Israel, the disappointment of Christian apocalyptic hope, the stresses within Israel between Hellenizers and Palestine-bound rabbis, the disappearance of the Jewish Christians of Jerusalem, the pressures of a Gentile slave society's attraction to the kerygma — we can hardly imagine that the story might have gone another way.

Yet it could have. A Christian must assert that the story could have gone in a way more consonant with the message of Jesus, toward its realization instead of its betrayal. That I am unable to say precisely how that might have happened — Jesus recognized within Judaism? his movement understood by both Jews and Christians as belonging firmly within the one Israel under the one covenant? — does not mean that an alternative outcome was impossible. That it came to seem so set in motion the chain of consequences we are following here, until the betrayal becomes irrefutably clear in the twentieth century. The triumphal planting of the cross at Auschwitz, which gave us our starting point, now reveals its meaning: the displacement of Jews by Christians as the true Israel requires displacement there too. Even the Shoah must yield before the inexorable supersessionism.

→ 15 ←

The Lachrymose Tradition: A Cautionary Note

CLARE BOOTHE LUCE IS said by the novelist Herbert Gold to have complained to a Jewish friend that she found all the talk about the Holocaust insufferably boring. Her friend said he knew just what she was talking about. "In fact," Gold writes, "he had the same sense of repetitiousness and fatigue, hearing so often about the crucifixion."[1]

At this point in the narrative, it may be useful to note a warning that certain Jewish historians register. One of them, the great Salo Wittmayer Baron of Columbia University, author of a definitive social and religious history of Jews, decries what he calls "the lachrymose conception of Jewish history,"[2] the seemingly endless litany of disasters that, starting with the New Testament anti-Jewish libel we have just observed, leads to attacks on Jews by early Church fathers and moves through the Crusades, the Blood Libels, the expulsions, the restrictions on choice of occupation and place of residence, and on to the modern nightmare of the Shoah.

Such a narrow recounting of Jewish history, as if only evil befell this people, can be exacerbated by the way that even individual episodes are recalled. Norman Roth points out that medieval Jewish chroniclers took as a model the Book of Lamentations, which "tended to portray every calamity which befell the Jews in apocalyptic terms."[3] A spirit of exaggeration does infect some of the sources: Communities that were "utterly destroyed" by one tragedy or another could be discovered in other sources to have survived more or less intact.

Reacting especially to the overwhelming shock of the Holocaust, and perhaps to the realization of how close Hitler had actually come to achieving the Final Solution, some Jewish observers have become impatient with narratives that, beginning as far back as late antiquity, emphasize victimhood as the enduring note of Jewish identity. Has the extreme suffering of the Shoah become the lens through which all things Jewish must be seen? Does Clare Boothe Luce speak for more than narrow-minded bigots in complaining, in effect, that such relentless tales of woe can be subtly dehumanizing? Does the perennially highlighted misery of Jews in fact slyly fulfill what we will see later as the Augustine-inspired prophecy that Jewish misery as a punishment for the deicide doubles as proof of Jewish guilt? In the hands of Christian interpreters, Jewish suffering thus becomes a new law of social organization, if not of nature.

That is why it is so important to emphasize that Jewish history includes the triumphs of the rabbinic communities in Palestine and in the Diaspora during late antiquity; the early urban settlements of northern Europe; the sages who, during the early Middle Ages, reclaimed the Hebrew language, which was all but dead for half a millennium;[4] the intellectual and linguistic inventiveness of the Jewish translation centers in Iberia during the period of Christian-Islamic-Jewish amity; the active Jewish participation in the coming of the Renaissance; the extraordinary enlivening of Jewish spirituality in eastern Europe at the dawn of the modern era; the profound impact of Kabbalah, not only on Jewish religion but on Enlightenment philosophy and science, and on the coming of democracy.[5] In each of these cases, and others, Jewish thought, culture, religion, and life took shape independent of the pressures exerted by the broader world of an empowered Christendom.

There are, to be sure, important aspects of this story that have nothing to do with theology or Church attitudes as such. The fate of the Jews has been shaped by numerous factors besides religion. The movement from a feudal economy to a mercantile one, with the arrival of a large Christian merchant class, set up conflicts with Jews whose ties to commerce were long established. Demographic shifts, urbanization, increased literacy and mobility all reshaped European culture — and had an impact on Jews. My ongoing focus on religious factors in this book is not a claim that other factors were not decisive. Yet I assume throughout that anti-Jewish religious ideology provides the central and motivating through-line of the narrative I am obliged to pursue.

And how is that through-line embodied? When the story of Judaism is recounted expressly in relation to the Christian world, it is inevitably, and at times overwhelmingly, negative. From one epoch to another, as we shall see, this narrative is embodied in the symbol of the cross. Jews, like Clare

Boothe Luce's friend, can tire of hearing of the cross, and so can some Christians, perhaps. But tensions surrounding the cross — at once a sign of compassionate love and of sacred violence — form the heart of this story. Compassionate love, including that exercised toward Jews in the name of Jesus, will be a part of it — and so will violence inflicted on Jews in the name of God. That Christians today may have difficulty imagining the cross as a symbol of hatred, and that many Jews cannot imagine it otherwise, is at the crux, so to speak, of the ongoing conflict over the cross at Auschwitz.

Martin Gilbert, the distinguished Churchill biographer, compiled *The Atlas of Jewish History.* In its preface he wrote:

> My original concern was to avoid undue emphasis upon the many horrific aspects of Jewish history. I wished to portray with equal force the construction, achievements, and normalities of Jewish life through almost four thousand years. In part, I believe that I have succeeded; for there are many maps of traders, philosophers, financiers, settlers, and sages. But as my research into Jewish history progressed, I was surprised, depressed, and, to some extent, overwhelmed by the perpetual and irrational violence which pursued the Jews in every century and to almost every corner of the Globe. If, therefore, persecution, expulsion, torture, humiliation, and mass murder haunt these pages, it is because they also haunt the Jewish story.[6]

From the Holocaust, of which Mrs. Luce complained, back through history to the crucifixion, of which her Jewish friend complained — on a hundred hinges in between hangs the indispensable question: How are the two related? The story takes a turn now in which an answer begins to assert itself, when the cross of Jesus is wielded as a sword by the Roman convert Constantine.

PART THREE

CONSTANTINE, AUGUSTINE, AND THE JEWS

The Heart of This Story Is a Place

D RAW A MAP OF Europe in your mind. Picture the boot of Italy, the rolled cuff of the Alps, and that country's western coastline curving around to the south of France. Cutting northward from Marseilles is the Rhone River, which in Roman times was a highway through the wilds of Gaul. Above Lyons, the river peters out, but not many miles away, another, the Saone, begins, leading on to the Meuse, which leads to yet another, the Moselle. Crossing into Germany as the Mosel, it intersects the mighty Rhine at Koblenz, a Roman city named for the *confluentes* of the two great rivers. More efficient as transport than the touted Roman roads, the network of rivers was the key to the expansion of the empire north — especially the Rhine, flowing from the Alps to the North Sea. Bisecting the continent, the river made it possible for the caesars to conquer as far north as England, even before the birth of Christ.

But the Rhine also marked the permanent eastern limit of the Roman sway. Caesar Augustus, who ruled at the time Jesus was born, proposed the expansion of the empire into the northern wilderness. He decreed that the River Elbe, jutting down from the Scandinavian peninsula, was to be the far boundary of Rome, but it wasn't to be. In the year 9 C.E., the Roman legions, pushing into the heart of what we think of as eastern Germany, were routed at the Battle of Teutoburg Forest, a clash that left twenty thousand legionnaires dead. The defeat kept the Roman line at the Rhine. That frontier hardened into Europe's cultural fault line, with Latin-derived Romance languages to its west and south, Germanic-Slavic languages east and north. If the Battle of Teutoburg Forest had gone the other way, citizens of present-day Berlin might be speaking French.

The Rhine was the defining boundary of the Reformation too, the front line of every major war fought in Europe, and the *casus belli* of the worst of them. Such history was foretold, perhaps, by the fact that the first Roman settlements on that river, among them Mainz (at the confluence of the Main), Koblenz, and Cologne, a city whose earlier name, Colonus, meant "colony," began as fortified military outposts. A civilian supply settlement to support those and other outposts was established safely back from the Rhine frontier, about seventy miles up the Moselle from Koblenz. Taking its name, Augusta Treverorum, from a local Celtic tribe, the Treveri — the name would evolve into today's Trier — this settlement became the capital of the empire's western territories (Gaul, Spain, Germania, and Britain). As such, it was the first real city north of the Alps. Early in the Common Era, mail routinely went from Trier to Rome in little more than a week, an efficiency that would be lost, after the empire's decline, for more than a thousand years.

Today Trier has a population of under a hundred thousand, and is known, if for anything, for the modest house on Bruckenstrasse in which Karl Marx was born. Marx graduated from the local gymnasium, or high school — as did, most of a century later, a lad named Klaus Barbie, who grew up to be a notorius SS officer. In the thread that binds together Catholics and Jews, Marx and that Nazi form separate knots. But the point here is what goes unnoticed in Trier. Karl Marx's house is now a museum devoted to what he did and what he meant. A few blocks away stand the stunning but less noted remains of the palace of the Roman emperor Constantine (288?–337). It is a hauntingly mammoth hall, stark bricks setting off the rounded arches of Roman windows, with a coffered oak ceiling. The structure is huge, like a hangar for the *Hindenburg,* but today it serves as a sparsely attended Lutheran church, the Church of our Savior. In guidebooks it is referred to as the *Konstantin-basilika.* In Constantine's time it was known as *Aula Palatina.* Like the city that grows out from it, the *Basilika* is far removed from today's beaten tourist trail; Michelin gives it no star. And so it was in the late 1950s, when as a teenage boy I came by chance to Trier with my mother. I did not see Constantine's palace then, although a postwar restoration was completed in 1956. For us Americans, the story of ancient Rome belonged in Italy. I would not know of Trier even now but for that accidental pilgrimage with my mother. I will explain below what brought us to Trier, and how that city returns us repeatedly to this book's great question of Catholics and Jews, providing an unlikely but certain geographical touchstone throughout the centuries. But for the moment, it is enough to say that what brought my mother and me to Trier was not Karl Marx.

*   *   *

I am sixteen years old, kneeling next to Mom on the cold marble step of a columned railing in a corner of the largest church in the world, St. Peter's Basilica in Rome — a religious version of Constantine's palace. My family is soon to have the private audience with Pope John XXIII referred to earlier. The privilege, as I said, was due my father as a general and a Catholic. My mother has status too. She will be congratulated by His Holiness, as she has been by Cardinal Spellman, for her work as president of the Military Council of Catholic Women. Her position involved, for one thing, arranging a series of members' pilgrimages to holy places. Mom had taken a few preliminary trips herself, and I had accompanied her to several Catholic shrines, mostly in Germany — journeys I would retrace for this book.

But now, at sixteen, beside her, I am staring at the wondrous face of another mother, for we are kneeling at Michelangelo's *Pietà*. I glance at Mom. Her eyes are liquid, and I guess that they are fixed on the nail hole in Jesus' otherwise perfect right foot. His calf muscles and knees and thighs are toned and slim like an athlete's. The skin is taut across his ribs. His lifeless right hand rests just off the fold of Mary's dress. His left hand falls toward her lap. Each hand has its hole.

The fingers of Mary's right hand press out from below his armpit. Who has ever touched you there? His head is cradled in the crook of her arm, which is why his face has fallen into its repose. Jesus is dead, but he knows she has him. Theology says that — *consumatum est* — he gave himself over into the hands of his Father, but Michelangelo thinks otherwise, and what sixteen-year-old son would disagree? Who needs a father with a mother like this? The magic of the *Pietà* is in Mary's youth. The law of generation requires her to be at least middle-aged. In first-century Palestine, middle age would be old. But not here. Michelangelo's sculpture is luminous, as if lit from inside by her youth. It is the girl who glows. She has the complexion, the untouched lips, the swan-like, unwrinkled neck of a fifteen-year-old. She is Juliet holding naked Romeo, yet chastely. Death was the only consummation to touch this flesh. Yet the intimacy between these figures is entirely sensual.

At sixteen, I had already begun looking for a female of my own. Girls just like this one — whether picking up a dropped book in the school corridor, sipping a Coke at a drugstore fountain, or staring out from a shampoo ad in a magazine — were my obsession. I could not speak of it with Mom. I was aware of the curve of her figure, but incestuous longings were a mile below the surface. Yet I was acutely conscious of the sexual pull toward girls my age as a betrayal of her. I could not imagine abandoning

Mom to the heartless world of male power, even as represented by my good but mostly absent father. The welter of an adolescent's inner life boiled down to the fact that I had no idea yet how to be a man and a son both. What I had learned from my mother by then, though, was that no intense worry, not even if vaguely taboo, need be left outside a Catholic church. Why else do they have kneelers in front of the cross and every statue? Being sinners was what qualified us, and what was it to be a sinner if not lost like this, confused, afraid? These feelings, with their roil of sexual restlessness, were the heart of my first real prayer.

Michelangelo's Mary — the artist was twenty-four years old when he created her — soothed that unarticulated ache in me by being so simply a girl and a mother both. Her exquisite sexuality was fully robed against her son's nakedness, yet when has the inside of a wrist ever seemed more dangerously exposed? What face has ever been readier to be transported by ecstasy? Her sexuality combined with moral purity was an adolescent's ideal of hope. Grace and sin, hope and doom, love and fear — Michelangelo's Mary succeeds as the balance of such opposites because she is the incarnation of grief. That was surely what my mother recognized, and what, at bottom, I identified with. It would be years before my understanding could match that feeling — the grief I'd felt from the moment I left my mother's womb, a grief that, since I was no longer hers, she was already no longer mine. This is the slap from which we never recover, yet we never stop trying, especially in the longing known as sex.

Jesus in the cradle of his mother's arms: I knew from the familiar welling in Mom's eyes that what she saw in the scarred body was my brother's. That was no offense to me by then. She had her grief, I had mine. I would be a man someday. I would always be her son. So being next to her before such a thing was enough. Behind the *Pietà* was a huge cross, the naked wood of which seemed to miss him. Jesus had just been lowered from its arms into his mother's. The name of the *Pietà* chapel was *Cappella del Crocifisso*. The cross was a permanent presence behind us, too. It had focused the religious landscape through which Mom and I had moved the last two years, on those preliminary pilgrimages ahead of the military women. Our day trips through the Rhineland brought to a kind of climax our custom of intimate sojourn to various churches. By sheer coincidence, they gave me a personal stake, which I only now see, in the field of battle between the Church and the Jews. This reminiscence of my mother may seem a long way from that, but it is not.

*   *   *

Our house in Germany was about a mile from the Rhine, but decidedly, for us Catholics, on its wrong side. We lived in the town of Wiesbaden, directly across the river from Mainz, which, as the metropolitan see of the largest ecclesiastical province of the Holy Roman Empire and as home of the most powerful archbishop elector, was once known as "the Rome of the North." The Mainz Cathedral, dating to the eleventh century, dramatically displayed the transition from Romanesque to Gothic to Baroque style, and its towers were long famous for stamping the city with Roman Catholic primacy. The several churches of Wiesbaden, on the other hand, were showily Protestant — brick instead of stone, solitary steeples instead of twin or triple towers, crosses without corpses. Our city's *Dom* ("cathedral"), in effect, was the Spielbank, or casino, which, with the Kurhaus, or hot spring baths, had made Wiesbaden a favorite resort of the Prussian nobility. The architect of the lavish Kurhaus designed several other notable buildings in Wiesbaden, including the requisitioned mansion that the U.S. Air Force assigned to my father as his family quarters. One of the kaiser's marshals had built it, we were told. The opulent digs were ours because of my father's rank, but also because of my mother's fertility: With five sons, our Irish Catholic family was too big for the houses on Generals' Row at the air base. Unlike Mainz, a mere two miles away, Wiesbaden had not been bombed, which is why Eisenhower had made it his headquarters after crossing the Rhine in 1944. It had evolved into the headquarters of the U.S. Air Force in Europe ("U-Safe," we said) when my father was named its chief of staff.

There were three places in the Rhineland to which our mother took us, all across the river: Cologne, for its cathedral and its precious relics; Koblenz, for nearby Maria Laach, the ancient Benedictine abbey; and Trier, which was significant to us as the site of the exquisite thirteenth-century *Liebfrauen-kirche*, but not even that was what brought us there.

The first major purchase my parents made in Germany was a tan VW convertible. My father was chauffeured in a blue Lincoln staff car with stars on the bumper, but the thrill of his status was matched by that of having a suddenly racy mother, liberated from the musty old Studebaker by that roadster Beetle. I still remember with pleasure my mother at the wheel of that car, with wisps of hair feathering out from her scarf as we bombed along the autobahn. She seemed another person from the grim worrier of my brother Joe's illness only a few years before. Now one or two or all three of my younger brothers might be bundled into the back seat, but with Joe away at college and Dad at work, there was no one to compete with me for riding shotgun. The wind feathered my hair too.

The trips along the Rhine were plunges into virtue and adventure both. We careered up the river valley, past hillside vineyards and cobblestoned villages, above island castles and below the fortresses of Rhenish barons. Passing the Lorelei, Mom would tell us the legend of the enchantress whose song lured boatmen onto the rocks. Passing the giant statue of Bismarck on a mountaintop, Mom would call it "the Watch on the Rhine," and we would joke that it was another of the clocks she'd taken to collecting. "Look at that!" she'd say, but what she meant was "Look at us!" If only the headset girls she had supervised at the phone company in the Loop could see her now!

Our visits to Cologne, perhaps four hours down the Rhine, were emblematic of all that was at stake for us. That city was living proof both of the savagery of which an unleashed America was capable — by 1945, 90 percent of Cologne's city center was reduced to rubble — and of our nation's sensitivity, for our skilled bombardiers had spared the great Cologne Cathedral, whose twin steeples, before the Eiffel Tower was erected in 1889, had been the tallest structures in the world. I would not realize it until years later, but one reason we drove all that way to Cologne, while almost never crossing into nearby Mainz, was that the even more sacred cathedral of Mainz had been half leveled by the same Allied bombers that spared Cologne's *Dom*. Even in 1959, a decade and a half after the destruction, the holy center of Mainz was not fully restored. We spared ourselves that refutation of American humaneness by pretending it was not there.

The other thing that took us to Cologne were the relics of the Three Kings, the Magi. Their bones were, and still are, enshrined in a triple pyramid of gold caskets on the high altar of the cathedral. How did the dust of Melchior, Balthazar, and Gaspar come to rest in that far city of Europe and not in Arabia, Mesopotamia, or Babylon? The answer hinges on the medieval politics of relics. Seeking to strengthen his hold on the northern realm, Frederick Barbarossa brought the remains of the Wise Men to Cologne in 1164. The subsequent influx of pilgrims, requiring the building of the new cathedral, lent prestige to the imperial center, solidifying its market and helping it to compete with Mainz and Trier. But where, twelve hundred years after the Epiphany, had Barbarossa obtained such relics? He found them in Milan, the imperial center to which they had been brought in the fourth century.

Around that time, the bones of saints and martyrs, and other relics, had

become central to the religious imagination of the Church. Things believed to be remnants of an earlier age, and associated with its heroes, enabled the faithful to feel connected to the sacred past, even to invoke its
magical power. When Constantine was buried, twelve empty coffins were
placed around his, one for each of the apostles. By the time his son died,
the bones of several apostles had been "discovered" and brought to the
imperial mausoleum.[1] Coffins no longer had to be empty. The Christian
hunger for the Incarnate God spawned a hunger for nearly unlimited in-
carnations of holiness.

I remember a young American priest explaining about the bones of the
Three Kings to my mother and me on our tour of the cathedral. What
jolted me, and what ties the memory of my mother to the knot of this
story, was that he credited the relics to the mother of Constantine, Saint
Helena, a woman I had heard my mother speak of as the discoverer of the
True Cross. Saint Helena had brought the bones of the Magi to Milan, the
priest said, and her name made it seem true. As the priest walked us
around that sanctuary, speaking of her — Helena was a general's wife, like
my mother — I felt the bond with my mother as something new.

The triple sarcophagus is large enough for adult corpses. It is elaborately gilded, bejeweled, and embossed with bas-relief biblical scenes. The
crest of the city of Cologne bears three crowns, for this. How does an uncertain teenage boy dismiss such accumulated piety? There is a hint of the
genius of the Catholic aesthetic in the tradition of reverence for relics, a
manifestation of the deep sacredness of the flesh, a refusal to treat the wall
separating the past from the present as impenetrable. The same human
impulse leads Americans to honor Plymouth Rock and the flag of Betsy
Ross. But what happens when reverence for relics becomes swamped by
superstition, when the past is treated as infinitely malleable, depending on
the needs of the present? Really — the Three Kings? I would surely have
dismissed it except for that priest's explanation. Saint Helena was an au-
thenticating hook on which to hang any story, and people like us would
believe it. If she had discovered the True Cross in Jerusalem, why could she
not also have discovered corpses of the Three Kings in the same city? Saint
Helena was central to the piety of Catholics of our kind. If you started to
disbelieve her, where would you stop?

In addition to celebrating the virtue of omnipotent America, our pilgrimages through the Rhineland implicitly honored the heroic integrity of Roman Catholicism, which, we were assured, had never been sullied by the

Third Reich. We knew the Catholic Church as a staunch opponent of to-talitarianism — in the 1950s, Pius XII was America's fiercest and most out-spoken ally against Stalin. We all assumed that Catholics had bravely defied Adolf Hitler. That Hitler was born and had died a Catholic, even if only a nominal one, was never referred to. The living witness to Catholic virtue in Germany was the West German chancellor Konrad Adenauer, who ranked in the postwar pantheon with Charles de Gaulle and Dwight D. Eisenhower. Adenauer was a living refutation of the Soviet emphasis on pan-German culpability, as opposed to a narrow American emphasis on Nazi guilt. The American position suggested that there were relatively few Nazis, and they were all gone. We wanted a revived Germany to stand with us against Moscow, and Adenauer's roots in the Roman Catholic Chris-tian Democratic Party — not the Social Democrats of, say, Willy Brandt — served that purpose.[2] I grasped little of this at the time, but I knew that Adenauer was a former mayor of Cologne and a staunch Rhinelander. He had had the new West German capital built in nearby Bonn. Such a com-mitment to a region we had adopted only made him, and his virtue, seem that much more like ours.

Adenauer was one of the reasons for our pilgrimage to Maria Laach, the Benedictine monastery about halfway between Wiesbaden and Cologne. In the western nave of the twelfth-century abbey church is displayed a modern stained-glass window showing figures from the Bible. The win-dow is inscribed, *Dr. Konrad Adenauer, Bundeskanzler, 1956.* He donated the window to the abbey in gratitude that year because in 1933, after defy-ing the newly empowered Hitler, and drawing down a death sentence on himself by refusing to fly the swastika in Cologne, he had taken refuge there. The abbot, Ildefons Herwegen, and Adenauer had gone to school together, and so the abbot had offered him refuge. Adenauer was able to melt into the monastic community. For most of a year, he hid in a monk's cell at Maria Laach, and he fled only when Herwegen alerted him that he was in danger of being found out. Ever after, the ancient abbey has been associated with Adenauer's anti-Nazi resistance. A film shown to visitors in the pilgrims' hall refers to the connection even today. We will return to this story later.

The nearby lake, which the monastery dedicates to Mary, is a water-filled volcanic crater, set dramatically in the Eifel Mountains a few miles back from the river. The abbey is a walled cluster of buildings in various styles several hundred yards up a gradual slope from the shoreline. Lush pastures and woodlands still in the abbey's domain surround the lake. For more than a thousand years, with few breaks, monks have been chanting the office here. The pillared arcade at the entrance to the Romanesque chapel dates to the eleventh century, and is a source of our most cherished, if stereotyped, image of cloister architecture.

When my mother and I prayed at Maria Laach, we would have heard the Dialogue Mass, the liturgical innovation for which the abbey was then famous. It involved the congregation in the Eucharistic prayer, an antiphonal recitation of the Latin verses. In the 1950s the Dialogue Mass (*Missa Recitata*) was sweeping the Church, marking a shift away from clerical domination toward a more democratic expression in worship. Instead of being mere spectators to the priest's act, the people participated in it. The Body of Christ was all of us. Begun at the abbey decades before and championed by Maria Laach's foundation in the United States, St. John's Abbey, Collegeville, Minnesota, the Dialogue Mass was resisted by the Church's old guard, but its democratic impulse would be fulfilled by Vatican II in 1964, not only by its liturgical reform but by its new definition of the Church as the People of God.

My mother and I would have been oblivious of all this. I could handle the recitation, despite its being in Latin, because of my time as an altar boy, but my mother preferred her rosary. Neither of us could have been unmoved, however, by the mystical lilt of the monks' voices, the timeless quality of their chant, and its antiphonal rhythm with silence. Before coming to Germany, I had attended a Benedictine school in Washington, St. Anselm's, and even as a young teenager I had joined the Oblates, a lay affiliate, which entitled me to spend the night in the cloister on occasion, to eat with the monks at the narrow table of the refectory. I remember the dark bread, the porridge, and that no one sat across from you. I remember getting up before dawn to listen to the song of matins, an order of hours going back to the seventh century. I remember that I loved it.

I felt at home in monasteries, and I still do. A favorite, forever-repeated family story tells of the time my mother brought me to a monastery when I was five or six — this would have been to pray for Joe. And I said to a bald, bearded monk, "Why do you have hair on your chin but not on your head?" His answer, if he made one, was not a feature of the story. We always laughed at my innocent impudence, and I could always picture the arches of the cloister colonnade. Years later, I saw that the peculiar revelation of the story, apart from its dead-on notation of a monastic propensity for baldness, was that a child should have been in such a place at all. Yet what the monks offered me was a quickening of that religious imagination I had from her. Now I see that my mother's offer was being responded to. I was being subtly recruited in those places. In time I was conscripted by the Benedictines of St. Anselm's, and then, because I loved it at once, commissioned somehow by Maria Laach. Not many years later, when I entered the religious life, it was to build an identity around the mystery — brothers in the choir, the balance of solitude and solidarity; a devotion to art, architecture, song; a hint of anti-Hitler heroism that defused the hint of the effete — the mystery I had glimpsed at that German cloister.

Maria Laach was tied to the web of our Rhineland pilgrimages, too, in the chain of consequence that began with Helena, for it was founded in 1093 by monks from the Abbey of St. Maximin at Trier,[3] which had been founded, in turn — yes, the tradition insists on this — by Constantine's mother.[4] No one explained how a Benedictine monastery could have been established more than two hundred years before Benedict. The point for us was Helena — and Helena, beyond everything else, meant Trier. Because of her, we could go there, her hometown, and nearly touch what had touched the very flesh of the Lord, the son of Mary.

In previous chapters, we followed the story as it ran from Jesus through the first generations of his followers, whose claim to the mantle of Israel was denied by the followers of the rabbis. Jews and Christians coexisted both as rivals and as overlapping communities on the margins of the Roman Empire, but that all changed with Constantine. Politics and theology were fluid until then, but boundaries were suddenly defined around the grid of the True Cross. A symbol then and ever after associated with Helena, it now became the touchstone of membership, not only in the Church but in the empire. That made it the touchstone of survival. Saint Ambrose, the greatest theologian of the age, would use the True Cross explictly against the Jews, finally urging violence as the proper response to their denial of Christian claims. Saint Augustine, the protégé of Ambrose, would demur, and Jews would live, but only in a certain way — one that stamps history still. All of this unfolds from where I stood, knowing nothing, in Trier.

ᐳᐳ 17 ᐸᐸ

The Story of Constantine

CAESAR AUGUSTUS DID not reach the Elbe, but his armies, and those of his immediate successors, planted the Roman standard all over Europe west of the Rhine, through central Europe south of the Danube, into the Near East, and in North Africa along the southern edge of the Mediterranean. These conquests would not be expanded upon, and indeed, from the first century on, the posture of Roman legions was defensive, largely holding on to what had been won. For nearly two hundred years, until the beginning of the third century, the Roman world was more or less orderly and prosperous. Spurred by the efficiencies of Roman transportation and communications, much of northern and western Europe was brought into a regional economy of trade, industry, and finance. But such consolidation brought its own stresses. Because the military was so well established throughout most of the empire, more and more power shifted to the armies. The makeup of the legions, meanwhile, had become less and less Roman, as the "barbarians" of the provinces and frontiers filled out the ranks, and ultimately the officer corps.

The third century was a period of civil war, barbarian invasion, and general social breakdown throughout the empire. As chaos mounted, so did the power of the military, which successfully asserted authority over the Roman Senate, and even over the seat of the emperors, who came and went so quickly (twenty between 235 and 284) that they were unable to establish power centers of their own. Rebellious generals and self-anointed general-emperors became features of the time. Militarization eclipsed all other aspects of Roman culture. Intellectual life collapsed, and the skills of classical art were lost. Archaeologists studying Rome from the early third century on, for example, find few inscriptions on public buildings and monuments.

Late in the third century, a general named Aurelius Valerius Diocletian, a commoner from Illyria, in the Balkan peninsula, was declared emperor by his soldiers. In 284, his claim was widely recognized, and he immediately applied what would prove to be his administrative genius to the task of drawing order out of the chaos into which the empire had fallen. In 285, Diocletian divided the empire in half, assigning the more vital and less conflicted East to himself, and taking the title Augustus. The thrust of his dividing line, running south from the Danube, is still more or less visible today on the much disputed border between the Roman Catholic territories of Croatia and the Orthodox territories of Serbia. Diocletian established his seat of government at Nicomedia, on the eastern side of the Bosporus.

As for the West, he designated as his fellow Augustus one of his fellow generals, Maximian. The idea was that each Augustus would be equal to the other, but in fact Diocletian was supreme. Each of the two Augusti had a deputy, with the title Caesar, with authority over a further division of the empire and a presumed right of succession to the office of Augustus. With four rulers in place, the period of Rome's tetrarchy had begun. It was an experiment in administration that would not last. Diocletian's Caesar was Galerius, who ruled in the East. Maximian named a general of the legions in Gaul, Constantius, who ruled from a capital at Trier. Maximian established himself not in Rome but in Milan, because it was closer to the threatened Alpine frontier of Italy. A military purpose thus dictated the momentous shift away from the ancient capital, but this is not surprising, since the entire rearrangement of power presumed the consent not of the Senate or of the citizenry, but of the armies.

At this point, therefore, the court of the emperor left Rome, never to return. Meanwhile, Christianity had grown, but slowly, with most of its converts being drawn from the lower classes of the Mediterranean world. The population of the Roman Empire in late antiquity is usually given as between fifty and sixty million.[1] Christians accounted for perhaps a tenth of that number.[2] From the early informality of a house-based network of communities that had sprung up in the generations after the Gospels were written down, and partly because those texts, once canonized, served as an organizing structure, the early Jesus movement had developed, probably by the mid to late second century, into something we can call the Church. It had imitated the highly efficient political system of the empire, dividing itself into dioceses and provinces, with local bishops serving as ecclesiastical equivalents of regional governors.[3] The Church had defined Rome as its administrative seat — a decision tied as much to organizational as to religious demands, even if the ancient connection to Peter was always emphasized.

In the late third century, Christians were a distinct minority in Rome, but the city was riven with factions of every kind. With the emperor gone, the influence of the Christian bishop, revered as the successor to Peter, would only grow. But there was another reason that power might flow to the Church at this time. Despite the fact that most Christians were of the illiterate poor, the Church had grounded itself in the studious work of an intellectual elite. The great exception to the third-century decline of intellect and culture in the Roman Empire had been the flourishing of Christian theology, with such figures as Tertullian (c. 150–225), Cyprian (c. 200–258), and Origen (c. 182–251). These and other thinkers transformed Christianity's self-understanding by applying the categories of the classics to affirmations grounded in Scripture. Thinkers like these flourished in Alexandria and Antioch, less so in Rome. In the intellectual ferment of the period, a variety of sometimes conflicting interpretations of the meaning of Jesus Christ took hold, but to outsiders the Church, with its common Eucharistic liturgy, its defined canon of sacred texts, and the relatively clear, if diffuse, hierarchy based on numerous bishoprics, appeared to be monolithic. These institutional innovations served the Church well in times of oppression, and would do so even more when it came into power.

Like Judaism, Christianity was a religion of the One God. Jews and Christians were equally determined to refrain from participation in the cult rituals of Rome's pagan civic religion. But going back to the first century B.C.E., Jews had been exempted from the requirements to offer sacrifices to and utter blessings in the name of pagan gods. When the Church grew apart from the synagogue, Christians lost that exemption, which posed a growing problem as the emperors themselves began, in the third century, to claim the prerogatives of deity. Jews were also exempt from military service, but Christians were not. Church members who were in the army, in particular, could face impossible pressures to drop incense in the bowl or put an offering of a bird on the fire. The religion of Mithras, a Persian god, had become popular in the military, and as the army's power grew — there were half a million men under arms by now — Christian soldiers found themselves pressed by their officers to participate in that cult, too. In general, they refused. The Church remembers this refusal as having resulted in a long tradition of martyrdom in ancient times, but in fact, violent oppression of Christians was relatively rare and sporadic.

There was a persecution under the emperor Decius (249–251).[4] Another began in 303, when Diocletian, as a part of his overall attempt to impose order, declared a crackdown on Christians, whose dissent could seem like atheism. He also ordered the destruction of all Christian churches and texts.[5] The destruction of churches was so widespread in the East in this period that archaeology tells us little or nothing about their design.[6] Under Diocletian, Christians were liable to be put to death almost anywhere in the empire, with the exception of the northwestern provinces over which Constantius ruled. This was probably because the Church in Gaul, Germania, and Britain was far less well established than in the East, but also because, as the general of an army made up in large part of tribal recruits who maintained loyalty to their own gods and cults, Constantius had learned the value of religious tolerance.

Judaism had found its own place in the empire, with concentrations of Jews to be found nearly everywhere. There were, by the beginning of the fourth century, something like a minimum of three million Jews, so their number, while probably less than that of the Christians, was still substantial. Two thirds of that figure lived east of the Balkan peninsula.[7] Jews lived in cities, especially Alexandria and Carthage, as well as Rome and the urban centers of Asia Minor. They also pursued agriculture in fertile areas like the river valleys of Mesopotamia and along the Nile. Many of these Jews were Hellenized, speaking the language of their neighbors and interacting with Christians and pagans. As we saw earlier, up until late antiquity, there was far more fluidity among these communities than is ordinarily imagined. We can presume that Hellenized Jewish communities were as intellectually and culturally vital as any. As in Christianity, the canonization of sacred texts had spawned among Jews a culture of text study and interpretation,[8] but it is a mystery that these Jews left almost no written records of their religious and cultural life. "After 100 C.E.," in the words of one historian of ancient Judaism, the Jews of the Hellenized Diaspora "appear to have become illiterate . . . Greek-speaking Jews read the Bible in Greek . . . but were not inspired thereby to write. Why, we do not know."[9]

The story was very different in the communities of rabbinic Jews concentrated in what from Rome could seem the backwaters of Palestine, in what had been known as Judea and Galilee.[10] An emblem of Jewish survival was the story told about the Pharisaic leader Yochanan ben Zakkai, who had been spirited out of the besieged city of Jerusalem inside a coffin. He had set up his community at Yavneh, on the Mediterranean coast, and, as we saw earlier, a rabbinic academy had flourished there.[11] By 300, the great literary tradition of Mishnah was well established. Throughout the preceding period of violence and dispersal, Jewish scholars and scribes, working quietly in schools under the leadership of a succession of prominent rabbis, based in Babylonia and Palestine, painstakingly recorded the oral traditions of commentary and law. The collected writings of the Mishnah were codified in the late fourth century, and they would spawn the further elaborations of Gemara, and the whole would ultimately be collected as the Talmud. In this way the spiritual legacy of Israel was not only preserved but built upon. Hebrew and Aramaic were the main languages used in these pursuits, but Greek, Latin, and Persian references in the ancient texts make it clear that translation was a central skill and that exchange with surrounding cultures was common. The rabbinic texts provide evidence of a rich, erudite communal life built around the study of Torah. As Christians revered their martyrs, rabbinic Jews revered their sages. Torah study, not open defiance of Roman religious cult, was what gave Judaism lasting strength. Indeed, Jews had less reason to resist than Christians. In addition to the exemptions from military service and pagan cult, Jews living in the communities of the rabbis exercised considerable autonomy, with a Roman-recognized Jewish patriarchate based in Palestine.

Thus, while both Christians and Jews consistently rejected all association with the pagan religions of Rome, Jews enjoyed a higher level of tolerance by the empire. Why is that? The answer involves a range of factors — for example, Judaism's status as an ancient religion set it apart from upstart cults — but perhaps one defining difference stands above others. Once the Church understood Jesus Christ as God-made-man, it seemed a corollary that all human beings were called to be united with him. Wasn't that why Jesus was remembered, in Matthew, as having commanded, "Go therefore and make disciples of all nations"?[12] Christian theology evolved in such a way that primary emphasis was given to the Church as the community of the saved. The affirmation that all who were baptized in Christ had access to God came to be understood exclusively — that *only* those who were baptized could be saved. This notion underwrote Christianity's aggressive program of proselytizing, which led to the Church's steady growth, but it also was the source of offense taken by Roman pagans who regarded such a theology as an intolerable violation of a necessary religious tolerance.

Rabbinic Judaism had no notion of God-made-man. "In Jewish

thought, God stayed strictly separate from man," Alan Segal wrote, "just as the Jews stayed strictly separate from Gentiles. For the Jews, purity categories could remain strong without sacrificing universality because, when Jews distinguished between themselves and the Gentiles, they were not distinguishing between the saved and the damned."[13] Roman pagans could accept the walls Jews erected between themselves and "impure" cults, strict Jewish marriage laws, and even prohibitions against taking meals with non-Jews, because such boundaries did not imply an assumption that pagans were damned. Jews engaged in proselytizing in the ancient world, but not for the reasons that Christians did. Soon enough, Jewish proselytizing would become illegal, Jewish distinctiveness would offend, and Jewish autonomy would be abolished.

In 305, Diocletian, sixty years old, abdicated the imperial throne — probably a signal of his serious purpose as a reforming ruler. He imposed the same decision on Maximian, his counterpart in the West. Constantius and Galerius became Augusti. To tie himself to the emperor's court in Milan, Constantius had divorced Helena, of whom we have already taken note, and married Maximian's daughter Theodora. Yet Constantius was still more the rough soldier than the courtly emperor; soon after his ascension to the rank of Augustus, he led his legions into Britain to maintain control over the island's perennially unruly natives. While there, in 306, Constantius was taken ill. He died at York. At his side was his son Constantine, who is commonly said to have been about eighteen years old. He was described by contemporaries as a large, impressive-looking man, and he certainly had impressed his father's troops. They spontaneously hailed him as the successor to Constantius, the Augustus of the Western empire. But in Rome, Maximian disavowed his forced abdication to reassert his claim to the position.

Constantine would have none of that. He ensconced himself in Trier, quickly consolidated his control over the northern legions, and ordered construction of a palace fit for a Roman emperor — the *Konstantin-basilika* referred to earlier. And he laid plans to take on Maximian.

Thus begins the remarkable story of the reign of the man who transformed the Roman Empire, the Church, and the place of Jews. As usually told, the story is quickly summarized.[14] A threatened Maximian sued for peace, displaying a surprising deference by coming to Trier to confer with Constantine. In 307, the wily Constantine recognized Maximian as senior Augustus, and sealed the arrangement by marrying another of Maximian's daughters, Fausta. He was prepared to wait to assume full control in the West. But the next year, Maximian's son Maxentius, seeing himself shunted aside, staked his own claim to be emperor of the West. Maximian, understandably, faltered in his deal with Constantine, who was quick to take offense. Their armies met in battle at Marseilles in 310. Constantine was victorious. He killed Maximian. In 312, Constantine stormed Italy, moving against Maxentius's army, fortified in Rome. The story is that Constantine's legions were spent by now, demoralized, and uncertain so far from home. In the coming battle against Maxentius, who would be fighting on his home ground, they would be the decided underdog. But the night before the battle at the Milvian Bridge, on the Tiber, Constantine saw a cross in the sky, above the legend *In Hoc Signo Vinces* ("In This Sign, Conquer"). With the news of this vision, a signal of favor from the Christian God, Constantine's troops rallied, went firmly into battle the next day, and won. Constantine himself threw Maxentius off the bridge into the Tiber, where he drowned. On the strength of that vision, and its fulfillment, the emperor became a Christian, so did his army, and, ultimately, so did the empire.

In a way, this is the second-greatest story ever told, at least concerning what we think of as Western civilization. After the death and Resurrection of Jesus, the conversion of Constantine may have been the most implication-laden event in Western history. If we rarely think so, that is because we take utterly for granted the structures of culture, mind, politics, spirituality, and even calendar (Sunday as holiday) to which it led. None of those structures was foreordained, and indeed, to grasp the epoch-shaping significance of Constantine's embrace of Jesus, his sponsorship of Jesus' cause, imagine how the history we trace in this book would have unfolded had the young emperor been converted to Judaism instead. It is a nearly unthinkable turn in the story, imagined in retrospect, but in prospect such a conversion would have been no more unlikely than what happened, and to entertain the idea is to wonder how Judaism, instead of Catholicism, would have fared as the locus of political and religious dominance. When the power of the empire became joined to the ideology of the Church, the empire was immediately recast and reenergized, and the Church became an entity so different from what had preceded it as to be almost unrecognizable. It goes without saying that the conversion of Constantine, for Church and empire both, led to consequences better and worse — although not for Jews, for whom, from this, nothing good would come.

↦ 18 ↤

The Cross and the
Religious Imagination

CHRISTIANITY and Judaism are religions of revelation. But how, exactly, is the content of our beliefs revealed? It is a long time since we took for granted the idea of theophany, a sudden and dramatic unveiling of mystery — an experience like that of Moses before the burning bush, or Moses coming down from the mountaintop with the tablets of the Law. One of the assumptions I make in a work like this, however, is that the truth of our beliefs is revealed in history, within the contours of the mundane, and not through cosmic interruptions in the flow of time. Revelation comes to us gradually, according to the methods of human knowing. And so revelation comes to us ambiguously. Certitude and clarity are achieved only in hindsight, and even then provisionally. That is the work of memory, which is the arrangement of incident and experience into a meaningful narrative with a beginning, middle, and end. The theophany of Moses is less a matter of what happened to him on Mount Sinai than it is of the story told by those who came after him.

The great question for Christians is, How is Jesus God? It can come as no surprise to one for whom revelation is a profoundly human, and therefore timebound, way of knowing to realize that the Jesus movement only gradually came to ask that question. It applied categories of divinity to him through the turmoil of argument, guesswork, estimation, imprecise language, and error far more than through sudden inspiration from above. For religious inspiration, like all things in history, evolves over time.

However gradually it takes shape, the painstaking construction of a commonly held narrative involves an ultimate recognition, which can indeed seem to be a sudden lifting of fog — Joyce's epiphany again — before a new kind of knowing. Such a recognition of the basic content of belief in Jesus occurred in the fourth century when, at last, a formerly divided, contentious, widely dispersed Christianity achieved agreement on an answer to the question How is this man God? That breakthrough in theology, honored in a creed that is still recited around the globe in every hour of every day, was accompanied by, enabled by, a breakthrough in the social organization of a formerly divided, contentious, widely dispersed Roman Empire. For political as well as religious reasons, the revelation came decisively to the pagan population too. Jesus is God in the way Emperor Constantine says he is.

Constantine wanted to unify the empire in every way. When he declared a freeze on wages and prices to control inflation, a chaotic system of competing local economies began to operate as one. When he ordered workers to remain in their fathers' occupations as a way of assuring basic services, from the bakery to the blacksmith shop, the social order coalesced. In a similar way, Constantine was the instrument of a revolution in the religious imagination of the Mediterranean world, and eventually of Europe. His political impact on Christianity is widely recognized, but his role as a shaper of its central religious idea is insufficiently appreciated. Latin Christians, anachronistically, have preferred to keep him, as a ruler, on the secular side of the sacred-profane divide, as if he were an early Charlemagne. In the Eastern Church, he is honored as a saint, but even there his role in shaping a new religious consciousness is downplayed. But at the time, Constantine was a kind of, well, Moses — an image I would not presume to apply to him. It originates with Eusebius of Caesarea, his biographer.[1]

Eusebius (c. 260–c. 339), the bishop of Caesarea, was born before Constantine and died after him. He is sometimes called the father of Church history. The author of several important works, especially *History,* the earliest telling of the ascendancy of the Church, he is usually a reliable recorder in the mode of Josephus.[2] But his *Life of Constantine* is a celebration of the divinely ordained union of the Church and the empire — Constantine as Moses — and not in any way an objective work of biography. Thus, for example, Eusebius emphasizes Constantine's youth when he takes his father's place at the head of the rough northern legion, as if he were aged eighteen or so, barely a man, and that is the age I cited in my summary of the story of Constantine. Some sources say he was about twenty-five. He was probably nearer thirty,[3] but the challenges he faced would have been daunting no matter how old he was. His ultimate achievement suggests that even Eusebius's obsequious praise may not have exaggerated his strengths — saying nothing here about his virtues.

Around the figure of the famously converted emperor, in partnership with his mother, developed a new notion not merely of the Church, as has often been noted, but of Jesus himself — of the kind of God he is. Theologians, as if by imperial fiat — or rather, precisely *by* such fiat — now found ways to put the heretofore ineffable mystery into words, while liturgists gave it expression by moving a peripheral symbol into the dead center of the cult. A previously inchoate feel for the identity of Jesus became sharply defined from now on.

The content of that definition is important for our purposes, because at this time it also emerges, in theology and cult both, that the default custodians of the *proof* of the truth of this more fully realized revelation about Jesus, after all these years and still, are none other than the Jews. In the fourth and early fifth centuries, beginning with Constantine and ending with the great theologian Augustine, heretofore marginal Judaism (marginal to the Church, that is) became central to the argument and language of a renewed Christian proclamation. The foundation of the conflict between Christians and Jews was laid, as we saw, in the first decade after the death of Jesus — that "healing circle." In subsequent centuries, its structure took shape behind "the clumsy scaffolding of Hebrew prophecies," in the words of Augustine's most admired biographer, Peter Brown.[4] But the post and beam of the conflict, as would become so clear in a field by a wall in Poland at the end of the twentieth century, was the cross.

Before Constantine, the cross lacked religious and symbolic significance. Paul had made the crucifixion essential to the salvation earned by Christ's death; being "crucified with Christ"[5] was an implication of accepting faith. But even in Paul, the cross as such did not compete, for instance, with the waters of baptism as the Christian community's metaphoric representation of dying with Christ. As he put it, "All of us who have been baptized into Christ Jesus were baptized into his death."[6] The Gospel of John has water flow from the side of Jesus after he has been pierced, a clear symbol of baptism.[7] Water had a vivid hold on the Christian imagination; wood did not. The fathers of the Church followed Paul in developing the idea of salvation through the death of Christ, but Justin, for example, even in discussing the cross, keeps it at a metaphoric remove by seeing it more as the shape of Passover blood on the lintel than as the literal execution device.[8] The blood of Christ, yes. The cross, not so much.

Thus, on the walls of the catacombs in Rome prior to the fourth century were to be seen representations of palm branches, the dove, the peacock, the bird of paradise, or the monogram of Jesus.[9] The sacred fish was a favorite symbol because of Gospel scenes, but also because the Greek word for fish, *ichthys,* renders an acrostic of "Jesus Christ, Son of God, Savior."[10] Such symbols were ubiquitous in early Christianity, but the cross is simply not to be found among them. Some early Christians signed themselves, touching the forehead, shoulders, and breast, but even that is ambiguous, since, as we saw, Jews were known to make a similar sign.

The place of the cross in the Christian imagination changed with Constantine. "He said that about noon, when the day was already beginning to decline" — this is Eusebius's account of Constantine's own report of what he saw in the sky on the eve of battle above the Milvian Bridge — "he saw with his own eyes the trophy of a cross of light in the heavens, above the sun, and bearing the inscription CONQUER BY THIS."[11] The story goes on to say that Constantine then assembled his army — "He sat in the midst of them, and described to them the figure of the sign he had seen"[12] — and gave them the new standard to carry into battle. "Now it was made in the following manner. A long spear, overlaid with gold, formed the figure of the cross by means of a transverse bar laid over it." As we saw, the army behind this standard did conquer, and Constantine, so Eusebius heard him say, was thus convinced of the truth of Christianity. "The emperor constantly made use of this sign of salvation as a safeguard against every adverse and hostile power, and commanded that others similar to it should be carried at the head of all his armies."[13]

Some early versions of the legend of Constantine's conversion had described the miraculous vision as having been not of a cross but of the Chi-Rho, the monogram composed of the first two letters of the Greek word *Khristos.* This version of the story would have been in keeping with the ancient Christian reluctance to render the cross literally, as the gibbet on which Jesus had hung. But from Eusebius's account, not of the vision but of Constantine's own description of it, the actual "figure of the cross" is clearly what is meant. Constantine put the Roman execution device, now rendered with a spear, at the center not only of the story of his conversion to Christianity, but of the Christian story itself.

When the death of Jesus — rendered literally, in all its violence, as opposed to metaphorically or theologically — replaced the life of Jesus and the new life of Resurrection at the heart of the Christian imagination, the balance shifted decisively against the Jews. This was so because sole responsibility for that now pivotal death had long since been laid at their feet.[14] For our purposes, the Age of Constantine can be said to extend from 306, when he replaced his father as one of the tetrarchy's four caesars, until 429, when a Constantinian successor, following in a direct chain of political and theological consequence, abolished the patriarchate of Israel.[15] Not even the caesars, who twice leveled Jerusalem, had thus eliminated Jewish political autonomy — an abolition that would not be reversed until 1948. One could almost say that for Jews, the Age of Constantine came to an end only with David Ben Gurion.

That pivotal 125 years not only illuminates the conflict between Christians and Jews, but escalates it. In the new era, Christians went from being 10 percent of the empire,[16] a despised and violently persecuted minority, to being its solid majority. Christianity went from being a private, apolitical movement to being the shaper of world politics. The status of Judaism was similarly reversed, from a licit self-rule, a respected exception within a sea of paganism, to a state of highly vulnerable disenfranchisement. What might be called history's first pogrom, an organized violent assault on a community of Jews, because they were Jews, took place in Alexandria in 414, wiping out that city's Jewish community for a time. Even in Palestine, Jews became a besieged minority. The land of Israel, long ignored by Christians who had happily left it behind for the centers of the empire, now became known as the Christian Holy Land. Christians returned to it, not for the last time, with a vengeance.

Jerusalem, a long-neglected backwater still known by its Roman name, Aelia Capitolina, again became the spiritual navel of the world. "Jerusalem," Augustine would say, "with my heart stretching out in longing for it, Jerusalem my country, Jerusalem my mother."[17] Even the Temple returned briefly as an emblem of faith, only to be superseded yet again — its ancient wall a screen onto which new meanings could be projected. For Jews, in the words of Jacob Neusner, "The world now had passed into the hands of their rivals, their siblings, sharing Scripture, sharing a claim to be 'Israel,' sharing the same view of history, sharing the same expectation of the Messiah's coming."[18] For Christians, the dramatic and unexpected conversion of Constantine was a proof of the Church's proclamation, but the change of fortune it led to was proof of even more. "The creation of the Christian state," Neusner says, "claiming to carry forward the ancient Israelite state, and to appeal to its precedents, brought to a critical stage the long-term Christian claim that Christians formed the new Israel."[19]

But if the Christian stake to that claim was now decisively driven in, what was to be made of — done with — the survivors of that old Israel who stubbornly refused to disappear? The problem was complex. When Christianity was finally in a position to present itself on favorable terms to the pagan world, it was important to be able to do so not as an upstart religion but as the fulfillment of an ancient tradition, one that predated pagan heroes like Cicero, Socrates, Homer. Christians had no choice but to invoke their Jewish provenance, but that raised another problem. What were pagans to make of the clear rejection of those same Christian claims by Jews? How could the Gospel base its validity on its being the fulfillment of Jewish prophecy, yet be repudiated by the holders of title to that prophecy?

Pagans were right to wonder. This Jewish recalcitrance threatened the project of Christian expansion — not in a new way exactly, but, in the changed circumstance, more powerfully than ever before. The other new circumstance, of course, was that now Christians were also in a position to do something about it, since their program of expansion was sponsored by the emperor, whose army marched behind that spear with its transverse bar. The gradual closing of the imperial vise on Judaism[20] — from Constantine's edict in 315 making it a crime for Jews to proselytize to the edict almost a century later making it a crime punishable by death — was driven by the real problem that Jewish dissent from Christian claims made overcoming paganism far more difficult. In addition to the vexation it caused among pagans, Jewish dissent constantly threatened to undermine the devotion of the many Christians who continued to value the Jewish roots of faith in the One God. Indeed, in an age marked by aggressive persecution of heresies — one bishop catalogued 156 of them[21] — the original heresy was understood to be derived from Judaism itself.[22] Jews posed a threat from within the faith as much as from outside it.

The Vision of Constantine

T HE MOMENTOUS SHIFT in the delicate balance between Jews and Christians, a shift in the moral imagination of the West, began in the *Aula Palatina,* the basilica or imperial palace Constantine had constructed for himself at the outset of his rule. He had set out to impress, and did. "For no one was comparable to him for grace and beauty of person, or height of stature," Eusebius explains, "and he so far surpassed his compeers in personal strength as to be a terror to them. He was, however, even more conspicuous for the excellence of his mental qualities than for his superior physical endowments; being gifted in the first place with a sound judgment, and having also reaped the advantages of a liberal education. He was also distinguished in no ordinary degree both by natural intelligence and divinely imparted wisdom."[1]

Here we see Eusebius at work not as a historian but as the emperor's mythmaker. In fact, the entire story of Constantine, as rehearsed above, comes to us half cloaked in myth, but much of it was self-created. From the start, Constantine wanted to be taken as a man with a mandate from the gods. In large things and small, he declared his purpose and revealed its scope. For example, upon succeeding his father, he immediately ordered new coins struck at the mints he controlled in Trier, London, and Lyons, changing the inscription from the traditional "To the Genius of the Roman people" to "To the Unconquered Sun my companion."[2] Constantine's overlarge sense of himself was nowhere more clearly manifest than in the palace he ordered built in Trier, a complex of numerous buildings attached to a massive throne room and audience hall. Such a palace was less an indulgence than a statement, for Trier was now to be an imperial capital fit for the ruler of the Roman world, not a barbaric northern outpost. The *Aula Palatina* was the perfect symbol of his purpose, a foreshadowing of his bold program.

The throne room remains. It is more than two hundred feet long and nearly one hundred feet high and wide. Its walls once would have been elaborately decorated, and the floor an intricately patterned mosaic. Today the stark purity of stripped hewn stone, emphasized by the clear glass panes of thirty huge arching windows, makes as much of an impression as a riot of color ever could have. To stand in the audience hall — having been gutted by bombing and fire during World War II, it was restored, as noted, in the 1950s — is to feel the capaciousness of Constantine's ambition. As mentioned earlier, my mother and I did not enter this magnificent relic during my visits in the late 1950s. Its designation as a Lutheran place of worship, which Protestant Prussians had imposed on it during the nineteenth-century Kulturkampf, had kept it off our pious Catholic itinerary. The Lutherans occupy the place lightly: a very large gilded cross is suspended in the apse, as if in the sky, but otherwise the space evokes empire more than church. It is easy to imagine a throne where the altar is.

How overpowering it must have been to traverse that enormous open space, approaching the Augustus. The hall itself — the great rounded arch of the apse, the double row of windows, the thick stone walls, the distance from the small entrance to the imperial seat — would have made a supplicant of everyone who crossed it. And wouldn't that have been the point? Almost nothing remains of Constantine's magnificent palace in Istanbul,[3] but this basilica in now obscure Trier stands essentially as he made it, a true relic of his rule. That is as it should be, despite the surpassing prestige of those other cities, since it was here that his stature first revealed itself beyond the circle of his father's soldiers. "In short, as the sun, when he rises upon the earth, liberally imparts his rays of light to all, so did Constantine, proceeding at early dawn from the imperial palace . . ." This is the propagandist Eusebius, but the *Palatina* suggests that even this verbosity accurately evokes the impression he'd have made, going out from here. ". . . and rising as it were with the heavenly luminary, impart the rays of his own beneficence to all who came into his presence."[4]

It is impossible to stand under the magnificent coffered ceiling and not see a throng of togas, great ladies in diadems lining the heated walls, bowing at his arrival. Below them, in subterranean caverns, slaves would have labored at boilers to heat the mosaic tiles on which he walked, creating an artificial climate intended to make chilly Trier feel like Rome. Every effort would have gone to enhance the impression made by this one man, and from what followed, we know that it all succeeded. "And now, all rising at the signal which indicated the emperor's entrance" — this is Eusebius describing an arrival that he witnessed — "at last he himself proceeded through the midst of the assembly, like some heavenly messenger of God, clothed in raiment which glittered as it were with rays of light, reflecting the glowing radiance of a purple robe, and adorned with the brilliant splendor of gold and precious stones. Such was the external appearance of his person; and with regard to his mind, it was evident he was distinguished by piety and godly fear. This was indicated by his downcast eyes, the blush on his countenance, and his gait. For the rest of his personal excellencies, he surpassed all present in height of stature and beauty of form, as well as in majestic dignity of mien, and invincible strength and vigor."[5]

To a world threatened by dissolution, the unifying impulse can only seem virtuous, yet the perennial human problem is how to keep the ideal of unity free of the burden of tyranny, and that problem reached a point of crisis in the Age of Constantine. For him, unification was by definition a matter of domination. And that played itself out in the wars he waged against his rivals. But military domination was only part of his agenda. At a deeper level, he wanted a spiritual domination too, and a fuller sense of that background can help us see his conversion to Christianity in 312 in a clearer light.

After he defeated his wife's father, Maximian, at Marseilles in 310, Constantine's fortunes were already being raised to the divine. On the way back to Trier from Marseilles, he stopped at the pagan temple in Autun a moment, before the oracle that Eusebius enshrines: "O Constantine, you saw, I believe, your protector Apollo, in company with Victory, offering you laurel crowns . . . You really saw the god, and recognized yourself in the appearance of one to whom the prophecies of poets have declared that the rule of the whole world should belong."[6] News of this vision, with its implication of heavenly anointing by Apollo, who was identified with the sun god,[7] would have been spread far and wide by Constantine's panegyrist. As the historian of antiquity Averil Cameron points out, such claiming favor of the pagan gods offers the context in which to see the story of his subsequent vision at Milvian Bridge. Caesars had habitually declared special sponsorship by gods, but in this era, the meaning of such piety was changing. The coming to the fore of Christian ideas was only part of a larger religious revolution, which our own simplistic notions of paganism fall short of explaining. For example, it is significant that Constantine's coins stated his devotion to the Unconquered Sun. Sol Invictus had already come to be understood, in a proclamation by the emperor Aurelian in 274, as "the one universal Godhead," as the historian J.N.D. Kelly summarized it, "which, recognized under a thousand names, revealed Itself most fully and splendidly in the heavens."[8] The Roman cult of the sun god, as the supreme being, already manifested a movement toward monotheism, and it means everything that Constantine's own instinctive piety, both as a pagan and as a converted Christian, should have had as its constant vision the bright light in the sky. Monotheism is regarded as having strictly herded pagans to one side and Christians and Jews to the other, but definitions at the time were anything but strict.[9] What never varied in Constantine's otherwise fluid religious self-understanding, something that carried over from Apollo to Christ, was that it was divinely commissioned "that the rule of the whole world should belong" to him.[10]

Of course others felt the same way — for example, Maxentius, the son of Maximian who, after Marseilles, took his father's place at war with Constantine. Like his father before him, Maxentius affiliated himself with the demigod Hercules.[11] Constantine's putative association with the superior Sol was another kind of usurpation: The contest between the human rivals was also now a contest between their sponsoring deities — just like the contest between Moses and Pharaoh with which the saga of the One God began. Maxentius controlled Rome, and that was what Constantine wanted next. The legend of Milvian Bridge says that Constantine was moving against an overwhelmingly superior force, that when his vision of the cross promised victory, such an outcome was unlikely. The legendary vision thus made the contest one between the Christian God and the Roman gods.

"The gods of Rome, then, had declared for Maxentius; whence in this crisis should Constantine seek aid?" This account of the legend, written in 1931 by N. H. Baynes, breathlessly renders the tale on which I was raised, and which we saw in summary in the previous chapter. "Against the advice of his generals, against the counsel of the augurs, with amazing daring Constantine invaded Italy."[12] He knew from his vision that he had more than a chance; he had a mandate. But it depended on his putting his faith, at last, in Jesus Christ. That is why he raised the cross on a spear. Commenting on Baynes's version of the traditional account, T. D. Barnes dismisses it as "a boy's adventure story."

An alternative narration, preferred by Barnes and most scholars now, debunks key elements of the legend and the uses to which it has been put. Approaching Rome, Constantine was no underdog. He knew that Maxentius, whose army had been decimated in an earlier battle in Verona, had no chance. In a superior position, Constantine denounced his rival as a bastard and no true ruler.[13] The battle at the Tiber was a predictable rout, with Maxentius unable even to mount an orderly retreat. As he withdrew across the Milvian Bridge — which was in fact a jury-rigged pontoon construction — he fell into the river. He died, perhaps by drowning. Constantine may or may not have ordered it, but his wife's brother's head was carried through the city on a pike.[14] It may indeed be that Constantine entered Rome with an army bearing the cross, although some contemporary accounts attribute his victory to intervention by pagan deities,[15] and others are vague in identifying his religious association. The inscription on the Arch of Constantine, which was erected within three years of the battle and still stands near the Colosseum, cites victory only "by the inspiration of the divinity."[16]

Although a public conversion to a despised religion on the eve of battle might be considered supernaturally motivated maverick politics on Constantine's part, there are compelling reasons to think it would have been infinitely shrewd. Remember that Diocletian's order that Christian churches be burned had been issued only in 303. Since then, the persecution had eased, but Christian property was still in danger of being confiscated. Though it served Constantine's later purpose to have emphasized how threatened Christians were before his coming, especially in Maxentius's Italy,[17] it seems clear that a true state of Christian dispossession played a part in shaping his strategy in 312. If Constantine was to succeed in imposing authority on a restless Roman populace whose loyalties were divided among contending tetrarchs, he needed a political base within the city. His arrival behind the standard of Christ would have instantly given him one — among Christians. They were a minority, but a well-organized one, and no claimant had the allegiance of a majority. Fierce Christian devotion to a conqueror whose miraculous conversion proved the truth of their faith would have made Christians powerful political allies.

Within a year of Milvian Bridge, Constantine controlled the entire Western empire. His one remaining rival was Licinius, who had replaced Galerius as Augustus of the East. Constantine shrewdly proposed an alliance, and offered his half-sister in marriage to Licinius, who accepted. Licinius assumed the marriage would consummate an equality between two caesars. Consistent with his new friendliness toward Christianity, Constantine proposed an end to the persecution of the Church, which he, like his father, had never carried out in any case. Licinius agreed. They met at Milan in 313 and jointly issued the Edict of Milan, granting universal religious freedom to pagans, Christians, and Jews. "Since we saw that freedom of worship ought not to be denied," the decree read, ". . . to each man's judgment and will the right should be given to care for sacred things according to each man's free choice."[18]

It is a moving, almost modern statement, but our assumptions are very different from what theirs would have been. Again, we think of the words "pagan," "Christian," and "Jew" as defining distinct groups, but the fluid interchange among them in that period of massive social mutation is striking. The potent movement toward monotheism among pagans is reflected in the fact that *Summus Deus* was by then a common Roman form of address to the deity.[19] As seen in Constantine's originating piety, that supreme deity would have been associated with the sun,[20] and pagans would have recognized, with reason, their own solar cult in such Christian practices as orienting churches to the east, worshiping on "sun day," and celebrating the birth of the deity at the winter solstice.

That Christian piety commonly included pagan practice and superstition would have been part of the broad appeal of the Gospel among the least educated. Constantine's famously converted army, for example, was made up of unlettered peasants and barbarians, and it is unlikely they would have grasped essential matters of their new religion. Indeed, to the Teutons and Celts among them — and an army mustered from Trier would have drawn heavily from such tribes — the cross of Christ as the standard to march behind would have evoked the ancestral totem of the sacred tree far more powerfully than it would have Saint Paul's token of deliverance.[21] Such an association may have figured in Constantine's instinctive grasp of the cross as a sign to rally to, since his army of barbarians, which grew with every conquest, was the first population he had to unify. Beginning with that army, a pragmatic tolerance, up to a point, would have been Constantine's modus operandi.

While Jews kept themselves apart from pagans, the line between Jews and Christians, even after two centuries, was still not hard and fast. That blurring was greater in some places than in others. We have seen, for example, that the large and influential community of Greek-speaking Jews in Alexandria — there were a million Jews in Egypt by the beginning of the second century[22] — shared a Greek translation of Hebrew Scriptures, the Septuagint, with the Church. The distinctive Christian act of worship was the Eucharist, but many Christians also observed the contemporary Jewish form of Psalm recital and readings, vestiges of which are preserved in the Christian Liturgy of the Word and in the Latin breviary. No doubt

some Christians and Jews during this time practiced this worship together. Symbols associated with early Christianity, like the fish, bread, and
the cup representing wine, were Jewish cult symbols.[23] Hellenized Jews of
the Diaspora would have had more in common with some Greek-speaking Christians like the Arians, whose strict monotheism made them suspicious of divinity claims for Jesus, than with the more inward-directed rabbis of Palestine. Some Jews of the Diaspora, to cite another example, did
not insist on circumcision for Gentile converts,[24] which means that some
Jews would not have seen Saint Paul's inflammatory position on this issue
as the cause for rupture it is taken to be. Furthermore, there is reason to
believe that some Jews in this period were religious in ways that, to the
rabbis, would have been unrecognizable as Jewish.[25] And, one needn't assume that all Jews were religious in any sense. Finally, in that ultimate in-
dicator we saw earlier, modern archaeology finds it difficult to distinguish
between Jewish and Christian tombstones in many places, even into this
fourth century.

But as a dominant culture begins to define itself more sharply, attendant subcultures inevitably do so as well. Blurred lines become anathema
to all, and there is no doubt that the process of rectifying those lines had
to begin, for Constantine, within the culture he was trying to make his
own, which was the Church. Thus, while he was ordaining tolerance
among religions, he was preparing to abolish tolerance within Christianity. In a letter written in 313, the year of the liberal Edict of Milan, he instructed his prefect in Africa to move against the Donatists, schismatic
Christians who posited sanctity as a prerequisite for valid administration
of the sacraments. "I consider it absolutely contrary to the divine law," he
wrote, "that we should overlook such quarrels and contentions, whereby
the Highest Divinity may perhaps be moved to wrath, not only against the
human race, but also against me myself, to whose care He has, by His celestial will, committed the government of all earthly things, and that He
may be so far moved as to take some untoward step. For I shall really and
fully be able to feel secure and always to hope for prosperity and happiness from the ready kindness of the most mighty God, only when I see all
venerating the most holy God in the proper cult of the catholic religion
with harmonious brotherhood of worship."[26]

Of course the "proper cult" of Catholicism was not yet clearly established, as the multiplicity of what would soon be termed heresies indicated. Once the impulse to establish a "harmonious brotherhood" within
a group is reified, discordances from outside, originating with distinct

groups, become intolerable. The very fluidity of practice, belief, and membership between Jewish and Christian communities thus contributed to a first reneging on the Milan Edict's promise of equality among the three religions.[27] In 315, Constantine issued the edict, referred to earlier, singling out Jews, making it illegal for them to proselytize. The decree signals the success Jews were having in attracting Christians to their cult and calendar. Moreover, the decree was prompted by a widespread Christian wish to maintain a lively connection with the Jewish origins of faith in Jesus. But the way the new law sought to protect the "harmonious brotherhood of worship" was to target Judaism, and not the "Judaizing" Christians. It therefore marked the decisive shift of weight in a balance that would now forever tilt against Jews.

The year 315 was decisive for Christian-pagan relations too. By then, Licinius, Augustus in the East, had realized that, despite similarities with the sun deity, the Christian God was different and would not readily take a place among the other gods of the Roman pantheon.[28] It may well have occurred to Licinius that he'd been had by Constantine, for whom tolerance was only the first step toward a new, Christian domination. Licinius saw, too late, that the Milan Edict itself gave a kind of primacy to Christianity: "Christian religion" was named first, and Roman paganism, like all paganism, was referred to as "any other cult."[29] The growing influence of Christianity would enhance Constantine's power and diminish his own. Seeing this, Licinius began to purge Christians from his civil service. The act gave Constantine the pretext he needed to declare war against yet another brother-in-law.[30]

If there was then a certain religious fluidity among the peoples of the empire — a vagueness about attachments and beliefs that reflected the dispersion of political power — there was also a lack of religious clarity in Constantine's own mind. But as his gradual accumulation of political power seemed tied to his affiliation with the Christian God, he became firmer over time in that affiliation, beginning, in all likelihood, before the mythic conversion date of 312 and continuing even after his revealing letter of 313. His soldiers, going from victory to victory, would have redoubled their devotion to the charm of their Christian standard. That Constantine's full embrace of a Christian identity — and of martial sponsorship by the Christian deity — took place gradually, and not all at once as in the legend, is revealed by the fact that Sol, the pagan sun god, continued to be honored on Constantine's coins until 321. By such a relatively slow process do social mutations usually occur, even if after the fact they are compressed, in the manner of boys' adventure stories, into moments of dramatic turnabout. What began, both in the empire and in Constantine's psyche, in the year 312 at Milvian Bridge did not reach completion until twelve years later.

In 324, at the Battle of Chrysopolis, on the eastern side of the Bosporus, Constantine defeated Licinius, his last political rival. Constantine became the sole ruler of the empire. The ambition he had set for himself in the *Aula Palatina* in Trier was, in this patient, almost plodding way, achieved. And as all could see more clearly in 324 than they could have in 312, it was achieved under the sponsorship not of Sol Invictus, not of Apollo, but of Jesus Christ. It was not the result of mystical vision or supernatural intervention, for Constantine's pragmatic alliance with Christian groups in various contested locations was really what had proved decisive. Christians had faithfully rallied to him, and made the difference. And he could see that his allegiance to Christ would continue to be useful as he set out to consolidate his power over Asia Minor, the Levant, and Africa, which could only regard him as a foreign figure from the rough northwest. Christians made up a greater part of the Eastern empire than they did of the West, so Constantine's cross standard would be more rallied to now than ever.

What the effect of all this was on the ruler's inner state is impossible to say, but from this point on, all apparent ambiguities in his own religious identity dropped away. After Chrysopolis, Constantine was firmly and publicly Christian. He was, of course, instantly the most important Christian in the world, and in that time of social and religious ferment, he was in a position to put his own stamp on Christianity — and he did. That stamp inevitably reflected what he had just been through.

The Church in 324 had to remind Constantine of the empire he had inherited in 306 — a seething caldron of contention and rivalry, with doctrinal differences, even schisms, defined by regional loyalties. Bishops vied with each other for influence, and worshipers openly disagreed on the meaning of their worship. In addition to the Donatists, there were Docetists and Manichaeans and Arians with their cat's cradle of disputes about ways in which Jesus was man or God, and about the nature, substance, and personality of God. All of this must have seemed arcane to the soldier-monarch, appearing like religious versions of the tetrarchic factionalism he had set out from Trier to overcome. As a politician, Constantine had put his trust in the universalist spirit which, from above, appears as the humane bringing of order to chaos, while from below often appearing as totalitarianism. His method was to tolerate diversity and share power for only as long as he had to. The unity of the empire — under himself — was to him the absolute political virtue. His string of successful conquests had confirmed its divinely ordained righteousness. So in turning to religion, unity of belief and practice, not tolerance of diversity, had to seem paramount.

If the young Constantine had felt chosen by the gods to unify the empire, the mature, Christian Constantine likewise assumed a divine mandate to unify the empire's religion. "We strive to the best of our ability to fill with good hope those who are uninitiated in such doctrines [as the Gospel of Jesus Christ]." This is Constantine speaking to an "assembly of saints," Christian leaders, about the year 320. "For it is no ordinary task to turn the minds of our subjects to piety if they happen to be virtuous, and to reform them if they are evil and unbelieving."[31] Constantine fully understands himself by now as "the vice-regent of God,"[32] and, as is clear from what he did as soon as he defeated Licinius, he did not hesitate to act as such, especially against the "evil and unbelieving."

Constantine moved at once against paganism. Pagans would continue to make up a majority of the empire until well after his death, and as his successors would learn, their resistance to Christian dominance would increasingly threaten an imperial power that defined itself as Christian. Once Constantine had cast his lot with the Christians, and once besieged pagans had looked to Licinius and his other enemies, Constantine knew that pagan submission would never mean loyalty. In some places he ordered pagan temples burned, as Diocletian had churches. He confiscated temple treasuries and outlawed the showing of sacrificial smoke — a jettisoning of the tolerance of Milan. "Hence it was that, of those who had been slaves of superstition," Eusebius wrote of the pagans, "when they saw with their own eyes the exposure of their delusion and beheld the actual ruin of the temples and images in every place, some applied themselves to the saving doctrine of Christ; while others, though they declined to take this step, yet reprobated the folly they had received from their fathers, and laughed to scorn what they had so long been accustomed to regard as gods."[33]

But Constantine knew the impossibility of forcing conversion on the pagan majority, and so, despite evidence of some such attacks, the main mark of his program was not violent persecution. That would come later in the century. Constantine wanted his pagan subjects to be won over as he himself had been — by seeing the benefit to the Roman world of a unifying affiliation with the Christian deity. But how could they see that if Christians themselves were not unified? Christians could not even agree on how to calculate the date of Easter, much less on how Jesus was God.[34] Thus Constantine's political problem opened immediately into his religious one. That led to his — for our purposes — most fateful action yet. Immediately upon coming to power as the sole ruler of the empire, but only then, Constantine asserted the right to exercise absolute authority over the entire Church. He did this despite the fact that he was not baptized, and, as was not unusual, would not be until shortly before he died. The necessarily blurred lines of mystical feeling and spiritual paradox — what our contemporaries would call the religion of the analogical imagination, as opposed to the univocal or one-dimensional faith[35] — would be erased now in favor of clearly drawn boundaries of dogma. As regionalisms of a once divided empire had to be deleted — a common calendar had to be enforced — so with faith and its calendars. Constantine saw, in other words, that only a unified, sharply defined, and firmly advanced Christianity would overcome paganism.

Suddenly tolerance of theological disagreement and ecclesiastical particularities, which had been a given among Christians since Saints Paul and James had reached a modus vivendi at the Council of Jerusalem in the first century, was now deemed unchristian. Religious diversity fell under suspicion of being an overly relativized polytheism, a mark of the Pantheon, not the Church — although for two centuries Christian monotheism, like Jewish monotheism, had included a multiplicity of meanings and traditions. If that multiplicity became an unacceptable choice — "heresy" comes from the Greek word for "choice"[36] — it was more because of a political requirement than a religious one. The aim was *E pluribus unum. Pluribus* would be defined not as a principle of coequality but as the expendable means to the self-justifying end that is *unum.*

How is Jesus God? We saw that this question, *as* question, had been the essence of Christian conversation since his first followers had allowed themselves, in grief, first to pray to Jesus, then to speak aloud their tremendous intuition about him. But now an answer would replace the question in discourse. The single, definitive, univocal answer that had so far eluded the Christian consensus — eluded, that is, finely tuned, passionate minds as variously engaged with the question as Irenaeus, Origen, and Arius — would now be imposed by imperial fiat. Unity would henceforth be the note not only of the political order but of a revealed truth. With holiness and catholicity, "unity" would henceforth be, in the argot, a "mark" of the Church — at least in theory.

Differences in Christian belief and practice were often rooted, as in New Testament times, in the regional differences between, say, an Antioch in Syria or a Corinth in Greece, where Saint Paul composed his hymn to diversity.[37] Differences were natural in such a world, but now an emperor with a "celestial" mandate for "the government of all earthly things"[38] was determined to change that world. For Constantine, religious differences were impediments to the power that had replaced Maxentius and Licinius. In this way, the choice ("heresy") to be religiously different became defined as treason, a political crime. But different from whom, and from what? For the first time in its history, the universal Christian Church was seen to need a defined orthodoxy, a word derived from the Greek for "right thinking." This resulted from what might be called the first law of exclusion: You can't say who is out unless you can say what it is to be in. "No heretic," as the proverb has it, "without a text."[39] It is important to emphasize that this need, which has so dominated Roman Catholicism that even now the Church cannot break free of it, was first defined not by the Lord, a Jew who identified with dissenters; nor by his apostles, who did not hesitate to differ from one another; nor by their successor bishops who defended regional interests; nor by evangelists who produced not one version of the Jesus story but four; nor by theologians who introduced innovative Hellenistic categories into Scripture study; nor by preachers who readily put their eccentric personal stamps on the kerygma — but by an all-conquering emperor for whom one empire had come to equal one religion.

Thus, the now absolute and sole Caesar, demonstrating an authority no one had ever exercised before, summoned the bishops of the Church to a meeting over which he himself would preside: "Wherefore I signify to you, my beloved brethren, that all of you promptly assemble at the said city, that is at Nicaea . . ."[40] Two hundred and fifty of them came.[41] He would not let them leave until they had begun to do for the Church what he was doing for the empire. This meeting was the Council of Nicaea, the first Ecumenical Council of the Church. It took place in 325, only a year after Chrysopolis. In response to the emperor's mandate, the bishops did, in fact, agree to a formulaic statement of belief, defining especially, and in explicit terms, how Jesus is God.[42] They did so unanimously — well, almost unanimously. Those who dissented were exiled by Constantine. (More than one bishop — and most famously Athanasius, banished later — would serve out his exile in Trier.)[43] Christians still recite this formula today, as the Nicene Creed. As we stand solemnly at the midpoint of a Sunday liturgy, letting the familiar words roll off our tongues, we think of the creed as a religious necessity, perhaps treasuring it as such, as I do. We give not a thought to its first function as a kind of loyalty oath, fulfilling a political necessity as much as a religious one.

But the creed we recite is not the same as the one the bishops approved, and the difference marks a turning point in our inquiry. "We believe in one God, the Father almighty, maker of all things, visible and invisible . . ."[44] For the first several verses, what the bishops approved and what we say are identical, including the key statement of how Jesus is God. To us, these phrases are an arcane litany, but to the Nicene prelates they were a precise confession, full of implication. "And in one Lord Jesus Christ, the Son of God, begotten from the Father, only-begotten, that is, from the substance of the Father, God from God, light from light, true God from true God, begotten not made, of one substance with the Father, through whom all things came into being, things in heaven and on earth, who for the sake of us men and for the purpose of our salvation came down and became incarnate, becoming man, suffered and rose again on the third day, ascended to the heavens, and will come to judge the living and the dead."[45] The original Nicene statement goes on to issue a condemnation — "These the Catholic Church anathematizes" — of those who hold to the Arian position that the Son was somehow inferior to the Father, but that needn't concern us here. The point of comparison is with the phrase "becoming man, suffered and rose again on the third day." Here is how an expanded Nicene Creed is recited in churches around the world today: ". . . and became man. For our sake he was crucified under Pontius Pilate; he suffered, died, and was buried. On the third day, he rose again in fulfillment of the Scriptures."

In the original version of this pivotal profession of faith, not only is the death of Jesus not mentioned, neither is the crucifixion. In the second version, equal emphasis on incarnation, suffering, and Resurrection has been replaced by a strong emphasis on death, with the elaboration "suffered, died, and was buried." That strong emphasis is redoubled when the means of death — the only concrete, historical detail in the entire formulation — is given as "crucified under Pontius Pilate." Explicitly holding the Roman procurator responsible contrasts with Gospel accounts that emphasize his reluctance before Jewish bloodthirst, a change that may reflect the Church's new status in the empire as favored instead of persecuted, and that avoids self-accusation because, of course, Pilate was a pagan, and pagans have now joined the Jews as enemies par excellence. But the introduction of the phrase "in fulfillment of the Scriptures" makes a creedal affirmation of the supersessionist pattern of "prophecy historicized." We have seen how easily the proclaiming of the story of Jesus as "fulfillment" opens into anti-Judaism. There is a hint of the anti-Jewish spirit of the Nicene fathers in their ban of the celebration of Easter in the same week as Passover.[46]

The text of what we think of as the Nicene Creed evolved through a series of subsequent councils, more than a dozen of them,[47] culminating in the Council of Constantinople in 381. (That council is known for its definitive condemnation of Arianism.) Finally, the creedal statement, as reflected in the text we know, put the crucifixion at the center of faith and the death of Jesus at the heart of redemption.[48] That this is a mid-fourth-century innovation is emphatically revealed by the fact that the first Nicene formulation, in mentioning neither death nor crucifixion, had, in line with the constant tradition of the Church, left the emphasis on Incarnation and Resurrection. This change means that the Son of God became man not to be one of us, not to take on the human condition — which includes suffering but is not defined by it — and not, for that matter, to undergo the Resurrection, as the affirmation of the Father's covenantal faithfulness to the Son. Instead, according to the theological shift reflected in the amended creed, the Son of God became man in order to be crucified. The crucifixion takes the place of the Resurrection as the saving event, and Christ the victim takes the place of Christ the victor as the symbol of God's love for the world.

This shift has important implications for relations between Christians and Jews. With the cross at the center of a theology of salvation, it becomes the means of salvation. In this altered context, the Gospel slander that shifts chief responsibility for that cross from the Romans to the Jews — the creed's indictment of Pilate notwithstanding — sets in motion a dynamic that will keep Jews at the heart of a quickened, and quickly armed, Christian hatred. "Tell me, do you praise the Jews for crucifying Christ," Saint John Chrysostom will ask, around 387, "and for, even to this day, blaspheming Him and calling Him a lawbreaker?"[49] Chrysostom (c. 349–407), the bishop of Antioch, still revered as the patron saint of preachers, was the master of the sermon genre known as *Adversus Judaeos*. Such words inevitably led to actions: assaults on synagogues, the exclusion of Jews from holding public office, expulsions. Can it be a coincidence that attacks on Jews, both rhetorical and physical, become a notable pattern of Christian behavior only after the cult of the cross is established, not at Nicaea precisely, but in its aftermath?

How did this happen? Part of the answer may lie, remarkably enough, with a postprandial speech delivered by Constantine to the fathers of Nicaea at a banquet marking both the conclusion of the council and the twentieth anniversary of the emperor's accession to power. Here is how Eusebius sets the scene, "the circumstances of which were splendid beyond description": "Detachments of the body-guard and other troops surrounded the entrance of the palace with drawn swords, and through the midst of these the men of God proceeded without fear into the innermost of the imperial apartments, in which some were the emperor's own companions at table, while others reclined on couches arranged on either side. One might have thought that a picture of Christ's kingdom was thus shadowed forth, and a dream rather than reality."[50] Those present at this banquet would all have just signed the creed that made no mention yet of the cross — but the cross was at the heart of what Constantine had to say.

Eusebius, having just attended the council as bishop of Caesarea, was present at this event. His account of what Constantine said is the first clear telling of the story of the vision that the emperor only now, thirteen years after the fact, claims to have had on the eve of the Battle of Milvian Bridge. Various traditions had already cropped up that explained Constantine's conversion. One writer, Rufinius, had described an apparition that was aural, not visual, with Constantine hearing angels singing "By this conquer."[51] Other accounts, as we saw, said the miraculous vision was of the Chi-Rho, a kind of divine monogram. But now, through Eusebius, we have Constantine's own description of what happened. I offer a fuller version now of what I cited in part earlier, to underscore the fact that this primal Christian myth of the cross has its origin not only in Constantine's own words but in his words spoken at Nicaea, meant to advance a political agenda.

> The emperor said that about the noon hour, when the day was already beginning to wane, he saw with his own eyes in the sky above the sun a cross composed of light, and that there was attached to it an inscription saying, "By this conquer." At the sight, he said, astonishment seized him and all the troops who were accompanying him on the journey and were observers of the miracle.
>
> He said, moreover, that he doubted within himself what the import of this apparition could be. And while he continued to ponder and reason on its meaning, night suddenly came on; then in his sleep, the Christ of God appeared to him with the same sign which he had seen in the heavens, and commanded him to make a likeness of that sign which he had

seen in the heavens, and to use it as a safeguard in all engagements with his enemies.

At dawn of day, he arose, and communicated the marvel to his friends; and, then, calling together the workers in gold and precious stones, he sat in the midst of them, and described to them the figure of the sign he had seen, bidding them represent it in gold and precious stones. And this representation I myself have had an opportunity of seeing.[52]

Eusebius then goes on to describe the making of the military standard, "the spear and transverse bar" we saw before.

What is going on here? This is mythmaking by the emperor himself. That the occasion for this first and only elaboration of that vision from years before, an explicit vision of the cross, was the Council of Nicaea tells us everything. It is at this moment, far more than in 312, that a unifying and universalizing symbol can serve the emperor's purpose. The cross, even apart from its association with the death of Jesus, is the perfect emblem of Constantine's program, with its joining of horizontal and vertical axes and with its evoking of the four directions: north, south, east, west. The cross of the compass unites the globe; a hand-held globe surmounted by a cross would be, with the crown and scepter, a symbol of the Christian king.

The public display of the cross as a religious symbol, especially as rendered in gold and jewels, would be a step away from the second-commandment prohibition of graven images. Indeed, a flowering of the Christian imagination would follow upon Constantine's innovation, with an elaborate iconography that would forever set Christianity apart from Judaism. But no creation of the Christian aesthetic would surpass the satisfactions of the cruciform image because of its subliminal but powerful evocation of the universal.[53] And it should be noted that, as Constantine was elevating the cross to the realm of the sacred, he was abolishing crucifixion as the Roman form of capital punishment. Soon enough, the memory of its true horrors would be smothered in pious stylization. Once unleashed, the impulse to raise the cross would lead not only to its hanging around necks and at the ends of strings of prayer beads, not only to placement on the walls of churches, but to the design of churches themselves, with the imperial basilica transformed into an apse by an intersecting transept. Christians would recognize the cross in the human body and in the tree, in the way light flares and in the conjunction of planets at the sun. Eventually they would see the cross, as I do, in telephone poles and in airplanes flying overhead.

The cross would become an object of adoration and a means of warding off evil. The thing itself would serve as a kind of primal sacrament. Even when Byzantine iconoclasts, years after Constantine, throw out the images of faith, they will make an exception of the cross,[54] the sign under which they, too, will seek to conquer. The letters IHS are ubiquitous in the Church — on vestments, altar cloths, baldachins, even impressed on the unleavened wafers of Holy Communion. The initials are the first three letters of the Greek word for Jesus, but after Constantine they also became understood as referring to his vision of the cross: *In Hoc Signo (Vinces)*. In my experience, that is the meaning most commonly attached to the monogram, a sign that the myth of Constantine's conversion remains firmly in Catholic memory. Once, however, kneeling beside my mother in St. Mary's Church, I asked her to explain the IHS above me, and she answered, "I Have Suffered."

It is not my purpose here to deny or establish the authenticity of Constantine's account, but only to observe that his choice of that first-ever council meeting at Nicaea as the place from which to promulgate his vision of the cross as a foundational myth of the church-state and state-church reveals a kind of imaginative genius. The cross and the creed *together* unified the Church. It seems at first only a nice coincidence, soldier that he was, that the cross so well lent itself to construction as a spear, but eventually that, too, would seem ordained. The appeal of the cross as a universalizing symbol would achieve its mobilizing critical mass as the emblem of the process begun at Nicaea only if the Christian sense of the cross's central place in the death of Jesus — and that death's central place in the redemptive plan of God — could be quickened. And for that, Constantine turned to his mother, Helena Augusta. Here enters the legend of the True Cross, which meant so much to my mother and me at Trier. Legend, yes, but the "discovery" is an event to which Constantine himself refers in a letter preserved by Eusebius.[55] The finding of the True Cross was a marvel Constantine rejoiced at and immediately publicized. What the emperor began with his speech to the bishops at Nicaea in 325, Helena carried forward with her pilgrimage to Jerusalem the following year.

✦ 20 ✦

The True Cross

J UST AS CONSTANTINE's battle-eve vision of the cross at Milvian
Bridge in 312 was not reliably recounted until 325, so the full story
of Helena's "discovery" of the True Cross was first told only years
later, by Saint Ambrose, the bishop of Milan, in the year 395.[1] As is
true of the vision, so with the discovery: the context in which each
story was first told lays bare its meaning. If the tide turned against the
Jews in the first instance, it began to flood in on them in the second, as
will become clear when we look at Ambrose's stance on the use of violence
against Jews.

Eusebius, our source for Constantine's Nicaean telling of his vision,
was, as we saw, the bishop of Caesarea in Palestine. In that role, he accompanied Helena on her pilgrimage, and he records the fact of that journey's
having taken place.[2] Attributing a pious motive to her, Eusebius says that
she wanted to pray on the very earth on which Jesus had walked. That is
an impulse the power of which I know from my own experience. But Helena's journey to the East seems to have been as much an exercise in diplomacy as piety. After the Council of Nicaea, Constantine had returned to
Rome, but the promulgation of the creed, unanimous or not, hardly settled the quarrels in the Church, with objections being raised especially in
the East. "It would have been Helena's task on her 'pilgrimage' to help
solve these problems," the scholar Jan Willem Drijvers has written. In his
biography *Helena Augusta*, published in 1992, Drijvers provides an exhaustive history of the legend of the True Cross, and in what follows I rely
on his account. "Helena's journey was not restricted to Palestine, but included in fact a visit to all the eastern provinces, as Eusebius himself states.
She did not travel as a humble pilgrim but as an Augusta."[3] Helena had become her son's regent — in effect the First Lady of the empire — only the
year before, upon the death of Fausta, Constantine's wife, an event to

which we will return. In Drijvers's view, Helena made her dramatic journey to further Constantine's effort to Christianize pagans.[4] Her related purpose was to help Christians overcome their reluctance to embrace his policy of unification of the Church.

Eusebius says that Helena visited the emperor's soldiers and distributed lavish bonuses to them. She presided over the release of prisoners and gave money from the imperial treasury to the poor. Everywhere she went, she presented the emperor's benevolent face, reinforcing a restive population's devotion to him. And not only that. Perhaps the most visible part of Constantine's Christianizing program was a hurried campaign to build large and resplendent churches everywhere, a strategy of demonstrating the triumph of Christianity over paganism. Constantine constructed the original of St. Peter's Basilica in Rome, a deliberate reverencing of the site of the Fisherman's martyrdom. Helena, too, on her son's behalf, funded the construction of churches in the cities she visited. The climax of this effort was her association with the building of the Church of the Holy Sepulcher in Jerusalem.[5]

The construction of a lavish basilica shrine on the site of the tomb of Jesus had been undertaken by order of Constantine shortly after Nicaea. He wanted this church to be the most beautiful in the world, and there are records that Helena herself saw to its decoration. The tomb's location had been marked by a temple dedicated to Aphrodite, dating to the early second century when the Romans had renamed Jerusalem Aelia Capitolina. Across generations, the knowledge of the temple site's origin as the tomb of the Lord had been preserved. If anyone was going to look for the actual place of Golgotha, much less for remnants of the True Cross, they'd have begun where such an unbroken tradition pointed.

There are reasons to accept as historical the underlying fact of the legend of the True Cross — namely, that under Constantine, within a short time of Nicaea, something thenceforth revered as the cross on which Jesus died was discovered in Jerusalem. Constantine, writing to the bishop of Jerusalem in 326, refers to a "token of that holiest Passion" that had only recently been rescued from the earth, and he implicitly defined the basilica, to be known as the Martyrium, as a shrine to the True Cross.[6] This is a geographical and physical extension of his placing the cross at the center of Christian symbolism at Milvian Bridge, and at the center of theology at Nicaea. As is reflected in the adjustments to the Nicene Creed in these years — "crucified . . . suffered, died, and was buried" — the idea of the centrality of the cross spread quickly.

Saint Cyril, a successor bishop of Jerusalem, writing in 351 to a successor emperor, Constantine's son Constantius II, connects the dots by tying the Milvian Bridge vision to the discovered True Cross in Jerusalem. "For if in the days of your imperial father, Constantine of blessed memory, the saving wood of the Cross was found in Jerusalem (divine grace granting the finding of the long hidden holy places to one who nobly aspired to sanctity), now, sire, in the reign of your most godly majesty, as if to mark how far your zeal excels your forebear's piety, not from the earth but from the skies marvels appear: the trophy of victory over death of our Lord Jesus Christ, the Only-begotten Son of God, even the holy Cross, flashing and sparkling with brilliant light, has been seen at Jerusalem."[7]

According to such sources, there is no reason to accept as historical that Helena herself, despite her certain presence in Jerusalem in 326, had anything to do with the discovery of the True Cross, whatever is referred to by that phrase. When I first learned that, it came as a shock, because the story had been poured into the foundation of my faith — by, of course, my mother. I remember a scene in our yard at that house in Alexandria, Virginia. I might have been seven, the age I was when I met my neighbor Peter Seligman. It was springtime, and she was showing me the white blossom of our dogwood tree. Dogwood, she told me, was the state flower of Virginia. She loved our new tract house as much for the tree the contractor had spared as for anything. It had grown wild in the woods, was mature, but, in the way of dogwoods, was not large. It had a pleasing shape, and when in bloom it was a marvel of white.

"Look here," she said. I peered into the cup of the blossom cradled in her hand, and I followed her gesturing fingers as she touched the four petals, each with its tiny, heart-shaped purple stain. "This is the tree of the cross," she explained. "Once the dogwood blossom had been pure white, without these purple marks. Once the dogwood had been the tallest tree in the forest. But then the killers of Jesus used the wood of the dogwood to make the cross. The wood that Saint Helena found in Jerusalem was carved from a dogwood tree, and that helped her to recognize it as the True Cross, because by then, dogwood blossoms grew to make a cross themselves, showing the wounds of Christ with stains. By then the mighty dogwood no longer grew to be so tall." Our dogwood tree was not so small that its branches did not overhang the Seligmans' yard. I never told the story of the tree to Peter.

When a story falls into such blatant folktale rhythms, it is easy to dismiss it. Those who are inclined to discount the whole business of a found crucifix have an ally in, of all people, Eusebius. As Helena's companion and chronicler, he is the reason to believe that her journey to Jerusalem in 326 was a historical event. No doubt that journey is the source of the legend connecting Helena to the True Cross, even if the connection is first made more than half a century later by Ambrose, who presents both the discovery and Helena's responsibility for it as factual. But in Eusebius's detailed account of Helena's progress through Palestine, there is no mention of the True Cross at all, which is a surprise, if only because the emperor himself referred to it ("token of that holiest Passion") in the same time frame.[8] In describing Helena's sojourn, Eusebius is concerned just with the uncovering and celebrating of the ancient tomb of Jesus — the Holy Sepulcher, which to Eusebius is the site of the Resurrection. To him, the Resurrection is what counts. He has no interest in Golgotha, site of the crucifixion. As for the True Cross — like most Christians, he'd have regarded it as a token of shame, not an object to be sought out and revered. The Resurrection was the point.

Eusebius refers to the already begun construction of the Church of the Holy Sepulcher, and implies Helena's role of supporting her son's sweeping program of church-building throughout the East. Eusebius's account makes it seem that only one thing was going on here, when, as the design of the church itself indicates, a second strain of the Christian impulse was already being felt, and it had the weight of Constantine behind it. The architecture of the church complex makes the thing clear: The tomb of Jesus was marked by a relatively modest rotunda, called the Anastasis, while the newly uncovered, adjacent site of Golgotha was marked by a much larger basilica, the Martyrium. The basilica resembled, in fact, the audience hall of the palace Constantine had built for himself in Trier, a subtle reference to his origins. The tension apparent in the church-building foreshadowed the difference in emphasis between the Eastern and Latin Churches that continues to this day, the one elevating the victory of the Resurrection, the other elevating the agony of death.

There is, one should add, another reason besides theology that Eusebius would have chosen to ignore any report of a recovered True Cross in Jerusalem. As bishop of Caesarea, he was the primate of Palestine. That he was the region's dominant religious — and now political — figure is shown by his place at the side of Helena Augusta. Jerusalem, until then, was a backwater town from which Jews were still banished and in which Christians had expressed no interest. That was changing. The attention given to Jerusalem by the emperor and his mother had to alarm Eusebius.

A shrine containing relics of the True Cross, drawing pilgrims and power, could only undercut the prestige of Caesarea. In the event, with the legend of the True Cross taking hold, Caesarea did fade as the world importance of Jerusalem grew.[9] It was an early lesson in the politics of relics, which would not be lost on, among others, the archbishops of Mainz, Trier, and Cologne.

Constantine traveled to Jerusalem in 335 to preside at the dedication of the completed Basilica of the Holy Sepulcher.[10] It was one of the most magnificent churches in the world at the time. He would die two years later, and all would marvel at the new city he had created in Constantinople, but the goal he had set for himself in his first grand basilica, the *Aula Palatina* in Trier, was really achieved here, in his last one. Nothing symbolized the unity he had created more powerfully than the cross, and perhaps nothing had more pointedly enabled that unity than the cross. This was its shrine. The Martyrium would stand until 1009. The Anastasis, many times repaired, stands yet. It is what pilgrims revere today as the Church of the Holy Sepulcher, but it is a pale shadow of what Constantine built.

His insistence on the cross, both symbolic and literal, sparked an immediate interest in relics of the True Cross. Fragments of wood appeared across Europe, supposedly from Jerusalem, to be venerated in churches and to be worn as talismans. A vestige of this obsession is preserved in our impulse to "knock on wood," to ward off bad fortune. A piece of the True Cross is contained in the bronze cross atop the obelisk in St. Peter's Square.[11] In the first manifestations of this cult, little attention was paid to the precise circumstances of the discovery of the True Cross, but soon enough — a familiar human pattern — a story began to evolve. Not surprisingly, it was a story featuring Helena. Hadn't she been the one to shower benefactions on soldiers and common people? If Constantine had made himself a godlike figure, didn't that make his mother like the mother who'd stood beside the cross of her divine Son? The cult of Helena would explode in the late fourth century around an elaborately imagined legend — or rather, set of legends[12] — that told of her devotion in tracking down not only the True Cross but its nails, the sign Pilate attached to it, various instruments used to torture Jesus, the thorns, the whip, and the Seamless Robe that Jesus wore, a relic to which we will return. How the bodies of the Magi fit into this is not clear, but Helena would also be credited with discovering the site of the Nativity cave in Bethlehem — relics from womb to tomb. Not incidentally, the potent narrative of this legend would assign a new, even more damning role of villainy to the Jews. And the True Cross itself, a fine and final reversal, would justify the Jews' long-overdue punishment.

The one to give first and masterly expression to this legend was Saint Ambrose (339–397), the bishop of Milan. The son of a Roman official, Ambrose had made his first reputation, curiously enough, as the provincial governor of Trier. He was a cultured man, educated in the classics, who had been serving as an imperial governor when the people of Milan spontaneously chose him as their bishop — a signal of the century's volatile mix of religion and politics. Ambrose was a slight man but an eloquent preacher, and he soon became one of the most influential figures in the Church.

Some of the vivid impressions of Ambrose come from the writings of Augustine, whose conversion to the Church is often attributed to Ambrose. We find, for example, this description of Ambrose in *The Confessions:* "When he read, his eyes scanned the page and his heart explored the meaning, but his voice was silent and his tongue was still. All could approach him freely and it was not usual for visitors to be announced, so that often, when we came to see him, we found him reading like this in silence, for he never read aloud. We would sit there quietly, for no one had the heart to disturb him when he was so engrossed in study."[13] From Ambrose, Augustine would learn what the contemplative act of reading enabled in the mind. It was to read without moving one's lips, an activity of the interior life entire.[14] From Ambrose, Augustine would learn to see more than what was before the eyes. "I noticed, repeatedly, in the sermons of our bishop . . . that when God is thought of, our thoughts should dwell on no material reality whatsoever, nor in the case of the soul, which is the one thing in the universe nearest to God."[15] Because of Ambrose, Augustine became convinced for the first time of the existence of a spiritual world, and by watching Ambrose, he found a way to enter it. "The story which Augustine tells in the *Confessions,*" says his biographer Peter Brown of this relationship, ". . . is one of the most dramatic and massive evocations ever written of the evolution of a metaphysician; and his final 'conversion' to the idea of a purely spiritual reality, as held by sophisticated Christians in Milan, is a decisive and fateful step in the evolution of our ideas on spirit and matter."[16]

Despite present-day assumptions about the naiveté of a mind susceptible to mere legend, the sophistication of Ambrose is on full display in the use he makes of the story of Helena's discovery of the True Cross. He tells it in the oration he preaches at the funeral of the emperor Theodosius, on February 25, 395, the oldest record of the legend. "The Spirit inspired her to search for the wood of the Cross," Ambrose declared. "She drew near to Golgotha and said: 'Behold the place of combat: where is thy victory? . . . Why did you labor to hide the wood, O Devil, except to be vanquished a second time? You were vanquished by Mary, who gave the Conqueror birth.'"[17]

The victory includes the dawning of a Christian empire, but that has been delayed until now — delayed, according to Ambrose, by Satan's sur-viving agents, the Jews. Because of the discovery by Helena, Ambrose says, "The Church manifests joy, the Jew blushes. Not only does he blush, but he is tormented also, because he himself is the author of his own confu-sion." The reign of Constantine and the reappearance of the Cross, which indicts them, undoes the Jew, who confesses, "'We thought we had con-quered, but we confess that we ourselves are conquered! Christ has risen again, and princes acknowledge that He has risen. He who is not seen lives again.'"[18] The Cross itself thus becomes a kind of second Incarnation, a salvific turning point by which the will of God is accomplished. Clever Jews knew the Cross had such power. They hid it over the centuries, not just because it was a proof that they had crucified the Lord, but because its revelation would bring about their final defeat.[19] One version of the Hel-ena legend has a Jew being tortured until he agrees to show her where the Cross is buried. This story is poignantly rendered in the *Legend of the True Cross* fresco in Arezzo, by the fifteenth century's Piero della Francesca. The elaborate painting, in one panel entitled *Torment of the Hebrew,* shows a man with a rope around his neck being lowered into a well. Under such duress, he agrees to give up his people's last secret. When he does, Juda-ism's last hope is gone.[20]

Drijvers summarizes Ambrose's argument against the Jews this way: "They thought they had defeated Christianity by killing Christ, but through the finding of the Cross and the nails, as a result of which Christ and Christianity had come to life again, they themselves were defeated. Now, even the emperors recognize Christ and they have made themselves subservient to his power. Ambrose evidently presents Judaism as a force by its nature opposed to Christianity . . . [and] is undoubtedly of the opinion that the emperors should combat Judaism and that the Church and the secular authorities should consider the ruin of Judaism their common cause."[21]

Thus the finding of the True Cross is the definitive victory over the

Jews, the end of a two-hundred-year-old sibling rivalry. An inch below the surface of piety, the discovery is a mythic sacralization of the momentous political event by which one of the siblings, for the first time, gained power over the other. Rivalry assumes a relative equality of force that would simply never exist again between Christians and Jews. So a shift here was inevitable, whether handled benignly or not. Alas, in this case, the newly empowered younger sibling, embodied in the *arriviste* Ambrose, reacted as if the very existence of the other were more a threat than ever.

Clearly, the uses to which Ambrose puts the legend of the True Cross mark a turning point in what will come to be known, in Jules Isaac's phrase, as the "teaching of contempt."[22] Because promulgated by one of the greatest minds of the era, this contempt, now tied directly to the cross, will take hold as never before. For a time, it threatens to underwrite a version of what will come to be known as the Final Solution. And this all takes place in the name of Helena, the saint, the queen, the friend to nuns and priests, the patroness of armies, the benefactress of churches, the devoted mother of the emperor, and — through all of this — a model for my own. Helena, with Constantine, was seen to preside over a version of the Holy Family, the amity of which was a sacrament of the unity of the empire. In the name of that unity, the empire was to be a univocal totality now, whose mortal enemies within and without were at last to be defined and named. And once defined and named, targeted.

The sad truth is that Flavia Julia Helena Augusta was no such woman. The irony would be only poignant if so much violence did not hang on her legend. She began as a jilted wife — as we saw, her husband, Constantius, had turned her out of his household in favor of another woman. Only the coming to power of her son rescued her from bitter disappointment. She was brought back into the center of his family. But then, no sooner had they been put forward as the familial version of the concord Constantine wanted from Nicaea, these people turned on each other.

Before marrying Fausta in 307 (recall that she was the daughter of Maximian, Constantine's rival), Constantine had had a son by a concubine. That son's name was Crispus, and he had grown up to rule the northern empire as his father's regent, based in Trier. The family implosion that took place just as Constantine consolidated his power was probably some kind of dynastic intrigue, with Helena favoring Crispus, who lived in the Trier palace associated with her, on the site of the present cathedral. As Constantine's wife, Fausta would have had good reason to oppose Crispus as Constantine's favorite, in favor of her own son. (Sibling rivalry now comes to seem a kind of cancer in the marrow of this story.) Some historians conjecture that Fausta hatched a plot to inspire Constantine's suspicions against Crispus.[23] All that is certain is that in 326, the year after the enforced love feast of the Council of Nicaea, Constantine ordered the murder of his firstborn son and the obliteration of the name Crispus from imperial history. That order may account for the destruction of Crispus's residence in Trier that year. The holy legend remembers this demolition as prompted by Helena's desire to replace her palace with the new cathedral built to enshrine the relic she brought to her hometown, which was the Seamless Robe of Jesus.

If Fausta did falsely conspire against Crispus, and if, after the murder, Constantine learned (from Helena?) that he had been misled by Fausta, that would account for what happened next. So would another, simpler explanation that some historians favor — namely, that Crispus and his stepmother Fausta were lovers.[24] What we do know is in that same fateful year, shortly after murdering his son, Constantine murdered his wife. It was then, and only then, that Helena assumed her sole place at her son's side, and it was then that she went out into the world to represent him — and the image of his family's unity. What could Helena's inner state have been when she made her pilgrimage to Jerusalem? Were her acts of charity, so celebrated by Eusebius, a kind of penance? Eusebius promoted only the happiest of images in all his accounts, and having designated Constantine as the new Moses, he makes no mention of the murders of his wife and son.

It was a ruthless time. We have already seen how, in his ascent, Constantine had not hesitated to dispatch a pair of rivals who were also his brothers-in-law. But a son! A father who slays a son! A father who slays his son in righteousness! It is impossible to consider the hidden tragedy of 326 apart from the glories of that year. Constantine's embrace of the ethos of the cross was already firm by then, but one needn't be a Freudian to sense the new power that the myth of the cross would have had over him. Evoking the binding of Isaac as it does, the story of the all-powerful father forced to put to death his beloved son — but for a redemptive purpose — must have obsessed the emperor at that moment. If God can kill his Son, so can God's coregent. Not that either need be left with a feeling of triumph. So, of course, the emotional appeal of the crucifixion would have outweighed the glories of the Resurrection. It was in 326 that Constantine insisted on the construction of the greatest church in the world, the Martyrium, on the site of that "token of the holiest Passion," which, against Eusebius, was decidedly not a token of new life but of death. And how could a father, after a year like that, have done otherwise?

In all of this, the family of Constantine was an authentic sacrament of the true state of the empire he had created — not in the holy concord of the legend but in its unleashed murderous violence. The irony was that the violence could be justified in the name of unity. After Constantine died in 337, his three surviving sons — Constantine II, Constans, and Constantius — were named by the Senate as coequal Augusti.[25] But they were immediately embroiled in a succession struggle that led to a blood-bath in Constantinople. At the end, apart from the three sons, only two males out of more than a dozen members of Constantine's household were left alive. Soon enough, the sons set upon each other. Constantine II challenged Constans in 340, and was killed. Constans ruled in the West for a decade, to be murdered by a rival in his own army. Only about 353 did the third, Constantius, reestablish control over the whole empire.[26] For more than two decades after Constantine's death, a kind of murderous in-ternecine chaos reigned. There was ample precedent for such a turn in Ro-man history, but this went by the name of Christianity, with various rivals outdoing each other in claiming pious motives for political machinations.

The result? In 361, a member of the family who had been raised in this pathological culture of holy violence succeeded to the throne. His name was Julian. He was the son of a half-brother of Constantine's who had been murdered by supporters of Constantine's sons. Julian had been six at the time and barely survived the massacre. As emperor, he reigned for less than two years, but his impact on Christian attitudes, and on the arc of the Jewish-Christian narrative, was explosive. Julian tried to overturn the Constantinian revolution. He is remembered as the last pagan em-peror, but it is important to note that he was raised a Christian — he is known as Julian the Apostate. Only after his army had saluted him as the new Augustus did he reveal that he had become a pagan, and that he in-tended to return the empire to paganism.[27] Given what he had seen in the household of Christianity, why not? But if his objection was to sacred vio-lence, one would not know it from the ruthless campaign he immediately launched against Christian churches. "The Church again had martyrs," T. D. Barnes comments.[28]

Julian was a well-educated man, schooled in Athens. To him, paganism was not, as to us, a matter of taking cues from the entrails of pigeons, but a matter more of the wisdom of Socrates. He had a genius for sensing the Church's weak point — and wasn't that the Jews? Since the entire inverted pyramid of Christian belief had come to rest on the point of "prophecy historicized," Julian understood that if he could demonstrate that the Christian claim to have replaced Judaism as the "true Israel" was false, he could undermine the Christian religion. That is, if he could show that the "fulfillment" of ancient Hebrew prophecy, on which the Church based every claim it made for Jesus Christ, was illusory, the Christian God would fail. How to do such a thing?

In the beginning of this story lies the answer, and it is the Temple in Jerusalem, which is why the end of the story — John Paul II reverencing the Western Wall — is so compelling. So much had come to rest on the initiating moment described in Luke: "And as some spoke of the temple, how it was adorned with noble stones and offerings, he said, 'As for these things which you see, the days will come when there shall not be left here one stone upon another that will not be thrown down.'"[29] And hadn't just such a thing come to pass? The Temple's destruction in 70 and again in 135 was concrete proof that God had withdrawn his favor from the old religion to bestow it on the new. "Destroy this Temple," Jesus was remembered as having said, referring to himself. That he was the new Temple was proven when the old was destroyed.

So Julian, right after declaring the end of the Christian empire, ordered the Jewish Temple in Jerusalem rebuilt, stone upon stone, to falsify the very words of Jesus. He ordered the city opened to Jews again, and he empowered Jews to govern it. All of this was a measure less of Julian's affection for Judaism than of his hatred for Christianity. And one can imagine how a Christianity newly enamored of the "Holy City" and of its own Temple, the Holy Sepulcher, took this reversal. The meaning of the survival of the Jewish people as rejecters of Jesus Christ had never been more powerfully on display. The whole Roman world would have understood what was at stake in the rebuilding of the Jewish Temple.

Jews, naturally, were overjoyed. Their long suffering was finally vindicated, and their restoration seemed at hand. They began to work on the reconstruction of the ruined Temple at once. To this day, Jerusalem's tourist guides point to the course of mammoth blocks they added to the Temple Mount, at the Western Wall. To place one stone upon another was a long-overdue rebuttal to the false Messiah.[30]

"The Church again had martyrs," Barnes wrote, but he added, "and again had vengeance from on high: Julian died during an invasion of Per-

sia which had failed."[31] Not only that. The Jews at work on new excavations for the Temple had touched off explosions in gaseous deposits,
which Christians saw as the mighty and miraculous intervention of
God.[32] There were even reports that the explosions were accompanied by
the appearance of the cross in the sky.[33] "So ended the last attempt to rebuild the Temple of Jerusalem, from then to now," Jacob Neusner comments. "Julian's successors dismantled all of his programs and restored
the privileges the Church had lost. We need hardly speculate on the profound disappointment that overtook the Jews of the empire and beyond.
The seemingly trivial incident — a failed project of restoring a building —
proved profoundly consequential for Judaic and Christian thinkers. We
know that a quarter of a century later, John Chrysostom dwelt on the matter of the destruction of the Temple — and the Jews' failure to rebuild it —
as proof of the divinity of Jesus."[34]

Proof! Proof! But never enough. After the near reversal of Julian,
Christians reacted with an unprecedented vengeance, both emperors and
bishops, against both pagans and Jews. Such reaction was undoubtedly
caused by fear and insecurity. It was only after Julian, through the succes-
sive reigns of the emperors Valentinian and Theodosius, that the empire
came to be formally proclaimed Christian; only then that Christian heresy
was pronounced a capital crime; only then that pagan worship was officially banned; only then that the authority of the Jewish patriarchate was
abolished forever. And it was then that the question of what to do about
the Jews who refused either to yield or to disappear surfaced in the official
discourse of secular and religious authorities. From one side, it seemed
simple. Once church and state had agreed that it was righteous and legal
to execute those Christians — Docetists, Donatists, Nestorians, Arians —
who dissented from defined dogma on relatively arcane matters of theology, why in the world should stiff-necked persons who openly rejected the
entire Christian proclamation be permitted to live?

Here is the relevance of the explicitly anti-Jewish use to which Saint
Ambrose of Milan finally put the legend of the True Cross. He recounted
it as a historical sequence of events — as it would be recounted from then
on, down to the time my mother told the story to me — complete with the
supposedly factual detail that it was a Jew who led Helena to the long-buried crucifix. The Jew who betrayed Jesus — by this time, Judas Iscariot was
remembered as the Jew among the Christian apostles — now betrayed his
own people. In Ambrose's hands, sweet Helena became the mother of real
Jew hatred, and she was the canonizer of his now open campaign to wipe

out Judaism. In 388, a Christian mob, led by the bishop in Callinicus, a small city on the Euphrates, attacked and burned a synagogue, destroying it utterly. They also destroyed the chapel of a Gnostic sect, despite the fact that its leaders had just agreed, under pressure from the emperor Theodosius, to accept Nicene Christianity. So Theodosius ordered the Christians of Callinicus to rebuild the Gnostic chapel and the synagogue. This is the emperor whom Hugh Trevor-Roper called "the first of the Spanish Inquisitors."[35] His command to rebuild the places of worship was a matter not of religious freedom but of imperial authority. Still, the action in defense of a Jewish community prompted an immediate and ferocious response from none other than Ambrose. In a direct written challenge to Theodosius — at whose funeral most of a decade later he would recount the Helena legend — the bishop of Milan declared himself ready to burn synagogues "that there might not be a place where Christ is denied." A synagogue, he said, is "a haunt of infidels, a home of the impious, a hiding place of madmen, under the damnation of God Himself."[36] To order the rebuilding of such a place, once it had been burned, was an act of treason to the Faith.

Theodosius yielded, but insisted that the Christians of Callinicus had to restore the sacred articles of worship they had plundered. He would rebuild the synagogue himself. Ambrose rejected this, too. The principle had to be established that the destruction of the "vile perfidy" of Jewish worship was a righteous act, in no way to be punished. Ambrose challenged the emperor to his face, during Mass at the cathedral of Milan. Rosemary Radford Ruether describes the scene: "Coming down from the altar to face him, the bishop declared that he would not continue with the Eucharist until the emperor obeyed. The emperor bowed to this threat of excommunication, and the rioters at Callinicum went unadmonished."[37]

21

Augustine Trembling

T HE PREVIOUS EASTER, in 387,[1] this same Ambrose had taken a thirty-three-year-old man naked into a pool of water, and three times, pushing by the shoulders, he had forced the man under, saying, "I baptize you, Augustine." After Constantine, the conversion of Augustine (354–430) may be the most momentous in the history of the Church. He was born seventeen years after Constantine died. He was a bishop in Hippo, a small city in North Africa, but it is as a writer that he is remembered. He wrote nearly a hundred books, by his count, and thousands of letters and sermons, most of which survive. Garry Wills describes his method: "Augustine dictated to relays of stenographers, often late into the night . . . He employed teams of copyists. His sermons, several a week, were taken down by his own or others' shorthand writers. In some seasons, he preached daily. His letters were sent off in many copies. He paced about as he dictated, a reflection of the mental restlessness and energy conveyed in the very rhythm of his prose."[2] His greatest work, to which we will turn, may be *The City of God,* a meditation on the relationship of the Church and the empire, of politics and virtue, of history and hope. But his most compelling work is surely *The Confessions,*[3] the Western world's first great autobiography. This book, with its realistic exploration of human psychology and its affirmation that subjective experience is of ultimate value, stamped the mind of Europe. Its search for God in an act of memory makes each person a center of Christian revelation. That idea is the birthplace of modern individualism, for good and for ill.

Augustine's solid grounding in the classical intellectual tradition prepared him for the task of applying categories of Platonic thought to Christian theology. To take only one example of the importance of his ideas, he marshaled the definitive argument against the Donatists, who held that saintly virtue was a prerequisite for full membership in the Church. Augustine's position was rooted in Plato's distinction between

the ideal and the real, and Augustine knew that the ideal would not be realized until God brought about the fulfillment of Creation at the end of
time. Therefore, he held, the human condition was by definition flawed.
Gospel was addressed to human beings, not to angels. Because Augustine
carried the day against the Donatists, Christians could come together before God, confessing sin, and knowing that the Church itself, too, remained imperfect. The Church would not be a sect of the saved but a
community open to all. Augustine is commonly credited as the father of
Western Christian theology, but he is, perhaps more basically, the father
of the inclusive Western Church we know, in both its Catholic and
Protestant manifestations.

Augustine took his baptismal instructions from the great Ambrose.[4]
For our purposes, it is worth noting that the mediating link between Augustine and Ambrose was Augustine's mother, Monica. She was a devout
Christian, but the young, unchurched Augustine had fled her, leaving her
standing "wild with grief"[5] on the pier in Carthage. But she followed him
to Milan. There, while he continued his preconversion life as a pagan,
she became a devoted follower of Ambrose. When the bishop was physically besieged by barbarian Arians in his basilica in 386, for example,
Monica was with him, sharing the mortal danger.[6] She formed the habit of
ending each day by chanting hymns that Ambrose had composed. The
pattern of such devotion, especially focused on a prelate — in my mother's
case, it was Cardinal Spellman — is familiar to sons who follow their
mothers into piety.

The Confessions tells a mammoth story, but a central theme is Augustine's flight from his mother. Like Helena, she was a disappointed wife of a
withholding husband, and she turned the laser of her need on her son.[7]
Her love seemed overbearing and suffocating until — well, until it seemed
like love. "Not long before the day on which she was to leave this life —
you knew which day it was to be, O Lord, but we did not — my mother
and I were alone, leaning from a window which overlooked the garden
in the courtyard of the house where we were staying at Ostia. . . . We
were talking alone together and our conversation was serene and joyful."[8]
Monica died in 387, not long after her son's baptism. Garry Wills takes the
view that "too much is often made of her role in Augustine's life,"[9] but Augustine's own testimony is poignant: "I closed her eyes, and a great wave
of sorrow surged into my heart."[10]

In the enclosed garden of his consciousness, Augustine watched as what
his mother had planted in him came to flower. "Words cannot describe
how dearly she loved me," he writes in *The Confessions*, "or how much

greater was the anxiety she suffered for my spiritual birth than the physical pain she had endured in bringing me into the world."[11]

"You were there, before my eyes," he says to God (and, one infers, to Monica). "But I had deserted even my own self. I could not find myself, much less find you."[12] When he found God, he put into a new kind of language what the experience of God could be for human beings. In his milestone work of theology, *The Trinity,* Augustine detects the very structure of God's inner life in the dynamics of human consciousness and human relationships — an approach that could have rescued Christian theology from the dead-end disputes that had racked the Church for much of the previous century, when Christians went to war over definitions of words like "essence," "substance," and "person" as applied to God. "The reader of these reflections of mine on the Trinity should bear in mind," he begins, "that my pen is on the watch against the sophistries of those who scorn the starting-point of faith, and allow themselves to be deceived through an unseasonable and misguided love of reason."[13] The point for Augustine was that whatever the *aspects* of the Godhead (or, as a Jewish sage might have put it, such *activities* of the Godhead as Word or Spirit) are to each other, they are in *relation* to each other. *Relationship* is the ground of divine being, an idea that opens up monotheism by moving the meaning of God's oneness away from "unit" and toward "unity." This tempering of the constant human temptation toward exclusivism could reasonably be expected to have tempered the universalist totalitarianism gripping the empire and the Church by then. *The Trinity* is a celebration of love as the basis of Christianity. As such, it may not be too much to detect its source in the love Augustine had experienced from and for Monica, the full range of which was revealed to him only in the writing of *The Confessions,* which he completed in c. 397. He completed *The Trinity* in c. 410, but in that same year Alaric's Gothic hordes sacked Rome. "When the brightest light was extinguished," said Saint Jerome of that event, "when the whole world perished in one city, then I was dumb with silence."[14] The culture-wide trauma of the Germanic tribes' arrival in Rome marked a turning point in Augustine's life and attitudes.

I referred to Augustine's assertion of the idea that the human condition implies a perennial state of finitude, weakness, and sin, all of which will be overcome, even for the Church, only with the end of time. Augustine's theology of original sin and the Fall has influenced all subsequent generations of Western Christians, none more so than Luther and Calvin in the Reformation era. Augustine is thus regarded as the father of a severe, flesh-hating, sin-obsessed theology, but that dark characterization misses the point of his insight. His honest admission of the universality of human woundedness is a precondition for both self-acceptance and forgiveness of the other, which for Augustine always involved the operation of grace, God's gift. Only humans capable of confronting the moral tragedy of existence, matched to God's offer of a repairing grace, are capable of community, and community is the antidote to human woundedness. Augustine sensed that *relationship* as being at the heart of God, and he saw it as being at the heart of human hope, too. This is a profoundly humane vision.

But hope faded. As was true of many of his contemporaries, Augustine's spirit was gradually weighed down as Alaric's armies began an inexorable movement east and south from Rome, while Attila's Huns took over the north, all the way to the Rhine. These invasions signaled what was even then taken to be the beginning of the end of the empire. With the coming invasions of the Vandals, clouds darkened Augustine's essentially positive outlook, marking his late writings with apprehension and unrest. By then Augustine was a man waiting for the end of the world, with reason. The Vandals destroyed the Roman order in North Africa in the summer of 429, wiping out all that Augustine had built and loved. Not long after his death in 430, they would overrun his city of Hippo.

Scholars draw a contrast between the early and late Augustine, between the life affirmer and the naysayer. It was the late Augustine who, no longer depending on the force of reason, justified the use of coercion in defending, and spreading, the orthodox faith: "For many have found advantage (as we have proved, and are daily proving by actual experiment)," he wrote in a treatise ominously entitled *The Correction of the Donatists,* "in being first compelled by fear or pain, so that they might afterwards be influenced by teaching."[15] He supported the passage of laws against pagans and heretics, and he offered a theological justification for a policy of *correctio.* He could not advocate the extension of such fierce evangelizing without a qualm, but finally he did. And now the fierceness was armed. "What shall I say as to the infliction and remission of punishment in cases in which we only desire to forward the spiritual welfare of those we are deciding whether or not to punish? . . . What trembling we feel in these things, my brother Paulinus, O holy man of God!" This is from a letter Augustine wrote to Paulinus of Nola around the time of Alaric's invasion of Italy. "What trembling! What a darkness! May we not think that with reference to these things it was said, 'Fearfulness and trembling are come upon me, and horror hath overwhelmed me. And I said, O that I had wings like a dove, for then I should fly away and be at rest.'"[16]

But the time when Augustine could flee was past. As a bishop now, he too had to make the hard decisions, in this brutal age, attendant on the proclamation of the gospel of Jesus Christ. He had taken his place with those prepared to use violence in stamping out heresy; indeed, he gave them their theological rationale. In *The City of God,* his last great work, written to rebut the charge that the empire's embrace of Christianity had led to the collapse implied by Vandal victories, Augustine firmly justified the harsh, even totalitarian policies of the Christian rulers. If anything, they had not been harsh enough. Now, for Augustine, the world was divided between those who lived in the flesh of the City of Man and those who lived in the spirit of the City of God. The latter could look forward to heaven, the former to hell, and if hell began for them on earth, so be it. The dualistic Manichaeism of Augustine's youth reasserted itself with a vengeance. The basic theme of *The City of God,* as Peter Brown puts it, is "that the disasters of the Roman Empire had come not from neglect of the old rites, but from tolerating paganism, heresy and immorality in the new Christian empire."[17]

Augustine's was a tragic vision, for it was authentically grounded — despite the shivers caused in us by his *correctio* — in the idea of God as love. The offer of that love, even to inhabitants of the City of Man, was permanent. If that was so, then violence could have no sacred significance, because it did not represent any attitude or action of the loving God. The City of God is based on love; the City of Man is based on war. Violence, Augustine felt, was not built into the nature of things, and so was not inevitable. Furthermore, while never to be seen as sacred, violence in defense of an endangered neighbor could be an act of love.

Despite the unbridled ruthlessness of his age, Augustine, building on the religious argument of the Hebrew Scriptures, initiated history's first political argument against war, an argument that has come down to us as his widely misunderstood theory of the just war. Instead of being a rationale for state-sponsored violence, as its critics are wont to say today, the theory is a rather desperate effort to curtail it, to hem war-making in, that is, by stringent conditions. The idea of the just war, the introduction of limiting principles, and a notion of war as always involving evil, even if a lesser evil, were profoundly humanizing innovations.

The tragic purity of Augustine's intentions — tragic because all too pure — was fully on display when he turned to the question of the Jews. Rampant violence, sanctioned by the Church and the state, was ubiquitous.

Jews were increasingly targeted, ominously so, because of all misfit groups they still posed to univocal Christianity the most mortal threat. In the year of Augustine's baptism — the year of his mother's death — Saint John Chrysostom, bishop of Antioch, had delivered a series of sermons that ratcheted up homiletic attacks on Jews. Ruether calls them "easily the most violent and tasteless of the anti-Judaic literature of the period."[18]

It is of secondary importance that Chrysostom's real targets were those Christians — "Judaizers" — who were drawn to Jewish cult and practice, because his assault carried beyond them to Jews as such. "I know that many people hold a high regard for the Jew, and consider their way of life worthy of respect at the present time. This is why I am hurrying to pull up this fatal notion by the roots . . . A place where a whore stands on display is a whorehouse. What is more, the synagogue is not only a whorehouse and a theater; it is also a den of thieves and a haunt of wild animals . . . No better disposed than pigs or goats, [the Jews] live by the rule of debauchery and inordinate gluttony. Only one thing they understand: to gorge themselves and to get drunk."[19] Ruether points out that nowhere in his sermons does Chrysostom directly order attacks on Jews, but did he need to? He said, "When animals have been fattened by having all they want to eat, they get stubborn and hard to manage . . . When animals are unfit for work, they are marked for slaughter, and this is the very thing which the Jews have experienced. By making themselves unfit for work, they have become ready for slaughter. This is why Christ said, 'Ask for my enemies, who did not want me to reign over them, bring them here and slay them before me.'"[20]

Should we be surprised that not long after these sermons were preached, there were several violent outbursts against Jews in Antioch, with its great synagogue demolished? Antioch is the site, in this period, of a first draft of the "ritual murder" charge brought against Jews.[21] Shall Jews be allowed to live as Jews? Increasingly, momentum built toward a new consensus: No. In 414, what might be termed history's first large-scale pogrom occurred, that savage assault, referred to earlier, on the large, ancient, and prestigious Jewish community in Alexandria. A historian of the time says the Jewish settlement there was destroyed.[22]

The abolition of the Jewish patriarchate in Palestine, tied as it was to the rediscovery by Christians of the Holy Land, emphasizes, like the fate of the community in Alexandria, that Jews living alongside Christians would from now on be at particular risk. One result of this would be the further flourishing of the rabbinic centers in relatively remote Babylonia, under

Persian dominance, where a so-called exilarch was recognized as the head of the Jewish people. Jewish academies in Persia, building on the Mishnah, would bring to full flower Jewish literary and spiritual impulses in the masterly Babylonian Talmud. Here is an important difference between Jewish and Christian development: Jewish study of Torah and commentary, conducted at a remove from Christianity, led to a more or less independent self-understanding.

Beginning in this period, Jews stopped acting like sibling rivals in a contest over a shared legacy and began to see their own legacy as having nothing to do with the developing theology or opinions of Christians. Jewish sages, commenting on the commentaries, interpreting the interpretations, had entered an entirely new room of the religious imagination. The discourse of rabbis became multilayered. They derived meaning as much from the nuances of text as from its obvious significance. Exegesis became a way of recovering the past, and Midrash, from the Hebrew word for "interpretation," became a way of infusing the present with awe. The elusiveness of God came to be reflected in the circumspection of the esoteric elucidation of God's Word. "In the Jewish tradition," Moshe Halbertal comments, "the centrality of the text takes the place of theological consistency. Jews have had diverse and sometimes opposing ideas about God: the anthropomorphic God of the Midrash, the Aristotelian unmoved mover of Maimonides and his school, the Kabbalah's image of God as a dynamic organism manifested in the complexity of his varied aspects, the *sefirot*. These conceptions of God have little in common and they are specifically Jewish only insofar as each is a genuine interpretation of Jewish canonical texts."[23] Israel, as the critic Sidra DeKoven Ezrahi put it, "was transfigured into texts-in-exile," and the "literacy of exile" would give shape to the Jewish religious imagination.[24]

The rabbinic method itself, in other words, was seen as a worshipful embodiment of the holy. Much of this was spoken in instruction, meditation, and prayer, as masters trained disciples, but nearly always there were disciples taking careful notes of what was said, and then editors compiling new texts, which themselves served as the touchstone of contemplation and, more prosaically, as instruction manuals in Jewish spirituality. Among this most literate people, an oral tradition quickly became a living sacred literature. At the heart of this enterprise, of course, remained the Pentateuch of Moses — the Torah. Mishnah, and ultimately Talmud, built a kind of moat around the Torah, as the study centers themselves served as a bulwark of the Jewish people.

But Jews in the crumbling Roman Empire remained at risk because their very presence challenged the integrity of both a transformed Church membership and a radically new Christian self-understanding to which Jews remained important. Augustine's treatment of the question must be seen against this backdrop. Among Church fathers, Augustine is remarkable for his sensitivity to the Jewish character of Christian faith, which derived from his close reading of Paul. Augustine was far less polemical in his reading of the Old Testament than other Christian thinkers. "Augustine forbears derogatory comparison," Paula Fredriksen has written. "If the Old Testament is a concealed form of the New and vice versa, then each is alike in dignity and religious value." Fredriksen also makes the point that Augustine argued "against Jerome that both Jesus and the first generation of Jewish apostles, Paul emphatically included, were, as Christians, also Torah-observant Jews."[25]

But Augustine's writing about Jews of his own time, especially his treatise in the *Adversus Judaeos* genre and in book 4 of *The City of God,* both of which date to about the year 425, is marked by a typical expression of Christian contempt. In one place, denouncing them for their rejection of the "obvious testimonies" of the prophets, he declares Jews to be "the House of Israel which [God] has cast off . . . They, however, whom He cast off . . . are themselves the builders of destruction and rejecters of the corner-stone."[26] In another, he asserts that "the Lord Christ distinguished between His faithful ones and His Jewish enemies, as between light and darkness." Jews were "those on whose closed eyes He shed His light."[27]

Augustine calls on Jews to repent and come into the Church. But if they refuse? The danger to Jews was that, in a brutal age in which the Church was finally in a dominant position, key Christian thinkers were openly concluding that the Jews' continued existence could no longer be justified. Whether out of an essential humanitarianism or not — and one would like to think he came to his position as a result of a firm attachment to God as a God of love — Augustine met that argument head-on, and rejected it. That is, he rejected not only Chrysostom but his mentor, Ambrose. Against those arguing that Jews were the enemies of Jesus, Augustine would insist, in effect, on considering the question in the light of Jesus' own Jewishness. And even if such enmity was to be established, he could ask, Where in Jesus does one find an execution order?

Ruether writes, "The difference between the treatise of Augustine and the sermons of John Chrysostom does not lie in any difference of basic doctrines about the status of the Jews, but in the fact that Augustine writes in the detachment of his study with no Jewish threat in sight, while Chrysostom speaks in the heat of battle."[28] But is that so? Nothing in

Chrysostom wants the survival of Jews as Jews, while in Augustine that very thing comes to be seen as "part of the providence of our true God."[29] At a crucial moment, writing at the height of his prestige, Augustine offers a new rationale for a limited Christian version of the long tradition of Roman tolerance of Judaism. This lengthy passage, a whole chapter in *The City of God,* summarizes the history of Jewish-Christian conflict. It includes a description of how this prophecy-fulfillment dynamic condemns the Jews and, in Augustine's momentous innovation, how that same dynamic requires, in a murderous age, that Jews be spared:

> When Herod was on the throne of Judea, and when Caesar Augustus was emperor, after a change in the Roman constitution, and when the emperor's rule had established a world-wide peace, Christ was born, in accordance with a prophecy of earlier times, in Bethlehem of Judah (Micha 5:2). He was shown in outward appearance as a human being, from a human virgin; in hidden reality he was God, from God the Father. For this is what the prophet foretold: "See, a virgin will conceive in her womb and will bear a son, and they will call his name Emmanuel, which is translated, 'God with us'" (Isaiah 7:14). Then, in order to make known the godhead in his person, he did many miracles, of which the gospel Scriptures contain as many as seemed enough to proclaim his divinity. The first of these is the great miracle of his birth; the last, his ascension into heaven with his body which had been brought to life again from the dead. But the Jews who killed him and refused to believe in him, to believe that he had to die and rise again, suffered a more wretched devastation at the hands of the Romans, and were utterly uprooted from their kingdom, where they had already been under the dominion of foreigners. They were dispersed all over the world — for indeed there is no part of the earth where they are not to be found — and thus by evidence of their own Scriptures they bear witness for us that we have not fabricated the prophecies about Christ. In fact, very many of the Jews, thinking over those prophecies both before his passion and more particularly after his resurrection, have come to believe in him. About them this prediction was made: "Even if the number of the sons of Israel be like the sand of the sea, it is only a remnant that will be saved" (Isaiah 10:20). But the rest of them were blinded; and of them it was predicted: "Let their own table prove a snare in their presence, and a retribution and a stumbling block. Let their eyes be darkened, so that they may not see. Bend down their backs always" (Psalm 69:22). It follows that when Jews do not believe in our Scriptures, their own Scriptures are fulfilled in them, while they read them with blind eyes. Unless, perhaps, someone is going to say that the Christians fabricated the prophecies of Christ which are published under the name of Sibyl, or any prophecies that there may be which are ascribed to others, which have no

connection with the Jewish people. As for us, we find those prophecies sufficient which are produced from the books of our opponents; for we recognize that it is in order to give this testimony, which, in spite of themselves, they supply for our benefit by their possession and preservation of those books, that they themselves are dispersed among all nations, in whatever direction the Christian Church spreads.

In fact, there is a prophecy given before the event on this very point in the book of Psalms, which they also read. It comes in this passage, "As for my God, his mercy will go before me; my God has shown me this in the case of my enemies. Do not slay them, lest at some time they forget your Law," without adding, "Scatter them." For if they lived with that testimony of the Scriptures only in their own land, and not everywhere, the obvious result would be that the Church, which is everywhere, would not have them available among all nations as witnesses to the prophecies which were given beforehand concerning Christ.[30]

The impact of this passage on those who read *The City of God* boiled down to that admonition ingeniously culled from the Psalms: Do not slay them! Augustine made it seem like the very voice of God. This was a direct contradiction of the imperative — Slay them before me! — that Chrysostom attributed to a brutal Christ. Subsequent history resounds with the cry of Augustine here: Do not slay them!

Why not? Because the Jews (unlike pagans, unlike Christian heretics) still had a role in the salvific plan of God. They were to be "as witnesses to the prophecies which were given beforehand concerning Christ." Fredriksen argues that Augustine saw Jewish devotion to the Law as a kind of sacrament, and because it was out of that devotion that Jews rejected Jesus, their "continuing 'fleshly' allegiance to their Law made Israel, even after the establishment of the church, uniquely witness to Christ. Thus God himself protects them from the duress of religious coercion."[31]

But the excerpt just given, perhaps reflecting the darkness of the later Augustine, nevertheless points to the precarious position in which Jews now found themselves. The irony in this passage is heartbreaking, as the entire misbegotten pattern of the Jewish-Christian disconnect is recapitulated. Those first, grief-struck followers of Jesus had created a narrative of his Passion and death in part out of reports of what had happened, but more out of the consoling Scriptures of their Jewish religion. All too soon, that creative narration had come to be understood as "history remembered" instead of "prophecy historicized." Later Christians, especially those not Jewish, could only misread the details of the narrative that had been gleaned from the Psalms and the Prophets as referring to things that had actually happened. Then, in generation after generation, such "fulfilled prophecies" were used against the Jews as "proofs." Augustine, as we saw, was disinclined to a polemical pairing of Old and New Testaments, and he saw the tradition of Jewish Law observance as a positive witness to Christ, yet here the meaning of Judaism was reduced to Jews' "witnessing . . . in spite of themselves" to those selfsame prophecies. A continuing Judaism would serve as a source of authentication for the prophecy-based claims of Christianity. As long as Jews existed, with their ancient texts, the ancient — and therefore noble — character of Christianity was apparent, because those texts "foretold" Christ. The dispersion of Jews helps with this, and so it is God's will — Scatter them! — that they be allowed to live as exiles everywhere. By this schema, they would be allowed to be at home, "at their own table," nowhere.

As this tradition took hold in the minds of Christians, it brought along what Fredriksen calls a "trail of pseudo-Augustinian anti-Jewish writings that grew in its wake."[32] It was not only the Diaspora that provided Jewish witness to the truth of Christian claims, but the negative condition of exile. Jews came to be seen as witnesses in the very desperation of their status. They must be allowed to survive, but never to thrive; their "backs" must be "bent down always." Their homelessness and misery are the proper punishments for their refusal to recognize the truth of the Church's claims. And more — their misery is yet another *proof* of those claims.

The legacy of Augustine's teaching on the Jews is a double-edged sword. On one side, against Chrysostom and even Ambrose, it requires an end to all violent assaults against synagogues, Jewish property, and Jewish persons. Jews are henceforth exempt from the Church-sanctioned, state-sponsored campaign to obliterate religious difference. Polytheists will disappear from the Roman world because they were given the choice to convert or die. Jews could have disappeared then, too. "Judaism endured in the West for two reasons," Jacob Neusner writes. "First, Christianity permitted it to endure, and, second, Israel, the Jewish people, wanted it to. The fate of paganism in the fourth century shows the importance of the first of the two factors."[33]

It is not too much to say that, at this juncture, Christianity "permitted" Judaism to endure because of Augustine. "His teaching on the special place of Israel and the Jews in the economy of Christian redemption," Fredriksen writes, ". . . protected Jewish communities in Europe for centuries."[34] As the eighteenth-century Jewish philosopher Moses Mendels-

sohn put it, but for Augustine's "lovely brainwave, we would have been exterminated long ago."[35] In contrast to other possibilities of the era, his
attitude is deeply humane, and indeed implies a critique of the by then triumphant Constantinian ideal, embodied in Constantine's sword. In this
passage from *The City of God,* there is more than an implication of critique of what the imperial Church, the Christian empire, has put in place:
"But think of the cost of this achievement! Consider the scale of those
wars, with all that slaughter of human beings, all the human blood that
was shed . . . a man who experiences such evils, or even thinks about them,
without heartfelt grief, is assuredly in a far more pitiable condition, if he
thinks himself happy simply because he has lost all human feeling."[36]

On the other side, Augustine's relatively benign attitude toward Jews
is rooted still in assumptions of supersessionism that would prove to be
deadly. The "witness" prescription attributed to him — Let them survive, but not thrive! — would underlie the destructive ambivalence that
marked Catholic attitudes toward Jews from then on. Ultimately, history
would show that such double-edged ambivalence is impossible to sustain
without disastrous consequences. For a thousand years, the compulsively
repeated pattern of that ambivalence would show in bishops and popes
protecting Jews — but from expressly Christian mobs that wanted to kill
Jews because of what bishops and popes had taught about Jews. Such a
teaching that wants it both ways was bound to fail, as would become evident at every point in history when Jews presumed, whether economically
or culturally or both, to even think of thriving. This is the legacy that
haunts the Catholic Church into the twenty-first century, a perverse legacy from which, despite the twentieth-century's jolts, the Church is not
yet free.

"Allow me this, I beseech you," Augustine prayed in the fourth chapter
of his *Confessions,* "to trace again in memory my past deviations."[37] So he
did, throughout the book. And so do we here. There is a kind of tracing
through deviation in such an understanding, requiring as it does a direct
look at abject failure — abject *Christian* failure. It also requires a restored
sense of longing, *Christian* longing, for another way. What could more
sharply prompt in Christians such a wish for forgiveness and redemption
than this story? Are we reduced to gratitude for the day when one of us
found a way, through a jury-rigged theology if ever there was one, to justify the cry "Do not slay them!"? Yes, we are.

22

The Seamless Robe

YEA, DOGS ARE round about me; a company of evildoers encircle me; they have pierced my hands and feet." The words are from Psalm 22, and we recall the way the first, grief-struck friends of Jesus, gathering in something like a healing circle, had found consolation and meaning in such passages. The stunning loss of Jesus and the shocking violence of his death at the hands of the Romans were somehow mitigated by the way the beloved old Scriptures could name such an unspeakable experience. "I can count all my bones — they stare and gloat over me; they divide my garments among them."[1]

We saw in an earlier chapter how, over a period of years in the immediate aftermath of the death of Jesus, a Passion narrative was constructed, and how many of its details were drawn not from events as they actually happened — the scattered followers of Jesus would have known little about such details — but from the Scripture passages that they were reading together in those early circles. And we just saw, in Augustine, how that blurring of "history remembered" and "prophecy historicized," in Crossan's terms, had come to form the supersessionist prophecy-fulfillment structure of Christian attitudes toward Jews.

A detail drawn from Psalm 22 for use in the Passion narrative has special poignancy for our story now. As we saw, that psalm was the source of what we read in the Gospel of John: "When the soldiers had crucified Jesus they took his garments and made four parts, one for each soldier. But his tunic was without seam, woven from top to bottom; so they said to one another, 'Let us not tear it, but cast lots for it to see whose it shall be.'"[2]

By the time the Gospel of John was written, at the end of the first century, it is likely that no one was still alive who had firsthand knowledge of how the Passion story had been composed, that the account was, in some large measure, the product of "prophecy historicized." And it was then, in

response to pressures from "the Jews," that the crucial interpretive flip occurred, with the claim that the Passion narrative was "history remembered."³ Thus John says about the throwing of the dice for the Seamless
Robe, "This was to fulfill the scripture. 'They parted my garments among
them, and for my clothing they cast lots.' So the soldiers did this."⁴

If the Old Testament prophesied it, and if the New Testament fulfilled
it, then how could the Jews deny the claim made in the name of Jesus?
We have seen how this essential concept of Christology — Christ as
fulfillment — stands, in Ruether's phrase, at the "left hand" of Christian
Jew-hatred. In the conflict between the Church and the Synagogue, every
detail of the Passion story can be turned into a debating point, even the
shirt of Jesus. Its seamlessness was a proof of his Messiahship. And how in
the world did his mother weave such a thing anyway?

We saw how the legend of Saint Helena's discoveries in the Holy Land
served the purpose of her son's campaign to Christianize the empire, and
indeed, for centuries, the univocal solidarity of Christendom was based
on the veneration of relics associated through her with Jerusalem. So relics were a bridge not only in time but in space. Not incidentally, Helena's
discoveries — the True Cross, the instrument of deicide long hidden by
Jews; the Magi, as far-off witnesses to what nearby Jews denied — sharpened the conflict between Christians and Jews. As the Scriptures of Israel
were used in the first and second centuries to "prove" Christian claims, so
were Helena's discoveries in the fourth century — and for centuries afterward. What matters here is that she is remembered as finding not only the
True Cross and the corpses of the Three Kings, but also that miraculously
woven robe, which in John's reading was itself proof that the Jews were
wrong. And what did Saint Helena do with that robe? She brought it back,
right then, to her beloved hometown of Trier.

The story, as still recounted by tour guides today and hinted at in Trier's
tourist brochure,⁵ says that Helena donated her palace to the young
Church, and that it was leveled, to be replaced immediately by the first
great Christian edifice in the north of Europe, constructed to enshrine the
Seamless Robe. Another view suggests, as we saw, that the palace, where
Crispus was living, was leveled on Constantine's order as part of his attempt to obliterate the memory of the son he murdered. Ultimately, the
palace was replaced by the sibling churches that stand there today: the
Liebfrauen-kirche, that small thirteenth-century gem, perhaps the first
Gothic church in Germany, whose cruciform rotunda is a sort of religious
womb, and the much larger, more imperial cathedral, dating in part to

Helena's fourth century, but mainly to the eleventh. The cathedral was built to house, and still houses in its sanctuary, the sacred Seamless Robe of Jesus. The tradition developed that the relic was kept hidden from public view, and today it rests behind the high altar in the *Heiltumskammer,* a kind of enclosed tabernacle from which a mystical light glows, but to which no one is admitted.

The hidden Robe was put on open display only three times in the twentieth century, each time for a period of weeks. One of those, as it happened, was in August and September of 1959. The archbishop had ordered the Robe's display, inviting Catholics to give thanks to God for the finally achieved recovery from World War II — that year, the restoration of heavily bombed Trier was complete. It was only in writing this book, and traveling to Trier again not long ago, that I remembered that 1959 display was the occasion of my youthful visit to the town. At last I understood that my mother, my brothers, and I were there to see the Robe of Christ, and to give thanks. For a long time, in my mind, I associated my glimpse of the Robe — it was a brown tunic, suspended above the altar as on a clothesline, looking to my willfully irreverent eye like a soiled extralarge T-shirt — with the German Passion play to which I referred in Part One. I assumed I had seen that Passion play here. But in August and September?

I had a distinct memory of a costumed Jesus bound hand and foot, wearing that very robe. I remembered Pilate turning away to wash his hands. I remembered Pilate's face, contorted with disgust at the Jews who wanted Jesus dead. I remembered Judas, the hook of his nose, his hands clutching at coins. All these images had fed my hatred of those who'd killed my Lord. When I tried to plumb those memories, returning to Germany recently, I learned that the Passion play tradition had not taken hold in the Rhineland. Holy Week services included the usual readings of Passion texts, but rarely as dramatizations. As for the display of the Robe in Trier, there would perhaps have been observances recalling the Gospel references to the garment, but no Passion play, and not in summer. Yet I was certain that I had seen the death of Jesus enacted in Germany. And I had seen the Robe.

This was true, but not in the way I first thought. My research trip took me back to Wiesbaden. The American enclave is still there, although now it bases the U.S. Army instead of the Air Force. The housing development, with its school and chapel, was spanking new in our time, but now, essentially unaltered and surrounded by the showy opulence of German prosperity, it has the neglected feel of public housing. Atop a hill that is still called Hainerberg is the tidy shopping center, now the PX, but in our time the BX, the base exchange. It is a small strip mall worthy of any midcentury American suburb. There was the snack bar where we hung out after school, a Burger King now, but otherwise just as I remembered it. And across the parking lot was the Taunus Theater, the movie house named for the nearby mountain range. The Taunus! One of the military's perks in postwar Europe was a steady flow from Hollywood, movies for a quarter, and I had been there every Friday and Saturday night.

I realized that I had seen that supremely detached but, compared to the Jews, benign Pontius Pilate on the screen of the Taunus Theater, probably with my girlfriend at my side, instead of my mother. The scene was not from a Passion play, as I'd thought, but from a costume epic starring Richard Burton. Pontius Pilate was played by Richard Boone, later famous as the cowboy carrier of a business card that read "Have Gun, Will Travel." Now I understood that I associated that film, in my memory, with the tunic in Trier because it was *The Robe*. I recently rented the video, described on its case as "an awesome, uplifting Biblical blockbuster." It says everything about the quality of filmmaking that *The Robe*'s two Academy Award nominations were for costumes and set decoration. "Richard Burton stars as the Roman centurion in charge of the crucifixion, Marcellus Gallio," the promotional copy said, "who wins the Robe gambling at the foot of the Cross — and whose life is changed forever by it." Marcellus, naturally, embraces the truth to which the Robe testifies, the truth that the Jews in the movie reject. Once again, Roman virtue — the Passion play theme as carried forward by Hollywood — stands in contrast to the stiff-necked recalcitrance of Jews. The Robe was thus fixed in my mind as a symbol, and in my memory as a madeleine, of Jewish evil.

Not long ago, I stood alone in the rear balcony of the Trier cathedral, where I had stood in 1959 with my mother for our viewing of the Robe. (We'd been shown to that spot as VIPs. It had offered a clear view above the crush, across the length of the nave toward the suspended tunic.) At last I could recognize in my own experience the foundational human flaw of faulty memory — how I had displaced one image of the Robe (Richard Burton's) for another (Saint John's). In this I myself had recapitulated the tragic pattern of this narrative.

As I focused on the gleaming *Heiltumskammer,* the tabernacle concealing the Robe, the welter of feelings I had experienced came back to me. Within days of being here in 1959, I would start my senior year at

Wiesbaden High School. Soon my mother, father, and brothers would return to the United States without me. I would stay behind to finish school,
living in the dormitory where, unknown to my parents, my girlfriend also
resided. I would be free to give myself to her, to football, to a new sense of
myself as something other than pious. This forbidden hope grew in my
throat, and I remembered looking across at the Robe of Jesus hanging
there, right there, and thinking to myself, Who are they kidding? The
doubt I had not allowed myself in Cologne blossomed in Trier. Corpses of
the Three Kings? Give me a break. Inwardly, "I chattered away," as Saint
Augustine described an equivalent moment, "as somebody in the know."[6]

Augustine emerges in my free association here perhaps because of his
mother, Saint Monica. "For she loved having me with her, as all mothers
do, only she much more than most."[7] When I read such lines, a shiver of
recognition runs through me. As I stood recently in the cathedral in Trier,
I remembered what it was to stand beside my mother, knowing she was
praying for me. I have never completely come out from under the mixed
feeling of being doomed by that love. Yet to be the son of such a mother is
to be discreetly but immeasurably blessed, for, as one sees eventually, the
winding round and round is the spiral of forgiveness that extends to both
of us. A son becomes a man when he sees his mother as a human being as
much in need of mercy as he is, and then when he extends that mercy
himself. And what else has he been longing to do all his life? What he can
at last offer to her, he can at last accept himself.

The question that hit me in the cathedral was, How could I have forgotten what my mother and I were looking at together while she prayed?
How could I have forgotten what had actually brought us to Trier? And
why had my glimpse of the venerated Robe slipped into a received memory of a generic Passion play? The answer, all at once, was obvious. Not
until I was in the presence of the suspended piece of cloth had I acknowledged my indifference to it. Everyone around me, including my mother,
was swept up in sacred emotion. "It is impossible," one reads in Augustine, "that the son of these tears should be lost."[8] But I felt nothing —
nothing, that is, in relation to the Robe. It seemed a secret declaration of
independence to have set myself apart from this particular form of piety,
and in relation to that, I felt exhilarated.

I was questioning, of course, whether the Robe was real — whether, in
other words, that Robe *there* was real. We were told that science had established its age and seamlessness, but had that cloth in fact wrapped the skin
of Jesus? If it had not, I was free. I was free, in my mind, to leave Mom,

Mary, and Helena behind, free to love a girl who was *not* somebody's mother. Everything rode on the Robe, and instinctively I had made my choice — even if later I would reenter the world of the *Liebefrau* by joining the *Kirche*. But for now I was out, young, free. It did not occur to me to ask, as Crossan would force me to ask years later, whether the Robe, as described by the Gospel of John — or Matthew's Magi, for that matter — had ever existed at all. It was enough to have my secret, and its liberation. A short while later, my family went to Italy where we had our audience with the pope. It was then that I knelt with Mom before the *Pietà,* secretly, shamefully aroused by the swan-like neck of the mother of God. From the Vatican, my mother, father, and brothers went to Naples, to embark on a ship for home, while I stayed behind for the rest of my senior year. I saw my family off at the Stazione Termini, waving my handkerchief as their train pulled away as if I were sad. Then I exploded out into the Piazza Barberini and up the elegant Via Veneto, past the American embassy, where I imagined myself a young Foreign Service officer, a spy. Free! My joy was shameful to me, but also it was precious, as were my unleashed unbelief and the lust I was determined to act on as soon as my own later train returned me to Wiesbaden. Of all this, my mother, in whom it was my solemn duty to confide everything, knew nothing.

Mother. The Catholic faith of Europe had bound us. And now I wanted the bond to break — "She wept bitterly to see me go and followed me to the water's edge." This is Augustine, except in his case Monica is the one doing the seeing-off. He is setting sail from Carthage, without her. But she was

clinging to me with all her strength in the hope that I would either come home or take her with me. I deceived her with the excuse that I had a friend whom I did not want to leave until the wind rose and his ship could sail. It was a lie, told to my own mother — and such a mother! . . . But she would not go home without me, and it was all I could do to persuade her to stay that night in a shrine dedicated to Saint Cyprian not far from the ship. During the night, secretly, I sailed away, leaving her alone to her tears and her prayers . . . The wind blew and filled our sails, and the shore disappeared from sight. The next morning, she was wild with grief . . . proof that she had inherited the legacy of Eve, seeking in sorrow what with sorrow she had brought into the world. But at last she ceased upbraiding me for my deceit and my cruelty, and turned again to you to offer her prayers for me. She went back to her house, and I went on to Rome.[9]

Oddly, it was in Rome that my version of this scene took place — an Irish American version, lacking in histrionics yet full of equivalent feelings. I loved the Via Veneto for its *palazzi*, the imposing mansions and villas of the richest people in the world. It was a street without churches — no churches for me. I returned to Wiesbaden, where I was happy to be, finally, on the wrong side of the Rhine.

In my recent visit, I discovered that the Trier Cathedral also possesses one of the three nails of the True Cross (one of the other nails Saint Helena had given to her son, who had it promptly melted down for use in a new battle helmet). I also learned that nearby stands the Church of St. Matthias, which entombs the remains of that apostle. Helena is credited with bringing what was left of him to Trier as well, no doubt to invincibly arm her hometown for the coming relic wars. Why Matthias? He was the apostle elected, according to Acts, to take the place of the suicide Judas.[10] Matthias, replacing the traitorous Jew, was supersessionism personified.

The great relics of Trier, and the city's all-trumping tie with Helena herself, enabled it to maintain its religious, and therefore political, primacy over Mainz and Cologne for centuries. But Helena's relics did something else, too. In part because of the cults attached to these particular totems of the Passion story, Trier developed as a center of Christian hatred of Jews. We will return to this region during the Crusades, the Enlightenment, and the Nazi period in subsequent sections of this book. Suffice to note here, for example, that in 1349, Trier was one of the places where the scapegoating of Jews for the Black Plague was most extreme — townspeople murdered the entire Jewish community. Jews gradually returned to Trier, but in 1418 they were driven from the city, well ahead of the 1492 expulsion from Spain.

For all these reasons, from its origin in "prophecy historicized," to its role as a "proof" denied, to its close association with the pointedly "non-Roman" deicide, the venerated Seamless Robe became an eloquent symbol of all that Christians hold against Jews. I said earlier that the archbishop ordered the Robe put on display as a way of giving thanks in 1959, and I learned recently that thanksgiving had been the constant religious meaning of the rare unveilings. But there is political meaning here as well. By displaying this relic only rarely, the pitch of popular interest in it — and in Trier — was maintained. The Robe spawned periodic pilgrimages that enabled a literally backwater town on the Moselle to compete with trading centers of the Rhine. The Robe reinforced Trier's connection to Helena, who had surpassed her omnipotent son in being a saint of the Latin Church. Political uses of the Robe are nothing new.

In 1959, I saw how it works with my own eyes. We understood the properly unspoken assumption from our place among the dignitaries in the balcony, looking across at the shirt of Jesus, that thanksgiving for the recovery of West Germany was offered as much to the United States as to God. But were we, perhaps, really being thanked for refusing until then — our Cold War strategy against Moscow required a virtuous ally in Bonn — to hold the German nation responsible for its most heinous crime?

In 1891, the last time save one that the Robe had been displayed, the archbishop of Trier had been thanking God for the end of the anti-Catholic Kulturkampf, or culture war, and the restoration of the rights of Catholics in the Rhineland. (The monks of Maria Laach were allowed to return in 1892 from an exile that had lasted most of a century, and their ancient title to the abbey was restored in 1893.) Clearly this was a world where no hard and fast distinction between religion and politics had been possible, even after the Enlightenment, so why shouldn't the unveiled Seamless Robe, a symbol of political joy, have been lifted up before the believing eyes of a relieved people? I said before that the display of the Robe in 1959 was one of three such occasions in the century. In fact, it was the second.[11] My mother and I did not know that. We did not know the date of the first, or what it implied. Neither the guides nor the cathedral's brochures mentioned it. We stood in the VIP section knowing nothing. Nothing about Germany — the SS an exception! And nothing about the Roman Catholic Church. By the time I returned to Trier to research this book, I had learned a thing or two, but I was still unprepared for what I learned then. The previous showing of the Seamless Robe had taken place before throngs of rejoicing pilgrims in the summer of 1933.

In that year of Hitler's coming to power, the Vatican signed its concordat with the Third Reich. By doing so, the Catholic Church became the first foreign power to enter into a bilateral treaty with Hitler. I knew that. I even knew that in 1933 the Roman Catholic hierarchy of Germany had overridden an earlier ban on Catholic membership in the Nazi Party. But the Robe? However dubious its claim to a strictly scientific authenticity, the tunic's having been venerated as Jesus' own garment for perhaps fifteen hundred years had invested it with sacredness of another kind. On the occasion of my recent visit, I was far from indifferent to that history. I could no longer stand in the presence of the Robe's tabernacle and feel nothing. So the question hit me with unexpected force: Had the

Robe been enlisted in a rapprochement with Hitler? I stood before the *Heiltumskammer*, and, in truth, I deflected the question by turning it into a prayer.

Later, I asked it of my guide: What was the archbishop of Trier expressing thanks for in 1933? What were all those devout Germans celebrating? The guide winced, sorry to be asked. "There was among Catholics," she said with a shrug, "a feeling that things would work out."

✦ 23 ✦

The Danger of Ambivalence

THE CROSS AT Auschwitz continues to be a flashpoint, and it symbolizes the complexity of Catholic attitudes. When the Catholic nationalist referred to at the beginning of this book was indicted in a Polish court in Oświęcim for having led the campaign to erect hundreds of small crosses in the field around the large papal cross at the wall of the death camp, he was charged with inciting hate against Jews. "I only said the truth," he proclaimed, "and will prove it in court." Later, in 1999, as we saw, the Polish senate passed a law requiring the small crosses to be removed, but making the papal cross permanent.[1] This despite the fact that a Vatican commission, in response to Jewish objections, had proposed the removal even of the papal cross "to an appropriate alternative site." But there was a telling ambivalence in the Catholic hierarchy's response, and now, perhaps, we can more fully take the measure of that ambivalence.

The Polish Catholics who had acted in defiance of the apparent intentions of the Polish pope, and of the explicit recommendation of the Vatican commission, could have pointed not only to local Church support[2] but to a strong signal that had just come from Rome on another, but related matter. Only three weeks before the new crosses had been erected, the Vatican had announced that Cardinal Alojzije Stepinac, the wartime archbishop of Zagreb, Croatia, was to be regarded as a martyr and would be beatified the following October, the penultimate step to sainthood. Stepinac died in 1962 while under house arrest by the Communist government of Yugoslavia. He was a heroic opponent of Stalinism, but his prior role as the primate of a national church in whose name unspeakable atrocities were committed by the pro-Nazi Ustashi made observers ask what the Vatican could be thinking. It was clear that Stepinac had been condemned by the Tito regime for political reasons, that he had been unjustly prosecuted for crimes he could not prevent. Exoneration, perhaps. But Jews and Catholics both could ask why a man who nevertheless embodied the Church's flawed responses to events of World War II should be elevated to sainthood?

As at Auschwitz, the conflict was over how the Holocaust would be remembered. This is the issue with which we opened this book, and now we can begin to see how the Jewish-Catholic conflict at Auschwitz crystallizes the competing rivalry that goes back to the generation after Jesus; to the decisive split illustrated by the distance between the New Testament and the Mishnah; to the habit of mind, born of the Hebrew Scriptures themselves, according to which the new supersedes the old. In Poland, the cross at the death camp wall was seen by some Catholics as a commemoration of the many Catholics who had died there; in the disputed field itself, it was said, the Nazis had executed some 150 Polish Catholics. But were they to overshadow the memory of about a million and a half Jews who died at Auschwitz?

Jews seemed sensitive to the complexities of the cross as a symbol of a redemptive notion of suffering and death that seemed a violation of a primary commitment to life, as an ultimate religious value, and as a symbol of a totalitarian universalism, rooted in Constantine, that violated pluralism, which was for Jews an ultimate social value. Thus the Christian planting of the cross in that place overrode all possible good intentions, and even suggested other intentions: "Christianizing" the Holocaust, using Christian categories to "redeem" the genocide, using the cross to deny the role of ancient Christian Jew-hatred in preparing the soil for the Holocaust — as if the Nazis were sprung as Teutonic pagans from the primeval forest and not from the heart of Christian Europe. All of this could have no other effect than the demeaning of the overwhelmingly Jewish presence at Auschwitz.

Memory was at issue in the Stepinac case, too. There is evidence of his courage in opposing the Ustashi program of forced conversion of Orthodox Serbs and related brutalities. A U.S. State Department report released in 1998 put the number of Ustashi victims at 700,000, "most of them Serbs." The report commented, "Croatian Catholic authorities condemned the atrocities committed by the Ustashi, but remained otherwise supportive of the regime."[3] That was true of Stepinac. He had welcomed the coming to power of the mini-Hitler Ante Pavelič in 1941, and he never overtly broke with the so-called Independent State of Croatia or its dictator.[4] Stepinac had supported Jews in Croatia. In 1937, he helped Jewish refugees from Germany. In 1941, he asked Pavelič "to treat the Jews as humanely as possible," and when the deportation of Croatian Jews began, he protested privately to the government.[5] In sermons, he denounced mistreatment of groups defined "by race or nation," but he did not preach openly about the fate of Jews. His defenders, like those of the even more reticent Pius XII, argue that the one resounding frontal assault by a Catholic hierarchy in defense of Jews, in the Netherlands in 1942, led to the rounding up even of the Jews who had converted to Catholicism. "The courage of Holland's Catholic bishops and clergy is undeniable," one defender of Pius XII wrote in 1998. "But their heroism came at a terrible price: 79% of Holland's Jews — 110,000 men, women and children — were murdered, the highest percentage of any Nazi-occupied nation of Western Europe."[6] That qualifier "Western" is apt, since in Croatia, to the east, where the hierarchy, including Stepinac, was circumspect, 85 percent of the Jewish population — almost 39,000 out of 45,000 — was annihilated.[7]

None of this marks Cardinal Stepinac as a war criminal. Perhaps he did what he could. But sainthood? Croatia was not the Netherlands; in Croatia the Nazis were welcomed as friends and allies. The Roman Catholic Church of Croatia, over which Stepinac presided, was associated with the pro-Nazi regime's policies.[8] Catholic newspapers were among its strongest supporters, and Catholic priests were key to the postwar survival of some of the Ustashi's worst murderers. As a postwar fugitive, Pavelič himself was sheltered for two years in Rome, for most of that time in the College of San Girolamo, the residence of Croatian priests working at the Vatican. Croatian clergy in Rome were part of the infamous "Rat Line" through which numerous Nazi war criminals, with the collusion of the U.S. Army, escaped to Latin America. The priests helped Pavelič get to Argentina in 1947.[9] "Although no evidence has been found to directly implicate the Pope or his advisers in the post-war activities of the Ustashi in Italy" — this is the conclusion of the 1998 State Department report — "it seems unlikely that they were entirely unaware of what was going on."[10] This dark episode hangs over the Catholic Church, and one must wonder if the move to canonize Stepinac is intended, finally, to dispel it.

The Polish Catholics who defied every Jewish expectation by planting crosses at Auschwitz in the summer of 1998 had to have noticed the Vatican's similar defiance of expectation with the nearly simultaneous Stepinac announcement. What both incidents lay bare is the ambivalence at the center of Catholic attitudes toward Jews. There is ambivalence even in the obviously troubled Catholic conscience about the Holocaust:

Stepinac's elevation to the threshold of sainthood follows the canonization of Maximilian Kolbe, the Franciscan friar who voluntarily took the place of another prisoner (not a Jew) in the starvation barracks, but who had also served as the editor of an antisemitic Catholic journal. The week after Stepinac was formally beatified in Rome, in October 1998, the convert Edith Stein — one of those rounded up in Holland after the bishops' protest — was canonized. "The canonization of Edith Stein," the novelist Mary Gordon commented in the Jewish periodical *Tikkun,* "is the wishful re-dreaming of Europeans who have a stake in believing that the Holocaust was something other than what it was: the determination to obliterate the Jewish people."[11] We will return to the story of Edith Stein later.

The positive side of contemporary Catholic ambivalence is vivid. Since the end of World War II, there have been the theological revolution of Vatican II, with its rejection of the deicide charge and its affirmation of God's ongoing covenant with the Jewish people; the remarkable grassroots flourishing of Jewish-Catholic dialogue; and the serious effort of the Polish pope to confront the legacy of Catholic antisemitism. But there remain rigid lines drawn around beliefs that may not be changed and around questions that may not be asked. Already we have seen the deeply problematic legacy of Jew hatred in foundational Christian texts, in the implicitly anti-Jewish Christian idea of revelation as prophecy fulfillment, and most damaging of all, in the dominant Christian theology of Jesus, not only as the enemy of the Jewish people but as the Son of God who obliterates the integrity of all other ways to God. Catholic ambivalence is nowhere more evident than in the way in which the Church now officially rejects supersessionism while firmly defending its scriptural and theological underpinnings.

Catholic ambivalence toward Judaism dates, as we have seen, to the beginning. Jewish followers of Jesus found consolation in their Scriptures; but then, forgetting how the crucifixion narrative was constructed in the weeks, months, and years after his death, successors began to use those same Scriptures against Jews who failed to recognize the crucified Jesus as the longed-for Messiah, or who failed even to long for a Messiah. Ambivalence is implied in the very name that came to be applied to those Jewish Scriptures — the "Old Testament," which was valued for being ancient but was superseded for not being "New."

The pattern of ambivalence became set as one generation's mistake was compounded by the next, and made more dangerous. Jewish-Christian conflict in the first century took on ominous new meanings in the fourth, by which time Christians had all but forgotten that those early conflicts had been among people *all of whom were Jews.* Jewish rejection became a source not just of feelings of being threatened, but of feelings of hatred. Even as they evolved, such reactions remained ambivalent because the Jewish enemy was still the intimate enemy; the Jew as other was still the brother, the sibling rival. Christians hardly noticed when, as the "parting of the ways" became dramatic and the centers of Jewish life shifted away from the centers of Roman and Christian life, Jews stopped thinking of the Church as competition. If one sibling opts out of the rivalry, the one remaining can feel it more intensely than ever. That, in effect, is what began to happen when Christianity tied permission for Jewish survival to the formal theological role of Jews as the permanent negative other.

All these manifestations of ambivalence became welded to the intellectual and political framework of the Church only with the Augustinian formulation: Jews may survive, but never thrive. A noble witness to the prophetic sources of Christian faith was also the witness of "bent backs" and "dispersal." That Jews suffered proved that Jews deserved to suffer. The circle of logic that began with Augustine was complete. In his time, the consequences of this position were benign compared to what befell heretics and pagans. But once again, following the now set pattern, a later generation — that "trail of pseudo-Augustinian anti-Jewish writings," in Fredriksen's phrase — applying the inherited principle in changed circumstances, would misunderstand its original meaning, and then the consequences would no longer be benign, not even relatively so.

"Theological negation, political toleration, and practical limitation" is the way one Jewish scholar, Robert Chazan, summed up the ancient legacy of Catholic ambivalence toward Jews. "These elements constituted a complex doctrine, and therein lay grave danger. In untroubled times, to negate Judaism while tolerating Jews was perhaps feasible; in periods of agitation and stress, the complex and contradictory doctrine was apt to disintegrate."[12] Disintegration, in this context, is another word for violence. It is no accident that this citation, elaborating the volatile inner meaning of the cross at Auschwitz and a Croatian cardinal's beatification, is from a book entitled *European Jewry and the First Crusade.* That the first organized murderers of Jews carried the cross of Jesus Christ on their shields has shamed the Christian conscience whenever it has learned the story. But the juxtaposition of symbol and deed was no coincidence. That the theological negation at the heart of ancient and respectable attitudes toward Judaism was bound to lead to violence against Jews becomes clear in the sequence of events that began in 1096.

Before turning to the eleventh century, however, here is one last note from the twentieth. The covert Croatian Rat Line, the escape route used by Nazis to flee Europe after the war, operating in Rome from a Vatican-related Catholic college, under the authority of Cardinal Stepinac, was put at the service of a fugitive from the Nuremberg war crimes tribunal. He was the German who had headed up the Gestapo in Lyons, France — Klaus Barbie. Like Pavelič before him, the "Butcher of Lyons" escaped to Latin America. In the 1980s, he would be captured, deported to France, convicted of crimes against humanity, and sentenced to prison, where he died in 1991. If Barbie has a place in this narrative, aside from the large debt he owed to the Roman Catholic ambivalence that had helped him escape, it is because of his place of origin. He was born, raised, and educated in the geographic and moral center of this story — Constantine's square one, Helena's hometown, the repository of the Seamless Robe, my mother's cherished pilgrimage site, the realm of my own awakening. And now we must recognize it as the place where crusaders first moved against Jews, launching a season of terror throughout the Rhineland, letting fly the exterminating angel that overshadowed the millennium. It is time to return to Trier.

PART FOUR

FROM CRUSADES
TO CONVERSIONISM

→ 24 ←

The War of the Cross

I T CAME TO PASS in the year one thousand twenty-eight after the destruction of the Temple that this evil befell Israel." So begins "Mainz Anonymous," one of the surviving Hebrew chronicles that recount events of 1096 as they were experienced by Jews.

There first arose the princes and nobles and common folk in France, who took counsel and set plans to ascend, and "to rise up like eagles" and to do battle and "to clear a way" for journeying to Jerusalem, the Holy City, and for reaching the sepulcher of the Crucified, "a trampled corpse" "who cannot profit and cannot save, for he is worthless." They said to one another: "Behold we travel to a distant land to do battle with the kings of that land. 'We take our souls in our hands' in order to kill and subjugate all those kingdoms that do not believe in the Crucified. How much more so (should we kill and subjugate) the Jews, who killed and crucified him." They taunted us from every direction. They took counsel, ordering that either we turn to their abominable faith or they would destroy us "from infant to suckling." They — both princes and common folk — placed an evil sign upon their garments, a cross.[1]

This is a description of the so-called First Crusade, the military expedition that set out from northwestern Europe in the spring of 1096, bound for the Holy Land. But the cross-marked army's first act of belligerence took place in the Rhineland, not Jerusalem, and its target was not the Muslim infidel but the Jewish one. The story of the Crusades is familiar to every schoolchild, yet it is rarely told from the point of view of those first victims, what they saw when the horde came.

Another Jewish chronicler of the crusaders' rampage through the Rhineland, Solomon bar Simson, also fixed on the symbol of the cross: "They decorated themselves prominently with their signs, placing a profane symbol — a horizontal line over a vertical one — on the vestments of every man and woman whose heart yearned to go on the stray path to the grave of their Messiah. Their ranks swelled until the number of men, women, and children exceeded a locust horde covering the earth."[2] This may have been no exaggeration. Medieval chroniclers put the number of first-wave crusaders as high as 600,000.[3] A more credible estimate still counts in six figures.[4] A multitude responded at once to Pope Urban II's clarion call for an army to defend the besieged Christian empire in the East — and to liberate the Holy Land.

Muslims had occupied Jerusalem since the year 638, a conquest that occurred only six years after the death of Muhammad (570–632). Islam subsequently revered Jerusalem as the site from which Muhammad ascended into heaven. To Christians, Jerusalem was sacred, above all, as the site of the grave of Jesus, and on the eve of the First Crusade, an upsurge of millennial piety rekindled Europe's readiness to take offense at the Islamic occupation of the land on which the Lord had walked.

That Christians viewed Islam as a threat was hardly new. Indeed, Europe came to understand itself as a distinct civilization in large part by defining itself against Islam, once the Muslim armies had stormed out of the Arabian Peninsula to conquer Syria, Persia, Egypt, all of North Africa, the Iberian Peninsula, and into Aquitaine. Europe's first great political dynasty, after the fall of Rome, began when the Frankish leader Charles Martel (c. 688–741) defeated the Muslims at Tours in 732, saving the heart of Europe for Christianity. The Germanic tribes that had swept across the Roman Empire in the time of Augustine had, during the intervening centuries, established numerous kingdoms, but eventually the Franks had come to dominate the north and west of Europe, and now that power was consolidated by the victory of Martel. After his death, his son Pepin was elected king of the Franks, and when Pope Stephen II went to Paris, in 754, to anoint him (the first pope to travel across the Alps), the show of deference to another monarch strained the papacy's tie to the emperor in Constantinople.

The pope had thrown in with the Frankish king because he needed help in fending off from Italy assaults by the Lombards, another Germanic tribe. The emperor in the East was doing all he could to fight the Islamic armies attacking through Armenia. Under a terrible siege itself, Constantinople would be no help to Rome. When a subsequent pope, Leo III, then crowned Pepin's son Charles, to be known as Charlemagne (c. 742–814), in Rome on Christmas Day in 800, he proclaimed him the Holy Roman Emperor. Charlemagne would guarantee the pope's position. Indeed, he quickly took control of all of Europe, except Spain, Britain, and Scandinavia. He would reward his allies with grants of land, the basis of European nobility. Encouraging especially the careful transcription of manuscripts, he would preside over a cultural renaissance, centered in Aachen, his birthplace, a city seventy-five miles north of Trier. But Charlemagne's reign would mark the final political division between East and West, and the papacy's support for Charlemagne, whom the emperor in Constantinople regarded as a usurper, would lead to the breakup of the Church, although that split would not become formal until 1054. All of these events were consequent to the assault on Christendom by Islam.

Now at last the moment had come for Christian Europe to strike back. The Christian *reconquista* had begun in Iberia; this was the time of the legendary El Cid (Rodrigo Díaz de Vivar, c. 1043–1099), whose capture of Valencia in 1094 had encouraged the Christian world. When Urban II (pope, 1088–1099), a Frenchman raised to the martial tradition of chivalry, spoke at a gathering of bishops at Clermont in November 1095, he lifted up the image of Jerusalem, and it instantly became a kind of screen onto which Christians could project an overpowering millennial fantasy. The legacy of Saint Helena, in particular the cult of the True Cross and relics attached to the Holy Land, had found niches in which to thrive in every devotional impulse of the Church, and the dream of things associated with the life and, especially, death of Jesus took on new power. Of the reconquest of Jerusalem Pope Urban cried, "God wills it!" He sparked an awakening that has left an imprint on the consciousness of Western civilization to this day.

A hundred thousand people dropped everything to join. As a proportion of the population of Europe, we might imagine a comparable response today prompting well over a million people, as the expression put it, to "take the cross."[5] Northwestern Europe had been devastated by bad harvests that autumn of 1095, and no doubt the crusading impulse rescued many serfs, but also landowners, from desperate economic straits. Populations had markedly increased in the previous century, expanded social networks had lifted gazes, and an ethos of violence, originating with marauding invaders from the north, had taken hold at all levels of society. No one knew it, but Europe was ready for something like the Crusades.

So were individual Europeans. Still traumatized by the spiritual dread associated with the millennium, and given to a cult of penitential abnegation, reflected in the new practice of secret confession of sins to priests, Latin Christians were obsessed with personal redemption. Urban II's

Clermont summons promised rewards in the afterlife, including a guarantee of eternal salvation to those who died in the struggle against the infidel. For the first time in Christian history, violence was defined as a religious act, a source of grace. And, as it had been before, so was suffering. "You shall help me carry my cross," Jesus said to crusaders in one lyric of the era.[6] Not surprisingly, such bloody mysticism had tremendous appeal in that rough world.

A political nerve had been touched as well, one that had lain exposed for centuries. After Charlemagne had been crowned by the pope on that Christmas Day in 800, his triumph had come fast. He was the most powerful ruler since the Age of Constantine. But the Carolingian Empire had quickly become overextended. The nobles and bishops whom Charlemagne empowered had soon enough turned on each other, and the Germanic custom of dividing estates among all male heirs — Charlemagne's domain had been partitioned among his four grandsons — had exacerbated the climate of dispute. The Germanic polity was not based on law, as Rome's had been, but on undefined tribal customs, which emphasized loyalty over justice but depended on an enforcement that now came sporadically. These stresses, when matched by new invasions from the north, with Vikings sweeping down from Scandinavia, had led to a disintegration of European unity. Charlemagne's heirs were still kings of the Frankish kingdom, and they carried the title of emperor, but they had little power.

Only recently, the papacy had been embroiled in a savage dispute with the emperor, who now was more rival than protector. In 1075, in a controversy over who had the right to appoint abbots and bishops, and therefore control their vast holdings of land and treasure, the reforming Pope Gregory VII (1073–1085) had excommunicated Emperor Henry IV. In the Apennine snows, the chastised emperor stood barefoot, in sackcloth, seeking the pope's pardon. Gregory required of Henry the ultimate act of penitence, a prostration. The emperor had to lie facedown on the frozen ground, his arms outstretched in imitation of the cross. (The cross is everywhere in this story.) Only then, on January 25, 1076, did the pope lift the excommunication, absolving the emperor. This humiliation seemed a victory for the papacy, but it also helped to prompt Henry's brutal invasion of Rome in 1083. Another tribe, the Normans, came to the pope's defense, but then they too sacked Rome, in 1084. With such disputes at the highest level of society, it is no wonder that the feudal lords of Christendom had made a habit of savaging each other in fratricidal wars for a century.

The pope's impulse was to unite the warring princes and the divided Church against a common enemy outside Christendom. In a sense, it was a replay of Constantine's effort to unify the divided empire, which involved the identification and condemnation of its enemies. Constantine's program had led immediately to Nicaea, where the unifying and univocal creed was first articulated. Ironically, the ignited crusading energy also led back to Nicaea. Situated on the eastern shore of the Bosporus, it was a kind of fortress outpost of Byzantium, guarding Asia Minor. For sixteen years, Muslim warriors had occupied Nicaea. This was a double outrage, given the city's status as a symbol of the One True Faith and — thinking of Constantine's oration at the Council of Nicaea — as the birthplace of the cult of the cross. In June 1096, thousands of crusaders laid siege to the city with rams and scaling ladders.[7] They set up their catapults and hurled over the wall, in addition to small boulders, the severed heads of Muslim defenders.[8] After six weeks, the Muslims surrendered. Nicaea was the first victory of the Latin crusaders, but their brutality — a thousand other decapitated heads were sent to the Greek emperor as a proof of the victory — had to seem ominous to the rescued Byzantines. Such unleashed ethnic and religious hatred would turn soon enough against Greek Catholics, making permanent the half-century-old East-West division of Churches.

Nicaea had featured in that schism too, a further irony, because a papal legate had accused the Christians of Constantinople of violating the sacrosanct Nicene Creed by eliminating the crucial word *filioque* from its definition of the Trinity. The deletion implied that the Holy Spirit "proceeds" from the Father alone, instead of from the Father "and the Son," which would undercut the full divinity of the Son. But were the affirmations of the original creed so cut-and-dried? "At Nicaea," as Jaroslav Pelikan puts it, "the doctrine of the Holy Spirit had been disposed of in lapidary brevity: 'And [we believe] in the Holy Spirit.'"[9] The eleventh-century Latin legate did not know, apparently, that (as we saw) the "faith of Nicaea" had evolved over decades and that *filioque* was not part of the original formulation at all. Yet on this issue the Church wrecked itself — another instance of that early pattern, how one generation's absolutism perverts a misremembered prior generation's considered relativism.

The Nicaean controversies of 1054 were not centered on the cross of Christ as such. Rather, the dispute between the Greeks and what they called the Frankish Church concerned the "nature" of Christ. To the Byzantines, the Latin insistence on the *filioque* implied an overemphasis on the Second Person of the Trinity at the expense of the Father and the Holy Spirit. In the Eastern Church to this day, the focus of worship is not

Jesus Christ but the Trinity. The Eucharistic prayer is clearly addressed not to Jesus, not to the Father, but to the triune God. But in the West, beginning now, Christian liturgy and theology became increasingly centered on Jesus, and this is surely reflected in the symbolism attached to the Crusades and in the heightened devotion to the idea of Jesus' death, as opposed to his life or Resurrection, as the key to salvation.

All this amounts only to a matter of emphasis, but that is true of the most savage disputes. What the Byzantines took to be a tilting away from the ancient tradition of Nicaea, reflected in the Latin legate's ignorant charge, had its real meaning in Rome's having already tilted away from the Eastern emperor. The schism between the Catholic Church and the Orthodox Church continues to this day.[10] By 1096, that schism had itself become a *casus belli,* as Crusaders, who had set out to defend Byzantine Christians, ended up by attacking them. That violence inflicted further scars, ones that still fester, as the Balkan wars of the 1990s demonstrate. The mid-twentieth-century religious violence in Cardinal Stepinac's Croatia, with Catholics targeting "schismatics," as the Serbian Orthodox were called, is also part of the crusaders' legacy.

If history shows us anything, it is that violence is the price of the totalitarian impulse, whether religious or political. Referring to Constantine's achievement at Nicaea and the political consolidation it enabled, Augustine had noted, as we saw, that absolute social and religious cohesion comes, in his word, at a cost: "But think of the cost of this achievement! Consider the scale of those wars, with all that slaughter of human beings, of all the human blood that was shed!"[11] The cost is borne mainly by those at odds with the new solidarity. By the eleventh century, there was a long history of marginalizing misfits of various kinds: lepers and cripples, vagabonds and prostitutes, magicians and jesters.[12] When society was ordered by the categories of Roman law, the idea of citizenship had enabled peoples of various classes and backgrounds to have a sense of common membership, but in the culture of Germanic tribalism, with custom replacing law as the basis of social structure, the category of "stranger" had taken on new force in Europe. "According to Germanic Custom, a stranger was an object without a master. Insofar as he was not protected, either by a powerful individual, or by inter-tribal or international arrangement, he did not enjoy the most elementary rights. He could be killed, and his murderer could not be punished . . . his property was ownerless, and his heirs had no rights of inheritance."[13] As the Roman Empire mutated into the Germanic Holy Roman Empire, individuals had learned to live in dread of being so identified.

Now marginalization would become exclusion, and its definitive note would be a rigid expression tied to religion — rigid as stone, since the new emblems of this development were the churches that began to be erected in burgeoning cities throughout Europe. Urbanization itself accentuated feelings of Christian solidarity, and, in the words of the historian H. Liebershütz, the "great city churches, designed especially to hold large audiences listening to popular sermons, became a lasting monument of this situation."[14] To stand outside the new Christian consensus of the crusading era was literally to stand outside the new cathedral, which was not only a temple of a self-consciously univocal society, but also a gathering place capable of holding an entire urban community. The outsider was now defined as such. As in the Age of Constantine, he was the heretic. There would be a violent papal crusade against Catholic heretics, the Albigensians, in the south of France in the thirteenth century, but in the late eleventh century, heretics were still hard to ferret out. Muslims were outsiders too, of course, but with the Pyrenees on one side and the stretch of Anatolia on the other, the borders between Saracen and Christian were well defined and, for most Europeans, far away. That left only one easily labeled category of outsider close at hand — the Jew.

The consolidation of a continent-wide European identity that was a mark of Charlemagne's reign in the ninth century had brought with it the final closing down of what remained of Jewish citizenship rights dating to Roman antiquity. In both eastern and western Europe, laws were passed to make sure that Jews did not exercise authority over Christians, and restrictions of numerous other aspects of Jewish life were enacted. Jews were, in the formulation of one early medieval Church council, "subject to perpetual serfdom."[15] This meant that Jewish communities were dependent on the benevolence of princes, bishops, and popes who, it is not too much to say, thought of themselves as owning Jews. The rights of an evolving feudal system, such as they were even for peasants, were not extended to Jews. Instead, to survive in Europe, Jews had to seek privileges granted by their Christian lords and prelates. "Court Jews" were those who found ways to be of particular use to such rulers, winning privileges for their extended families. Over time, with the coming of money-based economies, Jewish communities became necessary as financial centers. Numerous factors led to the implication-laden association of Jews with money: they had been forbidden to own land; frequently expelled, always marginal, Jews were more mobile than Christians, which made them a ready source of currency exchange; lending at interest was seen as sin-

ful by many Christians, yet the new economy required it, which led to
the Jew as designated usurer.[16] Recent scholarship has established that
Jews were not the only moneylenders in medieval society and that many
Jewish moneylenders, unlike Shylock, were magnanimous and widely respected.[17] Yet the unnuanced figure of the oppressive debt-holder Jew
took hold of the popular imagination, with special force during times of
economic contraction. This underwrote an entirely new reason for attacks
on Jews, not only by peasants but by petty merchants who could feel the
pinch of debt. If kings, princes, bishops, and popes protected Jews from
Christian mobs and the competing burgher classes, as with some consistency they did over many centuries, rulers did so, in part at least, in the
way they protected their valuable herds of cows and sheep.

Largely because of their economic function, Jews by the eleventh century usually lived near the marketplace, which was always near the church
or, in bigger towns, the cathedral. In an era when Christendom began to
define itself by opposition to those it excluded, to live in the shadow of the
cathedral would soon enough be dangerous if you did not rejoice in what
it symbolized. This would be true no matter what the bishop thought.

Cathedrals gave expression to the fact that the Christian insider had
never been more consoled by feelings of belonging. And such was the
tenor of the time that insider feelings could never be more intensely enjoyed than when attacking those who did not belong. As reports of the
Iberian *reconquista* made their way north, a heightened xenophobia took
hold, enforcing a new tolerance among Christians for each other. The
princes, barons, and common people of Europe found that the urgent
emotion of Latin Christianity's uniting new project against the infidel
overrode the former spirit of internecine vendetta. Thus Pope Urban II's
summons to war against the Saracen, when seen solely through the prism
of Christendom, could be celebrated as an act of peacemaking. As such, it
was related to the earlier mandating of Church-regulated tournaments as
an alternative to the mayhem of battle. Because it was war undertaken in
the name of Christ, an effect of this "peacemaking" was a heretofore unthinkable militarization of Christian religion. Knights formerly dubbed in
the halls of castles were now dubbed at the altar. Soon enough, knights
would be wearing tonsure, would be bound by the three vows, would be
living as monks when not in combat. Bishops would be warriors at the
heads of armies. In the Holy Land itself, one French bishop, side by side
with the king, would lead an army into battle carrying what he and his followers believed to be Saint Helena's True Cross.[18]

But first, in this initiating Crusade of 1096, it would be the laity donning the mantle and claiming license to kill in the name of the Gospel. Armed convert makers, they would wear the "horizontal-vertical sign." Those outside the consensus, outside the cathedral, would learn to see the cross with horror. Those "taking the cross," however, and those "bearing" it were, ipso facto, marked for salvation.

⤞ 25 ⤝

The Incident in Trier

J UDGING FROM THEIR unambivalent response to Clermont, the various aristocracies — Flemings, French Normans, Normans from Sicily, Provençaux, and men of Lorraine[1] — were ready to lay off each other. But in a culture and an economy defined by the martial ethos, it required a way of doing so without, in effect, laying off their retinues of knights. Each of these mounted warriors carried in his wake archers, foot soldiers, engineers who manned siege machines, servants, and the ragtag horde of deracinated peasants and their families. It was a mass of people — mounted and in armor, carrying lances; on foot, bearing clubs and knives. Almost all were crudely marked with the cross.

In the months after Urban II's autumn summons, the larger part of this force mustered in the northwest of Europe. Their route to Jerusalem took them first along the valleys of the River Maas, in present-day Netherlands, which becomes the River Meuse in France, then down the Moselle, which becomes the Mosel in Germany. This movement brought them to the great continental highways of the Rhine and the Danube. And as Nicaea stood at the forward edge of the crusaders' true field of conflict, as defined by Urban II, so our Trier stood at the edge of a first battlefield the pope had never intended, never foreseen, and never blessed.

"I have been told of the incident of Trier." This is a medieval Hebrew chronicler again, commenting on an event that the otherwise prolix Christian chroniclers of the Crusades never mention.

> It came to pass on the fifteenth of the month of Nisan, on the first day of Passover, there arrived an emissary to the crusaders from France, an emissary of Jesus, named Peter. He was a priest and was called Peter the prelate. When he arrived there in Trier — he and the very many men with him — on his pilgrimage to Jerusalem, he brought with him a letter from France, from the Jews (indicating) that in all places 'where his foot would

tread' and he would encounter Jews, they should give him provisions for the way. He would then speak well on behalf of Israel, for he was a priest and his words were heeded. When he came here, our spirit departed and our hearts were broken and trembling seized us and our holiday was transformed into mourning.[2]

The Jews of Trier paid Peter, as he asked, but the crusaders attacked them anyway. They broke into the Jews' "strong house" and "threw the Torah scrolls to the ground. They tore them and trampled them under foot." The Jews then "fled to the bishop," who at first offered to protect them. The bishop's palace stood on the spot where the bishop's residence stands today, abutting the cathedral in which the Seamless Robe of Jesus is kept. The palace was only several hundred yards from the narrow streets where the Jews would have been living. "The bishop sent and called to the important men of his city and his ministers. They stood before the gateway of his palace. In the gateway there was a door like the grate of a furnace. The enemy stood around the palace by the hundreds and thousands, grasping sharp swords. They stood ready to swallow them alive, body and flesh. Then the bishop's military officer and ministers entered the palace (where the Jews had taken refuge), and said to them: 'Thus said our lord the bishop: Convert or leave his palace.'"

In this drama unfolding over a considerable period of time, the bishop had done what he could. Finally his guard abandoned the palace. Crusaders forced two leaders of the Jews to bow before "an image," the cross. When instead the two Jews mocked the cross, they were killed. A Jewish girl "stretched her neck outside and said, 'Anyone who wishes to cut off my head for the fear of my Rock, let him come and do so.' The uncircumcised did not wish to touch her, because the young lady was comely and charming." Rather than convert, the girl escaped from the palace, ran to the Moselle, threw herself in, and drowned. "After these were killed," the chronicler concludes, "the enemy saw those remaining in the palace — that they were as firm in their faith as at the outset."[3]

The crusaders forced the baptisms of some, but Jewish resistance continued. In time, the "uncircumcised" evangelizers moved on. Even a history according to Jews would remember this particular contingent of crusaders under Peter the Prelate as benign, but only compared to what other brigades did in other cities. But as the chronicler understands, the incident in Trier was the beginning of an unprecedented turn in the story of Christians and Jews: Crusader attacks on Jews throughout the Rhineland that spring amounted to Europe's first large-scale pogroms. And Trier's knot in the narrative thickens: Constantine's fateful conformity campaign had begun here, as now did Europe's rehearsal for the extermination of Jews who would not conform.

The factors accounting for this sudden wave of anti-Jewish violence are often limited to the new forces of economics, such as the anti-Jewish bias of a nascent burgher class; to the pressures resulting from a century-long demographic explosion and related urbanization; or even to the social stresses of conformity, which made dissent of all kinds more offensive. But such factors fall short as explanations. Jews and Christians had lived more or less peacefully together for centuries. Augustine's "Do not slay them!" had been sanctioned by Pope Gregory the Great (Gregory I, 590–604) at the end of the sixth century. He had expressly forbidden any forced conversions of Jews, yet he had also sanctioned Augustine's ambivalence. The popes would forever be protectors of Jews, but they would also be steadfast denigrators of Jews. Gregory I's proclamation began with the words *Sicut Judaeis,* which thereafter named the genre of papal defenses of Jews. Its key passage read, "Just as the Jews must not to be allowed freedom in their synagogues more than is decreed by law, so neither ought what the law concedes them suffer any curtailment."[4] To maintain this combination of protection and curtailment required a delicate balance, and in 1096, it was lost.

Was there something about medieval Judaism that elicited the brutal new hostility? On the contrary, Jewish life at the millennium was humane and thriving. In the Arabic world, with centers in Iberia and in Baghdad, Jewish communities had reached unprecedented levels of intellectual and religious achievement. I read this history as a Christian, but it seems fair to say that the Talmudic system had shaped a way of thinking by the very seriousness with which the commentary of rabbis was taken. That way of thinking, in turn, shaped Jewish communal life. The problems and crises of Jews were addressed and resolved through commentary and further commentary — an inbuilt commitment to text, reading, imagination, and community. All of this was organized around an admired collective whose authority was rooted in study and in the proven wisdom of its "responsa," its responses to questions. Though based on the Law of Moses, Judaism had emerged as a community ordered not by legislation or decree but by the influence of its interpreters, reflecting on a compilation of the commentary of ancestral masters. This is the culture of Talmud, a culture not of codification but of conversation, written and oral; a culture not of hierarchy but of mutuality.

The emphasis on practical application of theory prepared Jews to prosper, and, when unfettered, they did. Among Muslims, Jews occupied leading positions in science, art, commerce, and government. Yet the culture of Talmud turned out to be as transferable across the boundaries of time and place as the texts on which it was based. Rabbis could bring it with them wherever they went. Thus the vital premillennial centers of Jewish life in the Arab world spawned a religious and cultural renewal in Christian Europe, especially in settlements along the Rhine. "How wonderful is your place," the leaders of Spanish Jewry wrote to leaders of German Jewry in this era, "praiseworthy and honored, a superior assembly of scholars and teachers."[5] In the Rhineland Jewish communities, the literate, scholarly class outnumbered the ignorant, the unlettered. By far the most influential center of Talmudic scholarship was Mainz. One of its leading figures in the eleventh century was Rabbi Simeon the Great, so called because of his Talmudic learning. Among Jews across Europe spread the legend that Rabbi Simeon's son was kidnapped by Christians, baptized, and raised to become a priest. Reflecting the true, if secret, genius of his lineage, he eventually became the pope. "When he finally learned of his origin," the scholar I. A. Agus recounts, "he sanctified the Name of the Lord and according to some accounts died a martyr's death."[6]

Despite rumblings of coming attacks against Rhineland Jews as usurers, their international connections were, in the eleventh century, highly valued as sources of exchange and trade. Prosperity, when it came to the center of Europe, underwrote an intra-Jewish cultural enrichment. An expressly Jewish practice of medical science was growing. Vernacular and Hebraic literatures were taught at Jewish schools and academies, like the one in Mainz, which ranked with the best in Europe. Because of the interchange among Jewish communities along the Iberian–central European–Persian axis, Jewish translation skills were unmatched, and eventually it would be Jewish translators who brought to Christendom the Arabic masters, and through them Aristotle. Christians, meanwhile, knew little or nothing about this Jewish high culture of the Middle Ages, both far away and near at hand — and that remains true today.

So the hated Jew of the crusader's imagination was unrelated to the actual Jews he came upon, which only emphasizes the fact that something besides the normal sway of social upheaval explains what began to happen. The source of Jewish-Christian violent conflict lay entirely on the Christian side of the hyphen — an obvious statement, but not one that can go without saying. The crusaders, suddenly obsessed with the "infidel," projected onto Jews a fantasy tied to an ancient memory that had little enough to do with the Jews of that bygone era, and nothing whatever to do with Jews as they existed in the crusaders' time. The age-old "Jewish problem," that is, was and remains a Christian problem, spawned by an ignorant Christian imagination. Its cause? The answer is so plain we can hardly see it as such, and it has been there all along. A mis-carried cult of the cross is ubiquitous in this story, from Milvian Bridge to Auschwitz. The "war of the cross," which is another way of saying "cru-sade," is the definitive epiphany, laying bare the meaning of what went be-fore and what came after, even to our own time.

Exactly because the cross was ubiquitous on the breasts of warriors, we take it for granted, but we should see its significance there with fresh eyes if we can. A religious misunderstanding, the one we have been tracking forward from the way that circle of grief-struck friends of Jesus were misunderstood by Christians who came after, is at the heart of Christian hatred of Jews. What the crusaders do, especially as unleashed not so much in the East — though in 1099, in the violent siege of Jerusalem, they drove all the Jews into one synagogue and burned them alive[7] — but in the cities of the Rhineland in 1096, is to make the thing clear as rain, albeit a rain of blood.

To see more clearly how this new violence sprang from what might be called the sacred mistake of an overemphasis on the Passion and death of Jesus, and the inevitably related mistake of the "Jewish murder" of Jesus, let us return to the Hebrew chronicles' figure of Peter the Prelate. He is more commonly known to history as Peter the Hermit, leader of the so-called Peasants' Crusade. That is surely a misnomer, since his Crusade preaching was almost exclusively done in cities.[8] He is the only preacher of the Crusade whose name we know, a figure of legend but also of his-tory.[9] "Tiny in stature," one chronicler calls him, "but great in heart and speech."[10]

By the Jews of Trier, Peter may have been remembered as relatively be-nign, but there are accounts of his Good Friday sermon that same spring transforming the Cologne Cathedral congregation into an anti-Jewish mob. The present cathedral dates to the thirteenth century, when its foun-dation stone was laid, but it replaced a ninth-century cathedral on the same site. There Peter preached his Crusade, tying it to the death of Jesus. His listeners stormed out into the street at once, looking for Jews, and finding them. Despite protective efforts of the archbishop, whose name was Hermann, many Cologne Jews were murdered.[11] The *Jewish Encyclo-*

pedia says they were dispersed, and that, in one instance, three hundred Jews were encircled and given the choice of baptism or death. With an echo of the ancient story of Masada, the encyclopedia says that they refused to convert, and instead "selected five men to slay the rest."[12] Jewish mass suicide reenters history.

I stood in the Cologne Cathedral not long ago, contemplating these events. I thought of Archbishop Hermann, who, like the bishop of Trier, tried and failed to protect Jews. In the cathedral, I saw on the wall beside the tomb of a thirteenth-century bishop, Englebert, a stone tablet engraved, in Latin, with a proclamation known as the "Jewish Privilege." Though that word "privilege" reminds us that Jews were without rights, it also recalls the more or less consistent effort of bishops to protect Jews from the consequences of what Christians heard in their cathedrals. The Latin translates: "We, Englebert, Archbishop of Cologne, assure you, the Jewish community of Cologne, that you have certain rights . . . You need not pay taxes in excess of what others pay. If we find a Christian doing money exchange, he must leave the city: that business is yours. You no longer must pay a tax to bury your dead. You do not have to bury your dead near the place of execution."[13]

Near the "Jewish Privilege" is a shrine to the Christian "place of execution," the so-called Cross Chapel, which is named for the crucifix of Gero, a tenth-century bishop. The cross he commissioned survives as the oldest rendering of the crucifix in the West, and hangs above a Baroque altar. Its dark wood embodies a life-size corpus whose collapsed muscles and sagging torso capture the body's expiration. To stand in that chapel is to sense the motes in the air stirring with the last breath Jesus took only seconds ago. Yet this same cross very likely hung in the air through which Peter's deadly words resounded more than a thousand years ago. The tradition in which Peter the Hermit stood has yet to die, as this commentary on the Gero cross in the recently published *Cologne Cathedral and City Guide* indicates: "The work depicts exactly that moment in which Christ, the Son of God, has just died. From the point of view of Christianity, this instant in time is the decisive turning point in the history of the world. Prior to this, mankind lived under the strict laws which God gave Moses on Mt. Sinai; thereafter, in the age of mercy inaugurated by Christ's Death on the Cross."[14]

What mercy? Peter the Hermit, too, saw Christ's death on the cross as pivotal. Moreover, the entire crusading impulse begins, according to the Christian chroniclers, with Peter's prior pilgrimage to Jerusalem, and with his fury at the fact that the holy places associated with the cross were being blasphemed by the occupying infidels.[15] Recall that, after Helena, the mystique of the cross had transformed the implement of Jesus' execution into a new kind of Incarnation — as if Jesus *were* his cross. The "discovery" of the True Cross, the fourth-century rescue of the Cross from the sly, perfidious Jews, had completed the work of salvation history and vanquished the Jews once and for all. Or so it had seemed in the Age of Constantine.

Once the Muslims took over Jerusalem in 638, both Christians and Jews survived in the city as tolerated minorities. When Jerusalem emerged as an Islamic pilgrimage site, the fervor of Muslims increased, and, at times, so did their intolerance. By the tenth century, for example, Jews were no longer admitted to the Temple Mount, and in the early eleventh century, all Jewish and Christian places of worship in Jerusalem, including the Holy Sepulcher, were ordered destroyed by the ruling caliph.[16] Jews were not allowed to reconstruct their synagogues, although Christians were able, in 1048, to rebuild an unimpressive remnant of the Holy Sepulcher.

By the time Peter the Hermit visited Jerusalem as a pious pilgrim in the late eleventh century, "some years before the beginning of the Way [Crusades]," the site of Jesus' death was regarded in Europe as having been defiled by its infidel occupiers. But the incarnational spirituality that saw the Word of God made flesh in a man and saw the crucified Jesus "made wood" in the True Cross, still saw the place of Jesus' death as consubstantial — to use a word applied to the Eucharist — with Jesus himself. The religious meaning of Jerusalem had by now been distilled into this one event, this one place, this knot of the Passion and death. Peter the Hermit was a mystic at the mercy of the ethos of the cross, which in his time was the ethos of the cross desecrated.

According to a history by Albert of Aachen, composed within four decades of the event, Peter found himself swept up in a mystical summons from the Lord. While asleep in the Church of the Holy Sepulcher, he had a vision of Christ, who ordered him "to rouse the hearts of the faithful to come out and purge the holy places at Jerusalem, and restore the holy offices. For through dangers and diverse trials the gates of Paradise shall now be opened to those who have been called and chosen." As a proof of the validity of this vision, Peter was led to "discover" the holy lance, the weapon that had been plunged into Jesus' side.[17]

With this authority, Peter went to Rome and, so Albert of Aachen says, successfully roused the martial ardor of Urban II, who agreed to preach Peter's Crusade. "For this reason," Albert asserts, "the Pope crossed the

Alps" to Clermont, where "bishops of all France and the dukes and counts and the great princes of every order and rank, after hearing the divine commission and the Pope's appeal, agreed to God's request for an expedition at their own expense to the sepulcher itself."[18]

What the True Cross was to the Constantinian wars of conformity, the Holy Sepulcher was to the Crusades. The two "visions" — Constantine's of the cross above Milvian Bridge, and Peter's of Christ on the site where the cross had stood — like the two "discoveries" — Helena's of the True Cross, and Peter's of the holy lance — stand in the same place in relation to the larger dynamics they simultaneously resulted from and unleashed. And as the cross had become the incarnational focus of God's presence in Constantine's world, Jerusalem itself, in the European imagination, became the incarnational locus in the crusaders' world. As the cross and Jesus were identified — to revere one was to revere the other — so with the holy place. To rescue "captive Jerusalem" was to rescue a kidnapped Jesus. And just as the fourth-century worship of the cross sparked immediate violence against Jews, as we saw in Ambrose, so this passionate renewal of obsessive concern for the crucifixion and its paraphernalia sparked attacks on Jews, as if their synagogues in Jerusalem had not also been desecrated during the Islamic occupation. In the Christian millennial fantasy, Jews instantly joined, or even replaced, Muslims as the defiling enemy. "We desire to combat the enemies of God in the East," the Christian chronicler Guibert of Nogent (1053–1124) wrote, "but we have under our eyes the Jews, a race more inimical to God than all the others. We are doing this whole thing backwards."[19] The Christian fantasy, turned forward, gave pride of place to Jews, especially when it came to the *holy* place, which the Christian imagination still tied far more firmly to Jewish perfidy than Muslim. Recall that a central tenet of Augustine's theology of Jewish "witness" was the Diaspora, the idea that Jews were never to return to Jerusalem. That they had been allowed to do so under the Muslims was essential to the Muslim desecration of the Holy Land.

Thus the True Cross involved a progression of beliefs that had run together by now with the idea of Jerusalem. God had become a person, who became a place, which became an object, before which every Christian believer could bow in the form of a locally revered relic. It all fit together almost too neatly, even to the Rhineland piety that depended on relics traced to Helena: the Seamless Robe in Trier, the corpses of the Three Kings in Cologne, the splinters of the True Cross in gilded reliquaries all over northern Europe.

Aside from levels of violence, there was another difference between what the preaching of Ambrose and John Chrysostom started and what Peter the Hermit's preaching unleashed. Crusader attacks in the eleventh century were not on Jews as they really existed by then, but on the imaginary Jews who, in the permanent present tense of the liturgical cycle, were still murdering Jesus in Jerusalem. This is a mystery not only of place, in other words, but of time. As Christianity had imposed its categories on Roman and then on Germanic cultures, the supersessionist understanding of history as a process of "fulfillment" took root. This was perfectly symbolized by the change in the calendar according to which the passage of time was measured against the birth of Christ instead of the founding of Rome, or instead of the Germanic system tied to the reigns of kings. When years were numbered as *anno Domini,* a usage popularized by the Church historian Saint Bede (c. 673–735) and observed throughout Christendom by the tenth century, it was not just the past that was being defined, but the present.[20] The "year of the Lord" means that the Lord, with dominion over time, is as present now as he was when he walked the earth.

And the Lord's presence was celebrated at the altar of those cathedrals, proclaimed from their pulpits. That the first violent outbursts against Jews were associated with Holy Week observances is the large and foreboding clue. Yes, the crusaders' main enemy was identified by Urban II as the "Turk" or "Saracen," but, the only infidel enemy of whom people in northern Europe had knowledge were Jews. The point to emphasize here is that their knowledge was *liturgical* knowledge, gained in the mysterious realm of the great churches to which Christians brought their inmost fears. That there was thus something fundamentally irrational about assaults on Rhineland Jews did not make the consequences of those assaults imaginary. "If you prick us," Shylock asks, "do we not bleed? . . . If you poison us, do we not die?"[21] Shakespeare put those words in the Jew's mouth four centuries later, by which time the fantastic figment of the Christian imagination had become a central thread in Western consciousness.

And so with Jerusalem. Beginning with the crusaders' fervor, that city took on an elusive mystical aura, captured eventually by William Blake and by the classic hymn sung in the Gothic chapels of British public schools as a way of praising not God but England. So Jerusalem would feed the fantasies of English settlers in the New World. When John Winthrop decreed in 1630, from the deck of a ship in what would become Boston harbor, "that wee shall be as a Citty upon a Hill, the eies of all people are upon us," he was envisioning the American self-image as a new Jerusalem. As history shows, that has, in turn, been shadowed by the image of America as, in Walter McDougall's phrase, the "crusader state."[22] Not for nothing did Dwight Eisenhower entitle his memoir of World War II *Crusade in Europe.*

The shimmering idea of Jerusalem, the holy city to die and kill for, planted itself in the Western mind with the summons, in the words of the medieval chronicler Anna Comnena, of "a certain Kelt, Peter by name . . . that they should all leave their homes and set out to worship at the Holy Sepulchre and to endeavor with heart and mind wholeheartedly to deliver Jerusalem."[23] The holy city seemed suddenly very close: "Is this Jerusalem?" the accompanying children would ask breathlessly at every town. That was not because the crusading hordes were so ignorant of geography, but, again, because their sense of urgency was rooted in liturgy, not history. Just as the mystery of religious proclamation broke down barriers of time, identifying "the Jews" of the Passion narratives with Jews of the Middle Ages, bringing the suffering of Jesus from the deep past into the eternal now — so with space. Jesus, held captive in the Holy Land, could be encountered at every altar, with its IHS, as in mortal jeopardy *here.* Every believer on his knees at the altar rail was a putative conscript.

So the mystery of sacred time played with the minds of Christians. The great contemporary symbol of that mystery was the millennium. In the tenth century, the literal-minded pious were bound to read chapter 20 of Revelation, also known as the Apocalypse, with a fevered chill:

> Then I saw an angel coming down from heaven, holding in his hand the key of the bottomless pit and a great chain. And he seized the dragon, that ancient serpent, who is the Devil and Satan, and bound him for a thousand years, and threw him onto the pit, and shut it and sealed it over him, that he should deceive the nations no more, till the thousand years were ended. After that he must be loosed for a little while . . . And when the thousand years are ended, Satan will be loosed from his prison and come out to deceive the nations which are at the four corners of the earth, that is Gog and Magog, to gather them for battle; their number is like the sand of the sea. And they marched up over the broad earth and surrounded the camp of the saints and the beloved city; but fire came down from heaven and consumed them, and the devil who had deceived them was thrown into the lake of fire and brimstone where the beast and the false prophet were, and they will be tormented day and night for ever and ever.[24]

Crusading fever meshed with millennial fever, and soon enough the present moment was widely experienced as nothing less than the dawn of the apocalyptic age. Christ, ransomed by the sacrifice of his army, would return in triumph for the Last Day. Those embarked upon the rescue of Jerusalem were thus ushering in the End of Time. But this spirit impinged directly on the Jews, who could all too easily be tagged as "the beasts and false prophets" deserving of a long-overdue damnation. Jews were those for whom time, literally, was up.

The year 1000 had come and gone, but the millennial mindset it spawned, if only in a literate minority, continued to shape European thought patterns. The millennial understanding of time, as laid out by a twelfth-century monk, Joachim of Fiore (c. 1132–1202), involved three ages: that of the Father, which was the era belonging to the Jews; that of the Son, the era belonging to the Church; and that of the Spirit — the time before the End of Time.[25] It was this trinitarian schema that gave Adolf Hitler his motif. The Third Reich succeeded the First, the Holy Roman Empire (962–1806), and the Second, the Hohenzollern Empire (1871–1918), but below this literal chronology, Nazi mythology exploited the idea of the dawning of the messianic era. The Third Reich corresponded to the Third Age of the millennium.[26] It was expected to endure, as Hitler said repeatedly, for a thousand years. Hitler worked to undermine the principles of Christian religion and targeted those who openly defended them, he perverted biblical hope by proclaiming himself the Messiah, but he also echoed the medieval Christian conviction that the obstacle to the inauguration of the glorious thousand-year reign, was the stiff-necked Jewish people. That conviction was based on a particular reading — given the use made of it, one could surely say misreading — of the Pauline forecast that the conversion of the Jews would herald the return of the Messiah: "A hardening has come upon part of Israel, until the full number of the Gentiles come in, and so all Israel will be saved; as it is written, 'The Deliverer will come from Zion, he will banish ungodliness from Jacob.'"[27]

Jews who defended their "ungodliness" by refusing to convert — never mind that they did so in the name of God — were a threat to the ultimate fulfillment of salvation history, a threat that had no precedent, a threat that could not be tolerated. Savage violence? Hadn't Revelation predicted exactly that? "I believe that I am acting in accordance with the will of the Almighty Creator." Christians would later dismiss these words as ingenuous, since their speaker cared nothing for any will but his own, but they remain rooted in the sacred tradition. "By defending myself against the Jew, I am fighting for the work of the Lord." Such is the true expression of the millennialist mindset of the marauding crusader, although the statement was made by the later millennialist Adolf Hitler.[28]

Mainz Anonymous

FROM TRIER, where my mother and I found ourselves on opposite sides of piety, to Cologne, where I knelt, dubious, before the Three Kings; from Kespen, near Maria Laach, where I learned the timeless vernacular of plainchant, to Rüdesheim, where I drank my first hock — in these sacred places of my youth, Jews were savagely assaulted during the spring of 1096. A map of the Rhine region published in the *Jewish Encyclopedia*[1] shows fourteen "Sites, with Dates, of Anti-Jewish Outbreaks During the First Crusade, 1096." The dates range from April 17 to July 1. The number of Jews murdered or forced to suicide in those weeks is estimated by scholars to have been as low as 5,000[2] or as high as 10,000,[3] perhaps a full third of the Jews living in northern Europe. When adjusted for demographics, an equivalent number of victims in our century would exceed 130,000.

This rampage fell on the Jews like "a thunderclap out of the blue."[4] So, perhaps, does this history fall on a modern Christian. In my case, the blue sky it shatters was stretched like a film of innocence above the place where I came into self-awareness — that golden city of my father's headquarters on the Rhine. My innocence was decidedly American: "This war was a holy war," General Eisenhower had said of his crusade, "more than any other in history this war has been an array of the forces of evil against those of righteousness."[5] One of the forces of righteousness, the Soviet Union (later to be known as the "evil empire"), had switched sides by the time I was at my station as a crusader's son, which made our war holy too. And my innocence was Catholic, since, as everyone knew in the anti-Red heyday of Pius XII, the Church militant was the custodian of the martial holiness Ike had prized. Cardinal Francis Spellman, known as the military vicar, embodied the union of our ideals: *Pro Deo et Patria*. My mother's work for Spellman, in her role as president of the Military Council of

Catholic Women and organizer of those Rhineland pilgrimages, was the perfect expression of our triumphant religious nationalism.

From the hill above Wiesbaden — in the American enclave of Hainerberg, which we took to mean "Higher City," or more resonantly, "City on a Hill" — the blue sky was like a shielding canopy over a postwar population center that had not been brought to ruin. The pristine steeples below — Protestant, not Catholic — were sharp against the green hills that cut off our view of the mighty river and of Mainz on its opposite shore. Mayence is what that city is called in older sources, reflecting its pull toward the Romance culture of Catholic Europe; in fact, in the Napoleonic era, Mainz was annexed by France. Today the skyline is dominated by the proud Romanesque tower of the cathedral — dominated literally, since the German word for cathedral is *Dom*. Part of the church dates to the eleventh century, and that was built on the site of an older cathedral, which had been erected during the reign of Constantine. In my time there, however, the cathedral was unremarked upon, and there was no skyline of Mainz. In adjacent Wiesbaden, we knew nothing of that city, nor of its past, neither recent nor distant.

Mainz, with Trier and Cologne, had long been one of three ancient seats of the bishop electors who helped choose the Holy Roman Emperor. For most of the Middle Ages, Mainz, strategically situated at the confluence of the Rhine and Main Rivers, was the most powerful of the three. As we saw, it was known as "the Rome of the North," and like Rome it carried the title of Holy See. In the *Dom*'s apse, which predates the First Crusade, the emperors were anointed. Yet my pilgrim mother never took us there. Why? For the simple reason, I see now, that in the late 1950s, war damage from American bombardment was still evident. The market square adjacent to the cathedral had not been completely cleared of rubble, and the cathedral would not be fully restored until 1989. Allied air bombardment killed 600,000 Germans during World War II,[6] almost all of them civilians, and the majority in the last months of the war when the Nazi machine was all but defeated. In one city, Dresden, with more than 100,000 killed,[7] there were not enough survivors to bury the dead. For Jews, as we saw, the crusaders' Holy Week assault in 1096 was like a "thunderclap out of the blue." The Allied air offensive against Dresden, carried out on Shrove Tuesday into Ash Wednesday in 1945, was called Operation Thunderclap. Such a coincidence of language invites a conflating of anti-Jewish violence in this region with the later anti-civilian violence, yet that is not what I intend. Clearly anti-Jewish violence has its own demonic relentlessness. The point of comparison is tied more to the inner logic of the crusading impulse, and it seems impossible to ignore that it was unleashed in separate episodes nearly a thousand years apart over this same territory.

The German military positions along the Rhine were the fabled "West Wall" of the Third Reich. In the final months of the war, they were subject to massive Allied carpet bombing — but so were population centers on the river, strategically placed or not. When the Germans had first targeted cities early in the war, especially Coventry and Rotterdam, Franklin Roosevelt denounced an "inhuman barbarism that has profoundly shocked the conscience of humanity."[8] But near war's end, the Allied conscience had changed. The commander in chief of the British Bomber Command said, "I would not regard the whole of the remaining cities of Germany as worth the bones of one British grenadier."[9] Berlin, Hamburg, Dresden, Essen, Nuremberg, Frankfurt, Düsseldorf, all were "bombed to rubble."[10] As we saw, the Cologne Cathedral was spared as a monument to Allied humaneness, but no such restraint was imposed on the thunderclaps from the blue above Mainz. A guidebook I obtained there recently refers to the bombing that Mainz endured as "the apocalypse of the Second World War," an eerie, if incidental, rebuttal to Ike's use of the term "crusade." In fact, the crusading mindset was given more apt expression by the new technology of aerial bombing. Commenting on the British and American campaign against German cities, when no such assault was necessary to win the war, the historian Paul Johnson wrote, "The bombing offensive appealed strongly to the moralistic impulse of both nations: What the British atomic scientist P.S.M. Blackett called 'The Jupiter Complex' — the notion of the Allies as righteous gods, raining retributive thunderbolts on their wicked enemies." In that final paroxysm of violence, 80 percent of Mainz was, in a phrase of the guidebook, "reduced to debris."

When Allied ground forces moved into Germany in September 1944, they retraced the route of Peter the Hermit. At the heart of the first territory they took was Trier.[11] On March 22, 1945, George Patton led his Third Army across the Rhine south of Mainz, beating out Bernard Montgomery, who would cross the river later, to the north. Upon learning of Patton's thrust, Hitler ordered an immediate counteroffensive, but he was told that nothing was left with which to resist.[12] And that was why, finally, our lovely spa city of Wiesbaden, on the eastern bank, was spared, and why, little more than a decade later, my youthful American conscience could also be spared — spared its confrontation with these complexities. The

map of the gratuitous Allied air war against Rhineland cities was as unknown to me then as the First Crusade map in the *Jewish Encyclopedia.* Undertaking this book terminates a lifetime's sparing of conscience.
Without drawing a moral equation between these thunderclaps of crusader violence, medieval and modern, I must still observe that at the center of each stands Mainz, a mere two and a half miles away from where
I lived, prayed, and learned to be a man and a son, an American and
a Catholic.

"When the saints, the pious ones of the Most High, the holy community
of Mainz, whose merit served as shield and protection for all the communities and whose fame had spread throughout the many provinces, heard
that some of the community of Speyer had been slain and that the community of Worms had been attacked a second time, and that the sword
would soon reach them, their hands became faint and their hearts melted
and became as water. They cried out to the Lord with all their hearts, saying: 'O Lord, God of Israel, will You completely annihilate the remnant of
Israel?'"[13] These words are taken from the "Chronicle of Solomon bar
Simson," which is one of four Hebrew chronicles ("Mainz Anonymous,"
cited earlier, is another) that tell what happened to Jews during the Crusades of the eleventh and twelfth centuries. Solomon bar Simson's account was composed within a few decades of the attack in Mainz, which
took place in late May 1096, coming to a staggering climax on May 27.
"Then, the [Jewish] community leaders who were respected by the local
bishop approached him and his officers and servants to negotiate this
matter. They asked: 'What shall we do about the news we have received regarding the slaughter of our brethren in Speyer and Worms?' They [the
Gentiles] replied, 'Heed our advice and bring all your money into our
treasury. You, your wives, and your children, and all your belongings shall
come into the courtyard of the bishop until the hordes have passed by.
Thus will you be saved from the errant ones.'"

The archbishop of Mainz who offered this protection to the Jews of his
city was named Ruthard. The chronicler is ambivalent about this figure,
asserting at one place that the bishop only wanted the Jews' money, and at
another that he solemnly promised, "We shall die with you or remain alive
with you."[14] Robert Chazan concludes from his study of the First Crusade
that Ruthard was sincerely determined to protect the Jews.[15] But his effort
was doomed. His force consisted of three hundred soldiers, while the besieging crusaders numbered some twelve thousand. For two days, that

force was kept out of Mainz by the city wall, but then the gates "were opened by sympathetic burghers."[16] A self-interested bishop might protect Jews because they were a useful counterweight to the rising merchant class. But Ruthard's support of the Jews of Mainz went beyond self-interest. He risked his own life, since the crusaders, as the chronicler says, "wanted to kill him, too, because he had spoken in favor of the Jews."[17] Once the city was overrun, however, the archbishop fled, taking refuge across the Rhine in Rüdesheim (where I, sitting in the wine garden of a half-timbered inn nearly a millennium later, would have my first legal drink).

The crusaders were unleashed, storming through the city, looking for "the circumcised." Jews who had eluded crusaders, or bribed them during the early phase of the Rhineland incursion, had been succeeded, especially in Speyer and Worms, by Jews who were murdered in cold blood. By the time of Mainz, crusader ferocity was at its peak, fueled by a cross-inspired righteousness, for, as the chronicler recounts it, they declared of their Jewish prey, "You are the children of those who killed our object of veneration, hanging him on a tree; and he himself had said: 'There will yet come a day when my children will come and avenge my blood.' We are his children and it is . . . therefore obligatory for us to avenge him since you are the ones who rebel and disbelieve him."[18]

The theology of anti-Jewish hatred could not be more clearly stated. Its meaning could not have been more firmly grasped than it was then by the Jews of Mainz. More than one thousand men, women, and children huddled in the courtyard of the archbishop's palace. They knew very well what had happened elsewhere in the preceding weeks, how bribes and flight had failed, finally, to protect even children. In Mainz, Jews had time to reflect on what was coming, and they knew that the only possible escape was through apostasy. Some few took that way out, but to most conversion to Christianity was more unthinkable than ever.

There is an ancient arcaded courtyard beside the cathedral that dates to within a century of 1096, and it is certainly at or near the place where the Jews awaited the crusaders. Not long ago, on a balmy summer morning, I sat on a stone bench in that courtyard, with the Gothic arches of the church on one side, the pointed leaded windows of the present chapter house on another. The ornate chapter house formerly served as the archbishop's palace, on or near the site of Ruthard's. A large granite crucifix dominated yet another side of the yard. A stone fountain, a vestige of a well, stood in the center of a grassy rectangle, altogether the size, say, of a basketball court. A pair of relatively young trees cast a filigree of shadows toward the fountain. The trees reminded me that everything I was looking at had been reconstructed from the rubble of World War II. A scattering of rose bushes was in bloom that morning, and the red shimmered against the gray stone, a contrast that emphasized the dark weight of a multilayered past.

Solomon bar Simson wrote:

> The hand of the Lord rested heavily on His people, and all the Gentiles assembled against the Jews in the courtyard to exterminate them . . . When the people of the Sacred Covenant saw that the Heavenly decree had been issued and that the enemy had defeated them and were entering the courtyard, they all cried out together — old and young, maidens and children, menservants and maids — to their Father in Heaven. . . . "There is no questioning the ways of the Holy One, blessed be He and blessed be His Name, Who has given us His Torah and has commanded us to allow ourselves to be killed and slain in witness to the Oneness of His Holy Name . . ."
>
> Then in a great voice they all cried out as one: "We need tarry no longer, for the enemy is already upon us. Let us hasten and offer ourselves as a sacrifice before God. Anyone possessing a knife should examine it to see that it is not defective, and let him then proceed to slaughter us in sanctification of the Unique and Eternal One, then slaying himself — either cutting his throat or thrusting the knife into his stomach."[19]

In April 1942, Nazis swarmed into the Warsaw Ghetto, hauling Jews to Umschlag Platz, where the boxcars waited. The yellow building behind the high fence at 60 Sienna Street was a children's hospital. One of its doctors was Adina Blandy Szwajger. She survived to tell what happened as the Germans began "taking the sick from the wards to the cattle trucks . . . I took morphine upstairs . . . and just as, during those two years of real work in the hospital, I had bent down over the little beds, so now I poured this last medicine down those tiny mouths . . . and downstairs there was screaming."[20]

Or, as Solomon bar Simson wrote of those in the archbishop's courtyard:

> The women girded their loins with strength and slew their own sons and daughters, and then themselves. Many men also mustered their strength and slaughtered their wives and children and infants. The most gentle and tender of women slaughtered the child of her delight. They all arose, man and woman alike, and slew one another . . . Let the ears hearing this

and its like be seared, for who has heard or seen the likes of it? Inquire and seek: was there ever such a mass sacrificial offering since the time of Adam? Did it ever occur that there were one thousand and one hundred offerings on one single day — all of them comparable to the sacrifice of Isaac, the son of Abraham? . . . For since the day on which the Second Temple was destroyed, their like had not arisen, nor shall there be their like again . . . Happy are they and happy is their lot, for all of them are destined for eternal life in the World-to-Come — and may my place be amongst them![21]

While Jews were responding, first, to Christian attacks, at a subliminal level it seems possible that Jews and Christians were responding, in some odd way, to the same currents. Crusaders thought they were ushering in the messianic age by forcing Jews to convert or die, while Jews believed that the long-awaited Messiah would come more quickly because of their willing act of self-sacrifice. In both cases, suffering and death had taken on new power as sources of salvation. The term for martyr in Hebrew means "to sanctify the Name" — to die with the words of the Shema on one's lips. For both Christians and Jews, dying for the faith was now sacred, although for the crusaders, killing for the faith was better.

The new cult of martyrdom swept through both communities. Nothing better illustrates the essential similarity than the figure of Isaac, Abraham's son, who had willingly been bound to the altar of sacrifice. But, as is so often true of Judaism and Christianity, the similarity serves only to underscore the difference. The entire history of conflict between Jews and Christians could be said to begin when Saint Paul declared that Jesus, as the sacrificed beloved son of the Father, had replaced Isaac.[22] It was the Jewish scholar Jon Levenson who drew my attention to Paul's foundational statement: "Christ redeemed us from the curse of the law, having become a curse for us — for it is written, 'Cursed be every one who hangs on a tree' — that in Christ Jesus the blessing of Abraham might come upon the Gentiles, that we might receive the promise of the Spirit through faith. To give a human example, brethren: no one annuls even a man's will, or adds to it, once it has been ratified. Now the promises were made to Abraham and to his offspring. It does not say, 'And to offsprings,' referring to many; but, referring to one, 'And to your offspring,' which is Christ."[23]

Jesus, like the classic younger sibling, usurped the place of Isaac, superseded him. And in Paul's reading, emphasizing that singular "offspring," Jesus superseded all of the people Israel. And how did he do this? By that tree, by means of the crucifixion. In Isaac's case, God allowed the father to spare the son — recall that, at the last moment, Abraham's blade came down not on Isaac but on a sacrificial lamb. But in Jesus' case, God himself was the father, and in a shocking reversal of the meaning of love, he showed no such restraint — Jesus became the sacrificial lamb. Because the Son of God died a brutal death at the Father's own hand — albeit by means of "the Jews" — the rest of humanity can be saved.

The Jews of Mainz saw themselves as Isaac too, but Jews then and now read differently the story of a father's readiness to kill his son. Christians read it through the lens of a resurrection faith, and see in Abraham's lifting of the knife a certainty that, even if Isaac dies, he will live. As Levenson points out, Søren Kierkegaard gave eloquent expression to this Christian reading, stating that Abraham "reasoned that God was able to raise even from the dead." That is why, for Kierkegaard, Abraham was the avatar of faith. For Jews, according to Levenson, Abraham's virtue is not faith — he does not foresee a resurrection of his son — but obedience.[24] The theological concepts of Jewish and Christian martyrdom are profoundly different, for Jews do not presume a triumph beyond the act of an offered death. Unlike an Easter-inspired Christian imagination, the Jewish religious imagination does not attempt to define how God keeps the promise of the covenant. Jewish obedience to God therefore assumes an existential confrontation with mortality that eludes a faith tied to resurrection. This difference in theological thinking is reflected in Jewish-Christian differences not only over Isaac but over Auschwitz.

Unlike Isaac, the Jews of Mainz were not spared at the last moment. A new cruelty had apparently now infected the God of Judaism. But to the same effect, for whatever the meaning of their acts of martyrdom to those who actually died, to the Hebrew chroniclers the deaths of all these faithful ones were redemptive. Yet still the thought differed from Christian ideas. It was not the definitive act of one man, in place of all others, that formed the core of this piety, as in Paul, but rather the willingly embraced suffering and death of the mass of Jews. This was salvation not *for* a people but *by* a people. This choice of death over apostasy by the whole of that prestigious Jewish community in the north of Europe was seen as a fulfillment of that single maiden's act in Trier, the "comely" girl who threw herself into the Moselle, and of the three hundred in Cologne who were the first to replay the tragedy of Masada. To die rather than convert — these were heroes treasured in Jewish memory. Their witness, which is the meaning of the Greek-derived word "martyr," changed the way Jews understood themselves in relation to the newly threatening dominant culture. After centuries of concerning themselves only minimally with Christianity, Jews now would define themselves by their defiance of it.

Robert Chazan calls this "the Jewish 'countercrusade' mentality," an unprecedented state of mind, conceived in Trier, it seems not too much to say, and born in Mainz. This mentality mirrored that of the crusaders, and consisted, Chazan says, in "the sense of cosmic confrontation, the conviction of the absolute validity of one's own religious heritage, the emphasis on profound self-sacrifice, the certainty of eternal reward for the commitment of the martyrs, the unshakable belief in the ultimate victory and vindication of one's own community and its religious vision."[25] And beginning here, the religious vision of Judaism would itself be a kind of bulwark, as the Christian vision redefined itself in this era as a kind of assault. This conflict, once joined, would shape the Jewish-Christian polarity for centuries.

An imagined Jerusalem would form the crux of the conflict for Christians as each side idealized the holy city in different ways. For both, the place becomes a sort of presence of God in the world. The Temple, too, resumes its centrality for both, but for Christians the *destroyed* Temple is the point. "Destroy this Temple," Jesus had dared, "and in three days I will raise it up."[26] The Resurrection presumes the destruction. Of course, medieval readers of this Scripture had no idea that it was written *after* the Roman destruction of the Temple in 70 C.E., and so they could only think of that destruction as proof of Christ's divinity.

For Jews, the *restored* Temple is the dream, and the way the dream will come true is by the faithful and resolute observance of God's Law. Now that observance is epitomized by the refusal to convert. More than ever, that requires a rejection of, in Solomon bar Simson's words, "a crucified scion who was despised, abominated, and held in contempt in his own generation, a bastard son conceived by a menstruating and wanton mother."[27] The more forcefully eleventh-century Jews reject Christianity, the more certainly Christians become convinced that these Jews are as guilty of the murder of Jesus as their ancestors were, for wasn't this rejection itself proof that they wanted Jesus dead? Jews weren't guilty of killing the Messiah only in the past, but in the present too.

It is a truism of the history of the West that the Crusades transformed the Catholic religion — we will see in the next section how that transformation reached even into the abstractions of theology — but the Crusades transformed Judaism as well. "The sudden ordeal of the summer of 1096, a thunderbolt out of a blue sky, had the effect of forging the power to resist," wrote the scholar Leon Poliakov. And resistance would be "characteristic henceforth of the European Jews."[28] The massacre of Jews in the Rhineland was an event of little or no significance in the Christian chronicles, although such sources confirm that it happened. But the Rhineland catastrophe would be a lasting marker in the mind of Judaism. Not only would martyrdom be regarded now as a central religious act among northern European Jews, but the symbolic martyrdom of a total withdrawal from the dominant culture — it is good, runs the Talmudic proverb, to ruin one's life in study — would shape Jewish asceticism and the Jewish aesthetic.[29]

Christian hate spawned Jewish hate, but with a difference. Christian hate would almost always, from now on, be armed. Since Christians controlled the armory, Jews had to find other ways to defend themselves and to express their antagonism. In the burgeoning new economy of capital, they did. It is in 1096 that we find the ultimate source of a sublimation of Jewish hatred toward the dominant culture in the potent symbol — and razor-edged weapon — of money. As Poliakov and others point out, money would be the medium of exchange between Jews and Christians, the coin of self-defense, but also of aggression, and, finally, the funding of a new level of Christian hatred.[30] We will return to the complex question of the association of Jews with moneylending below, but the thing to note here is that it is not purely accidental that, in relation to Christendom, finance became nearly the sole realm of Jewish power.

But the inner life of Judaism would always be far more concerned with something else: the wound God had permitted to be inflicted on God's people once again. That perplexity would fuel the renewal of Jewish theology, with the *via negativa* of Moses Maimonides (1135–1204) and the mystical innovation of Kabbalah, a spiritual system with which to survive in a hostile world, and which begins to take form here.[31] Such a development should not surprise, since Kabbalah nurtures the sense, in the scholar Moshe Idel's phrase, of "God's closeness to those of 'broken hearts.'"[32] Jews had to confront, as in the past, the harsh reality that the hope of the martyrs had been disappointed, for the catastrophe of 1096, like the turning of the millennium itself, had proved irrelevant to the longed-for coming of the Messiah, no matter how piously the faithful ones had offered themselves. But instead of giving in to dashed hopes, Jews did with that wound what they had learned to do long before, which was to wrap it in the consoling shawl of storytelling. And not just any storytelling. The memory of 1096 — events up and down the Rhine, but especially the self-binding of Mainz — would be kept alive in the liturgy, as holy acts of prayer. That memory influences how Jews see the cross, even today, as the sign of the crusaders. And why should there not be contention over this symbol?

For all these centuries, down through the millennium until the present, the memory of Mainz has been lifted up on the annual fast day of Tisha b'Av, the commemoration of the Temple's destruction. From that destruction, so much of this tragic story flows. On Tisha b'Av, parts of the Hebrew chronicles are recited as sacred text.

⇥ 27 ⇤

The Blood Libel

O N MY DESK before me are half a dozen 3 x 5 photographs I took on my recent journey, pictures of an old cemetery in Mainz. Here is what a recently published city guidebook says: "*Alt Israelitische Friedhof* (Old Jewish Cemetery) in Mombacher Strasse contains the only remaining medieval tombstones of Mainz — those in churchyards or cloisters have all disappeared. On this hill, below the city district *Am Judensand*, grave slabs remind us of famous rabbis, Jewish scholars, and poets, from ca. 1000 onwards — members of an important Jewish community in Mainz."

The old Jewish cemetery is on a street behind the train station, on a hill from which the Rhine can be seen. As a boy, I would have driven on this street, but I never noticed the tombstones on the grassy slope. Almost certainly they were neglected then. Even today, nothing on the spot announces what this cemetery is, or what it means here. In the Hebrew chronicle "Sefer Zekhirah," also known as "The Book of Remembrance of Rabbi Ephraim of Bonn," there is a description of an event, in Würzburg, equivalent to what happened in Mainz when more than a thousand died in the courtyard of the archbishop's palace. "On the following day," the chronicler writes, "the bishop ordered that all the slaughtered saints be collected on wagons — all the choice severed limbs: hips and shoulders, thumbs of hands and feet, sanctified with holy oil, together with everything else that remained of their bodies and limbs — and buried in his garden. Hezekiah, son of our Master Rabbi Eliakim, and Mistress Judith, his wife, purchased this Garden of Eden from the bishop and consecrated it as an eternal burial ground."[1]

It was at the Mainz version of such a Garden of Eden that I stood, my tourist pictures of which lay spread before me now. The gravestones still protruded from the grass. The inscriptions were worn too smooth to read, but the sharp-angled letters were Hebrew in any case, unknown to me. There was no entrance sign, no gate beyond a swinging wire door, nothing to identify the place as the sacred acreage it was. The hillside graveyard was enclosed by a mundane chain-link fence — mundane except for the coiled barbed wire that ran along the top, an eloquent implication. On the day of my visit, there were attached to the fence a pair of bright-colored posters, and it took no language skills to see what they advertised: "Mainz Volkspark . . . Circus."

Traffic roared by on Mombacher Strasse. No one gave the hillside or its stones a glance. I was the only visitor that afternoon. Modern-day Mainz makes nothing of its long-dead population of Jews — a sign, surely, of how few living Jews claim the city now. But the cemetery's very anonymity added to the marvel of its survival — and what it had survived! By the miracle of that association, the place of the dead seemed alive to me.

One of the stones I came upon was familiar, a striking jagged monolith growing out of the earth like a last tooth in the mouth of time. Its inscription was partly broken off, but a section remained intact, and made me sure it matched the tombstone I had seen in a photograph in a book of Hebrew chronicles, which placed it in Mainz. The photo caption offers this translation of the fragmented medieval Hebrew: ". . . daughter of Isaac (who was murdered) and drowned in sanctification of the oneness of God in the year 906 (1146) on the Friday, the fifth of Iyar (19 April). May she rest in Eden, the Garden."

That the daughter of Isaac died in 1146 indicates that she was a martyred victim of the Second Crusade, which was launched by a call of Pope Eugene III in March of that year. That the young woman died in April, within the month, suggests with what efficiency crusader violence returned to Mainz. But in the Second Crusade, something different happened, for the successors of the well-meaning but hapless Archbishop Ruthard were determined that the anti-Jewish horror of 1096 not repeat itself. Bishops of the Church, including the popes, had been uniformly appalled at the Rhineland violence unleashed in the First Crusade. That outbreak had prompted an ecclesiastical examination of conscience, which ultimately led to the promulgation of the landmark papal bull *Sicut Judaeis* by Callixtus II (1119–1124). An echo of Gregory the Great's intervention five hundred years before, this medieval defense of Jews would be reissued by more than twenty popes during the subsequent four centuries. Setting an iron precedent, Callixtus offered Jews "the shield of our protection. We decree," he said, "that no Christian shall use violence to force them [Jews] into baptism."² This prohibition was a strengthening of the bull of Pope Gregory, issued in recognition that, after the events of 1096, the tradition of papal protection of Jews had to be urgently reinforced, and it was.

When, twenty years after *Sicut Judaeis,* reports were heard of the first attacks on Jews — one of whose victims was the "daughter of Isaac" — a papal legate came to the Rhineland to speak forcefully against such attacks. He was Bernard of Clairvaux, known to us as Saint Bernard. A great monastic reformer and theologian, he was the main preacher of the Second Crusade — its equivalent to Peter the Hermit. Although an enthusiastic supporter of attacks on Muslims, Bernard published an important proclamation condemning attacks on Jews, and he traveled throughout the Rhineland denouncing all who would incite anti-Jewish violence.

Bernard was described by his biographer as a man "of graceful body, pleasant face, very polished manners, shrewd wit and persuasive eloquence."³ Clearly his preaching had an impact, as indicated even by at least one Hebrew chronicle, which portrays him — "a decent priest" — as a rare Christian hero. This is a passage from "Sefer Zekhirah":

> Upon hearing this [that crusaders were coming again], our hearts melted and our spirit failed us, because of the fury of the oppressor who intended to destroy us. We cried out to our God, saying: "Alas, Lord, God, not even fifty years, the number of years in a jubilee, have passed since our blood was shed in witness to the Oneness of Your Revered Name on the day of the great slaughter. Will You forsake us eternally, O Lord? Will You extend Your anger to all generations? Do not permit this suffering to recur."
>
> The Lord heard our outcry, and He turned to us and had mercy upon us. In His great mercy and grace, He sent a decent priest, one honored and respected by all the clergy in France, named Abbé Bernard of Clairvaux . . . [who] spoke raucously, as is their manner; and this is what he said to them: "It is good that you go against the Ishmaelites. But whosoever touches a Jew to take his life, is like one who harms Jesus himself. My disciple Radulf [the anti-Jewish Christian leader], who has spoken about annihilating the Jews, has spoken in error, for in the Book of Psalms it is written of them: 'Slay them not, lest my people forget.'"⁴

Bernard's interpretation of Psalm 59, verse 11, as the Lord's commandment not to kill Jews reproduces the use Augustine made of the same verse. Just as Augustine, with his tremendous authority, trumped the violent anti-Jewishness of Saint Ambrose, enabling Judaism to survive into the Middle Ages, so Bernard's intervention would prove crucial. "Were it not for the mercy of our Creator in sending the aforementioned Abbé and his later epistles," the chronicler says, "no remnant or vestige would have remained of Israel. Blessed the Redeemer and Savior, blessed be His Name!"[5]

And yet. We saw, in considering Augustine's defense of Jews, that it involved an ambivalence that would eventually prove tragic, and we asked whether unbridled theological derision could really coexist with respect for the lives of those held in such contempt. I have noted that more than twenty popes would reissue *Sicut Judaeis* over four centuries, a positive record of which the Vatican can rightly be proud. Yet why was it necessary for them to do so? Bishops, popes, and kings would more or less consistently oppose the anti-Jewish violence that would, from now on, more or less consistently mark the behavior of lower clergy, townspeople, and peasants. But were the people responding to the other clear message they heard from their leaders?

"The Jews are not to be persecuted, killed, or even put to flight," Bernard wrote in "Letter to the People of England." But in explaining why, again repeating Augustine, he plants the seed of the very violence he abhors. "The Jews are for us the living words of scripture, for they remind us always of what our Lord suffered. They are dispersed all over the world so that by expiating their crime they may be everywhere the living witnesses of our redemption. Hence the same Psalm [59] adds, 'only let thy power disperse them.' . . . If the Jews are utterly wiped out, what will become of our hope for their promised salvation, their eventual conversion?"[6]

This is a far cry from a defense of the rights of Jews, and it serves to confirm in the Christian every impulse of negation. "To label a group the most heinous of enemies and then to demand for them tolerance (albeit limited) and safety" — this is Robert Chazan's assessment of Bernard's intervention — "is probably to make demands that the human psyche, over the long run, must have difficulty in meeting."[7] Such ambivalence, in other words, has a fuse attached to it. This mode of thought survived well into the twentieth century. The primate of Poland, Cardinal Augustyn Hlond, issued a pastoral letter in 1936 that included a clear prohibition of anti-Jewish violence. "I warn against that moral stance, imported from abroad, that is basically and ruthlessly anti-Jewish. It is contrary to Catholic ethics. One may not hate anyone. It is forbidden to assault, beat up, maim or slander Jews. One should honor Jews as human beings and neighbors . . . Beware of those who are inciting anti-Jewish violence. They serve an evil cause."[8]

What more could a defender of Roman Catholic behavior during the Nazi era hope for? But alas — and true to Augustyn Hlond's namesake — this very statement, with its rejection of slander, begins with these words: "There will be the Jewish problem as long as the Jews remain. It is a fact that the Jews are fighting against the Catholic Church, persisting in free-thinking, and are the vanguard of godlessness, Bolshevism and subversion. It is a fact that the Jewish influence on morality is pernicious and that their publishing houses disseminate pornography. It is a fact that the Jews deceive, levy interest, and are pimps. It is a fact that the religious and ethical influence of the Jewish young people on Polish young people is a negative one."[9] I characterized this passage as "an attack on Jews" in print,[10] and was criticized for it by Catholics who wanted to emphasize Hlond's pro forma rejection of violence.[11] But what was the real effect of his pastoral letter? Does the negation of this tradition consistently outweigh the affirmation? The letter was read from the pulpits of Poland as part of an official Catholic endorsement of a Nazi boycott of Jewish businesses.

Saint Bernard is credited by Christians and Jews both with an intervention during the Second Crusade that prevented a recurrence of the savage anti-Jewish violence of the First Crusade. But his concurrent powerful negation of Judaism may have been related to the other momentous turn in the story that occurred just then. It is as if anti-Jewish crusader violence, once expressly forbidden, had been channeled into a slyer form. In 1144, within three years of Bernard's Rhineland preaching, and within even less time of his letter to Christians in England, Jews were accused of the "Blood Libel" for the first recorded time — and it happened in England.

The Blood Libel charges Jews with replaying the crucifixion of Jesus by murdering a Christian child, always a boy, and using his blood in perverse rituals that mock the Eucharist. This first accusation was made in Norwich when a tanner's apprentice, a boy named William, was found dead in a woods, and his death was blamed on Jews.[12] The false charge was brought during Holy Week, with the retaliatory murder of a Jew being carried out on Good Friday. The "informant" who brought the report of the murder was himself a Jew,[13] like Judas Iscariot, and like the Jew who led Helena to the hidden True Cross. The Blood Libel resembled a virus that then lodged itself in the Christian imagination. Jews were accused of crucifying boys in 1147 in Würzburg, near Mainz, and of the same or similar crimes in Gloucester in 1168, in Blois in 1171, in Saragossa in 1182[14] —

and again and again after that, all over Europe, even into the twentieth century. The ritual murder charge appears in "The Prioress's Tale" of Chaucer[15] and in James Joyce's *Ulysses*.[16] Numerous "victims" of the Jewish "murders," like Saint William of Norwich, would be revered as saints of the Church. The niche in which the virus thrived, of course — and here is what it means that the Crusades spawned it — was the unleashed cult of the cross.

A monk called Thomas of Monmouth wrote an account of that originating murder charge in *The Life and Passion of the Martyr St. William of Norwich*. Even the title, suggesting a Passion narrative, points to the first crucifixion, and Thomas's text makes the connection explicitly. The Jews declare their intention, as he interprets it, "to kill the Christian as we killed Christ." The monk relates the testimony of the informant Jew, an "apostate" named Theobald, who reported, "It was laid down by [the Jews] in ancient times that every year they must sacrifice a Christian in some part of the world to the Most High God in scorn and contempt of Christ . . . Wherefore the leaders and Rabbis of the Jews who dwell in Spain assemble together at Narbonne . . . and they cast lots for all the countries which the Jews inhabit . . . and the place whose lot is drawn has to fulfill the duty imposed by authority."[17] The scholar Marc Saperstein comments, "Thus the earliest recorded account of Jewish ritual murder . . . is embellished with the suggestion of an international Jewish conspiracy, sanctioned by ancient Jewish texts, which Christians ought to fear." Saperstein adds, "A chilling conclusion is placed by the author in the mouths of the 'populace,' which cried out 'with one voice that all the Jews ought to be utterly destroyed as constant enemies of the Christian name and the Christian religion.' Such a sentence indicates that a 'Final Solution' was at least conceivable in the Middle Ages."[18]

As with crusader violence against Jews in the Rhineland, the Blood Libel was promptly and resoundingly rejected by the hierarchy of the Catholic Church. (In our own time, a twist was given this tradition when, in 1999, a Vatican official denounced Jewish questions about Pius XII's "silence" during the Holocaust as themselves amounting to a "Blood Libel.")[19] Pope Gregory X's "Letter on Jews" (1272) was typical of numerous papal repudiations: "Most falsely do these Christians claim that the Jews have secretly and furtively carried away these children and killed them . . . We order that Jews seized under such a silly pretext be freed."[20] The silliness, in the pope's word, of the Blood Libel is emphasized by those who distinguish between the "normal" Christian hatred of Jews, which originates in the Gospel portrait of Jews as killers of Christ, and abnormal hatred, which features "chimerical belief or fantasy," in Gavin Langmuir's phrase.[21] Langmuir is a historian of antisemitism. He dates its beginning, as opposed to normal anti-Judaism, to the Blood Libel of Norwich: It is normal Christian anti-Jewishness to say that Jews murdered Jesus, and therefore to degrade them for it; it is abnormal antisemitism to say that Jews slay Christian babies, and therefore to kill them for it. There is a racial element in modern antisemitism, but we will come to that later. For now, the question is tied to the distinction between the "realities" of mainstream Christian tradition and the paranoid delusions of disapproved eccentrics. Antisemitism, for reasons having nothing to do with the real deeds or beliefs of actual Jewish persons, is usually regarded solely as a manifestation of the latter.

Most post-Holocaust Catholics honor the wall of separation between normal anti-Judaism, which traces itself, in Robert Chazan's summary, "back into the core disagreement between Christians and Jews," and abnormal antisemitism, which Chazan defines as "embellishments that are extremely harsh, that lack grounding in fundamental Christian texts and teachings, and that never gained the respectability of widespread ecclesiastical approbation."[22] Many Catholic Scripture scholars insist, for example, that the Passion narratives of the Gospels, while anti-Jewish in varying degrees, are not in any sense antisemitic — not, that is, based on "chimerical fantasies" or libels of who Jews are and what they do. But this entire investigation follows from the conclusion that the Gospel accounts of who "the Jews" were and what they did, as understood by later generations, may themselves be said to be chimerical. One might say, indeed, that the first Blood Libel appears in the foundational Christian story of the death of Jesus. Thus the Church-absolving wall between anti-Judaism and antisemitism teeters at its base, just as the wall moves unsteadily between the sadism of Christian mobs and the nonviolent but contemptuous teaching of the Church establishment.

This problem of mob violence incited by elite denigration is restricted neither to the Middle Ages nor to anti-Judaism. In 1998, a young gay man, Matthew Shepard, was murdered in Wyoming. His killers had tortured him and, in effect, crucified him by hanging him on a fence. They smashed his skull. This incident occurred amid heated anti-gay campaigns, some conducted by Christian groups. The question poses itself: What is the relationship between violent attacks on homosexuals and open contempt for homosexuals expressed by respectable people and organizations? One answer was offered by the *New York Times* columnist Frank Rich: "It's a story as old as history. Once any group is successfully scapegoated as a subhuman threat to 'normal' values by a propaganda machine, emboldened thugs take over."[23]

That the medieval wall of separation between anti-Jewish thugs and the Jew-protecting hierarchy may not have been as stout as claimed is indicated by the fact that popes and bishops, beginning in 1096 and continuing thereafter, even while forbidding forced baptisms of Jews, held that such baptisms, once carried out, were nevertheless valid. These baptisms, it was said, even if conducted under the threat of death, were recognized by God. The souls of those baptized, whether they had assented or not, were indelibly marked with the seal of Christ.

Not all agreed. In the Crusades period, this was a point of dispute between emperor and pope, with the former insisting that Jews were free to return to their own religion, an impulse one monk derided as akin to a dog returning to his vomit.[24] Popes held against the emperor simply that converted Jews were obliged to live as Christians, no matter the circumstances of their conversion. The pope was able to challenge the authority of the emperor in this matter because, even most of a century after the climactic, snow-bound encounter at Canossa between Henry IV and Pope Gregory VII, when the emperor yielded to the pope, if only temporarily, the balance of power between empire and papacy was still shifting. For example, Frederick I (1123–1190), also known as Frederick Barbarossa, was the avatar of the Germanic emperor. He was the first to emphatically claim the title Holy Roman Emperor, and he styled himself after Constantine. But when he sent his armies into the territory of the pope, he cut a breach between Italy and the rest of the empire that would never heal. What had begun to happen under Constantine between East and West began to happen under Frederick Barbarossa between North and South. The destiny of northern Europe would unfold independently from that of southern Europe. Among other outcomes, this development assured the relative permanence of the pope's political power, even if concentrated in a regional base. As earlier popes had fought off the East, now popes would fight off the North, and so what led to the Catholic-Orthodox split in 1054 would lead to the Reformation in 1517.

The political contest between empire and papacy continued to involve competing religious claims. The appointment of bishops and abbots remained at issue, but even matters of spirituality could be disputed. The emperor could reject forced baptisms of Jews out of a desire to win

Jewish support in local struggles with the rising burgher class, but the emperor also could grasp the fundamental maliciousness of conversions won through threat of death. The pope, on the other hand, whatever he thought of forced baptisms of Jews — and we know that popes consistently forbade them — felt obliged, no doubt, to uphold the principle that sacraments that fulfilled the outward form remained valid, even if illicit. This fundamental tenet of Catholic sacramental theology, which sees the pitfall of a puritanism that links validity with interior purity of motive, would be tragically tied to the question of forced or ambiguous baptism of Jews even into the twentieth century.

Here is the perfect emblem of Church ambivalence at the highest level: Forced baptisms of Jews were forbidden, yet they were nonetheless, after the fact, canonically sanctioned. In this way, an impression in the mind of the "Christian mob" that God wills such baptisms seems not altogether surprising, especially in periods when an End Time psychology took over, for then the conversion of Jews, as a prelude to the return of the Messiah, could seem an urgent matter of apocalyptic fulfillment.

Nor is the appearance of the Blood Libel surprising. The slander that Jews were in the business of crucifying boys eloquently dramatized what had evolved into a core, if implicit, theological principle: People who once so fatefully murdered Jesus are still inclined to murder him. There is a line of causality, in other words, between the Gospel indictment of "the Jews" for the murder of Jesus — as if the Romans were bystanders, as if Jesus were not a Jew — and the medieval indictment of Jews for the murder of Jesus in the person of a Christian boy. In the twelfth century and after, Jews were held guilty not for the crime of their ancient ancestors but for their own present crime of a continuing rejection of Jesus. Not incidentally, that rejection had been made indelibly clear to twelfth-century Christians by the choices Rhineland Jews had made in such numbers during the spring and summer of 1096 — choices to die, or even to kill themselves and their children, rather than to convert. If they would kill their own children, Christians reasoned, what would they not do to ours? Jews were still saying no to Jesus in the most passionate and at times violent ways imaginable. What else could such vital recalcitrance mean than that twelfth-century Jews affirmed in their hearts what first-century Jews had done: This is so even if it occurred a thousand years before — or rather, *because* it occurred a thousand years before. Affirming such a past meant Jews in the present were still prepared to murder Jesus. Logic was with the mob.

It was a small step in the Christian imagination from that newly sharpened sense of permanent Jewish culpability to a conviction that Jews were prepared to murder not only a surrogate Jesus, but "us." Jews were believed ready to poison wells, if they could, aiming to kill not just Christ, but Christians. Twenty-seven Jews were executed for well poisoning in Bohemia in 1163. The charges were repeated in Breslau in 1226, and in Vienna in 1267. In 1321, Jews were accused of a conspiracy to poison every well in France. Many Jews were burned at the stake as a result, and the Jews of Paris were expelled from the city. When the plagues struck, it was "logical" to think that the source of infection was poisoned wells. The 1348 Black Plague would result in anti-Jewish violence that far surpassed the First Crusade, with perhaps three hundred Jewish communities, including those in Mainz, Trier, and Cologne, being simply wiped out.[25] The anti-Jewish mobs may have waved the banner of an insane rhetoric, making it seem they were irrationally avenging a long-dead Jesus or defending kidnapped children, but their very ferocity and the longevity of the Libel show that they were defending *themselves*.

From what? Not from villains conjured by some chimerical fantasy based on nothing real, but from the threat logically deduced from a solemn doctrine of the Church, one dramatically reiterated — indeed, this liturgy was key to the development of Western drama — in every Holy Week of every year. Namely, that Jews are murderers. In a dozen ways, as we have seen, the cross itself had been conscripted into this campaign, which was as much self-defense as revenge. And now every cross in Western Christendom would become an infallible promulgation of that same doctrine. The crusaders who stormed the archbishop's palace in Mainz, and the urban mobs who lynched Jews, threw them in rivers, and burned them at stakes, were being rushed along in currents of meaning and belief that ran below the surface on which official ecclesiastical repudiations stood. These currents swept through theology and philosophy, through Church councils and papal convocations, erupting finally in an innovative Christian self-understanding at the same moment as the First Crusade. If the face of the man wearing the cross on his breast was cruel, so was the face of God, as defined then by the greatest Church council yet convened and as described by the greatest theologian of the age. This God was defined as a Father who revealed himself most fully by imposing the cross not only on his Son, but on all creation.

28

Anselm: Why God Became Man

T HE CATHOLIC CHURCH into which I was born, and with which
I fell in love, came into existence in these years — the period
of ferment and fervor that Church history calls the "twelfth-
century renaissance." As the Crusades sought to impose a
universalized Christian faith on those outside Christendom, so a simultaneous reform movement sought to impose a central control over doctrine, liturgy, piety, and politics within Western Christendom — and it
worked. The feeling that Christians were now able to have about themselves — by belonging to a cohesive and sacred community, each one
could draw close to God — was a feeling I knew well as a child. Kneeling
beside my mother before the crucifix in St. Mary's Church fixed in me a
certain kind of piety, and then my attachment to the monks at my prep
school, St. Anselm's, rescued me from the fear that such piety could belong only to women.

I didn't know it then, but what appealed to me about the monastic life
— the movement of the daily office through the marks of time, the order
of authority, the rationality of faith, the simplicity embodied in monk's
bread, the self-denial of the three vows, the veneration of beauty, whether
in chant or carved choir stalls — the very sum and substance of what I
loved was a product of the twelfth-century Cluniac and Cistercian re-
forms. From my weekly bouts in the confessional, I knew that the Catholic
Church, for all its moralizing obsessiveness, was trustworthy because its
laws were rigorously defined and mercilessly enforced. Now I know that
there were more Church legal pronouncements in the twelfth century
than in all prior centuries put together.[1] This was a humane program of
legislation. Not each proscription was humane, but in rescuing Europe
from the lawlessness of brigands and warrior barons, and the Church
from the corruptions of simony, nepotism, and greed, the overall program

laid the groundwork of Western civilization. Unfortunately, this success would atrophy in subsequent centuries around the laws themselves, and the Roman Catholic Church would settle into that same moralizing obsessiveness, which in truth could not be trusted.

The *Codex Iuris Canonici* in force in the Catholic Church today was spawned, embryonically, in the twelfth century.[2] Canon law became a kind of juridical equivalent to the Gothic cathedral. The Gothic cathedral, of course, is an architectural form embedded in the worldview and technical limitations of the long-ago, yet the Catholic imagination clings to its soaring arches and shadowed vaults as the stone ideal of sacred space. Just so, the Catholic Church can never quite shake its attachment to law as the fulcrum of faith. When the age of anarchy passed, and with it the need for an overemphasized code of law, that attachment calcified in a regulation of minutiae. The spirit of medieval legalism still blows, a chill wind in the Church, yet it still serves a purpose. The *Codex Iuris Canonici* enshrines, above all, the divinely ordained pyramid of the hierarchy, with the pope as supreme head not only of the Church but, implicitly now, of creation.

The exquisitely balanced tension of this Gothic social system sustained a vitality that even an American boy of the 1950s could happily respond to. Yet because that system depended on the tensions of balance, it could be upset. That was why every non-Catholic posed a threat, which even that American boy could sense. Why else was he subtly encouraged to stay among his own? For confirmation of the timeless truth of Catholicism, he needed go no further than his parish church, with its pamphlet racks in the vestibule stuffed with copies of *The Pope Speaks*. The periodical always featured the same cover: the stern, bespectacled face of Pius XII, a canon lawyer who had served as the major-domo of the 1917 promulgation of canon law, about which we will see more later. The merest glimpse of the pope's hawk-like profile always put the boy in his place. But the point was, in this threatening, doom-laden cosmos of ours — the Dark Ages were only yesterday — we exiled children of Adam and Eve were lucky to have a place.

My own childhood experience of the consolations of an all-encompassing religious community allows me to understand that what jolted Christendom awake in the twelfth century was an electric impulse fueled by basic human need. As we have seen, this was not the first time such a need had made itself felt. The same unifying impulse had motivated Constantine, but this time there was a difference in the way an overarching authority expressed itself. Constantine had demonstrated his authority over bishops by convening the Council of Nicaea. The empire was unified under Constantine as supreme head, with the leaders of the Church subservient to him.

But things changed. The power struggle between secular and ecclesiastical rulers, beginning with Canossa in 1076 and continuing with Frederick Barbarossa's invasions of Italy a century later, would be a permanent feature of European life, but now a definitive tilt in the pope's favor occurred. In 1184 Frederick convened the so-called Great Diet of Mainz, wanting to duplicate Constantine's achievement at Nicaea. At the cathedral in the city on the Rhine, he brought together, as legend has it, seventy princes and seventy thousand knights and most of the bishops of Germany. The climax of the pageant was the dubbing as knights of his two sons, prior to their taking up the cross on the Third Crusade, which Frederick himself would lead. It was beginning now that Mainz would be known as "the Second Rome," but this accumulation of power in the heart of Germany in fact allowed the pope to consolidate his power in Rome itself, absolutely focused in the papacy. Princes and emperors embarked on the Crusades, but these great expeditions, by empowering princes at the heads of armed contingents and by quickening a mass devotion to the cause of the Church as the popes defined it, undercut emperors and boosted popes, leaving a legacy in Germany of a weak monarchy. Thus the Crusades, launched by Urban II twenty years after Canossa, had been an opening salvo in a campaign for papal power that would culminate in the claims of Innocent III (1198–1216).

As Frederick Barbarossa had emphasized his title as Holy Roman Emperor, Innocent III embraced the title *Vicarius Christi,* Vicar of Christ, marking a shift away from the traditional and, by comparison, modest emphasis on the pope as successor to Peter.[3] Innocent's was an unprecedented claim to a place "between God and man, lower than God but higher than man, who judges all and is judged by no one."[4] Instead of standing in the Shoes of the Fisherman, the pope now was seen as standing at the right hand of God; the title of Vicar was an emblem of a new claim to absolute spiritual authority. Innocent's genius was in understanding that a putative renunciation of political and material power in the name of moral and spiritual power was the surest route to political and material power. No longer would popes vie with emperors as competing peers, with disputes limited, for the most part, to the lines of authority over bishops, abbots, and Church property. Now the pope would possess the universal authority proper to Christ's deputy. The pope's sway extended to the afterlife, a claim that, in a doom-shadowed era, decisively established his power over this life. Thus Innocent would order the king of France to be reunited with his estranged wife, and would be obeyed (1198). By laying a sanction on all of England (1208), he would require its king, John, to accept him as England's feudal lord. Acting as such, he would declare null and void the upstart barons' Magna Carta (1215), which nevertheless survived the pope's dismissal to become the foundation of constitutional government. And as for the emperor, Innocent asserted the right of assent over imperial elections, and accordingly chose one claimant over the other.

Like popes before him, Innocent III launched Crusades, but his were different. He wanted to assert his own power within Europe, as much as Christendom's over Iberia, Asia Minor, and the Levant. Instead of merely targeting "infidels," Innocent's crusaders attacked Christian heretics in the south of France. "Catholics who take the Cross," Innocent's council declared, "and gird themselves up for the expulsion of heretics shall enjoy the same indulgence ... as those who go to the aid of the Holy Land."⁵ The Holy Land still beckoned, of course, and under Innocent's aegis, the Fourth Crusade set out for Jerusalem in 1202. But this Crusade vented its fury on Christian — but schismatic — Constantinople, which fell to the Latin knights after a savage sacking. Innocent denounced the pillaging of Constantinople, but the armies he'd launched were still at the service of his vision. The Crusades had thus become a means of imposing doctrinal and political unity within the Church, instead of outside it. When Innocent appointed a Latin patriarch to rule in the East, he thought he'd ended the Christian schism, but in fact he and his crusaders guaranteed that Eastern hatred of the West would be permanent.

As there were early, familial shadows cast over Constantine's claim to authority, so too with Innocent, born Lothair of Segni. His noble Roman family, tinged with German blood, would produce eight popes. He was himself the nephew of a pope, who made him a cardinal even though he was not a priest. A subsequent pope shunted him aside, but such were the quick turns in Vatican politics that, when that pope died, Lothair was elected to succeed him. He was only thirty-seven years old, and before being consecrated as pope, he had to be ordained to the priesthood.⁶

As Constantine had sought to establish unity and control by means of the Council of Nicaea, Innocent, after laying the groundwork for a decade and a half, sought the same absolute power for himself at the Fourth

Lateran Council (1215). It would be simplistic to define these similar ambitions as driven only by a thirst for self-aggrandizement. The emperor and the pope can each be seen to have been attempting a humane response to chaotic and violent epochs. To draw order out of chaos can be the ruler's highest moral mandate, and no doubt Innocent conceived of his purpose in such terms, as Constantine did. That the new order in each instance involved, for some, a new chaos was no more the pope's concern than it had been the emperor's. Innocent's council was aptly named, since the Lateran Basilica in Rome was thought to have originated as Constantine's palace.[7]

The Fourth Lateran Council, sometimes called the Great Council, was the most important ecumenical gathering held to that point, with more than four hundred bishops and archbishops, eight hundred priors and abbots, and the ambassadors of Europe's kingdoms and cities. The Byzantine Church was unrepresented, but otherwise it seemed that the whole continent had come together in unity under the sway of the pope.[8] Innocent established with final clarity the papacy's claim to monarchical authority. The pope was the feudal overlord of the world — *societas christiana*[9] — and at last Europe's emperors, kings, and barons by and large agreed.

The legislation passed by the Fourth Lateran Council put in place the main elements of the Catholic culture as we know it. The seven sacraments, from baptism to extreme unction, were defined. The Eucharistic doctrine of transubstantiation, equating the communion bread with the real presence of Christ, was promulgated. The seal of confession, binding priests to secrecy, was imposed. Clerical discipline was established. An elaborated creed, taking off from the Nicene, was articulated. A program of spiritual uniformity was adopted to match the political uniformity of an absolute monarchy. "There is indeed one universal church of the faithful," the council's opening canon reads, "outside of which nobody at all is saved, in which Jesus Christ is both priest and sacrifice." The perfect symbol of this unity is the Eucharist, perfectly controlled. "No one can effect this sacrament except a priest who has been properly ordained according to the Church's keys, which Jesus Christ himself gave to the apostles and their successors."[10]

It was Innocent's council that first promulgated crucial Church resolutions designed to isolate, restrict, and denigrate Jews. What had until then been merely local indignities were now made universal. For example: "Jews and Saracens of both sexes in every Christian province, and at all times, shall be marked off in the eyes of the public from other people through the character of their dress."[11] We can recognize here the precursor of the infamous yellow badge.

The importance of the Fourth Lateran Council for the future of Jewish-Catholic relations cannot be exaggerated. "It was not the riots in connection with the First Crusade in 1096," Hans Küng writes, "but this council which fundamentally changed the situation of the Jews, both legally and theologically. Because the Jews were 'servants of sin,' it was concluded that they should now be the servants of Christian princes. So now, in Constitution 68 of the council, for the first time a special form of dress was directly prescribed for Jews, which would isolate them; they were banned from taking public office, forbidden to go out during Holy Week, and had a compulsory tax imposed on them, to be paid to the local Christian clergy."[12] It is striking that this unprecedented systematizing of anti-Jewish practices should have been achieved at the moment of the Church's arrival at an unprecedented universal authority. One of the questions lurking beneath the surface of this inquiry is whether the universalist absolutism of Roman Catholic claims is causally related to the unleashing of Catholic anti-Judaism. The more "total" the Church's claim on the soul of the world, the more dramatically Jews stand out as "the original and quintessential dissenters" from that claim, as I have called them elsewhere.[13]

As with the absolutizing program of Constantine, only more so, the Church's medieval movement, through Crusade and reform, to impose a radical new unity on the world, under the pope, had direct, negative, epoch-shaping consequences for Jews. And, as always, the emblem of that movement was the cross. As we saw, it was at the symbolic center of Constantine's culture-creating achievement, not only his vision at Milvian Bridge in 312, but his construction of a myth of that vision at Nicaea in 325 — followed by both the unifying Nicene Creed, which put the crucifixion at the core of faith, and Helena's "discovery" of the True Cross in Jerusalem. In Ambrose's later telling, that event named the Jews as the Church's last problem.

And something like all of this happened again in the age of the Crusades, the next great age of the cross. We have seen it: Peter the Hermit's vision in the Holy Sepulcher; Urban II's mandate to rescue the place of the cross; the cross as the martial standard and as indictment of the Jews. As the politics and theology of the cross mirrored each other in Constantine's era, so now. As Constantine's ecclesiastical partners were the fathers of Nicaea, so the popes would have the fathers of Fourth Lateran. The Constantinian project had Ambrose of Milan, the greatest theologian of his age; the Crusades had the equivalent in Anselm of Canterbury — the patron, as it happens, of my own adolescent absolutism.

Saint Anselm (1033–1109), a monk and bishop, a philosopher and theologian, ranks with the greatest figures in the history of the Church. It was he who developed a true theology of the cross, one that is still preached today. Anselm provided the ex post facto rationale for the cross-centered creedal affirmation of Nicaea. He supplied a justification that the ubiquitous cults of crucifix veneration and relic worship had heretofore lacked.

St. Anselm's School in Washington, D.C.: I can still picture the miter-headed portrait of the bishop-monk hanging in the terrazzo lobby. I passed it every day, and came to think of Anselm as someone I knew. The monks of my school were attached to a congregation of English Benedictines. They were Anglophilic to the core, and loved Anselm for having been Britain's primate. In fact, he was an "Anselmo," born to a noble family in Piedmont. He entered the Benedictines at an early age and became abbot of one of the great monasteries, Bec in Normandy, still not yet in England.

Anselm's theological writings, painstakingly copied in the scriptoria of monasteries all over Europe, made him one of the most influential thinkers of the age. It was Anselm who boldly offered proofs of God's existence, including the ontological proof that is still debated: "God is that greater than which cannot be conceived."[14] Therefore God must exist, because the idea of God is not greater than the reality of such a being. As the ecclesiastical legislation of the twelfth century began Europe's rescue from the anarchy of brigands, so Anselm's insistence on the primacy of human reasoning began a recovery from the superstition of an illiterate people not long removed from barbarism. Theology, he said, is faith in search of reason. I believe, he said, in order that I may understand.[15] Anselm is called the father of scholasticism, but he is better remembered as father of a faith that owes no apology to intellect.[16]

Anselm was an intimate friend of Urban II, who called the First Crusade. Before becoming pope, Urban had been a reforming monk. For a time they lived close to each other.[17] At the moment Urban was calling for the Crusade, at Clermont in the autumn of 1095 — God wills it! — Anselm was beginning work on a major treatise. Published in 1098, *Cur Deus Homo* (*Why God Became Man*) is a first, systematic attempt to explain the doctrine of the Incarnation in logical fashion. His purpose, as he says in the preface, was to answer "the objections of unbelievers who reject the Christian faith because they think it contrary to reason."[18] The unbeliever to whom Anselm addresses his argument is not the "infidel" against whom Urban has just launched his Crusade, but the Jew. Anselm's dialogue partner in *Cur Deus Homo* is a fellow monk named Boso, a stand-in not for Muslims or pagans, but for those who alone had considered Christian claims and rejected them, the Jews.[19] Prior to Anselm, the Christian case was always made by appeals to Scripture, which Jews so infuriatingly rejected. Now the appeal is to be made — this begins a new era between Christians and Jews — solely on the basis of reason. Anselm reshapes the patristic and Augustinian understandings of Christian revelation, reducing them to an apologetic purpose.

"For we have proposed to inquire by reason alone whether His advent was necessary for the salvation of men . . . ," Anselm tells Boso. "Let us proceed, therefore, by pure reason . . . [along a course] in which faith in Christ is put to a rational test."[20] The train of thought runs like this: After the Fall of Adam, human beings were in a state of sin, alienation, and misery. If God is all-powerful, and if God, in his mercy, wanted to forgive humanity, why didn't he do so by means of the sacred *Fiat!* with which he had created the world in the first place? This is the most basic question that can be put to faith. Anselm's answer is not an ontological argument but a more compelling social one — an argument, that is, from the structure of society as he and his readers would have experienced it. For our purposes, the point is this: God became a man expressly to die on the cross.

The epoch-shaping image of Henry IV prostrate in the snow before Pope Gregory VII, the event that took place only a few years before, gives Anselm his motif, for he applies the assumptions of a feudal power struggle to relations between God and human beings. His logic is drawn from the rigid feudal order, which squares with Anselm's accepted notion of creation as a hierarchy of finite goods under the infinite good of God. When Adam was expelled from Paradise, humans were banished from that hierarchy. The human problem then became not merely how to make amends to a being whose place in the order of existence is superior, but how to do so from outside that very order. Thus the ontological argument has been subsumed by the social one: The problem of salvation is defined as a matter of rendering satisfaction and restoring honor to a Supreme Being who has been insulted by an inferior being. According to feudal norms, only a person of equal rank within the hierarchy could make amends to the one offended. The analogy is ruthlessly applied: If the one offended was divine, then only a divine being could redress the offense.

Or, as *Cur Deus Homo* has it: "If, therefore, as is certain, it is needful that that heavenly state be perfected from among men, and this cannot be unless the above-mentioned satisfaction be made, which no one *can* make except God, and no one *ought* to make except man, it is necessary that one who is God-man should make it."[21] The first conclusion: Jesus, as the man come to reverse the Fall of Adam, *had* to be divine. Thus God *had* to become a man. The Incarnation is necessary. The beauty of this logic prompts the credulous Boso to exclaim, "Blessed be God! Already we have discovered one great truth on the subject of our inquiry. Go on, therefore."[22] And Anselm does. But he moves immediately to a new problem, for God's becoming man, in this scheme, is not enough.

The Incarnation, as realized in the human life of Jesus of Nazareth, involved many "saving events," as the tradition calls them. Jaroslav Pelikan reports that, for many centuries, the "seven seals" of the Apocalypse were taken to refer to the conception, birth, life, crucifixion, death, burial, and resurrection of Jesus.[23] Any one of these, or the whole course, could have been offered as satisfaction to the offended divinity as a way, in Anselm's word, of "atoning" for the sin of Adam. Since Jesus himself was divine, that should have been enough — a life well lived to compensate for a life squandered. But this would not work in a schema drawn from a rigid code of feudal honor. "The man who does not render to God this honor, which is His due, takes away from God what is His own, and dishonors God, and this is to sin."[24] The offense God took at Adam's freely chosen act of disobedience can be removed only by a contrary act of obedience, and it too must be freely chosen — which leads, in this logic, directly to the isolated moment of death. Suffering and death are the wages of sin, the result of Adam's act. But Jesus, though human, is free of sin. So he is the only human being who came into the world with no need to suffer and die. Every other "event" of his existence was normal to his dual nature, but death was not. Jesus was born exempt from the sentence of mortality, which meant that only by a supreme act of his own freedom could he die. Such an act of freedom was exactly what the feudal honor code required.

If for righteousness' sake He permitted Himself to be slain, did He not give His life for the honor of God? . . . Do you not see that when He endured with uncomplaining patience injuries, and insults, and the death of the cross with robbers, brought on Him (as we said above) on account of the righteousness which He kept with perfect obedience, He gave men an example . . . ? No man beside Him ever gave to God, by dying, what he would not at some time have necessarily lost, or paid what he did not owe. But this Man freely offered to the Father what it would never have been necessary for Him to lose, and paid for sinners what He did not owe for Himself.[25]

We are in a rigidly juridical world here, with God as an aggrieved feudal lord, carefully weighing out recompense on a finely calibrated scale. This was very much the world of Anselm, who was forced to play out in his own life, both in Urban II's behalf and in his own as archbishop of Canterbury, a version of the feudal dispute that set Pope Gregory VII against Emperor Henry IV. Honor, satisfaction, reconciliation, atonement — these notions were all forged in the crucible of politics before being so rationally applied to religion. The furies of the long-simmering "investiture controversy," which at bottom was nothing but a feudal power struggle, infuse this theology with an energy that can be felt even in our era of church-state separation. Anselm wrote *Cur Deus Homo,* in part, after having been forced into exile by the English king, William Rufus, over a question of offended honor. Anselm, as the feudal lord claiming primacy, would not have his own honor satisfied until William died and his successor, Henry I, agreed to pay the archbishop homage. The king, that is, had to disavow the royal claim to the right of investiture — the right to make appointments to monastic and ecclesiastical offices. Thus satisfied, Anselm could duly acknowledge the king's temporal authority. This feudal pattern of offense and atonement between king and archbishop would repeat itself intermittently. Only a few decades later, one of Anselm's successors, Thomas à Becket (1118–1170), would play it out, mortally, with Henry II.

God was the ultimate feudal lord, and therefore, in Anselm's schema, God's preeminent virtue was justice. But even Boso, toward the end of *Cur Deus Homo,* has to ask about mercy. Even in a brutal feudal world, an "economy of salvation" that requires as a kind of debt payment the savage death, however freely chosen, of a beloved son raises a troubling question about the nature of this God. As Hans Küng points out, fathers of the Church like Origen (c. 185–254) had similarly described the death of Jesus as a kind of ransoming,[26] but in their schema, the one being paid off was Satan. The brutality fit. But in Anselm, the brutality only jars. How can God be doing this?

"The mercy of God . . . ," Anselm asserts in reply, "is so great, and in such harmony with His justice, that it cannot be imagined to be either greater or more just. For what greater mercy can be conceived than when God the Father says to the sinner condemned to eternal torments, and having no power to redeem himself from them, 'Accept My only-begotten Son, and give Him for thyself'; and when the Son Himself says, 'Take Me and redeem thyself'? For it is as though They were saying these very words, when They summon us and draw us to the Christian faith."[27]

Anselm's motive, as we saw, is to draw to the Christian faith the unbeliever, which in his context always means the Jew. But could Jews of that or any age respond to such an image? "That God needs a human sacrifice to reconcile his own creation with himself," the Jewish writer Pinchas Lapide protests, "that he, the ruler of the world, cannot justify anyone without a blood sacrifice, is as incomprehensible to Jews as it is contrary to the Bible."[28] Perhaps Lapide is thinking here of Isaac, whom God spares from such a fate. Yet versions of the idea of a God-required blood sacrifice had entered the religious imagination of Christians beginning, perhaps, with Saint Paul, but mainly as a way of understanding the crucifixion as something other than a cosmic disaster. Anselm succeeded in bringing the notion of Christ's death as atonement to its fullest expression. The appeal among Christian believers of this cross-centered theology, if not among Jews and Muslims, was immediate and widespread. It explained the dominant religious experience that Christians were undergoing in that millennial era, for an atoning cross lent meaning to what life required in a brutish time. But the cross could be misunderstood. Had Jesus come to promote suffering or to oppose it? Could the cult of the crucifix and related phenomena, like the flagellant movements, be a surrender to the very powers of sickness, suffering, and death that Jesus had intended to overcome? Could God, in other words, be portrayed as a bit too invested in the misery, not only of the Son, but of the rest of us? Is there a curl of sadism in this economy of salvation?

Anselm's theology of atonement took root in the Catholic mind, and it remains a dominant paradigm. I embraced it myself as a young man without understanding why it reinforced my inbred fear instead of freeing me from it. Salvation? Judgment? Where is the Good News in such appeasement? This paradoxical and tragic idea of God's mercy, bound to the cross, is profoundly violent. Whatever the feudal origins of the system, however tenderly meant its composition, and however glibly we invoke the word "love," the God of such atonement can appear, in a certain light, to be a monster. It was inconceivable that I, bred to the consoling devotions of Irish Catholicism, should see the God of Jesus Christ in such a way. And it has become equally inconceivable to me, weaned from those devotions and informed by this history, that a Jew of Anselm's era could see this God in any other way.

Now that the death of Jesus had become fully rationalized as the central saving event, or even as the *sole* saving event, the place of Jews became all the more precarious. This was so despite the logical flaw adhering in a scheme that emphasizes both that Jesus' death was freely chosen by Jesus himself and that Jesus' death was caused by the Jews. When Jews are blamed for the event that makes possible Christian salvation, a new, more pernicious layer is added to the Augustinian framework of ambivalence. For Jews, the cross became the symbol of the ultimate cul de sac. Their doom, resulting from no decision of their own, was more complete than ever.

29

Abelard and Héloïse

WE TOOK NOTE OF a theology that was implicitly tied to violence before, in Saint Ambrose's rigidly allegorical reading of the Old Testament, which led to the literal conclusion that the synagogue had no place in the New Testament era of allegorical fulfillment. Ambrose, as we saw, supported a Christian mob in the burning of a synagogue. But we also saw how the protégé of Saint Ambrose, Saint Augustine, subtly reversed his master's position. Something like this began to take place after Anselm, as his most prestigious successor offered a critique of *Cur Deus Homo* and its punitive theology of atonement. In contrast to what occurred with Augustine, the successor theologian, Peter Abelard (1079–1142), did not carry the day. Augustine prevailed, and as a result Jews survived as a people. We will see now that Abelard could have represented an even more positive turn in the story. After a thousand years of misbegotten Jew hatred, climaxing just then, this profoundly Catholic thinker lifted the pike on a road toward Jewish-Christian mutuality, a road leading to an end to hatred and the beginning of real respect. Alas for the Church, and more so for the Jews, it was a road not taken.

Instead, Peter Abelard was condemned at a Church council, eliminating him as an influence on mainstream Catholic theology. Abelard's romantic tragedy as the doomed lover of Héloïse (c. 1100–1163) is well known, but because of the related failure of his effort to humanize Anselm's contract-ridden idea of atonement and, therefore, to deemphasize the place of the cross in God's plan of salvation, his is as much a theological tragedy as a personal one. And it would have lasting implications for the ever-darker story of Christian attitudes toward Jews.

The city is Paris. The year is 1118 or so. A school has been established at the Frankish cathedral on the island in the Seine. There are perhaps as many as five thousand students in Paris, centered here.[1] Combining skills of logic, disputation, mathematics, philosophy, and the study of Scripture, the scholars of Paris are, in effect, inventing the modern university. Their monument is the cathedral that is being erected, the Gothic masterpiece of Notre-Dame.

Preeminent in this community of geniuses is Peter Abelard, known throughout Europe as a charismatic teacher. He is "a fair and handsome man, slim and not tall."[2] He had been schooled in the thought of Anselm of Canterbury, and was an unlikely candidate to challenge Anselm's primary affirmation. Abelard's *Sic et Non* (*Yes and No*) developed Anselm's dialogical method, applying the faculty of reason to faith. But Abelard did so with an unprecedented boldness. "By doubting," he said, "we come to questioning, and by questioning we learn truth."[3] The thrill of this free play of the mind drew students to his chair, established his prominence, and made him wealthy. His renown put him in touch with other intellectual centers. Most important, Abelard seems to have been influenced by the intellectually vital centers of Spanish Jewry, and through them, by newly translated works of ancient Greek thinkers.[4] This contact would make Abelard aware of Judaism as a living tradition, not simply an Old Testament caricature, and it would prompt him to respond to it. Eventually he would portray the Jew in his writing in a unique way: respectfully. But neither his intellectual openness nor the breadth of his knowledge can account for what set him apart so starkly from Anselm on the question of atonement.

In his *Exposition of the Epistle to the Romans,* written around 1130, about three decades after *Cur Deus Homo,* Abelard roundly rejected the idea that "the death of the innocent Son was so pleasing to God the Father that through it he would be reconciled to us."[5] Why did God become a man? In Romans, Paul says that "both Jews and Greeks" are justified "through the redemption which is in Christ Jesus, whom God put forward as an expiation by his blood."[6] But how? Abelard's answer, given in one of the "*quaestiones*" of his *Exposition,* is that Christ came to show us how to live, not to die in submission to the brutal power of the Father. "We are made more righteous by Christ's death than we were before, because of the example Christ set us, kindling in us by his grace and generosity a zeal to imitate him."[7] The death is exemplary, Abelard insists, and not expiatory. This is not exactly a new idea, but it strikes a note rarely sounded before.

In order to grasp the full context of Augustine's innovations, we found it necessary to consider the influence of his mother. In order to understand how Abelard arrived at a position of hostility toward a rigid theology of the crucifixion as debt satisfaction, we must do something similar. "As the west portal of Chartres is the door through which one must of necessity enter the Gothic architecture of the thirteenth century" — this is the assessment of the American historian Henry Adams — "so Abelard is the portal of approach to the Gothic thought and philosophy within. Neither art nor thought has a modern equivalent; only Héloïse, like Isolde, unites the ages."[8] Héloïse is a brilliant young woman who, at eighteen, is less than half Abelard's age. She is the niece of Fulbert, the powerful canon of Notre-Dame. That the great Abelard should have taken her as his pupil testifies to her uncle's prominence, but also to her gifts. "She was a lady of no mean appearance," Abelard himself tells us, "while in literary excellence she was the first."[9]

To be a teacher in Abelard's position was to be a cleric, although not necessarily a priest with the vows of ordination. Still, it is a grave violation when Abelard and Héloïse fall passionately in love. "Under the pretext of work we made ourselves entirely free for love and the pursuit of her studies provided the secret privacy which love desired . . . There was more kissing than teaching; my hands found themselves at her breasts more often than on the book . . . And the more such delights were new to us, the more ardently we indulged in them."[10]

"Whatever you wished," Héloïse would write, "I blindly carried out." The two exchange a lifelong correspondence to which Abelard would refer in his *Historia Calamitatum (The Story of a Calamity)*. The love affair takes its tragic turn when Héloïse becomes pregnant. Secretly they marry, but her uncle learns what has happened and takes mortal offense. Fulbert becomes, in point of fact, very much the offended liege lord, and his response perfectly embodies the rigid feudal notion of expiation that undergirds Anselm's atonement theology, but that Abelard rejects.

Abelard was punished, he writes of himself, "in a cruel and shameful manner and one which the world with great astonishment abhorred." Fulbert orders an attack on him, dispatching thugs to settle the score — "namely, they cut off the organs by which I had committed the deed which they deplored . . . How just was the betrayal by which he whom I had first betrayed paid me back; now my rivals would extol such a fair retribution."[11] Abelard suffers a grievous punishment under a system of justice that defines itself as "paying back in kind." The physical offense is punished physically, and Fulbert's dishonor is compensated for by Abelard's disgrace. He is banished, and so is Héloïse. They enter separate exiles, he to become a monk, she to become a nun. But now, in an unprecedented way, their love proves itself. "We are one in Christ," he writes to her. "We are one flesh by the law of marriage. Whatever you have, I regard as mine. Now Christ is yours because you have become His spouse . . . It is in your strength at His side that I place my hope, so as to obtain through your prayer what I cannot obtain through my own."[12]

With prodding from Héloïse, Abelard reenters the fray of philosophical and theological disputation, only now his views are shaped by experience. His writing from here on displays a consistent skepticism about an idea of God whose justice leaves no room for mercy. For example, Abelard now denies that the person outside the Church could for that reason be condemned because of "an invincible ignorance [that] makes him similar to those for whom the Lord in his Passion . . . prayed."[13]

The Lord in his Passion is, for Abelard, a figure of love, pure and simple. But in this crusading age, the Lord in his Passion has too many other meanings as well, and was bound to become a point of dispute. Abelard rejects the idea of the crucifixion as an act aimed at transforming God's attitude toward the sin-ridden descendants of Adam from one of hateful damnation to one of loving mercy. In Abelard's view, God's loving mercy is constant. The attitude in need of change is not God's but the self-hating human's. As Jaroslav Pelikan explains it, "Christ did not die on the cross to change the mind of God (which, like everything about God, was unchangeable) . . . but 'to reveal the love [of God] to us.'"[14] To Abelard, the crucifixion, as J. Ramsay McCallum explains it, was "an explanatory gesture of the Second Person, the Wisdom or Word which has already been known under the name of 'Logos' or 'Word,' or as the creative impulse of God by Jews and Gentiles alike."[15] The crucifixion, therefore, is a word spoken not to heaven, as Anselm has it, but to earth.

Abelard is asking not How are we yet to be saved? but How do we know that we are already saved? The ancient Scriptures tell us, and so does the life of Jesus. The story Jesus himself told that has direct relevance to this question, that of the Prodigal Son, describes a father whose attitude toward his incorrigible son is one of constant love. The climax of that story is not the father's change, but the son's. The son's return home is the occasion not for his redemption, but for his recognition that, in his father's eyes, he was never *not* redeemed. Faithful to this aspect of the message of Jesus, Abelard succeeds, as Pelikan puts it, in "shifting the question from the topic of salvation to the topic of revelation."[16] Here the cross is not the *cause* of the love of God — the monster God who needs, like Fulbert, to be paid back in blood, the blood sacrifice of an only Son. Rather, the cross is an epiphany of the permanent and preexisting love of God that needs nothing from the beloved except existence. Even in their fallen state, the very existence of human beings remains the measure of God's love for them.

In all of this, Abelard manifests a unique — one could say revolutionary — positive regard for human beings *as they are*. By contrast, the prevailing theological assessment of the human condition is represented by Anselm's hopeless characterization of sinful man as "condemned to eternal torments, and having no power to redeem himself from them."[17] The robustly human Abelard is a figure of suspicion among a body of theologians who "affirmed an original guilt transmitted by Adam to the human race." Abelard's work, McCallum says, is "an acute revision of this point of view . . . [showing] that man is not by heredity guilty . . . that there are human weaknesses, but that these are not sinful in themselves."[18] Humans in themselves are not, by definition, forlorn.

So for Abelard the state of fallenness is no obstacle to salvation, even for pagans, Jews, or other "infidels" — all those routinely pronounced as damned by Abelard's contemporaries, although not yet by solemn pronouncement of the Church.[19] Things seem simpler to the rational Abelard, as he applies the criteria of human logic even to the divine. The God of whom Abelard speaks is a God whose mercy trumps justice every time. God's mercy is as unlimited as God is. Thus Abelard, in Pelikan's summary, "found it 'consonant with piety as well as with reason' to believe that those who strove to please God according to their best lights on the basis of the natural law would not be damned for their efforts."[20] Therefore God's people are defined not yet by membership in the Church but by existence on the earth. All of God's people are already saved, which is to say infinitely loved, just by virtue of God's having created them. All this takes place "in Christ," Abelard would say, keeping him orthodox, because God's creative action occurs primordially and perennially through the Word, the Second Person, the one whom we call Christ.

It remains for the human only to accept that love, which, in our fallen — self-rejecting — state, may not be easy, but it is never impossible. And the outcome by which that acceptance is measured is not only self-acceptance but acceptance of the neighbor, too. The mark of this religion, spanning cause and effect, offer and response, is not "satisfaction" but love, a position consonant with the religion of Israel, which always emphasizes right action in behalf of the neighbor as the content of faith. The historian of theology Karen Armstrong summed it up this way: Abelard "developed a sophisticated and moving rationale for the mystery of the atonement: Christ had been crucified to awaken compassion in us and by doing so he became our Savior."[21] Abelard was convinced, therefore, that the "Hebrew saints," and all those who, by living compassionately and using their reason, responded to the Word through which God had created the world, were offered salvation.[22]

It should be no surprise, then, to find in Abelard a rare manifestation of empathy not just for "Hebrew saints" but for the besieged Jews of his own day. In his *Dialogue of a Philosopher with a Jew and a Christian,* he puts these words in the mouth of the Jew:

> To believe that the fortitude of the Jews in suffering would be unrewarded was to declare that God was cruel. No nation has ever suffered so much for God. Dispersed among all nations, without king or secular ruler, the Jews are oppressed with heavy taxes as if they had to repurchase their very lives every day. To mistreat the Jews is considered a deed pleasing to God. Such imprisonment as is endured by the Jews can be conceived by the Christians only as a sign of God's utter wrath. The life of the Jews is in the hands of their worst enemies. Even in their sleep they are plagued by nightmares. Heaven is their only place of refuge. If they want to travel to the nearest town, they have to buy protection with high sums of money from the Christian rulers who actually wish for their death so that they can confiscate their possessions. The Jews cannot own land or vineyards because there is nobody to vouch for their safekeeping. Thus, all that is left them as a means of livelihood is the business of moneylending, and this in turn brings the hatred of Christians upon them.[23]

Abelard's assertions set off a great debate. Many support him, and many others condemn him. Always, the gossipy cluck of disapproval curls the tongues of his critics. No one has forgotten Héloïse, least of all Abelard. She is his constant ally, although always at a distance. She has by now become one of the great abbesses of Europe. Yet their letters have never stopped.

Abelard's fiercest opponent turns out to be Bernard of Clairvaux, the crusader monk whom we saw earlier, warning the Rhineland against anti-Jewish violence. Bernard is the author of *Against the Errors of Abelard,* a long treatise that, among other things, defends Anselm's core idea. Bernard affirms the necessity of restoring the honor of God by means of the crucifixion, in order to bring the universe into its right order.[24] He sends this treatise to the pope, jelling the opposition to Abelard. "Bernard heartily distrusted . . . Abelard . . . ," Karen Armstrong writes, "and vowed to silence him. He accused Abelard of 'attempting to bring the merit of the Christian faith to naught because he supposes that by human reason he can comprehend all that is God.'"[25] And if Abelard could so comprehend God, so could Jews and "other peoples and nations." What would the coming of Christ have been for then?

"His books have wings," Bernard complained of Abelard. "His writings have passed from country to country, and from one kingdom to another. A new gospel is being forged for peoples and for nations, a new faith is being propounded, and a new foundation is being laid besides that which has been laid."[26] And in another place, Bernard griped, "He is a man who does not know his limitations, making void the virtue of the cross by the cleverness of his words."[27]

For Abelard, through all the controversy, the thing remains clear: God is not a cruel overlord to be appeased with the death of his only begotten Son, but a Father who has sent that Son to reveal his constant love — his love for all. But at last, in this harshly feudal age, Abelard's view is formally rejected. The indomitable Héloïse denounces Bernard as a false apostle,[28] but he is still, in Armstrong's words, "arguably the most powerful man in Europe."[29] In 1141, he commands Abelard to come to the Council of Sens, before the king and all the bishops of France. The once robust Abelard is now ill, apparently suffering from Parkinson's disease, but he complies. He is badgered even in the streets outside the council meeting place.[30] Inside, Bernard leads the attack himself. In anticipating this confrontation, Bernard had called Abelard "Goliath,"[31] yet now, as the medievalist Étienne Gilson describes it, Abelard is "no more than a beaten giant, wounded to death but struggling violently to raise himself."[32] To no avail. In a climax of fierce rigidity, Bernard's supporters condemn Abelard as a heretic, destroying him.

Shortly thereafter, not long before his death, Abelard writes a final letter to Héloïse. In the words of Gilson, this farewell "recites for her the profession of faith which Bernard of Clairvaux was unable to wring from him." Abelard writes, "Héloïse, my sister, once so dear in the world, today still more dear in Jesus Christ, logic has won for me the hatred of men . . . I adore Christ, who reigns at the right hand of the Father . . . And to banish all restless solicitude, all doubt from the heart that beats in your breast, I want you to have this from my pen: I have established my conscience on that rock on which Christ built his Church. Here, briefly, is the inscription it bears."

Then Abelard recites on the page a creed of his own composition, a lu-

cid assertion of his orthodox faith as a Christian, despite the condemnation of Sens. And, of course, he is right. His theology of salvation and revelation, of God's limitless mercy, will remain a minority report, but one
vindicated again and again, down to the formal proclamations of Vatican
II in our own time. For the purposes of this inquiry, it is important to see
what Abelard's creed says — in contrast to Nicaea, as amended after Helena — about the death of Jesus. Abelard affirms "that the same Son of God
satisfied all the exigencies of the human condition which He assumed,
even death itself."[33] Thus Jesus did not come to die, but to live as a human
being, to embrace the human condition, which includes death. Death here
is a moment, not a purpose; a part of the life story, not the meaning of it.
The implications of these distinctions for every part of our concern —
from crusader violence based on death as salvific, to vengeful assaults on
Jews who are unjustly tied to the death of Jesus, to the accusation (which
first appears within three years of Sens) that Jews crucify Christian boys —
can hardly be overemphasized. In Abelard, the Church is offered the antidote to the poison of ambivalence toward Jews that had found its highest
expression in Anselm, for in Abelard's view the "deicide Jew" will be unnecessary, and the "witness Jew" will be released. The Jew's difference
from the Christian will be a measure of human tolerance. Alas, none of
this is to be. Given all that is going on around Abelard in the name of the
cross he would deemphasize, his being condemned for a theology that, in
Bernard's indictment, makes "void the virtue of the cross by the cleverness of his words" can be no surprise.[34]

That does not, however, make Abelard's defeat less tragic, either for him
or for the history that now unfolds. "The consequence of his condemnation for heresy," the historian John Benton writes, "was that by the thirteenth century his works were little studied, and his fame as a philosopher
was eclipsed by his reputation as a lover until his rediscovery as a philosopher in the nineteenth century."[35] What the Church lost in those intervening centuries was the influence of a humanist at home with dialectic and
at home with doubt, a believer who wanted only to shift the emphasis
from one side of the Catholic paradox to the other. What Jews lost was a
rare Christian interpreter prepared to see them on their own terms. The
clouds of an unleashed violence were gathering in Christendom, violence
that would change everything. That Abelard's would have been a tempering voice is apparent even in the words of a prayer he offered: "Come as a
Redeemer not as an Avenger, as a God of clemency rather than of justice,
as a merciful Father not as a stern Lord."[36] Not, that is, as a feudal master.

One of the reasons Anselm's atonement theology prevailed over Abelard's more humane understanding must be that it reinforced the political structure of monarchy just as the papacy was solidifying its hold on that kind of power. The reputation of *Cur Deus Homo* still stands as a measure of the Church's true attitude toward democracy. The fact that a medieval schema of atonement survives as the default of Catholic soteriology, or theology of salvation, says everything about the link between theology and politics. If God can be seen as a feudal lord — here is the thousand-year-old question — why can't the pope be? But all those years ago, Abelard knew what was wrong with this perception. From the prostration of Henry IV, which inspired Anselm, to his own castration, Abelard saw the limits of such acts as analogies for God's own. Two of the men who had castrated Abelard were themselves seized and castrated by men of Abelard's faction, in perfect counterpoint.[37]

Yet Abelard's brush with a ferociously applied feudal justice is less full of implication, finally, than his lifelong bond of love with Héloïse. She wrote to him late in life:

> God knows I would not have hesitated to follow you or to precede you into hell itself if you had given the order. My heart was not my own, but yours. Even now, more than ever before, if it is not with you it is nowhere, for you are its very existence. So, I pray you, let my poor heart be happy with you . . . Remember, I beg you, everything I have done; and weigh out all that you owe me. When I delighted with you in carnal pleasures, many wondered why I did it, whether it was for concupiscence or for love. But now my last state shows my true beginning, and I now forgo all pleasures only to obey your will. Truly, I reserved nothing for myself but to be yours before everything, and such I am to this very moment.[38]

Peter Abelard died in 1142, at age sixty-three, disgraced but apparently reconciled even to Bernard, which is a last proof of what Abelard believed.[39] Héloïse, at the peak of her power as an abbess, arranged to have him buried at her own monastery, sixty miles southwest of Paris. When she died twenty years later — apparently she too was sixty-three — she was buried beside him. Legend has it that, in death, they embraced. In their letters, they had prayed, "Those whom Thou has parted for a time in this world, unite forever in the next, O Thou our hope, our inheritance, our expectation, our consolation, our Lord who art blest forever. Amen."[40] In 1817, the remains of Abelard and Héloïse were brought home to Paris, from which, as lovers, they had been banished. They were interred in Père

Lachaise Cemetery, where lovers, believers, and thinkers still come to pay them homage.

Bernard, of course, became a saint. He was canonized only twenty-one years after his death in 1153. He was sometimes referred to as "the secret emperor of Europe,"[41] and his fame was tied above all to the Crusade launched not long after Abelard died, and of which he, Bernard, was the prime inspiration. Since the question at the heart of this inquiry concerns the relationship between the crusading impulse and a violent theology of the cross — remember that Anselm and Urban II shared a bond of friendship just before the First Crusade — Bernard's role in the Second Crusade seems emblematic because of his defense, against Abelard, of Anselm's brutal God. Theology and political history go hand in hand. The lasting implication of Bernard's triumph over Abelard was not that the latter was disgraced, but that the former was then even more powerful. "Bernard of Clairvaux was the first Christian theoretician of the holy war," Hans Küng has written, "and provided theological justification for the killing of unbelievers."[42]

But we have also seen how the Hebrew chronicles revered Bernard for preaching in behalf of Jews the Augustinian mantra, "Do not slay them!" Bernard's intervention in the Rhineland prevented a repeat of the massacres of 1096. We also saw that there was a lit fuse attached to Bernard's intervention. Perhaps now we can understand where it came from. What Bernard preferred to the death of Jews was, in Robert Chazan's phrase, "their endless degradation." In this way, "the great Christian protector of twelfth-century Jewry," David Berger concluded, "sowed seeds which would claim the life of many a Jewish martyr."[43]

Bernard's first reputation rested on a lyrical celebration of the Song of Songs. At the other end of his life, not long before he died, he made a more fateful — and calamitous — contribution to relations between Christians and Jews. By then he was an embittered man who had seen his precious Crusade woefully defeated. The current pope, Eugene III (1145–1153), was formerly one of Bernard's monks, and a protégé of his.[44] Bernard was determined to use what levers of power remained to him, and he addressed to this pope a lengthy instruction on the proper exercise of papal power. It comes to us as *Five Books on Consideration to Eugene III,* or more simply as *De Consideratione.* It is in this work that Bernard advances what Hans Küng calls "the pernicious theory"[45] that God has given to the Church two swords. Bernard writes, "Both swords, that is, the spiritual and the material, belong to the Church; however the latter is to be drawn for the Church and the former by the Church. The spiritual sword should be drawn by the hand of the priest; the material sword by the hand of the knight, but clearly at the bidding of the priest and at the command of the emperor . . . Now, take the sword which has been entrusted to you [the pope] to strike with, and for their salvation wound if not everyone, if not even many, at least whomever you can."[46]

Constantine had changed history, and the very meaning of Jesus Christ, by turning his cross into a sword. Following the crusader monk, vanquisher of Abelard, popes would soon enough change history and the meaning of Jesus Christ again. The violence of the rabble would become the violence of the Church itself. The one sword of Constantine would become the two swords of the Inquisition.

↦ 30 ↤

Thomas Aquinas: Reason
Against the Jews

R ATIONAL THEOLOGY CAME into its own in the twelfth century. What Anselm and Abelard began — explanation of Christian mystery by systematic intellectual effort — would be carried to new levels in the thirteenth century, especially by Thomas Aquinas (1225–1274). Since so much of the virulent Christian hatred of Jews, as manifested by the outbreak of the Blood Libel and well-poisoning conspiracy fears, was patently irrational, one might have hoped that the new emphasis on rational method would prompt a positive turn in the Christian-Jewish story. The opposite is the case.

Innovations in philosophical theology, stimulated in large part by the northern European rediscovery of Aristotle, were facilitated, ironically, by Jewish translators, working in Iberia to render Greek and Arabic texts into Latin. We have seen how post-antiquity Jewish culture flourished in the area around present-day Baghdad, especially with the consolidation of the Babylonian Talmud and with the work of such scholars as Saadyah ben Joseph (882–946), who affirmed the compatibility of philosophy and religion. But Jewish communities influenced each other across continents. Building on the Talmudic tradition and the affirmation of rational philosophy, there followed the formulations of the great Rashi (Rabbi Shlomo Yitzhaki, 1040–1105), the "Prince of Bible Commentators,"[1] whose commonsense distillations of esoteric and complicated Talmudic writings made them available to a broad population of Jews who came after him.

The Pyrenees were a thinner screen than the Bosporus, and the thriving center of Jewish learning that had the largest impact on Europe was in Spain. We shall see more of this in Part Five. Suffice to note here that classic works of Arabic philosophy, like those of the Andalusian Ibn Rashid, known in Europe as Averroës (1126–1198), were mediated by Jewish linguists and scholars whose tradition was well established by the millennium. Solomon ibn Gabirol (c. 1020–1070) was a Jewish Neo-Platonist whose portrait of creation as a cosmic struggle between, in Plato's terms, form and matter, was widely circulated in Latin under the title *Fons Vitae*. The work had tremendous influence among Catholic scholars, who did not know the identity of its author. In a way, the encounter with classical philosophy came more naturally to Jewish sages than to the early schoolmen attached to cathedrals. The ancient tradition of Talmudic commentary on sacred texts had prepared Jewish scholars both to take in what was written and to elaborate on it. This tradition in Spain would permanently stamp Jewish thought when it culminated in the genius of the philosopher Maimonides (Moses ben Maimon, 1135–1204) and of the Kabbalist Abraham Abulafia (d. 1290). It would have an equal, though less direct, impact among Christians, many of whom, like Aquinas, would imitate Maimonides's methods and retrace his lines of inquiry, knowing full well he was a Jew.

Among churchmen, the new intellectual confidence led to the conclusion that the rational truth of Christian doctrine, once properly expounded, could be grasped by all people. Now it would be possible to explicate the faith according to a logic that would be irrefutable. The syllogism thus became a missionary tool.

Perhaps more surprisingly, so did the respectful impulse to appreciate the religious and intellectual traditions of those labeled as infidels or unbelievers. The ordered methods of reason were introduced into the religious discourse of the Church by the liberals and humanists associated with new urban universities. Peter Abelard can be taken as a type of this group, standing against conservatives tied to the rural monasteries, of whom Bernard was a type.[2] Reactionaries wanted Aristotle, the pagan, to be banned. They regarded the scientific "theology" to be a kind of heresy. Thus Abelard was condemned as a heretic — but so was Thomas Aquinas, although obviously his condemnation would not stick.[3] The new Christian intellectuals distrusted the warm feelings of mysticism and the mindless pieties of the sodalities. Neither would sustain authentic religion in the coming age, nor would they break the chains of superstition that were still locked to Europe's recent past. The new intellectuals asserted that the Church had nothing to fear from the spaciousness of the educated human mind. Wasn't reason as much a gift of God as faith?

But there was a catch. Was the spirit of rational inquiry to be free, or was it to be placed at the service of a sacred purpose? This is a question with which the Christian intellectual must still grapple, and it posed itself at the start. Abelard's ecumenical argument, for example, that all people can glimpse traces of Christian revelation in the logic of their own experience — more specifically, that Jews can recognize the Second Person of the Trinity in the eternal Word by whom, in Genesis, God creates the world — this argument retains an ecumenical character only if used to advance a mutual understanding. If Christians and Jews are engaged in a common stretch toward the elusive mystery of God, such exploration of related but distinct analogies can illuminate. But if such analysis is used to "prove" an a priori Christian claim, or to demonstrate a Jewish doctrinal inadequacy — an "unfulfillment" — then even an apparently open-minded intellectual exercise is placed at the service not of truth but of domination.

As it happened, when the energy of the Crusades was channeled, at the beginning of the thirteenth century, into an unprecedented conversionist movement, the missionary impulse overwhelmed the goal of bringing faith and reason together. This was partly the result of the humane Christian rejection of violence against Jews — the *Sicut Judaeis.* Yet the Crusades of the twelfth century also exacerbated Christian impatience with the crucifiers, which is why the first universal restrictions against Jews were introduced at the Fourth Lateran Council in 1215. In the new era of absolute universalism, heterodoxy was intolerable. This may be the most lasting result of the crusading period: Society discovered the efficiency with which it could organize itself around the project of attacking an enemy.[4] Thus heretics are ferreted out and offered the choice of recanting or being killed. Jews are pressed on every side, with the clear purpose of the long-sought conversion of the whole people. And the new rational theology, with its irrefutable analysis — Anselm's ontological proof is perfected a century and a half later by the "five proofs" of Thomas Aquinas — forms the heart of this offensive of the mind.

The advent of logic as a missionary tool was a welcome relief to Christians because the tradition of arguing against Jews from their own Scriptures was such an abysmal failure. Each note of Catholic faith — from the Virgin Birth to the Seamless Robe to the darkness at noon on Good Friday — was part of a mystical harmony scored in the Hebrew Scriptures. So why couldn't Jews hear it? Augustine's answer, following Paul, had been that for God's own purposes, God had made Jews tone deaf. Neither Paul nor Augustine nor any who followed this train of thought could ever explain why Jews should be held responsible, in grotesquely condemnatory

terms, for enacting a role ordained by God, performing a function necessary to the salvation of the world.

Christians, for their part, could not hear the consistent Jewish answer
to their arguments, which might describe the Jewish habit of reading the
Scriptures in context. For example, when Christian apologists cited Isaiah
7:14 — "The virgin is with child" — as proof of the Virgin Birth and, therefore, the messianic character of Jesus, Jews might have drawn attention to
the next phrase in Isaiah, which clearly says that she "will soon give birth
to a son." Soon after Isaiah's proclamation, that is. What may have happened many generations later in Bethlehem was of no account.[5] Or, for
that matter, the Jewish response might have drawn attention to the fact
that in the original Hebrew, Isaiah had written, "The young woman is
with child." It was the Septuagint translators, rendering the Hebrew into
Greek, who introduced the word "virgin." To Jews, the Christian claims
could appear shallow.

Yet to Christian polemicists, such replies could only seem like splitting
the hair of the prophet, which left them asking, Why don't Jews get it? Positively assessing the Jewish refusal to recognize patterns of "fulfillment" in
Christianity, as Abelard saw it, one would regard Jews as "invincibly ignorant." A negative assessment would see the stubborn Jews as less than human. Here is Abelard's nemesis, Bernard: "A Jew might complain, perhaps, that I go too far in baiting him when I term his understanding 'ox-
like' . . . 'The ox,' he says, 'knows his owner, and the ass his master's crib:
Israel has not known Me, My people had no understanding' [Isaiah 1:3].
You see, O Jew, I am milder than your own prophet: I put you on a par
with the beasts, he puts you beneath them!"[6]

But now something new began to happen. Pope Innocent III, whom we
saw earlier as the avatar of the new Catholic universalism, commissioned
two new religious orders, the Dominicans and the Franciscans, to carry
out the conversionist program. Thousands of men joined these orders at
the beginning of the thirteenth century, a spiritualized, and one could say
domesticated, version of the Crusade impulse. Bands of these friars, as
they were known, from the word for "brother," spread out across Europe.
They traveled as mendicants, embodying the virtues of the apostolic life
and, not incidentally, channeling the religious enthusiasm of the age into
structures of Church control. Not for nothing would the Dominicans be
known as the Order of Preachers, for they excelled at applying the new rationalism to the mysteries of the Gospel. The friars were famously devoted
to Christ in his Passion — Francis of Assisi (c. 1181–1226) would have the

wounds of the stigmata on his hands, feet, and side — but they also embraced lives of serious study. It was their command of reason applied to faith that made them relevant at that moment in a coalescing, young, and increasingly univocal civilization.

An exemplar of this emerging civilization was the intellectual enterprise of a man who would soon become the greatest of the Dominicans and the greatest of the era's thinkers, Thomas Aquinas. He was trained, in part, at Cologne. Then he followed Abelard at the University of Paris. He set for himself the ambitious goal of assembling two *Summas,* summaries of all human knowledge in the only two spheres that mattered. The *Summa Theologiae* (1273) would be a complete statement of Christian belief, arranged according to Aristotelian logic and drawing on Aristotelian metaphysics. This *Summa* would quote Aristotle 3,500 times.[7] The *Summa Contra Gentiles* (1259), written for Christians engaged in the debate with unbelievers, would be a complete synthesis of the faith as it should be presented to those who reject it. Thomas argued, he said, using "natural reason, to which all are compelled to assent."[8] His ambition was the intellectual equivalent of the Gothic masterpiece that he saw completed in Paris in 1250, the Cathedral of Notre-Dame, which was one of eighty massive churches completed in France between 1180 and 1270. Such construction was an extraordinary achievement by a population of fewer than eighteen million, an irrefutable signal of the vitality of this culture.[9]

Thomas's ambition could also be said to be the intellectual equivalent of Innocent III's claim to universal power, for Thomas articulated a philosophical rationale for the hierarchical order that the medieval Church embraced. He offered a theological justification for the central papacy that is still a mark of the Roman Catholic Church.[10] Hans Küng points out that in the *World Catechism,* published by the Vatican in 1993, Thomas Aquinas is quoted 63 times, which is more than any other authority except Saint Augustine (88 times) and Pope John Paul II himself (137 times).[11] Thomas created an intellectual structure of faith that is so internally coherent, so logically consistent, and so religiously devoted that its advocates could not imagine how anyone could honestly consider its claims and not assent. Thomas, in other words, proved it.

Aristotle's idea of the necessity of truth, which compels assent, led Thomas to one of the most important innovations of his career — and it concerned the Jews. It was Thomas who overturned the idea of the Jew's "invincible ignorance," which had been held from Augustine through Abelard. Thomas concluded that Jews, confronted with the truth of Jesus, had not been ignorant at all. They knew very well that Jesus was the Messiah, Son of God, but they murdered him anyway. "The disbelief of Jews derived, therefore," the scholar Jeremy Cohen summarizes Aquinas, "not from ignorance, but from a deliberate defiance of the truth."[12]

Thomas's patron was the founder of his order, a Spaniard, Saint Dominic de Guzman (1170–1221), for whom the Dominicans are named. Dominic had been dispatched by Innocent III against the heretics in southern France. The expectation was that the preached word would overcome the Cathari, the various sects that defined the cosmic struggle, in the tradition of the Manichaeans, as between a good and an evil God, a belief that led to rigid puritanism and a concomitant rejection of the Catholic Church. When the preaching failed to convince the heretics — an ominous pattern reveals itself here — the Fourth Lateran Council sent its Crusade against them.

Dominicans and Franciscans were inevitably directed to preach to Jews. As always, Jews were easier to identify than heretics, and closer at hand than Saracens. Then, of course, it was necessary to forcibly require Jews to listen to the preachers. Here is an edict, issued in 1242 by King James I of Aragon: "Likewise we wish and decree that, whenever the archbishop, bishops, or Dominican or Franciscan friars visit a town or a locale where Saracens or Jews dwell and wish to present the word of God to the said Jews or Saracens, these must gather at their call and must patiently hear their preaching. If they do not wish to come of their own will, our officials shall compel them to do so, putting aside all excuses."[13] Jews were herded into churches and preached at. Disputations were arranged, great debates at which Jews were allowed to rebut the arguments of the preachers. The movement of organized anti-Jewish polemic would grow throughout the thirteenth century. Friars would enter synagogues uninvited. Kings would order Jews to cooperate with the missionaries, and when Jews did convert, they would often become anti-Jewish polemicists themselves.

Early in this process, though, a problem surfaced. Despite the unprecedented level of missionary organization, despite the fresh edge that rational argument lent the polemic, and despite the staggering intellectual achievement of the new Christian scholarship, Jews remained, by and large, unmoved. Some converted, but the vast majority did not. How was this possible?

The mass hysteria that led, in this period, to widespread belief that Jews had secret powers, rituals, and magic gave rise to the Blood Libel and to charges of well poisoning. As we have seen, the Church establishment roundly rejected such paranoid impulses, but now that establishment was overtaken by one of its own. If the Church knew anything, it knew what Jews were — in Augustine's phrase, "bearers of the Old Testament."[14] Jewish religion was what Jesus had set himself against. Christians had never attended to the post-Temple rise of rabbinic Judaism, nor understood the relationship of instruction, commentaries, legal teachings, and stories to the study of Torah.[15] Such expositions had been assembled in the third century by Rabbi Judah the Prince, a collection that came to be known as the Mishnah. But Jews had treated this, too, as a living text, and it inspired further rabbinic interpretations and commentaries, which came to be known as the Talmud. Rabbinic Judaism had developed a thorough tradition of Talmudic study by the thirteenth century, yet only now did Christians seem to notice. When converted Jews spoke to Christians of the sacred writings of the Talmud, prelates and polemicists reacted as if this unknown text were a kind of intellectual well poisoning. They seized on news of the Talmud as an explanation for Jewish recalcitrance, as if the work's secrets equipped Jews with the power to withhold the assent that the friars' preaching would otherwise compel. Once an irrational fear arises, it can take over, and that is what happened as Jewish secrets now became suspect, as the source not only of ongoing Jewish rejection of Christian claims but also of heresy among Christians themselves.

Gregory IX took the Chair of Peter in 1227, little more than a decade after the Fourth Lateran Council, which had fired such a resounding warning shot at Jews. It was this Gregory who, with the aptly named constitution *Excommunicamus* (1231), took the fateful step of establishing the first papal Inquisition. This new institution took its name from its stated mission: *inquisitio haereticae pravitatis*.[16] Initially, as the Latin indicates, the Inquisition was aimed at Christian heretics, who, once condemned, were handed over to secular authority to be burned at the stake — or, if they were lucky, as Hans Küng points out, to have their tongues removed.

From within a self-defined world of univocal orthodoxy, heretics and Jews began to look more and more like the same thing. Soon, the papal Inquisition was directed by Pope Gregory to launch an investigation into the Talmud. A convert from Judaism, one Nicholas Donin, testified in 1236 before the pope himself about the blasphemous and heretical content of this compilation of writings.[17] Gregory ordered the archbishops and kings of Europe, as well as the Franciscans and Dominicans, to expose the secrets of the Talmud, "the chief cause that holds the Jews obstinate in their perfidy."[18] The University of Paris was especially commissioned for the task.

This investigation was a matter not only of uncovering blasphemies —

indeed, certain passages in the Talmud denigrated Jesus and his mother — but of determining whether rabbinic commentaries were heretical *within the context of Judaism.* The Church, in other words, was making the unprecedented claim — "an entirely new development in the Christian theology of the Jew," Jeremy Cohen calls it[19] — to moral and theological authority over the content of Jewish belief.

Here is an indictment of the Talmud solemnly given by Gregory's successor, Innocent IV (1243–1254):

> Ungrateful to the Lord Jesus Christ, who, His forbearance overflowing, patiently awaits their conversion, they manifest no shame for their guilt, nor do they reverence the dignity of the Christian faith. Omitting or condemning the Mosaic Law and the Prophets, they follow certain traditions of their elders . . . In Hebrew they call them "Thalamuth," and an immense book it is, exceeding the text of the Bible in size, and in it are blasphemies against God and His Christ, and against the blessed Virgin, fables that are manifestly beyond all explanation, erroneous abuses, and unheard-of stupidities — yet this is what they teach and feed their children . . . and render them totally alien to the Law and the Prophets, fearing lest the Truth which is understood in the same Law and Prophets, bearing patent testimony to the only-begotten Son of God, who was to come in flesh, they be converted to the faith, and return humbly to their Redeemer.[20]

Only two blocks from Notre-Dame, on the right bank of the Seine, there stands a lovely plaza, spread like an apron before the dignified, mansard-roofed Hôtel de Ville. Not long ago, I spent a quiet afternoon sitting at a small table in one of the sidewalk cafés that line one edge of the square. Visible to my right were the soaring towers of the cathedral, their gargoyles alert. Just beyond was the needle spire of the exquisite Sainte-Chapelle, built as a reliquary for the crown of thorns,[21] which made me think of the Seamless Robe — Helena's legacy was as alive in Paris as in Trier. Anchoring the distance, across the square, was the congested bazaar of the weekend market. Despite this lively scene, my concentration was taken over by the layered history of the place. Near here was the mustering point for the Jews of Paris rounded up on July 16, 1942. Thirteen thousand were taken away that day, four thousand of them children. There was no protest. More than half of the eighty-five thousand Jews deported from France to Nazi extermination camps came from Paris — the streets around me. Their confiscated artworks, bank accounts, and apartments are still being adjudicated.

What is the line between that day and the day in 1242 when up to twenty-four cartloads of books, something like twelve thousand volumes,[22] were dumped onto the pavement of this same plaza? Those books were all the known copies of the Talmud to be found in Paris and its environs, brought here by the soldiers of King Louis IX, also known as Saint Louis.[23] His men had invaded and ransacked Jewish homes and synagogues to get at the books.

The faculty of the University of Paris, heirs of Peter Abelard and teachers of Thomas Aquinas, had held its trial in the form of a debate, with conscripted Jewish sages speaking for the Talmud and Dominicans speaking against. The faculty rendered its verdict: The Talmud was a work of heresy. The Talmud was the reason Jews were refusing to convert. Destroy the Talmud, and the truth of "fulfillment" arguments from the Old Testament, rationally offered, would be clear to them at last. The king's men took their stations around the mountain of books, to keep back the Jews as the torchbearers approached. The two-sword theory of Saint Bernard was here given its first mature expression, as the king carried out the physical sanction decreed by the spiritual court. The bonfire was lit. The Talmud burned. It would take one and a half days to consume all volumes.[24]

Jewish elegies would mark the event, an ongoing communal lament that would sear the memory of European Jewry "with a grief akin," as Marc Saperstein put it, "to that in the wake of the Crusade massacres."[25] What was begun at Trier and Mainz in the spring of 1096 was continued in Paris in 1242, but with this difference: The assault on the Talmud came not from a mob but from the established seat, intellectual and ecclesiastical, of Christendom itself. First the crusaders, then *Cur Deus Homo*. If Anselm had turned God into a slayer of the innocent, now Innocent III, Saint Bernard, and Gregory IX had prepared the way for as much to be done to the Church. Already the meanings of this transformation, seen in the torching of the Talmud, were clear. The Augustinian mandate — "Do not slay them!" — was a protection for an Old Testament Judaism that had survived only in the Christian imagination. Jews were to be protected as long as they were true Jews, as Christians defined what was true. And now that truth could be so rationally explained, the category of invincible ignorance that had held from Augustine to Abelard would be reversed. The Talmud debate in Paris was a mere prelude to great debates that would follow, especially in Spain, where the Moors had been vanquished thirty years before. In the age to come, Jewish ignorance would be defined, ipso facto, as willful. With the advent of an operational, double-edged Inquisition, the once blurred line between error and truth could be clearly drawn.

The public burning in the great square of Paris was a first indication that a living, growing Judaism would not be allowed to survive in a Europe ever more under the sway of the sword-perverted cross. And what was written on those destroyed pages? Here are lines "picked from the Talmud at random," as the distinguished rabbi Emil Bernhard Cohn put it, ". . . to lift a corner of the veil":

> Love of humanity is more than charity. The value of charity lies only in love, which lives in it. Love surpasses charity in three respects: Charity touches only a man's money; love touches the man himself. Charity is only for the poor; love is for both poor and rich. Charity is only for the living; love is for both living and dead. Love without reproof of error is no love. He who judges his neighbor leniently will himself be judged leniently by God. Let man always be intelligent and affable in his God-fearing. Let him answer softly, curb his wrath and let him live in peace with his brethren and his kin and with every man, yes, even with the pagan on the street, in order that he be beloved in heaven and on earth, and be acceptable to all men. The kindly man is the truly God-fearing man.[26]

PART FIVE

THE INQUISITION: ENTER RACISM

➤ 31 ◂◂

One Road

A T FIRST GLANCE, they made the most unlikely duo since Richard Nixon and Elvis Presley posed for that famous Oval Office photo. On Saturday, September 27, 1997, Bob Dylan appeared on the same platform with Pope John Paul II at a youth festival in Bologna, Italy. "In one of history's more surreal celebrity pairings," the story in *USA Today* said, "the leader of the Roman Catholic Church and the Jewish-born protest singer clasped hands and chatted before 200,000 spectators at the outdoor concert."[1]

Bob Dylan wore an embroidered black suit and a white cowboy hat, and the pope, as customary, was garbed in the papal white soutane and white skullcap. It was reported that Dylan appeared at the Church-sponsored rally at the pope's explicit invitation.[2] The rock icon sang "Knockin' on Heaven's Door" and "A Hard Rain's A-Gonna Fall" while John Paul sat behind him in a throne-like chair. One photo showed the elderly pontiff — he was seventy-seven at the time — resting his chin on the palm of his hand. Dylan, who at fifty-six was no spring chicken himself, seemed totally focused on the knob of the microphone in front of him.

The two have more in common than is readily apparent. When Karol Wojtyla was elected to the Chair of Peter in 1978, he was condescended to in the press as a guitar-strumming Boy Scout leader, and in fact he was known in Poland for his love of folk songs and his knack for composing lyrics. As a young man during the Nazi era, Wojtyla had combined art and resistance — although as an actor member of a nationalist Polish theater group, not as a singer. While Bob Dylan was first making his name as the bard of the civil rights and peace movements — who of that generation can forget the mandatory pulse of "The Times They Are A-Changin'"? — Wojtyla was making his first mark on the wider Church at the Second Vatican Council. One priest who was there told me that the bishops' rancorous debate on *Nostra Aetate,* the declaration that renounces the charge that all Jews are corporately guilty forever of the murder of Christ, took a definitive turn toward approval when the theretofore silent Pole spoke re-soundingly in favor. "I remember raising my head," this priest told me, "and thinking, Who is that prophet? Wojtyla spoke of the Church's obliga-tion to change its teaching on the Jews with a passion that could only have come from personal experience. For an unknown bishop from Poland, it was amazing. Wojtyla made the difference."[3]

The *USA Today* writer carefully described Dylan as "Jewish-born." His given name was Robert Zimmerman. In the 1970s, Dylan became what the press dubbed a "born-again Christian," which was inaccurate, since the phrase assumes an initial baptism. Nevertheless, his conversion to Chris-tianity was a surprise not only to his legion of aging, post-religious fans, but to many Jews, for whom such a turn understandably evokes a visceral reaction.[4] Within a few years of Dylan's conversion, he announced, on the occasion of his son's becoming a bar mitzvah, that he had returned to Ju-daism. Since then, he has declined to discuss his religious life in public. On the occasion of his appearance with the pope, he denied that the event had any personal spiritual significance. "Playing for the pope is just a show," he said. "I don't judge who asks me to play. That's not my position. I'm grateful to be asked for whatever reason."

John Paul II, on the other hand, seems to have had a ready reason for the joint appearance. At the conclusion of Dylan's brief set, the pope went to the microphone. "'The answer, my friend, is blowin' in the wind,'" he said in his heavily accented English, quoting Dylan's legendary lyric. For that large audience of Italian young people, His Holiness defined the wind as "the breath and life of the Holy Spirit." Then, as if justifying the presence of Bob Dylan and, not incidentally, defending Dylan's now re-nounced conversion, John Paul raised the epic question: "'How many roads must a man walk down before you call him a man?'" And he an-swered it: "One! There is only one road for man, and it is Christ, who said, 'I am the life'!"

The line His Holiness quoted comes from Jesus' answer to the apostle Thomas's question, "How can we know the way?" Jesus replied, "I am the way, and the truth, and the life; no one comes to the Father, but by me."[5]

Thus, at the Dylan concert, John Paul II was claiming for Jesus only what the earliest Church had claimed for him — the claim from which Jews dissent. Yet given the long history of ecclesiastical politics, John Paul's claim for Jesus could seem simultaneously, if implicitly, a claim for himself. There are mixed messages in recent Catholic history on the question of whether other religions offer "ways" to salvation. When John Paul II convened a congress of world religions at Assisi in 1986, for example, his patent respect for other spiritual leaders seemed to indicate a new level of Church ecumenism, although Vatican officials quickly sought to correct that impression. "This cannot be a model," said Cardinal Joseph Ratzinger.[6] Church theologians who are *too* respectful of other religions are still disciplined, or even excommunicated.[7]

The defense of the exclusivist and universalist reach of Christian salvation has, at least since the era of monarchical feudalism, been at the center of papal self-assertion. Whatever John Paul II's personal impulses of openness toward other religions amount to, his long tenure — at more than twenty years, he is one of the longest-serving popes — has been devoted to the restoration of the medieval monarchy as the model for Church authority, with tremendous consequences for relations with other faiths. Indeed, John Paul's emphatic proclamation of that "One!" in response to the Dylan lyric echoes the claim of Boniface VIII (1294–1303), even to the word. That pope's bull *Unam Sanctam* gave the claim to absolute papal authority its ultimate expression, as, in fact, those same words — "one . . . holy" — had done for Constantine at Nicaea. Efforts to assure the unity of the Church quickly, in Constantine's method, become efforts to centralize authority. Boniface, like John Paul II after him, came to the papacy following a period in which papal authority had been diluted, although in that era the struggle was less with dissenting theologians than with competing monarchs. Boniface was fighting what would prove to be a losing battle against nationalist feeling, much as today's Vatican resists the ideology of pluralism.

The Church had traditionally seated its absolutist claims in the authority of Jesus — *he* is the way! But with Boniface, the claim moved from the authority of Jesus to that of the Church. "Urged by faith," *Unam Sanctam* begins, "we are obliged to believe and maintain that the Church is one, holy, catholic, and also apostolic. We believe in her firmly and we confer with simplicity that outside of her there is neither salvation nor the remission of sin."[8] That pronouncement, made in 1302, would remain a watershed in the life of Catholicism, and its underlying assumptions still influence key figures in the Church establishment.

Only a few years before, Thomas Aquinas, following the train of thought set in motion by Anselm, and adding the new fuel of an Aristotelian notion of metaphysical necessity, had defined Jesus Christ as "the absolutely necessary way to salvation." Thomas himself grappled openly with the logic of such an assertion: Not only is Jesus the way, but the Church is; not only the Church, but its divinely established head. If Jesus is necessary as "the one road," isn't the Vicar who tends the gate also "necessary"? Doesn't the one who has authority over the creed of those who follow Jesus ipso facto have authority over all, since all are called to follow? As I first learned from Hans Küng, Thomas concludes as much, asserting that since "it is for the Pope to define what faith is," it must follow that "it is necessary for salvation to submit to the Roman Pope."[9]

And not only that. In *Unam Sanctam,* Pope Boniface VIII extends the two-sword theory of Saint Bernard, justifying the state's use of the temporal sword when it is completely submissive to, and under the judgment of, the spiritual sword wielded by the Church. That submission is compelled by Thomas's link between the authority of the Church and the authority of "Christ's Vicar, Peter, and Peter's successor." This link is made explicit when *Unam Sanctam,* in its last sentence, repeats the pronouncement of Thomas verbatim: "Furthermore, we declare, we proclaim, we define that it is absolutely necessary for salvation that every human creature be subject to the Roman Pontiff."[10]

Thomas had nowhere explained how this principle applied to him. In 1263, Pope Urban IV had formally outlawed the study of the pagan Aristotle, as his predecessors had in 1231 and 1245.[11] Two years after Urban's interdiction, Thomas began his *Summa Theologiae,* the direct application of Aristotle to Christian faith.[12] Ironically, this apparent act of disobedience to papal authority led to the most far-reaching definition of papal authority ever given by theology, before or since.

At the Dylan performance, Pope John Paul II made his claim not for himself or the Church, but only for Jesus Christ. He thus observed the new canon of ecumenical modesty. Catholics had renounced "No salvation outside the Church" in 1953, when Richard Cushing, the archbishop of Boston, at the direction of the Vatican, excommunicated the antisemitic priest Father Leonard Feeney for bludgeoning Jews with it. But Feeney had Saint Thomas Aquinas, logic, and exactly 650 years of Church history on his side. In the years since the close of Vatican II, Church reform has faltered, and the logical inconsistency in the Church's position — making universalist claims for Jesus as the "absolutely necessary way," but not for the institution that alone shows the way to Jesus — has not been fully dis-

mantled.[13] Non-Catholics, so far, have seemed grateful for this more limited absolutism, and have not pushed against its hollow part. Catholics
who have done so, like Hans Küng, have been silenced as teachers of Catholic theology. At Bologna, the ancient resonance of that "One!" seemed,
therefore, familiar.

As indicated by the echo of Nicaea in its title, *Unam Sanctam* was a new
plateau along the trail on which Constantine had first set out. The emperor's goal had been an absolute unity of politics and faith under his own
imperial power. Boniface VIII completed the work of his medieval predecessors in reversing that primacy from prince to pope. "*Ego sum Caesar,*"
he would resoundingly declare to his cardinals, "*ego imperator!*"[14] This
theological and political assertion, while a logical outcome of forces unleashed in the previous two centuries, would shape the two centuries to
come in ways no one could have anticipated — or wished. And this is nowhere more true than in relation to the Jews. If, in a fully realized universal society, there is, in the scholar Jeremy Cohen's phrase, "no room . . . for
infidels,"[15] what happens to them? In the case of John Paul II, who has
done more to heal the Christian-Jewish breach than any other pope, the
answer is nevertheless unclear. His friendship with Jews is one thing, but
his defense of absolute papal power is another. His rigid crackdown on
dissent within the Catholic Church is not unrelated to the fate of Jews, in a
milieu of univocal control of doctrine, any more than, in the past, campaigns against Christian heresy were.

By definition, Jews, the original and quintessential dissenters, call into
question the supremacist universalism of claims made for Jesus Christ. In
the present age, with its overlay of politesse, the depth of this conflict,
and the danger of it, are obscure. But the history of the time when its
structures were erected — structures that John Paul II has sworn himself to uphold — embodies a tragic warning. Beginning with the Fourth
Lateran Council's (1215) resolve to eliminate heresy, and Pope Gregory
IX's *Excommunicamus* (1231), which set up roving Dominican and Franciscan ecclesiastical courts, the early Inquisition had pursued its program
intermittently, with no central apparatus. With Pope Innocent IV's decree
(1252), torture was permitted. Boniface VIII's absolutism (1302) led to the
consolidation of both the ideology and the institution. The coming of
the Spanish Inquisition in the fifteenth century, as we shall see, would
brace the soul of Europe before becoming planted in Rome itself. The cruelty and narrowness of the Roman Inquisition are linked in the public
mind with the Galileo case (1633), but that was tame compared to what

had gone before. This unprecedented institution, whose abuses are now roundly denounced by all,[16] intended only to uphold the oneness of the Church.

Is it possible to repudiate the Inquisition without questioning what it sought to defend? Beyond its methods and abuses, what about the broader impact of the Inquisition on the Catholic mind? In fact, the Inquisition would fatally undermine the positive side of the long-standing Catholic ambivalence toward Judaism, and would fundamentally change the Catholic attitude toward "the Jewish-born," in the careful phrase a newspaper applied to Bob Dylan. The Inquisition would spawn the idea of "Jewish blood." In what follows, we will see how Catholic medieval absolutism exacerbated anti-Jewish religious hatred, fueled new levels of violence, and sponsored an ever more hysterical conversionism, which, when up against continued Jewish resistance, finally led to modern anti-semitic racism.

➤ 32 ◄

My Inquisition

MY OWN BRUSH with the Inquisition was trivial, but even a now humorous encounter with a mere vestige could make an impression. It came when I was not quite twenty years old. I had arrived at the seminary with a small cache of books, which I was resolved to read in the spirit of self-improvement. I have no idea how I had made my selection of titles, but one of the books was *The Age of Reason* by Jean Paul Sartre. Somehow my possession of this philosophical novel came to the attention of the seminary rector, who summoned me. He demanded to know if I had been reading Sartre. I recall that the first phase of my panic was tied to shame at being unable to understand the work of the French existentialist. My intellectual mulishness would be exposed. Then I realized the rector had read as little as I. He confiscated the book, announcing it as "on the Index." The word carried a jolt, evoking an image of heretics burning at the stake. The Index was the devil's own library, a store of ideas too dangerous to know about. The Index? Me? But what really seemed amazing was that books on the Index were available in paperback.

The Index of Forbidden Books, dating to the sixteenth century, was the Inquisition's list of publications deemed to be heretical. Catholics could not read these books without formal dispensation. The Index was not abolished until 1966. The Roman Congregation of the Inquisition, formally called the Holy Office, was renamed in 1965, becoming the Congregation for the Doctrine of the Faith. The prefect, or head, of that congregation today is Cardinal Joseph Ratzinger, to whom we have already referred. Ratzinger is the putative author of Canon 1436.1 of the Code of Canon Law, which states, "One who denies a truth which must be believed with divine and Catholic faith, or who calls it into doubt, or who totally repudiates the Christian faith, and does not retract it after having been warned, is to be punished as a heretic or an apostate with major excommunication."[1] This canon and others like it were added to the Code of Canon Law only in May 1998, by Pope John Paul II, with an apostolic letter, *Ad Tuendam Fidem* ("To Defend the Faith"). Cardinal Ratzinger wrote an accompanying explanation that gave numerous examples of causes for excommunication, such as affirming the right of women to be ordained to the priesthood and questioning the absolute prohibition on sex before marriage.[2] The pope's amendment to canon law and Ratzinger's commentary drew relatively little attention outside professional Church circles. An editorial in the Catholic newspaper *The Tablet,* published in Britain, commented, "The recent *moto proprio Ad Tuendam Fidem,* and above all the commentary on it from Cardinal Ratzinger, are clearly designed to shut down debate on matters about which there was much more to be said . . . Rome's desire to silence theological dissent contradicts the deeply felt commitment to the importance of freedom of speech and intellectual integrity that is characteristic of modern democracies. In the secular world, only dictators silence their opponents and demand unquestioning obedience."[3]

A few months before *Ad Tuendam Fidem,* in January 1998, Cardinal Ratzinger announced the opening to scholars of the archives of the Holy Office — the Inquisition. In making available these previously closed records, which amount to some forty-five hundred documents, Ratzinger referred to *Tertio Millennio Adveniente,* the pope's premillennial call for a thorough Catholic examination of conscience. "It is appropriate," John Paul II wrote in 1994, "that, as the Second Millennium of Christianity draws to a close, the Church should become more fully conscious of the sinfulness of her children, recalling all those times in history when they departed from the Spirit of Christ." Aware of the distinction between "the Church" and "her sinful children," Ratzinger confidently predicted that historians would find that the archival records "clearly affirm the role of the Roman Pontiff to 'confirm his brothers in the faith.'"

That distinction was central to "We Remember: A Reflection on the Shoah," the 1998 document in which the Vatican attempted to confront its own relationship to the Holocaust. "We Remember" and Ratzinger's announcement about the Inquisition archives were published almost simultaneously, which seemed odd given one of the former's omissions. While individual members of the Church were acknowledged, in "We Remember," as having been guilty of pro-Nazi collaboration or worse, the Church as such was exonerated. So were the popes (as we saw, Pius XII was praised for the "wisdom" of his diplomacy), and so was the Vatican. The document carried the distinction between "sinful children" and the "Church as such" back through history, summarizing the "tormented" record of relations between Jews and Catholics dating back, as it says with such implication, to "the dawn of Christianity, after the crucifixion of Jesus." In this summary, Christian "mobs" were guilty of abuses toward Jews, including "violence, looting, even massacres . . . expulsions or attempts at forced conversions." To "the Church as such," however, belonged only virtues, like compassion for Jews.

Two weeks after the Vatican announcement about the opening of the archives, the Brown University historian David Kertzer wrote in the *New York Times*, "We can learn much from the newly opened archives. The explanation of what made the Holocaust possible is to be found in no small part in the files of the Inquisition. Those documents will deepen our knowledge of how for centuries the Roman Catholic Church conditioned the European population to view the Jews as inferiors."[4] But in its statement about Christian abuses of Jews, the Vatican does not explain how the Inquisition, the Holy Office, was the work not of the "Church as such" but of individual members departing from the Spirit of Christ. In fact, "We Remember" never mentions the Inquisition.

⤞ 33 ⤝

Convivencia to *Reconquista*

I T ALL BEGINS in what some remember as a kind of paradise. The Iberian Peninsula, cut off from Europe by nearly impassable mountains, and spared the long darkness of northern barbarian domination, had been the locus of a rich intermingling of Moorish, classical, Christian, and Jewish cultures. Three geographically distinct regions pollinated one another economically, intellectually, and aesthetically: the seafarers in the west, the land tenders and silk makers in the south, and the castle dwellers and townspeople of the center and north. A common culture resulted from the balance of these various regions, and it even included an anomalous mixing of religious influences. Spanish historians refer to this period as *convivencia,* a word loosely translated as "coexistence,"[1] but one implying a far more creative interaction than that of, say, the United States and the Soviet Union during their time of coexistence.

In Córdoba, for example, under the rule of the Islamic caliphate, Christians were welcome to hold their worship services in the Great Mosque, and they did so. It was one of the grand building complexes in Europe, dating to the eighth century, proudly situated by a noble river, above an ancient Roman bridge. The mosque still stands, with its dramatic horseshoe arches and arcades, stone window grilles and battlements, although all of the Moorish elements are overshadowed now by the Christian cathedral that was built on top of the mosque in the sixteenth century.[2]

Muslim Córdoba was the site of what may have been the first medieval university, begun in the tenth century. The city dominated a high plateau in dramatic, rolling country. It was "built in tiers," as an early source described it, "one above the other, so that the ground of the uppermost was at the level of the rooftops of the middle, and the ground of the middle at the level of the rooftops of the lowest. All three were surrounded by walls. The palace stood in the uppermost region . . . in the middle region were orchards and gardens, while the Friday mosque and private dwellings were situated on the lowest level."[3] Today, the terraces of the caliph's Córdoba lie open to the sun in vast excavations. Intricate stone carvings, showing trees and leaves and patterns of intertwined vines, mark walls, gates, and the capitals of pillars. The rich blues and greens of mosaic tiles are set off by gold chips of script that elaborates the name of Allah. Ribbed vaults supporting domes, and complex tunneling that supplied water to the city, remain as evidence of premillennial Moorish engineering genius.

Jews were taught Arabic by Muslim scholars, and they mastered the Koran as well as Hebrew Scriptures. Mathematics, astronomy, and medicine were complemented by the study of philosophy, based on the entire corpus of Aristotle and much of Plato. Extant scholarly works by Jews, dating to the *convivencia* period, establish that many Jews mastered these subjects. The most familiar such figure is the Córdoba native Moses ben Maimon, whose writing proves the point: Perhaps the most revered of all Jewish sages, Maimonides wrote in Arabic, not Hebrew.

The scholar Norman Roth is one of my important sources for information on the life of Jews in Iberia. He writes, "The names cited by Maimonides in his work read like a *Who's Who* of classical and Muslim philosophy and science: Plato and Aristotle, of course; but also Alexander of Aphrodisias, Themistius, John Philoponus, Euclid, Ptolemy, Pythagoras, and almost all of the Muslim philosophers."[4] Maimonides would not have been Maimonides had he not lived in Iberia, no matter what his genius. "Were he to have been born in another land, France or Germany, for instance," Roth asserts, "he would at most have become another one of those almost anonymous rabbis who wrote endless commentaries on commentaries on the Talmud." Because his creativity and intelligence were nurtured by the richest diversity of influences in the world — among the richest in history — Maimonides became "the greatest genius ever produced by the Jewish people."[5]

So Maimonides is a kind of measure of the value of *convivencia*. And as Muslims were the teachers of Jews, so Jews were schoolmasters to Christians, particularly in Castile and Catalonia.[6] The three religious traditions influenced one another, and eventually, for a time, ethnic and creedal differences came to mean less than differences of caste and region, of social role and work. This was, in other words, a moment full of possibility, another of the roads not taken. Yet *convivencia,* that it existed at all, establishes that there is nothing monolithic about the history of Jewish-Christian relations, and nothing fated to lead inexorably to disaster. That Jews

and Christians, together with Muslims, can live in amity, respecting differences while honoring commonalities — that this is no pipe dream — is
proven by the fact that, for centuries, they did just that.

The richness of Iberian life in this period was partly due to its isolation from the rest of Europe — which was living through a broad cultural
stasis, marked especially by its loss of the classical tradition — and, conversely, partly due to its fluent contact with the distant East, especially
the thriving Islamic capital of Baghdad. That city and its environs, since
the sixth-century publication of the Babylonian Talmud, had also been
a center of Hebrew biblical and Talmudic scholarship.[7] By the time of
Maimonides, Christians and Jews held positions of political power in the
Islamic regime that controlled most of Iberia. All three religious groups
were embarked on similar, sometimes common programs of material and
spiritual renaissance. Vestiges of *convivencia* are evident in the striking —
to our eye Moorish — style of architecture that still distinguishes Spanish
churches, mosques, and synagogues.

As if shaken by a continent-wide seismic shift, *convivencia* broke apart
into violent imbalance around the time that the crusading fervor first
swept through northern Europe. A far stricter sect of militant Muslims,
who rejected Iberian intermingling and aesthetics — and the soft life of
beauty reflected in the elegant Moorish style — crossed over from North
Africa in about 1145, a turn in the story remembered as the Almohad Invasion. For two decades, this puritanical contingent of Muslims fought the
ruling Iberian caliphates, as well as Christians and Jews, before finally establishing control, in the south and center.[8] But by then, astir with a crusading fervor of their own, the Christian kingdoms in the peninsula's far
north had begun the campaign of *reconquista,* with the ambition of restoring all of Iberia to Christian control. The Spanish epic poem *El Cid*
dates to this period (c. 1140). Taken as a celebration of Christian resistance
to Muslims, it nevertheless carries the curves of *convivencia,* since the
Christian hero ends as a man in the middle, associated as much with Muslims as with his own kind.[9]

By the middle of the twelfth century, in the thick of the crusading era,
the time of tolerance was passing. When the Christian Alfonso VII conquered Córdoba in 1146, he ordered a cross put atop the Great Mosque, in
which, before the Almohads, Catholic Masses had been freely celebrated.
King Alfonso declared that henceforth the mosque would be a church.[10]
The Muslims would recapture Córdoba in short order, and would remove
the cross. They struck out at Christians and Jews alike, with unprece-

dented ruthlessness. Perhaps the most striking signal of the demise of *convivencia* was the decision, in 1159, by the brilliant twenty-four-year-old Maimonides to abandon Córdoba, because Jews there were being forcibly converted or murdered by the now fanatical Almohads. Maimonides fled with his family to Egypt, where he would become famous as a physician. He never returned to Iberia. In tribute to his stature, he became known as a second "Moses the Egyptian," although he always identified himself as an Iberian.[11]

Christian armies decisively defeated the Almohads in 1212.[12] Before long, Muslim rulers were vanquished throughout the peninsula, except for an enclave in the far south, around Granada. When Christians retook Córdoba once and for all, the cross went back on the Great Mosque, where it remained. The *reconquista* reestablished Christian dominance for the first time since the eighth century. By now, Iberia was populated by about three million people.[13] Many Muslims had retreated to Granada and to North Africa, while some had become Christians. A sizable minority remained where they were as Muslims. The well-established Jewish communities, totaling several hundred thousand, remained more or less in place, as Christians took over again. Aware of contemporaneous events in northern Europe, Jews in Iberia were braced.

Yet the spirit of *convivencia* in some ways held, and in some places it flourished anew. In Castile, by far the largest part of Iberia, extending in the center from Portugal to the eastern kingdom of Aragon, no one was forced to change his religion. Ferdinand III, the king of Castile from 1217 until 1252, called himself the "king of the three religions,"[14] as if coexistence had a future.

Castile's capital was Toledo, in the dead center of Iberia. The late-medieval city had a population of perhaps forty thousand, with as many as a third of them Jews.[15] The Castilian court was known for its Jewish sages and physicians. Toledo was identified with the legendary School of Translators, a century-old collaboration of Jews, Christians, and Muslims, which only now came fully into its own. In fact, the tripartite work of translation had been going on all over Spain, a natural outcome of *convivencia,* but it was an activity particularly associated with trilingual Jews. It was these translators who, in the late twelfth and thirteenth centuries, had rendered the great works of Aristotle, Avicenna, Averroës, and Maimonides into Latin, making them available to the rest of Europe and sparking the northern renaissance.

Toledo is about an hour's drive from Madrid, and I made the trip while writing this book. The city, with its crenelated wall, dominates a mesa that rises above a dusty agricultural plain. There is something whimsical about Toledo's high prominence in the otherwise spare landscape, and it is easy to conjure the mystical impression it must have made on the medieval imagination. Once inside the wall, however, the visitor is struck by the confining narrow lanes that wind around a central square, above which loom the cathedral, municipal hall, and bishop's palace. The alleys and by-ways create a maze that makes the city seem small, undoing the feeling of spaciousness inspired at first sight of the hilltop enclave.

Toledo was called the Jerusalem of Spain, and some accounts trace its founding to Jews well before the birth of Christ. One conjecture has it that the name itself evolved from Hebrew.[16] Among the Christians who so positively interacted with Toledo's Jews a tradition developed that they were consulted by the Jews of Jerusalem as to whether Jesus should be put to death, and Toledo's Jews said no.[17] An indication of the vitality of Jewish participation in the life of medieval Toledo can be seen in a beautiful cluster of buildings in the western part of the city. They originated as the villa, constructed in the Moorish style in the early fourteenth century, of one of the prominent Jews of the era, Samuel Halevy (1320–1360?), who served the king of Castile as chief minister and treasurer. Halevy's house, with its multilevel tiled roofs, its colonnades, arched porticoes, and soaring central tower, is a monument to the family's power and taste, but also to a world that would cease to exist. In Halevy's own lifetime, with deadly consequences for him, a paroxysm of anti-Jewish violence would sweep Europe, set off by the Black Plague (1348) and a paranoid targeting, in particular, of Toledo's Jews. The continent-wide plague would be said to have originated in Toledo.

Ultimately, Halevy's villa became the home of the Spanish painter El Greco (1541–1614), who did some of his greatest work there. The building now serves as the El Greco Museum. Halevy would no doubt have been forgotten except for the building he constructed next door, a synagogue that served his community and that is known today as Sinagoga del Tránsito. The building is now a museum that commemorates the Jewish presence in Iberia. The central hall is about the size of a basketball court. With its intricately carved stonework and coffered ceiling, the place suggests the mystery to which a Jewish assembly would once have been attuned. Windows high on the wall, interspersed with blind arches, are said to repeat a pattern of the Temple; "and its windows," an inscription reads, "are like the windows of Ariel."[18] Hebrew letters line the high balustrade, and one wall features a design based on the tablets of Moses. Pillars support the Moorish arches that have ever since been a mark of synagogue architecture. Despite the distinctively Jewish cast to the original work, there is reason to believe that Muslim and Christian craftsmen and artists, along with Jews, built the building and decorated it.[19]

On the day of my visit, a thin trickle of tourists came and went, glancing quickly at a lost world, apparently unsure what to make of it. If there are ghosts in the place, they are lost Jews, but also knights of a military order that occupied it for a time and whose bodies are buried under the floor tiles, and Jesuits who said Masses in its niches. The building is a shrine, finally, to the melancholy history we are about to retrace. Indeed, the synagogue served as a Christian church for longer than as a center of Jewish study and prayer. As Halevy's house became El Greco's, the synagogue stands as a monument to supersessionism. A Christian belfry imposed long after Halevy's architects did their work dominates the building's exterior, and its very name derives from the one it bore as a church, El Tránsito de Nuestra Señora. The phrase refers to the glorification of the Virgin, but it suggests irretrievable worlds now lost.

In 1260, the School of Translators in Toledo received a royal charter from Alfonso X, Ferdinand III's son and successor. Under Alfonso's guidance, these scholars began to render the great works into Castilian, and a creative flowering of the vernacular followed. Jews were centrally involved in the invention of the Spanish language.

Alfonso X (b. 1221) was known as "the Wise." His reign stands in marked contrast to contemporary rulers in the rest of Europe. While Saint Louis, for example, was seeing to the burning of the Talmud in Paris, Alfonso was sponsoring its careful translation.[20] Yitzhak Baer, author of the seminal *A History of the Jews in Christian Spain*, noted, "The friendly relations between Alfonso X, the Wise, and the Jews extended beyond the realm of politics. The king, himself a scholar and patron of learning, extended to Jewish scholars a hospitality not to be found in the courts of any of his contemporaries . . . A versatile aggregation of Jewish scholars and scientists thus surrounded the learned king."[21] When Alfonso had buried his father, he ordered the tomb inscribed with tributes in Hebrew, Arabic, Castilian, and Latin.

But the stresses of this tumultuous age — recall that the Fourth Lateran Council had already issued its anti-Jewish strictures, and the conversionist Franciscans and Dominicans were fanning out across Iberia as much as France — are nowhere more tragically dramatized than in the denouement of the story of Alfonso the Wise. He not only wanted a reconquered Iberia, unified under himself, but also had attempted, through dynastic alliances and wars, to expand the power of Castile north into France. Twice (in 1257 and c. 1275) Alfonso sought to be elected Holy Roman Emperor, to assert his vision of absolute unity over Europe. In all of this he was defeated. Had he succeeded in the period of his ecumenical open-mindedness toward Jews, the history of Europe could have been very different. On the other hand, there would have remained in a kingdom of such univocal sway the question of Jewish difference, which might only then have surfaced as something at which such a monarch could take offense.

As it happened, Alfonso the Wise took offense at Jews not when he was gathering power, but when he began to lose it. Toward the end of his reign, he was betrayed by his son Sancho, who led a revolt against him (1280–1281). Alfonso's fierce reaction included an apparently out-of-the-blue attack on the very Jews with whom he had been so intimate.[22] It is not clear what prompted such a response, but what followed would make it appear that *convivencia* was a house built on sand after all. Jews of Toledo were imprisoned in their own synagogues. The wealthiest among them were made to pay exorbitant ransoms. Many were tortured and forced to convert. "The Jewish community of Toledo was demolished," Baer says, "like 'Sodom and Gomorrah.'"[23] It would attempt a recovery in the next generation, when Samuel Halevy rose to prominence and a temporary amity reestablished itself between Christians and Jews. But, as we saw, that would not last either. The days of Jews in Toledo were already numbered. As even the "wisest" and most humane of the Christian rulers revealed himself, in the end, to be an enemy of Jews, so the Jerusalem of Spain went the way of its namesake.

Alfonso's attack was not merely a matter of an ancient anti-Jewish dormant gene asserting itself, which is the way his assault on Jews, and the Iberian nightmare it foreshadows, is often read. This analysis, in effect, reinforces the doom-laden expectation that Jews must always be victims. In this view, *convivencia* was a temporary aberration, a mistake in history, instead of a genuine opening to a new possibility. I would argue that Jewish-Christian-Muslim amity in Iberia was no mistake; it was a development grounded in the core meaning of each tradition, one that could have continued to thrive. That it did not do so was the result not just of inbred Christian Jew-hatred but of a complex interplay of factors, one of which was the agency of Jews themselves. Jews, in other words, are not mere victims here.

There were forces at work beneath the surface of the Alfonsine *convivencia* that began with a powerful Jewish rejection of all that the king claimed for himself. At the time that Alfonso was fighting off his son and attacking Jews, one of the great Jewish sages, Moses de Leon (c. 1240–1305), working in Castile, was composing what the critic Harold Bloom has characterized as "the only indubitably great book in all of Western esotericism,"[24] the *Zohar,* or Book of Splendor. As Bloom's word "esotericism" indicates, the *Zohar* is usually discussed as a mystical text. A multivolume work composed in Hebrew and Aramaic, it is defined by the scholar Gershom Scholem as "the central work in the literature of the Kabbalah."[25] Kabbalah, a labyrinthine Jewish tradition of teachings about God and God's creation, now began to coalesce as an identifiable vision. With Moses de Leon, long-buried currents of Neo-Platonic and Gnostic systems of interpreting the tradition and its texts surfaced, and from then on, the tradition of Kabbalah, as much mythmaking as mystical, would be a major force in Jewish spirituality. More than that, Kabbalah would have profound implications for the place of Judaism both in Christendom and in the Enlightenment, and we will see more of its religious and political significance later.

The point to emphasize here is that thirteenth-century Kabbalists, based in Iberia, and perhaps especially in Castile,[26] engaged in a daring act of intellectual resistance, for their vision was a direct, if subtle, repudiation of all that the king of Castile was just then claiming for himself. In the *Zohar* we find the figure of a second-century rabbi, Simeon bar Yochai, who is remembered as risking his life to organize a secret campaign of opposition to the Roman overlord during the period of the savage Roman wars against the Jewish people. He is known among devotees as the Rashby, an acronym for his formal name. The *Zohar* records his commentaries on the Torah, together with descriptions of covert assemblies he convened, at which he expounded the mysteries of God's life in creation. The Kabbalists living in the time of Alfonso X, centered around the figure of Moses de Leon, modeled themselves on the Rashby, and they saw the Castilian king of their own day, with his increasingly absolutist claims to power, as equivalent to the oppressive emperor of ancient Rome. So when they compiled the sayings of the heroic master who taught how the Torah offered a way to stand against a prevailing ideology, they were engaged in politics as much as religion. "These mystics saw themselves as the true heirs of the Rashby and his associates," the historian Neil Asher Silberman writes, "meeting in secret conclaves far from the centers of royal power, connecting with the divine forces and envisioning a radical change in the order of things. As radical opponents of the ideology of the *Reconquista,* they shaped the earlier kabbalistic traditions into a far more politically focussed myth."[27]

Taking off from the Neo-Platonic vision of creation as an emanation of God, the *Zohar* implies, in Bloom's words, that "all theories of emanation are also theories of language."[28] One of the most potent ideas of Kabbalah is that "turns of language," in Bloom's phrase, somehow substitute for God — that the names of God, beyond mere representation, make God available to those who know them. When this idea is later misunderstood, especially by Christians, there will follow a common denigration of Kabbalah as a kind of code-magic, but in fact it represents a profound affirmation not only of the way God is invested in what God has made — in Kabbalah, emanation occurs within God, not out from God — but of the way words themselves embody the things for which words stand.

Here is one example of this idea and its explosive implications. *Shekhinah,* usually translated "Spirit," is one name of God associated with the Wisdom tradition, rendered in Greek as *Sophia,* implying the way it is taken as a female principle of divinity. Another is *Tiferet,* which means "Glory." One spectacular vision laid out in the *Zohar* assumes the marriage of these two emanations of God, a physical coming together of divine attributes, which is nonetheless imagined within the context of a strict monotheism. Silberman, whose work especially informs me, writes:

> The sheer anthropomorphism and blatantly sexual imagery of this configuration . . . has scandalized countless religious authorities from the time of its composition to the present. It is certainly an understatement to say that its ascribed roles to male and female within the constellation of divine forces are, by today's standards, exceedingly politically incorrect. Yet the political point made in the ideal of the "marriage" of Tiferet and . . . the Shekhinah was a direct repudiation of the royal ideology of the Castilian king. For where Alfonso sang as a troubadour of his love and attachment to the Virgin, the Zohar described the great, painful rift that had been forced on the heavenly king and queen. As already expressed by earlier Castilian kabbalists, the Shekhinah — the regal, motherly guardian of Israel — had been abducted by the forces of darkness, who were now even more explicitly parallel to the Alfonsine ideal.[29]

When Alfonso's dream of empire began to collapse, even to the traitorous rebellion of his own son, Kabbalists could only behold the drama as

an enactment of divine intervention on behalf of Israel. This was so because "the worldview of the Kabbalah has always been that events in
heaven are closely mirrored by unfolding historical events on earth. Could
Alfonso's humiliation mean that the forces of darkness were being weakened?"[30] The coming year 1300 sparked an apocalyptic fervor in Europe,
among Jews as well as Christians, and that too played into Iberian Jewry's
sense that political events were fraught with religious meaning. This belief
among Jews of a benign cosmic order that required a rejection of its enemies on earth, even if those enemies were in a position to wreak havoc
with Jews, strengthened a spirit of Jewish resistance at a time when few
could have predicted how necessary it was about to become. Soon even
many court Jews, those once favored associates of the Crown — linguists,
scientists, financiers, philosophers — aligned themselves with the radical
Kabbalists. The Rashby, hero of Jewish resistance to Rome, was one figure
to rally around; his saga was a text with which to construct a new gyre of
commentary and inventive interpretation. Far more than an "esoteric"
mysticism, the Kabbalah was launched as a bracing source of Jewish identity, even if, increasingly, and for ever more obvious reasons, Jews would
celebrate it in secret.

Convivencia would not survive *reconquista.* Above Christians the old
Constantinian cloud — how Christians behave when they come fully into
power — crossed the sky again, throwing shadows. The Church, as we
shall shortly see, mobilized in a new way, wielding its spiritual sword and
blessing the king's decidedly unspiritual one. The Castilian regime's campaign against Jews, particularly against wealthy Jews from whom money
could be extorted or robbed, went on nearly unchecked through the turn
of the century. In response, one of Alfonso's former Jewish associates, Don
Todros, in a series of powerful sermons to Jewish congregations throughout Castile, denounced the king and decreed an era of Jewish separation
and purification based on renewed observance of the Torah. Don Todros
gave shape, if indirectly, to the Kabbalistic vision of cosmic conflict between light and darkness, which he defined as a conflict between the
Crown and Israel.

Jewish courtiers who tried to save their positions of influence and their
fortunes were denounced by Don Todros as vigorously as the oppressive royals were, and with that something new began to happen among
Jews themselves. A class distinction suddenly cut across the old religious
boundaries, and Jews were able to be named as enemies by other Jews.
"The passionate struggle for freedom and redemption was now to be

waged against the wealthy wicked by the forces of the righteous poor."[31] Wealth and poverty, independent of other factors, became categories of moral judgment.

Don Todros's bold leadership at this crucial time has led some later historians of Kabbalah to conclude that he was the real figure behind the *Zohar*'s hero, Rabbi Simeon bar Yochai.[32] However it is remembered, the story of Don Todros's powerful appropriation of Kabbalah to defend Israel and inveigh against unjust privilege makes clear that the Jewish communities of Iberia, and then the Mediterranean where the message spread, were not passively waiting for the sky to fall, as Christian memory often portrays this history. No, at the beginning of the fourteenth century, an enduring Jewish faith in Israel as God's chosen people was refracted through a new politics and a new spirituality, both of which would feed back into an old Christian animus, but in ways of which Christians would remain ignorant to this day.

➤ 34 ◂

Convert-Making: The Failure
of Success

WHILE THE DENOUEMENT of Alfonsine *convivencia* played itself out in Castile, events in Aragon, to the east, unfolded somewhat differently. In 1242, the year of the burning of the Talmud in Paris, King James I of Aragon (1213–1276) issued an edict requiring all Jews in his kingdom to attend the conversionist sermons of the Dominicans and Franciscans. Clearly, Europe's dark cloud was drifting south. The Talmud was condemned in France, as we saw, not mainly for its blasphemies but for its heretical character in relation to "the Old Law which God gave to Moses," as Pope Gregory IX's complaint put it.[1] Similarly, the sermon mandate was an implication of the Church's innovative claim to spiritual authority over the religious lives of Jews. But within two years of James I's edict, that implication was made explicit by the newly elected Pope Innocent IV, whose condemnation of the Talmud we heard earlier. Justifying the forcing of Jews to listen to Christian sermons, he said: "Indeed, we believe that the pope, who is the vicar of Jesus Christ, has authority not only over Christians but also over all infidels, since Christ had authority over all . . . Therefore, the pope can judge the Jews, if they violate the law of the Gospel in moral matters and their own prelates do not check them, and also if they invent heresies against their own law."[2]

Following upon the edict of James I, and similar edicts by other Christian rulers, the Dominicans and Franciscans escalated their campaign. They went about "forcibly entering synagogues," according to Jeremy Cohen, author of the exhaustive study *The Friars and the Jews*, "and subjecting Jews to offensive harangues, participation in debates whose outcomes had been predetermined, and the violence of the mob. The intent of the

friars was obvious: to eliminate the Jewish presence in Christendom —
both by inducing the Jews to convert and by destroying all remnants of Judaism even after no Jews remained."[3]

This explicitly undid the long-standing Catholic policy, dating to Augustine, according to which Jews were to have a protected, if restricted,
place in Christendom. But that political reversal was tied to the theological one referred to above. Saint Paul's assessment that Jewish leaders had
not recognized Jesus as the Messiah because God, for God's own purposes, made them deaf and blind[4] was overturned now, as we saw, by
Thomas Aquinas. In a section of the *Summa Theologiae* entitled "The
Cause of Christ's Passion," Thomas writes, "A distinction must be drawn
between the Jews who were educated and those who were not. The educated, who were called their *rulers*, knew, as did the demons, that Jesus was
the Messiah promised in the Law. For they saw all the signs in him which
had been foretold."[5] Jews, who killed Jesus anyway, were even more heinous than had been thought.

In this era of massive shifts in the scales of political power, as popes
looked to secure broad allegiances while bypassing kings, bishops, and
even local clergy, and as kings sought to consolidate power over barons
and other nobles, the Jews would prove to be decisive weights in those
scales. The friars were levers with which to move them.[6] In 1263, James I
summoned Rabbi Moses ben Nachman (1194–c. 1270), known as Nachmanides, a leading Jewish sage, to appear at the royal palace in Barcelona.
The rabbi was in his sixties, a figure whose stature rivaled that of Maimonides. At four meetings that took place over several days in July, Nachmanides was forced to "debate" a Dominican preacher, Pablo Cristiani, or
Paul Christian. A convert from Judaism, he had formerly been named
Saul. The master general of the Dominican order, a Catalonian named
Raymond of Penaforte, now revered as a saint, was present, as were the
leading clergy and nobles and prominent Jews of the kingdom.

James I officiated as the two religious figures argued the essential questions that forever separate Jews and Christians: Was Jesus the anointed
one? Was he God? Did he suffer and die for human salvation? Was the
"Old Law" of Israel — Jewish belief and customs — now superseded and
to be, in Cristiani's word, "terminated"?[7] Christian and Jewish sources
alike assert that Nachmanides held his ground. How could the Messiah
have come already, he asked with elegant simplicity, with so much violence and injustice still prevailing? The Dominican, claiming an intimate
knowledge of the Talmud, added something new to Christian anti-Jewish

polemic, as I first learned from Adam Gregerman, for the friar emphasized that the Talmudic tradition's own logic pointed to the Messiahship of Jesus. Nachmanides countered that Friar Paul's readings were shallow distortions. According to Robert Chazan, the rabbi had two purposes: to persuade "the Dominicans of the fundamental flaws in their new missionizing argumentation, hoping to convince them to abandon it . . .[and] to prove to his fellow Jews that the new missionizing arguments were as unconvincing as the old."[8]

Nachmanides specifically rebutted Friar Paul's assertions of rabbinic authority for Christian claims, and mocked the idea that traditional Jewish discourse unintentionally proclaimed Jesus as Messiah.[9] In the end, the king himself testified to the rabbi's success, if backhandedly: "For I have never seen a man who was in the wrong argue as well as you did."[10]

But Nachmanides was not cheered. He saw quite plainly what was at stake in the disputation. Later he would write his own account of it, probably to give fellow Jews a primer on how to rebut the arguments of the friars, for it was clear to him that the Dominican campaign against Judaism would only intensify. As if he had seen what was coming, Nachmanides had wanted to cut short his own contest. He had opened the fourth and final session by declaring, "I do not wish to continue the Disputation." This was a plea to the king. "The Jewish community here is large and they . . . have begged me to desist, for they are very much afraid of these men, the Preaching Friars, who cast fear on the world."[11]

What sort of fear would become apparent soon enough. The king demanded that the disputation continue. Within weeks, James I issued a set of decrees forcing Jews to attend Dominican sermons and giving Friar Paul new powers to missionize among Jews.[12] When Nachmanides's own, entirely self-assertive account of the Barcelona disputation was published, with its forthright denunciation of the Dominicans, King James ordered the text burned and the rabbi exiled for two years. For the Dominicans, that was not enough. They charged Nachmanides with blasphemy for what he had said during the course of the debate they had forced on him. Pope Clement IV, in 1266, supported the charge, and rebuked James I for failing to "repress Jewish mischief," especially that of Nachmanides, author of the "book full of flagrant lies."[13] Nachmanides might have been killed, but King James enabled his escape, and he fled to Palestine.

The affair demonstrates how power was flowing to the Dominicans. Within a few years, one of them was elected pope, as Nicholas III (1277–1280) — an extraordinary ascent for an order that had been founded only two thirds of a century before. His time as pope coincided with the collapse of *convivencia* in Castile and with the surfacing among Jews there of Kabbalah. We have already noted that secrecy was an inbuilt characteristic of the *Zohar,* and now it becomes clearer why that had to be so. Talmudic texts were being widely distributed among the missionizers, with the sacred meanings of rabbinic sources twisted against the Jewish people. Kabbalists did not want the same fate to befall their compilations, which were, after all, able to be taken as literary acts of treason. And if the Talmud could be distorted by Christians to argue for the truth of Christian claims, there was no doubt that Kabbalistic texts, if known, could be too. In fact, it may have begun to happen. Putting a new kink in the earlier comity of a tripartite translation culture, the nephew of Alfonso X wrote that his uncle the king had "ordered translated the whole law of the Jews, and even their Talmud, and other knowledge which is called *qabbalah* and which the Jews keep closely secret. And he did this so it might be manifest through their own law that all is a [mere] representation of the Law which we Christians have."[14]

Pope Nicholas III, in promulgating the by now customary *Sicut Judaeis,* altered this bull that was instituted to protect Jews. Not surprisingly, the Dominican pope added a new requirement for the whole Church, mandating "sermons and other means for the conversion of the Jews."[15] Now this preaching had the ultimate credential, and was undertaken throughout Europe. In what did such sermons consist? They were unlikely to be the highly reasoned discourses of a Thomas Aquinas, nor were they necessarily ordered arguments for Jesus' Messiahship, whether from the Old Testament or from rabbinic texts. One must assume that the mendicant proselytizers were well intentioned and, perhaps at first, better disposed toward Jews than toward heretics, their other target. But as time wore on, and as heresy proved elusive, and as their efforts failed to bring about the longed-for mass conversion of Jews, which would usher in a new age of holy conformity, one must equally expect to find the onset of a certain intemperance. As Chazan writes, "The most massive effort at winning over Jews ever undertaken had inevitably to produce a significant level of anger and frustration with its failure . . . Old stereotypes of Jewish blindness and obtuseness were inevitably reinforced. This occurred not out of a specifically anti-Jewish hue to the missionizing or out of an initially negative disposition on the part of the missionizers. The culprit was ultimately the new environment that spawned the conversionist ardor."[16]

Nevertheless, the friars were generally drawn from the new mercantile middle class, and their sermons in this climate increasingly reflected the prejudices of that class, particularly relating to commerce and money-lending.[17] Their sermons, that is, grew to depend more on negative arguments against Jews than on positive arguments for Christ. Ongoing Jewish refusal to convert spawned sermons aimed not *at* Jews, but at other Christians *about* Jews, a subtle alteration designed to increase the pressure on Jews. Such an approach required that the anti-Jewish negatives be drawn in ever darker hues, and they were. Drawn from Jeremy Cohen's *The Friars and the Jews,* here is an example of a sermon preached to Christians by a leading Dominican, Giordano da Rivalto, in Florence on November 9, 1304. After beginning with the traditional assertion that Jews murdered Christ, the friar goes on to charge that Jews are *still* murdering Christ. "I say first of all that they repeat it [the crucifixion] in their hearts with ill will — wherefore they are evil at heart and hate Christ with evil hatred; and they would, were they able, crucify him anew every day . . . They are hated throughout the world because they are evil toward Christ, whom they curse."[18] And how do Jews curse Christ? By refusing to convert.

As the pressure mounted, with an all-out campaign to overcome Jewish resistance to Christian claims, the continued assertion of that resistance became *experienced* as a new form of crucifixion. The friars were themselves passionately identified with Christ. Indeed, such identification was an element of their innovative piety. In Saint Francis of Assisi the theme was set with his own stigmata, referred to earlier, the appearance of the wounds of Christ on his hands, feet, and side, which began in 1224, two years before his death. The friars were self-described *alter Christi,* other Christs, and it would have been natural for them to interpret the frustrations of their own mission as a repetition of the frustration felt by the betrayed Jesus. And it would have been easy for them to think that the betrayers were the same.

The inbuilt momentum of such feelings opens to a new perversion when the Dominican Giordano goes on to make the charge of contemporary crucifixion concrete by declaring in his sermon that Jews steal the Eucharistic host to blaspheme it. Giordano claims to have personally witnessed such a desecration — and to have seen with his own eyes an apparition of the youthful Jesus, come upon the scene to stop it. By this miraculous intervention, as Jeremy Cohen summarizes Giordano, Jesus "rallied the local Christian population to slaughter 24,000 Jews in punishment for their evil deed."[19] At last Jesus himself has been recruited as a booster of mass killings of Jews.

Giordano stoops to another level of denigration by claiming that Jews continue to murder Jesus down to the present by kidnapping a Christian boy every year and crucifying him. When we saw this libel before, it was being spread by barely literate rabble-rousers, and was resoundingly condemned by representatives of the official Church. But now the promulgator is the authorized official himself. Such a development meant, of course, that the situation of Jews would worsen in the fourteenth century. Yet when the new conversionism intersected with an unpredictable natural disaster, the consequences were almost unimaginable.

"In the cities, men fell sick by thousands, and lacking care and aid, almost all died." This is Boccaccio writing of the Black Plague. "In the morning, their bodies were found at the doors of the houses where they had expired during the night." Boccaccio was in Florence, and he says that "in the course of four or five months, more than one hundred thousand persons perished, a number greater than that estimated to be its population before this dreadful malady."[20] Between 1348 and 1351, something like twenty to twenty-five million people died as the disease spread through Europe from the southeast.[21] The infection was caused by a bacillus that lived in the blood of rats, and that seems to have arrived in Europe on a merchant ship at Messina, in Sicily. By the time the plague had moved across the continent and into England, one in three of those living in Europe was dead. The bodies of victims were often left where they were, and many corpses were buried in large communal graves.[22] This catastrophe, understandably, set off a vast panic, and given what had gone before, it is not surprising that the mass of Christians were ready to blame the Jews.

Everyone was asking what had caused this disaster. Pope Clement VI (1342–1352), was stunned when, in 1348, eleven thousand people died in his own court city of Avignon, including seven cardinals.[23] He was a Frenchman who had earned a doctorate at the University of Paris, and he summoned his learned advisors. When told that the cause of the plague was some conjunction of planets and stars, he scoffed. Clement ordered the papal physicians to dissect the corpses of plague victims, "in order that the origins of this disease might be known"[24] — an act that can be seen as the beginning of modern medicine. But survivors in the cities thought they knew the cause: a well-poisoning conspiracy of Jews. There was a heartbreaking poignancy in the widespread belief that the conspiracy had begun in Toledo, the one-time home of *convivencia* and center of the culture-creating tradition of Iberian translation. It was as if the intellectual transformation of Europe that *had* been spawned a century before in Toledo, largely, although not exclusively, by Jews, had been inverted by an act of black magic. The fruitful seeding of Christendom's intellect was now perverted into the deadly pollution of its drinking water.

A masterly rumor identified a native of Toledo, one Jacob Pascal, whose name suggested Passover, as the initiator of the plot. A cabal (a word we have from "Kabbalah") of Iberian Jews was the supplier of poison to Jewish agents elsewhere in Europe — a first international conspiracy. Jews in Geneva, under torture, confessed that the rumor was true, which was all it took.[25] As had been the case during the Crusades, the first major conflagration of anti-Jewish violence took place in the Rhineland, where Jews were slaughtered in large numbers. One chronicler reported that twelve thousand were put to death in Mainz — an echo of 1096.[26] There was an echo, too, in the resistance the Jews of Mainz put up, and in their self-immolation when all was lost. "By the time the plague had passed," Barbara Tuchman observed, "few Jews were left in Germany or the Low Countries."[27]

Officials of plague-stricken towns and cities wrote to officials elsewhere, warning of Jewish well poisoners.[28] A contemporary chronicler wrote, "In the matter of this plague the Jews throughout the world were reviled and accused in all lands of having caused it through the poison which they are said to have put into the water and the wells — that is what they were accused of — and for this reason the Jews were burnt all the way from the Mediterranean into Germany, but not in Avignon, for the pope protected them there."[29] Clement VI was the fourth pope to live at Avignon. He had presided over a lavish court, noted for its splendors. But, as indicated by his rejection of astrological superstition, the catastrophe of the plague brought out something great in him. His story is yet another of those all too rare chapels of heart in this grim history. He ordered the papal curia to maintain its routine as a way of defusing panic in the city, and he gave away a fortune to help those who had been struck down. Most important, and most dangerous to himself, he quelled the anti-Jewish riots in Avignon. He denounced violence against Jews, displaying courage, but also logic. In a papal bull, he pointed out the obvious fact that the supposed instigators of the plague were dying like everyone else. "That the Jews have provided the occasion or the cause for such a crime," he declared, "has no plausibility."[30] Clement ordered bishops everywhere to instruct the people not to attack Jews, but unfortunately the provinces under the pope's direct control seem to have been the only places where Jews were not assaulted in large numbers.[31]

As always, a Jew could escape the torment by accepting baptism, but again, it seems that relatively few did so. As in 1096, the chroniclers re-port that some Jewish communities — for example, those in Worms and Oppenheim — preempted their tormentors by committing mass suicide.[32] "In some cities the Jews themselves," a chronicler noted, "set fire to their houses and cremated themselves."[33]

The plague was an accelerating moment in the downward spiral of Jew-ish-Christian conflict, one to match the First Crusade, which had set the gyre winding. After 1348, anti-Jewish stereotyping became more vicious, with the Christian mind fixed on the Jew not merely as an enemy, as be-fore, but also as a mortal threat. After the plague, Christians were more obsessed with death than ever, and a heightened fixation on the agonized death of Jesus, as always, brought with it a renewed scapegoating of the "deicide" Jews. Popes, bishops, and some princes, following Clement VI's lead, would continue to defend Jews from violence and forced conver-sion, but they would also intensify their sponsorship of the program of proselytizing, which itself became more coercive after the plague. The in-ability of ecclesiastical and political leaders even now to grasp, as Rose-mary Radford Ruether put it, "that the mob merely acted out, in practice, a hatred which the Church taught in theory and enforced in social degra-dation whenever possible"[34] was never more tragic or dangerous.

Because the Jewish community in Iberia had been extraordinarily co-hesive and powerful, it had been especially scapegoated as the source of plague poisons. Now it would be especially targeted by the preachers. The steady drumbeat of officially enforced anti-Jewish denigration was heard in churches and synagogues throughout Spain. Despite the tradition of *convivencia,* plague-traumatized Iberian Christians were as subject to a blaming hatred of Jews as any, but the resentment of the peasant class and the urban poor was exacerbated by the relative affluence and social privi-lege of many Jews in Spain. The post-plague dislocations of agriculture and trade led to a series of economic crises that would shape the daily lives of all classes for more than a century. The fate of the Jews would prove to be tied to something as fundamental as the hunger of peasants, but that hunger could now lead to reactions that once, in Spain, would have been unthinkable.

Through the decade of the 1380s, a particularly ferocious anti-Jewish preacher named Ferrant Martinez operated out of Seville. In his sermons, he identified Jews as the obstacle to the prosperity and amity that were properly due to the faithful followers of Jesus. If Martinez was restrained at all, it was only because neither the king nor the archbishop would tolerate open calls for violence, but then, in 1390, both the king and the archbishop died. Pressure had been building for half a century, and Martinez lit the fuse. "The first terrifying date in the Judeo-Spanish calendar is June 6, 1391." This is the comment of a Spanish journalist, Thilo Ullmann. "In Seville, the rabble-rousing preachings of Ferrant Martinez, the administrator of the archdiocese, incited the massacre of Jews, and the conversion of synagogues to churches. The horror spread to the rest of Spain."[35]

Henry Kamen, author of *Inquisition and Society in Spain,* says that hundreds of Jews were killed by rioters in Seville in June 1391, and then hundreds more in Valencia and Barcelona, in July and August respectively.[36] The Jewish community in Barcelona was so decimated it would never recover. Pogroms spread within weeks to dozens of other cities throughout the peninsula, as if coordinated. It was not a matter of coordination, however, but of the now ubiquitous nature of Spanish hatred of Jews, a result of numerous factors — a crucial one of which was the work of preachers.

But the enforced sermons had influenced Jews as well as Christians, as became clear when, for the first time in history, large numbers of Jews responded to the mortal choice — convert or die — by converting. One historian says that in the summer of 1391, Jews "did flock to baptismal fonts across Castile and Aragon."[37] There were, to be sure, many Jews who chose to die rather than apostatize, and, as in 1096 and 1348, even to commit suicide. But the decision by many others to become Christian is what makes 1391 a turning point in this story.

By then, educated Jews, like their Christian counterparts, had been influenced by the new rationalism that had swept Europe. Among Jews it was called Averroism.[38] This philosophy, with its fine distinctions and dialectical method, perhaps opened Jewish believers, as rationalism had Christians, to an unprecedented skepticism. Jews in Spain, having been more assimilated than Jews elsewhere, may have had their own version of the anticlericalism that prevailed among educated and prosperous Christians — this is the age of Dante — which could have led them to disdain the rabbis and the Talmud. The Kabbalistic assault on wealth and privilege, embodied a century earlier in Don Todros, may have reinforced a feeling of religious alienation on the part of aristocratic Jews, leading them to cast their lots with fellow Christian grandees instead of fellow Jews. In addition to such factors, the mass conversion of Jews reflects the effect of nearly two generations of being subjected to Christian preaching. In some cases the conversions surely represented genuine spiritual decisions, but more, they must have resulted from the simple experience of having been spiritually worn down by all those unrebutted black robes (or white, or brown). No single reason explains what happened, but the consequence was clear: The preacher-inspired violence of 1391 changed everything in Spain. It created a new class of people, the *conversos*. As a group, they would always be thought of in relation to the initiating crisis: *Conversos* were Jews who converted to avoid being killed.

The preachers saw the conversions of that summer as the beginning of the end, and indeed, the phenomenon stimulated yet another wave of widespread millennial fervor that assuaged the ongoing distress of dispossessed Christians. The coming of the Messiah appeared imminent; the proselytizing campaign was redoubled. Because their rhetoric now carried an at least implicit threat of force, the preachers continued to succeed. At a famous disputation in Tortosa in 1414, fourteen rabbis were forced to defend Judaism, as Nachmanides alone had done in Barcelona 150 years before. But this time, twelve of the fourteen converted on the spot, which thrilled Christians and terrified Jews. In the first twenty-five years of the century, one third to one half of the Jews living on the Iberian peninsula had become Christians,[39] a total number of *conversos* of perhaps more than 200,000. Given the long struggle to bring Jews around, Christians might ask, What could be better? Soon enough, however, in the most ironic reversal of this always startling narrative, the question about these same conversions would become, What could be worse?

⇥ 35 ⇤

Expulsion in 1492

THAT SO MANY "did flock" to baptismal fonts is a marker for Jews as much as for Christians. Martyrdom or apostasy? The answer had been given its ultimate expression in the story of the seven brothers and their mother in 2 Maccabees, written a hundred years before Christ. "There were also seven brothers who were arrested with their mother. The king tried to force them to taste pig's flesh, which the Law forbids, by torturing them with whips and scourges. One of them, acting as spokesman for the others, said, 'What are you trying to find out from us? We are prepared to die rather than break the laws of our ancestors.' The king, in a fury, ordered pans and cauldrons to be heated over a fire." With the siblings and mother watching, the first brother's torture culminated in his being fried alive. After him, the other brothers, one at a time, were brought forward. "Never!" each one replied to the demand to eat, and each was then subjected to being scalped, his tongue removed, his limbs amputated, his being burned — all while the mother watched. To each one she said, "The Lord God is watching." When her last son refused to eat pig's flesh, the king implored the mother "to advise the youth to save his life." She leaned close to her son and whispered, "I implore you, my child, observe heaven and earth, consider all that is in them, and acknowledge that God made them out of what did not exist, and that mankind comes into being in the same way. Do not fear this executioner, but prove yourself worthy of your brothers, and make death welcome, so that in the day of mercy I may receive you back in your brothers' company."

The boy did so, with a defiant "What are you waiting for? I will not comply with the king's ordinance. I obey the ordinance of the Law given to our ancestors through Moses." The mother watched as this, her youngest son, treated "more cruelly than the others . . . met his end undefiled and with perfect trust in the Lord." This seventh chapter of 2 Maccabees is perhaps the most violent passage in the Hebrew Scriptures, yet it ends with the most poignantly understated line in all the Scriptures, too: "The mother was the last to die, after her sons."[1]

With such a story anchoring the collective memory of Jews, it was no departure from tradition, however much it shocked Christians, when, as a Jewish chronicler of the First Crusade reported, "The women girded their loins . . . and slew their own sons and daughters, and then themselves."[2] Martyrdom, even self-immolation, was an affirmation of faith — Kiddush Hashem — a way as Marc Cohen puts it, "of reenacting on a human plane the sacrificial cult of the ancient Jerusalem Temple."[3] Jewish martyrdom was the steady ideal of Jews in Europe, however much, over the years, individual Jews fell short of it.

But there was another current in the river of medieval Judaism, and it had been given its most eloquent articulation, not surprisingly, by Maimonides. As we saw, the Islamic Almohad persecution drove him from Iberia in 1159. In response to the crisis prompted by the choice to convert or die, Maimonides wrote his "Letter on Apostasy." As it happened, this was not long after Jews were martyred by the thousands in the Rhineland. Maimonides wrote:

> Verily, one who preferred to suffer martyrdom in order not to pronounce the Mohammedan confession, has done nobly and well and his reward is great before the Lord. He may be regarded as supremely virtuous as he was willing to surrender his life for the sanctification of the name of God, Blessed be He. Should one, however, inquire of me: "Shall I be slain or pronounce the Mohammedan confession," my answer would be: "Utter the formula and live!" To be sure one should not continue to live in such an environment but until the opportunity presents itself to leave one should be confined to the privacy of his home and conduct his transactions in secret.[4]

Maimonides is talking here about Islam, which may or may not involve idolatry — the rabbis are divided. He is not talking about Christianity, which, by virtue of the claims made for the divinity of Jesus, is regarded as essentially idolatrous. But there are two important elements to his reasoning that carried over into the minds of Iberian Jews after the *reconquista,* when a range of pressures was already driving Jewish culture underground. First, he asserts that intention is crucial, and second, that one's private integrity as a Jew can be protected even while publicly disavowed. "We are not forced," Maimonides says, "to perform any acts of apostasy but just to recite an empty formula. And if one wishes to practice the six hundred and thirteen precepts in secret, he can do so without punishment unless he voluntarily desecrates the Sabbath. For this form of compulsion requires no action but the recital of a simple formula which the Moslems themselves know was uttered insincerely only to circumvent the King's whims."[5]

This is a long way from the mother and her seven sons, yet the position's common sense, rationality, and emphasis on intention are far closer to a modern sensibility than is the headlong rush to martyrdom. Maimonides had other advice — that those who could should flee "those places of hostility and go to a location where one could fulfill the Law without compulsion and fear."[6] Which is exactly what he did. But by the late fourteenth century, many an Iberian Jew was behaving as if he had internalized Maimonides's distinction between outward "apostasy" and interior faithfulness to the Law "confined to the privacy of his home."[7] Many Jews who became Christians did so with full sincerity, but there were also many, perhaps more, for whom the act of undergoing baptism was nothing but a ticket to survival. They remained Jews in everything but public observance. They were the secret Jews, who had adopted a duplicitous mode of survival — observing Sabbath at home on Friday evening and Saturday, attending Mass at the cathedral on Sunday — simply because they did not want to die. In less violent periods, this may have translated into not wanting to lose their possessions or social rank.

There were so many "converts" in such a short time that the Church found it impossible to properly instruct most in the ways of authentic Christian faith. Thus a good number of *conversos* occupied a muddled middle ground between Judaism and Christianity, without necessarily knowing who or what they were. In addition, some *conversos* were active Judaizers, believers who, out of conviction that Christian tenets could be reconciled with Mosaic Law, sought to combine the traditions. The Kiddush cup, for example, could now be raised in Eucharist. In that, they represented, in a way, a reincarnation of those doomed Jewish Christians or Christian Jews of the first centuries, believers whose identity — observing Torah while revering Jesus — was an offense both to Gentile Christians like John Chrysostom and to the rabbis of Yavneh. And as was true in the time of Chrysostom, those occupying this middle ground, defined not as infidels but as heretics, stirred the rage of Christian apologists in ways that Jews as such never did.

In many Iberian cities, *conversos* continued to live near and to work with their former coreligionists, those Jews who refused to convert. This proximity with the increasingly despised refusers would soon be regarded as the self-perpetuating source of heresy, and then the focus of suspicion would revert back to the Christ-rejecting Jews. These ambiguities fed on each other. As the century progressed, few of the "Old Christians" — so called to distinguish them from the *conversos,* or "New Christians" — could keep crucial aspects of the religious and racial identity of these people straight.

Jews who converted maintained their positions of power and affluence. Since they were no longer barred from offices in the king's service and the Church, and no longer subject to anti-Jewish occupational restrictions, *conversos* prospered more than ever. Many married into prominent Old Christian families, and others took up important positions in the Church, sometimes as the most zealous anti-Jewish proselytizers. Yet there were two persistent problems. Ongoing economic crises throughout Iberia kept the broad population off balance. In such periods of dislocation, the fifteenth century's urban poor and distressed peasantry transferred their age-old resentment of Jews onto the New Christians, whose evident prosperity galled as never before. Now when there were hunger riots, as in Toledo in 1467 and 1473, *conversos* were targeted as much as unconverted Jews were — an ominous blurring of religious and racial identity.

The Church, too, had a problem, which grew more grievous as the decades passed. Having coerced Jews to convert in large numbers, Christians began to suspect that the conversions must have been insincere, since they *were* coerced. The irony was doubled and redoubled. Judaizing, the mingling of Christian and Jewish elements of faith, cult, and calendar, was defined as a heresy. The Church now began to move against it in earnest. But that meant investigating the *conversos* as a class, which implied that anyone with "Jewish blood," whatever his or her religious identity had become, was suspect. "In fact," the historian Angus MacKay writes, "the hatred of the *conversos* and their success grew into racial hatred. As early as 1449, the idea was being propagated that the pure blood of the Castilian Old Christians was being defiled by that of the Jewish race."[8]

Ordinarily, such an idea would have been roundly rejected by all levels of official Catholicism. The Church had consistently emphasized the religious distinction between Judaism and Christianity, ignoring any racial distinction between Jews and Christians. But this was not an ordinary stretch of history. The division between those prepared to follow the logic of radical conversionism to its once unthinkable conclusion and those who maintained an attitude of restraint, even protection, toward Jews cut across the whole Church, including the papacy itself. Beginning about the time of the 1391 pogroms and the consequent forced conversions of large numbers of Jews, a succession of popes taking opposite sides of the question came to power, almost, as it were, alternating between sympathizers with Jews and sympathizers with the anti-Jewish friars. In effect, for the next century and a half, the Church, and the papacy, would be arguing with itself over what to do with the Jews.

The first of the era's papal defenders of Jews, Boniface IX (1389–1404), took office just as the anti-Jewish violence of the 1390s swept Iberia. While Jews were being massacred in Spain and expelled from France (1394), this pope was granting a new charter of protection to Jews in Rome. They had been subjected to the usual restrictions with fluctuating severity, but in a thousand years the Jews of Rome had never been violently attacked as a group, not even after the Black Plague.[9] The tradition of *Sicut Judaeis* held.

Pope Martin V (1417–1431) exhibited the usual negative attitudes toward Judaism, but overall, he must be counted as a strong defender of Jews. He forbade the baptizing of Jewish children without their parents' consent — a practice that often followed on the friars' sermons. As the violence mounted in Spain, this pope, in 1422, issued an edict criticizing the preaching of friars against Jews, ordering that "every Christian treat the Jews with a humane kindness."[10]

When the city council of Toledo, in 1449, passed an ordinance decreeing "that no *converso* of Jewish descent may have or hold any office or benefice in the said city of Toledo," Pope Nicholas V (1447–1455) reacted with a fury suggesting he saw what was at stake in such a move. The bull he issued bore, in Henry Kamen's phrase, "the significant title *Humani generis inimicus*." The enemy of the human race was not the Jew but the new conviction that the Jew could not be changed by his conversion. "We decree and declare," Nicholas wrote, "that all Catholics are one body in Christ according to the teaching of our faith."[11] Nicholas V excommunicated the author of the Toledo statute. Yet two years later, the king of Castile formally approved the regulation. Jews would be legally defined now in Spain not by religion but by blood.

If the beginning of what we think of as modern antisemitism can be located anywhere, it is here. The shift from a religious definition of Jewishness to a racial one is perhaps the most decisive in this long narrative, and its fault lines, reaching far into the consciousness of Western civilization, will define the moral geography of the modern age. The Church's worry, for example, that its very own *conversos* were corrupting Christians would find a near permanent resonance in the modern European fantasy of Jews as parasites — successful and assimilated, but feeding on the host society. The ultimate example of this image would emerge in Germany, of course, but the fear that led Nazis to regard Jews as bloodsuckers to be excised was anticipated by the Iberian suspicion that Jews were more to be feared as assimilated insiders than as dissenting outsiders. Thus hatred of the other became a society's scare-driven urge to eradicate an alien part of itself.

By the twentieth century, Christians, especially Catholics, would be vigorously distinguishing between the "normal" anti-Judaism based in religious dispute and the pathological antisemitism of race hatred. Yet because of these origins in the Church's own history, that line of argument could only smack of bad faith. Because religious dispute was the source of racial hatred, there are sweeping implications here not just for Christian-Jewish relations, but for fundamental Western attitudes about identity itself. The modern world, which prides itself on being a repudiation of the irrationalities of a culture that could give rise to an Inquisition, was in fact forged in the fires of those irrationalities, and we can still feel their heat.

If this development began in Iberia, it was at first vigorously opposed by the Church in Rome, perhaps because the implications of the shift from religion to blood were apparent. But Rome's opposition would prove to be ineffective. Nicholas V was one of the first of the Renaissance popes, the founder of the Vatican Library, and the patron of Fra Angelico.[12] But he was also an avatar of the papal corruption and intrigue that were the rot causing the Church to crumble from within. Heresy was no longer the aberration of individuals, but a set of movements, like that begun by John Hus, which foreshadowed the coming crisis of the Reformation. The words in which Hus was condemned by the Council of Constance (1415) foreshadowed something too: "O cursed Judas, because you have abandoned the councils of peace, and have counseled with the Jews, we take away from you the cup of redemption."[13]

By the middle of the fifteenth century, it was clear that nothing could check the rising tide of skepticism and dissent. Hus himself had been burned at the stake. So, for that matter, in 1431, had Joan of Arc. In 1442, the bishops of the Church gathered at the Council of Florence and, like youths pushing at a dike, struck their most severe blow yet at those who would not conform: "The holy Roman church firmly believes, professes and preaches that all those who are outside the catholic church, not only pagans but also Jews or heretics and schismatics, cannot share in eternal

life, and will go into the everlasting fire, 'which was prepared for the devil
and his angels,' unless they are joined to the catholic church before the end
of their lives . . . Nobody can be saved no matter how much he has given
away alms and even if he has shed his blood in the name of Christ, unless
he has persevered in the bosom and unity of the catholic church."[14] A
spirit of barely reined panic infuses this statement, and well it might. Only
a decade later, in 1453, Constantinople fell to the Ottoman Turks, whose
use of artillery in the siege would prove to be a turning point in the history of warfare, ending, for example, the era of the castle and the culture
that depended on it. More immediately, the fall of the city Constantine
had founded marked the definitive end of the Christian Eastern Empire
and of any hope of reconciliation between Roman Catholicism and the
Greek Orthodox "schismatics." Also, the exodus west of scholars from
Constantinople, after its fall, would be an important factor in the emergence of secular humanism in Italy, the heart of the Church. So there
were solid reasons for the institutional paranoia that was rampant in the
Church now. And Jews would suffer for it.

Not all Christians, however, gave in to these new forces, and at the highest
level both of the Catholic hierarchy and of the ranks of theologians a humane alternative to antisemitism appeared. It was embodied in one man,
a theologian and cardinal native to Germany, Nicolaus of Cusa (1401–
1464). He is not well known today outside the circle of scholars, which
hints at the fate that befell the alternative he represented, but the story of
Nicolaus of Cusa is another of those wayside chapels marking the other
track this history might have taken.

Nicolaus was a man of genius, not only an inventive philosopher and
theologian but a mathematician whose speculations anticipated Copernicus (1473–1543). The free play of this man's spacious mind led him to
apply the insights of one discipline to another. He titled one essay, for example, "The Theological Complement Represented in the Mathematical
Complements."[15] By means of such "complements," he developed from
mathematics a feel for what the Catholic theologian David Tracy calls "the
logic of the infinite." Tracy describes Nicolaus of Cusa as "the most balanced of the great Renaissance thinkers."[16] Instead of thinking of God in
constrained images equivalent to mathematical symbols of the sphere or
circle or triangle, Nicolaus proposed thinking of God in an image more
like the line, which is by definition unbounded, impossible to hem in or to
possess. The discursive reasoning of the scholastics, who slavishly imi-

tated the method of Thomas Aquinas without preserving his spirit, seemed the opposite of such logic of the infinite to Nicolaus, and he criticized the prevailing theology of his day, in effect, for doing too much with too little. Nowhere was that theology better expressed than in the anathemas issued by the Council of Florence, just referred to. Theologians spoke of God as if they understood God fully, and they sought to enforce a uniformity of thought that left no room for mystery, ambiguity, or paradox. Nicolaus of Cusa saw, on the contrary, that God is God precisely in escaping and transcending total comprehension by human beings. Just as a line is defined by its movement in two opposite directions at once, so God is "the coincidence of opposites," the one in whom maximum and minimum fall together.[17] In God, this coincidence occurs in such a way that the contraries maintain their differences, which, mathematically speaking, is why God is more like a line than a point.

Nicolaus of Cusa's masterwork was called *On Learned Ignorance,* and his approach to God is characterized as apophatic, which means to posit by negating (an apophasis: "I will not bring up my opponent's questionable financial dealings"[18]). Nicolaus argued not that God is unknowable, but that God's unknowability is the most profound and illuminating thing humans can know about God. This idea is the theological equivalent of the Copernican insight into the cosmos — that the earth revolves around the sun, not vice versa — that would come a generation later. Both ideas mean, as Tracy put it, that the old cosmology is finished, the closed system is collapsed, replaced by an open, infinite system.

We have seen repeatedly how basic theological assumptions translate into the political sphere, with importance — sometimes positive, sometimes negative — for relations between Christians and Jews. That is certainly true in the case of Nicolaus of Cusa, but like Abelard before him, his insights and their political implications would not carry the day. The political crisis that cast its shadow over Abelard's thought was the crusading movement. Nicolaus was challenged by the historic conquest of Constantinople by the Turks. This event is a marker on the arc of this narrative for several reasons. It brought to a conclusion the story begun when newly anointed Constantine left Trier to unify the empire. Constantine's city had stood against invaders for a thousand years before the Turkish artillery pieces rolled into place below its ancient walls. The last Christian defender of Constantinople was himself named Constantine, and fittingly his enemy was named Mohammed II.

By 1453, Constantinople was a city depopulated and impoverished by the numerous wars it had withstood. This last Constantine had only 10,000 soldiers to command, while the besieging Turks numbered between 100,000 and 150,000. The siege began in early April and went on, brutally, until the end of May. When the wall was breached, the Turks rushed in, and in the final battle Constantine was killed. He was the last Christian emperor of the East. Mohammed, established by this victory, would be regarded as the founder of the Ottoman Empire, which would last into the twentieth century.

Such was the savagery of these wars that the six hundredth anniversary of the previous victory of the Ottomans, at Kosovo on June 15, 1389, would give Slobodan Milosevic the occasion to whip up Serbian Orthodox resentment against Albanian Muslims, whom Serbs regarded as the descendants of the Turk conquerors. Milosevic's 1989 speech is usually charged with igniting the four Balkan wars of the 1990s, but the tinder Milosevic ignited was the long Serbian memory of those distant defeats.

After Constantinople fell, the Turks pillaged the city for days. Santa Sophia, the greatest church in Christendom, was made into a mosque. News of the violence, rape, and slaughter that came down on the Greek Christians traumatized Europe. Nicolaus was like most Christians in being horrified at the reports of the siege and fall of Constantinople.

He was unlike most Christians, though, in what he made of that news. He had been named a cardinal of the Church only five years before, but now he put pen to paper in a way that would set him apart from others in the Catholic hierarchy. He composed what remains one of the most poignant pleas ever written by a Catholic theologian and prelate, *De Pace Fidei* — "On Peace Among the Faiths," or, less literally, "Reconciliation Between the World Religions." What stung Nicolaus was the image of human beings savaging each other because of their opposing ideas of God — God who was, to him, unknowable. If that was so, how could men kill one another in the name of what they claimed to know of God? He began by asking the question of Muslims, but, no doubt with an eye on history, he addressed it equally to Christians and to those of other religions. It was a question that inevitably led him to confront the issue of the Church's relationship to the Jews. Here are excerpts from what he wrote soon after the fall of Constantinople:

> News of the atrocities which have recently been perpetrated by the Turkish king in Constantinople and now have been divulged, has so inflamed a man, who once saw that region, with zeal for God, that amongst many

sighs he asked the Creator of all things if in His kindness He might moderate the persecution, which raged more than usual on account of diverse religious rites. Then it occurred that after several days — indeed on account of lengthy, continuous meditation — a vision was manifested to the zealous man, from which he concluded that it would be possible, through the experience of a few wise men who are well acquainted with all the diverse practices which are observed in religions across the world, to find a unique and propitious concordance, and through this to constitute a perpetual peace in religion upon the appropriate and true course.[19]

Nicolaus assumed, of course, the truth of Christian revelation, and he was seeking to discover how that truth was embodied in other faiths, which from one point of view assumes a superior Christian authority. But what is notable about this work is its more basic assumption that all religions embody the truth and that all offer a way to the unknowable God. In his treatise, he goes on, addressing God:

Although the intellectual spirit, which is sown in the earth and is absorbed by shadows, does not see the light and the beginning of its origin, You have nonetheless created in him all that through which he, full of wonder over that which he attains with the senses, is at some time able to elevate his mental eyes to You . . . To the various nations, however, You have sent various prophets and masters, the one for this, the other for another time. It is a condition of earthly human nature to defend as truth lengthy custom, which is regarded as part of nature. And thus no small dissensions arise, when any community prefers its beliefs over another's. Therefore come to our assistance, You who alone are powerful. For this rivalry is on account of You, whom alone all venerate in all that they seem to adore.[20]

Nicolaus constructs a conversation among a Jew, a Muslim, a Tatar, an Indian, a Persian, a Syrian, a Spaniard, a Turk, a German, a Bohemian, an Englander, a Greek, an Arab, and an Italian. For Christians, he lets Paul speak. Here is an example:

Tatar: "It is proper to keep the commandments of God. But the Jews say they have received these commandments from Moses, the Arabs say they have them from Mohammed, and the Christians from Jesus. And there are perhaps other nations who honor their prophets, through whose hands they assert they have received the divine precepts. Therefore, how shall we arrive at concord?"
Paul: "The divine commandments are very brief and are all well known

and common in every nation, for the light that reveals them to us is created along with the rational soul. For within us God says to love Him, from whom we received being, and to do nothing to another, except that which we wish done to us. Love is therefore the fulfillment of the law of God and all laws are reduced to this."[21]

This is a long way from the burning of Hus, the hauling of *conversos* before inquisitors, and, for that matter, the decrees of the Council of Florence, issued barely a decade before. That may be why "On Peace Among the Faiths" and other works were published in a volume entitled *Toward a New Council of Florence.* As Nicolaus could entertain the elusive thought that the "contraries" united in the "coincidence of opposites" that is God nevertheless retained their distinctive identity, so he could imagine a concord among religions that celebrated what they had in common and still accepted their ongoing independent existence. This is not the difference-obliterating universalism that swallows all religious distinctiveness in a triumphant Christianity. Rather, it is an acknowledgment that before the unknowable God, all religions are finite. Only God is absolute.

Alas, this vision, prophetic in its pluralism, did not take hold. Perhaps it would have, but the absolutizing impulses set loose by the dawn of the Age of Discovery and the coming of the Reformation outweighed such nuance. The simplicities of preachers and radicals and conquistadors were preferred to the complexities of a first humanist theologian. He had reversed the usual method of religious reflection, drawing a theological conclusion about the nature of God from a passionate ethical insight. His moral outrage at slaughter committed in the name of God had forced a new theology, but neither method nor theology would take. His plea would not be heard, which is why the name of Nicolaus of Cusa remains obscure. Instead of his vision of peace among the religions being realized, the opposite happened. A massive cultural shift was under way, and it had deeply unsettling effects on all people. A spirit of agitated skepticism was spreading through Europe, just as the unidentified bacillus had spread a century before. And once again, many Christians, and most of their leaders, moved against doubt in the traditional way — by repressing existential anxiety, defining it as evil, and projecting it especially onto Jews.

As the detritus of the social upheavals of the late fifteenth century rained more and more on the heads of Jews — and, in Spain, on *conversos* — there were Christians who saw what was at stake. They may have lacked the vision and integrity of Nicolaus of Cusa, but in this one area of egregious abuse, at least, they were not indifferent. Nor were they silent. There was Pope Sixtus IV (1471–1484), for example, another worldly Renaissance pope. It was he who ordered the beautification of the Sistine Chapel, but it was also he who began the selling of indulgences. But like others of the hedonist pontiffs, and more than the puritanical reforming popes — an irony — Sixtus IV's inclination was to protect Jews.

In Renaissance Rome, Jews were thriving. The coming of humanism to Italy brought unprecedented collaborations, like that between the Christian philosopher Giovanni Pico della Mirandola (1463–1494) and the Jewish Aristotelian Elijah del Medigo (c. 1450–1493), who participated in friendly exchanges in Pico's home.[22] Pico was an audacious aristocrat who, at age twenty-three, published a work consisting of nine hundred *conclusiones,* attempting a synthesis of science and religion.[23] He learned Hebrew and was one of the first Christians to plumb the mysteries of Kabbalah. An apparent syncretist, he could seem to have caught the ecumenical spirit of Nicolaus of Cusa, who died within a year of Pico's birth. But in fact, Pico, like Christian Talmudists before him, sought, with Kabbalah, to prove the all-encompassing truth of Christianity, using Jewish texts, in effect, in a campaign to convert Jews. "The very fundamentals of the Hebrew sages . . . ," he said, "most decisively confirm the Christian religion."[24] Because thirteen of his nine hundred *conclusiones* were suspect, however, Pico himself was labeled a heretic, and arrested.[25] The times had blades. Even intellectual collaboration that Jews could welcome now invariably had an apologetic thrust, and mortal danger lurked in the most abstract of discussions. Still, the give-and-take between Pico and his Jewish masters would bear fruit. His appreciation of Kabbalah, and his appropriation of its method of decoding both texts and observed phenomena, would seed mainstream European thought, helping to lead, for example, to the next century's adoption of the scientific method.[26]

Renaissance Jews were advisors and physicians in the papal court. They were teachers of music, theater, and science. Rome was a center of Hebrew literature and publishing. To be sure, there were the usual limits, even special indignities, like the primitive foot race of Jews on the Corso, a feature of the annual carnival.[27] But Sixtus IV, like most of his predecessors, took his role as a defender of Jews from violence more or less for granted.

Yet Sixtus was politically weak. He had set out to consolidate the Papal States, but competition among regional dynasties made it impossible. The pope's troops were being humiliated by those of Naples and Venice. At the critical moment, he could not oppose the powerful young rulers,

Ferdinand of Aragon and Isabella of Castile, whose marriage in 1469 had united the two great Iberian kingdoms. When, in 1478, they asked the pope to authorize the establishment of ecclesiastical tribunals to ferret out "crypto-Jews" and Judaizers from among the *conversos*,[28] Sixtus IV would surely have been reluctant. More than twenty years before, the king of Castile, Henry IV, had applied to Rome for similar authorization. Pope Nicholas V (1447–1455), who in another context had cited Saint Paul's rejection of distinctions between Jew and Greek (Romans 10, 12) to reject distinctions between Spain's Old and New Christians,[29] simply never replied.[30]

The Inquisition had been active, as we have seen, against heresy in France, Germany, and elsewhere, but the Christian faith had always been regarded as unpolluted in Iberia — despite *convivencia* or, somehow, because of it. The Inquisition had never been wanted or seen as needed on the peninsula, but now, according to rulers and friars together, it was both. Either because he was convinced or because power politics made it impossible for him to resist, Sixtus IV yielded, and gave his approval. This marked the beginning of the Spanish Inquisition.

There was the matter of who would preside over the tribunals. Numerous Dominicans had undertaken investigations throughout Castile and Aragon, but a more ambitious campaign would require a central (*suprema*) administration. Perhaps Sixtus IV, a master of intrigue in his own sphere, knew that one of the Dominican inquisitors was in fact a man of Jewish blood; perhaps Sixtus hoped that such a man would have some capacity for sympathy toward the maligned *conversos*. As it happened, this Dominican was also the confessor to Ferdinand and Isabella. For whatever reason, Sixtus appointed him the first grand inquisitor — Fray Tomás de Torquemada (1420–1498). The secret of his Jewish ancestry would, if anything, fuel his hatred. Sixtus and his two successors would try, without success, to restrain him.

Almost immediately upon Torquemada's appointment, the Inquisition began issuing its findings, as the historian Benjamin Gampel put it, "that the New Christians were generally involved in Jewish rituals and obeyed precepts of the Jewish religion, and that their heretical behavior should not be tolerated."[31] In towns and cities, the tribunal sessions involved open-air processions, elaborate liturgy, and the hugely popular autos-da-fé ("acts of faith") in which heretics either recanted or were put to death. Not incidentally, such displays deflected a growing hostility toward the monarchy. The Old Christian peasantry and the urban poor particularly welcomed the campaign against New Christians and the spectacle of its procedures. But now the monarchy, as chief sponsor of the tribunals, had replaced the restive populace as the main antagonist of the hated New Christians. In other words, Isabella and Ferdinand's legendary popularity was based, in part at least, on their wily use of the Inquisition.[32]

"When the inquisitors began operations in a district" — this summary is from Henry Kamen's *Inquisition and Society in Spain* — "they would first present their credentials to the local Church and secular authorities, and announce a Sunday or a feast day when all residents would have to go to high mass, together with their children and servants, and hear the 'edict' read. At the end of the sermon or the creed, the inquisitor or his representative would hold a crucifix in front of the congregation and ask everybody to raise their right hand, cross themselves and repeat after him a solemn oath to support the Inquisition and its ministers. He would proceed to read the edict." The edict typically included a demand that all present denounce any Christian who "keeps the Sabbath according to the Law of Moses . . . using no lights from Friday evening onwards . . . or [has] eaten meat in Lent . . . [or any] parents placing their hands on the heads of their children without making the sign of the cross . . . or if they recite the psalms without the *Gloria Patri* . . . or if anyone on his deathbed turns to the wall to die."[33]

Torture was commonly used in criminal procedures in that era, and it was a method of the Inquisition, applied as a way of forcing confessions. The torturers, like the executioners, were agents of the Crown, not the Church. This distinction, which some cite to absolve the Church even today, was the ultimate fulfillment of the "two sword" theory promoted by Saint Bernard of Clairvaux three centuries before. When torture was deemed necessary, the accused of the Inquisition were suspended by their wrists with their bodies weighted (*garrucha*), had water forced down their throats (*toca*), were wrapped in ropes to be squeezed as they were tightened (*potro*).[34] Careful records were kept of the proceedings. Here, again from Kamen, is the partial transcript of the interrogation of one woman accused, in 1568, of refusing to eat the flesh of pigs and of refusing to do housework on Saturdays:

> She was ordered to be placed on the *potro*. She said, "Señores, why will you not tell me what I have to say? Señor, put me on the ground — have I not said that I did it all?" She was told to tell it. She said, "I don't remember — take me away — I did what the witnesses say." She was told to tell in

detail what the witnesses said. She said, "Señor, as I have told you, I do not know for certain. I have said that I did all that the witnesses say. Señores, release me, for I do not remember it." . . . She was admonished to tell the truth and the *garrotes* were ordered to be tightened. She said, "Señor, do you not see how these people are killing me? I did it — for God's sake, let me go."[35]

Kamen judiciously points out that the inquisitors' procedures, while no worse than those prevailing in other European tribunals, were in some ways less severe. Inquisitorial prisons could be relatively humane. Torture rarely resulted in death, or even permanent crippling. Confessions obtained under torture had to be reconfirmed by the suspect later, under "normal" conditions. For the most part, the many people put to death were found guilty of a clearly defined capital crime, heresy. Thus Jews as such were not officially targeted by the Inquisition, only those who had been baptized or were found to have encouraged the baptized to lapse into Judaism. This offense was so broadly defined, however — any Jewish "consorting" with a *converso* could be prosecuted — and so aggressively pursued that eventually the Inquisition did mount a frontal assault on Judaism itself.[36]

The Inquisition survived as an operating institution for three hundred years, and its methods varied widely during that long stretch of time. In its early years, when the as yet unnamed panic of the coming social and religious catastrophe we remember as the Reformation was the underlying driving force, thousands of unrepentant or relapsed heretics were burned at the stake. "Nothing, certainly," Kamen says, "can efface the horror of the first twenty holocaust years."[37] He comments elsewhere, "The savagery of the onslaught against the conversos was without equal in the history of any tribunal in the western world."[38] Statistics kept by contemporary observers suggest that in the first eight years alone, two thousand were burned at the stake. Thousands of others would follow in the next two decades. The vast majority of those put to death by the Spanish Inquisition during its entire three hundred years perished in that first savage paroxysm, which is why the name Torquemada lives in infamy.

Always in this story there is the cross. To a Jew, the cross's proximity, if not centrality, to each new round of violence is only a reminder of its negative meaning. To a Christian, it still must come as a shock and a source of sorrow, as if the cross had not already been fraught enough by what the Romans did with it. The cross, as we saw, featured as a sacramental object at the beginning of the inquisitorial procedures, the friar holding up the crucifix for the swearing of the informant's oath. At the other end of the process, in the climactic auto-da-fé, the cross featured as well. Repentant heretics were reconciled to the Church by being signed with the cross on the forehead, as the friar intoned, "Receive the sign of the cross, which you denied and lost through being deceived."[39]

The way this story keeps coming back, at its most violent moments, to the sacred symbol of the cross reminds us that religious politics are always reflected in the religious imagination. When the Renaissance in visual art came to Spain in the next century, its glories would be transformed by an almost sadistic concentration on physical torment, derived from the friar-driven cult of such torment as a source of salvation. There would never be any mistaking the aesthetic of Italy for that of Spain. The cross accomplished the sanctification of the Iberian spirit of repression. This is the meaning, for example, of the tone struck by El Greco, who, as we saw, took up residence in the Toledo villa that Samuel Halevy had built. His paintings captured the essential air of Inquisition culture. How else can his achievement be taken when he brings the embalmed flesh of the corpus into the hands, faces, throats, and fingers of his subjects, whether friars or mourners, *dons* or *doñas*. All of their figures seem, in that trademark El Greco elongation, to have been racked. In burial pictures, but also in his bread-and-butter portraits of grandees and their ladies, El Greco brought the palette of death to life, laying bare the soul of Spanish Catholicism in this period. No other Spanish artist could approach his genius, and after him painters and sculptors alike took to the physical agonies of the Passion, and the torture of the crucifixion in particular, with a vivid literalness that made all prior renditions seem impressionistic. The religious imagination of the Inquisition fixed itself in the liturgical taste of the Spanish Empire, and it still jars visitors to the older churches throughout that part of the world.

Spanish mysticism would be similarly stamped by the cross. Its leading voice was the aptly named Saint John of the Cross (1542–1591), whose greatest poetry was written in a prison in, as it happens, Toledo. (He was jailed by a faction of his own religious order, the Carmelites, which rejected his efforts at reform.) His spiritual masterpiece was *The Dark Night of the Soul,* which articulated the religious meaning of negation itself. A hundred years of Spanish history — taking into account the activities of the conquistadors, the most violent hundred years in world history to that point — had prepared for the mystical conclusion that God could be present only in absence. The idea can seem to echo the mysticism of darkness found in the Kabbalah, and it is likely that John of the Cross was influenced by the powerful undercurrents of the Jewish tradition that had been running through Iberia for centuries. But as Harold Bloom explains, Kabbalah must always be distinguished from Christian, and for that matter Eastern, mysticism because it is "more a mode of intellectual speculation than a way of union with God . . . a power of the mind over the universe of death."[40]

Saint John was confessor to the equally great Saint Teresa of Ávila (1515–1582), whose mystical "espousal" to Christ was sealed when Jesus, appearing in a vision, gave her not a ring but a nail from his cross.[41] The much reproduced Bernini sculpture *The Ecstasy of Saint Teresa* renders the full, lips-parted sensuality of the nun's affective, as opposed to intellectual, communion with her Lord.[42] It was Teresa who founded the order of Carmelites which, centuries later, would attract the converted Jewish philosopher Edith Stein, who took the religious name Teresa Blessed of the Cross because her conversion from Judaism was prompted by reading the mystic's autobiography. Edith Stein, of whom we will see more later, died at Auschwitz in 1942, and was named a saint of the Church in 1998. Partly in her memory, as we saw, the Carmelites established the controversial convent at the wall of Auschwitz, where the cross that gave this long narrative its starting point still stands.

Such history underscores the irony of the fact that Saint Teresa of Ávila was herself a New Christian. In 1485, her father, as a child, was hauled before an auto-da-fé in, as it happens again, Toledo. Not long ago, I stood in the central square before the cathedral, where such an event would almost certainly have occurred. Teresa's father, with *his* father, was given the choice of repenting his relapse into Judaism or being burned at the stake. He was one of five thousand people who denounced himself and repented, to save his life.[43] According to his biographer Gerald Brenan, Saint John of the Cross, too, had Jewish ancestry, but may not have known of it. Teresa did know. Brenan comments, "The knowledge of Santa Teresa's Jewish descent adds to the interest of her life and mission. It explains how a deep sense of guilt caused by her consciousness of belonging to the race of deicides, as they were called, helped to drive her against her will along the hard path of the mystic and religious reformer."[44] Edith Stein was like her patron in feeling the burden of what her people "had done to Jesus." In her spiritual last will and testament, she offered her life to God "for the atonement of the unbelief of the Jewish people."[45]

Torquemada's determination to eradicate the Judaizing heresy led him almost immediately to regard the presence of such "unbelieving" Jews as an intolerable obstacle. The mere existence of Jews in Spain supported crypto-Jews and Judaizers, reminding New Christians of their prior commitment and inviting them to resume it. The proximity of openly observant Jews was said to influence secret Jews in their observances of forbidden cult and study of Torah — this was the rationale for the Inquisition's heretofore unauthorized attacks on Jews as such.[46] In fact, this abandonment of restraint was an inevitable outcome of adopting religious purity as a widespread social goal. Despite a century of restriction and repression, numerous Jews had managed to cling to positions of importance in the economies of many towns and cities, but now they would be targeted. It was the same dynamic, though operating in reverse, by which Hitler's attack on Jews had inevitably to broaden to include those, like Edith Stein, who had renounced Judaism to become Christian. Here we see very clearly the specter of "blood" that will shape modern notions of race.

In 1490, the Inquisition crossed the line to bring charges against a Jew, one Yuce Franco.[47] It will perhaps not surprise the reader to learn that the crime of which Franco was accused was the ritual crucifixion of a kidnapped Christian infant, a male child, as the tradition of the Blood Libel required. Franco and his accomplices were tried and executed in 1491. The furor that these proceedings aroused in the *converso*-hating, Jew-hating population of Spain prepared them for what came next. In January 1492, the Muslims in Granada, the last vestige of Moorish Iberia, were brutally overrun by the army of Ferdinand and Isabella. A cross was mounted on the highest tower of Granada's fortress-palace, the Alhambra.[48] Iberia was finally free of Islam. Two months later, on the last day of March, the "Catholic Monarchs," as Ferdinand and Isabella were known, ordered the expulsion of Jews from Castile and Aragon. The descendants of Alfonso the Wise, who, with his father, had called himself the "king of the three religions," now defined the one nation they had achieved by its one religion. It was a late-medieval version of the impulse of Constantine, the final blow to *convivencia*.[49]

Expulsion of Jews was not new. They had been expelled from France a century earlier, from various principalities of Germany in the twelfth century, from England in 1290, from Provence in 1394, and from Austria in 1421.[50] But these expulsions involved relatively small Jewish communities, and were sometimes reversed in fairly short order. The rationale offered for the expulsion of Jews from Spain was also different. In their edict, the monarchs explained that they were banishing Jews, despite the economic cost to themselves, and despite human reluctance, as a way to protect *conversos* from being drawn back — "attracted and perverted to their injurious opinions and beliefs" — into Judaism. "We have been informed by the Inquisitors . . . ," they decreed, "that the mingling of Jews with Christians leads to the worst evils. The Jews try their best to seduce the [New] Christians . . . persuading them to follow the Law of Moses. In consequence, our holy Catholic faith is debased and humbled. We have thus arrived at the conclusion that the only efficacious means to put an end to these evils consists in the definitive breaking of all relations between Jews and Christians, and this can only be obtained by their expulsion from our kingdom."[51]

After decades of trying and failing to remedy the problem of the *conversos*, the Catholic monarchs accepted the logic of the grand inquisitor, concluding that the proximity of real Jews was the real problem. When a delegation of prominent Jews met with Ferdinand and Isabella and offered to pay to be allowed to remain, Torquemada is said to have burst in on the royal audience, thrown pieces of silver on the floor, and demanded to know what Judas was offering this time. The monarchs did not withdraw the edict of expulsion. It was issued in the names not only of "Their Majesties," but "of the Reverend Prior of the Holy Cross, Inquisitor General." The reference is to the convent, Santa Cruz at Segovia, of which Torquemada was prior,[52] but it means that the expulsion order, too, was stamped with the cross.

The Jews had three months either to convert or to get out of Spain. It is difficult to establish numbers with certainty. There were probably about 300,000 Jews in Iberia at this time, out of a total population numbering in the low millions. About half of the Jews became Christians rather than go into exile.[53] This, ironically — yet more forced conversions — was bound to make the *converso* crisis worse.[54] Many tens of thousands of Jews left Spain in the spring and summer of 1492. Yitzhak Baer puts the number at more than 150,000.[55]

One chronicler of the exile wrote:

> In the first week of July, they took the route for quitting their native land, great and small, old and young; on foot, on horses, asses, and in carts; each continuing his journey to his destined port. They experienced great trouble and suffered indescribable misfortunes on the roads and country they travelled; some falling, others rising; some dying, others coming into the world; some fainting, others being attacked with illness; that there was not a Christian but what felt for them, and persuaded them to be bap-

tized. Some from misery were converted; but they were very few. The rabbis encouraged them, and made the young people and women sing, and
play on pipes and tambors to enliven them, and keep up their spirits.[56]

Many Jews went from Spain to Portugal, only to be ordered by the Portuguese king, in 1497, to accept baptism.[57] Many left for lands controlled
by Muslims — in North Africa and the Ottoman Empire in the Levant.[58]
Some made their way to the Netherlands, others to central Europe. When
I visited the Ramu Cemetery in Kraków in 1996, the Jewish burial place
abutting the site of the city's oldest synagogue, I saw a gravestone dated
1493. I would later learn that Jews were expelled from Kraków in 1494, although not permanently, unlike Spain.[59] After Poland and the Ottoman
Empire, the most sizable contingent of Iberian Jews took refuge in the
only place in the rest of Europe that would have them: the papal territories
in Italy, especially Rome.

✦ 36 ✦

The Roman Ghetto

STAMP FOR INFAMOUS POPE" was the headline in a Catholic newspaper not long ago.[1] The story reported that the Vatican had just unveiled a new postage stamp honoring Pope Alexander VI (1492–1503). First known as Rodrigo de Borja y Borja, he was one of the notorious Borgia popes. He was also the nephew of a pope and the father of numerous children, including Lucrezia Borgia. His son, Cesare, whom he made a cardinal at age eighteen, was likely the murderer of his brother Juan. Alexander VI drew the demarcation line dividing the New World between Spain and Portugal, commissioned Michelangelo to design a new St. Peter's Basilica, and saw to the burning of Savonarola (1452–1498), the Dominican reformer who had challenged the Medicis in Florence.[2] Alexander VI's intrigues and appetites made him, in the words of the postage-stamp story, "an example of why the Church should pronounce a millennial *mea culpa* for historic wrongs." Apparently, the stamp was being issued only because of the parallel between the Vatican jubilee years of 1500 and 2000.

Oddly, there is one way Alexander VI may well be deserving of a respectful commemoration — his refusal to endorse the gravest of "historic wrongs." He was a man of Catalonia, and had been a subject of Queen Isabella. His admiration for her and Ferdinand, and his effort to ingratiate himself with them, is reflected in his having bestowed on them the honorific "Catholic Monarchs" not long after he ascended to the Chair of Peter. It may even be that Alexander did so, as one historian suggests, in appreciation for their having expelled the Jews from their realm.[3] But if so, that response was overridden in the pope's own heart when large numbers of desperate Iberian Jews began presenting themselves at the borders of papal territories in Italy, including the gates of Rome. The arrival of these Jews in Italy — all told, they would have numbered close to nine thousand[4] — was a jolt to Italian Christians and Jews alike. "You would have thought that they wore masks," one Christian who watched them wrote. "They were bony, pallid, their eyes sunk in the sockets; and had they not made slight movements, it would have been imagined that they were dead."[5] The historian Cecil Roth reports that in Genoa, friars greeted the starving refugees at the docks, "a crucifix in one arm, and loaves of bread in the other, offering food in return for conversion."[6]

But not in Rome. The Jewish community already living there probably numbered about a thousand people,[7] and suddenly nearly that many, or perhaps more, Spanish refugees decamped on the Appian Way, asking to be admitted. These may seem to be small numbers, but according to the historian Kenneth Stow, whose work informs my discussion of Jews in Italy, the entire population of Rome then was only about 50,000.[8] An equivalent in today's figures to the number of Iberian Jews arriving in Rome in the summer of 1492 would be about 100,000. The Roman Jewish community had roots extending back before the Christian era, but by now it included descendants of various European refugee groups. Rome had been a steady haven. Still, Jewish leaders seem to have been reluctant to welcome the mass of newcomers. If so, it was no doubt because their situation at that time of rising tension was precarious.

The record from Jewish as well as Christian sources is that Pope Alexander VI welcomed the Iberian refugees into Rome and pressed local Jews to do so as well. In contrast to his fellow Spaniards, and unlike the quayside friar in Genoa, Alexander declared that Jews in Rome "are permitted to lead their life, free from interference from Christians, to continue in their own rites, to gain wealth, and to enjoy many other privileges."[9] When Jews were expelled from Portugal in 1497, and from Provence in 1498, many of them, too, would make their way to the papal territories and to Rome. The pope's personal physician by then was the eminent Maestro Boneto, who from 1499 would also serve as the rabbi of the Roman congregation. The "notorious" Alexander VI was remembered by Jews as a magnanimous protector.

As such, the Borgia pope had fulfilled the best tradition of papal support for Jews. The Jewish community in Rome had concentrated itself along the Tiber, in Trastevere, in the shadow of Vatican Hill. Popes had sponsored anti-Jewish legislation, as we have seen, but in general such provisions as the distinctive badge were less strictly imposed in Rome than elsewhere. The abuse of Jews in the carnival was a feature of Roman life. The Talmud had occasionally been attacked. Friars had at times been allowed to pursue their aggressive conversions. But when medieval popes were strong enough to impose their will, they defended Jews with remarkable consistency. To repeat a point made earlier, *Sicut Judaeis,* the papal bull of protection, had been issued by twenty-three popes, from the twelfth to the fifteenth century.[10] It is in this context that Alexander VI's otherwise uncharacteristic virtue must be understood. He was responding to something that, by then, was deeply ingrained in the meaning of his office.

Not only the Jews were being protected by this tradition; so was something central to the idea of Christian faith. Since Saint Augustine and Gregory the Great, the Jews had functioned as a partner in a theological dialectic. As we saw, Augustine had called them the "witness people," positively affirming the tradition of Jewish faithfulness to the God of Israel. After Augustine, their witness was tied to the state of their degradation, which was itself taken as proof of the truth of Christian claims. Jews were degraded because they denied those claims. Christians who affirmed them could expect the opposite of degradation, which was salvation. Thus a Christian's sure expectation of his reward was reinforced by the felt experience of a Jew's quite palpable punishment. In order for this dialectic to be sustained, three things were necessary. First, Jews could not be allowed to thrive. Their perpetual punishment was a sine qua non. Second, though, their punishment could not be excessive, leading to their disappearance. Therefore violence was ruled out. Third, their place within the Christian community had to be protected so that each new generation of Christians could benefit from their witness. The impulse to kill Jews, or, now, to expel them, violated this system, which is why popes opposed it.

But in the fifteenth and sixteenth centuries, something new had begun to happen, undercutting the balance of this dialectic. The trauma of a massive collapse of the spiritual order of the Church had destroyed the former equanimity. The expulsion of Jews from Iberia was significant both as symptom and attempted cure, but then, it was also significant as an apparent unleashing of the virus of Jew hatred. At bottom, the Spanish Inquisition had provided a clear diagnosis that the cause of the Church's shaken faith was the very presence of Jews. Expulsion was not a first attempt at racial extermination, but it surely was the beginning of the strategy of elimination.

The amorphous spirit of heresy coalesced as a mortal danger to the Church around the figure of Martin Luther (1483–1546). Any examination of the civilizational roots of the Holocaust must take into account the impact of the Reformation, and of Martin Luther's own attitudes, on what Daniel Goldhagen called "the cognitive model of Jews that governed Germany."[11] My concern, as I said early on, is mainly with the Roman Catholic aspects of this narrative, but the Holocaust is the endpoint of a variegated European history, not a specifically Catholic one — or, for that matter, an exclusively Christian one.

As we move into the early fifteenth century, we must acknowledge the important, and expressly non-Catholic, turn the story takes in Germany. It was, as the historian Salo Wittmayer Baron describes, "in the territory of the Holy Roman Empire that the great drama of the Reformation immediately affected many Jewish communities and constituted a major factor in the subsequent destinies of the Jewish people, down to the Nazi era and beyond."[12] Martin Luther posted his Ninety-five Theses on the door of a Wittenberg church in 1517. In 1543, he published an antisemitic text, "On the Jews and Their Lies," and Hitler himself would appeal to anti-Jewish slanders that began with the great reformer himself. "The underlying cultural model of 'the Jew' (*der Jude*)," Goldhagen writes, "was composed of three notions: that the Jew was different from the German, that he was a binary opposite of the German, and that he was not just benignly different but malevolent and corrosive."[13] All these elements of Jew hatred were present in the long history of German Christianity, but they became solidified after Luther's diatribes.

The tragic character of Luther's impact on the fate of Jews in Germany is only fully apparent when "On the Jews and Their Lies" is read against an earlier treatise, "That Jesus Christ Was Born a Jew," written twenty years earlier, in 1523. During those twenty years, Luther had been seared in the fires of ferocious Catholic rejection. His bitterness poisoned much that began as good, including his attitude toward Jews. As "That Christ Was Born a Jew" shows, he began as a stout defender of Jews. He denounced the Blood Libel and the idea that all Jews were serfs of the emperor. In a commentary on Psalm 22, which, you will recall, provided the first Christians with much of the narrative detail used against Jews, Luther condemned the way "Passion preachers [during Easter week] do nothing else but enormously exaggerate the Jews' misdeeds against Christ and thus embitter the hearts of the faithful against them."[14] As one who felt the early sting of official Roman Catholic rejection, Luther manifested a remarkable sympathy for Jews, and he even averred that Jews had been right to resist Catholic efforts to convert them. "If I had been a Jew," he wrote in

"That Jesus Christ Was Born a Jew," ". . . I should rather have turned into a pig than become a Christian."[15] Luther hoped that Jews would come to see in his reformed Christianity the true faith of their fathers. He, too, proved to be a conversionist. He preached on the Five Books of Moses, expecting that Jesus, seen fully as a Jew, could finally be embraced by Jews as the Messiah.

That Jews, for their part, roundly rejected Luther's overture was part of what caused his bitter attack later, his version of the old pattern. Nothing generates Christian fury like the Jewish refusal, especially if what is refused is self-defined Christian kindness. But that rejection was only one factor in Luther's growing disenchantment with Jews, a disenchantment that would fester into a venomous hatred. "On the Jews and Their Lies" amounts to a homiletic massacre. In it, Luther advocated the burning of synagogues. Jews, he said, should be "forbidden on pain of death to praise God, to give thanks, to pray, and to teach publicly among us and in our country."[16]

But another cause stood behind Luther's hatred of Jews. To Catholics, his readiness to take the Old Testament on its own terms was proof that he was a Judaizer.[17] As ever, Catholics were ready to blame Jews, and now Jews could be blamed for the outbreak of heresy. Through Talmud, and perhaps through the secrets of Kabbalah, Jews were thought to have spread the deadly spirit of skepticism — what had enabled Jews to reject Christian claims from the beginning, and to turn aside the new rationalism with which Christian missionaries had learned to cloak their apologetics. The virus of Jew-spawned skepticism was thought to have found niches in the monasteries and universities of Europe, where the likes of Luther had been infected. But when he was charged by allies of the pope with propounding a Jewish heresy, Luther reacted by lumping Jews and the pope together as his mortal enemies: "Because the Papists, like the Jews, insist that anyone wishing to be saved must observe their ceremonies, they will perish like the Jews."[18]

The crisis of the peasant uprisings of 1524–1525 prompted Luther to throw in with the German princes, particularly his protector Frederick of Saxony, against peasants who were inspired by Luther's own attacks on authority, but whom he now perceived as a threatening rabble. The peasants had three targets, priests and lords — and also Jews.[19] In a savage war, the princes put the peasants down. Luther's die was cast. He supported the nascent regional nationalism of these German rulers not only against the universalist pope, but also against the transnational — and devoutly Catholic — Holy Roman Emperor. Thus, at the critical moment, Luther's religious purpose meshed with the political aims of the barons, and nothing symbolizes that juncture more powerfully than the role played by Luther's German translation of the Bible in the birth of German national consciousness. Luther's faith-versus-works reading of the Epistles of Paul, especially, would equate the dead legalisms of the papists with those of the Jews who rejected the Gospel. To oppose one was to oppose the other, and that dual opposition defined the core identity of his movement. In this process, as the great articulator of a new German self-understanding, Luther decisively influenced the creation of the "cognitive model of Jews," in Goldhagen's phrase, which would hold sway in Germany from then on. It was characterized by Luther's distinction between "ancient Israelites, whom he boundlessly admired, and the Jews of the Christian era, whom he hated with increasing venom."[20] It is important to emphasize that Luther's position on the Jews, however hateful it became, was grounded in the theological heart of Christian proclamation. "The basis of Luther's anti-Judaism," as the historian Heiko Oberman sums it up, "was the conviction that ever since Christ's appearance on earth, the Jews have had no more future as Jews."[21]

Because Jews were associated with their traditional protector the emperor, who was now defined as the political enemy, and because Jews involved in finance were even associated with the monies collected for indulgences for the hated pope, Jews became a catchall vessel for political hatred. Moreover, as the German culture began to define itself in terms of these enemies, Jews became the embodiment of enmity. "Know, my dear Christian," Luther said, "and do not doubt that next to the devil you have no enemy more cruel, more venomous and virulent, than a true Jew." Thus, as the new polities of what would become the regional states of Germany took shape, Jews were not only explicitly excluded from citizenship, but were cast in the role — more than the emperor, more than the pope — of the German people's negative other. The ambivalence that had mainly characterized Roman Catholicism's attitude toward Jews would not be a feature of politicized Lutheranism. Luther wanted Germany to be *judenrein.* "They are for us a heavy burden, the calamity of our being; they are a pest in the midst of our lands."[22]

Charles V (1500–1558) was already king of Spain when he was elected Holy Roman Emperor in 1519, two years after Luther's posting of his theses in Wittenberg. Charles presided at the Diet of Worms (1521), at which Luther was condemned, and he would later force the calling of the Council of Trent (1545) to deal with the catastrophe of the Reformation. But Charles was the grandson of Ferdinand and Isabella, the expellers of Jews, and he was pleased with Spain's being *judenrein* in his time. He was therefore an unlikely friend to Jews. Catholic princes of Europe were not generally more tolerant of Jews than Protestants, and in Rome, as we shall see, the anti-Jewish current was growing swifter. But as his conflict with the Protestant princes of Germany progressed, Charles V joined this fight as well, ultimately defending Jews as vigorously as Luther attacked them — as if for him, too, Jews now functioned as a symbol around which to wage this war.

In addition to the obvious negative trends, the Reformation also set loose forces that favored Jews, and that would contribute to their liberation — not least of which was the idea of individual rights. The positive side of the Protestant revolution for Jews would become clear particularly in places where the legacy of John Calvin outweighed that of Luther.[23] Born in France, ensconced in Geneva, Calvin presided over a movement that, unlike Luther's, did not get so swept up in the new spirit of nationalism. Calvinism's embrace of economic enterprise as a work of religion would lay the ideological groundwork for modern capitalism, and in that context Jewish collaboration in financial matters would be welcomed. Where Calvinist Huguenots and dissenters prevailed, especially in parts of France, the Low Countries, and North America, Jews would do far better than they would in most of Germany, with the important exception of banking families in the free cities of Frankfurt and Cologne.

These trends favoring Jews were already in evidence in the energy with which the emperor Charles V finally went to their defense. In 1544, not long before his armies and the Protestant princes went violently to war, Charles issued a new privilege for Jews, one that perhaps went further in establishing Jewish freedoms (not rights) than any previous decree. He outlawed the expulsion of Jews from imperial cities, forbade the forcing of Jews to wear distinctive badges in public, discouraged the charges of ritual murder, and proscribed the shutting down of synagogues. And, as Baron puts it, "the emperor quite bluntly stated here for the first time that '. . . they shall be allowed to invest and make use of their funds by lending them on interest . . . at much higher rates and greater profit than is permitted to Christians.'"[24]

That Christians now defined their opposition to each other, in addition to everything else, around Judaism was a new turn in the old story. The tale is usually told as if Jews were passive participants in this conflict, like an inanimate club with which Catholics and Protestants, peasants and burghers, prelates and princes, slugged each other. In fact, Jewish leaders continually found ways to manipulate their ever more dangerous situation, subtly navigating through these separate power centers. And if the emperor used his considerable power in defense of Jews, one reason was the traditional notion of Jews as the emperor's own serfs, but another was that Jews gave this embattled emperor every reason to do so.

The Christian pattern is to highlight the stories of Christian defenders of Jews, when they appear, as if Jews were as passive as beneficiaries as they were as victims. This shows up today in the book-and-movie saga of Oscar Schindler, the Nazi-era German Catholic who is given complete credit for the survival of the Jews on his "list" — as if his Jewish collaborator, the accountant Itzhak Stern, could not equally be remembered as shrewdly using Schindler to save his fellow Jews. The Itzhak Stern of Charles V was Josel of Rosheim, who, Baron says, was elected by German Jewry to represent them to the emperor. "A contributory cause of Charles' firm attitude was the great impression Josel of Rosheim had made on him," Baron writes. "Endowed with a quiet, tactful, and yet magnetic personality, Josel was well-versed in religious as well as political matters and was, at the same time, a realistic statesman . . . A most remarkable aspect of Charles' Jewish policies was that he issued his privileges without the customary special compensations . . . Exceptionally, the emperor's policy toward his Jewish 'serfs of the Chamber' was thus dictated less by purely fiscal considerations than by the desire to strengthen the declining power of his imperial office."[25] Josel helped the emperor to see how an alliance with Jews could help him, tilting the balance in cities, for example, where barons sought the support of the up-and-coming merchant class. Unfortunately, all of this was too little too late — for Charles V and for his Jews. Charles V would be the last emperor to be crowned by the pope, and though the designation Holy Roman Emperor would continue into the nineteenth century, the Constantinian ideal of a transcending imperial throne, established by Frederick Barbarossa in the twelfth century, would effectively end here. Exhausted by a succession of wars, the interminable Council of Trent (it would drag on until 1563), and the futility of efforts to turn back Protestantism, Charles abdicated in 1556. He took refuge in a monastery, where he died two years later.

The natural response of the Roman Catholic Church to this political and religious chaos was an urgent effort to impose a new uniformity of belief and practice. Despite the ways in which such uniformity had been held up as an ideal in the past, from Nicaea to *Unam Sanctam,* there was an unprecedented totalism — as in totalitarianism — in the Church's response to this crisis. And that had to impact Jews. Despite Charles V's practical alliance with Jews, the long-established Iberian conclusion had come to seem irrefutable among most who fought the heretics: Jews were the source of the corruption. It was a small step for Catholics to assume that, somehow, the Protestant Reformation itself was a result of Jewish influence, and many did. Rational arguments were attached to this deeply irrational fear. In Rome, Spanish clergy who were officials in the papal bureaucracy now came under suspicion of having Jewish ancestry. As Jews had been thought to have poisoned wells in the fourteenth century, *conversos* were now thought to have infiltrated the inner circles of the Church.[26] In 1556, the year of Charles V's abdication, his own son, Philip II, in one of his first acts as his father's successor as king of Spain, could already write that "all the heresies which have occurred in Germany and France have been sown by descendants of Jews, as we have seen and still see daily in Spain."[27]

These stresses are reflected in the record of the popes who came after Alexander VI, who had welcomed the exiled Iberian Jews to Rome. They were a succession of pontiffs who, in effect, badgered each other and themselves over what to do about — among so much else — the Jews. In 1520, Pope Leo X (1513–1521) condemned the works of Luther, which were fed to bonfires across Europe. Adrian VI (1522–1523), a Dutchman and the last non-Italian pope until Karol Wojtyla became John Paul II in 1978, had served as regent in *converso*-hunting Spain. He failed in his main project, to launch a new Crusade against the Turks. When Adrian died, the news was greeted with joy by factions that hated him as a "northern barbarian" and by Romans who hated the work of his Inquisition. Upon Adrian's death, his doctor was honored for having failed to keep him alive.[28]

Yet nothing demonstrates the insecurity of the papal position in this chaotic period more than the sack of Rome in 1527. Pope Clement VII (1523–1534) had angered the emperor Charles V by entering into an alliance with King Francis I of France, prompting even the devoutly Catholic Charles to send an army into Rome. Those forces kept the pope prisoner in Castel Sant'Angelo, the former tomb of Hadrian, for seven months. As we saw, the emperor forced a General Council of the Church on the next pope, Paul III (1534–1549). The Council of Trent, named for the small city in the north of Italy where it met, convened in three sessions (1545–48, 1551–52, 1562–63). It was preoccupied throughout with matters of Church reform and doctrinal definition. After all, with Nicolaus Copernicus (1473–1543) cosmology itself was being overturned, an intellectual equivalent, if not a cause, of upheavals in theology to which the council fathers had to respond. Politically, the council was dominated by prelates and rulers from north of the Alps. The pontiff rarely held the initiative at the council, but in any case, its first enemy was clearly defined as the Protestant movement.[29]

Jews were referred to dismissively at Trent, or hardly discussed. But the council fathers made one solemn statement on another subject that, over the centuries, would have a direct bearing on Catholic-Jewish relations. A remarkable demonstration of the complexity of Catholic attitudes toward Jews, the statement concerned the crucifixion of Jesus, which had so consistently been laid at the feet of Jews. That was never the whole story, however. The Gospels, and especially Paul, had made an equally emphatic point, which kept getting lost. But now it surfaced with unusual clarity, for Trent affirmed that responsibility for the death of Jesus belonged to sinners — to all persons, that is, in their having sinned. The old question Who killed Jesus? was explicitly answered: Human sinners did. And *our* sins, these Christians declared, mark *us* as responsible. And more than that. "This guilt," the fathers of Trent declared, "seems the more enormous in us than in the Jews, since according to the testimony of the same Apostle [Paul]: 'If they had known it, they would never have crucified the Lord of glory' [1 Corinthians 2:8], while we, on the contrary, professing to know Him, yet denying Him by our actions, seem in some sort to lay violent hands on Him."[30] If this perception had maintained its firm hold on the moral imagination of Christians, the history of Jews would be different. That something else happened, beginning with the Gospels' own scapegoating of Jews, only proves Trent's point, that "we" are sinners.

In the first half of the sixteenth century, some of the popes were not only sinners, but knew it. Consequently, even in that period, the Church could turn a relatively benign face toward Jews, as happened, for example, during the pontificate of Paul III, who presided at the opening of Trent.[31] His sister had been the mistress of his patron, Alexander VI, the pope who welcomed Iberian Jews to Rome. Paul himself had been a typically hedonistic member of the Borgia pope's court. But he changed, taking the Reformation as a personal challenge to reform his own life. It was he who excommunicated Henry VIII of England, but it was also he who commissioned Michelangelo's grand examination of the Catholic conscience, *The Last Judgment*. More to the point, Paul III was vigorous in his defense of the Jews. He banned performances of a wildly popular Passion play in the Colosseum because it incited attacks on Rome's Jews. His support for Jews was significant enough to draw acid criticism from other prelates.[32]

But just as the overriding effect of the Council of Trent (its pro-Jewish theology of the crucifixion notwithstanding) was the imposition of rigid Counter-Reformation measures to suppress all "unbelievers," including Jews, so even a Jew-protecting pope like Paul III embraced the era's movement — and machinery — of repression. Popes had generally opposed the Spanish Inquisition since its inception, but they had been unable to stop it, or even to temper it. Now, finally, a pope came to see the necessity of allowing a version of the same Inquisition to come to Rome. In 1542, Paul III authorized the establishment there of a Spanish-type Inquisition, which would pursue the agents of doctrinal impurity who were corrupting the Church from within. He appointed as its head the fearsomely ascetic Gian Pietro Caraffa, who had served as a papal nuncio in Spain. "Were even my father a heretic," Caraffa is remembered as saying, "I would gather the wood to burn him."[33]

In 1553, Caraffa saw to the burning at the stake in Rome of a Franciscan monk who had converted to Judaism. Caraffa presided at the burnings of dozens of Jews, whether *conversos, marranos* (a derogatory term meaning "pig," applied to secret Jews), "cryptos," or the vaguely suspected relapsed. All such Jews were regarded, in one way or another, as sponsoring heresy.[34] Under Caraffa, also in 1553, the Roman Inquisition launched a massive campaign against the Talmud, bringing to relatively tolerant Rome the violent obsession with rabbinic texts that had broken out in Paris three hundred years before. For the first time ever, but establishing a firm precedent, Jewish homes and synagogues in the city were invaded, and all copies of the Talmud and other texts were seized. As such volumes had been hauled to what is now the Place de l'Hôtel de Ville in Paris, they were piled in a mound in Rome's Campo dei Fiori, a broad square that still serves as the site of a sumptuous daily food market. A bonfire was lit; the burning of the Talmud had come to Rome.

"Once these books are removed," an advisor to the Roman Inquisition wrote, ". . . it will soon result that the more they are without that wisdom of their princes, that is, the rabbis, so much the more will they be prepared and disposed to receiving the faith and the wisdom of the word of God."[35]

In the center of the Campo dei Fiori today stands a morose statue of a hooded monk named Giordano Bruno (1548–1600), a monument raised only in 1887, after the Church lost control of Rome. In part out of admiration for Saint Thomas Aquinas, Bruno had entered the Dominican order, and he quickly distinguished himself as a thinker. Eventually he was influenced by the Kabbalah, in the somewhat fanciful Christian tradition of Pico della Mirandola.[36] In line with the speculations of Nicolaus of Cusa and the observations of Copernicus, he posited, for example, the infinity of the universe, a notion condemned by the Church of his time. When Bruno was summoned by the Roman Inquisition in 1576, he "shed his ecclesiastical garments and took flight from the Eternal City."[37] He believed that God was omnipresent, and available, in creation — not just in the Church. No doubt influenced by his exposure to Jewish texts, he held that people of differing religions should respect each other's freedom of conscience. Bruno's arguments with Church authority became increasingly vituperative, until he was seized in Venice, brought back to Rome, and given the chance to recant. He refused. He was burned at the stake in the Campo dei Fiori by the Inquisition on February 17, 1600.[38] To mark the day, citizens of Rome still come to Bruno's statue to lay flowers, and in the year 2000, on the four hundredth anniversary, a demonstration there was attended by hundreds of Italians.[39] It is impossible to look at the sculpture's shadowed face and not think of the fires that raged in that place. Caraffa, from a generation before, was the fire starter.

Paul III may have appointed Caraffa, and he may have authorized the coming of the Inquisition to Rome. But he did not approve the other, equally perverting innovation that now began to make its way from Spain to the center of Catholicism — though it did so, ironically, because of him. In 1546, Paul III had appointed a *converso* priest to a clerical position at the cathedral in Toledo. It should have been a routine matter, but the archbishop of Toledo, the reach of whose power can be seen in his having been a tutor to Spain's King Philip II, defied the pope by rejecting the appointed priest on the grounds that he had impure blood.[40] Recall that this sort of discrimination against "New Christians" and their descendants had been staunchly opposed by the papacy. Paul III vacillated before finally withdrawing the appointment. The emboldened archbishop carried the matter further than any prelate ever had, issuing, in 1547, the Statute of Toledo — the statute of so-called *limpieza de sangre,* or blood purity — according to which no one of Jewish blood could hold office in the cathedral. Paul III refused to approve the decree, and most other prelates, including many in Spain, denounced it. But the Inquisition began extending such *limpieza* statutes to other institutions. People of Jewish ancestry were banned from holding office in Iberian universities, in religious orders, in various guilds, and in some municipalities. As we have already seen, this emphasis on blood purity was a line in the sand of history. On one side of it stood the Inquisition and what would prove to be its most damning legacy, a turn of mind given over to racism. On the other side of that line, still, was the papacy, clinging, however tentatively, to an ancient responsibility. What would prove to be the succeeding era's most fateful question had set inquisitor against pope.

But then, in 1555, the story took a decisive turn, perhaps its most decisive, when the grand inquisitor Caraffa, the man who had burned the Franciscan Jew, Judaizing Christians, and the Talmud, was elected to fill the Shoes of the Fisherman. Gian Pietro Caraffa became Pope Paul IV (1555–1559). He was seventy-nine years old. Acting quickly, here is what he did: He ratified the blood purity Statute of Toledo.[41] He forbade Jews to possess any religious book except the Bible. From now on the Talmud would be on the Index of Forbidden Books. To enforce that proscription, he abolished Hebrew printing in Rome, which during the Renaissance had become its world capital.

Most momentously, in July 1555, Paul IV issued the bull *Cum Nimis Absurdum:*

> Forasmuch as it is unreasonable and unseemly that the Jews, whom God has condemned to eternal slavery because of their guilt, should, under the pretense that Christian love cherishes them and endures their dwelling in our midst, show such ingratitude to the Christians as to render them insult for their grace and presume to mastery instead of the subjection which beseems them; and forasmuch as it has come to our notice that in Rome and in other cities their shamefulness is carried so far that they not only make bold to dwell among Christians, even near their churches, and without any distinction in their dress, but even rent houses in the distinguished streets and squares of these cities, villages and localities, acquire and possess landed property, keep Christian nurses, maids, and other servants, and do much else that is for a disgrace to the Christian name; therefore do we perceive ourselves constrained to issue the following ordinance.[42]

Jews are to own no real estate. Jews are to attend no Christian university. Jews are to hire no Christian servants. Jews' mercantile roles are to be strictly regulated. Jews' taxes are to be increased. Jews are no longer to ignore the ancient requirement to wear distinctive clothing and badges. Jews are to refuse to be addressed as "sir" by Christians. "In no public document, until the advent of Hitler," wrote the historian Malcolm Hay, "have Jews been addressed with more unseemly language than that employed in this message to Christendom."[43] What makes *Cum Nimis Absurdum* a milestone of papal notoriety, though, is less its language than its central ordinance: Jews are to live on a single street, or in a distinctive quarter cut off from other sections of the town or city. This quarter is to have only one entrance. The bull, in other words, mandated that henceforth Jews in Christendom were to live in the ghetto.

Cardinal Edward Cassidy, head of the Vatican Commission for Religious Relations with Jews, said in an address to a group of Jewish leaders in Washington, D.C., in May 1998, that "the ghetto, which came into being in 1555 with a papal bull, became in Nazi Germany the antechamber of the extermination."[44] Before that bull, however, the ghetto already had a long tradition. The Fourth Lateran Council (1215) had issued orders isolating Jews, including residence in confined quarters, but such requirements had been irregularly enforced. Cologne had its ghetto as early as 1150; Frankfurt's dates to 1460. No sooner had refugees arrived in Poland from Iberia than a ghetto was established in Kazimierz, in Kraków, in 1496.[45] But never before had a decree ordering the establishment of a Jewish quarter been issued with such seriousness of intent, and never before, as subsequent history would show, was such a mandate to be so rigorously enforced. And never before had such a mandate been issued by a pope.

Cum Nimis Absurdum was promulgated on July 12. On July 23, male Jews living in Rome were required to begin wearing yellow conical hats (women had to wear veils). On July 26, all of Rome's Jews were rounded up and brought to the district beside the Tiber — about a mile square, about a mile from the Vatican — that would thenceforth serve as the ghetto.[46] (The word "ghetto" originated in Venice, where Jews had previously been confined to a district near the new iron foundry, or *geto nuevo*.) Work commenced immediately on an encircling wall, which took two months to build and for which the Jews themselves were required to pay. The restrictions of life inside the ghetto would lead to an almost immediate and complete physical and cultural — although not religious — impoverishment of the once proud Jewish community. Jews would be required to live within its confines, a cramped population that at times exceeded ten thousand, until late in the nineteenth century. Across the street from what served as the gate of the ghetto stands the Church of San Gregorio alla Divina Pietà, with an inscription from Isaiah above the door. An English translation of the verse reads, in part, "I spread out my hands all the day to a rebellious people, who walk in a way that is not good."[47]

The suffering caused by the ghetto was extreme, and as Cardinal Cassidy indicates, the ultimate consequences of this escalation, when joined to other historical currents, have been unspeakable. But there is reason to believe that even the remorseless Paul IV intended something else. In the preface to *Cum Nimis Absurdum,* the pope explained that the purpose of his restrictive policies was to lead Jews to conversion.[48] He had fully and finally abandoned the Augustinian idea that Jews served God's purposes by continuing to live, as degraded "witnesses," among Christians. The sole principle now would be that Jews had been allowed to survive only to glorify God and the truth of his Church by converting. Thus the innovative inhumanity of the ghetto was not intended to be permanent. Indeed, the very brutality of these new policies was designed to make them necessary only briefly. Some Jews did respond to the new regime by converting, but most did not.

To put the best face on it, the ghetto and all its restrictions were not intended as a kind of social torture, the organized application of pain designed to force the surrender of stiff-necked Jews. Caraffa and other Church officials would have learned from the *converso* disaster in Iberia that forced conversion is by definition untrustworthy, and would lead to an underground counter-religion of crypto-Judaism. What Paul IV imagined was that if the Jewish degradation was made complete, Jews themselves would recognize it as, in the words of the historian Kenneth Stow, "the fulfillment of the prophecies of servitude, and therefore, as a result of this recognition, they would convert."[49] Jews who had not recognized the fulfillment of prophecies about the Messiah embedded in the life of Jesus, in other words, would recognize that fulfillment in their own lives. What Paul IV was doing with *Cum Nimis Absurdum* was reducing to a new level — to the absurd? — the "fulfillment" mistake that the Jesus movement had made in the first generation when it claimed a "New Covenant" that fulfilled and therefore superseded the "Old."

While Paul IV was bringing the mind of the Inquisition fully into the papacy, he was also rejecting reconciling overtures from Elizabeth I of England (1533–1603), an element in what made her father's split with Rome permanent. Obviously, the culture-wide trauma of the Reformation was part of what prompted the shift in papal strategy toward Jews. For centuries the conversion of Jews had certainly been on the Catholic agenda, but never exclusively so, mainly because the insecurity that resulted from Jewish denial of Christian claims had been only subliminally felt. From the first generation of the Jesus movement, Jewish rejection of Jesus as Messiah had posed a mortal threat, but perhaps for that

very reason, it had been repressed. As an anxiety denied, it had served all
the more efficiently as the fuel of anti-Jewish hatred. Yet within the Catholic Church, prior to this shift, as the historian Heiko Oberman puts
it, "hatred of the Jews did not exist apart from protection of the Jews;
these were two sides of the same coin."[50] But now, with a papal-enforced
ghettoization, which would be imitated in cities across Europe, the balance of the age-old ambivalence was upset. It could not be maintained in
a Church under siege.

On the surface, it appeared that the Roman Catholic Church had been
essentially unchallenged in the West since Constantine. Even the quake of
the great East-West schism in the eleventh century had been shaken off by
the triumph of the First Crusade and the subsequent twelfth-century renaissance, the coming of age of Christendom. Church contests with kings
and emperors, and even between rival claimants to the Chair of Peter, had
sent aftershocks jolting through Europe, but it seemed the Church always
emerged from such struggles stronger, rescued in one age after another
by great-souled mystics and thinkers whose loyalties to God and the
Church were the same thing. But the Protestants were something else. So
were the continent-wide forces of social tumult and class conflict, of scientific revolution — Copernicus! — and nascent capitalism. The feudal
age, in which the Church had beheld its own ideal, was clearly dead. What
was replacing it? The Reformation, with attendant new nationalisms and
economies, had by now gravely shaken the confidence the Church felt in
itself as the inerrant Body of Christ. Perhaps for the first time since the
conversion of Constantine, the Church was in need of reassurance. Was
that the clue? As a conversion had provided the rescue before, so now. But
not the conversion of one man only. Nothing could have assuaged the Ref-
ormation-era insecurity of the Roman Catholic Church like the mass conversion, at long last, of the Jewish people.

For Christians attuned to their own Scriptures and to the intellectual
concept of "fulfillment," such a prospect necessarily evoked an image of
the Last Days. Stow argues that Pope Paul IV was at the mercy of just such
an eschatological hope.[51] The sweep of heresy through Europe was taken
as a sign of the Antichrist's coming, the climax of salvation history. To the
inquisitor pope, the Christian's duty at such a moment was clear — the
personal and institutional embrace of an absolute discipline. "Let there
be one faith," he declared, "and there will be one peace; let there be
one confession in the Church, and one path of brotherhood. Remove
the golden calves; remove the haughty; let there not be Rehoboam

and Jeroboam, Jerusalem and Samaria; let there be one flock and one pastor."[52]

Nothing better captures the spirit of the Counter-Reformation than Paul IV's urgent effort to bring about the purification of the Church at once, immediately. For an extreme ascetic like him, the swift conversion of the Jews was central to such a plan. In the face of the collapse of everything he believed in, there was only one thing to do, which was to impose order in every way he could, by whatever means were required. Therefore, *oppose* Protestants outside the Church, *impose* discipline within the Church. But especially, *convert the Jews*. Only that would close the fault line that had cracked the rock of the Church from the very beginning. It would not just signal but would accomplish the completion of salvation history, as foretold in Paul's Epistle to the Romans, where it is written that the conversion of the Jews will mean "nothing less than a resurrection from the dead!"[53] As Stow writes, "The conversion of the Jews would also establish order. But this order would possess a special virtue. With it would come an end to all anxiety about the validity of Catholic truth and the stability of the Catholic world. For the order which their conversion would establish was the millennium. The attempt to convert the Jews thus suggests that the desire for order as a solution predisposed men to seek the ultimate order."[54]

Paul IV's successors would make adjustments to the "discipline" he imposed, with one pope doing away with restrictions and another reimposing them. When Jews refused this new and ultimate "invitation" to convert, popes would react with a bitterness that recalls Luther's, although lacking his invective. Pius V (1566–1572) would expel Jews from the Papal States, all but Rome and Anconia, where they continued to be useful points of contact with trade. Gregory XIII (1572–1585) would send missionaries into the ghetto, requiring Jews to listen to conversionist sermons in the one synagogue left to them. Some popes would ease up on Jews — Clement IX (1667–1669) would do away with the carnival foot race of Jews — and others would crack down again. But for more than three hundred years, no pope, "not even the most humane and beneficent," in Hermann Vogelstein's phrase,[55] would act to dismantle the squalid ghetto at the foot of Vatican Hill. It would take the "godless" soldiers of the French Republic to do that in 1796. After the defeat of Napoleon, Pope Pius VII (1800–1823) would order the walls of the ghetto rebuilt. It was not finally abolished until the popes lost control of Rome to the "secular" forces of Italian nationalism in 1870,[56] an event to which we will return. Suffice to note here that on September 3, 2000, the last pope to maintain the Roman ghetto, Pius IX (1846–1878), a pope who referred to Jews as "dogs," was beatified by John Paul II. Beatification marks the penultimate step to sainthood.[57]

Long before losing control of the Roman ghetto, however, the popes had lost control of anti-Jewish conversionism and what it led to. Not even Paul IV's imposition of "discipline" and "order" had bent the ancient stiff-necks. In the next chapter, we will try to understand what went into the Jewish refusal, and what it meant. Meanwhile, the Church itself was undercutting the conversionist program with the inexorable spread from the Iberian fringe of *limpieza de sangre,* the new idea of blood purity. When Paul IV, in violation of tradition and the near-unanimous policies of his predecessors, ratified the 1547 Statute of Toledo, forbidding the appointment to that city's cathedral of any Christian descended from Jews, he was participating in the destruction of the one motive a self-interested, if not necessarily religiously pure, Jew might have had to convert. If accepting baptism did not enable Jews to escape pariah status within the Catholic culture, why would most convert? This may not have been a question for the eschatologically minded Paul IV — the Jew would convert because he had seen the light — but it had to be a question for those increasingly desperate Jews who were no more exempt than anyone from the demoralization and doubt of the era. In effect, the arrival of blood purity regulations spelled the end of the Church's anti-Jewish missionary effort that had begun in the thirteenth century.

But the arrival of *limpieza* regulations in the heart of the Church marked the beginning of something too. More and more of the central institutions of the Roman Catholic Church, from religious orders to Catholic guilds to dioceses, began to imitate the Toledo Cathedral in discriminating against those of Jewish blood. At bottom, this phenomenon represented a radicalizing of the mistrust of Jews, and an institutionalizing of it. As the embattled sixteenth century wore on, with the Reformation split widening instead of closing, and with the newly "disciplined" Jews still refusing to convert, resentful suspicion of Jews sank its taproot deeper than ever. A fatal paranoia about "Jewish blood" was next.

The age-old pattern was repeating itself: Fresh Christian initiatives toward Jews — rational apologetics, say, or Talmud-based argumentation — leads to fresh Jewish refusal — few converts, or converts who can't be trusted — which leads to a new level of Christian hatred — the violent Inquisition, the punitive *limpieza.* Finally, the Catholic Church went further than merely ratifying such regulations enacted by its subsidiary organizations. In 1611, Pope Paul V (1605–1621) decreed that the blood purity standard would apply in Rome too, that "persons of Jewish descent shall not be admitted to canonicates of cathedrals, dignities in brotherhoods, and offices entrusted with the care of souls."[58]

This violation of the essential openness of the Christian message to all, and of the equality before God of all the baptized, did not take. No Catholic would affirm it today. Blood purity regulations were eventually revoked, even in Spain, where they were made irrelevant by the passage of time and the complete absence of Jews. Nevertheless, this introduction of a distinction by race into the central institutions of Christianity — a distinction assuming not mere racial "diversity" but a biological divide of racial superiority and racial inferiority — stands as a watershed not just in Church history but in human history. "Nineteenth-century racial anti-Semites never claimed this as a precedent," Marc Saperstein comments, "but the Spanish 'purity of blood' legislation was an ominous venture into new conceptions of Jewishness."[59] We noted this earlier. The point here is that, for a crucial period, a time that served as the incubator of modernity, this narrowly "Spanish" idea — a heresy if ever there was one — became a Catholic idea.

When Cardinal Cassidy forthrightly acknowledged the connection between the Church-enforced ghettos of Europe and the death camps of the Nazi era, in May 1998 and again, in my presence, in March 1999, he was addressing groups of Jewish and Catholic scholars on the subject of the Vatican declaration "We Remember: A Reflection on the Shoah," of which he was the principal author. Having revisited the era in which violent anti-Judaism moved from the streets of the Christian mobs into the sanctuary of the Church, we should return to the Vatican's present-day assessment of this history. "We Remember," eleven years in the making, was promulgated as a definitive Catholic examination of conscience on the Church's relationship to the crimes of the Holocaust.

Regarding Cardinal Cassidy's stark acknowledgment, as he put it to me, of the Church-enforced ghetto as the "antechamber of Nazi death camps," it must be noted that the official statement itself makes no such direct connection. "We Remember" denies the causal link between the admitted history of Catholic anti-Judaism and the Nazi hatred of Jews. The document speaks of modern racial antisemitism as if it were unrelated to what had gone before. "By the end of the eighteenth century and the beginning of the nineteenth century . . . theories began to appear," the text states, and the impersonal, agentless diction seems full of implication, "which denied the unity of the human race, affirming an original diversity of races. In the twentieth century, National Socialism used these ideas as a pseudoscientific basis for a distinction between so-called Nordic-Aryan races and supposedly inferior races."[60] The statement firmly attaches such a racial distinction to unnamed sources outside the Church. "The Shoah was the work of a thoroughly modern neo-pagan regime. Its anti-Semitism had its roots outside of Christianity." The text goes on to cite "the difference which exists between anti-Semitism based on theories contrary to the constant teaching of the Church on the unity of the human race and on the equal dignity of all races and peoples, and the longstanding sentiment of mistrust and hostility that we call anti-Judaism, of which, unfortunately, Christians have also been guilty."

"We Remember" was followed up with "Memory and Reconciliation," the Vatican statement that appeared in March 2000. In a short passage of that document, entitled "Christians and Jews," the points of "We Remember" are simply repeated, with emphasis given again to the distinction between the Church and its members, and to the non-Christian nature of "the pagan ideology that was Nazism."

These assertions in the Church's most solemn attempts at self-examination raise numerous questions, including, again, that of the apparently exonerating distinction between "the Church as such" and "Christians." The point here, however, concerns the claim to a "constant teaching of the Church on the unity of the human race and on the equal dignity of all races and peoples." It is hard to see how the history of the fifteenth, sixteenth, and seventeenth centuries upholds such "constant teaching." The Inquisition-inspired adoption by "the Church as such" of the blood purity standard, in particular, would seem to undercut this central claim of "We Remember." Doesn't the *limpieza* legacy suggest that the Church itself was part of what enabled the movement from a religion-based hatred of Jews to a race-based hatred? The seventeenth century is a long time ago, but even in the twentieth, Catholics up for appointment to "offices entrusted with the care of souls" were at times required to "display their genealogical charts," as Rosemary Radford Ruether puts it, to show that there were no Jews among their ancestors. Blood purity regulations, Ruether asserts, "remained on the books in Catholic religious orders, such as the Jesuits, until the twentieth century. They are the ancestor of the Nazi Nuremberg Laws."[61]

Here, for example, is the text of a resolution passed by the Fifth General Congregation of the Society of Jesus, which met in 1593–1594: "Those, however, who are descended from parents who are recent Christians have routinely been in the habit of inflicting a great deal of hindrance and harm on the Society (as has become clear from our daily experience). For this reason many have earnestly requested a decree on the authority of this present congregation that no one will hereafter be admitted to this Society who is descended of Hebrew or Saracen stock."[62]

In the Sixth General Congregation, which met fourteen years later, the restriction was extended from "parents" back to "the fifth degree of family lineage," with the requirement that a candidate for admission to the order not be descended from a Jew or Saracen "within that degree of family relationship."[63] The restrictive regulation was allowed to stand by one General Congregation after another, although the exclusion of those of "Saracen" stock dropped away. Here is the regulation governing admission of candidates as it was approved by the Twenty-seventh General Congregation, in 1923: "The impediment of origin extends to all who are descended from the Jewish race, unless it is clear that their father, grandfather, and great-grandfather have belonged to the Catholic Church."[64] The Jesuits finally did away with this rejection of those descended from Jews, but this is how the fathers meeting at the Twenty-ninth General Congregation put it: "Regarding the impediment of origin, introduced by decrees 52 and 53 of the Fifth General Congregation, explained in decree 28 of the Sixth Congregation, preserved, albeit in mitigated form, by decree 27 of the Twenty-seventh Congregation but not contained in the Constitutions, the present congregation did not wish to retain it as a secondary impediment, but substituted for it a statement reminding the provincials . . . of the cautions to be exercised before admitting a candidate about whom there is some doubt as to the character of his hereditary background."[65] This is as close as the Society of Jesus could come that year to a ringing repudiation of *limpieza de sangre*. It was 1946.

In the fall of 1998, the Vatican sponsored a meeting of historians on the subject of the Inquisition, a follow-up to the earlier opening of the archives, to which I referred in chapter 32. Pope John Paul II asked the scholars to withhold moral judgments, and instead to "help in the most precise possible reconstruction" of the milieu within which the Inquisition developed. Revisionist historians emphasize that "the black legend," in historian Carlo Ginzburg's phrase, has been exaggerated, and it seems that the Vatican hopes for a tempering of history's profoundly negative judgment of the Inquisition. As we saw earlier, the worst abuses of Inquisition violence occurred in the first phase of its long existence. But questions of torture and execution as a mode of thought control, and even the historical context that might mitigate the harshest judgments, are one thing; the overall impact of the Inquisition on Jews, and those of Jewish ancestry, is another. The fact is that the Inquisition moved Christian suspicion of Jews to a whole new level of irrationality. Thus the positive assertions of "We Remember" seem of a piece with the document's failure even to mention the Inquisition, and with the later reliance on euphemism in "Memory and Reconciliation," where the Inquisition was referred to as "the use of force in the service of the truth." Nevertheless, the question remains: Was the Inquisition the hospitable organism to which the virus of modern antisemitic racism first attached itself?

Pope Paul V, who formally embraced the *limpieza* standard in 1611, was also the pope who presided over the start of the Inquisition's move against Galileo Galilei. Those proceedings were concluded by Pope Urban VIII (1623–1644), who sympathized with the scientist but condemned him anyway.[66] In 1992, Pope John Paul II apologized for that condemnation — the earth does indeed revolve around the sun — but that Vatican acknowledgment of error had something of the self-exoneration of "We Remember" about it. The pope cited "a tragic mutual incomprehension" between the Inquisition and the scientist — "as if," in Hans Küng's words, "there were errors on both sides." I was interviewing Küng in 1996 at his home in Tübingen, Germany. "What?" He banged his fist on the table. "Galileo was right. The others were wrong."[67]

It was Galileo's intimate nemesis, Urban VIII, who ended the Roman custom according to which a Jew, upon entering the pontiff's presence, was expected to kiss the Holy Father's foot. Urban required instead that the Jew kiss the floor on the spot where the pope's foot had stood. A story told by Jews in Rome had it that Urban VIII intervened when a convert-hungry friar was trying to take a Jew's child away, to baptize the child. But the Jew refused to let the child go. When the pope heard of it, he decreed that if the Jew did not hand over the one child to be baptized, all of his other children would be taken as well. To make the point, a second of the man's children was taken, and both were duly baptized. Freed from the ghetto, the first child was then carried through the streets of Rome, to be hailed.[68]

The Religious Response of the Jews

T HE TURN IN the story occasioned by the new restrictions of the Church-mandated ghetto in Rome and other cities should have been an instance par excellence of the "lachrymose tradition" of Jewish history. The ever-tightening vise of Christian paranoiac prejudice squeezed more and more life out of the Jewish community. The forced impoverishment that came with ghettoization entailed a shocking collapse of a once proud culture. The loss of books and the proscription of education led to sharp declines in literacy rates. Among Jews, the *convivencia*-era embrace of an Aristotelian rationalism, represented by the Maimonides school, was perceived now as a source of relativism that had led many to convert to Christianity. The disciplined intellectual life, as defined by the broader culture, became suspect. What looked to that culture like mere superstition replaced philosophy as the touchstone of wisdom. Indeed, the curtailment of significant interaction with that broader culture marked the onset of Jewish inwardness. The word "ghetto" may have originated with a Venice foundry district, but Jews recognized another word inside it — *get,* which in Hebrew means "bill of divorce."[1] Instead of being only lachrymose, however, this divorce, as sometimes happens among men and women, was the occasion of a remarkable renewal of the injured party.

On the Christian side, the ghetto symbolized the end of the long tradition of mixed messages, tracing back through *Sicut Judaeis* pronouncements, which both protected Jews and promulgated contempt for them; through Saint Augustine's dual proscriptions that Jews should survive, but not thrive; through Saint Paul's repudiation of the Law and his assertion that God does not revoke the Covenant; to the Jesus movement's scapegoating of Jews for the crucifixion and its self-definition as the "new Israel." After the Inquisition, the expulsions, the *limpieza,* and the ghetto, the Catholic Church's attitude toward Judaism would be relentlessly nega-tive. The "divorce" imposed by the popes was supposed, by the twisted logic of this relationship, to bring about the final Jewish submission. When it did not — Kenneth Stow says that the number of Jews accepting baptism in the Roman ghetto, with its population of 3,500 to 4,000, rarely exceeded twenty in any given year[2] — Judaism was cut off from life outside on the assumption it would die. To be sure, conversionist programs were continued, with friars making forays into the ghetto synagogue. As the story about Urban VIII's intervention in the case of the Jewish child indi-cates, not even children would be exempt from such pressures. Neverthe-less, with the twin policies of ghettoization and expulsion, embraced even by the papacy, a new age of Jewish isolation had begun.

Yet behind those walls, and through networks linking urban ghettos, Jews underwent a spiritual renewal that might be compared to the first flourishing of rabbinic Judaism at the onset of the Diaspora, after the dev-astating wars with Rome. For the first time, European Judaism was truly set apart from Christian culture. We saw in Part Four how the spirit of martyrdom had marked both crusaders and their Jewish victims. The twelfth- and thirteenth-century spiritual revival that showed itself on the Christian side in the monastic renewal of Cluny and its satellites, like Maria Laach, showed itself among Jews in the surfacing of Kabbalah and the appearance of the *Zohar,* attributed to Moses de Leon, at the end of the thirteenth century.

But what developed among Jews in response to the traumas of the sixteenth century had no equivalent among Christians, Catholic or Prot-estant. The Reformation and Counter-Reformation involved spiritual re-coveries of different kinds, but they shared a framework that had nothing to do with Judaism. In its own sphere, the Jewish religion underwent a spiritual and ethical renewal that was nuanced, original, and deeply effec-tive in terms of individual meaning and of communal sustenance. Such was the divorce that Christians would hardly notice this development, or if they did, they would misunderstand and condescend to it.

We have seen how, beginning in the twelfth century, Kabbalah had sur-faced as a source of a new Jewish mythology and a new Jewish mysticism. We have seen how some Christians, from John of the Cross to Pico della Mirandola and Giordano Bruno, were influenced by Kabbalah, but to the extent that most Christians were aware of it, they regarded it as supersti-tion, the mumbo-jumbo of numerology or magic or witchcraft. But the richness of this tradition is manifest by nothing more clearly than the fact that, in the crisis-ridden sixteenth century, Kabbalah reinvented itself, and flourished anew.

What Jews behind their ghetto walls were doing was nothing less than recasting, in a state of physical distress, the spiritual meaning of their situation. Jewish spirituality evolved on its own terms, of course, but in times of crisis, as now, dynamic interactions between the two communities were decisive. If the Christian world had cut them off, the Jews would turn their separation into a religious value. Christianity ceases to be mentioned now in Jewish texts. If, after the various expulsions and corrallings, they were once again a people in exile, they would define exile itself as holy, a kind of metaphysical truth of the human condition. If Jews seemed once again to have been abandoned by God, they reenvisioned creation as the work of God's self-abandonment. If Jews were forbidden even the remotest suggestion of sexual liaison with Christians, they would turn intra-Jewish matrimony into a dynastic principle of social cohesion, even across national boundaries, as families from various ghettos arranged marriages. If Jews were forbidden to leave the ghetto at night, then night would become not only the time for study and prayer, but an image of God's own darkness. (Jews in the ghetto, in the seventeenth century, drank newly imported coffee as a way of staying awake.[3]) This mysticism, Stow writes, "allowed Jews to transcend the physical limits of the ghetto. It permitted them to fantasize that things were the opposite of what they seemed to be in reality. Closure was really an opening. By being restricted to the ghetto, therefore, the Jews were being propelled mystically toward their rendezvous with the liberation of the messianic moment. Mystical speculation made them immune to the threats of the outside world."[4]

The prophet of the new Jewish mysticism, "the central figure of the new Kabbalah," in Gershom Scholem's phrase,[5] was Isaac Luria (1534–1572).[6] He was a contemporary of the ghetto-creating inquisitor pope, Paul IV, but Luria, "the Holy Lion," had a ferocity that expressed itself differently. He lived in Palestine, in Safed, a city that still draws mystical seekers. "Rising from the haze and fog of Upper Galilee's deepest ravines and valleys, Safed has no biblical pedigree, no deep roots in the scriptural or prophetic history of Israel . . . ," Neil Asher Silberman writes. "Yet after 1492, with the horror and uncertainty of the Spanish Expulsion and the increasing flow of Jewish immigrants toward the Ottoman Empire, Safed was one of the several towns in the Holy Land that received a significant number of refugees."[7] Silberman cites a "massive influx of sages back into the Land of Israel." By the time of Luria's arrival, Safed was a vital center of Jewish scholarship that ran the gamut from text-observant Torah study, to unbridled mystical theorizing, to feats of memorization, to pursuits in chemistry and astronomy along tracks laid down by Kabbalist texts. "In the span of less than three years — that seems in retrospect like a lifetime — the young kabbalist burst upon the mystical scene in Safed . . . He offered his followers a profoundly disturbing secret: he helped them understand the nature of *evil* and the means by which it would eventually be overcome."[8] God, too, was understood as grappling with evil. In Luria's view, as Harold Bloom summarizes it, creation itself is "God's catharsis of Himself, a vast sublimation in which His terrible rigor might find some peace."[9]

Refracted through Luria's genius, Kabbalah offered a bracing worldview that enabled its adherents to stand amid the swirl of individualism that marked the unfolding new epoch — without being swept away by it. Kabbalah was rooted in an enduring faith in Israel as God's chosen people, and that peoplehood was never more to the point. Thus Jews found a way to temper the individualism that would mark the coming modern age. Because exile was defined as essential to the human condition, the scattering of the Jewish people would become a condition of cohesion, not dispersal.

Luria's teachings spread quickly through the traumatized Jewish world. In an ingenious leap of religious imagination, Luria enabled Jews to transcend their recent experience of catastrophe by positing a primordial catastrophe — *tsimtsum* — in which elements of the Divine Being were splintered into an infinity of broken pieces. These "shards" are the stuff of creation. The purpose of creation, this splintering of God, was seen as nothing less than, in Silberman's words, "destroying the principle of evil from within."[10] Once this shattering of the divine has occurred, it becomes the responsibility not of a single Messiah but of the Jewish people to bring about the gradual restoration of cosmic unity and God's own being, the ultimate ingathering of those broken pieces — a redemptive process that is called *tikkun olam*. The Messiah will come when the work of the Jewish people has been accomplished, which will be done through faithful study of Torah, observance of the Law, and performance of works of justice. *Tikkun* is one of the most precious ideas ever to strike a human mind. It is the "restoration of creation [which] must be carried out by the religious acts of individual men, of all Jews struggling in the Exile, and indeed of all men and women struggling in the Exile that Luria saw as the universal human existence."[11]

Emphasis on redemption based on the response of the people set Judaism apart from Christianity more than ever, for in bringing about the fulfillment of time, the Messiah, in this scheme, takes second place to Torah. Jews found a way to believe that even in their degraded situation, they had a noble, uplifting function to perform, one entirely unlike the Christian mandate — one that was nothing less than contributing to the restoration of the fullness of the Godhead. By means of the lighting of candles on Shabbat, the study of Torah, the observance of *mitzvot* ("commandments"), and prayer, exiled Jews understood themselves to be preparing for a messianic future by redeeming the splintered past. It was a call to rebuild the cosmos so that the exiled God could come home.

Karen Armstrong, in her *History of God,* notes the stark contrast between this positive mythology, which defined the broken creation as partaking in the divine, and the dark contemporaneous visions both of Protestantism, with its puritanical emphasis on the doom of humanity without grace, and of Catholicism, which during the Counter-Reformation fell ever more under the sway of a morbid, cross-obsessed hatred of the world.[12] It is in this period, for example, that the Stations of the Cross, the mournful following in the imagined steps of Christ on the way to Golgotha, comes into its own as a dominant Catholic devotion.[13] In contrast, Luria's conception of God, according to Armstrong, "was able to help Jews to cultivate a spirit of joy and kindness, together with a positive view of humanity at a time when the guilt and anger of the Jews could have caused many to despair, and to lose faith in life altogether."[14]

As Luria's movement grew in Safed, other manifestations of Jewish vitality showed themselves. Messianic figures appeared, like David Reubeni and Solomon Molcho in Portugal, and *conversos* and unconverted Jews alike took heart from their bold rejection of the idea that Jews were fated to be oppressed.[15] In the next century, a Kabbalist from the Turkish city of Izmir emerged as the leader of one of the most potent religious-political movements in Jewish history. He was Shabbetai Zvi, a self-declared Messiah who found enthusiastic followers in Jewish communities around the Mediterranean, and in Europe as well, especially Poland. The political hopes that many had for Shabbetai came to nothing when, imprisoned by the Turks in 1666 — the combination of sixes in that year had made it portentous — he chose to convert to Islam rather than risk martyrdom. But his heroic movement had by then spawned numerous centers of enthusiastic Judaism, including one that would quicken in Poland and Ukraine in the eighteenth century. Spreading throughout eastern Europe, this movement was led by Israel ben Eliezer, the beloved Baal Shem Tov. Yet another charismatic leader, he "transformed the shattered hopes of the messianic movement, the surrealistic images of Lurianic kabbalah, and the centuries-old magic of the Jewish mystical tradition into the vibrant *modern* movement of the Hasidim."[16] Across geography and across generations, Jews were reinventing their ideology, renewing their commitment to the God of Israel, and finding ways to express joy, hope, and happiness while the world outside remained ignorant of these currents.

Eventually, just as contact with Jews had threatened the broader culture during the period of *convivencia,* the self-sufficient separateness of Jews would do the same. Both their friends and enemies in the Christian world consistently saw Jews as having no existence apart from their function either as witnesses to the flaws of the Church or as accusers. But the fact that Jews had an independent positive theology of their own, it came to seem, was the real affront. "All that the Jews of Europe asked," Leon Wieseltier explains, "was not to believe in Jesus, and to be left alone in Judaism. But it was too much to ask."[17] The choices of the past had consequences for the future. Patterns of rejection, acceptance, and ever-fiercer rejection kept repeating themselves. "Thus, in Spain in the sixteenth century," Rosemary Radford Ruether writes, "we have a dress rehearsal for the nineteenth-century European experience. The Jewish community, made to assimilate *en masse,* then is perceived as a shocking invasion of Christian society, and barriers previously thrown up against them on religious grounds are now reinstituted on racial grounds."[18] In Part Six, we will see how that nineteenth-century development, especially as embodied in the Dreyfus affair, constituted, in turn, as Hannah Arendt similarly dubbed it, "a kind of dress rehearsal for the performance of our own time."[19]

↣ 38 ↢

Shema Yisrael!

ORAL MATURITY LIES in the ability to see links between events — how choices lead to consequences, which lead to new choices, which set up even more fateful consequences. Such a concatenation of choice and consequence defines the narrative arc of every story, including this one, which curves from Jesus to the Holocaust. Yet the same question surfaces at every point of choice-and-consequence: Where does the Christian hatred of the Jews come from? This history invites a return to John Paul II's answer to the question put by the Bob Dylan song. "One!" the pope said. "There is only one road, and it is Christ!"

But for Jews, the word "one" has reference only to the Holy One of Israel. The post around which this entire narrative has turned is the ancient, enduring statement of Jewish faith, the Shema: "Hear, O Israel, the Lord is our God, the Lord is One!"[1] Age in and age out, from Jerusalem to Mainz to Toledo to Rome, then back to Mainz again, Jews do not yield on their affirmation of God's oneness, their affirmation of the way to God represented by "carefully"[2] obeying God's commandments. Their very existence as a people doing this denied the Christian claim, as Saint Thomas Aquinas defined it, that Jesus is "the absolutely necessary way to salvation." Their denial has had tremendous power over Christians. At some deep psychological level, it has felt like nothing less than crucifixion: The Jews who crucified our Lord crucify us. Obviously there is far more than a mere theological dispute here, as if the issue were a Nicaea-like conflict over Trinitarian monotheism. It is more than a mortal grudge tied to a crime, even deicide, from long ago. Choice and consequence. Is it that an early Christian choice — whether in Saint Paul's generation or in Constantine's, whether a choice for religious exclusivity or for absolute uniformity — undercut Christian certitude of belief in a Christian meaning that had become too constricted? Is it that subliminal anxiety about the Church's faithfulness to Jesus — his message of love betrayed precisely in *this?* — prompts the Church to make extreme claims for its own inerrancy? "Universalist absolutism," a Catholic veteran of the Jewish-Christian dialogue, Padraic O'Hare, has said, "thrives on the diminishment of the other." The more the Church shores up the reach of its claim, the greater the danger that, again — here is the lesson of the Inquisition — we will have "religion as a source of brutality."[3]

In addition to everything else about Judaism — its integrity as a religion affirmed on its own terms — Jews have perennially made visible the invisible mystery of such contradictions. Have they therefore become a kind of living epiphany of a restless Christian conscience? Jews survive as an unsettling figment of the religious imagination of the Church — which is the problem. Judaism has its own existence, of course, apart from any such link to Christianity, and I intend no reduction of Judaism here. I write as a Christian, from a Christian point of view, admittedly concerned with the meaning of these events for Christians. But their meaning has wider importance than that. In academia, the history of antisemitism is taught in Jewish studies departments, if at all, when it should be taught as a core component of the history of Western civilization. When the narrative of Jew hatred is recounted within the relatively narrow scope of Jewish studies, the structure of Jewish accusation and Christian guilt is reified, and antisemitism is defined as the Jews' problem, instead of that of Western civilization, the culture that came into being with the Jew defined as a religious, economic, social, and, ultimately, racial outsider. But when antisemitism is treated mainly as a Jewish problem, the Jew is condemned to play the role of either self-flagellant or denouncer, with obvious dangers attached to each. That is why this history must be recounted not as the history of Jews but primarily as a history of the Church.

I began this project by describing it as the story of "Jewish-Christian conflict," but I realized that the word "conflict" was too slight. I spoke then of "Jewish-Christian hatred," but that isn't it either, although hatred is an element. Oddly, the passion of Christian antagonism toward Jews achieves such a level not only of brutality, but of attachment, that it must be seen as including also a rare sort of intimacy, beyond that of any other pair of enemies known to history. It is as if Jews and Christians had begun not merely as rivalrous siblings but as Siamese twins, tragically set against each other in connected bodies that were one body, and sharing, perhaps, one sorely divided soul. This history is nothing but the story of a violent separation, and it prepares us, for one thing, to honor the ways in which Judaism and Christianity have grown radically apart. Obviously, these identities are quite distinct now, and that distinction is the ground on which stands the hope not of some reunion but of mutual respect. That assumes, of course, that talk of "One Way" has no place in this conversation.

Although the opposite is not the case, Christian identity depends on Jews, just as the Christian Scriptures depend on the Hebrew Scriptures. In the past, that has been taken to mean that Christian identity depends on winning the Jews over, or silencing their dissent, bringing order to religious disorder by converting Jews. In reaction to this violent history, trying to overcome it, some Christians now assert that the importance of Jews to Christianity consists in their being the first and last witnesses to the flawed humanity of the Church. If that is true, the position of Jews is still precarious, because the Church, as we have repeatedly seen, is continually tempted to deny its flawed humanity. In other words, the contest continues.

This is not to say that Jews have an investment in criticizing the Church or in bringing the Church around — say, by a full "apology" for the Holocaust — to a new understanding of itself. It is not to say that Bob Dylan had any need of Pope John Paul II that day in Bologna. On the contrary, what Jews are doing is only what Jews have always done, which, if a Christian may say so, is to affirm that only God is God. God's existence is the only absolute, and God's existence matters absolutely. As the late Edward Flannery, a Catholic priest and pioneer in the Jewish-Catholic dialogue, put it, "The hubris in the human heart cannot forgive the Jew for bringing into the world the idea of a transcendent God and a divinely sanctioned moral law binding on everyone." Flannery offers a classic statement of the problem: "Jews have suffered so long because they bear the burden of God in history. Anti-Semitism is symptomatic of an animus against God, an animus deeply lodged in every person."[4]

And, therefore, in every human institution. No Catholic is exempt from this judgment, and, as this narrative demonstrates, neither is the Church. Individuals deflect this damning truth with the shield of an unexamined self-righteousness. The Church does so by the absolute claims it makes for itself, even when it cloaks them in claims it makes for Jesus. The Catholic version of the Shema properly extends to him, but in what way? And does it properly extend to the Church as such, when it defines itself as the Body of Christ? A theology of Incarnation necessarily extends the worship of the holy and transcendent God to a creature of that God. This is the Catholic paradox, and it is somehow a source of the scandals we are rehearsing in this book. It is a source of the Vatican's determination to shore up univocal feudal controls over ecclesiastical organizations and over the thought of Catholics. The Incarnation means that God has come to live among us *as we are*. We may be tempted to deny our flawed humanity. God is not. But God's judgment is forgiveness, which is why there is no reason to fear the truth — not even the truth of this narrative. That is why, to repeat the millennial statement of John Paul II cited earlier, the Church is "not afraid of the truth that emerges from history and is ready to acknowledge mistakes wherever they have been identified."[5] Faith in the forgivingness of God makes self-criticism possible — which is another way of saying that it makes history possible.

"Listening to the past," Rabbi Abraham Joshua Heschel wrote, "attuned to the striving of ancestors, we perceive that to be a Jew is to hold one's soul clean and open to the flow of that stream of striving, so that God may not be ashamed of His creation." Is there a counterpoint between Judaism's emphasis on salvation history as *history* and Christianity's effort to define itself by what lies ahead? "The quest for immortality is common to all men," Heschel said. "To most of them the vexing question points to the future. We Jews think not only of the end but also of the beginning. We have our immortality in the past."[6]

The Christian story is equally time bound, as if, in the biblical vision, time itself has become a mode of God's presence. But think of Pascal's image, as George Steiner puts it, "of Christ's agony persisting until the end of time."[7] And yet from another point of view, Christians understand the meaning of the Lord's coming as a transcendence of time. Because the first followers of Jesus were convinced, within Jewish messianic categories, that time itself was about to end, they experienced the "drawing nigh" of eternity. That meant both that the past collapsed into the present — "In the beginning was the Word," the Word who is Jesus — and that, because Jesus would soon return, the future infused the present, too. The urgent expectation of those first followers was disappointed, but not before it changed the way they experienced time. For Christians, God had become, in a phrase of Rahner's, the absolute future. The future becomes absolute as it becomes ours.[8] The future, it can seem, is all we have. To Christians, Jesus is "eternity in time," to use the critic David Denby's term, but it is time as unfolding before us. Denby read the New Testament for his *Great Books,* and he summed up this development as "the version of time and history that Christianity brought into Western consciousness, a way of conceiving of time that had an immense influence on theology and literature at least through the Renaissance . . . The Christian mode of thinking had shaped literature and art and institutions, it had been woven through history and could not be shaken out. It had woven itself into me, too."[9]

As it happens, Denby is Jewish. Perhaps his sense of the distinctiveness of Christian time-consciousness notes too little the Jewish aspect of that first Christian mindset. I understand these things as a Christian, and I surely take Heschel's point about the primacy of the past. Yet it strikes me that in the chanting of the Shema there is no future, no past. Doesn't the classic Jewish proclamation transcend time as much as a theology of Incarnation? In the notion of *tikkun,* there is the hope that the broken shards of the past can open to a messianic future, establishing Judaism's vital redemptive character, but in the Shema past and future bow. There is only now. Only this. Only God. The Holy One of Israel transcends Israel, too, both as a mystical entity, the biblical people of God, and certainly as the modern state of Israel, despite all temptations of Zionism. If Catholics are not exempt from judgment, neither are Jews. The Holy One transcends — and Jews themselves insist on this — even the Holocaust. The Jewish absolute, in this sense, is "more absolute" than Christianity's, since Christians cannot bring themselves to say, quite, that God transcends the Church, which in the tradition is "mystically" identified with Jesus.

Israel has never identified itself with God. Indeed, the Shema is an affirmation of God's radical otherness. Ironically, the Christian imagination attributes a kind of materialism to Judaism — the legalisms of the Torah, an emphasis on the this-worldly importance of history, the money-grubbing stereotype, Marx's atheistic positivism, and so on — yet in this central religious act, Judaism is anything but materialistic. God is above all that is, including time and history, yet God cares for people in the here and now. Perhaps the ability to affirm that paradox is why the faith of Jews survives — survives everything. The Jewish proclamation of God's existence, God's oneness, and God's immediate relevance to human life, affirmed twice daily for thousands of years, is the spine not just of Jewish religion but of the civilization that springs from it. There need be no argument over whether Western consciousness owes more to Christians than to Jews.

Those who have gone at Jews brandishing the cross, in recent days as well as in ancient times, apparently regard this resolute Shema as the cross's competition. The cross is meant to be a symbol of love, but looked at from below, it can be a symbol only of domination. And it can even be a symbol, in Flannery's phrase, of the "animus against God." The cross drives this story, from its beginning at Golgotha to its end at what John Paul II called "this Golgotha of the modern world."[10] By the close of the crusading Middle Ages, the ambivalent Renaissance, the blood-tainted Reformation, and the tainted-blood Counter-Reformation, the cross had become an icon of all that Jews were required by the Holy One of Israel to reject. And what Christian, after Auschwitz, can say that they were wrong?

No matter how Christians take it, that rejection is not an act of negation, for the anguish it assumes itself opens to a holy recognition. "When thou hidest thy face," the psalmist prayed, "they are dismayed; when thou takest away their breath, they die and return to their dust."[11]

In the modern era, to which we turn now, when the face of God became hidden in the mists of secularism, could Catholics have recovered the cross as what it must have been for Jesus — since, after all, he too saw it from below? To him, the cross was the Shema made wood, Jesus' own witness to the Holy One of Israel, for that is what it meant when, despite not seeing God's face himself, he found a way to pray, "Into your hands I commend my spirit." If Catholics had seen this, could they have joined with Jews in announcing what they both still knew — that even when human beings leap from God's hiddenness to God's death, God is the One who does not die? Could Catholics have then recognized that the modern assault on hierarchy was not an assault on God? Indeed, this history suggests it was the work of God. Does the Catholic Church's blindness to the real meaning of Judaism have anything to do with Catholic blindness to post-medieval democratic values as a trace of God in time? Kabbalah, with its ideology of God's emanation in the souls of all people, planted seeds of tolerance in the Western mind, whether condescending Christian apologists knew it or not. Leibnitz and Locke,[12] perhaps through Spinoza, were beneficiaries of the spacious hopefulness of *tikkun,* and now science would flow from the currents of the Jewish mystical tradition. How little the Church would understand not only of the secular, as it broke in, but of the deepest meaning of its own spirituality.

In the new age, whether defined by the ascendancy of capitalism, by political revolutions, or by secularity, the battle would continue, as always, to be between the Church and the Jews, emphatically or subtly. In chapter 32

I recalled my own, admittedly ludicrous brush with the spirit of the Inquisition. At last I understand why the Indexed book they took from me should have been Sartre's *The Age of Reason*. Neither I nor my inquisitor had read the book. Its title and its author were enough to frighten us. If I recall *The Age of Reason* now, it is to draw this story forward into the Enlightenment, where we will see why fear seized the Church by its very soul.

PART SIX

EMANCIPATION, REVOLUTION, AND A NEW FEAR OF JEWS

39

Karl Marx, Second Son of Trier

W E RETURN TO this city again and again: Trier, on the Moselle, upriver from its confluence with the Rhine, site of the ancient Roman capital of the north, when the city was known as Augusta Treverorum, then as Treveris. We saw this as Constantine's first headquarters, how he launched his campaign to unify the empire from here, how his greatest palace is preserved still, how on the site of his mother's palace stands the present cathedral.

Because it was Saint Helena's home, Trier became the first episcopal see in Gaul, and subsequently the seat of powerful prince electors of the Holy Roman Empire. Helena, as we saw, is revered for having brought from Jerusalem a nail of the True Cross and relics of Saint Matthias, the apostle elected to replace the traitor Judas. But Helena's place of honor in Trier is due above all to the Robe of Christ, the tunic attributed to her discovery and preserved in the hidden reliquary of the cathedral. The tunic, you recall, is what had brought me to Trier with my mother. We had come as pilgrims for only the second showing in the twentieth century. As an object of Old Testament prophecy — "for my raiment they cast lots"[1] — the Seamless Robe, when centurions were remembered rolling dice for it, became a proof of the claims made for Jesus. As such, it had been a challenge to the thin piety of a self-doubting teenager. But far more than that, it was a permanent rebuke to Jews. It gave every baptized witness the right to nudge a Jew with "Don't you see?" Gazing across the bowed heads of Germans, I had been sophisticated enough to ask, "Is this the real Robe?" To ask if there had ever been such a thing at all — to ask, that is, if the friends of Jesus simply lifted the detail from a psalm they loved, for the sake of a consoling continuity — had been unthinkable to me. Even more so was the Robe's connection to Christian antisemitism.

It was here in Trier, as we saw, that Jews first suffered the insult of the crusaders, and it was here — that "comely" girl who threw herself into the Moselle — that Jews first set the pattern of their resistance. And 842 years later, it was near here that Allied armies first broke into Germany. Ike and Monty retraced the routes of Constantine and the crusaders, moving east. And now, as we track the story of Catholics and Jews into the darkest corner of the Enlightenment, we will see still more of the mystery of this place.

I am standing in a burgher's modest house at 10 Bruckenstrasse, in the center of the city, less than a five-minute walk from the market square and the cathedral in one direction, and a shorter distance from Constantine's palace in another. The house consists of three stories, on each of which are two or three small rooms. From the street, the building — its linteled doorway, its eight windows, each with its grid of panes, its capstone at the blushing crown of a timid arch — impresses like a self-important bureaucrat, cravat in place, vest properly gilded with the chain of a watch, the only thing of real value hidden. A courtyard in the rear separates the house from its one outbuilding, which in 1818 would have been a stable and carriage house. In that year, Trier was a country town, home to about 12,000 people,[2] compared to today's population of nearly 100,000. In the guidebooks of Trier, 1818 is always featured because that is the year Karl Marx was born, and this is the house of his birth.

Today Karl-Marx-Haus is a museum. The philosopher and revolutionary's letters and manuscripts are on display, as are first editions, in various languages, of *Das Kapital* and *The Communist Manifesto.* The domestic furniture has been removed from the former parlor and bedrooms, and the walls are decked with photographs and prints. There are pictures of the young Marx, a dandy with styled hair and a carefully trimmed beard and mustache; of the "Young Hegelians," a clique at the university in Berlin; of Friedrich Engels. There are broadsides and posters: *Workers Unite!* A defiant earnestness marks the display, and one assumes that the museum dates to a time when the ideas of Karl Marx were still threatening, and that even now its tone is set by true believers.

Except for this: I am standing in the second-floor room where Marx was born. To my left are a pair of large windows, overlooking the street, through which rivers of light pour onto the wall before me, illuminating a large genealogical chart. In the Soviet Union this family history was never referred to. The chart traces Marx's forebears back to the fourteenth century — to "Eliesar um 1370," a paternal ancestor who is identified as a rabbi of Mainz. I think of that city's ancient Jewish cemetery and imagine Eliesar buried there. Dozens upon dozens of Marx's ancestors are named. "Levi, Isak, Israel," we read. "Hirsh, Abraham, Chaim." Many of the males are identified as rabbis: "Moses Halevi Marx, Joshua Heschel Lwow, Josef ben Gerson ha-Cohen of Kraków." From this line of men were drawn rabbis to the congregation of Trier beginning in 1650. The rabbi of Trier in Marx's own time was his father's brother. Both of Marx's grandfathers were rabbis.[3]

It is impossible to look at those names and dates without thinking of others. The year 1096, of course, and this Jewish community's encounter with Peter the Prelate; 1155, when Saint Bernard of Clairvaux preached here against mob attacks on Jews, unaware of his own part in prompting them; 1349, when, after charges of well poisoning, the entire Jewish population of Trier was slaughtered. In 1418, ahead of Spain, though after England, the Jews of Trier were expelled, which is why the chart shows the family moving east for several generations, as far as Poland. "How lonely sits the city that was full of people!" begins the Book of Lamentations. It is impossible not to hear the echo of such verses here. "How like a widow has she become, she that was great among the nations! She that was a princess among the cities has become a vassal . . . among all her lovers she has none to comfort her; all her friends have dealt treacherously with her, they have become her enemies."[4]

The princess is the family tree itself, and the ladders linking mothers and fathers, children and grandchildren, sisters and brothers, and cousins to the tenth degree are precisely how she withstood her affliction. In fact, this lineage represents a positive history more than a negative one, a veritable sacrament of the self-renewing vitality of rabbinic Judaism. It means everything that the legacy of Karl Marx should be traced to the community that supported the great Talmudic academy of Mainz, where the exegetical imagination took hold in the heart of Europe. A genealogy gives us our genes, and the diagram before me charts the flow of lifeblood through the spiritual centers of Jewish revival. I think of Nachmanides, Moses de Leon, Don Todros, Isaac Luria, and the Baal Shem Tov here, in this room where Marx was born, whether they'd have been named that day or not. In the fifteenth and sixteenth centuries, members of this family had settled in cities north and south, east and west; this family's elders had continually tested tradition against the new experiences of intellectual alienation and exile. And, apparently, a center held. Marx had ancestors; so did his genius.

In other words, the family tree of Karl Marx, a web of distinctly Jewish names; of places stretching to the shtetls of eastern Europe, yet returning again to the Rhineland, and always Trier; of dates reaching back many centuries, but seeming to build toward the single date of May 5, 1818. The chart's stark specificity, like winter branches shorn of foliage, exposes the unspeakable implication that this one family survived. It illuminates the wonder that in generation after generation, despite pogroms and expulsions, Blood Libels and Inquisitions, book burnings and autos-da-fé, Jewish men and women — *these* Jewish men and women — found each other, loved each other, gave life to children, lit candles, studied Torah, all the while with a throng of rabbis proclaiming the Shema.[5] Seen in the skeletal truth of a family tree, the arc of this story reveals itself, transcending the instances, which are all we usually see, to the sum of their meaning. Some Jewish historians, as we saw, decry the "lachrymose tradition," as if what we have been recounting is a story only of misery. And there *is* an unbroken chronicle of suffering over time in the very names of this family, and in the places — Alsace, Ansbach, Cologne, Mainz, Kraków — where its women bore their children. The family tree is itself the Book of Lamentations. Open it to any verse, and it will weep. Yet open it and read what else is written there: suffering balanced by a history of affirmation of which outsiders are barely aware. One family's longevity in a world that did not want it manifests a triumph of political resistance and religious faithfulness, which for Jews were the same thing. And more. This chart, so crowded with names, reveals the Jewish secret: how kinship ultimately transcends itself; how one family becomes a people.

Since the time of Constantine — the time, that is, that the young, fiercely ambitious tetrarch left Trier to impose his unrelenting vision of unity first on his fellow tetrarchs, then on the empire, then on the Church — people who identified themselves as Jews, even when that identification was less than clear, were forced to stand apart. Unlike Christians, and unlike the Muslims who came later, they were not allowed to proselytize, and those who would join them as converts did so at their peril. Jews could abandon their religion, but they could not expand it, except through procreation. This meant that, over time, the religion did, in fact, become a people, as kinship became a kind of nationhood. While the various races of Europe, through the migration, conquest, and intermarriage, were blurring the lines of what had initially set them apart, and while Catholic Christianity was gathering itself around an absolutist universalism, Judaism was being reduced down to a narrowly defined kinship religion. This was happening as a result not of anything intrinsic to Torah, Talmud, or the "Israelite" character, but of the world of sacred intolerance in which Jews were forced to live.[6] Time, in other words, was putting its stamp on a people, giving them the cohesion that underwrites the wonder of their survival, while moving them, by virtue of that cohesion, ever more surely into the center of a target that had first been hung, yes, by Trier's own Constantine, only half a dozen city blocks away from here.

On May 5, 1818, however, the age of Jewish cohesion, kinship, and nationhood was presumed by many Europeans — including many Jews, including perhaps Heinrich Marx, that day's proud father — to have passed. Karl Marx would use his remarkable life to expand the idea, saying time was up for religion as such. Yet the conflict he ignited, raging for a century, would prove it was not so. One of his many biographers, Werner Blumenberg, emphasizes the significance of Marx's ancestral Jewishness, recalling Marx's own statement: "The traditions of all dead generations weigh like a nightmare on the minds of the living."[7] But I wonder, looking at the map of his human past, how could Marx have known what a nightmare of experience weighed on him? And once he so crudely turned his back on that experience, how could his soul not have been deeply troubled?

40

Spinoza: From Rabbis to Revolution

A
FULL APPRECIATION of Karl Marx presumes an understanding of his precise relationship to the rabbinic tradition that weighed on his living mind, whether he knew it or not. Yet that tradition came to him not directly, through religious channels to which he was only tenuously related, but indirectly, through the philosophical and political innovations that had reshaped society at the birth of modernity. The bridge figure standing between the rabbis and the philosophers was Benedict Spinoza (1632–1677), a philosopher who lived his entire life in Holland, less than two hundred miles from Trier. Like Marx two centuries later, Spinoza was born a Jew, but by the time he died he was branded an atheist, a materialist, an anarchist, and a revolutionary. In fact, his writings, derived from the mystical tradition of Judaism, gave shape to the authentic religious impulse of the post-Copernican age, and his call for political tolerance, born of his experience as a twice-exiled Jew, anticipated the idea of liberal democracy. And because his association with theological and political innovation was perceived by Christians through the lens of anti-Jewishness, Spinoza became a modern version of the ancient enemy, especially when the Church set itself against the Enlightenment, of which he was one progenitor.[1]

As is true of so much in this long narrative, Spinoza's story begins with the cross, and as his name indicates, it begins in Iberia. In 1596, in Portugal, Spinoza's grandmother had been denounced as a secret Jew by her own father and aunt. Her son, Spinoza's father, witnessed the autos-da-fé as a child, and "he would have told [Spinoza] with revulsion of the *sanbenitos,* yellow robes slashed with black crosses, which surviving 'penitents' had to wear thereafter at mass, and in the street on religious feast days."[2] We saw earlier that the Holy Roman Emperor Charles V had implemented at least some policies that were favorable to Jews, and in that tradition, but also because it meshed with his efforts to fend off Protestantism and to nurture support among the merchant class, he allowed new Christian refugees from Iberia to settle in Amsterdam, which was the beginning of the Jewish community there. Spinoza's father, while still a child, came as a refugee to Amsterdam. There, he married a woman of Portuguese and Spanish ancestry, some of whose own relatives had been pursued, and burned, by the Inquisition.[3]

The fires of such conflict were not limited, of course, to Iberia. The Thirty Years' War (1618–1648), a ferocious contest between Catholics and Protestants that raged from Bohemia to Scandinavia, was well under way when Spinoza was born, and would not end until the Peace of Westphalia, when he was sixteen. That treaty, which established the territorial sovereignty of states and the religious boundaries of Europe, is sometimes regarded as signaling the end of the Counter-Reformation.[4] During that period, sometimes regarded as having begun with the papal approval of the Jesuits in 1540, with the establishment of the Roman Inquisition in 1542, or with the opening of the Council of Trent in 1545,[5] Roman Catholicism pursued two purposes at once — a rigorous internal reform of the religion, represented above all by the intellectual and moral vigor of the Jesuits, and a fierce combat with those whom the Church regarded as enemies. The combat was waged figuratively, through a steady stream of anti-Protestant anathemas issued from Rome, and literally, through the Inquisition and the continent-wide conflicts we lump together under the rubric of religious wars. The St. Bartholomew's Day Massacre of Huguenots in Paris in 1572 would be a particular marker of the age.

And throughout the time both before and after Spinoza's birth, the Catholic Hapsburgs, from their solid base in Iberia, tried to reclaim imperial dominance over the French and Germanic realms, and even over Sweden and England. Their success in what we think of as Austria-Hungary would not be matched in northern Europe, and the disaster of the so-called invincible Armada (1588), when the Spanish fleet of more than 130 vessels was destroyed off the coast of England, would stand out as one of history's great turning points.

In the same period, the Hapsburgs lost control of the northernmost provinces of the Netherlands to the Protestant William of Orange. Once that happened, many *conversos* who had moved north from Iberia reverted to the practice of Judaism. The Dutch Calvinists established their own religion as the orthodoxy of their republic in 1619. They were not known for being tolerant, but they were so fiercely opposed to papists that they rather liked it when Jews renounced their ties to Catholicism. Jews were "welcomed at first as fellow victims of Spanish cruelty."[6] While the United Provinces of the Netherlands were still holding off the Spanish enemy to the south, the merciless rigidities of Calvinism were directed toward Catholics, not Jews. On one occasion, the Protestant police of Amsterdam raided a discreet gathering of worshipers whose use of a foreign language, presumably Latin, had been overheard. The Calvinist officials thought they were nabbing surreptitious Catholic Mass-goers, but what they found were Jews observing the Sabbath — in Hebrew, not Latin. Two Jews were arrested, but in short order they were released.[7]

Soon enough, synagogues were permitted in Amsterdam, and Spinoza's father emerged as a leader in the city's Jewish community, which numbered about a thousand when Spinoza was born. His father named him Baruch, which in Hebrew means "blessed," and is Latinized as Benedict. Young Spinoza's mother tongue was Spanish, but he learned Hebrew, too, and he received instruction in the Iberian tradition, studying Jewish and Muslim masters, including Maimonides and Averroës, who shaped his introduction to philosophy, and to Aristotle, far more than the Christian scholastics did — a background that would distinguish him, for example, from René Descartes (1596–1650).

Spinoza was schooled in Talmud, with its attachment to the idea that interpretation is essential to meaning, and in Lurianic Kabbalah, with its devotion to the emanations of God in creation. Spinoza's grounding in "the Jewish philosophical, literary, and theological tradition," as one of his biographers put it, was "something that no other major philosopher of the period possessed."[8] Eventually he learned Latin, and paired himself intellectually with a Dutch humanist and disciple of Descartes, Franciscus van den Enden. Like Descartes, Spinoza pursued a broad line of inquiry, ranging across what would later be termed the separate disciplines of physics, mathematics, philosophy, political science, and theology. It is beyond our scope to delve into the complex questions that formed the intellectual challenges of the time. Suffice to note that the great problem that presented itself to these thinkers concerned the relationship of spirit to matter, of mind to body, of God to creation. One solution to this problem, speaking generally, was to conclude that the relation between such entities was extrinsic. Descartes's apothegm, "I think, therefore I am," gives primacy to mind, with a consequent devaluation of body, a dualism that would stamp the modern age, and that can be recognized as dividing the emotional from the rational, the individual from the community, the sci-

entific from the artistic, the pragmatic from the moral. A key political innovation of the time, the separation of church and state, reflects this
dualistic spirit. A God conceived in such terms is the God of deists, the
Creator as clockmaker, who wound up the cosmos and set it going, to
work its way without God's participation or presence. The genius of
Thomas Jefferson depended utterly on the prior genius of René Descartes.

But Cartesian dualism comes at a cost, reducing the human being, the
soul, in a famous image, to a prisoner in the machine of the body. Much of
the negative legacy of the Enlightenment can be tracked to this idea, from
the "rugged individualism" of the capitalist democracies, to the spirit-de-
valuing materialism of Marxism, to the contemporary American confu-
sion about the relationship between public and private spheres in politics,
as if character can be divorced from virtue.

For our purposes, it is instructive to note that Spinoza, reflecting the
tradition that set him apart, resolved the question of the relationship of
matter to spirit differently than Descartes and others did. "Nothing exists
save the one substance — the self-contained, self-sustaining, and self-ex-
planatory system which constitutes the world." This is Roger Scruton's
summary of Spinoza's metaphysics. "This system may be understood in
many ways: as God or Nature; as mind or matter; as creator or created; as
eternal or temporal. It can be known adequately and clearly through its
attributes, partially and confusedly through its modes . . . All things that
exist, exist necessarily, in thoroughgoing interdependence."[9] This is a philosophy of "both-and," not "either-or," and it has tremendous implications for religion and for politics. If God lives in all that is, then a human
being may have no great need of the mediating institutions of church or
synagogue to be in contact with the divine. Similarly, a political society's
main goal should be respect for every member as equal to every other,
since all are instances of God's presence. The sovereign is to be valued no
more than any citizen.

These principles did not lead Spinoza to advocate doing away with institutions of religion or the state, as some of his critics maintained, but
only to seeing them *sub specie aeternitatis*, "from the point of view of eternity," to cite a well-known phrase of his, instead of from the point of view
of time.[10] Human institutions, as we might put it, are not absolute, and
our ultimate happiness is grounded in recognizing this. Not even the
Scriptures are absolute: Spinoza was one of the first to read the Bible with
a sense of how its composition reflected the contingencies of time and
place; he read in the light of what we call historical criticism. He argued

that the real test of religion was whether it prompted the love of the neighbor — hardly an original conviction, but one impossible to consider apart from the opposite experience he and so many of his contemporaries of various denominations were having in that era. Particular dogmas of whatever stripe, he said, "must all be directed to this one end: that there is a Supreme Being who loves justice and charity, whom all must obey in order to be saved, and must worship by practicing justice and charity to their neighbor."[11]

In a culture conditioned to think in categories of Cartesian dualism or of a pre-Copernican cosmology that split the heavens and the earth, Spinoza was taken either as an atheist who reduced everything to matter (at various times, of course, both Christians and Jews had been taken to be atheists) or as a pantheist who believed God was everywhere. Descartes saw everything from the point of view of the detached and thinking "I." Immanuel Kant (1724–1804), especially in his *Critique of Pure Reason*, would dismiss the idea that the world seen from the point of view of the thinking subject could be reliably known, since perception is always filtered through categories of perception like space and time. But Spinoza's hope, whether his critics grasped it or not, was to see the world from the point of view not of the self, not of its condition in space and time, but of God. Reason, he believed, pointed human beings toward nothing less. *Sub specie aeternitatis* defined for Spinoza the meaning of happiness and the content of salvation.

There were limits to his thought — for example, the leap to "eternity" takes the bondage of time with too little seriousness, and it misses the sacred character of time as well. In such a system, there can be an angelic flight from the world as it is, and the angelic can be as inhuman as the demonic. Gottfried Wilhelm von Leibnitz (1646–1716), his near contemporary, was like Spinoza in pursuing mathematics as a way of knowing the mind of God, but he missed the complexity of Spinoza's thought, which led Leibnitz to accuse Spinoza of reducing creatures to mere "modes or accidents"[12] of divine being. Such criticism notwithstanding, it is impossible to encounter Spinoza in a narrative like this and not be struck by the deep humanity of his vision. Because he took nature so seriously, effectively rejecting the distinction between the sacred and the profane, he influenced the development of mathematics and science, which in his system were nothing less than a pursuit of the holy. And because he affirmed the godliness of every person, he contributed to the growing acceptance of religious tolerance not only as a primordial public virtue but as a measure of true piety. But this is the way we read Spinoza now, aware that after him scientists lost a sense of the sacred, with deadly results, and that a thoroughly secularized politics proved to be, if anything, even more intolerant than the ancient theocracies.

In his own time, even in Calvinist Holland, Spinoza was investigated by the Spanish Inquisition, which sent spies to Amsterdam, perhaps anticipating a reconquest of the Dutch republics. In 1659, little more than half a century after Spinoza's father's mother was denounced as a Jew to the Inquisition in Portugal, a Dominican priest, Fray Tomás Solano y Robles, reported to the Inquisition of Madrid that he had met with Spinoza in Holland, and that Spinoza was "content to maintain the heresy of atheism, since [he] felt that there was no God except philosophically speaking (as [he] had declared), and that souls died with bodies, and that faith was unnecessary."[13] Not surprisingly, each of Solano's assertions fails to do justice to the nuances of Spinoza's thought, but others misread him too. For a time, he was banished from Amsterdam by the civil authorities, and in 1670, the Calvinist Synod of North Holland banned his recent *Theologico-Political Treatise*. This work affirmed what we recognize as basic tenets of human rights and constitutional polity, including the anti-theocratic idea that only a secular government can uphold the freedom of conscience of every citizen. Nothing had driven home the importance of that freedom in his own life more than the experience he had had years earlier in his own Jewish community.

Before being banned by the Calvinists and investigated by the Catholics, Spinoza had been excommunicated by the Amsterdam synagogue. That was in 1656, when the philosopher was just twenty-three years old, before he had published anything. It is not clear what offense of thought or behavior drew that wrath down on him. His pious father had died in 1654. Records show that until 1655, Spinoza himself was attending synagogue regularly and contributing to its support. The decree of excommunication begins, "The Lords of the Mahamad announce that having long known of the evil opinions and acts of Baruch d'Espinosa, they have endeavored by various means and promises to turn him from his evil ways."[14]

Clearly, Spinoza's later articulation of religious tolerance, based on the equality of sects, could have been taken to undercut Judaism's sense of itself as the chosen of God; his notion of God's immanence in nature could have been understood as idolatrous; his rejection of a three-tiered pre-Copernican cosmology could be read as a violation of Scripture; his dismissal of the anthropomorphic idea of God prevalent among both Jews and Christians could seem impious; and in any case, his study of Descartes and other heterodox thinkers would have been a grave violation. The rigidities of the age affected Jews, too, and it is easy to grasp the offense the mature Spinoza might have represented, and to guess that, even when young, he was an unconventional thinker. Still, there is something tragic in the way his Jewish contemporaries seem to have missed Spinoza's echoing of Luria's idea of *tsimtsum,* the self-emptying of God into creation, for it is here that the kernel of the philosopher's great idea can be found.[15] If those who knew him best dismissed him, it is no wonder that others would follow in a shallow reading of his work. "We order that nobody should communicate with him," the decree concludes, "neither in writing, nor accord him any favor, nor stay with him under the same roof nor within four cubits in his vicinity, nor shall he read any treatise composed or written by him."[16] Baruch would be Benedict from now on.

Perhaps Spinoza was driven to tolerance as an act of self-defense. In a later age, such would be said of Jews when they became advocates of civil liberties. What matters for us is that Spinoza composed a first draft of a pluralistic ideal, one that would take hold in the political imaginations of, among others, transients passing through Holland just then on their way to North America. For that matter, Spinoza's ideas seem to have influenced John Locke, who spent some years exiled in Holland not long after Spinoza's death, in 1677. Locke was in flight from the religious intolerance holding sway in England.[17]

Just as Catholic authoritarianism would be undone by a nascent liberal democratic spirit that Spinoza helped to shape, so the Protestant (both Calvinist and Lutheran) denigration of humankind as infinitely unworthy of an all-powerful and distant God gave way to an Enlightenment hope that humans could take responsibility for their lives and the world, a hope tied to Spinoza's idea that humans participate in the divine. To repeat, for much of the eighteenth and nineteenth centuries, Spinoza would be either neglected or dismissed as an atheist or misunderstood as having been a "God-intoxicated" pantheist[18] whose notion that everything is divine made scientific objectivity impossible. But in the years immediately after his death, an incubation period of modernity, Spinoza's influence was widely felt. His ideas, Leibnitz said in 1704, were "stealing gradually into the minds of men of high station who rule the rest and on whom affairs depend, and slithering into fashionable books, are inclining everything towards the universal revolution with which Europe is threatened."[19]

The century of revolution did, of course, break over Europe. If Spinoza is little credited with the beneficial effects of the birth of liberal democracy, not to mention of a theology freed from superstition,[20] it should not surprise us, given this history, that he would nevertheless be blamed for the negative aspects of a revolutionary era. Marxists, but not Marx, would claim him as a progenitor of their dialectical materialism. When Spinoza's celebration of nature was cut loose from its mooring in God, and when the shift from theological to secular states was accompanied by monstrous acts of violence, it could seem that the new intoxication was for blood. In that context, the fact of Spinoza's Jewishness — "a renegade Jew and the Devil," as a condemning synod of the Reformed Church had put it[21] — would always be highlighted. It would be as if by hating Spinoza as a father of modernism, his accomplishments could be reduced to an act of revenge on behalf of Iberian Jewry. Voltaire, to whom we turn now, is an exemplar of this racist reduction, a demonstration of how even the liberalizing forces of the Enlightenment could be turned, according to the ancient pattern, against the very people who had helped prepare for them. Of Spinoza the great French philosopher wrote in 1772: "Then a little Jew, with a long nose and wan complexion / . . . Walking with measured tread, approached the great Being. / Excuse me, he said, speaking very low, / But I think, between ourselves, that you don't exist."[22]

41

Voltaire and the False Promise
of Emancipation

EMANCIPATION," in its Latin root, refers to a son's being set free
from the domination of his father, and that was surely the essence
of it for Heinrich Marx, who, against his rabbi father, prided himself on being a man of the Enlightenment. He believed, with the
philosophes who came after the misread Spinoza, that the mysteries of existence could be accounted for by the methods of natural science, by reason alone. Thus, Heinrich Marx's Jewish religion was nothing to him. As a
young lawyer starting out in Trier early in the nineteenth century, he had
the tremendous advantage, at first, of perfect timing. The French Revolution had marked a new day. As is always true in history, all that preceded
the storming of the Bastille had prepared for it, yet the summer of 1789
was a true rupture in time. After the Revolution, the intellectual, political,
social, even the religious landscape would never look the same. One of the
great thresholds of history, transforming everything, including the human mind, the French Revolution was bound to alter the place of Jews,
and it did.

The Declaration of the Rights of Man — "Men are born and remain
free and equal in rights" — meant that rights would now be seen as resid-
ing in individuals, not in governments or institutions.[1] Therefore, rights
are not bestowed, and cannot be taken away. Power resides neither in tradition nor in any institution, whether of the social-political order or of
the Church, but in individual freedom. The principle, of necessity, extended to all persons. That included Jews, too, as was made clear by the
French National Assembly's Law Relating to Jews, passed on November 13,
1791. Not since before the destruction of Jerusalem in 70 C.E. had Jews
been full citizens of a state anywhere in the world, but now in France they

were just that. The human leap forward represented by the ideals of *Liberté, Egalité, Fraternité* nowhere proves its authenticity more powerfully than in its inclusion of Jews, the pariah people of Europe. Yet in relation to Jews, the dark side of such idealism would be evident as well. The Revolution's new age, as defined by its most extreme adherents, assumed a "new" human being. Those who proved to be "old" human beings, whether by attachments to the king, to the Church, or only to the wrong faction, were simply killed. In 1793, under Maximilien François Marie Isidore de Robespierre (1758–1794), the Reign of Terror showed what happens to those who prove unable or unwilling to reinvent themselves according to the demands of civic "virtue."[2]

In the case of Jews, the reinvention assumed the renunciation of Jewish "nationhood," as if, after fifteen hundred years of enforced separation, Jewish identity could be reduced to "mere" religion, as the philosophes had reduced Christianity; as if Jewish cult and culture could be reduced to Sabbath candles and circumcision, both of which are practiced in private. But custom and piety could no longer be publicly at the service of the group. "To the Jew as an individual — everything," one deputy of the National Assembly declared; "to the Jews as a nation — nothing."[3] Another participant in the assembly debate ominously defined the meaning of such a principle: "Let us begin by destroying all the humiliating signs which designate them as Jews, so that their garb, their outward appearance, shows us that they are fellow citizens." Was the Enlightenment offer of such uniformity all that different from Torquemada's? An optimistic Jew could think so. "Let us restore them to happiness," Robespierre said, summing up the program, "by restoring to them the dignity of human beings and of citizens."[4] It is useful to recall that the full title of the National Assembly's Declaration of Rights indicates a limited reach, since it refers to the "Rights of Man *and Citizen*." Robespierre, known as "the Incorruptible," enforced his idea of citizenship with the guillotine, the weighted blade of which soon enough took his head, too.

The structure of the Jewish kinship system, rooted in the biblical idea of peoplehood but shaped in the millennium-long experience of exclusion, was a mystery to those outside it. Jewish religion was attached to Jewish "nationhood" like flesh to bone, soul to body. The frame of reference of even avowedly secular figures was still Christianity, which had evolved differently. Jewish leaders, including the so-called Great Sanhedrin convened by Napoleon Bonaparte (1769–1821), would not, or could not, make such distinctions clear. Judaism would come to be seen solely as a religion, a category that, especially as diluted by the Cartesian dualism of the Enlightenment, would be far too thin to contain the multifaceted complexity of Jewish life.[5] There was a fuse attached to this miscomprehension, and eventually it would explode the ideal of emancipation, and much else. But in the early period, when the hopes of many were running high, and when the shifting tectonic plates of the new society were still settling, real openings appeared, and Jews moved to fill them. They were the greatest beneficiaries of the Revolution, as the Roman Catholic Church, after the monarchy itself, was its greatest casualty.

When the Man on Horseback arrived in 1799 to draw order out of chaos, the first promise of Jewish equality seemed fulfilled. Napoleon I ruthlessly imposed a dictatorial political dominance, but he also protected and extended the principle of equality before the law. The Napoleonic Code eradicated old barriers of social rank, religious supremacy, and racial distinction. Wherever Napoleon's armies went across the continent, they broke down ghetto walls behind which Jews had been confined — even in Rome.[6]

The liberation of the Roman ghetto, within sight of the Vatican, was Napoleon's way of demonstrating to the Holy See that his power would not be turned back. As the Church, dating to the Fourth Lateran Council, had used laws requiring special badges and clothing to dramatize its authority over Jews, so now Napoleon, abolishing the yellow badge (*sciamanno*) of Roman Jews, dramatized his authority over the Church.[7] Pope Pius VII (1800–1823) had humiliatingly traveled to Paris in 1804 to crown Napoleon emperor, only to be insulted when Napoleon placed the crown on his head himself. The pope would subsequently excommunicate the emperor, but the anathema was no Russian winter, and Napoleon weathered the Church's disapproval. Now he had taken Rome — the tricolor waved from a mast above Castel Sant'Angelo — and he sent his engineers into Trastevere to batter down the gates of the ghetto, freeing its residents.

After 250 years, conditions in the ghetto had become deplorable beyond anything Paul IV, who established it, could have anticipated. Remember that his primary purpose in imposing the harsh, restrictive regime had been to force the mass conversion of Jews. The ghetto should have been temporary. Instead, extended over time, it had led to "the complete abasement of the Jews of Rome," in the words of the scholar Hermann Vogelstein.[8] Ghetto Jews were the most degraded people in Europe. "Life in the ghetto," Kenneth Stow wrote, "was destined to degenerate on all levels, especially cultural and social ones." Not even the religious genius that had initially transformed ghetto exile into a new image of God survived the "irremediable stasis . . . The closed physical space of the ghetto vanquished the open fictitious one of the original holy community."[9] Illiteracy, the loss of the Italian language, multiple generations of chronic illness, grinding poverty, overcrowding, and regular inundations of the foul waters of an uncontrolled Tiber River had all ravaged the Roman Jew physically and mentally. To those who hated Jews, their condition confirmed the stereotype of their inferior status, while to the forces of the Enlightenment, their condition epitomized the irrational cruelty of the old order. Thus Jewish emancipation had become, even to the secularists who would have had contempt for the religion of Judaism, the most dramatic symbol of the end of the ancien régime. It would not be the last time that the Jewish enclave by the Tiber would be used to prove a point of absolute political and military control.

The Jews of Europe responded to this new situation in a variety of ways. Moses Mendelssohn's (1729–1786) earlier translations into German of the Hebrew Scriptures and rabbinic texts were harbingers of Jewish interest in a cultural rapprochement. Enlightenment Jews, like Mendelssohn, saw no contradiction between civic equality, cultural participation, and faithful religious observance. Some, like Benjamin Disraeli (1804–1881), would leave religious observance behind, although accepting baptism. Others, like the lyric poet Heinrich Heine (1797–1856), would formally convert to Christianity, less from religious or even political reasons than for broadly aesthetic ones. Heine called baptism the "entrance ticket into the community of European culture."[10] In the early days of Emancipation, with the grip of religion apparently broken, the pressure on Jews to convert seemed dissipated, and in fact relatively few Jews were, in Heine's word, "sprinkled." For example, between 1812 and 1846, fewer than 4,000 Jews out of Prussia's total of 123,000 formally embraced Christianity. Most of those were probably in Berlin, home of Mendelssohn, where a majority of Jews, apparently, were baptized.[11] Mendelssohn's own grandson, the composer Felix Mendelssohn, was "sprinkled."

Some Jews, like Karl Marx's father, would enthusiastically embrace the Enlightenment of the philosophes, shedding religious practice and particular creed as easily as Thomas Jefferson had, abandoning Yahweh for the God of deism. When Napoleon took control of Trier in 1803, folding it into his Confederation of the Rhineland, the senior Marx resolved to become his family's first full citizen of their hometown. A "man of reason," he set out to become not a rabbi but a lawyer. I am referring to him rather awkwardly here because there is a confusion about his name. Isaiah Berlin says that Heinrich Marx was born with the surname Levi, and his given name was not Heinrich, but Herschel.[12] Karl Marx's father's personal "emancipation" from *his* father, the rabbi Marx Levi, occurred when he rejected "Levi" in favor of the more neutral "Marx." As for "Herschel," that name would soon enough seem as much an obstacle to advancement as Levi would have been.

In 1808, Napoleon had surprised Jews by introducing anti-Jewish restrictions of his own — a sign of his devotion to the Enlightenment project of Jewish makeover. But Napoleon was still the continental emancipator of Jews, the demolisher of ghetto walls. Jews greeted his armies as liberators, an image Napoleon cultivated as he moved against Moscow. He hoped to draw support, in that campaign, from Polish and Russian Jews, and did. That is to say, Napoleon, even while attempting to suppress Jewish "nationhood" in the lands he controlled, was exploiting it in the territory he coveted. The strategy fell short, of course, and Napoleon failed.

The period of reaction that followed Waterloo was bad news for Jews. As obvious beneficiaries of the social and political revolutions dating to 1789, they could now be scapegoated for the negative consequences of those upheavals. This is the beginning (we will see its further development later) of the paranoid and near-permanent association in the popular mind of Jews and revolution. Rolling back the latter would mean roping in the former. The Emancipation suffered its biggest setback in 1815, as forces of the old order rallied. They dubbed themselves the Holy Alliance. In France and the Netherlands, the rights of Jews would be hedged, but would survive. In Germany, Austria, and Italy the Emancipation would collapse. In Rome, Pope Pius VII was restored as a temporal ruler by the Congress of Vienna, the conference of European powers that restored the monarchies with agreed-upon territorial adjustments. Pius VII celebrated the defeat of his mortal enemy — Napoleon had dared to take him prisoner — by reclaiming the Papal States, and by immediately reinstating the ghetto.

Ghettos were reestablished in other cities, but only in Rome and a handful of other places were the walls that Napoleon had demolished actually rebuilt.[13] This pattern would repeat itself. When the anti-papal revolutionaries of 1848 declared a republic in Rome, the pope was forced to flee, afraid for his life. This pope, Pius IX (1846–1878), had begun his reign inclined to abolish the ghetto, but when the revolution was overthrown, so were such liberalizing impulses, especially regarding Jews, whom the Vatican now blamed for its ordeal. As Vogelstein writes, "A deputation of the Jewish community which called on Cardinal Savelli was told that Jews were responsible for the long duration of the revolutionary government."[14]

In Trier, meanwhile, events had been less tumultuous after the Congress of Vienna, but they had been equally transforming. The Rhineland had been taken from France and assigned to Prussia, the beginning of its effort to draw the states of Germany together into one nation. Almost immediately, in 1816, Prussia abrogated the Napoleonic Code in the Rhineland, and prepared new restrictions against Jews.[15] Herschel Marx was informed that his chosen profession, the law, was no longer open to him because, deist or not, Marx or not, he was still a Jew.

Herschel Marx did not hesitate. In 1817, little more than a year before his son's birth, despite his family history and his brother Samuel's status as the chief rabbi of Trier, he renounced Judaism altogether and was baptized a Christian.[16] Trier, then as now, was overwhelmingly Roman Catholic, but its new Prussian overlords from east of the Rhine were Lutheran. The state religion was Lutheran. For a man of the Enlightenment, Roman Catholicism was an anachronism in any case. So when Marx, né Levi, changed his first name from Herschel to Heinrich, he did so accepting baptism into Trier's small Lutheran congregation. Later, the Prussian government, to bolster Protestant prestige in the Catholic pilgrimage center, would convert the *Konstantin-basilika* into the Lutheran Church of Our Savior, as it remains today, with a congregation of fewer than three hundred. On the Sunday in 1998 that I joined them for worship, they seemed lost in the vast space of the former imperial audience hall. Constantine's spirit was effectively evoked, though, by the shimmering gold cross that hung above the altar, where the emperor's throne would once have stood.

Karl Marx's mother, Henriette, would be baptized a Lutheran too, although not for eight years, in 1825, when her own father had died.[17] Thus Karl Marx, the son of a Protestant lawyer, was born to a woman still a Jew. According to Jewish tradition, Hitler would be technically correct in referring to him, a century later, as "that Jew Marx."[18] Of course, Marx was never any such thing to himself or, despite their poignant genealogy, to his parents. Heinrich Marx saw to the christening of Karl in 1824, at age six, when admission to the public school in Prussian Trier presumed it. The weight of the past pressing "like a nightmare"[19] on the young Marx was a distant past — those fiercely resistant rabbis — and an immediate one. His father was a "timorous lawyer," in Isaiah Berlin's phrase, "whose life was spent in social and personal compromise."[20] One needn't stretch Karl Marx on the psychoanalytic couch of his Freudian critics to see that his insight into the "contradictory"[21] character of human progress — the inevitability, for example, of class conflict — arose from the contradictions of his own condition.

But it was his sensitivity to the conditions of the dispossessed that made Karl Marx a historic figure. He was born at the dawn of a period of massive social change, and he became the voice of those who would be displaced by it. In the nineteenth century, the population of Europe would more than double. That increase alone would have accounted for the pressures of scarcity, not only of resources and land but of opportunity, that would make life miserable for the great majority. Adding in the economic shifts of industrialization, the cultural shifts of urbanization, and the deracination of secularism — why should a huge underclass not have felt abandoned? Why should they not have recognized their champion in a man who could write, as Marx did in the famous close of *The Communist Manifesto*, "Let the ruling classes tremble at a Communistic revolution. The proletarians have nothing to lose but their chains. They have a world to win. WORKING MEN OF ALL COUNTRIES, UNITE!"[22]

In a society divided into three estates — the clergy, the nobility, and all the others — it was the first two, of course, that had a world to lose. At the time of the 1789 Revolution, France was a nation of 25 million. The first estate, consisting of 100,000 clerics, owned 10 percent of the land. The second estate, including 400,000 aristocrats, owned 25 percent of the land.[23] The gross inequity of this division of resources, exemplifying the inequity that cut through every aspect of life, was underwritten by a religious claim of divine right. God himself — God would continue to be "he"; not even the most radical of revolutionaries challenged the idea of male dominance — was seen to have ordained the social structure. A challenge to its order, and this is implied in the identification of church and state, was sacrilege. If the Catholic Church was to be attacked, it had to be attacked not only for its property and privilege but, more importantly, for the theology that sustained both.

License to launch that attack came from those who followed the trail of Spinoza and Leibnitz, the eighteenth-century philosophers who addressed themselves not to the peasantry or the poor of cities but to the urban middle classes and marginal aristocrats. The epitome of Enlightenment philosophy was François Marie Arouet, better known as Voltaire

(1694–1778). After being imprisoned at age twenty-four, and then exiled for insulting the Crown, he devoted himself to justice, as the relatively privileged Enlightenment culture would define it. "It is the man who sways our minds by the prevalence of reason and the native force of truth," he wrote, "not they who reduce mankind to a state of slavery by force and downright violence . . . that claims our reverence and admiration."[24]

Voltaire made everything of the "force and downright violence" that had been used by the Inquisition against the Jews. For him, the Inquisition defined the Church as the venal opposite of all that he and the other advocates of reason stood for.[25] He focused on the Catholic Church because of its dominance, but his true target was religion as such. In an essay in the *Philosophical Dictionary*, Voltaire describes a vision in which, like a latter-day Ezekiel, he is transported to a "desert all covered with piles of bones." His guide, a genie, tells him what he is looking at. "He began with the first pile. 'These,' he said, 'are the twenty-three thousand Jews who danced before a calf, together with the twenty-four thousand who were killed while fornicating with Midianitish women . . . In the other piles are the bones of the Christians slaughtered by each other because of metaphysical disputes. They are divided into several heaps of four centuries each . . . Here,' said the spirit, 'are the twelve million native Americans killed in their own land because they had not been baptized.'"[26]

All of this leaves him repulsed by religion. Finally, in his vision, Voltaire is brought face to face with Jesus, "a man with a gentle, simple face, who seemed to me to be about thirty-five years old." Voltaire asks about the valley of bones he has just toured, and Jesus denies responsibility. Voltaire dares to press him.

"You did not then contribute in any way by your teaching, either badly reported or badly interpreted, to those frightful piles of bones which I saw on my way to consult with you?"

"I have only looked with horror upon those who have made themselves guilty of all these murders."

. . . [Finally] I asked him to tell me in what true religion consisted.

"Have I not already told you? Love God and your neighbor as yourself."

"Is it necessary for me to take sides either for the Greek Orthodox Church or the Roman Catholic?"

"When I was in the world I never made any difference between the Jew and the Samaritan."

"Well, if that is so, I take you for my only master." Then he made a sign with his head that filled me with peace. The vision disappeared, and I was left with a clear conscience.[27]

Voltaire's "clear conscience" had led him to denounce the slaughter of Jews. In that, he was a representative figure not only of the eighteenth-century Enlightenment but of the nineteenth-century revolution. Nevertheless, the conscience of both the Enlightenment and the revolution allowed itself to make a "difference between the Jew and the Samaritan" — between, that is, Jews and all other people. Heinrich Marx, who read approvingly from Voltaire to his son Karl, thereby sowing seeds of the young Marx's lifelong contempt for all religion, was fooled if he thought Voltaire and the other philosophes had a place in their brave new world for him. The spirit of rational tolerance, which did not extend to Jewish religion, did not extend to Jewish human beings either. It would fall to Heinrich's son to help make that deadly point clear.

When the origins of Nazi antisemitism are attributed to modern neo-paganism — and we have seen how they are — more than some Teutonic/ Aryan obsession with forest nymphs is being referred to. Voltaire was an anti-Semite, as indicated by the dismissive use of caricature in his assault on Spinoza, but he was an anti-Semite who defined Jewish inferiority in terms of classical antiquity. Greek and Roman pagans detected in the Jewish refusal "to eat at the same table with other men," as Arthur Hertzberg sums up the charge,[28] evidence of their innate inferiority. Their "obstinate attachment to each other" proved, as Tacitus asserted, "the implacable hatred which they harbor for the rest of mankind."[29] Hatred for Jews originates, that is, in a prior Jewish hatred. Voltaire praised Cicero's hatred of Jews, and, in a letter theatrically addressed to Cicero, notched it up. Jews "are, all of them," he wrote in 1771, "born with raging fanaticism in their hearts, just as the Bretons and the Germans are born with blond hair. I would not be in the least bit surprised if these people would not some day become deadly to the human race."[30]

Voltaire's main project was to liberate the human mind from the grip of irrational and violent religion, and so he has to justify his visceral rejection of Jews as such, a rejection to which he remained committed in other than traditional religious terms. "Voltaire had thus, being an ex-Christian," Arthur Hertzberg explains, "abandoned entirely the religious attack on the Jews as Christ-killers or Christ-rejectors. He proposed a new principle on which to base his hatred of them, their innate character."[31] Hertzberg summarizes the significance of this idea, planted in the heart of the Enlightenment: "The notion that the new society was to be a re-evocation of classical antiquity was the prime source of post-Christian anti-Semitism in the nineteenth century. The vital link, the man who skipped over the Christian centuries and provided a new, international, secular, anti-Jewish rhetoric in the name of European culture rather than religion, was Voltaire. The defeat of the emancipation of the Jews of Europe existed in embryo even before that process began."[32]

Is it true that the hatred of Jews could "skip over the Christian centuries"? Is it true that the coming defeat of emancipation could be laid at the feet of some pagan antisemitism, as if Tacitus and Cicero are guilty of crimes of which Torquemada, Isabella, and Paul IV are innocent? From the Jewish side, perhaps, ancient Roman hatred could seem like the same thing as later Christian hatred, since both were prompted, at bottom, by the Jewish refusal to renounce the oneness of God. In the former case, that required a boycott of tables where pagan deities were honored; in the latter, a rejection of the divinity of Jesus. But paganism never defined itself as a negation of Judaism, and, beginning with its second generation, Christianity did. That is the fatal difference, and it manifests itself throughout this story. Looked at from the side of non-Jews, there can be no doubt that the traditional demonization of Jews by Christians, beginning with the canonical New Testament, had a radioactive impact all its own, even if anti-Christian Voltaire had reason to deemphasize it — reason, that is, to "skip over the Christian centuries."

The intellectual structure of Cicero's anti-Judaism enabled Voltaire to imagine he had done so. But where could Voltaire's visceral, prerational, and "innate" mistrust of Jews have come from if not the culture into which he was born? That culture was decidedly linked by what Malcolm Hay, one of the first Catholic historians of antisemitism, called "the chain of error" to the deep Christian past.[33] That chain runs, as we have seen, back through the various popes to Saint Bernard, Saint John Chrysostom, Saint Ambrose, and ultimately to Saint John the Evangelist. In other words, the exclusive assertion of an ancient pagan justification for a contemporary and irrational reaction to a group of human beings, intended as a way of marginalizing the influence of Christian justifications for that same reaction, is itself irrational. Christian efforts[34] in our day to claim exoneration on the basis of Voltaire's paean to paganism are equally so.

In her monumental twentieth-century study of antisemitism, in *The Origins of Totalitarianism,* Hannah Arendt, for a different motive, would do much the same thing. She saw how Christian hatred of Jews for essentially religious reasons had been transformed in the modern era into a profoundly secular, indeed anti-religious, phenomenon. She posited a radical discontinuity between the hatred of Jews displayed by Nazis and that displayed over the centuries by Christians, locating the break in the Enlightenment. She did this because the idea of a *continuous* flow of such venom, from her stance as a post-Holocaust historian, was simply too horrible. "In view of the final catastrophe, which brought the Jews so near to complete annihilation," she wrote, "the thesis of eternal antisemitism has become more dangerous than ever. Today it would absolve Jew-haters of crimes greater than anybody had ever believed possible."[35]

On the contrary, seeing how the hatred of Jews in one era prepares for the hatred of Jews in another, refining it, perhaps, but always making it more lethal, absolves no one. Instead, the drawing of a clear narrative arc, naming each link in the "chain of errors," requires every participant so named in this almost, yes, eternal drama to be held accountable. At the beginning of this book, we compared its narrative to a drama, classically defined and causally determined, with a beginning, which leads to a middle, which leads to the end.[36] A drama is not a mere sequence of episodes: "The king died, and then the queen died" is the episodic sequence we saw before, the one given by E. M. Forster to make the point. No, a drama consists in "The king died, and then the queen died of grief."[37] The cause of the action, grief, is what we care about. Escapist entertainment, and episodic history, may ask of a narrative, "What then?" But drama, as Forster defines it, asks "Why?" The answer to that question is always found in the connection between cause and consequence. "Don't look at this as a bunch of little threads," as prosecutors tell jurors. "Look at it as threads in a rope."

This way of thinking, with attention to causality and consequence through a narrative unfolding over time, resists the spectacle of isolated incidents on which our sound-bite culture thrives. Reality perceived as uncaused instances is reality of which no moral account can be made. By this schema, for example, the bank deposits and artworks of murdered Jews exist only in locked Swiss vaults and on unprovenanced museum walls, and not also in a starkly untied rope of history. Such moral disconnectedness defines the contemporary anomie, suggests why accomplishing a true moral reckoning with the Shoah has proven so difficult, and represents the real moral paralysis of which Arendt was so properly afraid. And not incidentally, this impoverishment of the moral imagination, defined as causal disconnectedness, has its source in the self-satisfied illusion of an Enlightenment that regarded its age — Reason! — as superior to the point of being discontinuous with what went before.

If Voltaire claimed to have thoughts shaped exclusively by Cicero, that does not mean that he did. If Hitler's paranoia about Jews was fueled by the grafting of the secular and neo-pagan racism of modernity to the stock of ancient and medieval Christian Jew-hatred, why does that remove Christian history from the center of the story? The stock remains the stock. Modern secularists found a new language with which to slander Jews, but their impulse to do so — here is the point — was as rooted in the mystery of religion as any grand inquisitor's.

The habit of deflecting this truth is relevant to the pair of masterly elaborations of anti-Jewish stereotyping of the nineteenth century, one of which Karl Marx, the ex-Christian Jew hater, articulated more drastically than anyone, and the other of which "that Jew Marx," in Hitler's phrase, so well embodied. The images, negations of each other, came to define the modern Jew. Both images lived nowhere more vividly than in the Catholic imagination.

42

Jew as Revolutionary, Jew as Financier

AS A CHILD growing up in Trier, Karl Marx could well have known of the anti-Jewish pogroms that broke out in the Rhineland during the first decade of his life.[1] In 1834, at age sixteen, he was confirmed in the Lutheran Evangelical Church.[2] There is every reason to think that he "imbibed," in Padover's word, the Christian prejudice against Jews that would have typified his friends and neighbors, Protestant as well as Catholic. But here it is important to take note of the Lutheran tradition into which he was initiated, if only formally, because, as we observed previously, German antisemitism would prove especially lethal, in no small part because of shadows cast by Martin Luther. "The unmentionable odour of death" that W. H. Auden sensed above Europe in September 1939 he traced back to something rotten in the great reformer's program, the madness, as Auden put it, "from Luther until now."[3]

Luther's biographer Richard Marius comments on this perception of Auden and others who laid the Nazi pathology at Luther's feet: "Although the Jews for him were only one among many enemies he castigated with equal fervor, although he did not sink to the horrors of the Spanish Inquisition against Jews, and although he was certainly not to blame for Adolf Hitler, Luther's hatred of the Jews is a sad and dishonorable part of his legacy, and it is not a fringe issue. It lay at the center of his concept of religion. He saw in the Jews a continuing moral depravity he did not see in Catholics. He did not accuse papists of the crimes that he laid at the feet of Jews."[4]

But that "unmentionable odour of death" was even more decisive than the challenge posed by Jews, yet then the two became intermingled. The core of this entire narrative has involved the Church's too exclusive focus on the death of Christ, which began with Constantine and became progressively more emphatic with the Crusades, the atonement theology of Anselm, the *reconquista,* and the Inquisition, which turned death into an act of faith. All of this is symbolized by the way the cross replaced the face of Christ as the central Christian icon.[5] With death at the apex of theology and cult, the vulnerability of Jews, as the ones responsible for death, was axiomatic. Ironically, because suffering and death had been cast as the primary meaning of the life of Christ — the source of Christian salvation — the suffering of Christians became glorified as the "imitation" of Christ, while the suffering of Jews continued to be the proof of their sin in rejecting Christ.[6] This positive-negative reading of suffering and death remained a paradoxical note of Catholic attitudes, but with Luther the paradox broke, and the doom of death became absolute, with ever more dreadful consequences for Jews.

Martin Luther's religious vocation began in the terror Luther experienced during a storm, when fear of death prompted his youthful vow to become a monk. One way to understand him is as the embodiment of the death-obsessed Christian, and it was precisely his horror at the prospect of mortality that led the bile of his obsession to spill onto Jews. Marius points out, for example, that his *On the Jews and Their Lies,* which was published in 1543, came within months of the death of his beloved daughter Magdalena, who died in his arms. "Afterward his grief was intense, and he spoke feelingly of the terror before death while affirming his trust in Christ. This combination of woes may have driven him to lash out at someone, and the Jews were there, testifying to his worst fear, that Jesus had not risen from the dead, and that Christians would enjoy no victory over the grave."[7] Jews denied, therefore, not just an abstract set of Christian claims, but the only hope this man had. Luther's sense of doom was not theological, but intensely personal, literally physical.

Luther is commonly regarded as being preoccupied with sin, damnation, and salvation, but Marius makes a compelling case that what really drove Luther was this dread of death, and the Jews were those who stood between him and hope. Jews were at the center of Luther's perception because they contradicted the one thing that kept him from going mad. And this was true not only because of what they denied (negatively) about Christian faith or what they affirmed (positively) about the Law of Moses. The mere existence of Jews sparked the panic Luther felt. Even the way they had resisted every assault, survived the cruel horrors of anti-Jewish violence, fed his hatred. Living Jews had refused Christendom's every effort to convert them, which meant that neither they nor their forebears could possibly have regarded death with the terror it held for Luther. "I suspect," Marius comments, "that [Jews'] patient endurance of suffering and death in their adhesion to their own faith, necessarily rejecting his, made him afraid, and so created in his mind a fantasy called 'Jew' that was in part constructed of hated elements in his own soul."[8] That fantasy Jew would thrive in Lutheran Germany as nowhere else, even if the twentieth century, combining it with pseudoscientific racism to make what we call modern antisemitism, would reinvent the fantasy with unprecedented ferocity. "But the fact that Luther's hostility to Jews was not the same as modern antisemitism does not excuse it. It was as bad as Luther could make it, and that was bad enough to leave a legacy that had hateful consequences for centuries."[9]

The personal venom of Luther's hatred of Jews, and his perhaps psychotic experience of the Jew as standing between him and salvation — the Jew makes death absolute — are what separate Catholic antisemitism from that inspired by Luther. This is an enormously complex question; the point to emphasize here is that the shadow cast by Luther fell in a particular way over Germany, over Hitler, obviously, and perhaps over Marx.

When at last Luther was dying, in bed during the night, after having complained of chest pains, he declared that Jews had done this to him. He had condemned Jews in his last sermon. The date of his death was February 18, 1546.[10]

The date of his birth was November 10, 1483. Four hundred and fifty-five years later, the Lutheran bishop of Thuringia, Martin Sasse, exulted, "On November 10, 1938, on Luther's birthday, the synagogues are burning in Germany." The bishop was referring, of course, to Kristallnacht. His joy was expressed in the foreword to his collection of Luther's anti-Jewish writings, which the bishop was publishing in the hope that the German people would take to heart the words, as he put it, "of the greatest anti-Semite of his time, the warner of his people against the Jews."[11]

Such was the broad, if still evolving, cultural milieu into which Karl Marx was born. It is impossible to sort out Catholic and Lutheran influences on Marx, because it was more a matter of cultural spirit than of creed, and who is to say what the German Christian ethos, particularly in the Rhineland, was by that time? We know that, even as a child, he would never have had more than a formalized and shallow relationship to the Christian religion into which he had been sacramentally initiated, but contempt for Jews was by then in the German air. Marx would have learned other lessons about the values of Judaism by witnessing his own parents' capacity to shrug it off like an old cloak. "No one is proud to derive from an inferior people, and it is understandable that Marx — always conscious of his Jewish origin — tried to alleviate his burden by endeavoring to become non-Jewish." This is the scholar Edmund Silberner. "This endeavor — typical of his Jewish self-hatred — led him repeatedly to attacks on the Jews. His aggressiveness towards them was a means of convincing himself and the outside world how little Jewish he was, in spite of his rabbinical ancestors."[12]

Such attacks had special meaning coming from Marx, and special consequences. As a young man, he went to Bonn, and then to Berlin, for his university education. In Berlin, he was particularly influenced by G.W.F. Hegel and Ludwig Feuerbach. But by 1842, at age twenty-four, he was back in Trier, submitting articles to a Cologne newspaper, *Rheinische Zeitung*. By the end of the year, he would be the editor of that paper, but in these months in Trier, the shape of his future work showed itself in a startlingly ugly form. It was then that Marx wrote his first essay of note, which was published in 1843 with the title "On the Jewish Question." The article is a screed that takes off from his mentor Feuerbach's blasphemous description of Jehovah as "nothing but the personified selfishness of the Israelitish people."[13] Or, as Marx put it, "Money is the jealous god of Israel, beside which no other god may exist."[14]

It is important to note at the outset of any consideration of Marx's attitudes toward Jews that he was a steady supporter of Jewish emancipation. But he saw that cause in firmly secular terms. Like Voltaire, Marx was by now looking for ways to dismiss the cultural and historical significance of religion, and so he focused on what he called "the everyday Jew" instead of "the Sabbath Jew." Marx wanted to emphasize, as if against Christianity, that there was more to be detested in Jews than just their religion. The impetus for "On the Jewish Question" was the general question of Jewish emancipation, much debated in Europe as ghetto walls fell, and again as they were rebuilt. It was as a liberal that Marx naturally supported emancipation. So did *Rheinische Zeitung*, one of whose owners was Dagobert Oppenheim, of the up-and-coming Cologne Oppenheims, one of the Jewish families that would rise to prominence in the new world of finance.

But something in the subject of the Jew touched a raw nerve in Marx, short-circuiting his liberalism. Whether he could identify the source of his irrationality or not, we can. The rope of history, knotted in Trier, was choking him. Marx took off from the medieval complaint against the

Jew as usurer, carrying it to the level of character assassination. He indulged the same old medieval manipulation: Let's force Jews into moneylending and then hate them for it. Hating Jews for moneylending, let's define them by it. Marx's great work, of course, would be a critique of
heartless capitalism, and the kernel of his insight shows in this early essay.
But where later he will become famous for demonizing the capitalist, here,
occupying the same ground in an economics of exploitation, the devil figure is "the real Jew."

> Let us not seek the secret of the Jew in his religion, but let us seek the se-
> cret of the religion in the real Jew. What is the profane basis of Judaism?
> *Practical* need, *self-interest.* What is the worldly cult of the Jew? *Huck-
> stering.* What is his worldly god? *Money.*
>
> Very well: then in emancipating itself from *huckstering* and *money,* and
> thus from real and practical Judaism, our age would emancipate itself.
>
> An organization of society which would abolish the preconditions and
> thus the very possibility of huckstering, would make the Jew impossible.
> His religious consciousness would evaporate like some insipid vapour in
> the real, life-giving air of society . . .
>
> We discern in Judaism, therefore, a universal *antisocial* element of the
> *present time,* whose historical development, zealously aided in its harmful
> aspects by the Jews, has now attained its culminating point, a point at
> which it must necessarily begin to disintegrate.
>
> In the final analysis, the *emancipation* of the Jews is the emancipation
> of mankind from *Judaism.*"[15]

In less than five years from the publication of "On the Jewish Question," after having begun his collaboration with Friedrich Engels (1820–
1895), Marx would publish *The Communist Manifesto* (1848). In that work,
his call for "the abolition of the preconditions" of antisocial Judaism was
replaced by a demand for an end to the class society. With *Das Kapital*
(1867, 1885, 1895), his vile intuition about Jewish "huckstering" — a word
drawn, presumably, from the hawking of sellers in a market — was transformed into a substantial critique of the market economy. Instead of
writing of the necessary disintegration of Judaism through a natural "historical development," he writes of the "contradictions" in all social systems that, through history, lead to their destruction. His assertions about
the inevitable dispersal of the "insipid vapour" of Judaism prepared him
for insights into the fate of a bourgeoisie that "produced its own grave
diggers."[16]

One senses that Marx's visceral reaction to the Jew prepared him for his considered rejection of the capitalist. Before turning to the impact of Marx's reduction of the Jew to a shameless market man, it might be useful to note that such a polemic has characterized not only anti-Semites, but also Jews treading the blurry line between self-criticism and self-hatred. Theodor Herzl (1860–1904), for example, was a passionate Zionist in part because he believed that Jews had been deformed by their long status as an oppressed minority in Christian Europe, condemned to lives of hawking and haggling. That oppression had resulted in what he derided as "the crookedness of Jewish morality."[17]

To say that Marx's lasting ideas were grounded in the hatred of his own people can float above this story like yet another abstraction — but not when one recalls that his people included, say, that "comely" girl of Trier who, in 1096, broke away from her captors to fling herself into the swirling Moselle. Who was Karl Marx to condescend to her? He flattered himself to think his conclusions were drawn from the rational study of history and economics, but his condemnation of Jews, its high moral tone notwithstanding, was barely more than a glib rehash of the twisted charges of Christian preachers, made even as he sought to distance himself from their religion. Marx prided himself on a consideration of "the real Jew," yet his diatribe betrays, in Padover's words, "nearly total ignorance, possibly willful, of the lives and ideas of the people he had descended from."[18] He knew nothing real about the true character of Jews, in the past or in his own day.

Of overriding significance is the fact that, in "On the Jewish Question," Marx epitomized his charges in a figure that would become a durable nineteenth- and twentieth-century stereotype. He is not the originator of this particular strain of modern antisemitism — the Jew as the embodiment of materialism — but his is nevertheless an archetypal instance of it. The vitriol of his language thus becomes a symptom of society's disease. The words he used, whether original with him or not, were inflammatory: "The *chimerical* nationality of the Jew is the nationality of the trader, and, above all of the financier."[19] In his mature analysis, he would unforgettably label that hated figure not as the Jew but as the capitalist. In the European imagination, however, and in the socialist imagination, thanks in no small part to Marx, the figure of the Jew and the figure of the capitalist would be identical. The Jewish "financier," as a target of revolutionary hatred, would dominate the age. Once again, an imagined "jew" is made to seem pivotal for the salvation or damnation of the rest of society.

The association of Jews and banking, as is well known, grew out of medieval restrictions — Jews could not join guilds or own land — that had forced them into moneylending. The Church condemned usury, but that did not keep many Christians, including prelates, from engaging in the practice, often to the exclusion of Jews. Because of the stigma attached to moneylending, and the readiness of debtors to resent their creditors, it served the purpose of Christian usurers to encourage the myth of the Jewish dominance of the currency exchange and loan businesses. The myth was based not on the real origins of the association of Jews with money, but in a twisted slander — yet another — of Judaism's core beliefs. With its emphasis on what, to Christians, seemed the minutiae of the legislation of Leviticus — those 613 commandments — wasn't Jewish religion all about adding and subtracting? Wasn't the toting up of such observances a kind of spiritual avarice? And wasn't the emphasis on good works a kind of commercial exchange with God? Jews would bargain with God. Or rather, because they did, they bargain with everybody. In other words, observable characteristics of Jews, like their relative prominence in the realm of money, were attributed not to the contingent factors that produced them, including oppression, but to something innate in Judaism.[20] In this regard, Marx gave expression to the dominant anti-Jewish prejudice of his time. It seems not to have fazed him that one of his targets, implicitly, was the "financier" Abraham Oppenheim, a backer of the Cologne paper that gave him his first serious job.[21] Marx took over as editor of *Rheinische Zeitung* shortly after he wrote "On the Jewish Question" but before he published it. Before the essay appeared, as it turned out, *Rheinische Zeitung* failed because it was too liberal for Prussia.

The first half of the nineteenth century saw the rise of a group of Jewish investment bankers who had ties to each other and to family branches in various cities and nations. In addition to the Oppenheims, there were the Rothschilds, the Seligmans, the Warburgs, the Sassoons.[22] These commercial figures had been able to turn to their economic advantage the long-term disadvantages of enforced ghettoization, which served for these few as an incubator of success. They were quickly taken to be "typical Jews" by the mass of bigoted and resentful Europeans, including some clients, despite the fact that the vast majority of Jews were still burdened by the effects of ghetto dispossession. In 1800, for example, there were six hundred Jewish families in Frankfurt, most in the *Judengasse,* its ghetto. Almost half of their net worth was held by sixty families, several of whom would go on to dominate the finances of the city, and one, the Rothschilds, of the continent.[23] Instead of being typical Jews, such figures were successors to the court Jews of the Middle Ages, those physicians, advisors, and, yes, lenders on whom kings, bishops, and popes had relied from the feudal era through the Renaissance. In the myth of the financier, the tradition of "the exception Jew" was kept alive, but it was turned against the rest of Jews when the exception was defined as typical. Religion had become politics and economics, but once again, the Jew was held responsible for the fate of the general population — fate defined as doom. Thus Marx's early, Trier-composed essay "On the Jewish Question," when matched with the incendiary notions in his later writings, "made its small contribution," in the words of Lawrence Stepelevich, "to the formulation of that fatal equation between Judaism and exploitative Capitalism which bore its fruit in the doctrines of National Socialism."[24]

There would be irony enough in this turn in the long story — the Jew despised for his degradation becomes despised for his privilege — but the irony is redoubled by the other turn the story takes at almost the same time. Just as some Jews played leading roles in the invention of modern investment capitalism, others happened to play important parts in the intellectual and political opposition to it. Most socialists were not Jews, but some were, especially in Germany. Of the sixty Jews elected to the German Reichstag between 1871 and 1930, for example, thirty-five were socialists.[25] There were few Jews in the early stages of Russian revolutionary activity, but as Marxist socialism spread toward the end of the nineteenth century, more Jews joined the movement against the czar.[26] But antisemitism would stamp the culture of socialism too. Karl Marx's rival in the International, the Russian Mikhail Bakunin, supported Marx's theories, but referred to him as "that Jew," an ominous precursor — but in reverse — of the later Soviet policy of never referring to Marx's Jewish roots. Indeed, under Stalin, Marx would be cited against Jews as justification for state-sponsored antisemitism, while the anti-Stalinist Russian Orthodox Church would be stoking hatred of Jews as a way of opposing the state.

By the end of the twentieth century, Russian Communism, such as it was, distinguished itself in nothing so much as its antisemitism. Victor Ilyukhin, a leading Communist legislator in the Russian parliament, attacked Boris Yeltsin in December 1998 by characterizing the post-Soviet economic collapse as a "genocide." He said, "The large-scale genocide wouldn't have been possible if Yeltsin's inner circle had consisted of the main ethnic groups, and not exclusively one group, the Jews." As a *Boston Globe* writer said, Ilyukhin "used one big lie to explain another." There had been no post-Soviet genocide in Russia, and the vast majority of Yeltsin's much-rotated inner circle were never Jews.[27]

The revolutionary movements of the nineteenth century included socialists, Marxists, Communists, anarchists, and radicals of a dozen different stripes, yet increasingly, to those who felt threatened by them, these figures all began to transmogrify into a shape at once alien and familiar. If the "financiers" violated a basic tenet of the new nationalism by being "internationalists," lo and behold, so did the "socialists." If the word "cabal" applied to Jewish bankers secretly manipulating rates of exchange and interest, it applied equally to the surreptitious network of revolutionary cells. "Materialism" was the spiritual indictment brought against both kinds of Jews — simple greed in one case, "historical materialism" in the other. Each variant echoes the ancient charge, attributed to Paul, that Jewish "law" is opposed to Christian "spirit."

There were major revolutionary outbreaks across the continent in 1830, 1848, and 1871. With each one, masses of Europeans saw ever more sharply who the enemy was. At one extreme or the other, the enemy was the Jew. This dynamic ran diametrically against that of emancipation. Ironically, such omnidirectional hatred was fueled by emancipation. It was predictable, perhaps, that society would find a good reason to resist the authentic liberation of Jews. What could not have been predicted was that society would find two.

The 1871 conflict in Paris dramatized the mortal nature of the threat posed by revolution, and it solidified the image of the Jew as revolutionary. Both happened, in part, because Karl Marx, for whom the Jew was still the financier, celebrated the Paris Communard uprising with rare eloquence. In 1870, the forces of Napoleon III (1808–1873), a self-anointed defender of Catholicism, had been decisively defeated by the Prussian army. The chaos of the Franco-Prussian War's denouement was centered in Paris, which had suffered through a brutal starvation siege. When a settlement was imposed on Napoleon by the victorious Otto von Bismarck (1815–1898), the Iron Chancellor and creator of the modern German nation, the citizen army rebelled, joining forces with workers, liberal politicians, so-called bohemians, intellectuals, and others who feared a final return of the ancien régime. Thus the Paris Commune was declared, a revolutionary organization that was to control the city for barely three months. The Commune, in one Communard's words, "proclaimed death to all tyrants, priests and Prussians."[28]

The regular army, operating from Versailles, cut the city off, and once again starvation and terror stalked Paris, with familiar results. The Communards gave themselves over to a frenzy of executions and murders, to the horror even of liberals elsewhere in Europe, who had begun by supporting them. But Marx was not horrified. At this time he was an obscure haunter of the British Museum in London, where he had lived since being expelled from Germany and France after the failed risings of 1848. He had published a book on economic theory[29] and written numerous articles, many appearing in the *New York Herald Tribune*. He had worked with the International Working Men's Association, an organization in the vanguard of the trade union movement. But it was his articulation of the meaning of events in Paris that would make him famous.

After the Commune was crushed by the army on May 30, 1871, Marx delivered, from the safety of London, an address that would be much reprinted. It was a celebration of the Communards entitled "The Civil War in France." Marx said, "Working men's Paris, with its Commune, will be forever celebrated as the glorious harbinger of a new society. Its martyrs are enshrined in the great heart of the working class. Its exterminators history has already nailed to that eternal pillory from which all the prayers of their priests will not avail to redeem them."[30] This romantic defense of the Commune brought Marx his first international fame. Even from London, he became a lion of the European revolution, which would now have its scripture in *Das Kapital*. Marx became the living embodiment of revolution. To European reactionaries — monarchists, the military, Catholics (especially clerics), the landed gentry, the industrial *nouveau riche*, and much of the burgeoning middle class — one thing soon dominated the perception of Karl Marx, and it was not his fulsome beard. He was "that Jew."

The Roman Catholic Church, as the most tenacious element of the ancien régime, had been a special target of the violence of the Communards. They had taken hostage the archbishop of Paris, and in a frenzy of retribution they murdered him.[31] This was a blow that Catholics all over the world felt as something deeply personal. In Rome, where the Italian civil wars were reaching a climax, the killing of the French prelate could only have exacerbated an already monstrous paranoia. After this pivotal year, revolution would be seen as the greatest enemy the Church had ever faced.[32] And indeed, from the violence of the Communards to the bloodlust cruelties that followed wherever political economy was restructured according to the theories of Marx, revolution as defined by the international Communist movement would prove itself to be the enemy of the human. Yet now, in part because of the way Marx was perceived, this radical new threat was defined in the oldest, narrowest terms of all.

So deeply ingrained in the Catholic imagination is the identification of the revolutionary and the Jew that it keeps resurfacing. In November 1998, a Catholic priest attached to the Vatican Congregation for the Causes of the Saints responded to negative reactions by some Jews to the news that the "cause" of Pius XII had been progressing toward canonization by evoking this old canard. The priest — the relator, or official advocate — for the controversial pope's canonization was a Jesuit named Peter Gumpel. When Aaron Lopez, Israel's ambassador to the Holy See, asked that the canonization be delayed until the Vatican's full wartime archives were opened, Father Gumpel bristled. He was reported by the Austrian newspaper *Der Standard* as saying that such criticism "makes one wonder what the Jewish faction has against Catholics." Jews who criticize Pius XII, he was quoted as saying, may be "massive accomplices in the destruction of the Catholic Church." Father Gumpel was referring to the history of Jews in anti-Catholic Communism, from its origins to its flowering under Stalin. "The *Communist Manifesto* of Karl Marx and Friedrich Engels has Jewish origins, as well as the assertion that religion is the opiate of the masses. Eighty per cent of the initial Soviet regime was Jewish, so Jews were the managers of Communism."[33]

Putting Father Gumpel's statements together with the nearly simultaneous charges of Victor Ilyukhin in the Russian Duma, we have a contemporary replay of the full range of the tradition: Jews being blasted in Rome *as* Communists while being branded in Moscow *by* Communists as agents of anti-Russian genocide. In a subsequent interview with the *National Catholic Reporter,* Father Gumpel insisted his remarks had been taken out of context. "I have many Jewish friends," he said. He had not addressed his criticism "to Jews in general. That would be false and unfair. But since the Catholic Church is making an examination of conscience, what I said is that we would appreciate it if that would happen on the other side as well. Some Jews have greatly damaged the Catholic Church."

In the clarifying interview, Father Gumpel insisted on the relevance of his basic point. "It is a historical fact that many of the Bolsheviks who persecuted the Catholic Church, as well as the Orthodox Church in Russia, were Jews. That is the simple truth." It is also reminiscent of the Vatican's having characterized the Galileo affair as one of "mutual miscomprehension," as if there were errors on both sides. Thus, Father

Gumpel said, "it would be a good idea for both parties, Jews as well as Catholics, to admit guilt."

Gerhard Bodendorfer, the chief of the coordinating body for Christian-Jewish dialogue in Austria, protested Father Gumpel's remarks in a letter to the Jesuits and the apostolic nuncio in Austria: "I am amazed that an official collaborator in a highly responsible Vatican position could hold these old, obviously undistilled prejudices that are still hawked today. Conspiracy theories about world Judaism, combined with anti-Communist polemics, come out of the lowest drawer of antisemitism. Gumpel's behavior shows that he obviously did not find in the body of actual Church doctrine that such antisemitism is clearly and completely condemned."[34]

Father Gumpel's defensiveness for Pius XII is understandable, perhaps. What is instructive is that this pope's canonically appointed advocate should have such visceral convictions about Communism as a Jewish crime. Pius XII's defenders argue that, in all prudence, there was no overt action that he could have taken against the Nazis or against Hitler. He was limited to discreet, behind-the-scenes diplomacy. But the question arises: Why could he not have responded to the Nazis with the uncompromising ferocity of his responses to Communism? We referred in passing to this earlier: No Catholic-born Nazi — not Goebbels, Himmler, or Bormann; not even Adolf Hitler, who died with his name still on the rolls of the Catholic Church, and for whom the Catholic primate of Germany ordered the Requiem sung after his suicide — was ever excommunicated for being a Nazi. But, as Hans Küng observed, Pius XII "did not show the slightest inhibitions after the war, in 1949, about excommunicating all Communist members throughout the world at a stroke."[35] That decisive act, taken as a matter of moral absolutism, without regard for the consequences to the privileges of the Church, or even to the safety of Catholics behind the Iron Curtain, remains an unrefuted measure of what Pius XII could have done in 1943. The Catholic Church's strong opposition to Communism has never been in doubt.

The most important point of contact between Nazism and the Church was that twin identification of the Jew as financier and as Communist. On the Catholic side, the identification was given expression, to cite an example familiar to American readers, by Father Charles Coughlin (1891–1979), the radio priest who had an enormous following in the United States in the 1930s. In the threshold year of 1938, his newspaper, *Social Justice,* published *The Protocols of the Elders of Zion,* a forged document that first appeared in Russia in 1905, and that purported to be transcripts from a secret World Zionist Congress. Often characterized as a blueprint for world domination by Jews, the *Protocols* is a mishmash of commentary on the press, finance, government, and history. Its usefulness to anti-Semites — particularly in Germany during the 1930s — consisted more in the much-touted *idea* of proven conspiracy than in proof of anything real. The diabolical center of the plot, of course, was the international cabal of Jewish financiers, and world domination would be achieved by Jewish control of money. The *Protocols* was useful to Coughlin as part of his campaign of opposition to the gold standard. He preferred what he called "Gentile silver." The worship of gold had come from Jews, who believed, as the priest said in a broadcast sermon, "gold is sacred, gold is wealth, gold is more precious than men and the homes in which they live." That was, he said, "the theory of the European Jew." Closer to home, bankers on Wall Street were "modern Shylocks . . . grown fat and wealthy."[36]

Coughlin was a switch-hitting anti-Semite who also regularly denounced what he called "communistic Jews." In one *Social Justice* editorial, again in 1938, the priest wrote, "Almost without exception, the intellectual leaders — if not the foot and hand leaders — of Marxist atheism in Germany were Jews." The historian Alan Brinkley points out that this and other slanders in the editorial were in fact plagiarized by Coughlin from a speech given by Joseph Goebbels, the Nazi propaganda chief.[37]

↣ 43 ↢

Revolution in Rome: The Pope's Jews

FOR THE CATHOLIC CHURCH, the century of revolution culminated in Vatican Council I (December 1869–October 1870). It was the twentieth ecumenical council, and took its name from the place it met — St. Peter's Basilica in the Vatican. Nearly eight hundred bishops convened, almost all Europeans (forty-eight bishops represented the United States, but many of them would have been immigrants). The council was presided over by Pope Pius IX, who had set his face against everything associated with liberalism. As the archbishop of Paris would soon learn, there were good reasons why the Catholic Church was defining its struggle against the spirit of modernism as a fight to the death. The pope's authority over his own territories was being threatened by the movement of Italian nationalism, and nationalism itself was seen as incompatible with the Church's exercise of civil and theological authority across borders. Catholic theology was perceived as being undermined by liberal ideas. Pius IX's solution to all of this was to draw from the bishops gathered in council an unprecedented affirmation of his own authority as pope, and he succeeded.

Vatican I's declaration in support of Pius was issued as the constitution *Pastor Aeternus*. "When the Roman Pontiff speaks *ex cathedra*," it said, "that is, when . . . as the pastor and teacher of all Christians in virtue of his highest apostolic authority, he defines a doctrine of faith and morals that must be held by the Universal Church, he is empowered through the divine assistance promised him in blessed Peter, with that infallibility with which the Divine Redeemer willed to endow his Church."[1]

It is well known that the Catholic Church claims that its leader, the pope, is endowed by God with the charism of infallibility in matters of "faith and morals." What is not so widely appreciated is that the first formal declaration of this doctrine did not come until this moment of crisis when so much was tearing at the fabric of traditional faith and institutional power. This is not a book primarily about papal power, but we have already seen how absolutist theological claims and institutional universalism have led directly to Church oppression of Jews. We shall see in later chapters that the Church's relationship to the modern fate of the Jews is intertwined, in a particular way, with efforts to extend the spiritual and political power of the papacy. The declaration of the infallibility of the pope is therefore a pivotal event for this story. The context within which it occurred tells us everything we need to know about its meaning for Catholics and for Jews.

The doctrine of papal infallibility was defined on July 18, 1870,[2] only two days after Napoleon III announced his suicidal mobilization against Prussia and one day before the Franco-Prussian War was formally begun.[3] This Napoleon was heir to the ethos of the French monarchy, not to the republican spirit of the 1789 Revolution. As such, his soldiers had been stationed in Rome as the pope's protectors since 1866. He was the only thing standing between the Roman Catholic Church and the final disaster it had been staving off for centuries. Within weeks of the French declaration of war against Prussia, Napoleon III's army would be routed in a decisive battle at Sedan, a city on the Meuse in northeastern France. Within months, the war would end in the catastrophe of the Paris Commune — and the murder of the archbishop.

In Italy, the Risorgimento, the movement for independence, unification, and constitutional government, was on the rise. The anti-papal nationalists, who had succeeded in stripping the pontiff of temporal sovereignty over all the papal territories outside Rome and its environs, were closing in for what had to feel to the council fathers like the kill. Popes had exercised political authority over various domains since the fourth century, but the tide of history had turned. In 1791, papal territories in France, centered in Avignon and memorialized in the vintages of chateauneuf du Pape, had been ripped away by the French Republic. Then, in 1861, Italians under Giuseppe Garibaldi (1807–1882) and Victor Emmanuel II (1820–1878) had taken the swath of papal land across the midsection of the boot, sweeping up to the second papal city of Bologna.

The opening section of *Pastor Aeternus* makes the thing clear: "And seeing that the gates of hell, with daily increase of hatred, are gathering their strength on every side to upheave the foundation laid by God's own hand, and so, if that might be, to overthrow the Church: we therefore . . . do judge it necessary to propose to the belief and acceptance of all the faithful . . . the doctrine . . . in which is found the strength and solidity of the entire Church."[4]

The imminent "upheaving" of one kind of absolute Church authority therefore required the extraordinary promulgation of another. It was a case of responding, in the scholar Hans Kühner's phrase, to "the political nadir" with "the dogmatic zenith."[5] In reply to questions from reluctant Vatican Council fathers who saw little support in the tradition for the doctrine (some 20 percent opposed the definition of infallibility;[6] once it was voted, 61 bishops walked out in protest), Pope Pius IX declared, "I am the tradition!"[7] Nevertheless, *Pastor Aeternus* refers to the pressing political and social crisis of the moment — "in this very age"[8] — as a justification for its astonishing pronouncement: "Hence we teach and declare that . . . all of whatever rite and dignity, both pastors and faithful, both individually and collectively, are bound, by their duty of hierarchical subordination and true obedience, to submit not only in matters which belong to faith and morals, but also in those that appertain to the discipline and government of the Church throughout the world . . . under one supreme pastor . . . the Roman Pontiff. This is the teaching of the Catholic faith, from which no one can deviate without loss of faith and of salvation."[9]

Obviously, those who were inclined to "deviate" included a swelling population of liberals, republicans, nationalists, and revolutionaries of various kinds. The papacy had made itself the century's bulwark against the new idea. It is "false and absurd or rather mad," Gregory XVI had declared in 1832, "that we must secure and guarantee to each one liberty of conscience; this is one of the most contagious of errors . . . To this is attached liberty of the press, the most dangerous liberty, an execrable liberty, which can never inspire sufficient horror."[10] Viewed from the twenty-first century, such Church opposition to liberalism, and that opposition's late-twentieth-century renewal during the pontificate of John Paul II, can seem to have been about little more than power, yet the questions underlying this conflict went to the heart of what it is to be human. "The entire liberal world-view appeared to many leading nineteenth-century Catholic theologians," as the sociologist Alan Wolfe sums it up, "to be premised on the notion of the person as a solitary individual lacking connectedness to any sense of meaning or purpose."[11] Indeed, as the twentieth century showed, the legacy of nineteenth-century liberalism would be profoundly ambiguous, but Catholicism, at first, would be attuned far more to what it threatened than what it promised.

Ironically, Pope Pius IX had come to the Chair of Peter in 1846 as a kind of liberal himself, determined, as we saw, to loosen the siege mentality that had closed like a vise on the Church. He began his reign by announcing an amnesty for political prisoners and, most tellingly, by ordering the walls of the Roman ghetto torn down. "On Passover night in 1848, the seventeenth of April," Hermann Vogelstein writes, "the Jews in the Roman ghetto, in the midst of the celebration in their homes, were startled by the threatening sound of ax strokes. But anxiety soon changed into exultant joy . . . It was the end of three hundred years of what the Book of Joshua calls 'the reproach of Egypt.'"[12]

Before the liberation of Rome's Jews was fully accomplished, however, and before the pope's initial liberalizing impulse bore fruit, the revolution of 1848 struck in cities across Europe. As elsewhere, the workers, the urban poor, and the disgruntled took to the streets of Rome. Pius IX was forced to flee the city, disguised as a common priest, afraid for his life. While he was in exile in Gaeta,[13] the revolutionaries declared themselves a government. As it happened, several Jews were elected to the governing body of the Roman Republic.[14] The status of Jews was as much an emblem of the new order as of the old — by the rule of reversal.

Austria, Spain, and France under the emperor Louis Napoleon aligned themselves against the revolutionary movements, and they rallied to the pope. He was restored to power after the French army laid siege to Rome, a brutal struggle that lasted more than a month. Pius IX was traumatized by it all, and when he resumed control of the Papal States, he was a changed man. "And now the blackest reaction made its entry," Vogelstein writes of what happened in Rome. We already saw how Jews were now scapegoated. "Revolutionaries were persecuted, Jews thrown back in the Ghetto . . . violent regulation against the Jews followed." Now the one-time reconciler was a tyrant, and the Jew-imprisoning walls went up again.

Pius IX excommunicated Italian nationalists, including the entire Sardinian House of Savoy.[15] He swore his enmity to every kind of liberal. By 1864, Pius IX had compiled a "Syllabus of Errors," a list of eighty mistakes of philosophy, theology, and politics to which, in the encyclical *Quanta Cura,* he attached the anathema. In issuing the proclamation, he denied that "the Roman Pontiff can and ought to reconcile and align himself with progress, liberalism, and modern civilization." With that broadside, the Holy See had launched its counterattack against "Modernism," which eventually would be condemned as "the synthesis of all heresies."[16] Before

Pius IX was finished — his reign as pope would be the longest in history (1846–1878) — he would see himself in a fight to the death. And seeing himself as losing that fight, he would summon that First Vatican Council to rally all the bishops of the world as his defenders. The safety of the Church and of the pope had become the same thing.

But not only the Church. Liberalism and modernism were seen as bearing the seeds of the destruction of civilization itself, and the dark side of the new order would make itself all too clear in the twentieth century. There was much in the new age that the Church was right to suspect, so the Catholic strategy of arming the leader of the Church with the spiritual mace of infallibility made some sense. Joseph de Maistre (1754–1821) was a French royalist who had made the case for papal absolutism in his *Du Pape* (1819).[17] He had argued along a set of connected propositions, each of which was firmly tied to the tradition he wanted to defend. "No public morality and no national character without religion," he said, "no European religion without Christianity, no Christianity without Catholicism, no Catholicism without the Pope, no Pope without the supremacy to which he is entitled."[18] Catholics who made this argument would prove to be so fiercely devoted to it precisely because they understood themselves to be defenders of far more than the mere prerogatives of the institutional Church. De Maistre's logic could seem irrefutable to those who accepted it: "There can be no humane society without government, no government without sovereignty and no sovereignty without infallibility."[19] In this way of thinking, the pope is the lad with his finger in the dike, holding back the flood of — whatever one chooses to label the imminent social disaster. Infallibility is the pope's finger.

"The Council of the last century was called by Pius IX to condemn the errors of modern times," wrote the theologian Walter Kasper, "just as the Council of Trent was called to repel the false doctrines of the sixteenth-century Reformers. The object was to present the infallible authority of the Pope as the remedy for the crisis of modern society that was already beginning to take shape."[20]

Cardinal John Henry Newman (1801–1890) was one of those who had his doubts about such logic, and therefore about a conciliar definition of infallibility. For one thing, he knew Church history, as others of the bishops gathered in St. Peter's did. They knew that the line of popes had included not only moral degenerates but heretics — one pope, Honorius I (625–638), had been condemned by a Church council not for being a sinner but for getting doctrine wrong.[21] Newman predicted that a subsequent council would be needed "to trim . . . the barque of St. Peter," as Roland Hill summarized Newman's position, "in its unnavigable Infallibilist course."[22] That subsequent council was the one convened by John XXIII in 1962, and despite a resolute beginning, Vatican II would do little to alter that course. So profoundly had the contest with "Modernism" affected the mind of the Church that, even after Vatican II, which had implicitly affirmed much of what "Modernism" had been condemned for, a formal rejection of those "errors" was still required of young clerics, the "Oath Against Modernism." It would not be abolished until the late 1960s — I would be presented with it as a precondition of my own ordination. Even so, the Church would take up the anti-modernist fight again, rallying against "relativism." As Wolfe writes, "Pope John Paul II, for all his heroic opposition to communism, is one who harkens back to the Church's nineteenth-century crusade against liberalism."[23] It is he, more than anyone, who sponsored the beatification of Pius IX in September 2000.[24]

Yet Pius IX represented to Catholic liberals of my generation the Church's great stumble. We associated him with old battles that would never need to be refought, or so we thought. We had a first hint that we were wrong when the Vatican revoked Hans Küng's *missio canonica,* his right to teach as a Catholic, in 1979. Küng was the dominant theological model of our generation, and what brought the wrath of the Vatican down on him, revealingly, was his book *Infallible? An Inquiry.* Published in 1970, the work drew the Vatican's full fire only once John Paul II had come to the throne in 1978, and it soon became clear that he took Küng's challenge personally.

John Paul II, holding back a second tidal wave of liberalism, had reason to identify with Pius IX's resistance to the first wave. Both men were shaped by early traumas, both saw the very existence of the Church as at stake, and both, for that reason, when their authority to defend the Church was challenged, responded by claiming that authority more resolutely than ever. It was with survival in mind that Pius IX demanded the ultimate gesture of support from the bishops of his Vatican Council. Their solemn definition of the doctrine of papal infallibility, to be exercised outside the context of conciliar collegiality, makes sense only as an act of spiritual resistance against the direst of worldly threats.

To those bishops, many of whom had been targeted by revolutionaries, many driven from their palaces by mobs, modernism was no mere school of thought. It was an assault in every sense, and often it was an armed assault. And it was worldly indeed, as in worldwide, seeming to sweep from one nation — one diocese, one city — to another. With the collapse of

Catholic France, with Otto von Bismarck's anti-Catholic Kulturkampf coming within the year in Germany, followed soon after by a democratizing movement within the Church itself (to be condemned as the heresy "Americanism") and then Great Britain's support for anticlerical nationalism,[25] it could feel as if the world itself were turning against the barque of Peter. And not only the world, but now Italy. The pope and the bishops were braced.

Within days of the French defeat at Sedan, Italian nationalist forces mustered at the city limits of Rome. The French withdrew without a fight, but the pope's own soldiers vowed to hold the city. After a brief siege, however, the pope ordered the white flag of surrender flown. The fathers of the First Vatican Council dispersed, leaving their agenda to be picked up again ninety years later. On September 20, 1870, the soldiers of Giuseppe Garibaldi and Victor Emmanuel entered Rome.[26] That date is enshrined in the name of the proud boulevard, Via Venti Settembre, that runs past the Quirinale, the palace that since the sixteenth century had served as the summer residence of popes, but that — a further indignity — now became the residence of the new constitutional monarch. (Since 1947, the Quirinale has been the residence of Italy's president.) Pius IX became a self-styled "prisoner of the Vatican," where the popes would remain until Pius XI came to terms with Mussolini in the Lateran Treaty of 1929. The treaty's most important provision recognized papal sovereignty over the ninety-acre enclave of Vatican City.

What did all this mean for Jews? We have seen how the nineteenth-century ebb and flow of Risorgimento had a way of leaving Jews high and dry. In 1796, the ghetto of Rome was liberated, then quickly restored. That pattern repeated itself in 1808 and 1816, in 1830 and 1831, in 1848 and 1849. We have seen how authority over "the pope's Jews" became a potent emblem of the power struggle between the Church and the liberalism it opposed. The Jew was a familiar figure of opposition. The catch phrase used to describe the Church's mortal enemies became the triad "Freemasons, Protestants, and Jews." To a great majority of Catholics, the emancipated and resurgent Jew had become a symbol of all who despised the Church. Thus the politics of reaction in an age of revolution was indeed a factor in the unapologetic Catholic determination to keep the Jews subservient. Catholic ultramontanism, "a movement which sought to marginalize liberal tendencies within the Church," as the historian Jacques Kornberg put it, "mobilized antisemitism for its campaign against liberalism."[27]

But Catholic theology, stuck in its first groove, was an equally important factor. Saint Augustine's notion that the Jews were to be allowed to survive, but not to thrive assumed the continuance of Judaism as a distinct and restricted entity within the larger Christian culture. Emancipation was a negation of this theology, and the idea of assimilation without conversion was theologically unthinkable. Distinction, restriction, and palpable inferiority defined the Jews as "the witness people." Popes had taken this notion for granted as the ground of Church policy since the *Sicut Judaeis* was promulgated by Callixtus II after the First Crusade.[28] Then, and at other times, as we saw, popes made crucial interventions against murderous Christian mobs, although without ever confronting the relationship of the "official" theological denigration to the "unofficial" massacre. Nevertheless, most popes came to think of themselves as the protectors of Jews, and so it often appeared to Jews as well. But some popes, especially since Paul IV's *Cum Nimis Absurdum,* which established the Roman ghetto in 1555, had applied the theologically sanctioned restrictions so ruthlessly as to make any idea of papal protection absurd.

By 1870, when all this came to a climax, Jews took for granted "the violence of the Church's regime," in Vogelstein's phrase.[29] In fact, the papal policy of enforced ghettoization of Jews, whether its violence was overt or implicit, was an inevitable consequence of Catholic theology. That the ghetto seemed only more and more anomalous to non-Catholics as the modern era progressed did nothing to show Church authorities why, in this new age, with the Church in full retreat to the ninety-acre enclave of the Vatican, the ghetto did not make more religious sense than ever. The more besieged the papacy, the stouter the ghetto walls. Hence the Roman ghetto, practically alone of the urban Jewish concentrations in Europe, kept being restored in this period, its gates rebuilt after every destruction. This was so not despite the ghetto's cruel restrictions but because of them. The way to Jewish "emancipation" had always been clear in the eyes of the Church, and indeed the ghetto had initially been established to hurry Jews along that way. And the way, of course, was baptism.

"The pope's Jews" were still required to attend conversionist sermons. Jewish children were constantly at risk of surreptitious baptism, being claimed for Christ in Church-sanctioned kidnappings.[30] It should be noted that this dogged emphasis on conversion indicates that by now the Church had pulled back from the temptation represented by the blood purity laws of the Inquisition. A Catholic theology that still presumed a goal of Jewish conversion assumed the religious inferiority of Judaism, but decidedly not the biological or racial inferiority of individual Jews. Judaism, as a religion of the radical rejection of Jesus, might be defined as innately evil, but Jews, taken as persons, were not. This position had come to dominate nineteenth-century Catholicism, although not universally so, as we saw in relation to the blood purity requirements of the Jesuit constitutions, which were maintained into the twentieth century.

Still, a recovered conversionism separated the Church from the growing racial antisemitism of the era, even if that could trace at least one of its roots back to the Inquisition's blood purity idea that the Church had by now mainly rejected. Some of the new anti-Semites were themselves Catholic, but the movement was more secular than religious. The new "racialism" would not hesitate to apply the pseudoscience of biogenics to Jews, a rejection of any method of bringing "Semites" into the social or national mainstream. The word "antisemitism" was coined in 1879 by one of its proponents, Wilhelm Marr, a German journalist who warned that Jews were not only a threat to the superior Aryan race, but would take over the world if they could.[31] Such paranoia would be a hallmark of racial antisemitism. Another would be — and we saw it in relation to Karl Marx, and Spinoza before him — the belief that religious conversion did nothing to alter a Jew's identity.

As much as the Catholic Church had rejected that idea, it had rejected emancipation, which earned it the further enmity of Jews and liberal critics. The liberals argued that the degradation of Jews — what "proved" the inferiority of Judaism, making Jews "the witness people" — had been caused by the way Christians had treated them, instead of by the "blindness" of the Jewish religion. Some Catholic theologians advanced this "liberal" argument, as Abelard had done centuries before. Thus, in the words of Jacques Kornberg, characterizing the nineteenth-century opponents of papal absolutism, "Jews and liberal Catholics had a common enemy. Hatred of Jews was nourished by the same survivals of the Middle Ages that had produced the triumphs of Ultramontanism, the Syllabus of Errors (1864), and the decree on Papal Infallibility (1870), namely the belief that 'we alone are in possession of the full saving truth.'"[32]

For the Church establishment, the still valid — because ancient — proof of that saving truth could be seen in the deserved fate of Jews. Jewish emancipation untied to a prior renunciation of Jewish error was a violation of the order with which God, in Christ, had redeemed the world. That was why, every time the nineteenth-century popes retook control of Rome, the first thing they did was to reinstate the ghetto.

At each of these reversals, the situation of the Jews in the dank enclave by the Tiber worsened. In 1867, they were hard hit by cholera. Once the ghetto population had exceeded ten thousand, but now less than half that remained, and nearly half of those were supported by charity.[33] "The economic situation of the Jews of Rome was perhaps never so desperate" as on September 20, 1870. "Though the joy that greeted the Italian troops as liberators was general," Vogelstein writes, "no class of the population had better ground for gratitude and happiness than did the Jews. They had been held in the deepest degradation, with no liberty and in miserable poverty, not even protected against having their children stolen for baptism. Now they knew that the day of freedom had dawned, that it would bring them human rights and human dignity, that it would give them home and country along with the other inhabitants of Rome. For the new Kingdom of Italy recognized no differences in rights among its subjects. The hour of emancipation had now finally struck for the Jews, who had been longest and hardest pressed in the oldest community of the West."[34]

From 1555 until 1870, the popes of the Church, including saints, forced a rigid and at times brutal imprisonment on the Jews of Rome. Only forces hostile to religion and to the Church brought about the final destruction of that system. The impious Garibaldi's action raised an immediate question about the universalist moral claim a Vatican Council had just made for the papacy weeks before. There is no question of official doctrinal formulation — ex cathedra — in the record of the Church's relations with Jews, but how can the claim to an essential spiritual endowment implied by the doctrine of papal infallibility stand before this history? How could the Vicar of Christ, acting in his capacity as such, have enforced such policies over generations? These are questions put by the Roman ghetto to a Church that attributes fallibility to its "sinful sons and daughters," never to itself.

The pope's power to enforce the witness misery of Jews at the foot of Vatican Hill was taken away. But the powerful example of the Roman Catholic Church's will to degrade Jews would continue to have its effect across Europe. That effect would be both immediate and remote. It is enough to note here that on October 13, 1870, the new government of a unified Italy issued a decree abolishing all restrictions against Jews. Sometimes students of history wonder why Europeans, little more than a generation later, did not protest, or at least grasp its full significance, when fascist governments in Germany, Italy, and then France issued decrees restricting Jews — what they wore, where they lived, what jobs they could have, what they could read, with whom they could have children, and on and on. Many such citizens of Europe, observing the introduction of these restrictions in the 1920s and 1930s, had been alive in 1870, or were the children of those who had been. Europeans knew firsthand, that is, of a time when the harshest imaginable restriction of Jews had been imposed in the name not of Der Führer or Il Duce, but of Jesus Christ. The fascist/Nazi campaign of restrictions against Jews had been directly anticipated by the Catholic Church, not in the Middle Ages but recently. Indeed, even in 1933, Europeans knew very well that the Church had abandoned its anti-Jewish campaign only because forced to. In addition, the twentieth-century acquiescence before, and cooperation in, the fascist/Nazi campaign of Jewish degradation by the vast majority of non-Jews had equally been prepared for by the Church. That is what it meant, finally, that for three hundred years, the keeper of the keys of the Jews' first and, until modern times, last and most squalid concentration camp was the keeper of the keys of Peter.

But twentieth-century consequences of the papal policies toward Jews in Rome were remote compared to what happened more immediately, particularly in France, where Catholics had been as traumatized by the Communards in 1871 as the pope was by Garibaldi in 1870. Not surprisingly, as the next act of this tragedy unfolded, the chief victim of the traumatic denouement would be not only the one Jew whose name is permanently attached to the tragedy, but the whole community of his fellow Jews who had thought themselves, through all of this, set free.

⤙ 44 ⤚

Alfred Dreyfus and *La Croix*

CONSTANTINE, SAINT HELENA, the Seamless Robe, a nail of the True Cross, relics of the man who replaced Judas; a first battlefield of the Crusades and of Eisenhower's campaign; the birthplace of Karl Marx and of Klaus Barbie. What more could be subsumed under the name of Trier?

If Rome was vulnerable to the tide of invaders at the time of Saint Augustine, so was its northern capital on the Moselle. Germanic tribes had no trouble taking control of Treves, as Trier was known in the fifth century. (Recall that the name derived from the original tribe that Caesar's army had encountered in the region five hundred years before — the Treveri. The initial Roman settlement had been called Augusta Treverorum, which eventually shook down to Treves.)

There had been Jews in Treves from the beginning of the Roman settlement. With the coming of Germans, some Jews, presumably as a way of identifying themselves in language that the bearded new overlords would recognize, took a new name, a Germanic mimicking not of the meaning but of the sound of Treves. They put the word *drei,* which meant "three," together with the word *fuss,* which meant "foot." Thus the ancient name of the city of Trier provides, in the historian Michael Burns's phrase, the "linguistic skeleton for his family name"[1] — the name, that is, of Captain Alfred Dreyfus.

The Dreyfus family had migrated south from Trier, but not far. Settled near the Rhine, in Alsace, they would find themselves in the midst of conflict between France and Germany, as the forces of nationalism split Europe. Alsace had its eyes firmly fixed on France at the time of Alfred's birth in 1859. As his home city of Mulhausen had shed the Germanic by calling itself Mulhouse, so Alfred's father traded the Germanic "Dreyfuss" for the Frenchified "Dreyfus."[2] Yet the Franco-Prussian War, which had traumatized Paris and, indirectly, sealed the pope's fate in Rome, also put its stamp on the Dreyfus family's home region. As it would repeatedly, with such catastrophic effect, the border shifted, this time to the west, across the Rhine. In 1871, Mulhouse became part of the new Germany that Bismarck was shaping out of the alliances of principalities and city-states he had pulled together to fight France.

The German occupiers came when Alfred was twelve years old. It was, as Burns reports Dreyfus saying, his "first sorrow."[3] His family was Jewish, but his first identity was as French, and as was true for most Alsatians, the German occupation only reinforced him in that primordial loyalty. The Dreyfus family had made the most of emancipation. Alfred's grandfather Jacob, born before the French Revolution, had traveled the Rhineland as a peddler of used goods. But Alfred's father, Raphael, born in 1818 — on May 12, one week to the day after Karl Marx was born — became a prosperous merchant, then an even more successful manufacturer of textiles. Unlike Marx — perhaps reflecting what it was to live in France just then, not Prussia — both Raphael and his son were raised to take their Jewishness both seriously and for granted. But also, since they considered themselves French, never German, to see it as no barrier to full citizenship.

The family was affluent by the time of Alfred's childhood, and his older brothers were moving into the thriving family business. Alfred was educated at boarding schools in Paris. Though more inclined to intellect than action, his intense feeling for France led him boldly to aim for a career in the French army. The shadow of the Commune was still on Paris during the time of Alfred's schooling: in 1871, he would have been twelve years old. A dread of revolution as social dissolution was in the air. After the Commune had been destroyed, Roman Catholicism had found ways to reassert itself. A massive church, the Sacré-Coeur Basilica, was being built on the hilltop of Montmartre as a monument to the victory over the anticlerical Communards. At the same time, radicals, Freemasons, and a class of economically powerful Protestants opposed the restoration of Catholic influence. The parliament of the Third Republic was riven with factions reflecting all of this. Such discord only reinforced in the military an ethos of nonpolitical and nondenominational devotion to an ever more mystical *la France*. That devotion naturally meant support for the established order, whatever it was. Alfred's one intensely felt political opinion was tied to the recovery of Alsace and Lorraine from Germany — a conviction that fueled his military ambition.

As Burns recounts the progression, Dreyfus was admitted to the École

Polytechnique, a military academy, and upon graduation in 1880, he was commissioned. A decade later, having earned the rank of captain, he solidified his position with an admirable marriage. In a ceremony at the leading synagogue of Paris, and of France, Captain Dreyfus married the twenty-year-old Lucie Eugénie Hadamard. She was an elegant, well-educated pianist, a clear-eyed young woman from a distinguished family. Her father's diamond trade in Paris had made the Hadamards wealthy. Presiding at the wedding was Grand Rabbi Zadoc Kahn, who, as the leading spokesman for French Jews, had notably affirmed a commitment to "Fatherland and religion."[4] As we saw earlier, this tendency to reduce Jewishness to religion alone could and would be used against Jews for whom the identity was more comprehensive. But it served the purposes of the secular society to treat Judaism and Christianity as equivalent, since both were to be dismissed. Rabbi Kahn's role, however, was not to raise such points of contention, but to sidestep them. He said, "Jews above all feel a love for France without limit . . . They are proud . . . to work for her prosperity and to defend her flag."[5] That was exactly how Captain Dreyfus felt. He would happily leave his Jewishness out of it. In our terms, that part of his identity was private, and in this public-private dichotomy, as in that between religion and identity, we see the Enlightenment dualism that first surfaced in Descartes.

Lucie and Alfred settled into a comfortable apartment in the Eighth Arrondissement, between the Champs-Élysées and the Seine, an area where a good number of affluent Jews lived, a mile or two up the river from the district around the Hôtel de Ville, where poorer Jews were concentrated. It was in the Place de l'Hôtel de Ville that Saint Louis had burned the Talmud in 1242. The smoke from the flames could well have drifted across the needle spire of nearby Sainte-Chapelle, which the sainted king was then building to house relics of the Passion found by Helena, including the crown of thorns. A century and a half later, the Jews of Paris were expelled, not to return for nearly three hundred years.

But this was a new day in Paris. For a century, the promise of *liberté* had beckoned Jews. Nearly all Jews living in France had settled into French identity, speaking the language as their own.[6] By the late nineteenth century, forty thousand lived in the city, including many refugees from pogroms in Russia and Poland. Yes, the Jew-caricaturing tradition of Voltaire was alive here, but the code of liberalism by now required a certain circumspection in such expression. Yes, many Catholics, especially clerics, assumed a Jewish alliance with Freemasons and Protestants, but many other Catholics had grown into a benign indifference toward Jews. This tended to loosen society's grip on the tenets of faith and on its prejudices. All of which meant that the Third Republic, coming after Napoleon III's defeat in the Franco-Prussian War, upheld the new ideal. Like its economy, its social structures had proved to be more expansive than anyone could have predicted. In France, Jews no longer had to hope to be citizens; they already were. Their attachment to the republican ethos reinforced the impulse among defenders of the ancien régime throughout Europe to regard Jews as the living image of the hated Revolution.[7] As we have seen, Jews were perennially liable to be blamed for the excesses of that Revolution, which in Paris had included the savage desecration in 1791 of Sainte-Chapelle itself.

Captain Dreyfus, at the start of a promising career, seemed proof that the Jews of France had arrived. Admitted to the elite École de Guerre, the war college that groomed senior officers, he graduated ninth in a class of eighty-one. By contrast, as Burns points out, Napoleon Bonaparte had graduated from the École Militaire near the bottom of his class.[8] Dreyfus was rewarded in 1892 with an appointment to the army's general staff. It is often said that he was the first Jew to hold such a position, but that is not clearly so. As the historian Robert Hoffman points out, some Jews had become generals by then. As to Jews on the general staff itself, it is hard to say, but that very "uncertainty should be significant, for most of the French seem not to have paid close attention to who and where the Jews were."[9]

Nevertheless, one of Dreyfus's superiors protested his appointment because he was Jewish. But according to the minister of war, "The army makes no distinction among Jews, Protestants and Catholics, and any such division is a crime against the nation."[10] The appointment of Captain Dreyfus to the general staff stood. The event should have marked a fulfillment of the promise of emancipation. Instead, it was the beginning of its undoing.

The facts of the so-called *l'affaire Dreyfus* are quickly summarized.[11] In October 1894, Captain Dreyfus was arrested and charged with spying for Germany. For two weeks, Lucie was told nothing of his whereabouts, or of the charges. Finally, she was asked to provide letters in her husband's hand to investigators, which she did. The evidence against Dreyfus was one handwritten page enumerating the military secrets that had been passed to the Germans. The army charged that the writing was the captain's. His wife believed in his innocence from the start, and resolved to defend him.

When the arrest of Dreyfus was made public, the fact of his being a Jew set off an explosion of anti-Jewish invective in the press. In December, Dreyfus was brought to trial, convicted, and sent to Devil's Island, the notorious penal colony off the coast of French Guiana in South America. He was its only prisoner at the time. "My only crime," he cried, "is to have been born a Jew!"[12] The army rejected every suggestion that an injustice had been done, but the captain's family refused to abandon the effort to prove otherwise. The minister of war who had presided over the case, General Auguste Mercier, turned all criticism into a point of personal honor, and much of French society rallied to him. Those who supported Dreyfus, on the other hand, were seen by an increasingly agitated press and public as participants in a conspiracy against the nation. The case became politicized, with factions facing off across the clearly defined, but heretofore dormant, fault line separating right from left, monarchist from republican, Catholics from the new secularists. And all of those differences coalesced around the word "Jew."

A year and a half after the first charges were filed, an army supporter of Dreyfus uncovered a document in handwriting that matched the single page of script that had convicted Dreyfus, but this document was known to have been written by one Major Ferdinand Esterhazy. Supporters of Dreyfus, called Dreyfusards, demanded a new trial. That was denied, but charges were brought against Esterhazy. On January 11, 1898, he was acquitted by an army court. Two days later, the novelist Émile Zola published a broadside attack — "*J'Accuse . . . !*" — against those responsible for scapegoating Dreyfus. Zola condemned "the odious antisemitism of which the great, liberal, rights-of-man France will die if she is not cured."[13] But he also named names — "I accuse General Mercier of having rendered himself the accomplice . . . I accuse General Billot of having had in his hands certain proofs of Dreyfus's innocence . . . I accuse General de Boisdeffre and General Gonse of having made themselves accomplices . . ."[14] — singling out the ministers and generals who presided over the frame-up. As a result, Zola was charged with, and then convicted of, defamation, prompting his flight to England.

But Zola's charge transformed *l'affaire,* galvanizing that part of the population prepared to believe in Dreyfus. Pressure on the army mounted. In August 1898, one Colonel Hubert Henry admitted that he had forged supporting evidence against Dreyfus in the original trial. Then Henry committed suicide. A court of appeals ordered a new trial for Dreyfus. In the late summer of 1899, after the prisoner's return from

Devil's Island, the second trial took place. The army's entire high command now saw its honor at stake, as well as that of General Mercier. They were more determined than ever to stand by the original verdict. The board of officers presiding at the second trial, choosing, as it was put, between Mercier and the Jew, once again voted to convict.

There is every reason to believe that army officers knowingly covered up an initial mistake, especially once Mercier's honor became yoked to Dreyfus's guilt. But to the conservative segment of the public that supported the army, the matter was simpler, and since they were ignorant of the hidden facts, so was the choice. General or Jew? It was unthinkable to those upholding the honor of France that Mercier and the others would lie. Mercier was an embodiment of the old order. *L'affaire* was revealing that the old order was in some way corrupt.

The injustice of the second conviction was apparent. Immediately, the president of the Third Republic, Émile Loubet, pardoned Dreyfus. On September 19, 1899, he was released from prison. That did not satisfy Dreyfus or his family. They continued to press for a complete exoneration, an impulse that even some supporters saw as Jewish impudence. Finally, in July 1906, the high court of appeals, a civilian court, reversed the second conviction, decisively overruling the military. "Dreyfus Innocent!" one broadside proclaimed, a victory "*du Droit, de la Justice et de la Vérité.*"[15]

By then, however, some Jews had drawn conclusions from the Dreyfus affair. A Jewish journalist who had covered the case saw it, and the manifestations of extreme, widespread antisemitism it elicited, as cause to reject the goals of assimilation and emancipation. His name was Theodor Herzl, and the actions he took led to the founding of the World Zionist Organization and, ultimately, the state of Israel.[16]

Dreyfus was restored to the army and promoted to major. He remained a patriot. When the Great War broke out, he would serve as an artillery commander with the rank of colonel at Verdun and Aisne. Later, the army would refuse to acknowledge his frontline service with the appropriate decorations, a final indignity.[17] In 1931, documents made available from Germany proved once and for all that Esterhazy had indeed been the spy, but that did not remove the French army's difficulty in facing the truth of its crime against the Jewish officer. Even in 1994, that difficulty persisted. The French army marked the centenary of the arrest of Captain Dreyfus with the publication of a study that made the army itself the victim. In it, Dreyfusards were identified as socialists, republicans, Freemasons, and radicals opposed to "the military caste." As for Dreyfus, the most the army review could acknowledge was that his "innocence is the thesis now generally accepted by historians." The French army has never reversed its two verdicts against the Jewish officer. The *New York Times* story about the 1994 study was headlined, "Years Later, Dreyfus Affair Still Festers."[18]

What makes the affair so difficult to comprehend is that the antisemitic venom unleashed in France by the dispute seems at odds with the more or less progressive situation in which most French Jews had found themselves before Dreyfus was arrested. Clearly a hatred of Jews had been stewing below the surface of French society, from the reign of Napoleon III to the Paris Commune to the Third Republic, but no one could have predicted the strength it would have at century's end. Dreyfus's lawyer, Edgar Demange, took the case on at great cost to himself, not least because he was a fervent Roman Catholic, which would come to seem anomalous.[19]

Certain leading Catholic intellectuals would denounce the vulgar antisemitism of Dreyfus's opponents. Léon Bloy, for example, in his 1892 book *Salut par les Juifs,* had already ridiculed the ignorant but widely promoted idea that Jesus was not a Jew.[20] He did so not as a modern ecumenist would, but as a traditional Catholic who, while rejecting anti-Jewish violence, also saw Jews as cursed by God. To insist that Jesus was a Jew was not to ennoble Judaism but to emphasize its offense in rejecting one of its own. Nevertheless, Bloy's repugnance at the mindless antisemitism of the time has a ringing eloquence to it. Writing expressly as a Catholic, once the affair had begun, he attacked the opponents of Dreyfus, condemning their hidden motives: "All the leaden-cheeked Christian onion-eaters . . . understand admirably that a war against the Jews could, in the end, be an excellent dodge for healing up many a bankruptcy, or reviving many a decrepit business. We have even seen priests without number — among whom there must nevertheless have been sincere servants of God — fired at the hope of an imminent affray in which enough blood of Israel would be shed to make millions of dogs drunk."[21]

A minority of Catholic liberals, some of whom would be disciplined by the Church as "modernists," associated themselves with the ever-fiercer struggle against antisemitism.[22] The poet Charles Péguy was one. In reflecting on the Dreyfus case later, he offered his famous aphorism: "Everything begins in faith and ends in politics."[23] Such Catholics might have cited a letter written by Pope Leo XIII (1878–1903) in 1898 condemning an antisemitic movement in Algeria.[24] Leo was a relative liberal who, though he would condemn the heresy of "Americanism," also disappointed monarchists by urging French Catholics to support the Third Republic. The

Church, Leo wrote in the encyclical *Sapientiae Christianae* (1890), "holds that it is not her province to decide which is the best amongst many diverse forms of government . . . provided the respect due to religion and the observance of good morals be upheld."[25] Leo's most important encyclical, *Rerum Novarum* (1891), was a resounding defense of workers, although, as Alan Wolfe points out, it was written more in the traditional Catholic language of solidarity than of individual rights.[26] But Leo XIII was pulled in several directions, and he did not hesitate to support openly antisemitic organizations.[27] His condemnation of antisemitism in Algeria was contained in a private letter, and it is unlikely that such Catholics as Bloy or Péguy were aware of it.

Far more publicly aired were Vatican attitudes as expressed that same pivotal year, 1898, by the Vatican newspaper *L'Osservatore Romano:* "Jewry can no longer be excused or rehabilitated. The Jew possesses the largest share of all wealth, movable and immovable . . . The credit of States is in the hands of a few Jews. One finds Jews in the ministries, the civil service, the armies and the navies, the universities and in control of the press . . . If there is one nation that more than any other has the right to turn to antisemitism, it is France, which first gave their political rights to the Jews, and which was thus the first to prepare the way for its own servitude to them."[28] Given the long history of Vatican resistance to early French efforts to liberate the Roman ghetto, and Vatican insistence on the symbolic significance of a degraded Judaism for the maintenance of theological and social order, it is impossible to read this Vatican communiqué as anything other than an "I told you so." And it is remarkable for another reason, that it speaks of antisemitism as a right, especially since the Vatican was normally averse to discussion of rights at all.

The explosion of Jew hatred in France essentially ended the great turn in history that was the post-Revolution emancipation of Jews in Europe. Despite the witness of the exceptions cited above, that explosion was ignited, and then fueled, by Roman Catholicism. Later, the strategic use of overt antisemitism as a way to restore Catholicism was rejected by Leo XIII, but the French Church, for a crucial time, rallied around just such a policy. Hundreds, perhaps thousands of Catholic priests — "priests without number," in Bloy's words[29] — attended antisemitic congresses, gave Jew-baiting speeches, and, in their sermons, inflamed Catholic congregations all over France. The usual stereotypes were invoked: the Jew as revolutionary, as financier, as traitor, as the killer of Christ, as the ritual murderer of Christian children. These priests were never chastised or reined in by their bishops, who themselves never raised a protest, as one injustice followed another in *l'affaire Dreyfus*.[30] Catholic bishops in other countries, like Bishop John Ireland of the United States, spoke up for Dreyfus, but not in the country in which the scandal unfolded. "No authorized voice was raised in the Church of France against these judicial monstrosities," one Catholic Dreyfusard protested, adding, "The universal silence of the French episcopate appeared as a crime . . . The great moral authority which the Church represents was dumb . . . it did not protest, it did not wax indignant, when forgery, collusion and perjury combined in broad daylight to mislead the conscience of Christians."[31]

Most such Christians were misled, tragically, into regarding the campaign against Dreyfus as a holy cause. Another Catholic Dreyfusard wrote in 1902: "Too many Catholics, too many members of the clergy, too many so-called religious newspapers have allowed the cause of the Church to be identified with that of antisemitism. The upper clergy, it is true, and the episcopate in particular, has not gone so far; it is too careful for that. The bishops rather have kept quiet; their prudence has taken refuge in silence; but this silence itself, with which the anti-Semites have sometimes reproached them, has been taken by others as the sign of a tacit acquiescence in antisemitism."[32]

There was nothing tacit about the antisemitism of two attack-dog newspapers that led the charge against Dreyfus and Jews. *La Libre Parole* was published by a Catholic populist, Edouard Drumont. His hugely successful book of 1886, *La France Juive*, had struck like the first thunderclap of the coming storm: "The Semite is money-grubbing, greedy, scheming, subtle, sly; the Aryan is enthusiastic, heroic, chivalrous, disinterested, frank, trustful to the point of naiveté . . . The Semite is by instinct a merchant. He has a vocation for trade, a genius for all matters of exchange, for everything giving an opportunity to deceive his fellow man. The Aryan is farmer, poet, monk, and especially soldier . . . The Jewish Semite . . . can live only as a parasite in the middle of a civilization he has not made."[33] It was Drumont who first published the news that the officer on the general staff arrested as a spy was a Jew. It was Drumont whose newspaper's motto was "France for the French!" and who led the charge against Jews as "a nation within a nation."[34] This chord plucked strings that were tied to the initial idea of 1789 that Jews would get everything as individuals, nothing as a nation. Their treason now consisted in having maintained ties of kinship and peoplehood that violated the Enlightenment notion of a fully compartmentalized — marginalized — religion.

The deeper chord now struck evoked no mere treason but the arch-treason of Judas and the archcrime of deicide. The ancient religious content of Jew hatred was brought more powerfully into play than its watered-down secular offspring. Drumont concluded *La France Juive* by asking, "At the end of this book of history, what do you see? I see one face and it is the only face I want to show you: the face of Christ, insulted, covered with disgrace, lacerated by thorns, crucified. Nothing has changed in eighteen hundred years. It is the same lie, the same hatred, the same people."[35]

The face of the crucified Christ could literally be seen on the masthead of the second leading newspaper of the anti-Dreyfusard faction, a paper published daily in Paris and named, with tragic aptness, *La Croix*. The historian Stephen Wilson called it "the most important mouthpiece of Catholic antisemitism."[36] The newspaper stood as an especially authoritative voice of the Church because it was published by the Assumptionists, an order of priests in the Augustinian tradition. "Help! Help!" an editor of *La Croix* wrote on January 18, 1898. It was the paper's response to Zola's "*J'Accuse . . . !*" published five days earlier. "Are we going to leave our beloved France in the hands of Jews and the Dreyfusards?"[37]

The urgency in that question reflects the ignorance undergirding it. The anti-Semites referred to a population of Jews in France in excess of 500,000, when in reality, the number was not much more than one tenth of that, out of a total population of about 36 million.[38] Only five cities in France had more than a thousand Jews, few of whom were religious, and the vast majority of whom had worked to assimilate. Yet now French people began to feel overrun by an alien tribe, and Zola seemed the tribal spokesman.

The next day, January 19, *La Croix* evoked the threat of revolution, which always conjured up the chaos of 1789, but which, to this newspaper's readers, would also have meant the nightmare of the Commune, less than twenty years before. "The first revolution was by France on behalf of the Jews. The revolution which is in the making is waged by the Jews against the French. This is how Jews show their gratitude."[39]

In an issue published on January 28, *La Croix,* as was often done, leapt from the Dreyfus case to a larger social complaint, offering an analysis of all that threatened Catholic France in the Third Republic, from curtailments on religious education, to restrictions on clergy, to other institutional constraints implicit in a separation of church and state:

> We know well that the Jew was the inventor of our anti-Christian laws, that he put them on stage like the puppetmaster, concealed behind a cur-

tain, pulls the string which makes the devil appear before the unsuspecting audience.

The proof that the man hidden behind the curtain was the Jew emerges in the first battle engaged by Judaism — that engaged by the Syndicate [trade unions] . . .

You don't have to be a great scholar to understand that law which . . . removes the Crucifix from hospitals and schools comes from the same Pharisees who underhandedly persuaded people to free Barabbas and to vote for the death of the innocent Jesus.

The parents, the children of France have only benefited from the parochial schools just as the people of Judea only received healing from the Savior, while universal suffrage cried on all sides "death! Death!"

Who is whispering this cry today as they whispered it to Pilate?

The Savior died saying of the poor crew of opportunists, "They know not what they do."

But the organizers of the Jewish plan know well what they are doing . . . This is how the Israelite financiers, so adroit at ruining France . . . with clever phrases, are trying to persuade a naïve people that Jesus was condemned according to the law of the people . . .

The subtle alliance of all the makers of the anti-Christian laws, with the powerful Dreyfus syndicate, leaves no room for doubt. They are all of a piece. Destroy the army, destroy the religious orders and let the Jew reign! That is the goal.[40]

In Drumont's phrase, "The Jew is behind it all."[41] As has been discovered again and again by tyrants of all stripes, the great usefulness of mass antisemitism is its efficiency in offering an explanation for everything that people hate about their situations, if not their lives. In this *La Croix* diatribe, the nineteenth-century's masterly illogic is on display. The Jew is the revolution *and* the bank; the Jew is the trade union movement *and* the owner; the Jew is the solitary betrayer *and* the international conspirator. As if all this weren't enough, the Jew is also, and still, the manipulator of an innocent Pontius Pilate, the fooler of naïve crowds, the crucifier of Jesus. *La Croix* referred to the Jews as "the deicide people,"[42] and the invective of this newspaper, as well as that of many anti-Dreyfusards, shows that the judicial charge of murder, lodged against Jews, provided the electric jolt to awaken this Jew hatred. Even in a nonreligious context, the religious lie is at the heart of the loathing. Thus, in protesting the enactment of secular education laws, Drumont brought in the Blood Libel: "In the past, [the Jew] attacked the body of children; today, it is their souls which he is after by teaching them atheism."[43] Reflecting a resentment that had been festering since the Paris Commune, *La*

Croix, in January 1899, described French Catholicism itself as having been "betrayed, sold, jeered at, beaten, covered with spittle, and crucified by the Jews."[44]

At the time this was happening, *La Croix* was the most widely read Catholic publication in France.[45] It counted more than twenty-five thousand Catholic clergy among its readers.[46] It had been founded in 1880 as a vehicle for the new fervor that had taken hold in French Catholicism amid the traumas of social upheaval.[47] For example, in this period the pious had been flocking to Lourdes, a town in southwestern France where the Virgin Mary was said to have appeared in 1858. We will see more of such devotions later. Suffice to note here that they were encouraged by a clergy anxious to reconnect with an alienated populace.

The most visible manifestation of this essentially defensive fervor was the basilica of Sacré-Coeur, on Montmartre. The piety of the Sacred Heart of Jesus, emphasizing Christ's Passion, with an image of his heart pierced by his enemies, seemed to capture the mood of buffeted Catholics. Though the devotion originated during the Counter-Reformation, only now, beginning in France, were images of the Sacred Heart displayed in the homes of the pious — an indication of the assault under which Catholics felt themselves to be. Among the most active proponents of this cult were the Assumptionists, publishers of *La Croix.*

Sacré-Coeur is a white, neo-Byzantine, multitowered church that features a huge central cupola and, as acolytes, four smaller domes. Construction was begun in 1876, a monument to the defeat of the Commune, which had murdered the archbishop. The church would not be finally consecrated until after World War I, but during the Dreyfus affair it already loomed above the city like a chastising apparition, making its rebuke felt by being visible from everywhere, except, of course, from the peak of Montmartre itself. Wags say that is why the hill became the haunt of bohemians. Pablo Picasso would distort the lines of the church in one of his earliest cubist works, which had to seem to the pious like a rebuttal. On the skyline, Sacré-Coeur rivaled the Eiffel Tower, a monument to the other France, built for the 1889 centenary of the Revolution. Today the two structures still compete for the eye, but the Parisians who hated or loved the sight of the church during the affair were not responding to the lines of its architecture.

The priest then in charge of Sacré-Coeur was Père Dehon, a member of antisemitic organizations and a writer of wide influence. "The Church has no hostility against Jews individually," he wrote. "She prays for them and desires their conversion, but she cannot mitigate her basic suspicion of them."[48] Such suspicion was reduced to the question of the crucifix on classroom walls in the debate over the secularization of education. "Who was the first to throw the crucifix out into the street?" *La Croix* asked, then answered, "Hérold the Jew," referring to a Third Republic legislator.[49] Crucifixes were being removed from municipal buildings, but not from those controlled by the army. Both times that Dreyfus was found guilty, he heard the verdict while standing at attention, staring straight ahead, his eyes necessarily on the crucifix that adorned the front walls of military courtrooms.[50] At the announcement of the verdict at his first trial, the captain, ever the patriot, cried out, "*Vive la France!*" In the next day's edition, *La Croix* called this act the "last kiss of Judas."[51]

Such knee-jerk antisemitism was more than an expression of the racial hatred of Jews, and more than the traditional religious antagonism — though one priest claimed that Jesus himself was the first anti-Semite, since "He had driven out the Jews of his time."[52] Catholic antisemitism had now also become an affirmative catechetical tool. By the last decade of a century in which the Church had been rocked by one blow after another, not only in France but even in Rome, the cultivation in society at large of such prejudice served the purposes of Catholic restoration. Hundreds of thousands of people read *La Croix* and similar papers.[53] More than a hundred thousand had purchased Drumont's *La France Juive*. The powerful psychological revulsion these publications stirred against Jews simultaneously served to rekindle in a previously indifferent population feelings of attachment to the Church.[54] As the Dreyfus case dragged on into the new century, the furies it engendered did not dissipate. As French citizens chose between the general and the Jew, they also chose — because *La Croix* and *La Libre Parole* ingeniously defined the debate this way — between the Catholic Church and the enemies of France. This is why even Church leaders who might have disapproved of the vulgar antisemitism of the most vocal anti-Dreyfusards chose not to denounce it. *La Croix* expertly used, in Stephen Wilson's words, "antisemitism as a weapon in a campaign to re-Christianize the masses."[55] Furthermore, *La Croix*'s antisemitism proved to the many non-Catholic Frenchmen who stood with the army against Dreyfus that heretofore suspect Catholics were as loyal to France as they. From an institutional point of view, in other words, there were good reasons for the bishops not to muzzle *La Croix*, no matter how rabid it grew. The bishops of the French Church were silent in the Dreyfus affair, as we saw, but they were also silent on *La Croix*'s campaign of hate, which went on for years.[56] "Ordinary, human words are quite inadequate," Léon Bloy wrote of the religious order that published the newspaper, "to assess and appreciate the degradation of the priestly office represented by these terrible monks."[57]

We saw in the Dreyfus chronology that the officer was convicted for the second time in September 1899, and then almost immediately pardoned by the president of the Third Republic. The Dreyfusards in the government were no longer willing to tolerate the mischief of the extreme anti-Dreyfusards. After years of dispute, the French anticlericals were as gripped by irrational hatred as the Catholic anti-Semites. Now that they had the upper hand, the anticlericals played it. In November, police closed the offices of *La Croix*. The government ordered the Assumptionists dissolved. Most of the order went to the United States, where, among other things, they founded Assumption College in Worcester, Massachusetts. As the historian Robert Hoffman sums up what then happened in France, "Several prelates and other clerics who openly expressed sympathy with the order were punished by suspension of their salaries, which ordinarily were paid by the state. However, *La Croix* continued publication, because timely Papal intervention had secured the transfer to laymen of its ownership and operation."[58]

Because of Pope Leo XIII's last-minute initiative, *La Croix* is still published as a Paris daily, with a circulation of nearly 100,000. Its offices are in a modern building in the Eighth Arrondissement, between the Champs-Élysées and the Seine, not far from the apartment Lucie Hadamard and Alfred Dreyfus shared as newlyweds. Catholic priests own *La Croix* again, although when I visited its offices in 1998, the bright halls bustled with attractive young laypeople, men and women. My request for back issues was greeted cheerfully, and a miniskirted Parisienne soon handed me photocopies of the editions I sought, some of which I have cited here. But the issue of *La Croix* that had brought me there was published on January 12, 1998, to mark the centenary of Zola's *"J'Accuse . . . !"* That edition reviewed the coverage that *La Croix* had given to the Dreyfus affair a hundred years before. "Down with the Jews!" the paper quoted itself as having proclaimed.

"Yes, we wrote that," the editors now confessed, striking a tone entirely unlike that of the French army in 1994. "We must remember that. We must repent for that." The editors remembered as well that *La Croix* had labeled Dreyfus as "the enemy Jew betraying France," and Jews themselves as "ferocious enemies" of Christ. "The men who wrote those deadly lines are our older brothers," the present-day editors acknowledged, a straightforward statement and a judgment. "Whether Assumptionists or laymen, the editors of *La Croix* had at the time an inexcusable attitude."[59]

45

The Uses of Antisemitism

ANNAH ARENDT, quoted earlier, called the Dreyfus affair "a kind of dress rehearsal for the performance of our own time." She also called it "a foregleam of the twentieth century."[1] Perhaps both of these images suggest rather too much discontinuity between the events that preoccupied France for the decade between 1894 and 1906, and the events that dominated Europe from 1933 to 1945. Instead of a dress rehearsal, is there a way the Dreyfus affair can be seen as a kind of first act? Did the broad, successful campaign to paint Jews in the most hideous colors have direct consequences on Jews a generation later? Arendt herself suggested something like this in writing, "Certainly it was not in France that the true sequel to the affair was to be found, but the reason why France fell an easy prey to Nazi aggression is not far to seek. Hitler's propaganda spoke a language long familiar and never quite forgotten."[2]

In the great European social conflicts of the nineteenth century, the forces of reaction, especially when allied with the Catholic Church, not only in France, but also in Spain, Austria, and Rome itself, dusted off the "long familiar" language of Jew hatred. For reasons of its own ambition, the Church invested that language with new power. In the late nineteenth century, that is, antisemitism rose, like devotional piety, as a source of connection between Catholic clergy and people buffeted by modernity. They could reassert a Catholic identity, and take consolation in a new solidarity, by expressing love for Mary and/or hatred of Jews. The dynamic is clearer in France than anywhere else because of the peculiar circumstances of the Dreyfus case, but the emergence of the Roman ghetto as a last-ditch symbol of papal dominance makes visible the same invisible tragedy. The hatred of Jews, the restriction of Jews, the denigration of Jews, all of which had long served a religious purpose, had come now to serve a political purpose. And because the Church in its various organs — from publications to religious orders to the lower clergy — did so much to revivify vulgar and ignorant contempt for Jews as persons undeserving of basic human rights, and because it did so at the dawn of the new century, it bears a heretofore unacknowledged responsibility for the behavior less, in this instance, of Hitler than of his "willing" masses.[3] The Dreyfus affair stands, in other words, as a marker of the fact that Catholic antisemitism was alive and well, armed and dangerous, not just in the Crusades and the Inquisition, but at the crucial modern moment. An expressly Catholic antisemitism was a seedbed for the coming catastrophe.

France "fell an easy prey" to Nazi propaganda about Jews because many of the Vichy-era collaborators had themselves been prepared to see the Jew as the "ferocious enemy" by, among much else, reading those issues of *La Croix* which had so defined them.[4] When the editors apologize in 1998 for editorials written in 1898, they are not apologizing for an impropriety but for their newspaper's role in helping to prepare the way for heinous crimes.

Catholics all over Europe were being taught powerful lessons every time the Vatican rebuilt the gates of the ghetto, what Cardinal Cassidy has called the "antechamber" of the Nazi death camps. And the Church-enforced ghetto, far from being an item of ancient history, still stood, in sight of the pope's window, down to the year my grandfather was born. As he grew up in Ireland, then made his way to America, he'd have known, as his whole generation would have, that the Roman Catholic Church had firmly set itself against the Jews of Europe.

Compared to developments in, say, central and eastern Europe, where Jew hatred continued to have overt, widespread manifestations, antisemitism collapsed as a political force in France after 1906, when Dreyfus was vindicated. Antisemitism did not continue to define reactionary attitudes, nor did it find expression as the dominant concern of the Church, into the twentieth century. Yet the extremes of Drumont and *La Croix*, and a Catholic readiness to benefit from them, had flourished for just the wrong period of history. An irrational readiness to suspect the Jew as the original source of disorder bore the imprimatur across a generation, and before that generation passed, its readiness to suspect the Jew in that way would be quickened and exploited by the propagandists of National Socialism.[5]

The Dreyfus affair — with the crucifix on the military courtroom wall, with the perjurer Colonel Henry swearing on the crucifix, with *La Croix* leading the charge, with the Church hierarchy silent and an anti-Semitic priesthood unrestrained, with the face of Christ portrayed as turned against his own people — offers a crucial lesson for those who revere the cross. For once, the connections between Catholic theology and Catholic power, and the negation of Jews that both assume, are clear. And as we have seen repeatedly, the connection between the cross of Golgotha, as misremembered in the Christian narrative, and that negation is anything but incidental. Georges Bernanos (1888–1948), the French novelist, a reactionary himself, nevertheless summed things up, writing in 1931: "The Dreyfus Affair already belongs to that tragic era which certainly was not ended by the last war. The affair reveals the same inhuman character, preserving amid the welter of unbridled passions and the flames of hate an inconceivably cold and callous heart."[6]

46

Lucie and Madeleine

A FIGURE WHO bridged "that tragic era," felt its inconceivable cold throughout, and carried in her own experience the direct links between *La Croix* and the "Golgotha of the modern world"[1] was Lucie Hadamard Dreyfus. Twenty-four years old when her husband was first arrested, a pampered wife, she was in no way prepared for what was to come. Yet as Michael Burns's stirring account reveals, she drew on a depth of courage and savvy intelligence that enabled her to save her husband and steady her family through a tumult that never ended.[2]

When Dreyfus was sentenced to Devil's Island, Lucie sought authorization to accompany him.[3] She was denied, but allowed a visit before his departure. She wanted to hold his hand. The prison warden, fearing a secret communication through a "cabalistic sign," refused to permit it. When Dreyfus was shipped off into exile, Lucie immediately wrote a letter that she hoped would arrive at Devil's Island before he did. "Take quinine as soon as you feel feverish," she wrote, displaying the research she had done. "And moderation . . . I know that you neither eat nor drink too much, but don't work too hard; it seems that for Europeans who are not accustomed to hard labor, it's the most dangerous thing they can do . . . Above all, write to me, that's all that I desire."[4]

More than a year later, in 1896, she wrote, "I am strong, my dear Alfred, so have no fear; when you feel most discouraged, most sad, tell me all your thoughts and describe all the bitterness in your heart."[5]

"My thoughts never leave you for an instant," Dreyfus wrote back to her, "neither during the day nor at night, and if I listened only to my heart, I would write you every moment of every hour."[6] As it was, the couple exchanged hundreds of letters.

Lucie wrote letters to every person of influence she could think of. She remained at the center of the Dreyfus family's unflagging effort to get the case reopened. Some, like Hannah Arendt, would later criticize the family for being too deferential, too reluctant to raise a furor or challenge the military directly,[7] yet Lucie and her brother-in-law succeeded in recruiting an ever-wider circle of supporters, including Zola, who would do just that. In 1896, nearly two years after her husband's arrest, Lucie wrote a letter to Pope Leo XIII. With the help of a friend, she drafted it in Latin. "The wife of a Captain of Jewish extraction," she wrote, seeks in all humility the "pity and compassion of the Father of the Catholic Church." As Burns summarizes the letter, she related what had happened to Dreyfus, then added, "Christians were beginning to greatly fear that anti-Semitic prejudices have had to do with this affair." Perhaps displaying the spirit of ingratiation that would offend Arendt, she described herself as kneeling before "the Vicar of Christ . . . just as the daughters of Jerusalem had turned to Christ himself."[8] Lucie might have known of this pope's relative liberalism. She might have sensed in him the thing that, two years later, would lead to a denunciation of antisemitism; Arendt credited Leo XIII with stopping "the 'grand strategy' of using antisemitism as an instrument of Catholicism."[9] But on Alfred Dreyfus the pope maintained a strict neutrality,[10] and he never answered Lucie's letter.

An anti-Dreyfusard broadside that appeared in Paris the same year announced, "How the Dreyfus Affair Will End." All of Israel, it said, "will be chased from France, disappearing in a cloud of dust and smoke . . . engulfed forever. It is the ruin, the death, the horrible slaughter of a race butchered by the hatred it had created across the centuries."[11]

Alfred Dreyfus died in Paris in 1935 after a long illness. Lucie had nursed him through his decline. In 1940, as the Nazis closed in on Paris, a million Parisians fled the city, tens of thousands of Jews among them. Lucie was now a woman of seventy-one, slowed by age and respiratory illness. Nevertheless, without hesitation she packed what she could carry and left the city with other members of her family, including her granddaughter Madeleine Dreyfus Lévy, a twenty-two-year-old social worker. The family traveled in several automobiles, in tandem, until they finally had to split up. Lucie's two grown children, their spouses, and her eight grandchildren dispersed through the south of France. For a time, Lucie took refuge in the crowded city of Toulouse, moving into a single room in a boarding house. Madeleine was nearby, living with friends. For two years, Lucie worked to stay in touch with her scattered family — sisters, in-laws, children, grandchildren, nieces, nephews. Mainly, she wrote letters. But then, even as the anti-Jewish campaign of Vichy intensified, she began to travel, to visit them. Careful not to draw attention to herself, she stayed in cheap hotels. She wanted to be a source of encouragement for her loved ones, as she had been for her husband. A practical woman, she had brought a large supply of cash with her from Paris, money she now used to keep her relatives safe. "Don't worry about the question of money," she wrote to her grand-daughter Simone. "Tell me what you need and I will send it."[12] Madeleine returned to Paris, then went back to Toulouse. Lucie supported her as she joined the Combat underground group, helping to smuggle fugitives out of France, via the Pyrenees, into Spain.

But in 1942, Lucie's relatives began to disappear. The roundup of Jews had begun in earnest. "The world has gone mad," Lucie wrote that summer. "We have lost our way in the midst of all these massacres, of all this universal unconsciousness."[13] Most members of the Dreyfus family would make their way to the United States or England. One who refused to leave was Madeleine. Determined to stay with the Resistance, she remained in Toulouse. By now, as Burns tells the story,[14] all three of Madeleine's siblings had joined Resistance organizations, a risky venture for anyone, but especially so for these members of the best-known Jewish family in France. Lucie, for her part, also declined to flee. It is easy to imagine her wanting to stay near her courageous grandchildren.

As the pressure mounted in 1943, she began using the married, non-Jewish name of her sister, Duteil. Lucie's sister arranged a contact with a Catholic convent in Valence, a city in the southeast of France, on the Rhone River south of Lyons. Valence was a Roman settlement, on the route that Constantine would have followed in travels to and from Trier. There was another connection with that mythic center of this narrative's geography. At the time Lucie was hiding in Valence, the Jews of nearby Lyons were being terrorized by Klaus Barbie. Barbie, as we saw, was born and raised in Trier, graduating from the same school as Karl Marx. In Valence, Lucie was known only as Madame Duteil, even to the nuns in whose convent she now began to live.

Madeleine, meanwhile, refused to leave her rescue work in Toulouse, helping more and more Jews out of France. Eventually, after a curfew violation, she was arrested, and the police kept her in custody, "because of her name."[15] She was taken to Drancy, outside Paris. This was the transit camp from which more than seventy-five thousand Jews were deported to death camps. It was at Drancy, now the site of a workers' housing block, that the Roman Catholic bishops of France, represented by the cardinal archbishop of Paris, in 1997 issued a formal statement about what had happened there. "We beseech the pardon of God, and ask the Jewish people to hear this word of repentance."[16]

The bishops asked no more of Jews — not forgiveness or understanding — than that they hear. This was not a request or a new demand. The bishops were referring only to events of the war years, but the words represented a profound reversal of a century-old position. Their repentance was for the fact that, though the plight of Jews was well known to them at the time, the Church leaders of France, who had said nothing against the anti-Semites of the Dreyfus era, had said nothing again. There was, in the words of Pierre Pierrard, a "total silence of the Catholic hierarchy in the face of anti-Jewish legislation."[17] Indeed, with reference to the *Statut des Juifs*, the Vichy ambassador to the Vatican had reported back to Marshal Henri Philippe Pétain that "there is nothing in these measures that can give rise to criticism, from the viewpoint of the Holy See,"[18] an observation that was borne out as the Vichy government tightened the noose around the Jews. From the Catholic Church there was a near-total silence in 1940 and 1941, and even in 1942, as the open roundup of Jews proceeded.[19]

But now, in 1997, they saw what they had done. The cardinal archbishop of Paris, Jean-Marie Lustiger, himself born a Jew and the son of a mother who died in Auschwitz, read the statement for the others. "Today," he said, speaking in French, "we confess that this silence was a *faute*." The word was mistranslated in some English-language press accounts as "transgression" or as "fault," but the word means "sin."

"This silence was a sin."

Of the Jews taken to Drancy, ten thousand were children. Upon her incarceration, Madeleine Dreyfus Lévy turned her attention to some of them. "I can be useful and help others through my *métier* as a social worker," she wrote in a message that was smuggled out to a friend. But soon enough, in November 1943, Madeleine was taken from Drancy to Auschwitz. Three months later, weighing less than seventy pounds, she died.[20]

Meanwhile, the Catholic nuns who protected Lucie did not know who she was. Because of them, the most famous Jewish woman in France survived until Liberation. Upon returning to Paris, Lucie and other family members embarked on a new campaign, one that recalled the family's effort fifty years before to learn the truth behind the lies told of Alfred

Dreyfus. This time the family was trying to learn what had happened to Madeleine. In July 1945, Lucie, Madeleine's parents, and the others found out.

A few months later, on December 14, 1945, Lucie Hadamard Dreyfus, aged seventy-six, died in Paris, of heart disease and tuberculosis.[21] Her beloved granddaughter's body was never found, of course, but Madeleine's name and fate are carved into the headstone that Lucie shares with her husband in the Montparnasse Cemetery.[22] The marker for Captain Dreyfus is an emblem of the links in this chain — a chain of coincidence but also of consequence: from Treves to "Dreifuss"; from Herschel Marx Levi, who was embarrassed by his name, to Madeleine Dreyfus Lévy, who died for hers; from the Roman ghetto to the Paris Commune; from the True Cross to *La Croix*. Because of Lucie's large and faithful heart, the stone that remembers Alfred Dreyfus remembers Madeleine, and therefore bears forever the word "Auschwitz."

PART SEVEN

THE CHURCH AND HITLER

From Christian Anti-Judaism to
Eliminationist Antisemitism

T HIS STORY REACHES its climax in Germany, where, in the
twentieth century, the last act of Europe's hatred of Jews was
played out. The Catholic Church is faulted for its silence in the
face of the Final Solution, even for its tacit sponsorship of the
virulent Nazi antisemitism that drove the machinery of genocide. But our
inquiry must go deeper, to ask how the Church's choices led to consequences that put Jews *as Jews* at risk, and to what further Church choices
did those consequences lead, and how did they affect the fate of . . . Jews
as Jews?

Thinking of the care with which social scientists distinguish between
"strong causality" and "weak causality," with which philosophers distinguish between "necessary causes" and "sufficient causes," I have assumed
all along in this book that it would be simplistic to argue that Hitler
was "caused" by Christianity. There was nothing deterministic in the
coming of Nazism, as if it were the inevitable and preordained result of
factors beginning with the deicide charge and proceeding through the
Crusades, the Inquisition, and finally the intermingling of antimodernism
and antisemitism. Without this strain in Europe's past, Nazism, a fascist
movement organized around Jew hatred, would not have occurred, of
course, but history is not dominoes in a line, and we have seen repeatedly
how this story could have gone another way.

The peculiar evil of Adolf Hitler was not predictable, nor was Christianity his only antecedent. He was as much a creature of the racist, secular, colonizing empire builders who preceded him on the world stage as he
was of the religion into which he was born, and which he parodied. But in
truth, the racist colonizers, before advancing behind the standards of nations and companies, had marched behind the cross.

When "the Church as such," as opposed to its "sinful members," is absolved of any guilt in relation to Nazism, and when what Christian failures there were are reduced to sins of omission, as if the only crime were silence, then the real meaning of this history is being deflected. However modern Nazism was, it planted its roots in the soil of age-old Church attitudes and a nearly unbroken chain of Church-sponsored acts of Jew hatred. However pagan Nazism was, it drew its sustenance from groundwater poisoned by the Church's most solemnly held ideology — its *theology*.

In this narrative, we have watched as the ambivalence that followed Augustine was transformed into a murderous paranoia, a fear of Jewish blood invisibly corrupting a host society. That society's attempt to purge itself of "foreign" but parasitic elements, as happened with the *conversos,* involves a different — and far more lethal — kind of hatred than hatred of the mere other, which is how Christian anti-Judaism is more often discussed. That this diabolical hatred of Jews ran mostly below the surface of "normal" hatred does not change the fact that it was essential to what Nazism inherited from the Church. That is why attempts to exonerate "the Church as such," or even to reduce the Church's failure to what it did not do between 1933 and 1945, are so evasive and, finally, immoral.

To imagine that the Catholic Church was craven in the face of the challenge posed by Adolf Hitler, that it failed to oppose him out of cowardice, is to ignore, as we shall see, the brave history of Church resistance in the not too distant past — this Church was not cowardly. Nor does the Church's anxiety about Bolshevism adequately account for its relatively more benign stance toward Nazism. Not even the other usual explanation, that the Church was too concerned with its own power and prerogatives to risk defending the Jews, is enough to account for what happened. No: Nazism, by tapping into a deep, ever-fresh reservoir of Christian hatred of Jews, was able to make an accomplice of the Catholic Church in history's worst crime, even though, by then, it was the last thing the Church consciously wanted to be.

Obviously, there were precedents to Hitler's attempted genocide of the Jews — Stalin's terror-famine aimed, in 1932–1933, at the people of Ukraine[1]; the extermination of Armenians by Turkey during World War I[2]; the brutal reductions of native peoples in remote lands colonized by Europeans, beginning with the Canary Islands in 1478 and continuing in the Americas, Australia, Asia, and finally Africa at the turn of the twentieth century.[3] That an effectively genocidal exploitation of the New World was launched around the time of Ferdinand and Isabella's expulsion of Jews from Iberia is not lacking in significance, to put it mildly. A religious assumption underlies both events. The record of European imperialism from the fifteenth century on is the record of the movement from aliens defined as condemned in the afterlife to aliens defined as condemned in this life, from aliens defined as less than worthy to aliens defined as less than human. The Church, at the onset of the colonial era, was conditioned, and was conditioning others, to see unbaptized strangers as belonging to the company of devils.[4]

And the scientific Enlightenment, pursuing its decidedly nonreligious agenda, added its own twist to this legacy, especially in the figure of Charles Darwin (1809–1882). He applied his own idea of the survival of the fittest to racial, ethnic, and national groups of human beings. Like certain species of grass, some racial groups are destined to survive and thrive, while others, like less hardy grasses in the scorched savanna, are destined to wither and disappear. "At some future period not very distant as measured in centuries," Darwin wrote in *The Descent of Man,* "the civilised races of man will almost certainly exterminate and replace throughout the world the savage races."[5]

The Swedish writer Sven Lindqvist, reflecting on this legacy of European colonialism, commented, "We want genocide to have begun and ended with Nazism."[6] But it didn't. Hitler was less the beneficiary than the product of religious and racial assumptions that had their origins, perhaps, in the Jew-hating sermons of Saint John Chrysostom or Saint Ambrose, and certainly in the blood purity obsession of Torquemada. The line between these two phenomena carves the narrative arc that achieves its apogee with the "Germanizing" of Darwin, especially in Nietzsche,[7] at least as he was caricatured by the Nazis. Hitler's all-encompassing ideology of race was "a vulgarized version," in one scholar's phrase,[8] of the social Darwinism that held sway in the imperial age among both intellectuals and the crowd. It was the dominant cultural and political idea of the day. "The air he [Hitler] and all other Western people in his childhood breathed was soaked in the conviction that imperialism is a biologically necessary process, which, according to the laws of nature, leads to the inevitable destruction of the lower races. It was a conviction which had already cost millions of human lives before Hitler provided his highly personal application."[9]

So however much Hitler twisted what preceded him, it is also the case that he emerged from it. Nowhere is this more true than in the way Jews served him in that "highly personal" way. When Nazism defined Jews as the negative other, in opposition to which it defined itself, it was building on a structure of the European mind that was firmly in place before Hitler was born. If nothing else is clear by now, it is that that structure of mind had its foundation in Christianity, and moreover, that defining the Jew as the negative other had served as a self-protecting Church's modus operandi down the centuries, from the Gospel of John to the sermons of Luther, from Saint Ambrose to the anti-Dreyfusards. Antisemitism was a consistently exploited organizing principle, a pillar of Protestant and Catholic identity. Individual Jews and whole Jewish communities were periodically sacrificed to this principle. We have seen that again and again. And we have seen, too, the even more pathological turn in the European imagination when the Jew went from being the hated other to being the attached parasite that was attacking society from within.

Now we must ask the question that has run beneath the surface of this entire narrative. Since we are tracking not the flow of an impersonal force of fate but a sequence of freely made, if conditioned, human choices, how, finally, did such choices culminate in the abyss in which, among millions of others, Madeleine Dreyfus Lévy was lost? In order to answer that, we must stay in the nineteenth century a little longer, to see how, at the pivotal moment and in the decisive place, the ancient hatred of Jews combined with a newly vulnerable Church's desperate effort to survive, and to see how the choices forced by that combination directly led to the most terrible consequences.

⤞ 48 ⤝

Setting a Standard: The Church
Against Bismarck

ARL MARX DIED in 1883, at age sixty-four. By then he was an icon of the social conflict that had preceded him throughout the century of revolutions and that was widely feared to follow. "Men make their own history" — to repeat what he wrote — "but they do not make it just as they please; they do not make it under circumstances chosen by themselves, but under circumstances directly found, given and transmitted from the past. The traditions of all dead generations weigh like a nightmare on the minds of the living."[1] We saw earlier how the dead generations of Marx's rabbinic ancestors may have weighed on him, but, equally, he could have been talking here about the weight of the — to him — anachronistic religious forces that had rallied to oppose everything he hoped to bring about. What appalled Marx was the way that forces loyal to the past could conjure up the "names, battle slogans and costumes"[2] of the old ways, using them as new centers to rally around. What must have seemed his worst nightmare at the end of his life, if he allowed himself to grasp it, was the success with which his nemesis, the Roman Catholic Church, had done just that.

"Religion is the sigh of the oppressed creature," he had written in 1844, "the sentiment of a heartless world, and the soul of soulless conditions. It is the *opium* of the people."[3] Subsequent generations of revolutionaries would reduce this acute observation to a slogan with which to denigrate otherworldly faith as worse than useless in bringing about political change. But like, say, the Polish Communist regime that would condescendingly dismiss the significance of the million-strong congregation that gathered in a field outside Kraków to hear Karol Wojtyla celebrate Mass as John Paul II in 1979, those revolutionaries failed to grasp the real-world impact of unleashed religious hope.

The nineteenth century was the century of nationalism, and usually the Catholic Church is defined as its great enemy. But it is perhaps more accurate to say that the Catholic Church, in fiercely opposing nationalism, simultaneously reinvented itself around the nationalist idea. Beginning almost exactly when Marx offered his religion-as-opium nostrum, the Catholic religion launched a counterrevolution that cloaked itself in surface devotions of prayer, cult, and superstition, but that also involved an ingenious use of potent symbols, banners, rallies, and demonstrations — its own version of the "names, battle slogans and costumes" that energized the new national movements of France, Italy, and Germany. What Marx derided as otherworldly escapism — those prayer rallies and miracle celebrations and a state-defying medievalism — would, in the Catholic case, prove over the rest of the century to be a spectacularly successful exercise of wily politics, the genius of which involved a steady denial that the movement was at all political.

We have seen some of this already in the career of Pius IX, who, upon election in 1846, was regarded as the pope of progress. But in 1848, he was forced to flee from Rome when revolutionary Italian nationalists took the city. He could return in 1850 only when French and Austrian forces routed the Roman republicans, which made him the permanent enemy of Italian nationalism and, by extension, of the spirit of modernity that underwrote it. Pius IX is remembered for his two salvos fired at the age: the "Syllabus of Errors," in 1864, which condemned all of the ideas most precious to democratic pluralism, from freedom of conscience to the very idea of tolerance; and the doctrine of papal infallibility, defined by the Vatican Council in 1870. The effect of these two pronouncements was to make the pope the central figure of an unbowed Roman Catholic identity, much in the way that nationalist movements were defining themselves around strong leaders, from Napoleon to Garibaldi to Bismarck. Ironically, as the state-inventing forces hostile to the Church had, over the decades, confiscated church property in various nations, disenfranchising abbots and bishops, they contributed to the growing power of the pope[4] and the strengthening of ultramontanism, as more and more Catholics in France, Germany, and Austria looked "beyond the mountains" toward Rome for support and guidance. The broad, although not universal, acceptance by Catholics of the doctrine of papal infallibility cannot be understood apart from its character as a defensive, and essentially political, act to shore up a besieged figurehead.

The "Syllabus of Errors" and the dogma of infallibility would draw quick, even violent reaction from the enemies of the Church in France, as we saw, but also in Germany. "How many divisions has the pope got?" Joseph Stalin would mockingly ask, but as the Soviet leader's successors would learn, especially beginning in that field near Kraków, the pope has other ways of wielding power. (One might have said, Don't underestimate the Legion of Mary.) Thus, well before the "Syllabus" and infallibility, Pius IX had fired an earlier salvo, perhaps a more potent one, even if his antagonists did not recognize it as such. In 1854, he had defined the dogma of the Immaculate Conception as an article of Catholic faith, an act widely regarded as his first formal invocation of infallibility, but in any case it was the first time a pope had presumed to make a declaration of dogma apart from his fellow bishops meeting in General Council. Not all Catholics welcomed the pope's claiming such authority.

The idea that the Virgin Mary was conceived free from original sin (the dogma does not refer to Mary's conception of Jesus) was long believed by the Church, but the pope here brought it forward as a way of elevating the cultic and theological status of Mary, a move that served, not incidentally, to identify the pope with her. Mary's celebrated primacy among creatures would enhance the pope's primacy, but even more to the point, the Virgin would now be a figure around whom an insecure, alienated, and defensive Catholic population could rally.

That the apparently religious act of promulgating this dogma was equally an ingenious political response to the assault the pope had experienced only four years before became clear when, four years later, the Virgin herself "interceded" to affirm it. On February 11, 1858, the mother of Jesus is reported to have made herself visible to a peasant girl named Bernadette Soubirous in a French town named Lourdes. Over the next six months, Saint Mary is said to have shown herself to the girl another seventeen times. Within weeks of the first apparition, twenty thousand pious Catholics had converged on the village, although only Bernadette could see the Blessed Mother.[5] Most significantly, the girl reported that, in the Virgin's first appearance, she had identified herself by saying, "I am the Immaculate Conception." Pius IX made it clear that he regarded this as "a sign that vindicated his promulgation,"[6] and that confirmed his dominion as sole authority above all others in the Church. Catholics began showing up in Lourdes by the tens of thousands; even now, two million visitors a year make the pilgrimage,[7] and the miraculous stream flowing nearby has by now been credited as the source of thousands of cures. (Fifty-eight "healings" have been officially recognized as miracles by the Church. In

1999, the Church recognized a 1987 healing as having been "accomplished through the intercession of Our Lady of Lourdes.")[8]

A renewed and widely sung emphasis on the miraculous could only have been seen in the mid nineteenth century as a resounding rebuttal to the science-minded naturalism of modernity. Catholics responded to the sneering liberals' dismissal of their religion as primitive superstition by elevating in an unprecedented way what outsiders could see only as superstition. Apparitions of the Virgin suddenly became a feature of Catholic life in Europe, with hundreds[9] of her appearances reported across the continent. To keep such popular enthusiasm in hand, and to channel it in ways designed to serve the Church's social and political purposes, prelates were careful to impose standards of credibility on the phenomena, which helped maintain clerical control over the powerful manifestations of a new kind of Roman Catholicism.

In addition to Lourdes, and beginning about then, officially sanctioned apparitions over the next several decades drew thousands of Catholic pilgrims to La Salette and Pontmain in France, Pompeii in Italy, and Knock in Ireland, to name only the most famous.[10] That the background of social anxiety caused by political upheaval is an important element in such a trend is perhaps best revealed in the apparition of Mary at Fátima, Portugal, which occurred in 1917. The Virgin's prophecy, made to three shepherd girls, that Russia would be "reconverted" after spreading "errors" around the globe[11] was instrumental in rallying Catholics against the nascent forces of Communism. At the Fátima Virgin's behest, every Catholic Mass would now be concluded with a special prayer for the conversion of Russia, a tradition maintained until the 1960s. It was a coincidence when a would-be assassin gunned down John Paul II in St. Peter's Square on May 13, 1981, the Feast of Our Lady of Fátima, the anniversary of her first apparition, but this pope, too, would make powerful political use of his association with the Virgin. He made it clear that the timing of the event was no coincidence to him, and that he regarded his survival as a miracle of Mary's intervention.[12] After that, his efforts to "reconvert" Russia would prove unstoppable.

In the mid to late nineteenth century, the threats to the Church were the various nationalisms, with their own "names, battle slogans and costumes," in Marx's phrase. According to the Harvard historian David Blackbourn, whose study of the religious situation in Bismarck's Germany informs much of what follows, "The pilgrimage badges, Marian hymns, and miraculous spring-waters of the apparition crowds were a rival set of emblems."[13] More to the point, intensely felt piety among Catholics became a vital source of identity that rivaled the identity others — the Church's enemies — were finding in the intensely felt patriotisms of the newly emerging states. And though the new Catholic piety was focused on Mary, its immediate political beneficiary was the pope, who had made Mary's cause his own. The pope could use the forces generated by the apparitions to advance his own position. As Blackbourn puts it, "The pontificate of Pius IX showed that the church could successfully channel powerful currents of popular piety; that it could take up the fears and as-pirations unleashed by the apparitions of the Virgin and give them insti-tutional shape. In a period bounded by the anticlerical challenge of 1848 and the European-wide church-state struggles of the 1870s, Marian appa-ritions were a symptom of popular Catholic sentiment; they were also a potentially powerful weapon in the hands of the church."[14]

In discussing the Dreyfus affair, we noted that one group behind the re-surgence of Catholic antisemitism in France were priests of the religious order that published *La Croix,* the Assumptionists. We also noted that those priests were among the most active in promoting Lourdes as a pil-grimage site. They established the French Pilgrimage Committee, and un-der its auspices, more than three million pilgrims visited shrines in France in one year, 1873.[15] It is probably not by chance that such an outpouring of Catholic piety followed close on the heels of the Communards' murder of the Paris archbishop, and, for that matter, of Karl Marx's celebration of it.

The fact that the Assumptionists were organizers of massive exhibi-tions of Marian piety as well as sponsors of a virulent campaign of Jew ha-tred indicates that antisemitism bubbled beneath all this. As the Vatican, through the century, had repeatedly restored the ghetto of Rome as a way of resisting modernism, and as the Church in France appealed to ancient suspicions and new prejudices against the Jews as a way of reasserting its ties with an alienated population, so the entire movement of ultramon-tanism, which aimed at solidifying the papacy's central place in the Cath-olic imagination — and over the levers of Catholic control — exploited antisemitism as part of its strategy. As I first learned from the University of Toronto historian Jacques Kornberg, this was a charge made at the time, in fact, by a leading theologian of the German Catholic Church, Johann Ignaz von Döllinger (1799–1890). A professor of ecclesiastical his-tory at the University of Munich, Döllinger first gained a reputation as a vigorous critic of Luther and the Reformation.[16] Later, in articles and speeches, especially after Pius IX's campaign against modernism was in full swing, Döllinger condemned the ways that the modern errors against which the pope had set the Church were so cavalierly identified with Jews. Döllinger shrewdly analyzed the long history of Church abuse of Jews, drawing the connection between antisemitism and a Christian pursuit of power. "The fate of the Jewish people," he wrote, "is perhaps the most moving drama in the history of the world."[17] Reflecting on his own era, Döllinger set himself against the dominant twin motif of Church resistance to revolution defined as Jewish socialism and Church resistance to materialism defined as Jewish greed.

Döllinger railed against Pius IX's decision in 1867 to raise to sainthood one of sixteenth-century Spain's notorious grand inquisitors, Don Pedro Arbues de Epilae. According to Kornberg, it was Döllinger's conviction that canonizing the inquisitor "served the pope's campaign of riding roughshod over liberal Catholics. The pope was celebrating a man who had sanctioned compulsory baptism of Jews, then inflicted judicial torture to make sure these conversions were sincere. Döllinger saw the origins of the Inquisition in a drive to enhance the papacy's 'worldly dominion and compulsory power over the lives and property of men.' . . . In this sense, the decree on Papal Infallibility was the logical culminating point of the Inquisition."[18] Not surprisingly, given such an attitude, Döllinger openly opposed the Vatican Council's decree on infallibility, and was promptly excommunicated (in 1871) for doing so.[19] His position, however, was clear. As Kornberg sums it up, "Döllinger had linked medieval anti-Jewish hostility to the papacy's coercive temporal and religious dominion as well, thus emphasizing that Jews and liberal Catholics had a common enemy. Hatred of Jews was nourished by the same survivals of the Middle Ages that had produced the triumphs of Ultramontanism, the Syllabus of Errors (1864) and the decree on Papal Infallibility (1870), namely the belief that 'we alone are in possession of the full saving truth,' coupled with a lack of respect for the 'right of independent action' of others."[20]

One of the things that makes the Döllinger episode another of those all too rare sanctuaries of a better way in this otherwise unrelieved narrative is the fact, as Kornberg puts it, that this German Catholic theologian "considered nineteenth-century Catholic anti-Jewish hostility no inevitable outcome of Catholic doctrine, but rather the result of Ultramontanism's fortress mentality. Not 'essential' Catholicism, but those who wished to prevent Catholics from being contaminated by modern ideas, had made an unholy alliance with antisemitism."[21]

In 1881, Döllinger delivered an address to the "festal meeting" of the Academy of Munich, a major convocation of German Catholic intellectuals. His subject was "The Jews in Europe," and his purpose, as he said at the beginning of his remarks, was "to show how the skein [of Jew hatred] was gradually twisted which none at the present day can hope to unravel."[22] But attempt to unravel it he did. After a long description of the very history we have traced in this book, Döllinger returned to the baseline source of Christian antisemitism: "The false and repulsive precept that mankind is perpetually called upon to avenge the sins and errors of the forefathers upon the innocent descendants, has ruled the world far too long, and has blotted the countries of Europe with shameful and abominable deeds, from which we turn away in horror."[23] As a historian, he had set for himself a purpose I attempt to emulate here, to show "how History, the guide of life, points to her mirror in which past errors are reflected as warnings against fresh mistakes which may be impending."[24] Little did he know.

Döllinger was unusual. Far more than from within the Church, opposition to Pius IX's absolutist claims came from outside, and nowhere more violently than in Germany, where the complaint had nothing to do with the Church's antisemitism. In Germany's story, the nineteenth century had begun, in 1805, during the upheavals of the Napoleonic Wars, with the Austrian emperor Francis II putting aside the crown of the Holy Roman Emperor. This effectively abolished the last vestige of a dynastic tie to the medieval kings of Germany, a line that had held, however unevenly, from the time of Frederick Barbarossa, six hundred years earlier. As the century unfolded, the various Germanic states vied with one another until Prussia's decisive victory over France in 1870 put Chancellor Otto von Bismarck in the position to establish a new German empire. Bismarck, born in 1815, the pivotal year of the Congress of Vienna, was the son of Prussian aristocrats. He was a cynical visionary who put everything second to the restoration of German glory. On January 18, 1871, with Bismarck calling the shots, the king of Prussia, William I, was crowned emperor of Germany in the Hall of Mirrors at Versailles. A new Reichstag was convened in Berlin. It would be an elected body, drawing representatives from the more than two dozen states, kingdoms, duchies, and free cities that Bismarck would now begin to stitch together into one nation.

He immediately hit upon a way to do that, by uniting the various political and regional factions against what he called "the enemy within," which was the Catholic Church. Recall that the Peace of Augsburg in 1555 had ended the religious wars of the Reformation by drawing clear lines between Protestant and Catholic states within the German world, and those divisions were still rigidly observed. Prussia was the Protestant stronghold and Austria the Catholic stronghold, but Bismarck had deliberately kept Austria out of the new empire, to keep Catholics a decided minority in his Germany. The proportion was two-thirds Protestant, one-third Catholic, most of whom were concentrated in border regions like the Saar, the Rhineland, Alsace and Lorraine, all of which had been in dispute with France, and in Silesia, which was culturally attached to Catholic Poland. The Germanic patriotism of border Catholics was readily called into question, and indeed, many of them hated Prussia. Bismarck already controlled the Protestant churches, and he knew that in order to control his empire, he was going to have to control the Catholics.

Bismarck was a conservative, and much of his appeal was as a defender of the old order against the "decadence" of liberalism, yet he needed the support of liberals in the new Reichstag, so he had to find a way to make common cause with them — which was another reason to define the Catholics as an enemy. Since Pius IX had so resolutely defined the Church as a bulwark against modernism, that was easily done. Liberals, for their part, were looking to restrain Bismarck's authoritarianism, and despite this campaign's violation of the basic liberal principle of tolerance, it served their purpose to have the Iron Chancellor direct his domineering will away from them. Thus liberal and conservative elements in the new Germany joined together in attacking Catholics.[25]

The assault can be said to have begun with the elimination, in mid 1871, of the Catholic bureau in the Prussian education ministry, and then with the so-called Pulpit Law, passed by the Reichstag late in the year. This statute outlawed criticism of the state from the pulpit — a statute aimed at Catholic priests. From then on, the anti-Catholic campaign was carried on at many levels, and would involve the banishing of priests and nuns from the country, the driving of bishops from their chairs, the closing of schools, the confiscation of church property, the disruption of Church gatherings, the disbanding of Catholic associations, and an open feud with the Vatican. The campaign was called the Kulturkampf, a word invented, ironically, by a progressive politician[26] and meaning "cultural struggle," or, as the conservative American politician Patrick Buchanan might put it, "culture war." The Kulturkampf lasted from 1871 until about 1887, and was characterized by a Catholic who lived through it as "Diocletian persecution."[27] Among the reasons to consider it closely is to see the kind of resistance the Roman Catholic Church can mount, both locally and from the Vatican, when confronted with a ruthless, calculated, and systematic attempt to destroy it. The Church's response to Bismarck, in that sense, sets a standard against which its later behavior, in response to Hitler, must be measured.

In 1871, the wily Bismarck appointed as imperial Germany's first ambassador to the Vatican an aristocrat named Gustav von Hohenlohe, an appointment that on its face seemed rather politic, since Hohenlohe was a Roman Catholic cardinal. But the pope was furious at the appointment, since this cardinal had vociferously opposed the doctrine of infallibility at the General Council the year before. (Döllinger had just been excommunicated for his similar position.) The pope rejected Hohenlohe, and, following further Vatican protest, Bismarck severed diplomatic relations with the Holy See in 1872. "We shall not go to Canossa," he said, displaying the long German memory: Henry IV had been humiliated in the mountain snows of Canossa by Pope Gregory VII in 1076. Instead, the anti-Church campaign escalated. In 1872, priests and nuns were banned from teaching posts in schools, and all Jesuits were ordered out of Germany.

The next year, other religious orders were expelled, and in May the so-called May Laws were passed in the Prussian legislature. These statutes gave to the government authority to oversee the training and assignments of priests, and put bishops under the direct control of the state. Nearly the entire Catholic clergy of Prussia reacted to these laws with adamant rejection, simply refusing to obey. The state responded ruthlessly, arresting, jailing, and exiling priests and even bishops. Eighteen hundred priests were imprisoned or banished from the state, and a vast fortune in church holdings was confiscated by the government.[28] The Catholic people supported their clergy, and in many towns spontaneous rallies occurred as angry demonstrators gathered to protest when police or soldiers hauled away curates.

In 1875, Pius IX issued an encyclical from Rome that amounted to a counterattack on the Kulturkampf, and its fierce provisions remain striking. The pope declared the May Laws null and void, "since they are completely contrary to the God-given institutions of the church."[29] He urged the Catholics of Germany to engage in a strategy, as he called it, of "passive resistance."[30] And, most telling, he decreed that priests who cooperated with the German government's implementation of these policies, the so-called state-priests, were ipso facto excommunicated.[31] "Many millions" of German Catholics, in the phrase of one contemporary,[32] did just as the pope asked, and passive resistance became the prevalent response even to the escalations of the Kulturkampf.

Before long, nine of twelve Prussian bishops were in exile, but perhaps the most dramatic resistance by a bishop came, in yet another uncanny coincidence, in Trier. That city, the senior Catholic diocese in the north of Europe (a status dating back to Saint Helena), was a hotbed of opposition. The seminary had been ordered shut in 1873. Two hundred and fifty Trier priests were hauled before Prussian judges, and many were, in Blackbourn's words, "on the run disguised as peasants or riverboat captains and in one case as a Jewish hawker; others slipped into villages in the early hours of the morning to celebrate mass illegally."[33] Their bishop, Matthias Eberhard, openly defied the May Laws, and in March 1874 he was arrested. Government officials could hardly take the bishop away, however, because the Catholics of Trier immediately gathered to protest. In the words of Eberhard's contemporary biographer, "The people threw themselves to the ground, tore their hair, and one heard lamentations that pierced the soul." Bishop Eberhard raised his hand to offer a blessing to his people, at which point, "the agitation of the masses at this final moment was so great, their wailing and moaning so heartrending, and the emotion that seized even sturdy men so powerful, so overwhelming, that the whole scene is indescribable."[34] The bishop was in prison for nine months.

The Trier Cathedral, as we saw, incorporates the *Liebfrauen-kirche,* a Gothic gem dedicated to Mary. After being freed from the Prussian jail, Bishop Eberhard spoke of Trier as standing "under the protection" of the Virgin,[35] but only a few months later, he died. It is certain that his flock was devastated, especially since the government could block the appointment of any successor.

Precisely a month later, on July 3, 1876, the same day that 100,000 French Catholics gathered at Lourdes to dedicate a statue to Mary, three eight-year-old girls went picking berries in Marpingen, a village outside Trier but in the same diocese. "Above all," Blackbourn observes, "the Catholic longing for divine intercession against worldly troubles attached itself to the Blessed Virgin."[36] And that day their longing was answered when the three girls reported seeing a beautiful lady dressed in white. "Who are you?" they asked. And the lady replied, "I am the Immaculately Conceived." When reports of the apparition spread, thousands of pilgrims made their way to Marpingen. Within a week, Blackbourn says, reports put their number at more than twenty thousand. A nearby stream was found to have miraculous water, and soon Marpingen was spoken of as a German Lourdes.[37]

But this was the Kulturkampf. In summary, drawing on Blackbourn's exhaustive and impressive account, here is what happened. On July 13, Prussian soldiers moved into the village in force, and among the places they requisitioned as a billet was the priest's house. The soldiers were met with hostility and recalcitrance. When bayonet-wielding soldiers tried to clear the apparition site of pilgrims, local miners fought back, and the soldiers withdrew. The pilgrims kept coming, more than ever. The Virgin's apparitions were reported as continuing. In the first three days of September, thirty thousand pilgrims came to Marpingen, and on September 3, the Virgin made the last of her appearances to the girls. Prussian officials, meanwhile, tried to undercut the phenomenon, confiscating religious paraphernalia and trying to intimidate the devoted Catholics, who responded with the unprovocative but unmovable mulishness that had come to characterize their "passive resistance." In the fall, state authorities took the three girls into custody, interrogated them mercilessly, and sequestered them in a Protestant orphanage for more than a month.

All of this only had the effect of drawing German Catholics more firmly behind the girls and the apparitions they reported. There was no bishop in the see of Trier, and wouldn't be for five years; most priests were underground, so Church authorities could have done little to shape the response of Catholics to these extraordinary events. Even Catholics who might otherwise have been skeptical of such an outbreak of popular piety found good reasons to lay their questions aside. Especially once the children were seen as victims of the state, Marpingen became the occasion of a broad exposure of the oafish cruelties of the Kulturkampf, and as such it became a point of German Catholic pride and, increasingly, of liberal and Protestant embarrassment. "The emblems of the apparition movement — the cross that marked the spot and the flowers that adorned it, the lighted candles and pictures, the Marian hymns — became potent symbols of non-compliance with the dictates of the state," Blackbourn observes. "Again and again, Catholics in Marpingen were able to seize the moral initiative and place the authorities in a vulnerable, even laughable position. 'Innocent children' became a symbol of moral superiority against the weapons of soldiers and gendarmes."[38] Marpingen, of course, did not become a German Lourdes. In the 1950s, my pious mother would have made a beeline for it if it had. But there is a reason why she, like most Catholics, never heard of Marpingen.

For a time, it became a meeting place of numerous associations of German Catholics and a center of organization. Sodalities, rosary and prayer groups, and young people's clubs feverishly nurtured the cult of the Virgin. Liberals and Protestants regarded the whole business as proof of the primitive character of the Catholic religion, but for Catholics this devotion was a source of sustenance, identity, community, and commitment — all the things the state was trying to destroy. Catholic miners who would refuse to be unionized by socialist labor organizers formed powerful associations around the cult of the Virgin. (Catholic miners in the region went on strike in 1871, but not over working conditions or wages; they refused to work when their daily prayer meetings were canceled.)[39] Marpingen, in sum, was instrumental in the surprising German Catholic ability not only to survive, but to thrive.

Years later, as a young adult, one of the three girls would confess that their reports of the Virgin's apparitions were "one great lie,"[40] and it would become clear that, whether ill intended or not, much coaching had gone into what the girls had had to say. By the time Catholics had reason to question the apparition openly, however, the Kulturkampf was over. Marpingen had served its purpose. When the local hierarchy was reestablished, the Church had reasons not to stamp the apparition site and its miraculous waters with the imprimatur of authenticity reserved for Lourdes, Knock, and a few others. If Marpingen had become a permanent, officially sanctioned pilgrimage site, it would have competed with Trier itself, and as we shall see, drawing pilgrims to venerate the Seamless Robe, if only on rare occasions, had a value that the Church wanted to protect.

Our interest in the potent Catholic resistance to Bismarck, recall, lies in its providing a standard against which to measure Church responses to Nazism. Not all such resistance to the Kulturkampf was mystical. Anticipating Bismarck's assault on the Church, Catholics had formed the Center Party in 1870, an opposition political organization that immediately put forth candidates for election to the new imperial Reichstag. Bismarck tried to outflank the party by appealing to the Vatican, hoping Rome would disown it in return for other liberties. But the Vatican refused.

The Center Party had only one aim — to defend the Catholic population of Germany (not the institutional interests of the Church, a preference that, as we will see, would lead to problems between the Holy See and the party in the next century). In the Reichstag election of 1874, it drew 83 percent of the Catholic vote,[41] but even that bloc was a minority, so the party set about making alliances across regions and classes, joining other factions, for example, to argue for a federalist government instead of the centralized state that Bismarck wanted. As the Conservative and Liberal parties, representing Protestant and socialist factions, fell in with the restrictive Kulturkampf legislation, the Center was reduced to protest — but protest the Center politicians did. Their strong, visible participation in the political debate served as a counterpoint to the resisting mulishness of the Catholic population, but more, their organizing had specific results in the institutional ability of Catholics to respond. For one thing, the Center Party contributed to the impressive growth of the German Catholic press in the 1870s, as more and more newspapers found readers eager to know about the maneuvers of politicians who were fighting for them. When the government tried to prevent the publication, in 1875, of Pius IX's encyclical condemning the May Laws, a Center Party representative took to the floor of the Prussian legislature and read the pope's decree for all to hear, cleverly taking advantage of the constitutional provision that guaranteed the right to reprint what was said in that forum.[42]

The story of the Center Party also brings to light one of the more curious aspects of the Kulturkampf. Because Catholics found themselves in a vulnerable position, their response to the plight of the other besieged minority in the new Germany, the Jews, was not what readers of this narrative may have expected. In 1873, an economic depression jolted the young nation and soon engulfed much of Europe. Unemployment and widespread financial loss hit Germany hard. Predictably, many Germans instinctively scapegoated "Jewish swindlers" as the cause of the crash. Jewish emancipation in Germany dated only to the 1860s, and the official support of Jewish participation in German life now proved to be fragile. Economic pressures meshed with the racism of the new, pseudoscientific eugenics movement that had such appeal to intellectuals, and that reignited the rationalist antisemitism we first saw with Voltaire. At the other end of the cultural and social scale, the nascent *volkisch* nationalism that was already defining the Jew as the German negative other was spreading quickly. If you recall, it was in 1879 that the word "antisemitism" was coined by the German racist Wilhelm Marr, whose widely read *The Victory of Judaism over Germanism* served as a battle cry for what would follow.[43] The Anti-Semitic League became active in this period, laying the groundwork for the Anti-Semitic Party, which would win seats in the Reichstag in 1882. That year, the age-old ritual-murder charge would resurface in the Rhineland.[44] Adding fuel to all this was Bismarck's strategy of using a hated enemy as a means of uniting and controlling otherwise diverse political elements. As the Catholics withstood the pressures of the Kulturkampf, the Iron Chancellor willingly shifted the pressure onto the Jews.

To some extent, Catholics were like all Germans in their hatred of Jews, with peasants exhibiting the "gutter" antisemitism that stereotyped Jews as moneygrubbers, and with the middle class manifesting the "respectable" antisemitism that shunned "cosmopolitan" Jews as endemic outsiders or socialist inciters. In 1871, at the start of the Kulturkampf, a Catholic priest named August Rohling had begun circulating an anti-Jewish diatribe, "The Talmud Jew," a rehash of the old prejudices.[45] And as Catholics sought ways to reestablish ties with the majority culture, many of them, like their coreligionists in France during the Dreyfus era, would ride antisemitism's swift current back into the mainstream. None of this is particularly surprising. What could not have been predicted was the fact that, as the Prussian government pursued its repressive anti-Catholic campaign through the decade of the 1870s, a pro-Jewish countertrend developed among German Catholics, a social equivalent of the theological affirmation we saw from Döllinger. In fact, this development reinstated the positive side of the chronic Catholic ambivalence toward Jews, which we saw reflected in Augustine's intervention against Ambrose and in the papal tradition of *Sicut Judaeis*. The defense of Jews was part of the Catholic tradition too.

While hardly free of prejudice, German Catholics would prove to be considerably less antisemitic in this pre-fascist period than either German Protestants and liberals or Catholics of Austria and France. The difference was the German Catholic experience of repression at the hands of the state. In imperial Germany, Catholics and Jews alike were branded by the political establishment as sources of decadence. Catholic loyalty to the Vatican was equated with Jewish internationalism as a violation of patriotism. Perhaps despite themselves, Jews and Catholics were thrown together in the same vat of hate — one political party published an exposé showing that eight popes were actually Jews.[46]

The Catholic politicians of the Center Party would prove themselves capable of exploiting antisemitic stereotypes — for example, in their electoral competitions with the Social Democratic Party — but the Center Party would also distinguish itself by its refusal to join in the legal and political assault on Jews, especially as led by the Anti-Semitic Party. Center members had to take positions on numerous pieces of anti-Jewish "exceptional legislation," and they consistently voted to oppose, even after the Kulturkampf had ended. Referring to the various Catholic constituencies to which the party was primarily responsive, the historian Ellen Lovell Evans showed how the Center, willy-nilly, became an advocate for others. "In defending these minority elements, the Center became a party which championed the civil rights of other minorities as well: of Poles and Alsatians who were discriminated against not primarily as Catholics but as aliens; of Protestant groups like the Danes and Hanoverians; and even the rights of Marxists and Jews threatened by exceptional legislation of the type condemned by the Center. Thus this essentially conservative party was led to a surprisingly liberal position on civil rights in general."[47] The Catholic position was summed up by Ernst Lieber, the Center Party leader from 1893 to 1902: "We, as a minority in the Reich, have not forgotten what happened to us, and for that reason, even if more elevated considerations and more fundamental motives did not restrain us, we cannot offer to forge the weapon to be used against the Jews today, the Poles tomorrow and the Catholics the day after that."[48]

As the years of the Kulturkampf wore on, it became clear to most Germans that the Catholics were not going to yield. In particular, the vast majority of Catholics were not going to distance themselves from the Vatican. On the contrary, the longer the struggle with the repressive Prussian government lasted, the more devoted the German Catholic Church became to the pope. As the conflict continued, Catholic voices critical of the Vatican simply ceased to be heard. Among Germans, the Center Party was making its argument by appealing to Germany's own tradition of suspicion of state absolutism, chipping away at the Protestants' and liberals' assumption that authoritarian oppression would not be directed at them — and chipping away at the solid anti-Catholic alliance in the legislature. In response to increasingly anxious hopes by some in the government that a compromise with the Catholics might originate with a compliant gesture from Rome, the Center deputy Ludwig Windthorst declared in 1875, "Prince Bismarck is the only person who can possibly restore peace, and he will restore it on the day when he is convinced that he is on the wrong track. [Laughter from the house.] And this conviction *will* come to him, believe me, gentlemen, even though he may as yet have no suspicion of it."[49]

In 1878, the uncompromising Pius IX died, and Berlin hoped that a new pope might accept some of the restrictions on Church life that the German government had imposed. Leo XIII, the pope to whom Lucie Dreyfus would write her pleading letter for support, was a pragmatist compared to his predecessor. Intent on defusing the Kulturkampf, Leo nevertheless joined with the German Church in insisting on a full restoration of its rights and property. In the same period, Bismarck found that, on a number of legislative and budget matters, he needed the support of the by then pivotal Center Party. Gradually, Bismarck yielded. The Church had successfully resisted to his face the man who, according to an admiring Henry Kissinger, was "outmaneuvered" by nobody.[50]

The restrictive anti-Catholic measures were taken off the books, expelled priests and bishops were allowed to return to Prussia, the Church's de facto supremacy in matters of ecclesiastical discipline and appointments was reestablished, and the vacant sees and pastorates were filled. In 1881, Michael Felix Korum, known as a vigorous defender of the papacy, was consecrated as the bishop of Trier.[51] In the end, because of effective Catholic resistance at every level, and because of its own essential injustice, the Kulturkampf proved, in Blackbourn's summary, to be "an embarrassment to Prussian state and liberalism alike. Conversely, the Catholic Church emerged from the conflict unbowed, even with enhanced moral authority."[52] In 1882, the Vatican and Berlin resumed diplomatic relations. When Karl Marx died the next year — recall that his international reputation, following his celebration of the Paris Commune, dated to the year of the Kulturkampf's beginning — the tide could seem to have turned in the Church's favor, although in Germany it would take the rest of the decade for remaining anti-Catholic measures to be diluted or lifted altogether.

By 1891, the Catholic Church in Germany was secure, and a great celebration occurred in Trier, presided over by Bishop Korum. As one of two dioceses whose bishop had actually been jailed (the other was Cologne), the prestige of Trier was high. The solemnities evoked the former glories of Constantine's northern capital and of the seat of the senior elector of the Holy Roman Emperor. For only the second time in the nineteenth century, the Seamless Robe was taken out of the *Heiltumskammer,* the hidden chamber that floats above the high altar of the cathedral, and put on display. The last time the sacred relic had been shown, in 1844, half a million pilgrims had come to Trier to venerate it, but now more than four times that number came.[53] This outpouring of publicly expressed and massively organized devotion amounted, of course, to far more than a religious affirmation. Because of all that the Church had suffered, and in light of its unmitigated triumph, the cultic celebration of the Seamless Robe that brought throngs into the squares and streets of Trier, at the feet of one of the most ultramontane bishops of Germany, was nothing less than an ongoing political victory rally, an unforgettable revelation of how the Church, when it wants to, can resist.

⇥ 49 ⇤

Eugenio Pacelli and the Surrender
of German Catholicism

EUGENIO PACELLI WAS born in 1876, the year after Pius IX's encyclical challenging Bismarck. Raised in a family closely tied to the Vatican, he entered the seminary as a young man, but instead of being trained in theology, his education concentrated on canon law. He was ordained in 1899, the year after Leo XIII had condemned the heresy of "Americanism,"[1] the latest in the papacy's salvos against what it perceived as the corruptions of the modern world. Leo XIII is remembered as a social liberal (his 1891 encyclical *Rerum Novarum* was read as an endorsement of the labor movement), and he successfully defused various anticlerical campaigns like the Kulturkampf, but he regarded the Church as "a perfect society," and the Vatican was to be the living embodiment of that perfection. Thus he ruled the Church as a rigid authoritarian. He devoted his time as pope to marshaling a spiritual and ecclesiastical dominance of the Vatican to replace its loss of temporal sovereignty over the Papal States. The young Pacelli was tapped to play a role in the next phase of that effort.

Leo died in 1903. His successor, Pius X (1903–1914), continued the campaign to make the papacy spiritually sovereign over the religious lives of Catholics everywhere. But more than that, the aim was to control Church activities in every nation, from the licensing of schools to the appointment of bishops. Such a vision required nation-states to deal with the Church through the Vatican rather than through local institutions, many of which had, in any case, been weakened by the property seizures and clergy expulsions that had marred church-state relations during much of the nineteenth century. Key to Pius X's program of centralizing Church authority in an absolutist papacy was a new Code of Canon Law that would give the pope unprecedented power over every aspect of Church life. (Other popes, like Innocent III, had made absolutist claims, of course, but not over the minutiae of Catholic ritual, practice, and piety.) Pacelli was one of two Vatican priests who spent more than a decade developing the code, which was finally promulgated in 1917. Canon 218 defines the pope's authority as "the supreme and most complete jurisdiction throughout the Church, both in matters of faith and morals and in those that affect discipline and Church government throughout the world."[2]

In Europe, where church and state were traditionally intermingled, with much overlap of political and religious authority (schools, the appointment of those bishops), the implementation of the new code required the cooperation of governments, which led to Pacelli's next assignment. John Cornwell, Pacelli's biographer, points out that the task of negotiating treaties (concordats) that recognized the freshly claimed prerogatives of the papacy fell to Pacelli. In 1917, shortly after his consecration as bishop, and after having successfully concluded treaties with Serbia and other countries, Pacelli went to Munich as papal nuncio. Cornwell writes that his "principal task in Germany was now nothing less than the imposition, through the 1917 Code of Canon Law, of supreme papal authority over the Catholic bishops, clergy, and faithful."[3] To that end, he set out to renegotiate existing concordats with the German regional states. Ultimately he hoped for a concordat with the German nation itself, one that would solidify Vatican power, especially in the matter of the appointment of bishops, which, as we have seen, had dogged papal-German relations going back to the eleventh century.

The anti-Catholic suspicions of Protestants and liberals of the Weimar Republic, which governed Germany from 1919 until 1933, were not the only obstacle to the new definition of Church authority. Even taking into account the legacy of ultramontanism, Germany's bishops were accustomed to holding sway in their own sphere, and the Catholic Center Party, soon to be one of the most powerful institutions in Weimar, had always defined itself as a defender of the Catholic people, not simply of the institutional Catholic Church[4] — a distinction that might not serve the Vatican's purposes under the new code.

Since the Kulturkampf, the Center Party had become a truly successful political organization. In 1919, it drew six million votes, second only to the Social Democrats. Occupying the contested middle ground in the mounting chaos of the Weimar era, the Center would provide five chancellors in the ten governments that came and went from 1919 to 1933.[5] Alas, this rise to influence in forming coalitions was accompanied by a lessening of the party's need, and readiness, to see its fate linked with that of other vulnerable groups, in particular the Jews. The responses of the period are complex. The Center Party had continued to oppose legislation aimed at Jews, and its leaders consistently rejected the gutter antisemitism that began more and more to infect public discourse as Weimar's economy faltered. Indeed, these manifestations of more bitter Jew hatred drew criticism from the Vatican, too, in ways that would not happen after 1933.

But at the local level, in the crisis years of the 1920s, Center politicians proved as capable of exploiting the antisemitic prejudices of Catholics as the party's rivals did of their constituents, and the Center press was increasingly given to appealing to the anti-Jewish instincts of readers, with emphasis, say, on "usurious Jewry."[6] Nevertheless, throughout the twenties, the Center Party was a moderating influence on German politics, and Catholics concentrated in rural areas and smaller cities kept their distance from the kind of rabble-rousing antisemitism that began to appear in big cities like Berlin.[7] Still, many Catholics, especially among the peasantry, the workers, and the petty bourgeois, were increasingly drawn into the scapegoating of Jews, and more and more local Catholic priests began featuring attacks on Jews in their sermons. Such manifestations were, in Blackbourn's words, a "serious embarrassment" to the Center leadership, and eventually, as the antisemitic political parties gained power and began openly to seek Catholic support, they became a serious threat to the Center as well. Yet it successfully maintained its base through this crucial period. As Adolf Hitler emerged in Germany, but before he took control, he and his party could count hardly at all on Catholics for their votes.[8]

But the leaders of the Center Party were not uniformly as malleable as Pacelli wanted them to be. For example, they consistently ignored Pacelli's and the pope's express wish that they keep the party out of coalitions with the left-wing Social Democrats.[9] Once the new Code of Canon Law was imposed on German Catholics, with the approbation of the German state, it would end such defiance. That is the fateful background to what followed when Hitler, soon after coming to power in early 1933, entered into treaty negotiations with Eugenio Pacelli, by then the powerful cardinal secretary of state.

A seismic shift had occurred in Catholic attitudes toward the Nazis, partly related to Hitler's having taken over the government, but also related to the Vatican's eagerness to deal with the Führer. Within a week of his first cabinet meeting, in early March 1933, Hitler received a friendly message from Pacelli, who was moving quickly to take advantage of a long-awaited opportunity to achieve the *Reichskonkordat*. The message included, as the Vatican envoy told Hitler, "an indirect endorsement of the action of the Reich chancellor and the government against Communism."[10]

Even an indirect endorsement meant everything to Hitler as he sought to establish his legitimacy at home and abroad. In these early months of 1933, Catholic leaders went from being Hitler's staunch opponents to his latest allies. This transformation was dramatically symbolized by the fact that in 1932, the Fulda Episcopal Conference, representing the Catholic hierarchy of Germany, banned membership in the Nazi Party[11] and forbade priests from offering communion to anyone wearing the swastika; then, on March 28, 1933, two weeks after Pacelli offered his overture to Hitler, the same Fulda conferees voted to lift the ban on Catholic membership in the Nazi Party.[12] The bishops expressed, as they put it, "a certain confidence in the new government, subject to reservations concerning some religious and moral lapses."[13] Swastika bearers would now be welcomed at the communion rail. Cornwell writes, "The acquiescence of the German people in the face of Nazism cannot be understood in its entirety without taking into account the long path, beginning as early as 1920, to the Reich Concordat of 1933; and Pacelli's crucial role in it; and Hitler's reasons for signing it. The negotiations were conducted exclusively by Pacelli on behalf of the Pope over the heads of the faithful, the clergy, and the German bishops."[14]

Pacelli's negotiations must be seen in the full context of the siege under which Roman Catholicism had found itself in Europe in the previous decades, but there was a distinction in his mind, and in his purpose, between a defense of the Catholic Church in Germany and a defense of the Vatican. Indeed, his disregard for the prerogatives of the local Church is indicated by his readiness to ignore, and even to deceive, important figures in its hierarchy.[15] Whatever its stated goal, the effect of Pacelli's maneuvering was hardly to advance the standing of the German Catholic Church. "When Hitler became Pacelli's partner in negotiations," Cornwell observes, "the concordat thus became the supreme act of two authoritarians, while the supposed beneficiaries were correspondingly weakened, undermined, and neutralized."[16]

The first true beneficiary was Hitler himself. The *Reichskonkordat*, agreed to on July 8, 1933, was his first bilateral treaty with a foreign power, and as such gave him much-needed international prestige, whether the

Vatican intended it or not. (The Vatican newspaper *L'Osservatore Romano* published a statement on July 2 saying that the concordat should not be taken as a moral endorsement of Nazism,[17] and Pacelli would make the same point later.) Yet the price Hitler demanded for the concordat was stiff: the complete withdrawal from politics (and therefore from any possible resistance to the Nazis) of all Catholics *as Catholics*. In negotiations with German officials, Pacelli had offered the 1929 Lateran Treaty between Italy and the Vatican as a model for the concordat, and Hitler would surely have been aware that the pope had agreed there to Mussolini's demand that the antifascist Catholic political party, Partito Popolare, be suppressed.[18] Bismarck had sought to have the Vatican disown the Center Party, which it refused to do. Now Hitler made that a key demand, and the Vatican acquiesced. On July 4, in the final runup to the agreement, the leader of the Center Party, Heinrich Brüning, who had served as Germany's chancellor from 1930 to 1932, consented "with bitterness in his heart to dissolve the party."[19] Hitler wanted the Center Party gone because it represented the last potential impediment to his program. In truth, Pacelli wanted it gone for the same reason — for the sake of his own program. But there is evidence that the unseemly rapidity of the Center Party's demise startled Pacelli, and, perhaps, embarrassed him.[20] Even before the Concordat was formally signed, the Center Party ceased to exist.

Hitler was not Bismarck. As would quickly become clear, the Nazis were prepared to stop at nothing to achieve their goals. Soon enough, blood would be flowing in the streets, the opposition press shut down, and the constitution abrogated. But in 1933, Hitler was not remotely what he would become, and the connivance of the Roman Catholic Church in these months of transition is part of what enabled him to emerge as a dictator. The Catholic people — there were more members of Catholic youth associations than there were of the Hitler Youth — were the last possible obstacle in Hitler's way. As a baptized Catholic himself, he would have been intimately aware of the courageous and wily history of the victorious Catholic campaign during the Kulturkampf. But instead of being called by the Church — by the pope himself — to "passive resistance," as their parents and grandparents had been, Catholics were encouraged to look for what they had in common with Nazis. And they would find it.

The *Reichskonkordat* effectively removed the German Catholic Church from any continued role of opposition to Hitler. More than that, as Hitler told his cabinet on July 14, it established a context that would be "especially significant in the urgent struggle against international Jewry."[21] The deep well of Catholic antisemitism would be tapped, to run as freely as any stream of hate in Germany. The positive side of the long-standing ambivalence, which had again and again been the source of impulses to protect Jews, would now be eliminated, allowing the negative side to metastasize. "This was the reality," Cornwell comments, "of the moral abyss into which Pacelli the future Pontiff" — he would become Pius XII in 1939 — "had led the once great and proud German Catholic Church."[22]

50

The Seamless Robe in 1933

I N THE HOLLYWOOD EPIC *The Robe,* a Roman centurion, Marcellus, played by Richard Burton, wins the tunic of Jesus in a dice game. The garment is "his first battle trophy, a victory over the King of the Jews." It is at this point that the centurion's troubles begin. Later, a Greek slave, Demetrius, played by Victor Mature, warns him, "You think it is the Robe that has cursed you, but it is your conscience." The film ends with a chastened Richard Burton declaring of the Robe, "It changed my life. In time it will change the world."[1]

Tradition tells us that the Seamless Robe was brought to Trier by Helena, the mother of Constantine, after her True Cross pilgrimage to the Holy Land. The Robe as a gambler's prize had its origin in the psalmist's reference, "They divide my garments among them, and for my raiment they cast lots."[2] We saw how it emerged as one of the imagined details that owed its presence in the original Passion narrative to the phenomenon defined by John Dominic Crossan as "prophecy historicized," rather than as "history prophesied," as such details are more traditionally understood. Once embedded in that narrative, a later generation used the Seamless Robe as a proof of Jesus' foretold Messiahship, a proof to be held against "the Jews," who, despite its source in one of their own texts, nevertheless denied it. The Robe, that is, emerged early on as a symbol of what first went wrong between the followers of Jesus and the post-Temple remnant of Israel that chose another way.

Thus the poignance of the Robe's presence in Trier at the time of the First Crusade, Europe's first pogrom, with its starting point in Trier; at the time of the medieval banishing of Jews, some of whom carried away a family name taken from the place; at the time of the great struggle to define the culture of Europe univocally under the Holy Roman Emperor, one of whose electors was the bishop; and at the time of the dawning of the secular Enlightenment, whose political champion, Karl Marx, was born within a few blocks of the Robe.

Through all of these centuries, the mystique of the Robe increased by the garment's being rarely seen. On occasions of jubilee, the bishop ordered the tattered garment to be taken out of its bejeweled vault. There were only three such occasions in the twentieth century. Recall that on one of them, I was present as a boy of sixteen, admitting a first doubt about the thing itself, a qualm that would live in the vault of my unnerved devotion for years. It was 1959, at the end of the postwar occupation era, and the Catholics of Trier were giving thanks for the reconstruction of the city, including its ancient churches, which symbolized the reconstruction of West German virtue in the great contest with demonic Communism. I can still see the coarsely woven tunic, pressed like a lab specimen between plates of glass that floated in the air above the throng of heads — the men hatless, the women in mantillas and scarves — across which I gazed from beside my stunned mother in the balcony reserved for American VIPs. Perhaps the size of the Robe caused me to doubt. It seemed a glorified T-shirt, only large enough to fit a child.

The century's prior jubilee when the Robe was on display, as I learned from a tour guide on my recent trip, occurred in 1933. "German Catholics," she had said with a wince, "thought things would work out well." My visit was in July, and I have since learned that sixty-five years before, the festive demonstration took place in July as well. In fact, the occasion for the 1933 celebration, the first since the 1891 display in honor of the end of the Kulturkampf, was the *Reichskonkordat.* Initialed on July 8, the treaty was formally signed on July 20. The signatories were the negotiators: for the Vatican, Eugenio Pacelli; for Berlin, Franz von Papen, the German vice chancellor, the man who, not seven months before, had persuaded the senile Weimar president Paul von Hindenburg to appoint Adolf Hitler as chancellor. Papen was a Catholic aristocrat, a victim of his own condescension, for he apparently thought that he could control the peasant politician from Austria.

The bishop of Trier, Franz Bornewasser, had been one of Hitler's strongest Catholic supporters, having, for example, urged voters in the decisive March 1933 election to support Catholic National Socialist candidates instead of the Center Party slate.[3] Bornewasser, it can be said, at least came to these views honestly, for his selection as bishop in 1922 had already been a political act designed to tilt the Church toward the nationalist purposes of a recovered Germany.[4] After World War I, France administered the region around Trier, which was nearly as Gallic as Teutonic. In Paris, it was known as "Rive Gauche du Rhin," and when the bishopric of Trier fell vacant in 1921, France wanted the Church to appoint a prelate who would favor its territorial designs over the Rhineland and the Saar, a coal-rich area with a population of 800,000. As it happened, the bishopric of Cologne, too, had just fallen vacant, and the same pressures were applied there. The Vatican at this point had one eye fixed warily on Russia, now led by Bolsheviks, and the other on France, which loomed on the continent. Though nominally Catholic, France was still a bulwark of anticlerical liberalism, and the wounds of the Dreyfus affair were far from healed. The Holy See, in other words, had reasons for wanting the political counterweight of a recovered Germany, whether dominated by Junker Protestants or not.[5]

After the chaos of the postwar Weimar years, the overwhelmingly Catholic population of the Rhineland was politically split, with some favoring full union with France, some favoring Berlin, and most, like the Center Party's regional leader Konrad Adenauer, angling for independence. Adenauer was the *Oberbürgermeister,* or mayor, of Cologne. He defined himself as a Rhinelander first and a German second, an attitude that would cause him trouble when the times demanded an uncritical nationalism. That a Catholic leader like Adenauer and the bishop of Trier were on opposite sides of the increasingly bitter struggle is emblematic of the tradition of Catholic ambivalence, the balance of which was quickly lost when the Vatican shifted its weight. And one ready lever in the shifting of such weight, as always, was antisemitism. To take only one example of the still lively power of on-the-ground Catholic hatred of Jews, waiting for Hitler to exploit it, consider that the Catholic Peasant Association in Trier (a kind of grange), had, between 1884 and 1918, brought 13,500 cases of complaint against various traders, merchants, and moneylenders, all charging usury. The association exploited peasant insecurities focused on the deadly stereotype of money and Jews as an organizing strategy.[6]

The significance of the mostly hidden struggles in the districts around Trier would become quite apparent in 1935 when Hitler abruptly reclaimed control of the Rhineland for Germany. Though a first step toward war, his move was widely supported in the region because his local allies had helped prepare the people for it. One of those allies was Bishop Bornewasser, who himself marked the distance German Catholics had come from the day when his predecessor, Bishop Eberhard, had suffered an imprisonment that probably killed him. That is why Bornewasser's support of the Nazi slate in the March 1933 election — again, opposing the Catholic Center Party — was so important. Once Hitler came fully into power that spring, however, Bornewasser's support, among Catholics, would become far from unique. In the Trier Cathedral, before a congregation of Catholic youth, the bishop declared that "with raised heads and firm step we have entered the new Reich and we are prepared to serve it with all the might of our body and soul."[7]

This is the context in which to understand how the impulse of Bishop Korum, who in 1891 brought German Catholics to Trier to celebrate the Church's victory over and against the government, could be reversed in a generation by Bishop Bornewasser's invitation to Catholics to come and celebrate the Church's alliance with the government. The bishop gave ultimate expression to his enthusiasm by inviting Hitler himself to come to Trier for the solemn exhibition of the Seamless Robe. On July 20, the very day the *Reichskonkordat* was signed in Rome, Hitler sent his regrets.[8] Ironically, his declining to join the celebration probably had to do with his reluctance to be too closely identified with the Catholic Church, which, after all, had unsuccessfully lobbied for just such a concordat throughout the thirteen years of the Weimar Republic. German Catholics, aware of Hitler's own Catholic roots, had reason to take the treaty as a signal that their long ordeal of second-class citizenship, dating to the Kulturkampf, was coming to an end.

In Trier, Catholics were disappointed that Hitler would not attend. In his place, however, he sent the Catholic favorite, the man who had negotiated the *Reichskonkordat*. "Vice Chancellor Franz von Papen was among the pilgrims to the Cathedral of Trier," a contemporary account reports, "where the holy vestments of the Savior were exhibited late in July in the presence of 25,000 other pilgrims from all parts of the country. Colonel von Papen officially represented President von Hindenburg and Chancellor Hitler at Trier."[9] Bishop Bornewasser and Papen together sent a telegram to Hitler on July 24 reconfirming their "steadfast participation in the work of resurrecting the German Reich."[10]

The concordat's significance to Hitler at that crucial moment is hard to overemphasize. "The long drive against the alleged atheistic tendencies of our Party is now silenced by Church authority," one Nazi Party organ crowed. "This represents an enormous strengthening of the National Socialist government."[11] We saw that *L'Osservatore Romano* had refuted the claim that the concordat meant Church approval of Nazism, but the German bishops made it seem otherwise. The full import of the Vatican agreement with the Third Reich was perhaps best described by a later dispatch from those same bishops. They sent it from their formal meeting at Fulda two eventful years later. On August 20, 1935, the prelates defended Pius XI (1922–1939) by presuming to remind Hitler that His Holiness had "exchanged the handshake of trust with you through the concordat — the first foreign sovereign to do so . . . Pope Pius XI spoke high praise of you . . . Millions in foreign countries, Catholics and non-Catholics alike, have overcome their original mistrust because of this expression of papal trust, and have placed their trust in your regime."[12] Cardinal Michael Faulhaber of Munich, in a sermon in 1937, declared, "At a time when the heads of the major nations in the world faced the new Germany with reserve and considerable suspicion, the Catholic Church, the greatest moral power on earth, through the Concordat, expressed its confidence in the new German government. This was a deed of immeasurable significance for the reputation of the new government abroad."[13]

Hitler had other reasons for welcoming the concordat, one to do with his plans for the army, and the other with his plans for the Jews. A "secret annex"[14] to the treaty, finalized some months after the promulgation and not publicized, granted Catholic clergy an exemption from any conscription imposed on German males in the event of universal military service. Since Germany was still expressly forbidden by the terms of the Treaty of Versailles to raise a large army, Hitler could regard this provision as the Vatican's tacit acquiescence before a campaign of German rearmament. As Papen wrote to Hitler at the time, this provision was important for Germany less "for the content of the regulation than for the fact that here the Holy See is already reaching a treaty agreement with us for the event of general military service."[15] Papen concluded his brief on the secret annex with a note of smug ingratiation. "I hope this agreement will therefore be pleasing to you."[16]

We noted earlier that an article in the July 2, 1933, issue of *L'Osservatore Romano* had insisted that no Vatican endorsement of Nazi teachings should be inferred from the concordat,[17] but Hitler himself saw it otherwise. The treaty with the Holy See had both spiritual resonance and political implication, for it was a world-stage rebuttal to those who accused him of being antireligious, and it established diplomatic recognition from the famously neutral Vatican at a time when other powers were still eyeing him with suspicion.[18]

Especially in hindsight, defenders of the Vatican's readiness to enter into such a treaty with Hitler insist that it was nothing more than realpolitik diplomacy designed to safeguard the political and social rights of Catholics in a hostile climate, a way in which the Church hoped to temper Nazi extremes to the benefit of all concerned. In this view, Pacelli's own wariness at the time of the treaty is emphasized. But is it conceivable that Pacelli would have negotiated any such agreement with the Bolsheviks in Moscow? Gordon Zahn, the American scholar of Hitler-era German Catholicism, reports that Cardinal Faulhaber and other bishops dismissed such a notion, and in the act defined the concordat as a Church endorsement of the Nazi regime.[19] Pacelli's defenders say he wanted the treaty as a basis for future protests against Nazi excesses, and indeed the Church would use it as such. But to Catholics in Germany at that pivotal time, including leaders like Bornewasser, the concordat was, and would remain, the soul of a compliant Catholic conscience that saw the way clear to support Hitler and his program. Even after the true nature of that program was laid bare, and after numerous provisions of the treaty had been violated, the Vatican would never repudiate the concordat. Many bishops and priests, even through the paroxysms of the war, cited the intact Vatican treaty as a sign of the Third Reich's ongoing legitimacy, allowing — no, requiring — German Catholics to carry out its orders.

Despite the contrasts with the city's earlier prelates, it is probably no surprise that one of Hitler's most enthusiastic backers in 1933 should have been the bishop of Trier. Taking the long view, many Catholics saw the Vatican-Berlin agreement as promising a return to the Sacrum Imperium[20] that had been given its first expression by Trier's own Constantine, and that had reached its apogee under the Holy Roman Emperor, whom Trier served as an elector. The shadow of Constantine had never fully lifted from Trier. The *Aula Palatina,* the enormous throne hall of his otherwise ruined palace, had been restored, as we saw, and transformed by the Prussians into a Lutheran church. The golden cross that hung in the vast imperial basilica had never seemed more full of implication. *In hoc signo:* Constantine's vision had changed the religious and martial imaginations forever.

The Eagle and the Cross, about which we will see more, was the name of the Catholic group — consisting of bishops, priests, theologians, and politicians, including Papen — that saw the advent of the Third Reich as a way to restore the medieval ideal of a united throne and altar. That ideal had been lost to the hated forces of Enlightenment liberalism, which, as Catholics told themselves, invariably led to godless Bolshevism. If Hitler was anything, wasn't he the enemy of that?

So Catholic euphoria was widespread in the summer of the concordat. The Te Deum was sung in Catholic churches across the country.[21] Once the treaty was formally ratified by both governments in September, a pontifical Mass was celebrated by the papal nuncio in an overflowing cathedral in Berlin. Above the worshipers, flags emblazoned with the papal colors and the swastika hung side by side. It was a long way — although a short time — from the prohibition of the Nazis' wheel of a broken cross in Church. The preacher at the Berlin Cathedral that day praised Hitler as "a man marked by his devotion to God, and sincerely concerned for the well-being of the German people."[22] At least one bishop enlisted in the SS.

Obviously, these churchmen had been deluded by Hitler, and they had deluded themselves. Soon enough, Hitler's pressure on Catholic youth groups, his assault on confessional schools, and his curtailment of Church prerogatives theoretically protected by the concordat would prompt criticism from a minority of bishops, including Cardinal Faulhaber of Munich, who delivered a series of Advent sermons rebutting Nazi assaults on "Jewish Scriptures."[23] A number of heroic priests, like Alfred Delp and Bernhard Lichtenberg, would boldly challenge Nazi policies: Delp was hanged in Berlin, and Lichtenberg "died en route to Dachau."[24] But in the end, a very small percentage — 1.5 percent — of German priests were imprisoned during the war.[25] About a thousand priests died in Dachau, but of those nearly nine hundred were Poles,[26] almost certainly interned not for protests but as part of the Nazi campaign against the Polish intelligentsia. Where nine of twelve bishops of Prussia alone had been exiled in the Kulturkampf, the total number of Catholic bishops driven from their seats during the twelve years of the Nazi onslaught was three.[27]

The spirit of resistance that had given rise to the fervor around the apparitions at Marpingen would even be rekindled when Catholics began to feel Hitler's vise closing on them, too, with Catholic pilgrims returning to the village, but not in anything like the original numbers.[28] Ultimately, with the 1937 encyclical *Mit Brennender Sorge* ("With Burning Sadness"), the Nazi regime would draw chastisement from Pope Pius XI himself, a rebuke the news of which Hitler tried to keep from Germans, perhaps especially Catholics. The encyclical complains primarily about Hitler's violations of the concordat.[29]

Only in hindsight is it possible to grasp the truly demonic character of Hitler's ambition, and it is possible to see early Church support for him as an attempt, however naïve, to influence the course of his movement. But it is important to acknowledge that the real nature of Hitler's purpose in one regard was evident at the start — his purpose with regard to Jews.

His declaration of war on "non-Aryans" was blatant. Not only was the rhetoric of his earliest writings and speeches built around attacks on Jews, but the very first organized action of the National Socialist government, on April 1, 1933 — less than a month after the election and little more than a week before the Enabling Act exempted it from all constitutional restraints — was an open assault on Jews everywhere in Germany. An apparently random Nazi brutality had been demonstrated before, especially by the party's private armies, the SA and the SS, but now the so-called boycott of Jewish businesses was launched across the nation. Jewish establishments and individual Jews were subjected to cruel and often violent pressures. The Nazis, that is, celebrated the final unification of the party and the state by going after Jews. Shops were not just boycotted but burned. Jews were not just shunned but attacked. It was a "dress rehearsal," to use Arendt's phrase, for the awful assault of Kristallnacht five years later.

The Catholic Church's response to this display of government-sanctioned Nazi brutality consisted of a foreboding silence and of an effort to protect Catholics, particularly Catholic converts from Judaism, at the expense of Jews. One cardinal, defending his refusal to condemn the April 1 boycott, declared that it was "a matter of economics, of measures directed against an interest group which has no very close bond with the Church."[30] Nor was there any recorded Church protest against the next large spectacle of anti-Jewish violence, which took place a month later, while the concordat negotiations were in their final stage. As the regime moved to control every aspect of life in Germany — the policy of "coordination," *Gleichschaltung*[31] — the works of non-Aryan writers, however loosely defined, were quickly targeted. Jewish authors — Brecht, Kafka, Heine, Hesse, and dozens of others — were declared "degenerate." In early May, books were burned by the cartload, as copies of the Talmud had been over the centuries, in city squares across Germany.[32] The burning in Cologne occurred on May 5, in Berlin on May 12. Huge rallies accompanied the orgiastic destruction, with professors joining brownshirts to denounce the authors. Some ordinary Germans protested these actions. They were arrested. Within weeks of the end of that summer of the concordat, more than twenty-six thousand "police prisoners" were being held in cellars, pens, and the first rudimentary concentration camps, which were hovels surrounded by stretches of mud and barbed wire.[33]

The cardinal whom I cited earlier as declining to protest the April 1 boycott of Jewish businesses was Adolf Bertram, archbishop of Breslau, a city east of Berlin, now Wroclaw, Poland. Bertram's position as head of one of the six archdioceses in Germany, as one of only three cardinals, and as the chief of the Fulda Episcopal Conference made him the leading Catholic prelate in Germany. After the concordat was initialed by Pacelli and Papen in early July, Bertram worried that it had not included sufficient protection for "non-Aryan Catholics," who were often targeted by Nazi thugs as if baptism had not removed them from the company of Jews. Though the Church of the Inquisition had flirted with the racial definition of Jewishness, and though some Catholic institutions like the Jesuits were still applying blood purity restrictions into the twentieth century, the ancient Catholic insistence on the *religious* note of difference as decisive had been reasserted. Otherwise the Church would have had to yield its hope that the Jews as a group would be converted yet, for if baptism did not wash a person clean of Jewishness, why would he submit to it? If conversion was not ontologically as well as religiously respected, then the End Time conversion of Jews would not signal the Messiah's return. Something central to eschatological hope would be lost. So Church figures like Bertram and others saw the biological racism of Nazi antisemitism as a lethal threat less to Judaism than to Christianity. This insistence on religion, not race, as the defining note of Jewishness would permanently separate the Catholic Church from Nazism. A baptized Jew was no longer a Jew, but try telling that to a member of the Hitler Youth.

Cardinal Bertram wanted it told to Hitler, and he wanted the principle set down in the concordat. On September 2, 1933 Bertram wrote to Pacelli, "Will it be possible for the Holy See to put in a warm-hearted word for those who have been converted from Judaism to the Christian religion, since either they themselves, or their children or grandchildren, are now facing a wretched fate because of their lack of Aryan descent?"[34] The cardinal's urgency in this plea indicates his firm grasp of the jeopardy the new situation of *Gleichschaltung* represented for Jews. Pacelli agreed with Bertram's concern and raised the issue with Berlin. His note in defense of "non-Aryan Catholics" was careful to acknowledge that the Vatican's concern was not with the fate of other "non-Aryans." The note began, "The Holy See [has] no intention of interfering in Germany's internal affairs." That is to say, the Holy See recognizes that the fate of non-Aryans is a matter outside the circle of Vatican concern, with one exception. "The Holy See takes this occasion," Pacelli wrote, "to add a word in behalf of those German Catholics who themselves have gone over from Judaism to the Christian religion, or who are descended in the first generation, or more remotely from Jews who adopted the Catholic faith, and who, for reasons known to the Reich government, are likewise suffering from social and economic difficulties."[35]

Thus, right at the outset of the Nazi regime, and after its savage anti-Jewish intentions were indicated, the Catholic Church at its highest level sent a signal both to Hitler and to the German Catholic Church that the Jews, "facing a wretched fate," were on their own. The Church laid a tentative claim to authority regarding baptized Jews, which would be reflected in its occasional objections to Nazi "racism," as opposed to "anti-semitism," but otherwise, it would have nothing to say. As, indeed, it did not. Obviously, Hitler was not waiting for this signal before resolving to eliminate the Jews one way or another, but it surely helped him realize that the way ahead of him in this campaign was clear. The Church, for its part, had come to a decision it would stick with, almost without exception — that the "wretched fate" of the Jews was unconnected to its own fate, or that of anyone else.

This decision was the result of an inability and a refusal to see Jews except through the clouded lens of the religious hatred that is the subject of this book. This decision also amounts to the climax of our narrative, which is why the return to Bornewasser's Trier is so full of implication. It is the revelation at last of where all the roads of this story have been leading, from the first century's complex reading of the meaning of the Seamless Robe, to Helena's claim of it, to the bishop of Trier's wish to display it for Adolf Hitler. To Marcellus, the Robe was a battle trophy, proof of the Roman "victory," as he put it, "over the King of the Jews." In 1933, the Robe had been brought out of its secret place for Hitler, and now its secret was exposed whether Hitler had come to see it or not. The Robe had been twisted by this history into a Christian battle trophy too. Hitler, in other words, had not started the war against the Jews, even if it was his central purpose now to finish it.

51

Maria Laach and *Reichstheologie*

THE MOMENTOUS 1933 shift in official Catholic attitudes toward the Nazi movement, from disapproval to an acceptance that ranged from reserved to euphoric, certainly reflected the traditional Catholic bias in favor of state authority. In Germany, the Catholic impulse to defer before the power of the state had only been sharpened since the Kulturkampf, which had left Catholics eager to prove their good citizenship. In that case, Hitler's election as chancellor in March was decisive. But there were other, underlying factors at work as well. Pacelli's concordat with the Reich, like the 1929 Lateran Treaty, which had achieved rapprochement between the Vatican and fascist Italy, was born of the quiet desperation that had marked the institutional Church since the mortal challenges of 1870: Garibaldi in Italy, the Paris Commune in France, the Kulturkampf in Germany.

But there was something else. For more than a century, the Church had been thrown off balance by liberalism or modernism, that post-Enlightenment confluence of political revolution, intellectual skepticism, and cultural secularism. In their early stages, fascism and then National Socialism each displayed what a German Catholic theologian would recognize as a "fundamental kinship" with the Catholic Church.[1] Of primary significance was the fact that both fascism and National Socialism opposed Bolshevism. Since the murder of the archbishop of Paris, which would be repeated in the mid 1930s with the Republican murders of a dozen bishops and hundreds of priests in Spain, Communists had evolved into what they would remain for most of the twentieth century — the Catholic Church's archenemy. The fascists and Nazis opposed other liberal phenomena as well, from parliamentarianism to feminism to the "decadence" of modern culture. Catholics could see in the Lateran Treaty and the *Reichskonkordat* the first steps, however tentatively taken, toward the restoration of a premodern European ideal. The fascist and Nazi visions of society were alike in emphasizing the primacy of corporate unity — in Germany, the *Volk;* in Italy, a recovered empire — which could seem to Catholics an antidote to the rampant individualism of the post-Enlightenment age. In addition, the Church still harbored the dream of a reunited Christendom, with a healing of the Protestant schism, not by denominational reconciliation but by the marginalization of the other denominations.

The fierce calls for totalitarian unity that would overcome all divisions, calls that marked the rhetoric of Mussolini and Hitler — *Totalitätsanspruch* was the Nazi slogan, "claim of the Whole"[2] — could fall on Catholic ears like a promised return to the medieval ideal of one nation and one church. The liberal doctrine of the separation of church and state was as detested by the two dictators as by the pope. That there was no true common ground for the ultimate social union — would His Holiness agree to a subservient Church? — could be deflected.

In sum, many Catholics recognized Il Duce and the Führer as inherent allies in the fight against modernism, and saw them adopting common strategies. For example, the Vatican's response to the crisis of Garibaldi's occupation of Rome, which was an unprecedented assertion of authority personal to the pope, could seem to one German Catholic theologian, Robert Grosche, a foreshadowing of what Hitler did in demanding the extraordinary powers of the Enabling Act after the "crisis" of the Reichstag fire in 1933. "When in 1870 the infallibility of the Pope was defined," Grosche wrote, "the Church anticipated on a higher level, that historical decision which is made today on the political level: for the Pope and against the sovereignty of the Council; for the Führer and against the Parliament."[3] The German Reich, proclaimed as the Total State, embodied in the realm of politics what the Church, as of 1870, was reduced to embodying in the realm of spiritual authority. Or, as Grosche put it in 1934, "The *Reich* is the secularization of the Kingdom of God."[4]

It is hard to read such a statement now without thinking it mindlessly crude, but in 1934 German Catholics were still, as that Trier tour guide said to me in 1998, "hoping things would work out." In fact, they were having their own separate and positive experience of the *Volk, Vaterland, und Heimat*[5] idealism that was fueling the Nazis. In the 1920s, a Catholic liturgical movement had taken hold in Germany, inspired by such figures as Romano Guardini (1885–1968), a theological giant of the century, whose 1918 masterpiece *The Spirit of the Liturgy,* as much as any single work, sparked the renewal of the Church that would culminate in Vatican II. We saw this before. Instead of seeing the Eucharist as the sacred act performed by a high priest before a congregation of spectators, this movement began to see the liturgy as the act of the community itself. The priest, no longer above the community, would be its spokesperson, its servant. Christ was present in the Church not through the ordained minister, but through the Mysterium of the entire people at prayer. The whole Church thus becomes defined, in the title of a 1943 encyclical, as "The Mystical Body of Christ." The priest's claim to authority is as the embodiment of the community. This ideology changed the way the Church thought of itself, and it did so mainly through the liturgy. When, twenty years after that encyclical, the priest turned away from the wall to, as we say, "face the people," he was stepping down from the medieval ladder of being. The operative image was a ladder no more, but a circle.

The end result of this liturgical movement, when it came to the United States, would be known as the folk Mass, a form in which the breezy, if inexpert, participation of congregants in the singing of common folksongs would be preferred even to magnificent performances of the Fauré and Mozart Masses, performances that had so long reduced congregations literally to audiences. Yet in the context of the movement's origins — as a religious version of what was going on in Germany at that time, the *volkisch* impulse — the tag "folk Mass" cannot seem quite so innocent.[6] Or rather, perhaps the liberating and humane outcome of the liturgical movement suggests that the *volkisch* movement, had it not been seized by the diabolical Hitler, might have had another outcome.

Even though the power of a fascist dictator can seem like a return, as Mussolini abstractly imagined it, to the imperial system, it is something else. As Mussolini showed he understood, his power derived not from the gods, not from a dynasty, but from the approval of a mass culture. That is why the rituals of Nazism and fascism — think of those rallies in Nuremberg and before the Palazzo Venezia — required the collective hysteria in which the individual self was subsumed in an all-engrossing identification with the group. The dictator was all-powerful because of that group's recognition of him, not as a king but as a "leader" — Duce, Führer.

The liturgical movement represented the Church's benign version of this phenomenon, even though, at the abstract level of doctrinal assertion, the Church remained committed to monarchy, the authority that comes from above, not below. Thus the liturgical movement amounted to a kind of democratic countercurrent in the Church, which is why, from an early time, the hierarchy regarded it with suspicion. The form of the Mass, with every syllable and gesture precisely defined, was stuck in the amber of the Counter-Reformation. If the ritual could change — here was revolution — perhaps the Church could. The tradition of the "underground Mass" began literally in the crypts of churches, where the first rubrically irregular worship services were held. Because monasteries, with their independence from diocesan control and their ancient, relatively democratic traditions, had always stood as exceptions to an otherwise strict feudal order, it is not surprising that a monastery was where the first major innovations in Catholic liturgy took place. Oddly enough, that monastery was Maria Laach, the Rhineland pilgrimage center to which, for unrelated reasons, my mother brought me as a boy.

Early in this book, I described my recent visit to that Benedictine foundation, a midpoint among Cologne, Mainz, and Trier. I described how, partly for its name, my mother loved the place, and how, listening to the chant of the monks in choir, I had felt a first faint tug toward religious life, the genius of Catholicism. I described how the mystical ideal of monasticism still enthralls me. The reader may remember that Maria Laach dates to 1093, when monks from Trier established it as yet another outpost of burgeoning Cluniac monasticism. The monastery was no doubt known to Saint Bernard of Clairvaux, promoter of the two-sword theory of church-state power. Maria Laach probably hosted Bernard when he came to the Rhineland to exhort Second Crusaders not to attack the settlements of Jews that had survived the First Crusade. The abbey church of Maria Laach, with its paradigmatic colonnaded portico and Romanesque towers, was dedicated in 1156. Including a dozen or more buildings, the monastery sits in the midst of a thousand acres of rolling farmland and forests above the crater lake that gives the place its name. The soft curves of the Eifel Mountains ripple away to the east, while the western land slopes gently toward the valley of the Rhine some miles away. The church itself, with its soaring central belfry and multiple apses, is made of rough sandstone, the mostly curved surfaces of which are broken only by the smallest of windows, some round, others shaped like archers' niches.

As I reported earlier, on entering the church I was drawn immediately to one of the windows in the nearby western apse, not knowing why until I stood close enough to read the letters in the colored glass: *"Dr. Konrad*

Adenauer, Bundeskanzler, 1956." The name took me back to the time I'd stood there with my mother, when Adenauer was the chancellor of West Germany. She had explained to me that Adenauer was the donor of the window, and I would later learn it had been installed only the year before. The association with the monastery of *Der Alte* (the Old Man), as he was called by then, had made the place seem doubly sacred because of Adenauer's postwar status as a hero of resistance to Hitler. Not only Catholics but Germans too had snuggled beneath the blanket of Adenauer's virtue, which was continually asserted by the unelaborated statement that he had ended the war in one of Hitler's concentration camps. During my recent visit, I noted that the window depicted a scene of Adam and Eve stunned in the gaze of a slyly tormenting serpent. In fact, Adenauer had been one of the first to criticize the hierarchy of the Roman Catholic Church for its failure to oppose Nazism. "I believe," he declared in 1946, "that if all the bishops had together made public statements from the pulpits on a particular day, they could have prevented a great deal. That did not happen, and there is no excuse for it. It would have been no bad thing if the bishops had all been put in prison or in concentration camps as a result. But none of that happened and therefore it is best to keep quiet."[7] As indeed, on this subject, Adenauer mainly was. His fierce declaration was made in a private letter, and by 1956 Catholics like my parents had no knowledge of his position.

Near the window he sponsored is the entrance to the church crypt below. It is a dark, low-ceilinged chapel with a dozen dwarf pillars holding up the vaulted stone. Despite kneelers and an altar, it can seem more like a *Ratskeller* than a sanctuary. Yet it was here, at liturgies attended by only dozens of people during the 1920s, that the first so-called Dialogue Masses were celebrated. The liturgical text was still in Latin, but the laity recited it antiphonally with the priest, a first, powerful step toward the new ideal of universal participation that has now become a Catholic norm. No longer do we attend Mass as a collection of *isolatos,* each on his or her knees, face buried in hands from which dangle rosary beads. We do not approach God alone but as members of a praying community, members of a "folk," also known as the Communion of Saints, Mysterium of Christ.

The prophet of this movement was the Maria Laach monk Odo Casel (1886–1948), whose work *Theology of Mystery* had a great impact in the Church, nowhere more than in America. A monastery that monks from Maria Laach had founded in Minnesota (St. John's, in Collegeville) became, in turn, the center of the liturgical movement in the United States.

The most influential American liturgist was the St. John's Benedictine Godfrey Diekmann, longtime editor of *Worship* magazine. Father Diekmann was familiar to me when I was a seminarian at the Paulist College at Catholic University. In the early 1960s, he was often at CU, a burly, overpowering man whose brilliant white hair and masculine ruddiness underscored the sense we all had that a new spirit was blowing through the Church. Diekmann's magazine was a rallying point, and it exerted a life-changing influence on Catholics of my generation. The man himself, in my several glimpses of him, had no less an impact. As a classically trained and fully credentialed Benedictine, Diekmann legitimized what critics dismissed as an arcane set of fads, but which the old guard astutely recognized as a revolutionary movement in midcentury Catholicism. We embraced one liturgical innovation after another — unheard-of modifications of vestments; a once unthinkable use of the vernacular; communion in the form of ordinary bread (Wonder bread indeed!) instead of sterile wafers, that bread placed in the communicant's hands instead of, infantilizingly, on the tongue; those renditions of "Kumbaya" replacing Tantum Ergo. The unstoppable sequence, like waves at a crumbling dike, broke down the everlasting Catholic resistance to change.

Unknown to us, Godfrey Diekmann came to his role as the Pied Piper of "folk" reform no stranger to the enthusiasm of such a movement. As a theology student a generation earlier, he had lived at the mother house, Maria Laach, from 1931 to 1933. The time there solidified his identity as a disciple of Odo Casel and a committed liturgical innovator. But Diekmann was alive to what else was happening at that moment in Germany. His biographer, Kathleen Hughes, cites a letter young Father Diekmann wrote to his abbot back home in Minnesota during that fateful spring. "Today is election day in Germany," it begins, enabling us to know it was March 5, 1933. Two days before, the Reichstag in Berlin had been set ablaze, an act of arson the Nazis succeeded in blaming on the Communists. What is striking about Diekmann's letter is the glimpse it offers of the anti-Communist hysteria that was sweeping even through the cloisters of Maria Laach. "All manner of the wildest rumors are floating around about 'discovered' plans of the communists. Maria Laach was officially warned by police that the Reds have evil intentions, and that a thorough nightly guard must be kept. Accordingly, every night a patrol of four or more men keep watch: the 'fire-department' has had drills, and large electric lights are strung all about the premises, so that the entire surroundings can be flooded with light, should any nightly emergency arise. Everybody is all excited: the abbot gave a conference on the proximate end of the world last Wednesday."[8]

That abbot was Ildefons Herwegen, and his palpable sense of panic, as reflected in Diekmann's letter, may partially account for his urgent embrace that spring of a pro-Nazi Catholic movement. Abbot Herwegen is credited with being a father of the worldwide Catholic liturgical renewal. Yet in him, perhaps more than in anyone else, can be seen that "fundamental kinship" between Catholic and German impulses of the time: Abbot Herwegen was also a father of what came to be known as *Reichstheologie.*

That chillingly named school of theology included some of the greatest Catholic theologians of Germany. They would promote not just an accommodation with National Socialism, but an alliance reaching to the deepest levels of religious meaning. Such instinctive pro-Nazi enthusiasm on the part of Catholic intellectuals would, for the most part, be relatively short-lived. Within a few years, talk of the "fundamental kinship" would be silenced by the onslaught of Hitler's brutality. But the importance of the intellectual and spiritual connections made in the name of a common longing for a "total" society in that crucial early period should not be overlooked. It was the theological equivalent of the pragmatic deal-making that brought Pacelli and Hitler together.

Our interest in *Reichstheologie* goes beyond its significance as one of the sources of Catholic accommodation with Nazism. Indeed, our concern remains less with the Church's failure to oppose Nazism than with the ways in which Nazism was able to tap into the fundamental currents of the Christian imagination. *Reichstheologie* is a manifestation par excellence of that phenomenon. It was also, of course, a root cause of Catholic acquiescence. What makes early theological and political accommodation of Catholicism with Nazism an unfinished matter of moral quandary is the fact that it was clear to all from the start that the "totality," whether defined religiously or politically, would, by that very definition, exclude the Jews. The Nazis were explicit in defining the Jews at the outset as the rejected group against which the "totality" defined itself. If the Church was not offended by this, it was because Christianity had done the same thing.

Protestant theology has its own history as an incubator of Nazi ideology, and figures like Paul Althaus, Emanuel Hirsch, and Gerhard Kittel have been subjects of searching examination. "The Protestant theology they inherited and shaped allowed them," as Robert Ericksen has written, "to endorse enthusiastically the rise of Hitler and to accept without complaint the removal of Jews from German life."[9] The most notable of the Nazi-friendly Catholic theologians was Karl Adam of Tübingen. His *Spirit of Catholicism,* published in the mid 1920s, an important text in my own training forty years later, was a prophetic statement of the new idea of the Church as a community. That Adam was perhaps the most notable Catholic theologian of his generation is why it matters that it was also he who said that the Nazi movement and the Catholic Church complement each other like nature and grace. As for Hitler, Adam wrote in 1933, "Now he stands before us, he whom the voices of our poets and sages have summoned, the liberator of the German genius. He has removed the blindfolds from our eyes and, through all political, economic, social, and confessional covers, has enabled us to see and love again the one essential thing: our unity of blood, our German self, the *Homo Germanus.*"[10] When my seminary professors introduced me to the work of Karl Adam, no reference was made to such ideas.

Another notable Catholic "Reichstheologian" — the scholar Michael Lukens calls him "the most pivotal figure"[11] — was Joseph Lortz, publisher of *Reich und Kirche,* a series of short books arguing for the compatibility of Nazism and Catholicism. Lortz, a priest and theologian at Braunsberg, actually became a Nazi Party member in 1933. He articulated more clearly than anyone the intellectual basis for the new compatibility. He argued that German Catholics "were obligated in conscience," in Guenter Lewy's phrase, "to support National Socialism wholeheartedly."[12] Lortz offered this summary of his analysis:

. . . insofar as [our present situation] is constructive, it is so in reaction against those spiritual factors and attitudes to life which laid the foundation of the modern age, which fashioned modern development, and then dominated it until the turn of the century. The new trend is (a) *Philosophically,* a turn from doubt, hypercriticism, historicism, or subjectivism, to a form of objectivism . . . (b) *Ethically,* the trend is from unrestrained freedom to authority, from the egoism of individualism to communal thinking. (c) *Politically,* the liberal and democratic idea together with its most concrete political manifestation, parliamentarianism, is yielding to the principle of leadership in the form of dictatorship, or government without parliamentary majorities, or nonparty government (Fascism, Nazism). (d) *Religiously,* there is a better understanding of the value of institutional religion, of the value of a Church as such, and an appreciation also of the unique character of religion and its special claims.[13]

Because of his association with Nazism, Lortz was tried by the Allied tribunals after the war, and barred from teaching. In 1950, he was appointed director of the Institute for European History in Mainz, a position he held while I was living only three miles away. He regained his respectability and held his position in Mainz until 1975, the year of his death.

A milestone gathering of the Catholic proponents of *Reichstheologie* took place at Maria Laach on April 3, 1933, with Abbot Herwegen as host.[14] This was two days after the Nazis' nationwide boycott of Jewish businesses, measures from which the Church had officially distanced itself. The group at the abbey included Catholic intellectuals, journalists, and professionals, organized around theologians. It called itself *Kreuz und Adler,* Cross and Eagle[15] (once again the cross in a context far from any meaning it could have had for Jesus or his followers). Maria Laach, presumably freeing itself from that Communist-induced panic about the "proximate end of the world" on which Abbot Herwegen had preached the month before, now became a center of the effort to join, in Lortz's phrase, the Reich and the Church. One *Kreuz und Adler* leader described its obligation to support the Third Reich as a "Christian counterrevolution to 1789."[16]

In July 1933, three months after the *Kreuz und Adler* meeting, the abbey hosted the convention of an association of Catholic academics, with prominent Catholic theologians in attendance.[17] One of those was Robert Grosche, whom I cited as having seen the parallel between the papal infallibility declaration of 1870 and the Enabling Act of 1933. The meeting turned into a German Catholic festival celebrating the recently announced *Reichskonkordat* between Berlin and the Vatican. Festivity may have been the note in any case, but the arrival at Maria Laach of Franz von Papen guaranteed it. He had just returned from Rome, where he and Cardinal Eugenio Pacelli had signed the concordat. As we saw, the Te Deum was being sung at nearby Trier, where Papen had represented Hitler at the solemn showing of the Seamless Robe.

An English translation of the text of the concordat, published at the time by a group calling itself the Friends of Germany, indicates its significance to Germans by citing this comment from the Augsburg newspaper *Postzeitung:* "No document will command such widespread attention as the text of the Reichs-concordat, the origin and object of which Vice Chancellor von Papen interpreted in response to an invitation of the Catholic Academic Union at Maria Laach before a crowded executive meeting of representatives from all parts of Germany. It proved an historic event, never to be forgotten by those present . . . Papen regaled his audience with an elucidation of various background details, as for instance, the reaction of the Holy Father to the treaty."[18] It was here, on July 22, that Papen drew the connection between the dissolution of the Center Party and the concordat.[19] The pope, Papen said, was especially pleased at the promised destruction of Bolshevism.[20] Indeed, Pius XI had agreed to the treaty "in the recognition that the new Germany had fought a decisive battle against Bolshevism and the atheist movement."[21]

Franz von Papen was a Catholic with a history of attendance at Maria Laach retreats.[22] He and the abbot were close friends, and it was at this celebration of an anticipated union of the Church and the Reich that Abbot Herwegen made what remains a distilled statement of the basis of that hope. "What the liturgical movement is to the religious realm," he said, "fascism is to the political. The German stands and acts under authority, under leadership — whoever does not follow endangers society. Let us say 'yes' wholeheartedly to the new form of the total State, which is analogous throughout to the incarnation of the Church. The Church stands in the world as Germany stands in politics today."[23]

Papen had to be pleased to hear these words from such a figure, but the abbot had a secret. It involved Konrad Adenauer. Recall that during our visits to Maria Laach, my mother and I never heard Papen referred to. To our knowledge he was no Catholic; to us he was a notorious war criminal who had been condemned at Nuremberg. For his role as a Nazi, he had been sentenced to eight years in prison,[24] which means he had almost certainly been released by the time we visited the monastery. I now know that in 1959, Papen, the man who had encouraged Paul von Hindenburg to appoint Hitler as chancellor in the first place, was quietly honored by the Vatican, raised to the order of papal privy chamberlain.[25] We Americans in Germany in that same era heard nothing of that.

From German Catholics we heard instead about *Der Alte,* the window donor — how, as mayor of Cologne, he had defiantly refused to allow swastika flags to be flown when Hitler came to the city; how he had sent a minor functionary in his place to greet Hitler at the airport; how, as a result, the Gestapo had targeted Adenauer.[26] All of this had taken place in late February and early March 1933. Hermann Göring declared that

Adenauer was to be made an example of swift Nazi retribution. At the time, Adenauer was a fifty-seven-year-old father of four small children. Gathering up his family, he fled and went into hiding. Then, knowing that his presence endangered his family, he fled again, alone. He went to Berlin, but was unsafe there. "In despair," his biographer Charles Wighton writes, "he was wandering from refuge to refuge." Finally, he wrote in desperation to an old boyhood friend, Ildefons Herwegen. "At once came a telegram," Wighton writes of the abbot's reply. "'I shall be delighted to have you with me.'"[27] In this way, the pro-Nazi monk offered the anti-Nazi politician refuge in Maria Laach. As the monastery's ideological sympathies became known, it proved to be the perfect hiding place. The fugitive mayor lived there secretly, in a monk's cell, from late March or early April 1933 until April 1934, when, alerted to suspicions of local Nazis, he was forced to flee.

This means that while *Kreuz und Adler* met at the monastery in April, and while the *Reich und Kirche* assembly took place in July, Adenauer was hiding nearby. So while Papen was celebrating the *Reichskonkordat* in the Maria Laach refectory, Adenauer was eating his monk's bread only rooms away. Papen and Adenauer were old enemies, with the former having accused the latter of the grievous offense of preferring the Rhineland to the nation as a whole. That Adenauer had not bought into the spirit of totalism is emphasized by the fact that one of the first of those who sought to aid him while he was a fugitive was a Jew.[28] Secluded in his room, he seemed on the wrong side not only of history but of Roman Catholic piety.[29]

Given this fuller story of Adenauer's time at Maria Laach, that stained-glass window with its serpent slyly assaulting Adam and Eve takes on a different meaning. The odd juxtaposition of Papen and Adenauer at that decisive moment of the Third Reich provides a dramatic instance of the ambivalence that had for so long marked Catholic attitudes toward Jews, with some Catholics seeking to protect them, and others to attack them. The ambivalence was always a matter of official Church reluctance to embrace violence, but at crucial times the balance was lost, when Augustine's dictum that Jewish survival served God's purpose was replaced by a radical conversionist purpose of eliminating Judaism as a competing religion. Hitler's transformation of that impulse into a program of elimination of Jews as a people was unprecedented, but not unprepared for.

When on April 1, 1933, Hitler ordered the boycott of Jewish businesses, he made his "Jews out!" plan crystal clear even without the smashing of glass that would come later. At that early date, not even Adolf Hitler, much less his Catholic admirers, could have known into what abyss his impulse would carry him. As late as 1938, in a furious public rebuttal by Hitler to the world leaders who had denounced the Kristallnacht pogroms, his decidedly unfinal solution to the Jewish problem was still "Jews out!," not "Jews dead!" His proposal, at that point, was the moral and political equivalent to Queen Isabella's, the expulsion of all Jews from the lands controlled by the Reich.[30] Jews were offered immediate exit visas — but exit to where? The same world leaders, notably Neville Chamberlain and Franklin D. Roosevelt, who had denounced the anti-Jewish violence of the Nazis declined to receive Jews as refugees.

The movement toward the Final Solution came to seem to have been inexorable, but it was not. As we have repeatedly noted, it is simplistic to say that Christian anti-Judaism caused the murderous policies of the Nazis, however much it sowed seeds of the Nazis' lethal antisemitism, but here the moral question is something else. The Church's failure to denounce publicly or privately early Nazi violence aimed at Jews, a failure rooted in the Church's own antisemitism and its own theology, was part of what allowed that violence to become genocidal. Crucial to its building to a point of no return was Hitler's discovery (late) of the political indifference of the democracies to the fate of the Jews, and his discovery (early) of the moral and religious indifference of Christians to that fate. Nothing laid bare such indifference more dramatically than the Nazi-Vatican concordat and the *Reichstheologie* of the German Catholic Church — both of which sought the restoration of a civilization that excluded Jews. The steps from "Jews out!" to "Jews dead!," from religious elimination to physical elimination — from elimination, that is, to extermination — would prove all too small.

52

Pius XII: Last Days of the
Roman Ghetto

I CROSSED THE Tiber not far from the site of the Milvian Bridge, where Constantine had pushed this story into second gear with his vision of the cross and its legend, "In this sign, conquer." I entered the district that is still sometimes called the ghetto, and that is still marked by the Hebrew letters of shopkeepers' signs. A block from the river, I came to the towering synagogue. A high, iron-spiked fence surrounds the building, which evokes the sensuous Moorish style instead of the stricter lines of classical Rome or the Renaissance. A dome rises majestically from the squared-off building, a worthy, if modest, counterpoint to the *cupolone* of St. Peter's. Jews were living in Rome before there were Christians.

When John Paul II came to this place in 1986, the first time a pope had ever visited a synagogue, he forthrightly condemned antisemitism "by anyone." In particular, he expressed his "abhorrence for the genocide decreed against the Jewish people during the last war." He added, "The Jewish community of Rome, too, paid a high price in blood."[1] This was a direct reference to the event that, as we saw early in this book, served Rolf Hochhuth as the indicting climax of his play *The Deputy*.

"Your Eminence, we now have come to this!" the play's Riccardo says to the Cardinal. "Citizens of Rome — outlaws! A manhunt for civilians underneath the windows of His Holiness!" All of the accusations against Pius XII, from his overreadiness in 1933 to negotiate the Nazi-legitimizing *Reichskonkordat;* to his indifference to the fate of unbaptized Jews, as reflected in the "secret annex" and the record of other Vatican initiatives limited to converted Jews; to his 1939 cancellation of his predecessor's encyclical condemning Nazi antisemitism;[2] to his refusal to condemn the brutal German invasion of Catholic Poland; to his tacit acceptance of Nazi and fascist anti-Jewish legislation;[3] to his failure to mention the Jews, or even the Nazis, by name in his Christmas message of 1942;[4] to his meeting repeatedly with Croatian Ustashi leaders, including Ante Pavelič, a mini-Hitler who found refuge in the Vatican after the war; to his declining ever to excommunicate Hitler, Himmler, Bormann, Goebbels, or other Catholic Nazis — all these accusations pale beside this one, dating to events in October 1943. As the Hochhuth character Riccardo wails, "Will no action be taken even now, Your Eminence?"[5]

The Germans had occupied Rome in September 1943. Until then, Jews had been relatively safe, but at 5:30 A.M. on October 16, the noise of gunfire broke the night silence of the ghetto. By then it was home to about four thousand Jews. The streets leading out of the quarter were blocked. SS officers drove residents from their homes, and in a few hours the Germans had arrested more than twelve hundred people. The Jews were taken to a temporary jail in the Italian Military College, which stood a few hundred yards from Vatican City. Yet from the Vatican, no voice was raised in public support of the Jews.[6]

Two days later, the prisoners were put on trucks, taken to the railroad station, and loaded into boxcars. Again, no voice was raised in protest. The arrested Jews were gone. Five days later, this entry appears in the meticulously kept log at Auschwitz: "Transport, Jews from Rome. After the selection 149 men registered with numbers 158451–158639 and 47 women registered with numbers 66172–66218 have been admitted to the detention camp. The rest have been gassed."[7]

On his visit to the Roman synagogue in 1986, John Paul II recalled the 1943 fate of Roman Jews, but he made no reference to the Vatican's silence. After Hochhuth's play had been performed around the world between 1963 and 1965, the Vatican had released documents showing that many thousands of Jews were rescued during the war by various officials of the Catholic Church.[8] John Paul II praised the Roman priests, monks, and nuns who opened "the doors of our religious houses, of our churches, of the Roman seminary, of buildings belonging to the Holy See and of Vatican City itself . . . to offer refuge and safety to so many Jews of Rome being hunted by their persecutors."[9] The pope made no mention of his predecessor, but defenders of Pius XII credit him with having directly sponsored this multitude of individual acts of heroism. The 1998 Vatican document "We Remember: A Reflection on the Shoah" honors Pius for what he did "personally or through his representatives to save hundreds of thousands of Jewish lives."[10] Acts of rescue performed in secret by the lower clergy and Catholic laity are defined as acts of the pope, although no records directly tying such heroism to Pius XII have ever been uncovered.[11]

In response to John Paul II's remarks at the synagogue, the president of the Jewish community of Rome, Giacomo Saban, acknowledged the truth of much of what the pope had said. Nevertheless, he included in his reply this rebuke: "What was taking place on one of the banks of the Tiber could not have been unknown on the other side of the river, nor could what was happening elsewhere on the European continent."[12]

Defenders of Pius XII insist that his initiatives, even in this case, took place behind the scenes. They assert that his response to events of October 16, 1943, was not mere silence but an urgent diplomatic intervention in behalf of the Jews. "It was not just coincidental," says one papal defender, "that the round-up of the Jews of Rome ceased after only one night. What took place the next morning was a dressing-down of the German ambassador by the Holy See's secretary of state."[13] Advocates for Pius XII define this meeting as an unambiguous act of pro-Jewish papal heroism, and for that reason it merits close attention.

The Vatican secretary of state was Cardinal Luigi Maglione. The German ambassador to the Holy See was Ernst von Weizsäcker, who, until shortly before, had been chief state secretary in the Nazi Foreign Office in Berlin, and whose son Richard would serve, decades later, as the president of the Federal Republic of Germany.[14] Maglione summarized what took place in their meeting:

> Having learned that this morning the Germans made a raid on the Jews, I asked the Ambassador of Germany to come to me and I asked him to try to intervene on behalf of these unfortunates. I talked to him as well as I could in the name of humanity, in Christian charity.
>
> The Ambassador, who already knew of the arrests, but doubted whether it dealt specifically with the Jews, said to me in a sincere and moved voice: I am always expecting to be asked: Why do you remain in your position?
>
> I said: No, Ambassador, I do not ask and will not ask you such a question. I say to you simply: Your Excellency, who has a tender and good heart, see if you can save so many innocent people. It is sad for the Holy See, sad beyond telling that right in Rome, under the eyes of the Common Father, so many people have been made to suffer only because they belong to a particular race.

The Ambassador, after several moments of reflection, asked me: What will the Holy See do if events continue?

I replied: The Holy See would not want to be put into the necessity of uttering a word of disapproval.

The Ambassador observed: For more than four years I have followed and admired the attitude of the Holy See. It has succeeded in steering the ship in the midst of rocks of every kind and size without colliding and, even if it has greater confidence in the Allies, it has known how to maintain a perfect balance. I ask myself if, at the very time that the ship is reaching port, it is fitting to put everything in danger. I am thinking about the consequences which such a step of the Holy See would provoke . . . The order came from the highest source . . . Your Eminence will leave me free not to report this official conversation?

I remarked that I had asked him to intervene appealing to his sentiments of humanity. I left it to his judgement to make or not make mention of our conversation which was so amicable.

I wanted to remind him that the Holy See, as he himself has perceived, has been so very prudent so as not to give to the German people the impression that it has done or wished to do the least thing against Germany during this terrible war.

But I also had to tell him that the Holy See should not be put into the necessity of protesting: if ever the Holy See is obliged to do so, it will rely upon divine Providence for the consequences.

In the meantime, I repeat: Your Excellency has told me that you will attempt to do something for the unfortunate Jews. I thank you for that. As for the rest, I leave it to your judgement. If you think it more opportune not to mention our conversation, so be it.[15]

In what way this conversation, as recorded in the cardinal's own notes, can be construed as a dressing down is not clear. The Vatican's concern for the fate of the arrested Jews is apparent, but so is a trust in indirection. Mainly what comes through is Maglione's anxiety.

Our concern is not to sit in judgment on the decisions made in such circumstances, only to insist that a failure of nerve not be recast as heroic, if subtle, diplomacy. Assessing Maglione's meeting with Weizsäcker, John Morley, the Catholic scholar who made the first thorough study of what diplomatic archives have been published, said, "There was neither confrontation, nor criticism, nor a plea for justice."[16] The Vatican secretary of state explicitly authorized the ambassador to regard this communication as private — the opposite of protest. The ambassador was authorized to refrain even from reporting the meeting to Berlin. Maglione trusted Weizsäcker to "do something for the unfortunate Jews," but without pressing him in any way. According to Maglione, this intervention led to the release of many Jews, and the pope's defenders have made much of that claim, but the record does not bear it out, to say the least.[17]

Other Church officials weighed in as Maglione did. It should be no surprise that the only beneficiaries of these interventions were the "fortunate" minority among the arrested who had converted to Christianity, or were married to Jews who had. This one effect of the Vatican strategy seems clear: About two hundred baptized Jews and Jews married to Catholics were set free before the rest of the Jews were transported north. In his own report to Berlin of his contacts with the Vatican, Weizsäcker seems to have been concerned to protect the pope from Nazi retaliation. He may actually have sought ways to mitigate the campaign against the Jews, but not because of Maglione's intervention. There is reason to believe that Weizsäcker was the one taking the initiative on behalf of Jews. His communications to Berlin have been published, and it is hard to know what game he was playing. Saving Jews may have been one purpose, but maintaining his standing with his superiors was surely paramount. In his communiqués, he emphasized more than once his success in keeping the pope from issuing any protest. For example, on October 28, Weizsäcker sent this message:

> By all accounts, the Pope, although harassed from various quarters, has not allowed himself to be stampeded into making any demonstrative pronouncement against the removal of the Jews from Rome. Although he must count on the likelihood that this attitude will be held against him by our opponents and will be exploited by Protestant quarters in the Anglo-Saxon countries for purposes of anti-Catholic propaganda, he had done everything he could, even in this delicate matter, not to injure the relationship between the Vatican and the German government or the German authorities in Rome. As there will presumably be no further German action to be taken in regard to the Jews here in Rome, this question, with its unpleasant possibilities for German-Vatican relations, may be considered as liquidated.
>
> On the Vatican side, at any rate, there is one definite indication of this. *L'Osservatore Romano* of October 25/26 gives prominence to a semi-official communiqué of the Pope's loving-kindness which is written in the characteristically tortuous and obscure style of this Vatican paper, and says that the Pope lavishes his fatherly care on all people, *regardless of nationality, religion, or race* [emphasis in the text]. The manifold and increasing activity of Pius XII (it continues) has been intensified of late because of the augmented suffering of so many unfortunate people. No objection can be raised to this public statement, the less so as its text . . .

will be understood by only very few people as having special reference to the Jewish question.[18]

Defenders of the pope note that this communiqué "has been cited against Pius. But read in context, it indicates that the pope would have gone public had the deportations not stopped."[19] In any case, was the suspension of a massive roundup of Jews in Rome the result of Vatican indirection or of an alerted Jewish community's having dispersed and gone into hiding around the city, with the aid of the Catholics who gave them refuge? These and other records suggest that the pope wanted reasons *not* to "go public," and with the help of the clever Weizsäcker, he found them. John Morley drew this conclusion about the events in Rome of October 1943: "The Vatican's efforts on behalf of these Jews failed, principally because the steps taken were so slight as to be out of all proportion to the crime committed."[20] And as for the further roundup of Jews stopping because of Vatican pressures, more than a thousand additional Jews were arrested after October 16. Neither Pius XII nor his secretary of state openly protested any of this, to the great surprise even of high-level Germans in Rome.[21] This failure the historian István Deák labels "deplorable." The pope, Deák says, "did nothing."[22]

The Deputy concludes portentously with an announcer's reading four stark sentences about the gas chambers continuing "to work for a full year more," as if Pius XII were responsible for that crime. The play's indictment of the pope stands as one extreme of how he is remembered. Morley studied the eleven volumes of Vatican documents made public after *The Deputy* caused its stir, and in 1999 he was appointed to a joint Jewish-Catholic commission to examine those and other archives further. He rejects Hochhuth's portrayal, but his conclusion is still critical. He ended his book *Vatican Diplomacy and the Jews During the Holocaust, 1939–1943* with this paragraph: "It must be concluded that Vatican diplomacy failed the Jews during the Holocaust by not doing all that it was possible for it to do on their behalf. It also failed itself because in neglecting the needs of the Jews, and pursuing a goal of reserve rather than humanitarian concern, it betrayed the ideals that it had set for itself. The nuncios, the secretary of state, and, most of all, the Pope share the responsibility for this dual failure."[23]

In an earlier chapter, I referred to a meeting with Cardinal Edward Cassidy, the chief author of "We Remember," convened in 1999 to "build upon" that document, a meeting at which I was present. Also in attendance was a *New York Times* writer, who suggested that if *The Deputy* offers one distortion of Pius XII, his canonization would amount to another. Yet even as worldy a figure as the novelist Graham Greene once portrayed Pius XII as "the servant of the servants of God, and not impossibly, one feels, a saint."[24] Greene was famously a convert, but he was never a sentimental Catholic. For him to have such an opinion of Pius XII, expressed in a *Life* magazine article in 1951, evokes a lost sense of the filial devotion that pope once inspired. His death on October 9, 1958, prompted a plethora of tributes, including some from prominent Jewish figures.[25] I have in front of me an illustrated book on the life of Pius XII, published on the occasion of his death. It includes a 78 rpm record, "The Voice of Pope Pius XII with the Vatican Choir and the Bells of St. Peter's."[26] The photos show Eugenio Pacelli as a boy of twelve, as a newly ordained priest, as a papal delegate to the 1911 coronation of England's King George V. Pacelli is pictured as the nuncio to Berlin, as the papal secretary of state, and as "Head of Christendom." One photo shows him in the triple tiara, sitting on the ornate portable throne, balanced on the shoulders of helmeted guards. The pope aims a blessing at the camera. The caption reads:

> . . . he loves the world as another man may love his only son. The enemies whom his predecessor pursued with such vigor he fights with the weapon of charity. In his presence one feels that here is a priest who is waiting patiently for the moment of martyrdom and his patience includes even the long drawn conversations of the nuns who visit him. From another room one hears the long stream of aged feminine talk while the Monsignors move restlessly in their scarlet robes, looking at their watches or making that movement of the hand to the chin forming an imaginary beard. This is the Latin way of exclaiming at a bore. Out comes the last nun, strutting away with the happy contented smile of a woman who has said her say. And out from his inner room comes the Pope with his precise vigorous step ready to greet the next unimportant stranger "with deep affection."
>
> All the people of Rome feel him to be like the great Popes of past ages whose images are frescoed on the walls and ceilings of the basilicas, their Bishop and incomparable warrior, far from Vatican Hill he defended not only the city, but the cause of righteousness and goodness.[27]

The portrait of Pius XII at prayer is familiar to me from childhood. The bespectacled man in white skullcap and red, ermine-trimmed cape, hands folded at an angle like a steeple falling toward the brocaded cushion of the prie-dieu — he really did seem a living saint to us. Thumbing through a tribute book like this, we would have made nothing of its failure to refer to World War II or to mention Jews. By 1958, Pius XII was, above all, an icon of the West's resistance to "the propaganda of hate of Atheistic revolt,"[28] also known as Communism. The only photo in this book not of Pius or St. Peter's shows a throng of nuns and bowing laity in a vast coliseum. The caption reads, "German Catholics Join in Mass Worship." The scene is Olympic Stadium in Berlin, with "many of the worshippers . . . from the Soviet Zone." West Germany, led by the Catholic Adenauer, was the anti-Soviet bulwark, which is one reason why questions about the Holocaust were not yet being asked. "Catholics all over Germany joined in the prayer hour which was broadcast over the radio. The Pope in Rome joined the prayer, also."[29] So we have the last word on Pius XII and Germany: The unofficial canonization of the one meant the rehabilitation of the other. This book's fulsome, uncomplicated praise seems lifted from a lost world of order and innocence.

The renewed impulse to restore the image of Pius XII, reflected in the Vatican's *fin-de-siècle* advancing of his "cause" toward beatification, preliminary to an official canonization, is no doubt related to a wish to reclaim that world. In the light even of the most favorable reading of Pius XII's World War II history, the move to canonize him is, in the words of István Deák, "a very strange undertaking indeed."[30] The Church official in charge of promoting the cause of Pius XII's elevation to sainthood is a German Jesuit, Father Peter Gumpel, to whom we referred earlier, and will again in other connections. In June 1997, he told an interviewer:

> After having studied all the depositions of all the witnesses in Pius XII's cause, I can say that very rarely have I found evidence so persuasive of heroic virtue . . . He was a man of extraordinary charity, laboring ceaselessly not only for the Jews, but for all those who suffered from persecution . . . Out of solidarity with the miserable conditions of the people, he did not drink even a single cup of coffee . . . Sister Pasqualina, his assistant, has said that even his linen was tattered . . . He spent [his patrimony] in works of charity . . . In sum, the cause is going forward, and the prospects of Pius's beatification are excellent.[31]

Such reports from Rome that Pius XII was to be honored as a saint prompted further waves of criticism from Jewish groups and from Catholics. The Vatican did not, as expected, advance the wartime pope's cause toward beatification when it put forward Pius IX and John XXIII in 2000. It was unclear what the status of that candidacy was, although Father

Gumpel and others in the Vatican insisted that the Church would not be deterred from declaring Pius XII a saint, and sooner rather than later. In 1999, Gumpel said, "The cause of the beatification and canonization of Pope Pius XII, who is rightly venerated by millions of Catholics, will not be stopped or delayed by the unjustifiable and calumnious attacks against this great and saintly man . . . May truth, justice and fairness finally prevail with regard to Pius XII, to whom so many Jews and their descendants owe their lives."[32]

By continuing to promote the image of Pius XII as a saint, whether he is ever formally canonized or not, is the Vatican trying to do for itself what it tried to do for German Catholicism in the immediate aftermath of the war? As a boy, I saw how this worked. In a letter to the bishops of Bavaria, in August 1945, Pius XII praised "those millions of Catholics, men and women of every class" who had resisted Nazism in Germany. Heroes like the Berlin Cathedral provost Lichtenberg and Father Delp were lifted up not as exceptions but as exemplars of Catholic behavior. Pius XII's praise of German Catholic resistance ignored the fact that such resistance was, as Lewy puts it, "not only discouraged by the Church, but condemned. Catholics who actively fought against the Hitler regime were rebels not only against the State, but against their ecclesiastical authorities as well."[33]

As the Catholic Church seems determined to negate *The Deputy*'s slander of Pius XII by raising him to sainthood, impeding, if not foreclosing, the ability of future historians to arrive at dispassionate judgments of these events, one wonders: Should the question of Pius XII's "silence" be this important? In remembering the fate of Jews living "under his very windows," words the historian Susan Zuccotti uses as the title of a recent book,[34] perhaps the more important piece of unadjudicated business concerns how those Jews came to be there in the first place. The Roman ghetto, from the middle of the sixteenth century to the last quarter of the nineteenth century, stood as a palpable sign not only of the Church's attitude toward Jews but of the pope's own claim to absolute authority. Traditional religious anti-Judaism was transformed when oppressive dominance of the Jew became a particular note of papal authority. It is instructive to recall here that it was through "restrictions, enslavement, and humiliations" of Jews — in the phrase the Jewish leader Giacomo Saban addressed to John Paul II during his visit to the Rome synagogue[35] — that the Vatican put its temporal authority on display for the world to see. This was especially true during its last embattled phase, when popes repeatedly celebrated their return to power during the on-and-off revolutions of the

nineteenth century by rebuilding the ghetto walls. The Roman ghetto thus
became the perfect symbol of the way that forces rallying to the threatened pope "reinvented antisemitism," in the words of one historian, "as
central to the Catholic tradition."[36] That is what made the ghetto, in Cardinal Cassidy's word, the "antechamber" of the death camps. In that connection, one must ask — and we will — what it means that the Church has
even now gone forward with the cause of canonization of Pius IX, the last
pope to defend, and rebuild, the ghetto walls.

By focusing so much of the Jewish-Catholic dialogue on the question of
Pius XII, the broader question of a massive Catholic failure is deflected.
One example of this surfaces in the work of Daniel Jonah Goldhagen,
whose book *Hitler's Willing Executioners* caused such a sensation in 1996.
He deals extensively with the failure of the Christian churches in Germany. Following the historian Guenter Lewy, he shifts the focus from
what the churches did not do — the "silence" — toward their positive
role in the Nazis' genocidal project, that of supplier of crucial records.
Goldhagen writes, "The foundational element of the Nuremberg Laws
was the regime's capacity to distinguish and demonstrate the extent of a
person's Jewish ancestry, to know who was a Jew. Enforcement therefore
depended upon the use of the genealogical records in the possession of local churches."[37] Lewy quoted a priest who defined this identification activity as a "service to the people," but that was in 1934. Once the function —
and the result — of this role became clear, did the churches stop performing it? Lewy says no. "The very question of whether the Church
should lend its help to the Nazi state in sorting out people of Jewish
descent was never debated." A few heroes among the clergy, including
Angelo Roncalli, the future Pope John XXIII, exploited the Church's function as a racial-certification agent to provide false identity documents to
Jews, but the institutional Church never renounced this role. "The cooperation of the Church in this matter continued right through the war
years," Lewy writes, "when the price of being Jewish was no longer dismissal from a government job and loss of livelihood, but deportation and
outright physical destruction."[38] This fact leads Goldhagen to include certain Church officials among the agents of destruction. "What defines a
perpetrator?" he asks. "A perpetrator is anyone who knowingly contributed in some intimate way to the mass slaughter of Jews . . . Perpetrators
include railroad engineers and administrators who knew that they were
transporting Jews to their deaths. They include any Church officials who

knew that their participation in the identification of Jews as non-Christians would lead to the deaths of the Jews."[39]

Pope Pius XII, without violating his tactic of diplomatic prudence, could have quietly instructed parish priests throughout Europe to destroy baptismal records once their diabolical function became clear. He never did.

Critics of Pius XII, like Hochhuth, have accounted for his failure to challenge Hitler more directly by charging him with cowardice, or with Nazi sympathies, but his biographer John Cornwell shows that the former was never the case, and by the late 1930s neither was the latter. Pius XII's courage and his contempt for Hitler were demonstrated by his active participation, early in his pontificate, in a plot to overthrow the German dictator. From late 1939 through March 1940, Pius XII served as a channel of communication between a group of anti-Hitler German army chiefs, led by General Ludwig Beck, and the British government, represented by Britain's Vatican minister, Francis d'Arcy Osborne. The Germans indicated their readiness to stage a coup and end the war, but only with assurances from London that the Munich settlement would be honored. For whatever reason, the British failed to pick up on the initiative, but not before the plotters and the pope himself had acted in ways that Hitler, had he learned of them, would have savagely punished. This episode leads Cornwell to a firm conclusion about Pacelli: "Pusillanimity and indecisiveness — shortcomings that would be cited to extenuate his subsequent silence and inaction in other matters — were hardly in his nature."[40]

So what accounts not only for the silence of Pius XII, but for Eugenio Pacelli's complicity with Hitler in the early years? The early years offer the clue, for it was then that Pacelli's determination to put the accumulation and defense of papal power above everything else showed itself for what it was. Above the fate of the Jews, certainly, but also above the fate of the Catholic Church elsewhere in Europe. "Was there something in the modern ideology of papal power," Cornwell asks, "that encouraged the Holy See to acquiesce in the face of Hitler's evil, rather than oppose it?"[41] The answer to this awful question, it seems increasingly clear, is yes, which makes even more problematic, too, the Vatican's current wish to make a saint of Pius IX, whose claim to infallibility and whose "Syllabus of Errors" made him the supreme modern ideologue of papal power.

It almost goes without saying that Pacelli would have shared the broad antisemitism of his culture, the Christian contempt for Judaism that would not be repudiated until Vatican II. But the pursuit of papal power in the modern era had come at the expense of Jews, and that too is part of what led to Europe's acquiescence before the Final Solution. We just recalled how this played out in the Roman ghetto, but it affected theology as well. When the "Syllabus of Errors" (1864) was defined by a leading Catholic journal as a set of detested "modern ideas . . . of Jewish origin";[42] when European liberal movements in politics and education were denounced as a demonic Jewish conspiracy; when Church organs led the way in branding Jews simultaneously as revolutionaries and financiers; and when all of this is centered in vengeful Catholic policies toward Jews in the Roman ghetto, under the pope's windows, a far graver issue arises than the silence of one man. The question rather becomes, How did a succession of popes prepare the way for the "silence" of an entire civilization?

"The Pope's silence," Father Edward Flannery wrote, "is better seen as the apex of a triangle that rested on the much wider acquiescence of the German episcopacy, his most immediate 'constituents,' which, in turn, rested on the still wider apathy or collusion with Nazism of German Catholics — or Christians — themselves so ill prepared for any better response by accustomed antisemitic attitudes so often aided and abetted in the past by the churches themselves. The triangle continues to widen, as we include a Europe and a Western world, impregnated with an indifference, if not an antipathy, to Jews."[43]

If Pius XII had done what his critics, in hindsight, wish him to have done — excommunication of Hitler, revocation of the concordat, "a flaming protest against the massacre of the Jews," in Lewy's phrase[44] — it would have been only a version of what Pius IX did in 1875 against Bismarck, and in 1871 against Garibaldi when he excommunicated all Italians who cooperated with the new Italian state, even if only by voting in its elections.[45] As before, Catholics would have had to choose between a Church-hating government and the Church. But in the 1930s, there is reason to believe, vast numbers of Catholic Germans, and perhaps other Catholic Europeans as well — those who had celebrated the *Reichskonkordat,* and those who had baited the Dreyfusards — would have preferred Hitler to Pius XII. "Shall I bring them into conflicts of conscience?" Pius asked, referring to Catholic Germans, in explaining why he could not protest the extermination of Jews.[46] Because of the "dark symbiosis"[47] of ancient Christian Jew-hatred and modern racism, Hitler's anti-Jewish program, even at its extreme, was simply not that offensive to the broad population of Catholics. As the scholar of antisemitism Léon Poliakov put it, "The Vatican's silence only reflected the deep feeling of the Catholic masses of Europe."[48]

And in fact, the Vatican's preference for its own power, as it pursued its vision of an absolute papacy, was only a version of the choice countless Europeans made to pursue their own welfare without regard for those outside the circle of their concern — the Jews.

That choice had been nearly two thousand years in the making. It is the last consequence of the long story this book has told, from the Seamless Robe of Christ to the cross of Constantine to *La Croix* to *Kreuz und Adler,* to the cross at Auschwitz. This story is itself the source of the pope's silence, and the meaning of it. This is the moral failure of Catholicism, and of the civilization of which it is so centrally a part. The pope's silence is better seen, that is, not as the indictment but as the evidence.

53

Edith Stein and Catholic Memory

ECHT IS A Dutch town near the River Maas, not far from Maas-tricht, the symbolic center of the new Europe, and even closer to the German border. I visited Echt as I made my way to the Rhine-land, revisiting the scenes in which the story of this book unfolded. But my trek to the small Dutch town took on the character of a solitary pilgrimage. It surprised me to find the contemplative's chapel I'd come looking for at the edge of a shopping district; just beyond the stout brick façade of the chapel's adjoining cloister was the Café Apollo, announcing in English, *Dancing*. Far less obtrusive was a stone tablet on the wall near the Gothic-arched chapel door. The tablet featured the chiseled face of a woman in the veil of a Carmelite nun, Edith Stein, who had fled to this monastery in Echt in 1938, and from which she was snatched by the SS in 1942.

My visit was late in the afternoon of a rainy Tuesday. The chapel door was unlocked, and it opened onto a stark room. The place was vacant, but the sanctuary candle flickered. Twelve pews divided the space, room for perhaps fifty people. A grainy photograph of the famous nun was on the wall to the left, behind a vase holding two craning birds of paradise. I had come here with my three questions. The first: How did the history of Christian antisemitism contribute to the Holocaust? The second: How did the Church abet, or oppose, the Holocaust as it unfolded? And the third: How does the Church today negotiate that layered past, both the deep past of antisemitism and the recent past of the Holocaust? With Edith Stein, that third question moved to the forefront of my mind. In the small cha-pel organized around her image, I knelt down to ask.

Edith Stein was born a Jew in 1891 in Breslau,[1] to whose archbishop we referred as wanting the *Reichskonkordat* to defend not Jews but Catholic Jews. Stein left Breslau, but her mother, to whom she remained devoted, lived there, an observant Jew, all her life. Stein was a gifted young woman who made her mark as a philosopher, earning a Ph.D. under the phenomenologist Edmund Husserl. Often described as his protégée, she made significant contributions to his thought, although they are rarely noted.[2] Her dissertation, "On the Problem of Empathy," which she defended in 1916,[3] was the first of several important philosophical works, but her dramatic life and her later devotional writing have been more widely acknowledged. Having abandoned Jewish religious practice in her student years, Stein became a Catholic in 1922, at the age of thirty or thirty-one. She reports having been moved to do so by reading the autobiography of Saint Teresa of Ávila,[4] the sixteenth-century Spanish mystic and Carmelite reformer. In 1933, Stein herself entered the Carmelite order.

Among the Carmelites, she was known as Sister Benedicta of the Cross, but on October 11, 1998, in a solemn canonization in St. Peter's Square, Pope John Paul II was the first to refer to her as Saint Teresa Benedicta. She was made a saint of the Church not because of her groundbreaking work in philosophy, her feminism, or her devoted life as a religious Catholic, but because a week after being hauled away from Echt, she was gassed in Auschwitz. In his sermon at the canonization of the woman he called "this eminent daughter of Israel and faithful daughter of the Church," John Paul II said, "May her witness constantly strengthen the bridge of mutual understanding between Jews and Christians."[5]

But the canonization of the convert from Judaism elicited more antagonism than mutuality,[6] and was taken by many Jews as an insult. Vatican officials reacted defensively. One fired back with the reminder that the Church has long suffered from attacks by Jews, especially Bolsheviks — a rejoinder that seemed especially pointed, being made by Father Peter Gumpel, who, as we saw, is the priest advocating for the canonization of Pius XII.[7] But presumably most Catholics were mystified and saddened by the dispute, for they recognized in Edith Stein the story of an innocent woman whose spiritual hunger led her to identify with the cross of Jesus Christ, and who then, as Christians thought of it, underwent a contemporary crucifixion. Like many Catholics, I was led to a new awareness of the Holocaust because of her. I was a young seminarian in the early 1960s when I picked up a book in the seminary library entitled *Walls Are Crumbling: Seven Jewish Philosophers Discover Christ,* by John M. Oesterreicher. One chapter was "Edith Stein: Witness for Love."[8] What Anne Frank was just then doing for society at large — making real the horror of the still deflected genocide by giving one victim a name, a face, a voice, and a story — Edith Stein did for me and many Catholics. The complexities of her witness never entered our minds.

The complaints of some Jews about the canonization of Edith Stein amounted to questions about an implicit supersessionism, the idea that Judaism has been replaced by Christianity. As we have seen, the Catholic Church had officially rejected supersessionism,[9] but when Stein was routinely referred to by Catholics as "a young woman in search of the truth," a phrase the pope used in his sermon,[10] Jews were hard put to deflect the suspicion that even now the truth was being defined in exclusively Christian terms. At first, Stein had been put forward as a candidate for sainthood in the category of "confessor," meaning that her exemplary life was what had qualified her for reverence, but Pope John Paul II had insisted on honoring her as a formally declared "martyr" for the faith.[11] Once again, the old Christian tendency to move death to the forefront of identity had asserted itself, but of course in this instance the means and place of death were essential. Another factor may have been at play. In order to be named a saint of the Catholic Church, a candidate must be credited with having caused two miracles, or, in the case of a martyr, one. So by declaring Edith Stein a martyr, the pope was simplifying what was needed to declare her a saint.

In proclaiming Edith Stein a martyr, the Church emphasized that she was killed as a Catholic, in retaliation for an anti-Nazi protest by Catholic bishops. But to Jewish critics, she died as a Jew, pure and simple. If she was a martyr, weren't all who died with her martyrs as well? And doesn't the very idea of Christian martyrdom, with its opening to the infinite consolations of redemption, do a further violence to Jewish victims for most of whom such consolations would have remained forever unthinkable? In these ways, didn't her canonization amount, as some Jews put it, to a "Christianizing" of the Holocaust — the ultimate supersessionism? Edith Stein, in other words, could be taken by Jews, and was, as the symbol of a theology of resurrection imposed on their dead. The cross at Auschwitz is a sacrilege.

Pope John Paul II had indicated in his sermon at the canonization that Stein's feast day, August 9, the presumed date of her murder, was to be a day on which "we must also remember the Shoah." Jews asked why Catholics could not have remembered the Shoah on the late April day that Jews themselves had already long marked as the observance of Yom Hashoah. Was the liturgical calendar also to be a realm of supersessionism?

For Jews, though, the implications of the canonization had become more problematic because of other events. One week before the Edith Stein ceremony, the pope had named as "blessed" Cardinal Alojzije Stepinac, the wartime primate of the Catholic Church in Croatia. We already took note of Stepinac's beatification, but seeing it in the context of the Stein canonization suggests more fully why questions keep surfacing. After the war, Stepinac was condemned by Tito's government as a Nazi collaborator, and while he may not have been a collaborator, the church over which Stepinac presided during the war had been mortally compromised by the pro-Nazi Ustashi regime and was implicated in many crimes, especially against the "schismatic" Serbs.[12] It did not assuage such suspicions when, not long after Edith Stein's canonization, reports surfaced — I was the main reporter — that the Vatican had dishonestly manipulated its own saint-making procedures, certifying as a Stein-sponsored "miracle" (the single one that was needed) the recovery of a sick child that a supervising medical expert insisted — in formal but secret testimony to Church investigators — was routine. The child was cured not by a miraculous intervention but by standard medicine, an outcome that "was what was to be expected."[13] The canonization itself was based on a knowing deception at the highest levels of the Catholic Church.

The canonization of Edith Stein, in other words, revealed the lengths to which the Church was prepared to go to renegotiate its own history during the Holocaust. This woman's story is being told to make Catholics victims of the Nazis along with Jews, and it is being told to reinforce, again, the centrality of martyrdom in faith, and to reaffirm the religious superiority of Christianity over Judaism. But there is another way to tell the story of Edith Stein — as an object lesson in Church denial.

The saint's story as a Catholic began with Teresa of Ávila as the source of her conversion, and as her namesake. But nothing reveals the painful complexity of a Jew's conversion to Catholicism more sharply than Saint Teresa's own history, which we touched on earlier. Her grandfather Juan Sánchez de Cepeda was a *converso*, but he had "relapsed" from Christianity back into Judaism. In 1485, he appeared before the Inquisition in Toledo, along with his wife and children, including Teresa's father, who was a child of six at the time. They were given the choice of reconverting to Christianity or being burned alive. As Saint Teresa's luminous career shows, they decided in favor of the former.[14] Edith Stein's story casts the Catholic memory back into that panorama of forced conversion of Jews by Catholics, of which the Inquisition was only one peak in a range.

Here we find the full significance of the move to make a saint of Pope

Pius IX — the nineteenth-century antimodern pope who issued the "Syllabus of Errors" and demanded that Vatican I proclaim his doctrinal infallibility. For our purposes, the thing to note about this putative saint is that he approved the unwilled baptism of Jewish children in territory under his control, and that he personally joined in sponsoring the kidnapping of a Jewish child.[15] The great-great-niece of that child called the beatification of Pius IX the "reopening of a wound."[16] That and other recent moves show that the Church, despite a contrary rhetoric, has yet to purge itself of a deep antagonism to the independent integrity of the Jewish religion, and that is why honoring a Jewish convert as a saint was bound to raise questions.

In 1933, a decade after her conversion and only weeks after the Fulda Episcopal Conference lifted its ban on Catholic membership in the Nazi Party, Edith Stein took her first extraordinary initiative as a Catholic, one that received little attention in the Vatican's 1998 canonization celebration. Before Easter in 1933, as she would later date it, she wrote to Pope Pius XI to request a private audience during which to plead for an encyclical condemning Nazi antisemitism.[16] At about the same time, probably while she was waiting for a reply, she was informed by her employer, a Catholic teachers' college in Münster, that she could no longer keep her position as a teacher because she was "non-Aryan,"[17] although, as a Catholic institution, this college would not yet have been required to take such a step.[18] That spring, the philosopher Martin Heidegger, who had interviewed Stein for a professorship and rejected her,[19] gave his notorious pro-Nazi speech at Freiburg.

We do not know what such events meant to Stein, but it was now that she began to consider acting on a long-deferred wish to enter the contemplative life. That same April, she applied for admission to the Carmelite convent in Cologne.[20] In philosophy, she had demonstrated, as the scholar Rachel Feldhay Brenner put it, "the tendency to incorporate, rather than eliminate, to reaffirm, rather than reject."[21] Her contemplative vocation, if anything, would sharpen that method, enabling a plunge into Christian spirituality, while events simultaneously forced a deepening of her Jewish identity, even as she redefined it according to the dominant supersessionism of the Church.

Around the time of her application to the Carmelites, Edith Stein received her answer from the Vatican. She was invited to attend, with numerous other people, a purely ceremonial audience with the pope. There was no question of a private word with His Holiness; uninterested in the honorific, she declined the invitation, appealing the refusal of her request. She then received a papal blessing in the mail.[22] This effort of Stein's to elicit a Vatican statement in defense of Jews is often assumed to have been an attempt to get the pope to influence the Nazis, which defenders of the papal silence always assert would have been impossible, given Hitler's diabolical character. But in 1933, Hitler was not "Hitler" yet. And Edith Stein would have already understood that it was her fellow Catholics who needed influencing. As an encyclical had mobilized them to "passive resistance" once before, might not a firm word from Rome have done so again?

After Kristallnacht in November 1938, Edith Stein fled from the convent in Cologne to Echt. It was on December 19 that she wrote to a friend, "I have often wondered since, whether my letter" — to the pope — "may sometimes have come to mind."[23] On July 6, 1942, Anne Frank's family moved into the hidden attic. A week later, a group of Dutch churchmen sent a telegram to the Nazi authorities denouncing the deportation of Jews from Holland. They added a special plea for baptized Jews, which proved to be a mistake, because it put the Nazis in a position to bargain with the Church. The Nazis replied that if the clergy ceased its protest, baptized Jews would be exempted from deportation. The open arrests and deportation of Jews continued, and at least some of the Dutch Catholic bishops could not accept the tacit agreement. The archbishop of Utrecht, perhaps in cooperation with other Catholic bishops, wrote a pastoral letter to the Catholics of the Netherlands that included the text of the telegram, denouncing "the measures already undertaken against Jews" as "contrary to the deepest conviction of the Dutch people and . . . to God's commands of justice and mercy." The Nazi reaction was swift. Something like two hundred Catholic-baptized Jews were promptly arrested, including, on August 2, Edith Stein and her sister Rosa.[24]

Years later, a Dutch official who had met the Carmelite nun in the transit camp at Westerbork, in northern Holland, reported that he asked if he could help her, apparently referring to her obvious status as one of the baptized (she was wearing a full habit). She demurred, saying, "Why should there be an exception made in the case of a particular group? Wasn't it fair that baptism not be allowed to become an advantage?"[25] The point of the story is not to honor Sister Benedicta for going willingly to her death, an emphasis the Vatican gave it in naming her a martyr. This is especially so since there are also reports that she sought in Westerbork to provoke an intervention by the Swiss consul.[26] What is notable, and what the Vatican fails to emphasize, is that, at the end of her life, Sister

Benedicta of the Cross, Edith Stein, rejected the distinction between baptized and nonbaptized Jews as defining the circle of Catholic concern. And more important, that she tried to fight Nazism in the only way she knew, via the Church. The Dutch bishops had joined her in that, but few others in the Catholic hierarchy ever did.[27]

The true epiphany of Edith Stein's story is that, in a visceral rejection of Christian theology, she refused to see the Jews as disadvantaged before God. Because of the world into which she was thrust, she was forced out of the supersessionist mold.[28] That said, it is also important to acknowledge that many of Sister Benedicta's earlier assumptions about the guilt of her "unbelieving people" reflected Christian religious antisemitism. "It is the shadow of the Cross which is falling upon my people," she is reported to have said in 1939. "If only they would see this! It is the fulfillment of the curse which my people called upon its own head."[29] In drafting her will some years before she died, she is understood to have offered her life in atonement for Jewish unbelief.[30] On the occasion of her canonization, *L'Osservatore Romano* honored her for saying to Rosa, as the SS took them off, "Come, we are going for our people." That "for" implies not only an expiation, but two thousand years of superiority, which is why the saint's niece, Suzanne Batzdorff, who is Jewish, insists that her aunt's fate was "to die with her people, not for her people."[31]

Edith Stein began her intellectual life with a study of empathy, the capacity of one person to find something in common with another, very different person. Nearly sixty years after her death, she remains a source of dispute over the meaning of conversion and martyrdom, and a source of doubt about the motives of the Church. Because of her and other candidates for sainthood,[32] the uses of canonization and their effect on how the Holocaust is remembered have come powerfully into question. Her death at Auschwitz spurred her fellow Carmelites to establish the convent there, and the cross erected in the adjacent field remains the poignant and outrageous symbol of all that still divides Christians and Jews.

Such contradictions gave shape to the life of Edith Stein. "For now, the world consists of opposites . . . ," she was reported to have said en route to Auschwitz. "But in the end, none of those contrasts will remain. There will only be the fullness of love. How could it be otherwise?"[33] But we are not at the end yet. The cross still stands at Auschwitz.

That the Catholic Church has sought to confront the meaning of the Holocaust through a hedged version of the memory of Edith Stein; that the Church has, through Stein, sought to place Catholics in the position of having been Nazi victims; that the Church's expressions of sorrow for the Holocaust have been self-exonerating — all of this shows how deeply inadequate these well-intentioned gestures have been. And, as this book shows, the Catholic Church's ongoing refusal to face honestly and fully the long history of its contempt for Jews is what has made it impossible for the Church to face its own complicity, remote and proximate, in the Holocaust — much less to authentically repent of that contempt, or to renounce it.

For these reasons, Edith Stein is the saint who, instead of advancing Jewish-Christian relations, impedes them. Until the Church accomplishes a complete reckoning with a past that reaches far beyond the Holocaust, Edith Stein, instead of blessing the Church, will haunt it.

PART EIGHT

A CALL FOR VATICAN III

⤞ 54 ⤝

The Broad Relevance
of Catholic Reform

ND THE END of all our exploring / Will be to arrive where we
started."[1] What I did not know at the beginning of this exploration was that the Church's attitude toward Jews is so central
to everything. The Christian fantasy of "the jew," with its bipolarity, its association with images of revolution and of finance, its attachment to myths of wandering, exile, and expiation — all helped shape the
Western imagination. So this book is more than a chronicle of religion,
and has as much to say to nonreligious readers as to Jews and Christians.
Certainly, more than Catholics have a stake in this story's past and future.

In recognizing the place where I arrive as the place where I started, I am
thinking of that decidedly Roman Catholic event, the Second Vatican
Council, which shaped my life as a young priest. When I described myself
early on as a child of Vatican II, I thought that the greatest significance of
the reforming council of the early 1960s was its concern with various aspects of Church renewal, but after this exploration of connections between theology and politics, I see its significance for an entire society beyond the Church. Even among non-Catholics, for example, the figure of
Pope John XXIII is linked in memory with that of John Kennedy, and for
good reason. Pope John's *aggiornamento* within the Church helped stimu-
late the transformation of cultural attitudes that swept Europe and the
United States in the 1960s. The liberalization of Catholic theology reflected that social mutation and advanced it, and that process is not complete. As the forces of religion have become, by the early twenty-first century, ever more fundamentalist, yoked to political reaction and ethnic
chauvinism, and as scientific rationalism has proven to be a woefully incomplete ideology, there is more need than ever for a revived Catholicism

committed to intellectual rigor, open inquiry, and respect for the other. This seems especially true in recognizing Roman Catholicism as the only world institution that bridges Northern and Southern hemispheres, rich and poor, and disparities between knowledge elites and mass illiteracy. To use a past Vatican Council that humanized the Church as a model of what a future council can be is to put the prospect of progressive societal change before a wide audience. And in nothing is this more true than in relation to the task of ending antisemitism forever.

The Second Vatican Council represented the beginning of the long-overdue demise of a Constantinian imperial Catholicism, as it had been shaped by a medieval papalism hardened in the fires of the Counter-Reformation. Vatican II signaled a truce in the Church's war against modernity, its final desperate revolt against a rapidly changing world. At the time, I thought that improving the Church's relations with Jews was one agenda item among others, some of which seemed more important. The rights of women, the end of patriarchal autocracy, the restoration of simple honesty, the recovery from clericalism, the place of the laity, the abandonment of denominational narcissism in relation to other churches, an affirmation of sexuality — not to mention my hopes as a young priest for the right to marry. What were the Jews among all these issues?

I embraced a first ideal for myself, defining it consciously in terms of the Church into which I was born. When I entered the Paulist Fathers' novitiate in 1962, I lived according to a daily schedule that had been set by the Council of Trent in the sixteenth century, observing rubrics of contemplation, scholasticism, and manual labor that preserved a puritanical regimen. And the truth is, I loved it. But also, equally consciously, I had been drawn to that life by my brush with Pope John XXIII, who had taken me in his arms. When my family had its audience with the pope I was a sixteen-year-old boy, but I towered above him, and bent to accept his embrace. I never forgot his red velvet shoe next to my penny loafer, the soapy aroma of his shaven face, his whiskers scraping my cheek. The curl of the words he whispered remained in my ear; their intimate affection had conscripted me, though I did not understand what he had said. What drew me to him, to the Church, and to what I thought of as God was the clear fact of Pope John's being anything but a puritan.[2]

The world loved him so, and I did, simply because he was not a misanthrope. We could not have admitted it, but the Catholic Church, with its Constantinian legacy, was institutionalized and bureaucratized misanthropy itself.[3] We took the weight of its world hatred so much for granted that a life-loving man like Pope John could seem a miraculous exception. He was not interested in being a museum keeper, he said. Instead, he wanted "to cultivate a flourishing garden of life."[4] The enthusiasm with which the Church, and those outside it, took to him was itself a grievous, if implicit, indictment of what we Catholics had allowed ourselves to become.

This was the pope who left for others the question of infallibility, declaring that he, for one, would never speak infallibly.[5] He was given to spontaneous remarks and jokes at his own expense. He disliked the pomp of office. To avoid being cheered like a potentate as he entered St. Peter's Basilica, he ordered the choirmaster to lead the throng in singing. When he visited the Regina Coeli prison in Rome, his biographer Peter Hebblethwaite reports, he eschewed the condescending piety that usually marks such encounters, and quietly told the inmates of his own uncle who had served time. In the middle of the Cuban Missile Crisis, in October 1962, he addressed an unprecedented message to the leaders of the United States, the Soviet Union, and the rest of the world. His words were reported the next day on the front page of *Pravda*, in Moscow, under the headline, "We Beg All Rulers Not to Be Deaf to the Cry of Humanity." "This was unheard of," Hebblethwaite commented. "John's appeal enabled Nikita Khrushchev, the Soviet leader, to back down without losing face."[6] Only months later, in his encyclical *Pacem in Terris,* he broke with Cold War orthodoxy and raised the question of whether nuclear weapons could ever be used as an instrument of justice, sowing the seeds of a new Catholic conscientious objection. John XXIII did not exactly initiate the peace movement of the 1960s, but his anticipation of it would serve as a powerful inspiration. Similarly with détente, for he embraced the nephew of Khrushchev at a time when other Western leaders were still demonizing Communists. Equally significant, he was one of the first to recognize the coming power of the women's movement, which he flagged, together with the demise of colonialism and the rise of workers, as one of the welcome signs of the times.[7]

All of that, and the steady work of practical change within the institution over which he presided. When he issued his surprising summons to the Vatican Council, barely six months after being elected, he said it was not for the purpose of condemning errors. The world didn't need the Church for that, he said, for "nowadays men are condemning them of their own accord."[8] When, at the beginning of Vatican II, he denounced the "prophets of doom," everyone knew that he was speaking of those who had set the tone in his own Church for generations. He was himself an alternative example of what the Church could now become. "As unforgettable as his person was," Hans Küng wrote of Pope John, "what he achieved for the Catholic Church was unforgettable too. In five years he renewed the Catholic Church more than his predecessors had in five hundred years . . . Only with John did the Middle Ages come to an end in the Catholic Church."[9]

But now I see all this in a different light. Angelo Giuseppe Roncalli was just turning seventy-seven when he assumed the papacy in 1958, elected as a compromise candidate whose great age was expected to keep him from doing much as pope. But he came to the office from a particular experience. For the previous six years, he had been the archbishop of Venice, but for the quarter of a century before that he had served as a Vatican diplomat in Bulgaria, Turkey, and France. The dominant experience he had had as a priest was of the devastation of World War II. He saw it not from the perspective of the sacristy, or for that matter of Vatican City, but of ruined cities, refugee centers, the camps. Roncalli, as we saw, was one of the only Catholic prelates in Europe who, as a legate in Bulgaria and in Turkey providing counterfeit baptismal records to thousands of fugitive Jews, had actively resisted the Holocaust.[10] Hence the relevance of Hannah Arendt's anecdote, cited earlier, about Hochhuth's play *The Deputy*. When asked what should be done against the play, with its devastating portrait of Pius XII, Arendt reported, Pope John allegedly replied, "Do against it? What can you do against the truth?"[11]

The Church's failure in relation to Adolf Hitler was only a symptom of the ecclesiastical cancer Pope John was attempting to treat. The long tradition of Christian Jew-hatred, on which Hitler had so efficiently built, was the malignant tumor that had metastasized in the mystical body. John XXIII had instinctively grasped this. Hence his open-hearted response to the Jewish historian Jules Isaac (in June 1960), who traced the Church's antisemitism to the Gospels, and John's subsequent charge (in September) to those preparing for the council that it take up the Church's relations with Judaism as a matter of priority.[12] Hence his elimination from the Good Friday liturgy of the modifiers "faithless" and "perfidious" as applied to Jews,[13] an implicit rejection of supersessionism. Hence his greeting to a first Jewish delegation at the Vatican: "I am Joseph, your brother," he said, then came down from his throne to sit with them in a simple chair.[14] To appreciate such a gesture, one need only think of the "pope's Jews" kissing the ground trod by the velvet slipper before returning to their "hole," as Pius IX, speaking not long before Roncalli was born, had called the ghetto at the foot of Vatican Hill.

As we have seen, for hundreds of years popes had defined their power in terms of their sovereignty over Jews, and for nearly two thousand years Catholic theology had projected almost every affirmation of the Church against the negative screen of a detested Judaism. Here was the Church's first, and permanent, mistake — an unbroken chain of choice and consequence that crossed the centuries. That narrative arc, traced here, cuts through time as a refutation of the core idea, expressed in various ways, that the Church is a "perfect society," that as the Bride of Christ it is spotless, that the claim to infallibility in matters of faith and morals is more than wishful thinking or rank denial. It is not too much to assume that for John XXIII, the Holocaust, which he saw up close and experienced as a trauma of his own, exposed this deeply entrenched assumption to profound questioning.

At bottom, what was so urgently required of the Catholic Church was a change in what it said, thought, and believed about Jews. A reform that addressed the problem of Catholic antisemitism could be anything but peripheral, and the Church's relations with Jews could be anything but just one more item on the council's agenda. This was so not only because the ongoing faith of Jews called into question absolutist claims made for Jesus Christ, not only because steady Jewish affirmation of the Shema apparently contradicted central tenets of the Christian creed, and not only because the universalist exclusivism of the Catholic Church was incompatible with authentic respect for Israel's unbroken covenant with God. The council's mandate to reform the Church was rooted in the history of its relations with Jews because that history, more than anything else, established the Church's radical sinfulness. And Pope John saw it.

Pope John died of stomach cancer in June 1963, not long after the promulgation of *Pacem in Terris* and after presiding at the first session of Vatican II. There would be three more sessions, presided over by Pope Paul VI (1963–1978). As Giovanni Battista Montini, he had worked as a devoted factotum to Pius XII, and that background showed in his pontificate. Pressed to establish the "cause" of John XXIII's candidacy for sainthood, Paul VI at the same time established that of Pius XII, as if the two men were in any way comparable. Acting out of the old (but not that old) instinct of papal primacy, Paul VI undercut the council when he refused to let its members consider the pressing questions of priestly celibacy and birth control. Defying what could easily have been opposite outcomes if the council fathers had taken up those questions, he issued independent encyclicals upholding the traditional requirement that priests not marry (*Sacerdotalis Caelibatus,* 1967) and banning contraception (*Humanae Vitae,* 1968). I was ordained to the priesthood in 1969, not appreciating yet the damage the pronouncements had done. I was then one of many thousands of Catholic priests who left the priesthood once that damage became clear. The disconnect between the teachings of these encyclicals and the lives Catholics were leading was too great, and the blow that the condemnation of birth control was to Church authority and integrity is well known.[15]

Given the ideology of papal absolutism that he inherited from his mentor Pius XII, Paul VI thought he had no choice but to reaffirm teachings that had been firmly adhered to by popes for a thousand years or more. His was the first effort to turn back the tide of Church reform that the Vatican Council initiated, and that program of medieval restoration has been vigorously continued by Pope John Paul II. The question of the Church's relations with Jews was far more fundamental than these matters of sexuality, but on that the council was able to take only the smallest step. I have already described the perplexity with which we seminarians greeted *Nostra Aetate,* the council document approved in October 1965, which stated that "what happened in his [Christ's] passion cannot be blamed upon all the Jews then living, without distinction, nor upon the Jews of today." I say perplexity because, while *Nostra Aetate* was put forward as if it were rebutting a marginal slander of gutter antisemitism, we young students of the New Testament knew that the sacred texts of the Church placed just such blame on the Jews then living and "on [their] children."[16] We knew that, from what we thought of as its origins, the Church had defined itself as the replacement of Judaism, and that because Judaism had refused to yield to that claim, the Church had further defined itself as the enemy of Judaism. *Nostra Aetate* took up none of this, but by defining as a lie an affirmation at the center of the Gospel, it clearly put such basic questions on the Church's near-term agenda. Indeed, *Nostra Aetate* implicitly raised the issue of whether, in its first generation, the Church had already betrayed its master.

We did not know it at the time, but *Nostra Aetate,* as promulgated by the council, was a considerably watered-down document when compared to earlier drafts. It probably fell far short of what John XXIII, responding to Jules Isaac, had wanted. For example, the first thought was that the council would make a stand-alone statement, entitled *Decretum de Judaeis,* about relations between the Church and Judaism, but *Nostra Aetate* is a declaration on all non-Christian religions, with only one small section devoted to Judaism. In the initiating spirit of Pope John, many council fathers expected the statement to include an acknowledgment of Church culpability. "Why can we not draw from the Gospel," one bishop asked during debate in the nave of St. Peter's, "the magnanimity to beg for forgiveness, in the name of so many Christians, for so many and so great injustices?"[17]

But it was not to be. *Nostra Aetate* "deplores the hatred, persecutions, and displays of anti-Semitism directed against the Jews at any time and from any source,"[18] but, of course, it seems not to know what the main source of the hatred, persecutions, and displays had been. As with the rejection of the deicide charge, the declaration here seems oddly incomplete, as if saying, We can go into this so far, but no farther. And sadly, the apology for sins against the people of Israel that Pope John Paul II offered in the momentous ceremony in St. Peter's on March 12, 2000, also avoided a direct confrontation with the source of antisemitism. We will turn to that apology's positive aspect later, but here we must note its shortfall. "We are deeply saddened," the pope prayed on that occasion, "by the behavior of those who in the course of history have caused these children of yours [Jews] to suffer." It was possible to hear that apology as regret for behavior that was inconsistent with core Church teaching, instead of set in motion by it.

In such difficult matters, any step toward authentic reckoning is to be welcomed. The papal apology in March 2000 built on what was said at the council, but honesty requires the acknowledgment that the early pattern of deflection has been continued. Here is how one historian of the council sums up what happened. "The Declaration *Nostra Aetate* had a very difficult and troubled development in the council, which recalls in many ways the tragic bimillennial history of relations between Christians and Jews and makes it seem almost miraculous that the declaration ever appeared. Indiscretions, intrigues, near-eastern misunderstandings and fears, especially of a political nature, all became entangled. In addition to this, there was what could be called 'Christian obstinacy,' a certain inability to understand, found among some Christians at the council. They were mentally unprepared for the topic."[19]

Or perhaps not. Maybe the council fathers had such difficulty because

A Call for Vatican III

they grasped, if only subliminally, how far into the ground of theology the spike of this question goes. And perhaps that still accounts for the Church's inability to face this history more directly. The "topic" of the Jews, unlike most other topics, has truly far-reaching implications. Neither the fathers of Vatican II nor Pope Paul VI was prepared to examine the foundational assumptions of Christian faith, the prophecy-fulfillment structure of salvation history, the construction of a Passion narrative requiring the Messiah to be rejected by "his own," and atonement Christology itself, as this all implied a denigration of the Jews. Instead, acting from good intentions, Church fathers hoped to renounce the denigration, but without facing what made it inevitable.

And so with Pope John Paul II. Continuing the pattern, he seems to have assumed that heartfelt gestures of friendship toward Jews, combined with sincere sympathy for Jewish suffering and abstract acts of repentance, would suffice. When Jews seemed to say otherwise, they were slapped down for being ungrateful. And always, from discussions of Holy Week pogroms to the Inquisition to the Final Solution, there has been the commitment to keep any shadow of moral culpability or accusation of sin away from, in John Paul II's phrase, "the Church as such." Thus, as we saw, the 1998 "confession," "We Remember: A Reflection on the Shoah," acknowledges the failures of some of the Church's children, but not of the Church. Similarly with the subsequent declaration, "Memory and Reconciliation: The Church and the Faults of the Past," issued just before the repentance ceremony in St. Peter's.

The examination of conscience for which John XXIII had called required more than was possible at the time, probably more than even he envisaged. It is one thing to consider allowing priests to marry or couples to practice contraception — and the Church has so far proved itself incapable of doing even that — but really to eliminate the contempt for Jews that lives not in the hearts of prejudiced Christians but in the heart of "the Church as such" requires fundamental changes in the way history has been written, theology has been taught, and Scripture has been interpreted. Indeed, in this context, the very character of Scripture as sacred text becomes an issue. Not even the Reformation, as traumatic as it was, sought to go this deeply into the meaning of the tradition, as is clear from Martin Luther's masterly appropriation of the tradition's antisemitism. So, yes, the reforming impulse of Vatican II fell far short of what was needed, and yes, in the years since, the authorities of the Church have done their best to dampen any return of that impulse within Catholicism. How, given this history, could it have been otherwise?

But the reforming impulse refuses to die, even in the Church, because the event that set it moving has only continued to grow in force in the conscience of the West. This is what it means that, at the most basic level, Pope John XXIII was responding to the Holocaust. The Final Solution has refused to remain unadjudicated in institutions everywhere. If Bayer, Swiss banks, the Louvre, owners of apartments in the Eighth Arrondissement, the Ford Motor Company, the U.S. Treasury Department, and the *New York Times* are made to confront their relationship to this unfinished business of the twentieth century, so with the Catholic Church. If Argentina can repent, as its president did in June 2000, of having offered refuge to Nazi war criminals, why can't the Vatican repent of having helped some of those same war criminals escape to Argentina? As a Catholic, I have been raised with the intuition that such moral reckoning is essential to the life of conscience, whether the individual's or the community's. I now understand better than I did before that Church history is itself the record of such moral reckoning, if accomplished in fits and starts.

In reaction to the Protestant Reformation, a defensive Catholicism adopted the attitude that, sinless in itself, "the Church as such" had no need of reformation, yet that was an anomalous mistake, in violation of a much older Catholic tradition. Ironically, in rejecting the spirit of modernity, the Roman Catholic Church, with a certitude to rival that of the crassest sort of Enlightenment science, had perfectly embodied that spirit. John XXIII's greatest achievement was to declare the time over when the Church could so blithely stand as a monument of self-contradiction, if decidedly not of self-criticism. The council he called was the twenty-first "ecumenical" gathering of Church leaders, and though that means such an event had happened, on average, more than once each century, the only council that had met since the defensive Trent was the hyperdefensive Vatican I, where papal primacy and papal infallibility were defined as dogmas. But the tradition of the councils itself was a proclamation of the Church's ongoing fallibility, its permanent need for reformation. That charged word was introduced into Church parlance not by Martin Luther but by the fathers of the Council of Constance (1414–1418), which called for "reform in faith and practice, in head and members."[20] *Ecclesia semper reformanda,* the Church forever being reformed, is another old slogan. The hope that resides in this enterprise, "firmly grounded in the Catholic tradition," is caught by Hans Küng when he points out that the Latin *reformare* means "to shape something according to its own essential being."[21]

The first General Council was the one we considered near the beginning of this book, at Nicaea in 325, and it was nothing but an effort to overcome disputes, factions, and fractures — notes of a community that saw itself as anything but perfect. Subsequent councils were called to heal schisms, to settle feuds, and to resolve absolutely contradictory claims made absolutely. The councils always took up the business of the Church's imperfections, and they often had to respond to the imperfections of the popes. The Council of Constantinople (680–681) condemned Pope Honorius I as a heretic. The Council of Constance, just referred to, when confronted with three claimants to the papacy, forced the resignation of one, deposed the other two, and elected a new pope of its own. Constance issued the proclamation *Sacrasancta,* which established the superiority of council over pope. The assumption took hold that the Church council exercised ultimate authority in the Church, and so there is something wonderfully absurd — something "modern" despite itself — about a council vesting just such authority in the figure of the pope. (How do we know that pope is above council? The council says so!) After Vatican I, with its decree of papal primacy and infallibility, the operative assumption of the papal absolutists was that there would never be a need for another council, which is why John XXIII's convening of Vatican II was itself seen at the time as such a revolutionary act. In fact, it was deeply traditional. The Church lives through the self-criticism implied in the conciliar process, and not only self-criticism, but self-criticism in response to history. John XXIII's summons was, ipso facto, the call to conscience, and it was an act of hope that I am only now able to appreciate as such.

John Henry Newman (1801–1890), the brilliant Englishman who made his name as an Anglican but converted to Catholicism in middle age (1845), was one of those who opposed the move to define papal infallibility as doctrine at Vatican I. When his faction lost out, he found in this long conciliar tradition the reason to remain a Catholic. "Let us have a little faith in her [the Church] I say. Pius is not the last of the popes. The fourth Council modified the third, the fifth the fourth . . . Let us be patient, let us have faith, and a new Pope, and a reassembled Council, may trim the boat."[22] Newman embodied the central Catholic idea that the faith is reasonable, which means that the faith is always subject to reconsideration, and doctrine always subject to development. Hence the conciliar tradition.

When one reads of a Newman, who was able to criticize the Church from within, one feels the sad tug of the absence of all those who were lost to Catholicism's endless argument with itself, especially when they were hounded out by a rigid Church establishment. The conciliar tradition, like the narrative we have traced, suggests that there are places among this people for an Abelard as much as for an Anselm, for a Nicolaus of Cusa as much as for a Thomas Aquinas, for a hedonistic Renaissance pope friendly to Jews as much as for a puritanical grand inquisitor pope who establishes the ghetto. Michelangelo could place a pope in hell in his *Last Judgment*, and as he acted from within the Church, the weight of his critique could be felt, as it is today whenever anyone enters the Sistine Chapel; while Voltaire, say, damning the entire apostolic succession, but from outside, remains forever ignored by those who most need to hear his complaint. The great tragedy of the Reformation is that Martin Luther, apparently by a combination of his own impatience and the Church's intolerance, launched his strongest challenges to a decadent Catholicism from outside it.[23] In part for that reason, the Reformation is still waiting to fully happen within the Catholic Church, and it came not enough to the so-called Reformed churches, which, cut adrift, became all too sectarian. Nothing demonstrates that twin set of disappointments better than the post-Reformation fate of the Jews, at the hands of Catholics and Protestants both.

Luther should have been at the great council of the Church that was convened to take up his challenge. At Trent, he might have made his case in a way that prompted something positive from Catholics. Alas, he was long excommunicated by the time that council convened in 1545, and in any case, Luther died the next year, with, as we saw, an anti-Jewish slur on his lips. It is impossible to look back at the Council of Trent without regret that its genuine and partially successful effort at internal reform of Church theology and practice was overshadowed by all that it did to "counter" its enemies outside the Church. Trent responded to the challenge of the reformers by shoring up the battlements — embodied in the rigidity of the Roman catechism, the casuistry of canon law, the violence of the Inquisition, the censorship of the Index, the hatred of nonconformist outsiders, the obsessiveness of rubrical liturgy, the elitism of the clerical estate, and, above all, in the formal establishment of the Roman ghetto — instead of addressing the continent-wide spiritual crisis that Luther, Calvin, and the others had made so dramatic.

Because of the chaos of post-Reformation denominational conflict, the contingencies of revolution, and the philosophical and cultural mutations that accompanied the Enlightenment, the next council, when it finally came in 1869–1870, was unable (to stay with Newman's metaphor) to trim the boat at all. Instead, Vatican I hauled the Church higher into the misanthropic wind, a course from which not even John XXIII, given his successors, was able to bring it about. Still, in this post-Shoah era, there are reasons to look not only for trimming but for a major tack in fundamental beliefs and practices of the Church, which is why the first conclusion a faithful, if critical, Catholic draws from this narrative is that the time has come to reenvision this religion and the way it relates to the world. The time has come for a gathering of those invested in the future of this Church, which, as is clear by now, means a gathering more broadly defined than any in Church history. Centrally Catholic, it will also include Jews and Protestants, people of other faiths and of no faith, clergy and laity and, emphatically, women. The time has come for the convening of Vatican Council III.[24]

55

Agenda for a New Reformation

O NE REASON to be grateful to the Church of the Counter-Reformation is its resounding rejection, not of Martin Luther — I agree with Hans Küng, who proposes a formal lifting, even now, of Rome's excommunication of the reformer,[1] despite his antisemitism — but of Luther's primal idea that the Christian is to be guided by *sola scriptura,* Scripture alone. In reaction to the abuses of Church authority that drove Luther to his radical stance, he appealed to the ultimate authority of the Bible, as if the texts preceded the community that reads them. But the Catholic position was, and remains, that the community, albeit an inspired community, produced those texts *as* inspired texts, and they are nothing without the readers who take them in. To Luther, Bible readers are individuals who submit to the Word of God as each one understands it, but also as each one bows before it. Luther rejected what appeared to him to be the Church's idolatry of its own hierarchy, but despite his best intentions, he replaced it with a deference to the Word that slips all too easily into an idolatry of its own. Biblical fundamentalism is a manifestation of this. The Catholic-Protestant disagreement goes far deeper than any complaint over indulgences or any political arrangement made with competing princes. Luther "brought the very essence of the Catholic Church into question when (this was the real innovation) he set his personal, subjective, and yet (by his intention) universally binding interpretation of the Scriptures *in principle* above the Church and her tradition."[2]

To Catholics, the understanding of the Scriptures is mediated to the individual by the teaching authority of the Church, which claims primacy over the Word. The Church, after all, began as the communities to which Paul wrote his letters and out of whose oral traditions the Gospels evolved. The Catholic Church understands itself as having canonized

(literally, "made a list of") the Word of God, not vice versa. In the twentieth century, when Scripture scholarship blurred the lines between denominations, and when the critical-historical method made many of the
arguments of the Reformation moot, the Catholic-Protestant difference
could seem more a matter of emphasis than substance. But even into the
twenty-first century, this difference remains, and is apparent, for example,
in the continuing divergence in practice and liturgy, if not theology, that
still separates the "Catholic" tradition, with its sacrament-centered cult,
from the more "Protestant" tradition, with its Bible-centered cult. But this
difference also means that now the community of the Catholic Church,
with its claim to authority even over the inspired Word of God, is in a position to confront the problem of foundational texts that have proven
themselves to be sources of lethal antisemitism.

   That brings us not only to the first item of the agenda a Vatican III must
at last take up — the anti-Jewish consequences of the New Testament —
but to the recognition that such a council's agenda has, in fact, already
been indicated by the history of Church hatred of Jews. What we have
illuminated throughout this history, despite its overwhelmingly negative
character, are the signposts of the roads not taken, those times and places
when other choices might have been made, leading to consequences of
love instead of hate. The purpose of retracing a way to such forks in the
road is not to deny the givenness of history, but to suggest that history
is not finished. The possibility of human recovery from the tragedies of
the past adheres, permanently, in the future. Thus, in addition to anti-
Jewish texts, a Vatican Council III would take up the unfinished questions, perhaps even in the order of the chronology we followed, of power
(Constantine, Ambrose, Augustine), of Christology (Crusades, Anselm,
Abelard), of Church intolerance (Inquisition, Nicolaus of Cusa, the
ghetto), of democracy (Enlightenment, Spinoza, modernism), and only
then of repentance (Holocaust, silence, Edith Stein). As this book has
demonstrated, the Church's attitude toward Jews is at the dead center of
each of these problems, and a fundamental revision of that attitude is the
key to the solution of each problem, too. "Salvation is from the Jews," Jesus said in John,[3] a problematic formulation, perhaps, if it means Jews are
blamed for conditions short of salvation. But it seems clear that authentic
Church reform, defined as shaping something according to its own essential being, is tied to the Jews, if only because the perversion of that essential being, the perversion, that is, of the message of love preached and
lived by Jesus — has so clearly been tied to the Jews from the beginning.

56

Agenda Item 1: Anti-Judaism in the New Testament

H OMO SAPIENS is the species that invents symbols in which to invest passion and authority," the novelist Joyce Carol Oates once commented, "then forgets that symbols are inventions."[1] The first followers of Jesus were no less human than the rest of us, and we saw that this is more or less what they did. Recall that after Jesus died, his friends quickly came to understand him in Jewish apocalyptic terms, expecting him to return soon, ushering in the End Time. This is why, for example, Paul counseled his readers to forgo marriage, not because he was antisex but because so little time remained that procreation, an ultimate investment in the open future, had ceased to have meaning. The assumed imminence of Christ's return informed the first Christians' readiness, even eagerness, to offer their lives as martyrs. The cult of martyrdom and apocalyptic longing go hand in hand.

It may help to review here what we saw before. The first true crisis facing the Jesus movement was that its first generation began to die off without seeing the return of the Lord. The Second Coming had proved to be not nearly so imminent as expected. What did it mean, in light of this new experience, to say that Christ's Kingdom had already been established? All at once, this became a pointed question, since whatever else that Kingdom was, the Jews who identified with Jesus assumed it involved a liberation of Israel from the oppression of Rome. Around 70 c.e., of course, Rome's oppression intensified, with the destruction of the Temple, which compounded the Jewish-Christian crisis of faith. Throughout these years, his followers were telling each other the story of Jesus, in terms taken in part from his biography as they knew it and in part from the Scripture. We saw that the seed of Christian Jew-hatred was planted here, with the old set against the new, with Jews defined as the enemy not only of Jesus but of God, and with Judaism defined as the religion that had outlived God's covenant. Thus the story, especially the core of it known to us as the Passion narrative, was, in Oates's term, "invented." We saw how the Seamless Robe of Jesus featured in this sacred exercise of imagination.

But after the crisis of the Temple's destruction, after the followers of Jesus had begun to adjust to the obvious fact that the Lord's return was not imminent, and after the expressly "Jewish" character of the movement was changed by the loss of the cult center of the Temple and by the influx of Gentile converts, the followers "forgot" that the Passion narrative was invented. Since Jesus had not returned, they had to do something the first generation had never expected or sought to do, which was to create an apologetic kerygma, or Jesus story, designed to bolster the faith they had in Jesus, both as a way of reassuring each other through the period of crises and as a way of explaining what they believed of Jesus to others, whom they now had to recruit to the movement.

It was at this point that the details of the narrative that had their origins not in the historical life of Jesus but in the Jewish Scriptures were reimagined as "facts." Now the Seamless Robe of Jesus, say, was understood as having actually existed, and the "facts" of its seamlessness and of the centurions' having rolled dice for it were understood as "fulfillments" of the Jewish Scriptures in which those details had first appeared. This perception was pressed into service of the apologetic impulse, and all at once the details of the Passion narrative and the pattern of Jewish "foreshadowing" and Christian "fulfillment" became understood as proving the claims that followers of Jesus were making for him. Such proof would have been unthinkable in the first years after the death of Jesus, not only because the invented character of the story was so well known, but because proof was unnecessary in any case, since Jesus was coming back so soon.

Once the story of Jesus took this shape, its rejection by other Jews — who themselves were responding to the trauma of the destruction of the Temple — had unprecedented bite. Recall that, in this post-Temple period, only the synagogue-based movement generally associated with the Pharisees had survived to compete with the Jesus movement for the legacy of Israel. When these rabbinic Jews, who were building their identity around the Scriptures, rejected the claims being made by the Christian Jews, the Christians felt threatened because those same Scriptures functioned as their proof. This conflict found its way into the second, third, and fourth iterations of the story Christians were telling each other and newcomers, which is how the Pharisees came to be pressed into service as the main antagonists of Jesus, even though they had been no such thing.

As Christians died, the excruciating death of Jesus took on a meaning, in isolation from his message and life, that it had not had at first. In Luke, Jesus says to the men on the road to Emmaus, "O foolish men . . . Was it not necessary that the Christ should suffer?"[2] Of course, this is not the voice of Jesus but that of his followers, confronted years later with the problem of how to make sense of the suffering they themselves were undergoing. Surely it was suffering at the hands of Rome, as ever. But even more, at the level of meaning they were so desperately clinging to in that traumatic time, it was suffering at the hands of their fellow Jews who alone could call that meaning into question. So as Christians felt themselves and their movement to be mortally challenged by the refusal of their fellow Jews to affirm their messianic understanding of Jesus, it was a small step to lay the actual death of Jesus at the feet not so much of Rome as of these rejecting Jews. Christians accounted for the rejection they were experiencing by making a version of that rejection — "his own people received him not"[3] — central to the experience of Jesus, not just in his Passion but throughout his life.

In this way, by the time the text of the last Gospel is written, "the Jews" are defined as the ontological enemy of Christ. In a contest with antagonists at first identified in John as "Pharisees," but then as "the Jews," Jesus is remembered as saying to them, "You are from below, I am from above . . . but now you seek to kill me, a man who has told you the truth which I heard from God . . . If God were your Father, you would love me . . . Why do you not understand what I say? It is because you cannot bear to hear my word. You are of your father the devil, and your will is to do your father's desires. He was a murderer from the beginning, and has nothing to do with the truth, because there is no truth in him. When he lies, he speaks according to his own nature, for he is a liar and the father of lies."[4] Jews are cast as the devil. But still — and this remains crucial — it is mainly Jews who are saying so.

If the first followers of Jesus, whom we called the healing circle, had in their grief invented the first draft of the story in part out of the Jewish Scriptures, subsequent generations invented third and fourth drafts out of what they had already heard, but also out of their own experience. The literary genre that came out of this complicated, profoundly human process of invention is not history, nor is it fiction precisely. It is, rather, gospel, and in addition to its being profoundly human, it is profoundly Jewish, for the creative interaction between inherited sacred texts and mundane experience is at the heart of what might be called the Midrashic imagination. The violence of human experience has often been reflected in the works created by such imagination, and the anti-Jewish polemic of, say, John, because of its character as a Jewish invention, stands comparison with the "troubling texts" that imbue the Jewish Scriptures with blood, from those slaughtered firstborn male children in Egypt to the Canaanites driven from Palestine.[5] When the anti-Jewish polemic of John, and the entire New Testament, is read outside the context and in ignorance of the Jewish community that produced it, the words become truly lethal.

The tragedy built into this process is the one Oates identified, namely, that people — especially those Gentiles who had no knowledge either of Jewish Scriptures or of the ways Jews used them — forgot that the Gospel was invented. They forgot not only that it was invented in its details, but that it was invented in its structure. Here we begin to see why *Nostra Aetate* did not go nearly far enough, and what a Third Vatican Council must begin to take up. Yes, the damage done to Jews by the slanderous assertion that they, more than the Romans, put Jesus to death has been incalculable, and as a first order of business that slander has to be repudiated. But the role of "the Jews" as villains in the climactic act of the Passion narrative comes right out of the dramatic structure of the kerygma itself, which puts Jesus in ontological conflict with his own people — a conflict, as I argued throughout Part Two of this book, of which he would have known nothing. The primal Christian slander against Judaism, rooted in the foundational Christian text, is that Judaism is Christianity's negative other. It is not enough to absolve Jews of the deicide. Is it possible to ask if the entire structure of the Gospel narrative can be criticized as being unworthy of the story it wants to tell?

Similarly with the basic framework of New Testament–Old Testament, which gives form to the Christian construct of salvation history. According to that scheme, Israel's prophetic "foreshadowing," which is by definition insubstantial and inferior, is contrasted with the Church's "fulfillment" as the new Israel, or, more polemically, the "true Israel." Although we cannot assume that Jews and Christians will ever approach the Scriptures in the same way, surely Jews have a right to ask: Must the Christian understanding of the very structure of God's Word include the derogatory "replacement theology"[6] that is so often found in the New Testament? When the wrath of an Old Testament God is "replaced" with the love of a New Testament God — and this formulation remains basic to Christian preaching — how can Jews not take umbrage at the insult to the Jewish heart such a contrast implies and at the distortion of the fundamental proclamation of Torah, which is God's love?

Throughout the book we have referred to this habit of mind by its technical term, supersessionism, and a number of Christians, aware of what it can lead to in the post-Holocaust era, have sought to repudiate it. *Nostra Aetate*'s attempt amounted to a first, tentative expression that cried out for elaboration, which, in subsequent commentaries, various officials have tried to supply.[7] Such scholars as the Lutheran Krister Stendahl insist, with similar sensitivity to consequence, that it is wrong to read Saint Paul, as Christians often have, as defining the Church, either in his own life or in history, as a replacement for Israel.[8] "I ask, then, has God rejected his people?" Paul wrote toward the end of his life. "By no means!"[9]

Thus the Church seeks increasingly to affirm, against a dominant Christian tradition, that God's covenant with Israel has never been repudiated. If that is the case, what is the relationship of the "new covenant" of which Jesus speaks at the Last Supper[10] to the preexisting covenant God had made at Sinai? Are there two covenants? Separate but equal? Or, if there is one covenant, how do these two divergent experiences of it mesh? As we saw, some scholars insist that what Jesus, if he used such language, would actually have been talking about was the "renewed covenant" referred to in Jeremiah,[11] but Jews can still detect in that formulation, offered from outside Judaism, an assumption of replacement. The German Jesuit biblical scholar Norbert Lohfink proposes a single covenant but "a twofold way to salvation,"[12] but the very idea of salvation introduces the question of whether Jews are subsumed in a Christian covenant in the afterlife, which amounts to a postponed religious imperialism. In other words, after nearly two thousand years of reading such texts in one way, we have barely begun to imagine how to read them in another.

It is impossible to imagine that the members of a new Vatican Council could return to the early second century and undo what was done after Marcion — the "tragic mistake," as some scholars call it, of the formalizing of the New Testament canon, which institutionalized, from the Christian side, the split between Judaism and Christianity. The road not taken then might have led to a religious collaboration between evolving rabbinic Judaism and nascent Christianity, with some kind of mutual notion of the one covenant, binding both currents to the broader stream of the one Israel. But only in science fiction do people get to relive such choices and follow such roads to other, wished-for outcomes. There is no changing the fact, in other words, that Christianity and Judaism are separate religions, each with distinct integrity that the other must respect. But by recalling that this real outcome, which after all was imagined neither by Jesus nor by Paul, was the result of contingent human choices made in response to accidents of history, the members of Vatican III could understand that no purpose of God's was served by the "parting of the ways," and that no conclusions about the superiority of one religion or the other should be drawn from it. Furthermore, Vatican III must affirm in the clearest terms what has so far been indicated only obliquely, at the level of theology, not official Church teaching — namely, that while Judaism exists without essential reference to Christianity, the reverse is not the case. The God of Jesus Christ, and therefore of the Church, is the God of Israel. The Jews remain the chosen people of God. The Jewish rejection of Jesus as the Son of God is an affirmation of faith that Christians must respect.

The task of Vatican III will be to reorder the Church's relationship to the "troubling texts" that deny all of this. There is no question of simply eliminating them, nor of rewriting them to purge the Epistles and Gospels of what the contemporary ear finds offensive. To some extent, translations can properly soften the edges of the anti-Jewish polemic, substituting, for example, "the leaders" for "the Jews" as the protagonists at the crucifixion, but it would be a mistake to do more to let the Gospels off the hook. Indeed, their offensive character is part of what the Church must learn not only to admit but to claim. The anti-Jewish texts of the New Testament show that the Church, even in its first generation, was capable of betraying the message of Jesus, establishing once and for all that "the Church as such" can sin. The Church as such stands in need of forgiveness. The Church must therefore preach the anti-Jewish texts of the Gospels — not against the Jews, but against itself.

In doing such a thing, the Church would be true to its oldest tradition. Christianity has inherited its theological method from Judaism, and that method, perhaps despite itself, is self-critical because biblical faith is self-critical. The prophetic tradition — the prophet Nathan, say, criticizing King David himself — is only the most obvious manifestation of this method, but it is constant. Biblical faith, that is, contains within itself the norms in terms of which biblical faith confesses to having continually fallen short. The Christian problem here, in other words, is a Jewish problem. And the solution is Jewish too. That the first followers of Jesus violated his message by slandering their rivals, even demonizing them, establishes better than anything else that the Church, at its core, is as sinful as any other institution.

Therefore, we must have a structure of understanding that enables Christians to read the foundational texts not as divine, as if partaking in the perfection of God, but as invented, to use Oates's word again. That God's Word is "inspired" does not mean it is free of self-contradiction or of tragic consequences. Surely the wonder of inspiration lies in God's use of the inherently flawed medium of the word in the first place. The sin to be repented of, and resisted, is the sin of forgetting that God's Word is human. Much contemporary biblical scholarship assumes this. Vatican III must make the work of such scholarship more widely available in the Church, which means that Christians must be called to a more sophisticated relationship to God's Word. So when they hear the Passion narrative read during Holy Week, they must be helped to hear it not as history but as gospel. To the extent that the texts involve more hate than love, they must be proclaimed as a revelation also of the flawed nature of those who created them. That proclamation of a flawed Gospel, created by flawed believers, leads to what is, after all, good news — that the one whom the Gospel proclaims is the one who will return again to bring this flawed beginning to its completion.

Vatican III, against the long Church tradition of claiming already to be in possession of the fullness of truth, must renew the Christian expectation that there is more to come, exactly because the Kingdom of God is unfinished. Among Jews such an expectation informs messianic hope, but among Christians it takes the form of faith in the Second Coming of the Lord. The measure of this desire is our own present need for it, and the effect of it is self-transcendence. The need for this perspective becomes clear in a study of history such as we have undertaken here. The obvious flaws of a Church that has so readily given itself over to hatred reveal the ways in which the "already" is simply not enough. Any Christian proclamation that says that salvation, redemption, grace, perfection, whatever you call it, has already come is unbelievable on its face. It is also unchristian, because it denies, in the Catholic theologian David Tracy's phrase, "the overwhelmingly 'not-yet' actuality of history itself."[13] A Church that believes it is "as such" incapable of sin — exempt, that is, from the actuality of history — believes it has no need of the return of its Messiah, which may be why the Second Coming of Jesus is rarely the subject of Catholic sermons. But such a Church is also incapable of surpassing itself, which is another way of saying it is dead.

That alone justifies the repudiation of any pretense that the Church, as now constituted, is perfect. "God's revelation in Jesus remains incomplete, unfinished, oriented toward the final manifestation." This is the Vatican II theologian Gregory Baum. "The redemption brought by Jesus to mankind in the present . . . is a token, a pledge, a first installment of the complete redemption promised in the Scriptures . . . But since divine redemption is not finished in Jesus, except by way of anticipation, the Church is not the unique vehicle of grace: room remains in world history for other ways of grace, for many religions, and in particular for the other biblical faith, for Judaism."[14] A renewed Christian longing for the return of the Messiah would rekindle a sharp appreciation for what still binds Jewish and Christian hope.

The future beckons like the horizon, but the past imposes its harsh judgment, and, likewise, one paramount duty: The Church must be responsible for the real-world consequences — all of the tragedy this book relates — of its most troubling texts. Never again must worshipers leave a church on Good Friday looking for Jews to attack. Therefore the act of reading such texts must now involve the act of arguing against them. The inherently supersessionist terminology of "Old" and "New" must be replaced.[15] Likewise "Law" and "Gospel." Instead of an inherently contemptuous tension between Jewish "prophecy" and Christian "fulfillment," Vatican III must invite a new sensitivity to what Stendahl calls the "tender typology," according to which Christians and Jews both could recognize the shape of God's way of acting in history and through time. There must be a resonance between Jewish and Christian narratives (Passover and Easter) that does not involve the superiority of one over the other.

Specifically, in moving beyond *Nostra Aetate,* the distortions that appear in the New Testament, whether of the behavior of "the Jews" or of the theology of Torah, would be flagged as such — and confessed as such. Vatican III must help Christians learn to read anti-Jewish texts as if they were themselves Jews (and anti-female texts as if they were women, and, for that matter, as I heard a Jewish scholar say, anti-Canaanite texts as if they were Canaanites).[16] The texts themselves call the Church to this, because finally they do enshrine the authentic presence of Jesus Christ — not the "historical" Jesus exactly, but the real and living Jesus as confessed by those who knew him, confessed above all as the embodiment of love. Remembered as one who called every act of hatred into question, therefore including hatred of "the Jews," Jesus is nevertheless remembered also as one who never assumed that his adherents would follow his example perfectly. The Church's memory of Jesus Christ "releases the theological knowledge that there is no innocent tradition," as David Tracy puts it, "no innocent classic, no innocent reading."[17] Indeed, the figure of Jesus presented by the Gospels, the one who forgives not once, not seven times, but seventy times seven, is clear on the point that all humans, and therefore all human texts, stand equally in need of forgiveness.

Jesus is never more "Jewish" than here, never more faithful to the one covenant with the One God. Vatican III could call as a witness Rabbi David Hartman. "The confirmation of human beings in their human limitation is the soul of the covenantal message," Hartman says. "The covenant is not God's desire for humanity to escape from history, but God's gracious love saying that humanity in its finite temporal condition is fully accepted by the eternal God . . . Can we love God in an imperfect way and in an imperfect world? . . . History is not the revelation of eternal truth, but God's ability to love us in our imperfection."[18]

The fear, envy, insecurity, despair, grief, and, finally, hatred that corrupted the authors of the New Testament do not destroy the Church. The marvel is, they establish it.

57

Agenda Item 2: The Church and Power

THERE ARE FEW things we can say with more certainty about Jesus than that he defined his mission in opposition not to Judaism but to the imperium of Rome. Rome's contempt for the peoples it had subjugated, Rome's ruthless violence, Rome's worship of itself, Rome's substitution of Caesar for God — Jesus said no to it all. Whether his message is understood to have been messianic, apocalyptic, magical, cynical, revolutionary, or "merely" spiritual, it is clear that he invited his followers to join him in rejecting Rome. The ambiguous nature of the early Church's relationship to Rome — one reason the Gospels highlighted Jews, instead of Romans, as enemies of Jesus was to avoid trouble with the empire, perhaps especially after Nero's brutal scapegoating of Christians in the decade of the 60s — takes nothing, finally, from the primal Christian critique of power. Once Paul turned the tragic fate of Jesus against those who had caused it — turned the cross, that is, against the legion's standard — the story of Jesus swept the world over which Caesar held sway because it spoke intimately to those whose throats were under Rome's heel. The Gospel took root in the soul of powerlessness, which is why, to this day, it beckons the dispossessed in ways it does no other group.

If the history traced in this book shows anything, it is that the Church has never come fully to terms with the contradiction it embraced when the Roman imperium and Roman Catholicism became the same thing. That tremendous reversal, as we saw, occurred when Constantine accepted the Christian faith and used it as the unifying ideology underwriting the extension of his imperial sway from Trier to the Levant. He ordered the abolition of crucifixion as a means of capital punishment, thinking of Jesus, but he also taught his soldiers to shape the cross by tying their knives to their spears. And his mother, just then finding the True

Cross, led to it by a treasonous Jew, helped to put that symbol where Caesar's eagle had been. The transformation of the cross was complete — not a sign of real suffering any longer, nor even, with Paul, of spiritualized victory, but a sign of power in the world. "The power of the cross of Christ," Athanasius of Alexandria declared, "has filled the world."[1]

The point is not to wish sentimentally that the Christian religion, in order to maintain its purity, had remained the marginal cult of a despised minority, with an ad hoc organization; more charismatic than catholic; possessing nothing; being more acted upon than a spur to action; and innocent, not in the sense of sinless but in the sense of untested, untouched. The glory of the Church includes what its institutionalization has enabled — a transcending of time and culture, a triumph over history that stands alone. Every Catholic is proud to be part of a two-thousand-year-old tradition that still lives. But such longevity presumes a weighty bureaucracy. It presumes possession, even wealth. It presumes the great contests of will between rulers and popes, princes and bishops, masters and monks. It presumes the wily strategies that survival required. It presumes the yoking of intellect to piety, and the adaptation of faith to Plato's separation of form and matter, to Aristotle's rational quest for universal order, and ultimately to Kierkegaard's leap into the arbitrary. It even presumes the admission of politics to pulpits, and perhaps the conscription of cloisters into service as bastions. The ruins of Europe, the museums of Europe, the cathedrals and castles and Gothic-towered universities of Europe, are the stone record of this story, and though there is cold shame in it, there is carved beauty too. The history of the Church, not above the world but in it, only continues what we just saw revealed by the Church's troubling foundational texts — that the Church is of the human condition, not against it.

But a Vatican III could ask the question of whether the Church, responding to an emperor's self-interest, assumed too much the emperor's ethos. Assumed it so much, in fact, that the emperor's ethos — more, say, than Augustine's adaptation of Plato, Aquinas's of Aristotle, Francis's of Jesus — is what most indelibly stamps the soul of Catholicism. Why is that? Pope John Paul II took a first stab at asking this troubling question when, at his millennial Mass of repentance in March 2000, he acknowledged that "Christians have often denied the Gospel, yielding to a mentality of power."[2] That confession, strong as it is, points beyond itself to what has not been confessed yet. Obviously, more than the behavior of "Christians" is at issue here, and, for that matter, more than a "mentality" is too.

A Vatican III could push further into this problem, asking if it is at last possible to reverse Constantine and reclaim the cross for Jesus Christ, and for those who are left out of every imperial victory, or rather, defeated by it.

Regardless of whether such a council would take up the question, history does. That is the meaning, finally, of the "interruption" of history experienced during the Holocaust. In light of that event as the outcome of the long narrative begun at Milvian Bridge, heretofore unquestioned Christian assumptions suddenly seem tragically problematic — and not only in relation to Jews. "Christian biblical theology must recognize," the Catholic feminist theologian Elisabeth Schüssler Fiorenza has written, "that its articulation of anti-Judaism in the New Testament goes hand in hand with its gradual adaptation to Greco-Roman patriarchal society. Christian as well as Jewish theology must cease to proclaim a God made in the image and likeness of Man. It can do so only when it mourns the 'loss' of women's contributions in the past and present and rejects our theological 'dehumanization.' Moreover, white Christian and Jewish theology must promote the full humanity of all non-Western peoples and at the same time struggle against racism wherever it is at work. In short the memory of the Holocaust must 'interrupt' all forms of Western patriarchal theology if the legacies of the dead are not to be in vain."[3]

Altering the Church's "mentality of power" presumes a fundamental shift in its attitude toward the other, which in turn involves the issue of women's equality. A power structure that denigrates women is the most basic manifestation of the binary opposition that has so blatantly oppressed Jews. While it may seem unrelated to Jewish-Christian conflict, a feminist critique of theology and practice is central to it, because feminism seeks not a mere substitution of female privilege for male privilege, but a dismantling of the entire structure of binary opposition in favor of authentic mutuality. Specifically, a feminist reading of the New Testament, as we have in a scholar like Elisabeth Schüssler Fiorenza, reveals, for example, that the women who followed Jesus, unlike the men, "understood that his ministry was not rule and kingly glory but *diakonia,* 'service' (Mark 15:41). Thus the women emerge as the true Christian ministers and witnesses."[4] The mentality of power is the issue, and as the Gospels display a treasonous anti-Judaism, they also reveal, in the anonymity of these very women, assumptions of male dominance that must equally be rejected.

The readiness with which the Church put itself at the service of the self-preserving and patriarchal imperium remains an untied knot of the Catholic conscience, from Constantine in his wars against his rivals, to the brown robes at the side of Spanish conquistadors, to the priests who blessed King Leopold's African loot, to the display in Trier of the Seamless Robe in honor of Adolf Hitler. Recall the conclusion of Part Seven — that central to the Church's failure to oppose Nazism was, in John Cornwell's phrase, "something in the modern ideology of papal power."

Again, if the long history we have seen demonstrates anything, it is that the "modern" pursuit of such power drives relentlessly along the unbroken shaft of apostolic succession, from Leo I (440–461), with his initiating universal claims; to Gregory VII (1073–1085), who bested the emperor at Canossa and, against the Greeks, claimed sovereignty over the whole Church; to Urban II (1088–1099), who started a holy war, launching Europe's first pogrom and sacralizing violence with the cry "God wills it!"; to Innocent III (1198–1216), who extended the claim of papal sovereignty to the whole world (and imposed the yellow star on Jews); to Boniface VIII (1294–1303), who decreed that every king, indeed every creature, is a vassal of the pope; to Paul IV (1555–1559), who, asserting authority over the human mind, established the Index (and the Roman ghetto); to Pius IX (1846–1878), who claimed papal primacy over the council, and papal infallibility over "faith and morals" (while kidnapping a Jewish child); to Pius XII (1939–1958), who put papal power above the fate of the German Catholic Church, to say nothing of the fate of the Jews; to John Paul II (1978–   ), who, against the great exception John XXIII, and despite his own evident good will, devotes himself to the continuation of this tradition. "Power corrupts," Lord Acton is well known for saying, "and absolute power corrupts absolutely." What is less well known, as Garry Wills points out, is that the British aristocrat was a Catholic opposed, in 1870, to the dogma of papal infallibility, and the power he was warning of was the pope's.[5]

Let us suppose that the members of Vatican III meet in St. Peter's Basilica, as the fathers of Vatican I and Vatican II did. On the subject of power, the place itself can be a prod to action. In my dictionary, "basilica" is defined as "a privileged Catholic church," but the word comes from *basileus,* for "king," and among Romans it referred to Caesar's palace — quite literally, as we saw, to Constantine's palace, the *Konstantin-basilika.* The soaring central nave of St. Peter's, with the semicircular apse at the far end, is modeled after the palaces Constantine built for himself. The design is perfect for enhancing the stature of the figure who occupies the throne in the

distant apse, and in St. Peter's that throne, behind and above the altar, belongs not to God but to the popes. Lining both side aisles of the mammoth hall are the massive imperial tombs in which Roman popes are buried, sarcophagi worthy of the potentates so many of them aspired to be. In
the towering cupola above the transept is the mythic inscription *Tu es
Petrus..*, as if the peasant Jesus ordained all this.

Whatever historical contingencies led to the cult of papal omnipotence
— from the empire of antiquity to the investiture disputes with medieval
kings, from the Renaissance glorification of genius to the assaults of reformation and revolution — can a member of Vatican III cast his or her eyes
around this shrine to the imperium and ask if its time has finally gone?
When John XXIII stepped down from his throne to sit as an equal among
a delegation of Jewish visitors, was he hinting at the necessary shift? And
when his council transformed the Catholic liturgy by eliminating the. secret language of the court in favor of the language spoken by all, and by
replacing the high altar with a simple table, which required the priest to
come down as Pope John himself had done, was the shift being further
prepared for? "Power to the people," we learned to say in our youth, and
because of a revolution begun at the Church's top, we Catholics had a first
taste of the "popular" religion that subsequent popes would try to turn
back. But how do you turn back a tide? "It is quite clear," David Tracy told
the *New York Times* in 1986, "that Catholicism is going through the greatest change since its passage from a Jewish sect to a Greco-Roman religion.
The ways of being a Catholic will necessarily multiply and the Church will
be more diverse; pluralism in religious expression will increase, not de-
crease."[6] Vatican II defined the Church as the People of God, and Vatican
III must make the definition real by reordering the Church according to
its new self-understanding.

The papacy must be restored as an office of *diakonia,* service, to be exercised in partnership with other Christians (not just Catholics, not just
bishops and priests, and not just men). For the purposes of this book, and
extending Elisabeth Schüssler Fiorenza's insight into the link between patriarchy and anti-Judaism, it is notable that the pope who instituted the
Sicut Judaeis tradition of defending Jews and forbidding their forced conversion, Gregory I (590–604), was also the pope who defined his function
as being not *Papa,* an ultimate patriarch, but, as he put it, "servant of the
servants of God."[7] As Hans Küng points out, Gregory was the author of
perhaps the most influential work written by a pope, *Pastoral Rule,* which
located the soul of ministry in personal example and in service, real acts

of meeting human needs — not in the concentration of control and not in the preempting of local leadership. The phrase "pastoral rule" can be taken as a rebuttal to "holy rule," which is the meaning of "hierarchy."[8] That this pope is called "the Great," one of only two so honored, suggests that the witness of such a life, as with John XXIII, weighs more in the balance than the witness of popes who take their greatness for granted. That Gregory's rejection of patriarchal triumphalism was accompanied by a sense of obligation to the well-being of Jews is no coincidence. As we have seen again and again, as long as the Church defines itself triumphalistically, Jews remain a living contradiction to all such claims, and the offense taken by Christians at their "prophetic critique refused"[9] is squared. It is then that Christians become most dangerous to Jews.

St. Peter's Basilica enshrines the problematic history we have studied, but it also enshrines the "dangerous memory" of Jesus Christ, which remains the "countermemory to all tales of triumph," Tracy says. "Christianity is always a memory that turns as fiercely against itself as against other pretensions to triumph . . . To become historically minded is to seize that memory for the present and to recall the past in that memory's subversive light."[10] Among Catholics, the main custodian of the anti-triumphal impulse has been the tradition of Church councils that have steadily, if imperfectly, checked the temptation to papal imperium. Therefore, in the name of the authentic Catholic tradition, and to counter the universalist absolutism that underwrites all "pretensions to triumph," the conciliar principle — the bishop of Rome exercising authority accountably, within the college of bishops — must be reestablished. Due regard for the regional autonomies of bishops, the cultural distinctions of local churches, and the idea that all Christians share the priestly office must be retrieved. It is in this context that the Catholic Church can finally honor the various regional differences that gave rise to most Protestant and Orthodox denominations. The primacy-enforcing ideas of Roman supremacy and papal infallibility, based as both are on a shallow urge toward certitude, reflect the universalizing pseudoscience of the Enlightenment more than the Gospel.

The members of Vatican III owe it to themselves "to become historically minded," in Tracy's phrase, including becoming more fully acquainted with the bizarre political and personal circumstances of Vatican I that prompted its fathers to issue *Pastor Aeternus*. Knowing of the nationalist siege that was closing in on them, we can honor their good intentions, sympathize with their fears, and salute their loyalty to the pope

while still forthrightly acknowledging that the definition of papal infallibility was a mistake. Twentieth-century Church history, with the Holocaust as its epiphany, establishes it as such, down to and including the
inability of Pope John Paul II to say of Pius XII, "What my predecessor
did, and what he failed to do, in the crucible of 'faith and morals' was
wrong."[11] The defining of the doctrine of papal infallibility amounts to
the low point in the long story of patriarchy, a legitimation of Church
exceptionalism, a reversal of the meaning that Jesus gave to ministry, and,
finally, an abuse of power. Instead of trying to slide past the embarrassment of the blunder, or hoping that the doctrine will wither into disuse
over time, Vatican III — since the point is to acknowledge fallibility —
should repeal it.

58

Agenda Item 3: A New Christology

G OD IS GREATER than religion . . . ," Rabbi Heschel wrote. "Faith is greater than dogma."[1] If the human species is constitutionally inclined to forget the created character of its creation myths, it is also true that its most absolutely asserted dicta are the products of relative intellectual constructs that are rarely recognized as such. Theology is profoundly tied to real-world political consequences, and for that reason Vatican III must initiate a Church-wide reimagination of sacrosanct theologies, or rather, sponsor the Church-wide dissemination of the inventive work that theologians have already been doing. Such a project is necessary because, however much intended as timeless acts of devotion, sacrosanct theologies have underwritten violence, intolerance, sexism, and, in particular, antisemitism. An example of this theological reconsideration of basic texts and dogmas, in light of the Church's historic negation of Judaism, is the work of Rosemary Radford Ruether, referred to earlier, whose classic formulation of the problem — Christology as "the other side of anti-Judaism"[2] — remains unaddressed by the Church. The Church has yet to face, in David Tracy's phrase, "the revolting underside of Christology in the history of Christian antisemitism."[3]

A summary return to the era of the Crusades, when politics and theology came together in tragic ways, can illuminate the source of this problem as it still exists and how we might leave it behind. Recall that 1096, the beginning of the First Crusade, which nearly coincided with the writing by Saint Anselm (c. 1033–1109) of *Cur Deus Homo,* is widely regarded as the year Europe began to wake from the slumber of its Dark Age. The Crusades both reflected and advanced a vigorous new social movement. Intercultural exchange, and with it the return of rationalism, reflected in Anselm's proofs for the existence of God, led to a renaissance in the West.

But recall further that the Dark Age itself was, in part at least, an unintended consequence of powerful but ambiguous developments occurring in Christian theology, an intellectual equivalent of the Church's political accommodation of the imperium in the aftermath of Constantine's conversion. The theological formulations that jelled between the Council of Nicaea (325) and the Council of Constantinople (381) had reflected an accommodation with Greek thought, and so had the work of the great Augustine (354–430). In this period, the metaphors that early Christians used to describe their experience of and faith in Jesus of Nazareth were reinvented in the categories of Hellenistic metaphysics. Obviously, the movement from religious expression which began, essentially, as poetry, which prizes ambiguity and allusiveness, to religious philosophy, which values precision above implication, represents a decisive shift.

When the Church fathers found the mysteries of revelation to be illuminated by their understanding of Plato's dichotomy between form and matter — between the world, that is, of ideal perfection and the inherently flawed material world of everyday experience — a new idea of the cosmos braced the Christian vision. Less a construct of Plato than of his syncretist interpreters of late antiquity, especially Plotinus (c. 205–270), Neo-Platonism posited a dualism that would become Christianized as between grace and sin. This was one culture's form of the perennial human temptation to binary thinking, as evidenced among Gnostics of various kinds in the ancient world. The Neo-Platonic divide between soul and body would have its later equivalents in the post-Descartes alienation between the self and the world, and even in the postmodern deconstruction of the bond between the self and the self's expression.

Now God was understood to be the True, the One, the Holy; the material world — enigmatic, chaotic, profane — could only be ontologically unrelated to such a God. Creation was merely the Creator's shadow. For a people with roots in the biblical view of reality, this was a massive mutation, for the God of Israel, while very much a transcendent God, was the Lord of human history who had chosen to be intimately involved in that history. Among Christians, a new idea of the person took hold too, one equally foreign to the biblical idea, with a split between the body and the soul, which in nature could not be reconciled. This split posed large problems for theologians who sought to define exactly how Jesus could be both God and man, and disagreements over the formulas constructed to answer the question — "begotten, not made," "hypostatic union," "*filoque*" — became violent, leading to the first great condemnations of heresy.

But perhaps the most damaging consequence of this new dualism was the devaluation of the physical world that seemed logically to flow from a Neo-Platonic suspicion of "matter." This led not only, say, to the distrust of sexual pleasure — original sin defined as the sex act — which has been a mark of Christianity ever since, but to the idea that human beings, mired in the material world, were inherently unable to arrive at a state of happiness — in religious language, salvation — that was natural to the realm of the ideal. The body, that is, condemned the soul to live in permanent exile from the realm for which it was made. It is only when such Hellenistic categories shape Christian theology that the idea of the immortality of the soul becomes the content of religious hope — a notion that has nothing in common with biblical hope, which is based on personal wholeness, not dichotomy; on God's promise, not the soul's indestructibility. But in the scheme of Christian Neo-Platonism, even the soul's intrinsic immortality was no hope, because its pollution by the body left it doomed.

The gulf between body and soul was itself a pale shadow of the infinitely larger gulf between God and the human person. For the purposes of this book, it cannot be emphasized enough that one effect of this thoroughgoing Hellenization of the meaning of Jesus, whatever positive results it had as an intellectual construction, was the final obliteration of the Jewish character of that meaning. With the Christian adoption of Greek intellectual categories, the parting of the ways became turnpikes set in concrete. From now on, most ominously, since there was nothing intrinsically Jewish about Jesus, there would be nothing to prevent Christians from defining themselves in opposition to Jews.

Despite the intellectual monuments created by Church fathers from Tertullian to Augustine, a collapse of intellectual pursuit and scientific inquiry was an ultimate consequence of the Christian adoption of a dualistic worldview, since there was no reason to take the experience of the senses seriously. On the contrary, the senses became the enemy, and where once the sexual body was celebrated as the very image of God — "So God created man in his own image, in the image of God he created him; male and female he created them."[4] — the sexual body now became an "occasion of sin" to be subdued. Among Christians, the Greek idea of soul became entirely removed from the biblical idea of spirit, which, since it literally means "breath," is intrinsically physical. Indeed, now the body, even with its breath, was defined as the source of all evil. Christian piety became penitential — the self-flagellation of body hatred became the highest form of devotion — and even work of the mind, like reading and study, because dependent on the senses, became defined as worldly distraction. A culture based on such assumptions was bound to shrivel, and the culture of Western Europe did just that.

And so too with Christology. The memory of Jesus was pressed into service as the antidote to the despair that flowed from such dualism. If the gulf between heaven and earth, between soul and body, was infinite, then the infinite Son of God alone could bridge it. The coming of Jesus was now defined as God's effort to repair the fallen creation, and consistent with the new attachment to flagellation, the flagellation of Jesus — the punishment of his body — took on a centrality it had not had for early Christians. The Son of God could bridge the gulf between Creator and creation, between soul and body, only by the destruction of his body. The Passion and death became the heart of the meaning of Jesus' life. The cross became the essential icon of faith, and the fact that these systems of belief affected the realm of politics is revealed by the coming of the war of the cross, the Crusades. We also took note of the way this combination of theology and politics inevitably escalated the Church's war against the Jews.

Ironically, the highest form of this philosophically dualistic Christology came with *Cur Deus Homo,* Anselm's explanation of "why God became human." I say ironically because it is also true that Anselm's embrace of the rational method, and his trust in the essentially physical process of thought, marked a turn away from anti-intellectualism and anti-corporeality. Indeed, Europe's recovery from the legacy of a rigid Neo-Platonism would be tied largely to its reacquaintance with Aristotle — his celebration of the unity of being as opposed to its dichotomy. In contrast to Neo-Platonic "idealism," Aristotle's "realism" defines the sensed world as "real" and not just as the insubstantial and inferior shadow of a higher realm. Such a real world is worthy of careful scrutiny, and only such a system of thought can support scientific inquiry. The return of Aristotle meant the return of *scientia,* which was the precondition for the thriving of the universities. Anselm, with his own trust in the rational method, marks the beginning of Europe's reacquaintance with Aristotle. Anselm, as we saw, was among the first outside Iberia to benefit from the *convivencia* that would restore Aristotle to Europe, as he came to be filtered through Maimonides (1135–1204) and Averroës (1126–1198). Only with Thomas Aquinas (1225–1274), nearly two hundred years later, would an Aristotelian alternative to the Neo-Platonism of the patristic era be fully constructed, not as a replacement but only as a counterweight. Dualism survives vigorously in the Church, as its attitudes toward sexuality reveal.

Here is how the Catholic theologian Elizabeth Johnson summarizes Anselm's significance:

> In the eleventh century the biblical and patristic pluralism so characteristic of interpretations of Jesus and salvation began to recede in the West due to Anselm's brilliant restructuring of the satisfaction metaphor into a full-fledged ontologically based theory. To wit: God became a human being and died to pay back what was due to the honor of God offended by sin. I sometimes think that Anselm should be considered the most successful theologian of all time. Imagine having almost a one-thousand-year run for your theological construct! It was never declared a dogma but might just as well have been, so dominant has been its influence in theology, preaching, devotion, and the penitential system of the Church, up to our own day.[5]

Anselm's idea is that the work of Jesus was "salvation" — saving those who believed in him from the impossible abyss that separated God from humanity, bridging it with his own body. But just as previous generations had forgotten the invented character of their sacred narratives, the heirs of the world shaped by Christian Platonism assumed that the gulf across which Jesus had to lay his body was created by God in reaction to the Fall, and not by the ancient interpreters of Plato. Religiously, they would have said it was the sin of Adam that had made an enemy of God, but actually their religious language was conditioned by a philosophical presumption that was enshrined by now in piety, if not dogma, that divided heaven from earth. Just because an intellectual schema dubbed God as hostile and unavailable did not mean God was any such thing. But who was to say that?

We saw that, because Anselm was operating out of the belief system of feudal politics, he took God to be an overlord whose insulted sense of justice required an act of "satisfaction" equal to the initial affront he had suffered, the original sin. Since the one affronted was infinite, Anselm reasoned, the one offering satisfaction had to be infinite, which is why Jesus had to be divine. And since the affront was an abuse of human freedom, it could be overturned only by an act of human freedom, which is why Jesus had, equally, to be human. Death is the wages of sin, and since Jesus was without sin, he in no way deserved to die. Therefore only by his free choice could he die, but that free choice was the only thing that would satisfy the affronted God. So ran the links of Anselm's chain of reason.

By choosing his fate on the cross, Jesus was, as Jaroslav Pelikan helped us to understand, getting God to change his mind about creation, getting the punitive God of the Old Testament, that is, to stop being the enemy of all that he had made. Jesus, the bridge between the otherwise irreconcilable human and divine, was "saving" creation by getting God to love it again. The Gospel replaced the Law. Grace replaced sin. The new Adam replaced the old. This dualistic progression perfectly matched the supersessionist assumption that by now was the central pillar of the Church. And not incidentally, the locus of this transformation was a particular place. The execution precinct outside Jerusalem, where the cross was planted, was itself the site of the defeat of doom, but doom defined as within the scope of Judaism. When Pope John Paul II called Auschwitz the "Golgotha of the modern world," he was thinking of Anselm's Golgotha, where God had intruded in time, turning time against the Jews. At Golgotha their time was up. And why should Jews not have been offended to hear Auschwitz so referred to?

The first result of Anselm's theology of salvation (soteriology) was, as we saw, to solder the faith to the cross, and to make the death of Jesus more important than anything he had said, despite his clear statement that "the words that I have spoken to you are spirit and life."[6] His death counted for more than his having been born, having lived as a Jew, having preached a gospel of love in the context of Israel's covenant with a loving God, having opposed the imperium of Rome, even having been brought to the new life of Resurrection. The death obsession of the flagellants was deemed holy, and the blood lust of the crusaders was sanctified. God, too, had blood lust. Christ's agony on the cross would now become the black flower of the Western imagination — on armor, in Passion plays, in paintings, in altar carvings, in rituals like the Stations of the Cross, and ultimately in the cross at Auschwitz.

But the second result of atonement soteriology was even more damaging — for Jews and for everyone else who declined to put Jesus at the center of hope. Jesus Christ was defined as the one solution to a cosmic problem. Understood as reordering creation, as redeeming an otherwise doomed world, he was seen as the only way to God. Because of this cosmic and ontological accomplishment of Jesus Christ, understood as bringing about an "objective" adjustment in creation and a change in the Godhead, Christianity understands itself, in the words of Karl Rahner (1904–1984), the great twentieth-century Catholic theologian, as "the absolute and hence the only religion for all men."[7] When the Vatican issued its apology in 2000 for using "methods not in keeping with the Gospel in the solemn duty of defending the truth,"[8] it seemed content to acknowledge the flawed character of "methods" without confronting the problem of the "truth" that was being defended, which was this absolute claim for the Catholic religion. In fact, the flawed character of the "methods" (the Crusades, the Inquisition) revealed the flawed character of the "truth."

Karl Rahner saw this. He was a German Jesuit whose first professorial post, at Innsbruck, was eliminated when the Nazis closed the Catholic universities in 1936. He spent the war years teaching religious education in Vienna,[9] and after the war his openly expressed appreciation of the need for a basic reconsideration of Catholic dogma led to his being silenced by the Vatican. No theologian's rehabilitation by Pope John's Vatican II was more dramatic. Rahner's great effort, toward the end of his life, was to reconcile the traditional claim for Jesus as the universal source of all salvation with its plainly negative effects. "The West is no longer shut up in itself," he wrote; "it can no longer regard itself simply as the center of the history of this world and as the center of culture, with a religion which . . . could appear as the obvious and indeed sole way of honoring God . . . Today everybody is the next-door neighbor and spiritual neighbor of everyone else in the world . . . which puts the absolute claim of our own Christian faith into question."[10]

Puts into question, that is, the idea that only the freely chosen death of Jesus appeased the condemning wrath of God. If Anselm is right, in other words, then there is no salvation apart from the Church (as the popes would say), or, at the very least, apart from an "anonymous" (as the more liberal-minded Rahner dubbed it) relationship to Jesus — a relationship, say, that a Torah-revering Jew might have, even without knowing it. The "absolute religion" must regard all other religions as inferior, if not venal. "Anonymous Christians," by virtue of their good conscience whatever its religious context, are conscripted into the Church without knowing it, whether they want to be or not.[11]

Here is where the work of a Vatican III would begin, for it is impossible to reconcile this Christology, these cosmic claims for the accomplishment of Jesus Christ as the one source of salvation, with authentic respect for Judaism and every other "spiritual neighbor." The Church's fixation on the death of Jesus as the universal salvific act must end, and the place of the cross must be reimagined in Christian faith. We will return to the starting point of this long reflection, but here we should note that nothing calls the traditional Catholic emphasis on the cross more powerfully into question than its presence at the death camp. "Perhaps the greatest question that Auschwitz raises for the tradition of Christian teaching about the cross," Paul van Buren wrote, "is whether we can continue to say with Hebrews (and perhaps with Paul in Rom. 6:10), that it happened 'once for all.' The price of doing so is to set God's authorization of Jesus on a radically different plain from his authorization of the Jewish people . . . A Church that affirms the Jewish people as the continuing Israel of God cannot coherently define the authorization of Jesus so as to undercut God's authorization of the people Israel. In a world that has known Auschwitz, consequently, the cross can only be presented as a world-redeeming event in more qualified terms than those of 'once for all.'"[12]

As long as an understanding of God as having been changed from wrathful to loving by the freely chosen death of Jesus maintains itself near the center of Church attitudes, any effort at interreligious amity will be false, for below the universalist claim of this "absolute religion" abides the flinty substratum of the old contempt. This is why Rahner could observe that "the pluralism of religions . . . must therefore be the greatest scandal and the greatest vexation for Christianity."[13]

And so, among key Catholic prelates, it is. In October 1999 there convened a synod of European bishops. A working document (*instrumentum laboris*) prepared by Vatican officials included this statement:

> Pluralism has taken the place of Marxism in cultural dominance, a pluralism which is undifferentiated and tending toward skepticism and nihilism . . . In the context of the present increasing pluralism in Europe, the synod also intends to proclaim that Christ is the one and only savior of all humanity and, consequently, to assert the absolute uniqueness of Christianity in relation to other religions . . . Jesus is the one and only mediator of salvation for all of humanity. Only in him do humanity, history and the cosmos find their definitively positive meaning and receive their full realization. He is not only the mediator of salvation, but salvation's source.[14]

The Vatican of John Paul II was so intent on defining religious pluralism as the great modern evil that, in 1997, it excommunicated a Sri Lankan theologian, Tissa Balasuriya, an "Asian Rahner" whom the Church he had served for half a century denigrated as a "relativist." Balasuriya's offense? Daring to imply that Hinduism and Buddhism might be authentic ways to God. Not even Hans Küng had been excommunicated (nor, for that matter, as we saw, had Hitler).[15] This campaign against "the rapid spread of the relativistic and pluralistic mentality" was carried forward even more vigorously in September 2000 when the Vatican issued "*Dominus Iesus:* On the Unicity and Salvific Universality of Jesus Christ and the Church," a surprising reiteration of the Roman Catholic triumphalism most thought had been buried at Vatican II.[16]

We will have more to say about pluralism in the next chapter. What is important here is that the first shift required toward a genuinely "open Catholicism" (in Rahner's phrase), a Catholicism that is, first, no threat whatsoever to Jews, involves what is believed and proclaimed about Jesus. An initial stab at that shift occurred, in fact, not long after Anselm had constructed his theology of Jesus as the universal source of salvation. Recall that Anselm was rebutted almost at once by Abelard, and the issue between them was the question of whether salvation was what Jesus came for in the first place. Salvation, as we just saw, is the solution to the hopeless divide between Creator and creatures, but Abelard, the author of *Sic et Non* (*Yes and No*), was not readily given to such discontinuities. For him, the natural world and, more to the point, the natural power of reason were occasions of connection with God, not division from God. The coming of Jesus was for the purpose of revelation, not salvation — revelation, that is, that we are all already saved. Creatures are saved not by virtue of the loving act of Jesus but by virtue of God's prior and constant love. The love of Jesus was "exemplary," a manifestation of God's love.

If this is so, then respect for human beings follows, whether they associate themselves with Jesus or not. This affirmation of the basic principle of pluralism brought to Abelard the opposition of the powerful Bernard, who accused him of opening up the "One Way" to Jews and other infidels, regardless of their attachment to Christ. "A new gospel is being forged for peoples and nations," Bernard complained. When Abelard was formally condemned, the new gospel was unforged. It would appear again with Nicolaus of Cusa's vision of peace among religions. Mostly the currents of the new gospel remained hidden, yet this is the very gospel that Vatican III must retrieve. As Genesis declares, God looked at everything God had made and saw that it was very good. That goodness remains, and so does God's unconditional positive regard for it. God loves the people no matter who they are, what they believe, or how they worship. Or, as Jesus himself put it, God "makes his sun rise on the evil and on the good, and sends rain on the just and on the unjust."[17] And recall that, for Jesus, being good or just was not a matter of being a believer but of caring for the neighbor. There is no ontological difference between the evil and the good, nor is there, with God, a hierarchy of the loved.

All that exists, and in particular all persons who exist, participate, by virtue of mere existence, in the existence of God. There is no question here of an unbridgeable gulf between the human and the divine. Christian Platonism yields to biblical faith. In this view, the Creation, more than salvation, is the pivotal event of being and of history, because the Creation is nothing less than God's self-expression. As Rahner explained, "God does not merely create something other than himself — he also gives himself to this other. The world receives God, the Infinite and the ineffable mystery, to such an extent that he himself becomes its innermost life."[18] Human beings are the creatures who instinctively respond to that innermost life. "This mystery," Rahner writes, "is the inexplicit and unexpressed horizon which always encircles and upholds the small area of our everyday experience . . . We call this God . . . However hard and unsatisfactory it may be to interpret the deepest and most fundamental experience at the very bottom of our being, man does experience in his innermost history that this silent, infinitely distant holy mystery, which continually recalls him to the limits of his finitude and lays bare his guilt yet *bids him approach;* the mystery enfolds him in an ultimate and radical love which commends itself to him as salvation and as the real meaning of his existence."[19]

For Christians, Jesus Christ is a revelation of that mystery. But Jesus did not come to put a fence around it, defining the corral gate as the way to salvation. There are numerous revelations of the mystery of God, and the shift initiated by Vatican III will be from, at most, a grudging tolerance of other religions to an authentic respect for other religions as true expressions of God "beckoning" the human heart.

Yet we saw that there was a kind of corralling of the meaning of Jesus when Hellenistic philosophical categories were pressed into service to explain it. The same would be true today, of course, if the new Christology were a product only of a reinterpretation in terms of the philosophical categories that have currency now. The most obvious such approach would take its cues from, say, the language philosophy of Wittgenstein, the existentialism of Kierkegaard, or the political gravity of Marxism. Evidence of all of these systems salts this book. The project of narrative theology, reflected in my method; the theological preoccupation with hermeneutics, which gives me my interest in social and political context; my preference, in defining Christ's purpose, for the "subjectivity" of a change in human knowing over the "objectivity" of a change in the structure of the cosmos — these are manifestations of current philosophical assumptions. Nevertheless, the emphasis I am giving to Jesus the Revealer as opposed to Jesus the Savior — giving, that is, to Jesus as the "expressive Being" of God, to cite the term the Anglican theologian John Macquarrie uses[20] — is rooted in the Christian tradition. Nothing I assert about Jesus, or the new way we should think of him, is unrelated to the theology we have explored in this book. Indeed, my call for a revised Christology comes from within the countermemory of the tradition itself.

Moreover, the retrieval of a Christology that does not assume anti-Judaism for its other side requires a careful measuring of every affirmation about Jesus against what can be known of his life as a faithful Jew. The categories of philosophy, however instructive, are not enough to tell us who Jesus was — and they never were. In Anselm's schema, as in Nicaea's for that matter, the Jewishness of Jesus was lost, and so was the context of Israel's hope, apart from which Jesus can have no meaning. This is the essential part of what Vatican III must retrieve with its new Christology. It is impossible to understand the disclosure Jesus offers without knowing that the One being disclosed is none other than the God of Israel. Likewise, the suffering and death of Jesus must resume its place along the continuum of his entire experience. If the death of Jesus is no longer seen as the trigger of a transformation of a wrathful God, then the false idea of "the Jews" as perpetrators of that death will cease to have weight — then and only then. That is why the cross must be reimagined, and deemphasized, as a Christian symbol.

A new Christology, faithfully based in the Scriptures and available from a tradition that includes an Abelard, will in no way support supersessionism. A new Christology will banish from Christian faith the blasphemy that God wills the suffering of God's beloved ones, and the inhuman idea that anyone's death can be the fulfillment of a plan of God's.

Equally important, a new Christology, celebrating a Jesus whose saving act is only disclosure of the divine love available to all, will enable the Church at last to embrace a pluralism of belief and worship, of religion and no-religion, that honors God by defining God as beyond every human effort to express God. In Rahner's image, God is the horizon, equally bidding all people to approach, yet equally distant from all people, Christians included. Vatican III will thus return to Jesus by returning to Rabbi Heschel and his liberating affirmation: "God is greater than religion . . . faith is greater than dogma."

59

Agenda Item 4: The Holiness
of Democracy

MY DEAR FELLOW CITIZENS, for forty years on this day
you heard from my predecessors the same thing in a number of variations: how our country is flourishing, how
many millions of tons of steel we produce, how happy we
all are, how we trust our government, and what bright prospects lie ahead
of us. I assume you did not propose me for this office so that I, too, should
lie to you."

So began the address with which the playwright and dissident Václav
Havel assumed the presidency of Czechoslovakia. The speech was delivered on the first day of 1990. The momentous events of the previous
months in the nations of eastern Europe, symbolized by the breaching of
the Berlin Wall in November 1989,[1] had amounted to an unpredicted outbreak of democratic fervor. As Havel put it, "Humanistic and democratic
traditions, about which there had been so much idle talk, did after all
slumber in the subconscious of our nations and national minorities."[2] In
that period, the social structures of totalitarianism were transformed not
only in the satellite states of the Soviet Union but in Russia itself, not only
in Europe but in South Africa. And the dramatic changes came about almost completely without blood in the streets, because the masses of ordinary people in many nations discovered within themselves an irresistible
civic identification, an urge to participate in the public life of society, a
readiness to claim those nations as their own.

Citizens of the nations of western Europe and America, where democratic traditions were already established, could only behold the political transformations of the Velvet Revolution with an unbridled sense of
wonder. What we saw played out again and again in those years, often

with staggering courage — Havel declining a strings-attached release from prison, Lech Walesa openly convening meetings of the outlawed Solidarity movement in Poland, Boris Yeltsin standing on that Russian tank, saying, in effect, You will have to kill me first — was the drama of democracy itself, entire peoples taking responsibility for themselves and their societies. We in the West had never before seen so clearly how the political system under which we lived, and which we took for granted, counted as a moral absolute. Democracy was a value of the highest order, and the impulse to embrace it, at great cost, lived unquenchably in the human heart. In 1989, the world beheld something sacred, and the business of Vatican III must be to honor that sacredness. Vatican III must end the Church tradition of opposition to, or at best ambivalence toward, democracy. Vatican III must, that is, celebrate the dignity of every human life. Vatican III must uphold the importance of treating each one equally. Vatican III must affirm the holiness of democracy.

To their everlasting credit, the Christian churches of Europe supported, and in some instances sponsored, the 1980s flowering of the democratic spirit. The churches were especially helpful in keeping violence at bay. Lutheran pastors in East Germany played crucial roles in challenging the German Democratic Republic. And the Catholic Church, especially in Poland, was a source of spiritual, and at times political, inspiration and sustenance to the dissidents. Pope John Paul II was himself an avatar of anti-Communist resistance. His biographers uniformly credit him, sometimes with Ronald Reagan, as the man who did the most to bring down the totalitarian system he had opposed from his youth in Kraków.

Opposition to Stalinism is not the same thing as support for the principles of constitutional democracy, however, and the Roman Catholic Church has yet to shed its suspicion of, and even its hostility to, governments that invest the people with ultimacy — or rather, governments in which the people do the investing. This has been especially true in the Vatican's suppression of liberation theology, which is a religious affirmation of the political ideal of rights for all. Thus, in opposing Soviet totalitarianism, the Church nevertheless maintained its internal commitment to methods that undergird totalitarianism, which was why, even as the Soviet system crumbled, the Church was doing its part to shore up Latin American oligarchies.

The same John Paul II who sponsored the most politically engaged Church of modern times in Poland, even to the extent of funneling large sums of money from the Vatican to Solidarity, condemned, silenced, and disciplined priests and nuns in Nicaragua, El Salvador, Guatemala, Brazil, Haiti, and Mexico because of their so-called political activity. The pope who wants to make Pius XII a saint is reticent about Oscar Romero, the bishop of El Salvador who was slain at the altar. The pope who railed against the ruthless dictators of Communism was the first and only head of state in the world to recognize the legitimacy of the military junta that overthrew the democratically elected president of Haiti (and former priest) Jean-Bertrand Aristide.[3] I say "so-called political activity" because the priests and nuns of the liberation insisted that their actions had more to do with their reading of the Gospel than any political tract. Observers of the difference between responses by the Catholic hierarchy in, say, Poland, where the Church lent support to Solidarity, and in Nicaragua, where the Church was a putative channel for money from the CIA during Ronald Reagan's Contra war,[4] were left with the feeling that it wasn't totalitarianism as such that the Church opposed, only totalitarianism that was unfriendly to the Church.

It was one thing for Pope Innocent III to declare the Magna Carta null and void in 1215 because it violated the divinely instituted order of hierarchy, and quite another for the Vatican, in its *instrumentum laboris* for the European synod of 1999, to equate pluralism with Marxism. It is impossible to reconcile a rejection of pluralism with an authentic commitment to democracy, and a Catholic devotion to the eradication of pluralism remains dangerous. Internal Church policies have relevance here because the use of anathemas, bannings, and excommunications to enforce a rigidly controlled intellectual discipline in the Church reveals an institution that has yet to come to terms with basic ideas like freedom of conscience and the dialectical nature of rational inquiry.

As we saw in our consideration of Spinoza, the very idea of constitutional democracy begins with the insight that government exists to protect the *interior* freedom of citizens to be different from one another, and to cling, if they choose, to opposite notions of the truth. The political implementation of this insight requires a separation of church and state, since the state's purpose is to shield the citizen's conscience from impositions by any religious entity. And we saw that Spinoza's arrival at this position came as a direct consequence of his family's experience with the Inquisition. The Church repudiated the violence of the Inquisition, but it continued to hold to the ideas that had produced it. The panic-stricken Vatican's sequence of condemnations in the nineteenth century — socialism, Communism, rationalism, pantheism, subjectivism, modernism, even "Americanism" — added up to a resolute denunciation of everything we mean by democracy. From the standpoint of the hill overlooking the Tiber, all of this was simply an effort to defend the key idea that the worlds of science, culture, politics, and learning — all worlds that could be easily associated with Jews — were apparently conspiring to attack. Spinoza himself had seemed to attack it — the idea that there is one objective and absolute truth, and that its custodian is the Church.

Again, we think of the papal apology of March 2000. That was the beginning of a process, not the completion of one, because, while John Paul II confessed the sin of "the use of violence that some have resorted to in the service of truth,"[5] the apology did not confront the implications of that still maintained idea of truth. Universalist claims for Jesus as the embodiment of the one objective and absolute truth, launched from the battlement-like pulpits of basilicas, have landed explosively in the streets for centuries. Nothing demonstrates the links joining philosophical assumptions, esoteric theology, and political conflict better than the course of the story of Christology that we traced in the previous chapter. The violence of the heresy hunts of the fourth and fifth centuries is tied to that story, and so, at its other end, is the violence of Europe's imperialist colonizers who, even into the twentieth century, felt free to decimate native populations — "poor devils" — because they were heathens. Hanging from the line joining those two posts, in addition to the Inquisition, are the religious wars waged in the name of Jesus, not only against heathens and Jews, but against other Christians who believed, but wrongly.

Underlying all this is a question that Vatican III must confront, a question the answer to which shapes attitudes toward democracy, a question the answer to which has profound relevance to the Church's past and future relations with the Jews. It is a question the answer to which shapes the meaning of Judaism's notions of monotheism, election, and chosenness, as well as of the Church's self-understanding as, in Rahner's phrase, the "absolute religion." It is the question that was put most famously by Pontius Pilate, in the Pilate-exonerating Gospel of John. This was an instant before Pilate told the Jews that Jesus was innocent, preparing the ground for Judaism's permanent blood guilt. "Everyone who is of the truth hears my voice," Jesus had just told Pilate. To which the Roman replied, "What is truth?"[6]

Latin philosophy had long answered that question by appealing to an objective and external order. We have seen that the various traditions claiming Plato and Aristotle as patrons had given shape to Christian theologies. The dualism of Christian Platonism posited a divide between nature and grace, with grace the realm of truth approachable only through faith. The more rationalistic tradition of Thomas Aquinas affirmed the compatibility of nature and grace, the knowability of God through reason. But in asserting the absolute character of truth, Thomas took note of the problem that occurs when a contingent, nature-bound creature attempts to perceive it. Truth, he said, is perceived in the mode of the perceiver. Human perception can take in the absolute truth, but not absolutely. Thus Thomas makes a modest claim for human knowing, with room for ambiguity — which means room for diverse claims made in the name of truth. Alas, this aspect of Thomas Aquinas's subtlety would be lost in the rigidities of the Catholic response to the Reformation.

René Descartes's *Discourse on Method* (1637) asserted that truth can be arrived at only on the basis of what is immediately self-evident, which eliminates knowledge gained through the unreliable senses. Therefore it is impossible to really know the truth — an impossibility that condemns the human mind to skepticism. It is this skepticism that the Catholic scholastics of the eighteenth and nineteenth centuries went to war against, and though they wrapped themselves in the mantle of Thomas Aquinas, calling themselves Thomists, they narrowly defined truth as the unambiguous conformity of the mind to the objective truth, without any sense that ambiguity might be a property of that mind. Enlightenment science had adopted a mechanical view of the universe that eliminated God (Nietzsche's *Thus Spake Zarathustra* announced the death of God in 1883). Ironically, to defend God the Thomists assumed an equally mechanical view of the universe, with a gear-like correspondence between nature and grace, subject and object, mind and truth. Imprecision, ambiguity, paradox, doubt, and mystery had as little place in the mind of a Catholic scholastic as in the mind of a catalogue-obsessed nineteenth-century naturalist.

Both are instances of what the Jesuit philosopher William Lynch calls the "univocal mind." A univocal word has only one meaning, and a univocal community has only one voice. "The basic drive behind the univocal mind," Lynch wrote, "is the tendency to reduce everything, every difference and particularity in images, to the unity of a sameness which destroys or eliminates the variety and detail of existence."[7] This Catholic view of truth meshed perfectly with, indeed required, the nineteenth-century view of Catholic authority, whose role was to guard against ambiguity — which it could do, after 1870, infallibly. Once the Church, in its hierarchy, and in particular in the pope, had defined the objective truth, the duty of the Catholic was univocally to conform his or her mind to that truth.

But history has a way of challenging such ideas. The implications of Darwin's theory of evolution outran its first adherents and soon frustrated the most compulsive cataloguer. Human knowing is as dynamic as the development of species is. The absolute truth can in no way evolve or change (God as the Unmoved Mover), but what if everything else does? Then, in 1918, Albert Einstein published *Relativity: The Special and General Theory,* suggesting that neither the ground on which one stands while thinking nor the time in which one pursues a thought to its conclusion is free of ambiguity, paradox, contradiction, movement — relativity. Suddenly thinkers had a new language, based in physical observation, with which to describe the fact that every perception occurs from a particular point of view and that not even the point of view is constant. Every person is a perceiving center, and every perception is different. There is no absolute conformity of the knowing subject to the known object. Therefore truth can be known only obliquely, and, yes, subjectively.

Change is built into the way truth is perceived, and every person's perception has something to offer every other's. Therefore revision, criticism, dialogue, and conversation are far more relevant to truth-seeking than conformity to dictation from above. This flies in the face not of Catholic tradition but of *recent* Catholic tradition. For example, this existentialist framework fulfills the apophatic impulse of Nicolaus of Cusa, whose *Learned Ignorance* (1440), affirming that God, and therefore truth, can be approached only indirectly, set the stage for his celebration of pluralism, *Peace Among the Religions* (1453). Unfortunately, Nicolaus of Cusa stood by another of those roads not taken. Catholic theology spent much of the twentieth century recovering from the defensive rigidities of Counter-Reformation scholasticism, but the recovery is not complete. Vatican III must retrieve for the Church the deep-seated human intuition that mystery is at the core of existence, that truth is elusive, that God is greater than religion. "The heart of the matter is mystery in any religion," David Tracy said. "The Law is there for the Jew to intensify that sense of mystery, not to replace it. The Church is there for the Catholic to do the same."[8] If mystery is at the core of religion, then ambiguity, paradox, and even doubt are not enemies of faith, but aspects of it.

This is what Abelard saw, and Nicolaus of Cusa, and John Henry Newman, for whom the truth was like a tapestry, but seen from the reverse side, with all the imprecision that implies. Newman, who, after the fact, assented as an obedient Catholic to the infallibility decree he had opposed, nevertheless insisted that the nature of truth required modesty toward oneself and respect toward all others. "He was capable of holding a position," as the theologian Gerald Bednar observes, "while at the same time admitting the validity of a system very different from his own."[9]

But how? Are we condemned to a mindless pluralism that is ready to equate the shallow with the profound, the stupid with the wise, the cruel with the kind, all to avoid the monotony of the "one voice," the tyranny of the univocal? Does subjectivity condemn the person to the tyranny of the self? Does subjectivity condemn the community to, in David Tracy's phrase, "the void of sheer fascination at our pluralistic possibilities"?[10] Fearing the answer to those questions had to be yes, the Church set itself against democracy, and still openly regards pluralism with suspicion. But Lynch, Tracy, and others suggest that the antidote to the equivocation of modern skepticism is not the univocal but the "analogical imagination," which, in its approach to truth, as Lynch puts it, "insists on keeping the same and the different, the idea and the detail, tightly interlocked in the one imaginative act." Instead of a dualistic universe, with nature and grace impossibly alienated, or conformed into the mold of one or the other, the analogical imagination posits a world in which every affirmation contains its own "difference, without ever suffering the loss of its own identity."[11] Difference, therefore, is to be respected, not condemned.

This idea, rebutting the excommunicating either-or of scholasticism, returns us to the both-and mind of Abelard, whose *Sic et Non* affirmed doubt and ambiguity as essential to the theological method. And recall that, in that crusading era, Abelard stood apart from his peers in his inbuilt positive regard for Jews, as reflected in his *Dialogue of a Philosopher with a Jew and a Christian.* Alas, he too stood by a road not taken, but, with Nicolaus of Cusa, he lives on in the memory of the Church as a reminder that the road is still there.

Tracy explains the vivid connection between such a frame of mind and the respect for a formerly hated other: "We understand one another, if at all, only through analogies. Each recognizes that any attempt to reduce the authentic otherness of another's focus to one's own with our common habits of domination only seems to destroy us all, only increases the leveling power of the all-too-common denominators making no one at home. Conflict is our actuality. Conversation is our hope."[12]

Conversation is our hope. In that simple statement lies the kernel of democracy, which is based not on *diktat* but on the interchange of mutuality. The clearest example of conversation as the sine qua non of democracy is the electoral process, in which candidates literally engage in conversation with the citizenry, opening themselves so that voters can judge them, but also changing their minds in response to interaction with the public. The proliferation of town meetings and debates in recent American political campaigns exemplifies this social equality and supports it.

There is a special tragedy in the fact that, for contingent historical reasons, the Catholic Church set itself so ferociously against the coming of democracy — tragic because Christianity began its life as a small gathering of Jews who were devoted to conversation. This was, of course, characteristically Jewish, since Judaism was a religion of the Book. Indeed, that was what made Judaism unique. That the Book was at the center of this group's identity meant that the group was never more itself than when reading and responding to texts, and while the rabbinical schools may have presided over such a process, all Jews participated in it, especially after the liturgical cult of sacrifice was lost when the Temple was destroyed. Gatherings around the Book became everything. Conversation became everything. The assumption among the followers of Jesus was that they were all endowed with the wisdom, insight, maturity, and holiness necessary to contribute to the pursuit of the truth of who Jesus had been to them.

The religious language for this assumption had it that all believers were endowed with the Holy Spirit, which was seen to reside in the Church not through an ordained hierarchy but through all. That is why the apostolic writings are nothing if not manifestations of pluralism. Indeed, there are four Gospels, not one. Each has its slant, and each slant, in this community, has its place. "That there is real diversity in the New Testament should be clear to any reader of the text," David Tracy comments, and he goes on to note that the first Christians could admit the validity of positions not their own — from the charismatics to the apocalyptics to the zealots to the prophets.[13] There is even a diversity of images that disclose the meaning of Jesus' life, with some giving emphasis to the ministry, some to the death, some to the symbolic assault on the Temple, some to the expected return. There are those who emphasize bringing the Gospel to the Gentiles and those who insist on the Gospel's place within the hope of Israel. And because the texts gather all of this, honor it, and declare it *all* sacred, nothing could be further from the mind of the early Church than making its subjects conform to a narrowly defined "objective truth." The

Spirit was seen to be living in all, and the truth, for all, remained shrouded in mystery.

It would be anachronistic, of course, to read this as evidence of an early Church polity that was what we would call democracy. That does not mean, however, that democracy, by taking each member of the community as of ultimate worth, equal to every other, is not a fulfillment of the biblical vision that attributes just such valuing of each person to God. Isaac Hecker, the American who founded the Paulist Fathers, the religious order to which I belonged, argued that America and Catholicism were inherently compatible because of this. To Hecker, the equal rights of citizenship was a secular expression of the religious "indwelling of the Spirit" in each person. When this idea was brought to Europe at the end of the nineteenth century, Leo XIII condemned it as the heresy "Americanism." In particular, the pope denounced the idea "that certain liberties ought to be introduced into the church so that, limiting the exercise and vigilance of its powers, each one of the faithful may act more freely in pursuance of his own natural bent and capacity."[14] The anathemas were nearly pronounced over Hecker himself. My own life as a twentieth-century Catholic, in dissent from a nineteenth-century Catholicism, began with my falling under Hecker's spell. Vatican III should rescind the condemnation of "Americanism," acknowledging that the "pursuit of happiness" assumes the "pursuance" of one's natural bent and capacity, and that nothing better defines the purpose for which our Creator made us.

So the answer to Pilate's question, What is truth?, matters. If truth is the exclusive province of authority, then the duty of the people is to conform to it. That answer to the question fits with the politics of a command society, whether a monarchy, a dictatorship, or the present Catholic Church. But if truth is, by definition, available to human beings only in partial ways; if we know more by analogies than syllogisms; if, that is, we "see in a mirror dimly,"[15] then the responsibility of the people is to bring one's own experience and one's own thought to the place where the community has its conversations, to offer and accept criticism, to honor the positions of others, and to respect oneself, not in isolation but in this creative mutuality. The mutuality, in this community, has a name — the Holy Spirit.

The implication here is that truth is not the highest value for us, because, in Saint Paul's phrase, "our knowledge is imperfect and our prophecy is imperfect."[16] Which is why the final revelation of Jesus is not about knowing but about loving. This, too, places him firmly in the tradition of Israel, which has always given primacy to right action. "Beloved," the author of the First Epistle of John wrote, "let us love one another; for love is of God, and he who loves is born of God and knows God. He who does not love does not know God; for God is love." This statement of a biblical faith in the ultimate meaning of existence *as love* is a classic affirmation of what one might call the pluralistic principle: Respect for the radically other begins with God's respect for the world, which is radically other from God. In other words, God is the first pluralist. "In this the love of God was made manifest among us, that God sent his only Son into the world, so that we might live through him. In this is love, not that we loved God but that he loved us and sent his Son to be the expiation for our sins. Beloved, if God so loved us, we also ought to love one another. No man has ever seen God; if we love one another, God abides in us and his love is perfected in us."[17]

Religious pluralism begins with this acknowledgment of the universal impossibility of direct knowledge of God. The immediate consequence of this universal ignorance is that we should regard each other respectfully and lovingly. But our clear statement of Christian openness to the other is its own revelation. The epistle just cited is attributed to John, the author of the fourth Gospel. It was written, apparently, about the same time as the Gospel, around the turn of the first century. It was addressed to Christian communities that were riven with the disputes that had come after the destruction of the Temple and with the first serious conflict between what was becoming known as the Church and the Synagogue. This plea, whatever else it referred to, concerned the tragedy then beginning to unfold — it is John, as we saw, whose Gospel demonizes "the Jews" above all. And the tragedy is underscored by the fact that in this same letter John, as if understanding already what is at stake in the conflict, begs his readers to "not be like Cain who was of the evil one and murdered his brother. And why did he murder him? Because his own deeds were evil and his brother's righteous."[18] The tragedy, and the sin, and what must forever warn us off cheap talk of love, is that all too soon, and all too easily, the followers of Jesus were content to read these words and identify Cain with Jews.

That sin, embedded in the Gospel itself, is proof of why the Church needs democracy, for the assumption of democratic politics, in addition to the assumption that all citizens can contribute to the truth-seeking conversation, is that all citizens are constitutionally incapable of consistent truth-seeking and steadfast loving. God may be love, but the *polis* isn't, and neither is the Church. So we come full circle and recall that the language of love is often used by those in power, while the language of justice is used by those who suffer from the abuse of power. The language of love is not enough. Because the language of love does not protect us from our failures to love; only the language of justice does that.

Democracy assumes that a clear-headed assessment of the flaws of members extends to everyone. But even the leaders of democracies, especially in the United States, salt their speeches with Christian chauvinism or an excluding religiosity, assuming that a democratic polity could be called univocal — no voices, that is, for religious minorities or those of no religion. And that, finally, is why a democracy assumes that everyone must be protected from the unchecked, uncriticized, and unregulated power of every other, including the well-meaning leader. The universal experience of imperfection, finitude, and self-centeredness is the pessimistic ground of democratic hope. We saw that in Spinoza's story,[19] which was, after all, the story of a man constructing the democratic ideal out of the cruelties inflicted in the name of God. The Church's own experience — in particular, of its grievous sin in relation to the Jews — proves how desperately in need of democratic reform the Church is.

Vatican III must therefore turn the Church away from monarchy and toward democracy, as the Catholic people have in fact already done. Vatican III must restore the broken authority of the Church by locating authority in the place where it belongs, which is with the people through whom the Spirit breathes. Vatican III must affirm that democracy itself is the latest gift from a God who operates in history, and the only way for the Church to affirm democracy is by embracing it. The old dispute between popes and kings over who appoints bishops was resolved in favor of the pope, but bishops now should be chosen by the people they serve. The clerical caste, a vestige of the medieval court, should be eliminated. Vatican III must establish equal rights for women in every sphere. A system of checks and balances, due process, legislative norms designed to assure equality for all instead of superiority for some, freedom of expression, and above all freedom of conscience must be established within the Church — not because the time of liberalism has arrived, but because this long and sorry story of Church hatred of Jews only lays bare the structures of oppression that must be dismantled once and for all.

Vatican III must finish the work that Vatican II began in its implicit, but ever more clear, reaction to the events of 1933–1945. Otherwise, we Catholics are condemned to ask, with David Tracy, "How can we stand by and continue to develop theologies of the church and the tradition as if the Holocaust did not happen?"[20]

60

Agenda Item 5: Repentance

P ULL OUT HIS EYES," the children chant in the mind of Stephen Dedalus. "Apologise, / Apologise, / Pull out his eyes."[1] The impulse to apologize for the Holocaust is properly distrusted, because words are cheap and apology has become an arrow in the well-equipped politician's quiver. An American president apologizes to Africans for failing to stop a genocide, while the United States, the richest nation in the world, ranks ninth in the percentage of national wealth given to combat worldwide AIDS, which kills more Africans than all the continent's wars put together. British Prime Minister Tony Blair acknowledges the failure of "those who governed in London at the time" to avert the famine known to the Irish as the Great Hunger, but Blair was hooted at by Ulster Unionists who said, "The Irish mentality is one of victimhood — and to ask for one apology one week, and another on a different subject the next."[2] The Vatican issues "We Remember: A Reflection on the Shoah" as an "act of repentance," yet puts responsibility for failure on the Church's children, not the Church; it never mentions the Inquisition, and it praises the diplomacy of Pius XII. John Paul II offers a millennial mea culpa early in the year 2000, and while, as we have noted, there was a profound significance in that apology, as far as it went, it revealed how far is the distance that must be traveled yet.

As the document "Memory and Reconciliation" put it, "Memory becomes capable of giving rise to a new future."[3] But the current leadership of the Church seems interested only in partial memory and a limited reckoning with the past. Otherwise John Paul II would not have devoted so much of his papacy to maintaining the very modes of thought and governance that were the historic sources of Church failure. Apologies offered too glibly, in other words, can be a sly way of asserting one's own moral superiority while reifying the victim status of the group to whom apologies are offered. This is especially so if the structures of that victimization remain in place.

"When Willy Brandt fell on his knees on the site of the Warsaw ghetto in 1970," the scholar Ian Buruma has written, "it was a moving and necessary acknowledgment of a great crime. But such symbolic gestures are too precious to become routine. Official tears have become too cheap, too ritualistic. Piety is often a substitute for knowledge and understanding."[4] Knowledge and understanding have been our purposes here, and the next council will accomplish nothing if it falls back, as the Church has so regularly done, on piety. But something else seems possible now, in the aftermath of John Paul II's millennial call for "the purification of memory."

That is more than a matter of mere words. Far more important than uttered apology, for example, was his momentous act in Israel only two weeks after the liturgy of repentance, an event that transcended the routine symbolic gestures of which Buruma warns. In Jerusalem, John Paul II left his wheeled conveyance to walk haltingly across the vast plaza before the Western Wall. For two thousand years, beginning with the Gospels, Christian theology has depended on the destruction of the Temple as a proof for claims made in the name of Jesus, the new Temple. Nothing signifies Christian anti-Judaism more fully than this attachment to the Temple in ruins, which prompted the pagan emperor Julian to order it rebuilt in the fourth century, and which underlies Vatican ambivalence toward the state of Israel in the twentieth. So when John Paul II devotedly approached the last vestige of that Temple, and when he placed in a crevice of that wall a piece of paper containing words from his previously offered prayer for forgiveness — "We are deeply saddened by the behavior of those who in the course of history have caused these children of yours to suffer" — more than an apology occurred.

Though the news media missed its significance, this moment outweighed even the pope's later, emotional visit to Yad Vashem. By bending in prayer at the Western Wall, the Kotel, the pope symbolically created a new future. The Church was honoring the Temple it had denigrated. It was affirming the presence of the Jewish people at home in Jerusalem. The pope reversed an ancient current of Jew hatred with that act, and the Church's relationship to Israel, present as well as past, would never be the same. Referring to the sight of the stooped man in white with his trembling hand on the sacred stones of the wall, a senior Israeli official said, "This is a picture that will appear in the history books — both Catholic and Jewish."[5]

*   *   *

An authentic confrontation with history results in the opposite of self-exoneration. That is why the members of Vatican III, in taking up repentance as an agenda item, must do so only after having confronted the questions embedded in this narrative, and the consequent questions of antisemitic texts, power, Christology, and democracy, all of which point to attitudes and structures of denigration that must be uprooted if the Church is truly going to turn toward Jews with a new face. Remorse over the silence of the Church in the face of the Shoah — the *faute* to which the French bishops confessed — is not enough. Neither is guilt over the ways two millennia of Church antisemitism prepared for the Shoah.

Authentic repentance presumes what we Catholics used to call "a firm purpose of amendment," which Jews call "desisting" from what led to sin.[6] Simply put, repentance presumes change — at every level of the Church's life, because it is at every level that the poison of antisemitism has had its effect. *Teshuva* is the word Jews use to describe the process by which repentance and forgiveness take place. The word means "return," and here is Rabbi David R. Blumenthal's summary of what *teshuva*, in this context, implies: "All the words, documents, and genuine expressions of contrition will avail naught without concrete actions . . . The way the Church deals with terrorist incidents, antisemitism, Church files on the period of the Shoah, Judaica deposited with various Church entities and not returned, Catholic education about Jews and Judaism, the nature of Catholic mission, relations with the State of Israel, relations with local Jewish communities everywhere, etc. are, thus, the action-yardsticks by which Catholic teshuva is measured."[7] Such changes — education, mission, relations — require the changes in doctrine and structure I have indicated. I call for those changes as a Catholic, but in fact I am following, as Tracy put it, "Jewish theology [which], in its reflections on the reality of God since the *Tremendum* of the Holocaust, has led the way for all serious theological reflection."[8]

Why would it take a Vatican Council to accomplish Catholic *teshuva*? Because more than one moral failure is at issue here. How do we measure the offense of the Church against the Jews? Perhaps by returning to a figure cited early in this book — that, since Jews made up about 10 percent of the population of the Roman Empire when this story began, their worldwide population today — but for intervening tragic factors — would have been, as a percentage of the total, about 200 million, instead of 13 million.[9] The Church, while not the sum of those factors, was their driving spirit, their engine, their sanctification. And the symbol of that sanctification was the cross. From Constantine forward, the cross became the symbol of all that Christians must repent in relation to the Jewish people. Mary Boys, a Catholic theologian and veteran of the Jewish-Christian dialogue, wrote, "The cross is a symbol Christians have been given to image their hope that God is with them even in pain and tragedy and ambiguity. It is a symbol of the longing to give themselves over to a project larger than their own self-interest . . . Yet it is not a symbol that can be re-appropriated without repentance."[10]

Thus we "arrive where we started," in T. S. Eliot's line, "and know the place for the first time." The cross at Auschwitz, when I beheld it on a dark November day in 1996, was what inspired this long examination of a Catholic conscience. I vaguely grasped the necessity of learning, as Paul van Buren put it, "to speak of Auschwitz from the perspective of the cross . . . by first learning to speak of the cross from the perspective of Auschwitz."[11] And how does that cross look now? I have in front of me a pair of maps, "The Auschwitz Region" and "Auschwitz I." The first offers a diagram of the locality. The Vistula and the Sola Rivers, indicated by wavy channels, intersect above the center of the map. Railroad tracks, black lines with teeth running in four directions, intersect just below the center. These intersections, I confess, look like crosses to me. There are symbols for houses and factories, and the three camps are indicated by hash-marked rectangles: Auschwitz III, the Monowitz Labor Camp; Auschwitz II, Birkenau; and Auschwitz I, the main camp.

The Auschwitz I map shows a carefully drawn compound with guardhouses, sentry towers, a crematorium recognizable by its chimney, and twenty-eight barracks buildings, arranged like peaked-roofed dominoes around three avenues. The camp wall is indicated by tiny crosses on a line, like barbed wire. At one end of the camp is the largest building of all, identified in the map key as the "Old Theater, then storehouse for valuables removed from bodies, site of the Carmelite Convent." Next to that building, along the wall that abuts Barracks 15, the starvation bunker, is an unmarked area that I recognize as the field in which the cross now stands.

I began this book at the mercy of an instinctive wish that the cross at Auschwitz could be made simply to disappear. I would have been relieved to learn that it had been spirited away in the middle of the night by anonymous agents of some Vatican commission or the World Jewish Congress. The cross at Auschwitz: the object of furious controversy, not only between Jews and Christians but among Christians themselves; a new symbol of Polish national revival; the vestige of argument over the convent, which has been moved, and over other crosses, which have been removed; the symbol of the practical impossibility of reconciliation among conflicting claims that are all absolute. And the cross there is a heartbreaking symbol of Pope John Paul II's tragic ambivalence, his longing to identify with the Jews who were crushed around him when he was young, his blindness to the weight of a Catholic past that helped make that crushing lethal. We return to our basic idea, that Catholic history, while not causing the Shoah, was a necessary, unbroken thread in the rise of genocidal antisemitism as well as the source of the Church's failure to openly oppose it. The Catholic past and the cross at Auschwitz are profoundly connected.

My wish is different now, the product not of instinct but of this history. The cross at Auschwitz, transcending whatever benign intention attaches to it, embodies supersessionism, medieval absolutism, the cult of martyrdom, the violence of God, the ancient hatred of Jews, and the Christian betrayal of Jesus Christ. This is the cross that was stolen by the emperor Constantine, perverted by the crusaders, and blasphemed by the editors of *La Croix*. Pius XII, in the encyclical *Mystici Corporis Christi*, issued in June 1943 as the roundup of Jews was peaking, declared, ". . . but on the gibbet of his death Jesus made void the Law with its decrees, [and] fastened the handwriting of the Old Testament to the Cross, establishing the New Testament in His blood . . . On the Cross then the Old Law died, soon to be buried and to be a bearer of death."[12] In the name of the cross, even in 1943, Jews were implicitly being accused of causing death, and not just Jesus'. And in recent years, by self-proclaimed Christian friends of Jews, the cross has been imposed on them, whether they wanted it or not. "Like the cross of Christ," the German theologian Jürgen Moltmann declared, "even Auschwitz is in God himself. Even Auschwitz is taken up into the grief of the Father, the surrender of the Son and the power of the Spirit."[13] The cross has thus been twisted into an apologetic tool and a source of slander. It has consistently been made to serve the purpose of power. Auschwitz is the final disclosure of this truth.

Therefore the Christian Church should come here and perform a simple penitential rite. This rite must be conducted in silence, to compensate for the sinful silence of the Church, but more, to push beyond all the words that have come too easily. The most precious Christian words — Golgotha, redemption, sacrifice — have no place here. Therefore, in silence the sin of the Church is acknowledged as the sin that was part of what led to genocide. There is no more talk that exempts "the Church as such" from this judgment. Instead, with Rahner, who wrote generally of the "sinful Church of sinners," the confession is made that the failures that brought the Church here are "the actions and conduct of the Church herself."[14] The piety of the Church herself is renounced as the piety that has kept the structure of victimization of the other so firmly in place, even until now. Rivals in victimization no more. Rivals for the blessing of God no more. Rivals no more at Auschwitz.

Silence does not preclude expression. The acknowledgment of sin requires expression, but the proper word of acknowledgment here is an act. A sacrament of the Church accusing itself. The penitential rite would consist of a dismantling of this cross, a removal of the horizontal beam, an uprooting of the vertical, a reversal of the instruction Constantine gave his soldiers. In this way, the cross would be returned to Jesus, and returned to its place as the cause of his death, not the purpose of his life. For Jesus, the cross could have been nothing of conquest or power. For Jesus, therefore, the cross could not conceivably have become a symbol of triumphalism, nor a sign of the defamation of his own people. To remove this cross is to begin the reversal of all that we Christians here confess. And to remove this cross is to retrieve the cross as a sign that God has come to a failed and sinful Church, and only confessing itself as such can the Church fulfill its mission as witness to God's unconditional love for all.

More important, to remove the cross from Auschwitz, deliberately, reverently, and in the presence of living Jews, would restore Auschwitz to those who were murdered here, asking nothing of them in return.

Epilogue: The Faith of a Catholic

W HEN OUR CHILDREN were young, my wife, Lexa, and I traveled with them through Europe on a Eurailpass, which let us hop on and off trains with abandon. It was 1989. Lizzy was nine, and Pat was seven. Beginning in Amsterdam, we passed through Brussels, then made our way to Paris for the centenary celebration of the Eiffel Tower, which our children dubbed the birthday tower. In that pre-euro era, what we loved most was crossing borders, and we decided to cross as many as we could.

Lizzy had a preoccupation that tracked us like a cloud. In Amsterdam, we had visited the Anne Frank House. The small rooms of the hidden annex had left us all short of breath, but it was our daughter who carried away the image of Anne as a locating compass rose. Lizzy's identification with the young girl, whose diary she had begun to read, was complete. When our train crossed from Holland into Belgium, Lizzy asked, "Whose side were these on?" The Belgians, she meant. Were they on Anne's side or Hitler's? Anne's, we answered. Then, the same thing when we crossed into France. "Whose side were these on?" Anne's, we said again, giving France a large benefit of the doubt. At each border she asked again. And when we said, at the crossing from Switzerland, that Italy had been on Hitler's side, we could see judgment seize her gaze as she turned to look out the train window, as if surely the landscape itself would tell her how such a thing had been possible. All of history was present to her as she stared out at the Italian countryside. For the first time, regarding the fate of Anne Frank and her people, I felt completely ashamed.

The next summer, we began in Amsterdam again, but now we went where we hadn't gone the year before, which was Germany. I had to overcome Lizzy's implicit objection — I wanted my family to see Wiesbaden, where I had been as a boy. The previous November, the Berlin Wall had been breached. Large vestiges of it still stood, and Lexa and I agreed that for history's sake we should all see it. We began our tour of Germany with a dreamy cruise down the Rhine, but soon it became a grim trip. As we sailed upriver from Cologne, passing Koblenz and the confluence of the Moselle, I thought of Maria Laach and Trier, but my family was already impatient, and I didn't tell them my stories of those places. When we disembarked directly across from Mainz, we turned our backs on that "Rome of the North" to go the short way to Wiesbaden. Its elegance no longer stood out from the ruins of the rest of the Rhineland's cities, as it had in my day, and so neither Lexa nor the children could see it. I insisted on the extravagance of staying in what had been the best hotel in town — in my time, reserved for senior American officers. But it was adjacent to the famous spa, and its rooms reeked of the sulfurous hot springs that Germans still regarded as an indulgence. When I showed my family the mansion in which my parents, brothers, and I had lived, no one was impressed.

We took the train from Frankfurt to Berlin, as I had in 1959 with a group of chums, traveling on a U.S. Army train, with gun mounts. On that trip, at the East-West border, we had seen Soviet tanks, and the train had been searched by "Vopos" (*Volkspolizei*) carrying machine guns. Even in 1990, the trip felt adventurous. The German Democratic Republic was not quite dismantled, and at the old border between East and West Germany our train was halted. I told Lizzy and Pat about the tanks I'd seen there once, explaining about the Iron Curtain. Pat spied an old rusting corrugated fence bordering the railyard, and cried, "There it is!" And I thought, What the hell, he's probably right. A new crew got on the train, and their shabby blue uniforms and peaked hats marked them as last-gasp functionaries of the GDR. One was a ticket-checking conductor who, when I showed him our Eurailpasses, snorted, *"Nein, nein."* He seemed to be threatening to throw us off the train, and for a minute I felt the blast of a Cold War fear. I gestured pathetically at my wife and children, asking for mercy. The East German waved me away in disgust, and soon the train was moving again. I looked out the window from then on with a feeling of relief and wonder.

In Berlin, the railroad station was swarming with people hauling televisions and mattresses and small refrigerators, cartons and baskets containing all kinds of consumer goods. These were Poles and Silesians and Prussians and Pomeranians, until recently prisoners of the East. Their first rush of freedom was to go shopping, although to us they looked like looters. We checked into our hotel on the Kurfürstendamm, then went right away to what I remembered of Checkpoint Charlie. Its metal shed was there, but the barriers were gone. The infamous wall — cinderblocks and cement with a large concrete sewer tunnel on top — was still standing, but in ragged, graffiti-covered pieces. Huge gaps had been opened in the wall, and across the way lay a wasteland several hundred yards wide, stretching half a mile or more between the Brandenburg Gate at one end and Potsdamer Platz at the other. This dusty vacancy was what remained of no man's land, the barrier zone between East and West Berlin that had, until the previous fall, been spiked with tank obstacles, laced with barbed wire, and studded with concrete pillboxes from which unmanned machine guns were trained at the level of the human heart.

Berliners, tourists, refugees from the East, and military personnel variously uniformed; punk rockers, hawkers in purloined Soviet officer caps with sleeves full of Red Army pins and medals for sale, and waif-like girls smoking cigarettes — a defiant chaos of strangers milled about in the acreage once known as the death strip. I saw the remnant of an isolated wooden platform and recognized it as the lookout staging onto which Westerners had once climbed to gaze out over the wall. Bellevue, it had been called, I remembered suddenly. I had mounted that platform myself, in 1980, when I had come here to write a magazine article. But now the section of wall in front of the platform was entirely gone, and the platform looked like a beached wreck.

Lizzy and Pat had run ahead, and I called after them. They ignored me, cavorting away, taking no man's land to be a playground. I began to be afraid even before I realized there was a reason. It was not the ghosts of Soviet machine guns that frightened me, the Vopos' klieg lights, the dogs. It was the shadow of a memory of what my guide had told me for that article in 1980. We had been standing on the lookout platform at Bellevue. Here is how I recounted it then:

> "Do you see that mound?" Jorg asked me. He pointed to a low dark hill, a weathered pile of dirt, really, halfway across the forbidden strip. "That is what remains of his bunker."
>
> "Whose bunker?" I stared at it. I could see the vestiges of streetcar tracks and pavingstones and I imagined ladies with parasols and vendors and the great coaches of Potsdamer Platz, not this wasteland. Then I tried to picture the Nazi headquarters and that bunker, but couldn't.
>
> "It's where he killed himself," Tramm said.[1]

The memory brought my head up, and my eyes went right to a low hill in the middle of the death strip. The mound that my official guide had pointed to in 1980 was still there. And now so were my children. There they were, in their yellow and red, their blue, Pat in his flashing Michael Jordans, Lizzy in her barrettes. My children were heading right for Adolf Hitler's bunker. I screamed "No!" and began to run. Lexa called after me, then began to run too.

The *Führerbunker* was a tunnel complex below the Reichskanzlei. Hitler, his new wife, Eva Braun, a few trusted aides, and a guard made up of an elite SS unit had watched American movies while the city above them was battered and torched by the storming Russians. The rooms were well furnished. There was a wine cellar. Precious paintings lined the concrete walls. I knew all of this. But to me the *Führerbunker* was a chamber of hell. And like hell, I hadn't been sure until now that it existed.

"No!" I screamed again, and I closed on them. They were at the mound, and like beagles going after prey, they had zeroed in on a small opening at the base of the low hill. Pat was already nosing into the hole. I saw a slab of concrete protruding from the dirt, and I thought, Pat is now going to touch what Hitler touched. "Get away from there," I ordered, swooping down on them, grabbing each one by an elbow and dragging them back.

"What's wrong with you?" Lexa demanded. My children looked up at me, mystified. And it seemed ridiculous, what I had to say by way of explanation. I said it, hardly believing it myself. "This was Hitler's place!" And I led them away.[2]

What was I afraid of? My children falling into the hole? My children sucked into the vortex of an abyss? Why is it that the innocence of our children is what finally forces us to face the flawed condition of our lives? I had never sensed how thin the membrane is between us and death until I watched my toddlers crossing the street or skied after my teenagers down the double-black-diamond slope of a mountain in Maine. In the former death strip of Berlin, I saw that I had brought my children into the zone of evil from which I had always assumed I would protect them.

Hitler is our Prince of Darkness. We would have liked to go on thinking that he alone was responsible for the monstrous crimes committed in Europe between 1933 and 1945. When I inadvertently took Lizzy, Pat, and Lexa to the very threshold of his lair, I think I still hoped to protect the illusion into which I had been initiated as a conqueror's son in the Rhineland, that the Nazis were of another species entire. I think that was why I screamed so, to keep my children on this side of the other Berlin Wall, the one I wanted to remain intact forever, the one that ran between the innocent and the guilty, the good and the bad. The Cold War had imposed its dualism on our minds, and we could still think that way, even though it was already clear that Mikhail Gorbachev was no Joseph Stalin. Perhaps in 1990, I needed Hitler's moral isolation from the rest of humanity more than ever, his abject evil as proof of our relative virtue.

The virtue of my children was absolute, of course. Part of what I wanted to protect us all from, in my panic, was the threshold of knowing that my own virtue was anything but. Now I see what I was afraid of that day: the shock of my own complicity with evil. How to protect them from that? I do not mean here to wrap myself in a blurring guilt, as if the perpetrators of the anti-Jewish genocide are not uniquely to be condemned. I have taken pains throughout this book to observe the distinction between the crime of the Nazis and the attitudes of Christians that prepared for it. But to accept responsibility for those attitudes, as a Christian, is to go much farther along the road of moral reckoning than I ever imagined I would have to. Having faced the anti-Jewish content of beliefs in which I was raised, and in which my Church is still entangled despite itself, I have had yanked away from me the right to imagine that I would have certainly behaved "virtuously" if confronted with choices at almost any point in this long chain of consequence.

When I was a boy of Pat's age the day he rushed toward the *Führerbunker,* I was rushing through the woods of Virginia with my buddy Peter Seligman at my side. I knew nothing of his Jewishness, and he and I together knew nothing of the real significance of the Johnny Rebs we emulated. Jeb Stuart, Stonewall Jackson, the Gray Ghost, Robert E. Lee — all devoted to keeping in place the right of white people to own black people as chattel slaves. Within a year or two of our discovery of each other as playmates, and our dedication to the lost cause of the South, the U.S. Supreme Court would rule on *Brown v. Board of Education.* Only by the fluke of my growing up in the era of that decision, instead of, say, the era of the Dred Scott decision, can I indulge the self-affirming integrity of a man devoted to civil rights for all.

Hindsight often opens us to hubris because we imagine, in looking back over the wrecked landscape of the past, that we ourselves, had we been there, would have done things differently. We would certainly never have owned slaves. We would certainly never have stormed into a Jewish district wielding a club. But such certainty presumes that we would have occupied our places in the past knowing what we know now. The moral meaning of behavior is understood completely only after the connection between choice and consequence has revealed itself. Or, as Hannah

Arendt, with whom we began this book, put it, "Action reveals itself fully only to the storyteller, that is, to the backward glance of the historian, who indeed always knows better what it was all about than the participants."[3] For that reason, one comes to the end of a story like this purged of any feeling of moral superiority one might have begun with. The shame I feel as a Catholic Christian, aware in detail of the ways that the Church sanctified the hatred of Jews, not only betraying Jesus but tilling the soil out of which would come the worst crime in history, is shame not only at what my people did, but at what I can now admit I might well have done myself.

When, on one of our European adventures, I found myself in Rome with Lexa, Lizzy, and Pat, I took them to St. Peter's Basilica, wanting them to see Michelangelo's *Pietà*, the work that had so moved me when I saw it as a boy. Entering St. Peter's was a problem, because our daughter, still a child, was wearing a skirt that the guard at the entrance deemed too short. It is hard to convey what witnessing Lizzy's humiliation did to me. I had not drawn attention to the border of Vatican City as we crossed it, and so the question of the Church's alliance — with Anne? — had not come up, a question I could not have answered. But the Vatican functionary, offended by the sight of my little girl's knees, represented every Catholic failure I could think of.

We retreated, but my savvy, non-Catholic wife was unintimidated. She helped Lizzy pull the skirt down to her hips, hiding the gap at her waist with a sweater, so that her knees were covered. The guard let us pass. St. Peter's had never seemed more like an emperor's palace.

But soon we were standing before the statue of Mary holding her son, and it still worked a spell on me, and perhaps it did on my family. Despite its subject, there is an unrestrained spirit of optimism in the *Pietà*, the human form never rendered more lovingly, the possibility of meaning in the midst of anguish never affirmed more directly. The guard at the door could not have approved of the sensuality of the youthful Mary's turned-out wrist, her son's perfect torso. Michelangelo created the *Pietà* as a young man, and it was as a boy on the threshold of manhood that I had found it irresistible. In the statue's presence I entered the presence of the young man I had been. That was the spell. I realized that the *Pietà* was not what it had been to me all those years before.

Was I already preparing for a task I had barely begun to imagine, but which Lizzy, with her border question, was sponsoring? Whose side were these stone figures on? Only now do I see why I then instinctively turned away from the high Renaissance triumphalism of Michelangelo's celebration of the death of Jesus.

We moved through St. Peter's, stunned less by its beauty than by its mass. In Maine, we had been on a mountain; here, we were inside one. It was when, on another occasion, I stood before *The Last Judgment* in the Sistine Chapel that I experienced another realm of the artist's work as the place where I belonged, and it is in that realm I find myself now. To enter the chapel, with its remarkable frescoes on the ceiling and walls, is to enter a jewel box. The cardinals of the Church meet here to elect the pope, an ultimate act of historical continuity. But the huge painting behind the high altar, toward which the room is oriented, portrays nothing less than the end of history.

Michelangelo was an old man when he mounted the scaffolding to paint this last great masterwork, and you can see how time had flogged him. In the years since he had created the serenely poignant *Pietà*, Luther, Copernicus, Magellan, Henry VIII, and several Borgia popes had all helped to upend the moral universe. The grand inquisitor Gian Pietro Caraffa had come to Rome, and soon, as Pope Paul IV, would establish the Roman ghetto, the antechamber of Auschwitz. *The Last Judgment*, painted between 1534 and 1541, reflects the era's loss of faith in the human project, and it is a certain window into Michelangelo's soul. His scathing vision is staggering, especially because it so contrasts with the earlier hopefulness of the scenes on the ceiling just above, with their triumphal rendition of the Creation. *The Last Judgment*, as it were, rebukes *The Creation*, for the beautiful creature to whom God had entrusted the spark of divinity, with that unforgettably outstretched finger, is now repudiated. Sinners and the righteous alike cower below the upright figure of the judging Lord. It is as if Michelangelo, looking afresh into the soul of humanity, had glimpsed the coming religious wars, slavery, Inquisition, genocide, death camps, and the black hole of the *Führerbunker*.

To me, the most heart-rending and fearsome aspect of Michelangelo's dark masterpiece is not despair overtaking the created world, but a smaller and more personal statement. Among the multitude of figures in *The Last Judgment* is a rare Michelangelo self-portrait. It is so discreetly done that his contemporaries failed to see it as him, and no wonder. Michelangelo, the genius celebrant of the human body, the creator of *David* and *Moses* and the *Pietà*, chose to put his own face, at last, on a shriveled, limp, formless skin that had been flayed from the body of a martyr.[4] Apparently the artist had lost all sense of the noble things he had done, and was still doing. The self-portrait of a face ripped from its bones is an abject confession of sin, impossible to behold out from under the crushing weight of conscience. The portrait says, "I stand as accused by God as anyone in this scene." As the artist who, in fact, conjured the devastating judgment of his own era, Michelangelo is saying, through his portrait, "There is nothing of which I accuse any other person here — popes, Borgias, Medicis — that I do not accuse myself of."

"You have utterly betrayed me," one hears the damning Lord declare — and what Christian, mindful of the story we have recounted here, would not know what, among all else, is being referred to? But *The Last Judgment* is not thereby a *Christian* vision. It is biblical faith that is fully in touch with the mystery of evil as it lurks in the human heart, and it is biblical faith that includes, always, the call to judgment. In the supersessionist rewriting of biblical narrative, the judging God stands in contrast to the redeeming God of the New Testament, but that is a total fabrication, unfaithful to the history of Israel and the story of Jesus. Despite the darkness with which Michelangelo renders it, judgment is the opposite of despair. Judgment, which is "action revealing itself fully," in Arendt's phrase, is the source of meaning. That is why visitors to the Sistine Chapel, after marveling at the grandeur of the Creation scene above, stand transfixed before the fresco on the wall behind the altar.

What do they see? In the burly nakedness of the majestically centered Christ figure, whose right arm is raised above his head, poised for one cannot say what, the doomed and the saved equally search for, in Arendt's phrase, "the possible redemption from the predicament of irreversibility — of being unable to undo what one has done though one did not, and could not, have known what he was doing." If the past is irreversible, then we are all doomed. No one can be saved. Is the history of Christian anti-Judaism reversible? That is a far more potent question than Is it forgivable? But only apparently so. For as Arendt goes on to point out, "Forgiving serves to undo the deeds of the past, whose 'sins' hang like Damocles' sword over every new generation . . . Without being forgiven, released from the consequences of what we have done, our capacity to act would, as it were, be confined to one single deed from which we could never recover; we would remain the victim of its consequences forever."[5]

Arendt is not talking here about the easy forgiveness we disparaged in the previous chapter, nor, in the context of the ancient crime of antisemitism, does forgiveness like this necessarily come from Jews, for whom forgiveness may equate with denial. The premature request for forgiveness, made by a Christian to a Jew, may constitute presumption at best, a further oppression at worst. That is why the act of repentance offered to the Jewish people by a council of the Church must carry no hint of a required or expected response, as if Jews have to accept it for the act to be complete. But there is another problem. Emmanuel Levinas, among others, has warned that the erasure of the past through cheap forgiveness, whereby the soul can "free itself from what has been," can slide all too easily into a valueless individualism according to which "no attachment is ultimately definitive."[6]

In Arendt's view, the human disposition to seek forgiveness, which responds to the otherwise irreversible predicament of the past, is protected from presumption and from irresponsibility when it is paired with the quest for a "remedy for unpredictability, for the chaotic uncertainty of the future, [which] is contained in the faculty to make and keep promises." In other words, there is no recovery from the past without a commitment for the future. More concretely, there is no apology for Holy Week preaching that prompted pogroms until Holy Week liturgies, sermons, and readings have been purged of the anti-Jewish slanders that sent the mobs rushing out of church. The capacity to be forgiven resides in the simultaneous capacity to make and keep a promise that "serves to set up in the ocean of uncertainty, which the future is by definition, islands of security without which not even continuity, let alone durability of any kind, would be possible in the relationships between men."[7] Forgiveness for the sin of antisemitism presumes a promise to dismantle all that makes it possible. Holy Week, that is, must become an island of Jewish security. We saw in the previous chapters what this means for the Church.

What does it mean for me? To be suspended between past and future, in Arendt's phrase, is to stand between the world into which my beloved parents brought me and the world to which I am sending my beloved children. How do I get out from under the irreversibility of my past, which is another way of asking, How do I get out from under the sword of my self-doubt? How is the chaotic uncertainty of the future to be tamed? The most deadly prospect at this point would be to find myself alienated from the community that has been the focus of my "backward glance." Instead of telling this story from the position of moral purity I may once have imagined myself occupying, I have felt flayed by every word. Like Michelangelo, I find myself unable to accuse my Church of any sin that I cannot equally accuse myself of.

Seeing the action of this awful narrative from the point of view of the participants, even while recounting it from the detached point of view of the storyteller, has left me readier than ever before to claim membership in this community, if only because I recognize myself *at the time* as much in Ambrose as in Augustine, as much in Anselm as in Abelard, as much in Pius XII as in Edith Stein. "Do we really have the right to cast the first stone at the sinful woman who stands accused before the Lord and is called the Church — or are we now accused in her and with her, and delivered up to Mercy for good or ill?"[8] It is only through this communion of saints and sinners that I have my connection to the biblical people for whom judgment, forgiveness, and the promise-making of covenant are all the same thing. And as Arendt writes, "No one can forgive himself and no one can feel bound by a promise made only to himself; forgiving and promising enacted in solitude or isolation remain without reality and can signify no more than a role played before one's self."[9] Therefore, in the presence of my dear family, in the presence of my Church, and in the presence of the imagined communion of my readers, I have told this story in the hope of forgiveness, and as a promise.

Peter. The name of my Jewish friend. The name of my imperial basilica. Yet always, Peter is something else. I return again and again to the story of Simon Peter spying a stranger on the beach. It is some days after the death of Jesus, the one whom this Peter betrayed not once but three times. Simon Peter is in his fishing boat with the others. They have worked through the night. In the haze of dawn, he watches the figure on the beach. The boat draws closer to shore. The figure is bent over a fire, preparing a meal. When Peter steps from the boat and approaches the man, he seems familiar. The meal is the first hint. The second is the act of judgment, for this stranger faces Peter with the truth of his condition as fiercely as the Christ of Michelangelo will the human world with the truth of its condition. The irreversible act that stands between these two is betrayal. Peter had loved Jesus, but also, three times — "and at once the cock crowed"[10] — he denied him.

    Here is the real power of the Church's ancient association of itself, centrally, with Peter — not that he was a rock of virtue, not that his authority was absolute, but that his failure of the Lord was so complete. Peter at its mythic center — this is how the Church defines itself as a Church of sinners and betrayers: the cowardly Church, which has so often put power over service; the threatened Church, which has used its old feud with the Jewish people to wall itself off from the fear that its faith in Jesus is misplaced. As the story of Jewish-Christian conflict renders undeniable, the Church, having betrayed Jesus in its first generation, has been betraying Jesus ever since. That a flawed Peter is the patron saint of this Church is the principle of its self-criticism.

For each time that Peter denied Jesus, the figure shrouded in the haze of dawn puts to him the question "Simon Peter, do you love me?" And each time, Peter replies, "Yes, Lord, I love you."

Then, "Feed my sheep."[11] Three times the figure calls Peter to this service. The threefold betrayal is reversed by a threefold ritual of forgiveness, built upon a promise.

That meals and feeding are central to this story, that the mysterious figure of Jesus is recognized in the breaking of the bread, gives shape to my faith. It is in attending Mass, partaking of the meal as one of a number of people who are almost always strangers to me, that I draw near to the figure whom I recognize. His story is mine, and I have it through the Church. Human history is a story told by God, and by attending to history, even tragic history, I draw near to God. Attention to the story is the structure of prayer, without which I am dead. At the offertory of the Mass I hand over to God, especially, the ones I love. I confess my sin three times, and hear the word of hope three times. The Eucharistic bread keeps me alive, and I believe it always will.

In other words, Jesus offers me, a non-Jew, access to the biblical hope that was his birthright as a son of Israel. Not that the Church in any way surpasses Israel, or supersedes it. The Church is how God's promise to Israel is available to me, a Celt, whose ancestors could have been among the northern tribal peoples recruited to the army of Constantine. Certainly, I have my Catholic faith through my Irish American mother and father, first exemplars of the movement from forgiveness to promise, from repentance to commitment. This is how the loving, forgiving, and challenging God of Abraham, Isaac, and Jacob — and of Sarah, Rebecca, Rachel, and Leah — has become available to me. My now grown children, Lizzy and Pat, who may or may not associate themselves, as believers, with the long story of this religious people, teach me that this God is available to all human beings, religious or not. Certainly, I believe God is available to them. Available as the undoing of the irreversible past; available as the securing of the unpredictable future, in which we must never repeat a Holocaust of any kind.

This has been the story of the worst thing about my Church, which is the worst thing about myself. I offer it as my personal penance to God, to the Jewish dead, and to my children, whom I led, by accident, to the threshold of Hitler's pit. Nietzsche warned that if we stare into the abyss, it may stare back, and this book proves Nietzsche right. My faith is forever shaken, and I will always tremble. The Christian conscience — mine — can never be at peace. But that does not say it all. This tragic story offers a confirmation of faith, too. God sees us as we are, and loves us nevertheless. When the Lord now turns to me to ask, "Will you also go away?" I answer, this too with Simon Peter, "Lord, to whom shall I go?"[12]

ACKNOWLEDGMENTS

CHRONOLOGY

NOTES

BIBLIOGRAPHY

INDEX

ACKNOWLEDGMENTS

Twenty-eight years ago, the playwright William Gibson and the psychoanalyst and writer Margaret Brenman Gibson were among the first to affirm my work as a writer, a connection that led to my meeting Donald Cutler, who became my literary agent, advisor, and friend. Bill, Margaret, and Don have sustained me ever since, offering particular support as I wrote this book. I dedicate it to them in gratitude and love.

This book begins with the cross at Auschwitz, which I saw while on assignment for *The New Yorker*. The sight of the sacred symbol there focused this work, so I want to begin by gratefully acknowledging my editor Jeffrey Frank and his colleagues at *The New Yorker*, where parts of this book appeared in somewhat different form. Early versions of parts of this book also appeared in *The Atlantic Monthly*, where my editors are Jack Beatty, Cullen Murphy, and Lucie Prinz, and in the *Boston Globe*, where my editors are H.D.S. Greenway, Renée Loth, Robert Turner, and Marjorie Pritchard. I am grateful to these editors and publications for sage advice and for encouragement.

I began this work in earnest while I was a fellow at the Joan Shorenstein Center for Press, Politics, and Public Policy at the Kennedy School of Government at Harvard University. I am especially grateful to my colleagues there: Marvin Kalb, Edith Holway, Richard Parker, Nancy Palmer, Pippa Norris, Julie Felt, Thomas Patterson, Connie Chung, Barbara Pfetsch, David Farrell, and Al Simpson. I was able to continue my research, and begin writing, as a fellow at the Center for the Study of Values in Public Life at Harvard Divinity School. There, I received tremendous support from colleagues David Little, Brent Coffin, Nancy Nienhuis, Laura Nash, Donna Verschueren, Margy Rydzynski, Missy Daniel, Will Joyner, Lawrie Balfour, and Kathleen Sands. Divinity School faculty were generous with time and advice, especially J. Bryan Hehir, Harvey Cox, Ronald F. Thiemann, Peter Gomes, Diana Eck, Gary Anderson, Jon D. Levenson, Sarah Coakley, Elisabeth Schüssler Fiorenza, Francis Schüssler Fiorenza, Helmut Koester, and David Tracy during his time as a visiting scholar at Harvard. I acknowledge a particular debt to the librarians of Harvard University, especially of the Andover-Newton Library. I gratefully acknowledge the Boston Public Library. Heartfelt thanks to Susan Sherwin and Thomas Jenkins of the Harvard Divinity School Development Office for their encouragement and for the funding they secured to support my work.

At the Divinity School I benefited from discussions of the year-long forum that I conducted on the subject of this book. I acknowledge my debt to the forum's participants. Parts of this work were also taken up by a seminar of biblical scholars led by

Professor Bernadette Brooten of Brandeis University. I very much appreciate their thoughtful response. In addition, Professor Brooten generously read a large section of this work and offered important suggestions; I am in her debt. Professor Paula Fredriksen of Boston University kindly read parts of this work and helped me improve it. Professor Harold Stahmer of the University of Florida introduced me to some of the complex history I have written about, and I am grateful.

I presented early drafts of this material in lectures at Colgate University, Holy Cross College, Merrimack College, Dartmouth College, Harvard Hillel, the Harvard Center for European Studies, the Harvard Jewish Faculty Luncheon Group, the Burke Lecture at the University of California at San Diego, the Lowell Lecture at Harvard, and the Lowell Lecture at Boston College. I learned from feedback on each of those occasions. While writing the book, I was privileged to participate in the annual theological seminar of the Shalom Hartman Institute in Jerusalem. I acknowledge a special debt to Rabbi David Hartman and to his longtime collaborator Professor Paul van Buren of Temple University. Paul's recent death came too soon in every way. Many years ago, I participated in Jewish-Christian dialogue at the Tantur Ecumenical Institute in Jerusalem, under the sponsorship of Father Thomas Stransky, C.S.P., whose work as an ecumenist was an early inspiration and whose support has nurtured me over the decades. And for some years I was a member of a Jewish-Christian Bible study group led by Bernard Avishai, Christopher Lydon, and Ilona Carmel. These discussions enriched my understanding of this history and theology, and I am grateful.

Early drafts of the entire manuscript were read by Eugene Kennedy, Bernard Avishai, Askold Melnyczuk, Padraic O'Hare, Susannah Heschel, Martin Green, James O. Freedman, the Reverend John F. Smith, and Kevin Madigan. For their thoughtful criticism I am especially grateful. Ken Schoen of Schoen Books was a tremendous help in tracking down sources. The late Adele Dalsimer and James Dalsimer helped me see the importance of this work and encouraged me throughout the writing; I carry Adele in my heart. I owe a special debt to the late Sharland Trotter and to Robert Kuttner and the members of the healing circle that gathered as Sharland died. May she rest in peace.

My brother Joseph Carroll generously supplied me with useful references — and steady encouragement. I am also grateful to Eugene Fisher for his regular e-mail bulletins on matters of importance to Jewish-Christian relations. For varied expressions of support, I offer thanks to Frederick Busch, the Very Reverend James Parks Morton, Leslie Epstein, Larry Kessler, Father Robert Bullock, Dan Terris, Ellen Birnbaum, Jacques Kornberg, Father Michael McGarry, C.S.P., Father Paul Lannan, C.S.P., Father Robert Baer, C.S.P., Rachelle Linner, Father John Morley, Ronald Modras, James Heffernan, the Reverend Milton McC. Gatch, Rabbi Ben-Zion Gold, the Reverend John Stendahl, Laurence Davies, Ruth Langer, Rabbi Leon Klenicki, Larry Wolff, Father Gerald O'Collins, S.J., David McCullough, Jacqueline O'Neill, Thomas P. O'Neill III, Joshua Marshall, Doris Kearns Goodwin, Richard Goodwin, Sidra DeKoven Ezrahi, and David Rush. I had the invaluable help of two superb research assistants at Harvard Divinity School: Christine Lehmann's work early in the project enabled me to bring it into focus, and Adam Reilly's work later on enabled me to bring it to completion, with far fewer errors than would otherwise have been the case. Their colleagueship was a gift and a privilege.

I acknowledge the encouragement and wise counsel, especially, of Professor Padraic O'Hare of Merrimack College, whose long experience as a Catholic participant in Jewish-Christian dialogue was an invaluable resource. And I owe a particular debt of gratitude to Krister Stendahl, who participated in the forum discussions I led, read the entire manuscript in several drafts, and generously shared his knowledge of Scripture, theology, and history. Bishop Stendahl's commitment to Jewish-Christian reconciliation and his love of the Church were my constant inspiration.

At Houghton Mifflin Company, I have been exceptionally supported. Nader Darehshori affirmed this project. My longtime editor and friend Wendy Strothman was its first and staunchest backer. Her wise counsel, sharp editorial eye, and publishing wit have been my greatest resources. My manuscript editor, Larry Cooper, with unfailing grace and acute insight improved this book, as he has other books of mine. And in the unstinting work of my editor Eric Chinski this book had the benefit of a rare intelligence and generous spirit, while I had the benefit of a patient friend. My first reader and strongest support remains my wife, Alexandra Marshall. To her, and to our daughter, Lizzy, and son, Pat, who keep me centered, I offer my profoundest thanks and love.

CHRONOLOGY

Middle Bronze Age (c. 2800–2200 B.C.E.) The Foundation Stone of the future Jerusalem Temple may have been revered as a holy place.

10th century B.C.E. The Temple is constructed in Jerusalem.

6th century B.C.E. The Temple is rebuilt after the Babylonian conquest.

63 B.C.E. The Roman general Pompey imposes military rule on Israel.

37 B.C.E. Herod the Great becomes king of Israel, will begin reconstruction of the Temple.

27 B.C.E. Caesar Augustus comes to power in Rome, declares himself "savior of the world."

c. 4 B.C.E. Jesus is born, perhaps in Bethlehem. Herod the Great dies, sparking unrest, which leads the Romans to crucify about two thousand in Jerusalem.

c. 30 C.E. Jesus is crucified under Pontius Pilate.

c. 40 The story of Jesus has begun to take shape, constructed partly of historical memory and partly of imaginative readings of the ancient Scripture.

c. 50s A first written document, Q, now lost, compiles the sayings of Jesus.

c. 50–c. 60 The letters of Paul are composed. The earliest (1 Thessalonians, c. 51) rebukes Israel for not accepting Jesus, but the latest (Romans, c. 60) warns followers of Jesus not to lord it over Israel.

c. 68 The Gospel of Mark is composed.

70 Romans attack Jerusalem and destroy the Temple. Flavius Josephus (c. 37–100), in his *Jewish War,* puts the number of Jewish war dead at 600,000.

c. 80–100 The Gospels of Matthew, Luke, and John are composed.

132–135 In response to a Jewish uprising, the Romans level Jerusalem and rename it Aelia Capitolina. Jews are driven from the city and from most of Judea, which is renamed Syria Palaestina. The Jerusalem community of Jewish Christians is eliminated. The tally of Jewish war dead reaches as high as 850,000.

167 Melito, bishop of Sardis, brings the first recorded charge of deicide against the Jewish people.

c. 200 Rabbis compile commentaries and legal teachings, a collection associated with Rabbi Judah the Prince and known as the Mishnah. Further commentaries and interpretations by rabbis will develop into the Talmud (Palestinian Talmud, 5th century; Babylonian Talmud, 6th century).

285 Aurelius Valerius Diocletian, a general newly come to the emperor's throne, reorganizes the Roman Empire, beginning the rule of the tetrarchs, one of whom is Constantius.

303 Diocletian, as part of his effort to impose order on the empire, decrees the destruction of Christian churches and texts.

306 Constantine, said to be about eighteen years old, replaces his father, Constantius, as one of the four ruling tetrarchs and immediately sets out from Trier to unite the Roman Empire under his sole authority.

312 Constantine attacks and defeats the forces of his rival Maxentius at the Milvian Bridge near Rome. Before the battle, Constantine had a vision of the cross, and he spurs his troops under the sign of the cross. The victory confirms his faith in Jesus Christ. Constantine's armies march behind the unifying insignia from now on.

324 At the Battle of Chrysopolis, on the eastern side of the Bosporus, Constantine defeats his last rival, Licinius, finally imposing sole political control over the whole empire.

325 Seeking a religious unity to match his newly won political unity, Constantine convenes the Council of Nicaea, which "unifies" Christian theology and belief with its Nicene Creed. At a council banquet, Constantine first relates the story of his vision of the cross and his "conversion" at Milvian Bridge. The cross comes to the center of Christian cult, theology, and symbolism.

c. 326 Constantine's mother, Helena, during a pilgrimage to Jerusalem, "finds" the True Cross.

335 Constantine presides at the dedication of the Church of the Holy Sepulcher in Jerusalem.

337 Constantine dies, not long after being baptized. A period of bloody dynastic rivalry among his surviving sons ensues.

361 Julian, a nephew of Constantine, becomes emperor. He will reject Christianity and order the Temple in Jerusalem rebuilt as a way of refuting Christian claims.

363 Julian, the last pagan emperor, is killed in Persia. The Temple restoration fails, which Christians take as proof of their claims. Subsequent emperors outlaw pagan worship, make heresy a capital crime, and formalize the Christian character of the empire.

c. 387 Saint John Chrysostom of Antioch initiates and perfects the *Adversus Judaeos* sermon genre. In the same year, Ambrose, bishop of Milan, baptizes the convert Augustine.

388 Ambrose defends the righteousness of synagogue burning, putting the very existence of Judaism at risk.

c. 400 Augustine completes *The Confessions*.

410 The Gothic hordes of Alaric sack Rome.

414 History's first organized assault on Jews *as Jews* takes place in Alexandria. Around the same time, history's first charge of ritual murder is brought against Jews in Antioch.

427 Augustine completes *The City of God*, which argues decisively for the survival of Judaism within the Christian world, but which also defines the dispersal of Jews as their proper condition.

429   The emperor abolishes the patriarchate of Israel, marking the end of Jewish political sovereignty until 1948. But it also leads to a further flourishing of Jewish academies in Babylonia and Persia. Jewish self-understanding develops ever more independently of Christianity.

590   Gregory I ("the Great") becomes pope, begins a papal tradition of defending Jews, especially against forced conversions.

638   The Muslims conquer Jerusalem, and against the wishes of the Christian patriarch, they invite Jews back into the city.

c. 900 Jewish culture in Iberia thrives. Saadyah ben Joseph affirms the compatibility of religion and philosophy. What might be considered the first university is begun in Córdoba in a period of *convivencia* among Jews, Muslims, and Christians.

1054   The Eastern Schism, the split between the Byzantine Church and the Latin Church, becomes formal.

c. 1070 *Fons Vitae,* a Neo-Platonic portrayal of the cosmos by the Iberian Jewish poet and philosopher Solomon ibn Gabirol, gains wide readership in Europe among Christian scholars who do not know the author's identity.

1076   Emperor Henry IV prostrates himself in the snow at Canossa before Pope Gregory VII.

1096   With the beginning of the First Crusade, the Church defines violence as a sacred act. Crusaders attack Jewish communities in the Rhineland. Many Jews choose to die rather than convert.

c. 1098 Anselm completes *Cur Deus Homo,* asserting that God became man in order to suffer and die on the cross.

1119   Pope Callixtus II issues the papal bull *Sicut Judaeis* in defense of Jews; it will be reissued by more than twenty popes in the following four centuries.

1130   Abelard rebuts Anselm, insisting that Christ came to show humans how to live, not to submit to a brutal death willed by a sadistic Father.

1141   Bernard of Clairvaux denounces Abelard at the Council of Sens and has him condemned as a heretic. A few years later, Bernard orders crusaders not to attack Jews, but also reiterates the idea that their degradation serves God's purposes.

c. 1144 Jews are accused of ritual murder of a Christian child in England, a "blood libel" that will be endlessly repeated.

1159   Maimonides (Moses ben Maimon) leaves Iberia for North Africa during a period of Islamic repression signaling the end of *convivencia.* His work as a philosopher and physician contributes to an intellectual revival in Europe.

1184   Emperor Frederick Barbarossa convenes the Great Diet of Mainz, to replicate Constantine's unifying achievement at Nicaea. He is the first to call himself Holy Roman Emperor.

1215   Pope Innocent III declares the Magna Carta null and void. In the same year, he convenes the Fourth Lateran Council, which decrees "Outside the Church there is no salvation." It also introduces laws to denigrate and isolate Jews, the ancestors of the yellow star.

1231   Pope Gregory IX issues *Excommunicamus,* empowering Dominican and Franciscan courts, the beginning of the Inquisition.

1242   King James I of Aragon forcibly requires Jews to listen to convert makers' sermons. Jews are herded into churches; friars are empowered to enter synagogues uninvited. Christians blame Jewish recalcitrance on the secrets of the Talmud. King Louis IX of France orders the Talmud burned in Paris.

c. 1260 The Dominican Thomas Aquinas publishes *Summa Contra Gentiles*, a summary of Christian faith as it should be presented to those who reject it, especially Jews. Now Jews who refuse to convert are regarded as deliberately defiant, instead of "invincibly ignorant."

1263 King James I of Aragon requires Nachmanides (Rabbi Moses ben Nachman) to debate Dominicans in Barcelona. Nachmanides refutes Christian claims. The Church moves in earnest to convert Jews.

c. 1280 Moses de Leon composes the *Zohar*. It will form the heart of Kabbalah, which will transform Jewish spirituality, underwrite Jewish resistance to the new conversionism, and influence the mind of Europe.

1302 Pope Boniface VIII promulgates *Unam Sanctam*, claiming ultimate papal authority.

1348 The Black Plague that devastates Europe brings with it a new level of Christian violence against Jews, with perhaps three hundred communities wiped out. A rumor is circulated that the plague originated in a Jewish well-poisoning scheme in Toledo. Pope Clement VI defends the Jews against the charge.

1391 A massacre of Jews in Seville, and then pogroms elsewhere in Iberia, result in unprecedented rates of Jewish conversion, which in turn lead Christians to suspect all *conversos*.

1449 The Statute of Toledo is issued by the city council, banning anyone of Jewish descent from holding office, introducing the idea of "blood purity." Pope Nicholas V condemns it.

1453 Constantinople falls to Muslim Turks, who use new artillery weapons in the siege. Nicolaus of Cusa responds with *De Pace Fidei* ("Peace Among the Religions"), arguing for religious respect, including respect for Jews.

1478 The Spanish Inquisition is established to ferret out secret Jews. A period of conflict between the Inquisition and the papacy begins.

1492 Jews are expelled from Spain; more than 150,000 are driven out. Pope Alexander VI welcomes Jewish refugees to Rome.

1517 Martin Luther posts his Ninety-five Theses in Wittenberg. His "That Jesus Christ Was Born a Jew" (1523) and "On the Jews and Their Lies" (1543) recapitulate the terrible ambivalence of Europe. He defines the Jew as the born enemy of the German Christian.

1545 Emperor Charles V presses Pope Paul III to convene the Council of Trent to combat Protestantism. Trent declares that all sinners, not Jews, are responsible for the death of Christ, but Trent also imposes new strictures on "unbelievers," including Jews.

1555 The century-long conflict between the Inquisition and the papacy is resolved when the grand inquisitor Caraffa becomes Pope Paul IV. He ratifies the blood purity Statute of Toledo and issues *Cum Nimis Absurdum*, which establishes the Roman ghetto. The Peace of Augsburg ends religious wars by dividing the German realm into Protestant and Catholic states.

c. 1570 Isaac Luria embodies the creative Jewish response to catastrophic events. His renewal of Kabbalah introduces the ideas of creation as God's self-exile and of *tikkun olam,* Israel's role in restoring God through acts of justice and study of Torah.

1608   The Jesuit order forbids admission to anyone descended from Jews to the fifth generation, a restriction that will be maintained until the twentieth century. Three years later, Pope Paul V decrees that the blood purity standard will apply to the Church in Rome as well as elsewhere. This will be reversed by subsequent popes.

1632   Baruch Spinoza is born in Amsterdam. He is schooled in Talmud and Kabbalah, and grows up to become one of the first great Enlightenment thinkers.

1771   Voltaire embodies a new, racial antisemitism, defining Jews as "deadly to the human race."

1789   The French Revolution begins. The Declaration of the Rights of Man and the Citizen applies to Jews, too — but only as individuals.

1799   Napoleon, in extending the principle of equality before the law, breaks down ghetto walls across Europe, including in Rome. But he, too, will introduce restrictions designed to stifle Jewish "nationhood."

1815   After the defeat of Napoleon, the Holy Alliance restores elements of the old order. When Pope Pius VII is reinstated as ruler of the Papal States, he immediately reestablishes the Roman ghetto.

1818   Karl Marx is born in Trier of a long line of rabbis, although his father had become a Christian. One of his first works will be "On the Jewish Question" (1843): "Money is the jealous god of Israel."

1854   Pius IX defines the dogma of the Immaculate Conception. Four years later, the Virgin Mary is reported to appear to a girl near Lourdes.

1861   Italian nationalists seize most of the papal territories, isolating the pope in Rome and its environs.

1869   The First Vatican Council convenes.

1870   *Pastor Aeternus* proclaims papal infallibility. Weeks later, Italian nationalists take control of Rome.

1871   Revolutionaries take over Paris, proclaiming the Paris Commune and murdering the archbishop. Charles Darwin publishes *The Descent of Man,* which predicts that "civilized" races will "exterminate . . . the savage races." The Kulturkampf, Bismarck's campaign against the Catholic Church, begins in Prussia.

1894   Captain Alfred Dreyfus is arrested in Paris, charged with spying for Germany, and jailed on Devil's Island.

1898   Émile Zola publishes *"J'Accuse . . . !"* Pope Leo XIII condemns antisemitism, but in a private letter. Most Church elements, like the newspaper *La Croix,* are aligned with antisemitic forces as a way of reconnecting with the masses.

1905   *Protocols of the Elders of Zion,* a document purporting to be records of a Zionist congress, appears in Russia.

1917   The Code of Canon Law, centralizing authority in Rome, is adopted by the Church.

1929   The Lateran Treaty between Mussolini and the Vatican assures the pope's autonomy in Vatican City. The Vatican agrees to the suppression of the Popular Party, a Catholic political party opposed to fascism.

1933 Hitler comes to power. His first bilateral treaty is the concordat with the Vatican, negotiated by Cardinal Eugenio Pacelli.

1939 Pacelli becomes Pope Pius XII. He cancels Pius XI's in-progress encyclical condemning antisemitism.

1942 Dutch bishops denounce the Nazi roundup of Jews. Edith Stein is arrested, and later dies in Auschwitz.

1943 Madeleine Dreyfus Lévy dies in Auschwitz. When Jews are rounded up at the foot of Vatican Hill, Pius XII does not openly protest.

1948 The state of Israel is established. *Jesus et Israel* is published by the Jewish historian Jules Isaac, linking contempt for Judaism to central Christian teaching.

1960 Pope John XXIII meets with Jules Isaac, calls for a change in the Church's relationship with Jews. He eliminates the words "perfidious Jews" from Catholic liturgy.

1962 The Second Vatican Council convenes, an implicit Church response to the Holocaust.

1965 Vatican II issues *Nostra Aetate*, deploring antisemitism, rejecting the idea that the Jews can be charged with the death of Jesus.

1978 Karol Wojtyla becomes Pope John Paul II and immediately sets out to heal the breach between Catholics and Jews. He also begins a program of rolling back the reforming spirit of Vatican II.

1979 John Paul II, at Auschwitz, calls the death camp the "Golgotha of the modern world."

1993 The Vatican recognizes the state of Israel.

1998 The Vatican issues "We Remember: A Reflection on the Shoah." Edith Stein is canonized, despite Jewish objections. Reports surface that, inside the Vatican, the "cause" of Pius XII is advancing toward sainthood.

2000 John Paul II issues an apology for the historic sins of members of the Church. He visits the Western Wall in Jerusalem. Five months later Pius IX is beatified.

NOTES

Epigraph

Rahner, *Theological Investigations,* vol. 1, 151–53.

1. Sign of Folly

1. John Paul II, "Homily at Auschwitz, June 7, 1979," in *Spiritual Pilgrimage,* 7.
2. For a discussion of this convent, see Bartoszewski, *Convent at Auschwitz.*
3. Ibid., 87.
4. Ibid., 91.
5. Ibid., 92.
6. For a discussion of the varied Jewish responses to the Holocaust, see Katz, *Post-Holocaust Dialogues.*
7. See, for example, Levinas, *Totality and Infinity.*
8. Quoted by Helmut Peukert, "Unconditional Responsibility for the Other: The Holocaust and the Thinking of Emmanuel Levinas," in Milchman and Rosenberg, *Postmodernism and the Holocaust,* 155.
9. Adorno, "Education after Auschwitz."
10. Elie Wiesel, "Art and Culture after the Holocaust," in Fleischner, *Auschwitz,* 405.
11. Quoted by Küng, *Judaism,* 585.
12. For an example of a work of Christian theology that does this, see Möltmann, *Crucified God.*
13. Elie Wiesel, "Talking and Writing and Keeping Silent," in Littell and Locke, *German Church Struggle,* 274.
14. Melito of Sardis, *On Parcha,* cited in Küng, *Judaism,* 152.
15. See *Nostra Aetate,* in Abbott, *Documents of Vatican II,* 660–68.
16. Rubenstein, *After Auschwitz,* 20. The "depth and persistence" of this charge against Jews is indicated by its having been repeated by a senior Vatican official, Father Peter Gumpel, S.J., the "relator" of the cause of the canonization of Pius XII. He said that "it is a fact that the Jews have killed Christ. This is an undeniable historical fact." Father Gumpel repeated this officially discredited charge in a CBC interview in March 2000, just days after Pope John Paul II presided at the historic liturgy of Catholic repentance in St. Peter's Basilica. See *The Globe and Mail* (Toronto), March 18, 2000.
17. I prefer to use "antisemitism" over the traditional "anti-Semitism." The latter, as

Padraic O'Hare, citing Professor Yehuda Bauer of Hebrew University, explains, "subtly grants the existence of something called 'Semitism,' in response to which one might well assume a posture of opposition." The hyphenated word thus reflects the bipolarity that is at the heart of the problem of antisemitism. See O'Hare, *Enduring Covenant*, 5f.

18. For an example of the complicated Jewish attitudes toward crucifixion language, see Maybaum, *Face of God*, 77–80. Maybaum strikes a note different from John Paul II: "Owing to the weakness of Christianity in our time, the Golgotha of Auschwitz was nothing other than the slaughtering bench where pagans threw off their Christian teaching. Owing to Christian failure, Auschwitz as a modern Golgotha was a place of cruel paganism" (80). For a Jewish response to Maybaum, see Katz, *Post-Holocaust Dialogues*, 248–67.

19. Michael Lerner wrote, "To think that God willed the brutal and senseless murder of more than a million children is to think that God is either a sadist or mad." *Jewish Renewal*, 177.

20. Genesis 1:2. See also the discussion of "Holocaust" in Novick, *Holocaust in American Life*, 133–34.

21. The Jewish philosopher Jean-François Lyotard distinguishes between Western civilization's figment "the jews," with a lowercase *j*, and what he calls "real Jews." This entity "the jews" exists only in the consciousness of Europe as a principle of negativity, denial, hatred, and guilt, which is why Europe wants to be rid of it. See, for example, Lyotard, *Heidegger and "the jews,"* 3.

2. Stumbling Block to Jews

1. *Boston Globe*, February 24, 1998.
2. Ibid.
3. See Blackman, *Seasons of Her Life*.
4. Quoted by Michael J. Horowitz, correspondence, *New Republic*, March 2, 1998, 4.
5. Leon Wieseltier, correspondence, *New Republic*, March 2, 1998, 5.
6. Wiesel, *Sea Is Never Full*, 193.
7. The theologian Bernard J. Lee, S.M., titles his multivolume work on the Jewish origins of Christianity *Conversations on the Road Not Taken*. See *Jesus and the Metaphors of God*.
8. Arendt, *Origins of Totalitarianism*, 8.

3. The Journey

1. This phrase originates with the Catholic theologian Karl Rahner, who used it to describe all people of good will, attributing to them a kind of membership in the Church whether they knew of it or not, wanted it or not. See, for example, Rahner, *Theological Investigations*, vol. 5, 115–34.
2. Cited in Burroway, *Writing Fiction*, 14.
3. Aristotle, *The Poetics*, 11.2.
4. 1 Corinthians 1:23.
5. The Vatican document "We Remember: A Reflection on the Shoah," issued in 1998, deflects responsibility away from "the Church as such" in this way, saying, for exam-

ple, that "the Church should become more fully conscious of the sinfulness of her
children" (http://jcrelations.com/stmnts/vatican3-98.htm; the Web site jcrelations.
com is a good source for documents concerning Jewish-Christian relations). In explaining this, the document's chief author, Cardinal Edward Cassidy, later stated in
various discussions, including one of which I was a part, that the Church, as the Bride
of Christ, is incapable of sin, but the fathers of Vatican II can be understood as having
taken another view. Article 8 of its "Dogmatic Constitution on the Church" reads, in
part, "The Church, however, clasping sinners to its bosom, at once holy and always in
need of purification, follows constantly the path of penance and renewal." The Catholic theologian Richard McBrien, an expert on Vatican II, noted that "there is no theological or doctrinal impediment to attributing sin to the Church as such in this whole
terrible matter of the Shoah and of the Church's complicity in it." Quoted by Rudin,
"Reflections," 523. We will see more of this question later.
6. See, for example, Fisher, *Seminary Education.* In a career spanning three decades, Eugene Fisher, of the National Conference of Catholic Bishops, has done more to root
out antisemitism from Church educational materials than any other Catholic, and
this volume shows that. See also Cunningham, *Education for Shalom.*

4. My Mother's Clock

1. In the winter of 2000, as I was revising this, the Israel Museum in Jerusalem announced that its *Montmartre in Spring,* by Camille Pissaro, which had been looted by
the Nazis, properly belonged to the heirs of a Jew who died at Theresienstadt in 1942.
The painting had come into the collection of John and Frances Loeb in New York in
1961, and in 1985 the Loebs had donated it to the Israel Museum in honor of its
founder, Teddy Kollek. After the rightful owner retook title to the painting, her attor-
neys permitted it to remain at the museum on extended loan, saying that "all members of the family that perished in the Holocaust would find comfort in the knowledge that the citizens of the State of Israel can experience this magnificent work of
art." *Ha'aretz,* English edition, February 18, 2000.
2. See, for example, "Victims No More: Auschwitz Survivor's Suit Aims to Expand Human Rights Law by Hitting Companies Where It Hurts," *National Catholic Reporter,*
May 7, 1999.
3. The word "genocide" appears in Lemkin, *Axis Rule.* See Fein, *Accounting for Genocide,* 3.
4. George Will, "Fifty Years of Existential Anxiety," *Boston Globe,* May 8, 1998.
5. James Carroll, "Shoah in the News: Patterns and Meanings of News Coverage of the
Holocaust," Discussion Paper D-27, October 1997, Joan Shorenstein Center for Press,
Politics, and Public Policy, John F. Kennedy School of Government, Harvard University.
6. See, for example, Dershowitz, *Vanishing American Jew.*
7. *Tertio Millenio Adveniente,* cited in Szulc, *Pope John Paul II,* 443.
8. "Memory and Reconciliation: The Church and the Faults of the Past" (http://
jcrelations.com/stmnts/vatican12-99.htm).
9. I heard Eva Fleischner make this point at the meting with Cardinal Cassidy.
10. For my criticism of "We Remember," see "Vatican Response to the Holocaust: A Bell
Has Been Struck, with No Sound," *Boston Globe,* March 31, 1998. For my analysis of

"Memory and Reconciliation," see "The Pope's Call for Forgiveness: Plaudits and Some Questions," *Boston Globe*, March 14, 2000.

11. Paul Elie, "John Paul's Jewish Dilemma," *New York Times Magazine*, April 26, 1998, 37. The article's title reveals the ancient bias, as if the "dilemma" here has ever been Jewish, and not Christian. ("How does it feel to be a problem?" W.E.B. Du Bois sarcastically asked his fellow blacks.) When the problem is defined as belonging to the victim group, the "solution" becomes that group's removal. "There will be the Jewish problem," Cardinal Augustin Hlond, the primate of Poland, declared in 1936, "as long as the Jews remain." Quoted by Modras, *Catholic Church and Antisemitism*, 346–47.

12. Introductory letter, "We Remember: A Reflection on the Shoah."

13. Allen, "Objective and Subjective Inhibitants," 122.

14. "Statistics on the Membership and Finances of the Churches, 3 July 1944," in Matheson, *Third Reich and Christian Churches*, 99.

15. Allen, "Objective and Subjective Inhibitants," 122.

16. Quoted by Helmreich, *German Churches under Hitler*, 360.

17. Quoted by Allen, "Objective and Subjective Inhibitants," 122.

18. Helmreich, *German Churches under Hitler*, 360.

19. Lipstadt, "Aryan Nation."

20. Cynthia Ozick, "Of Christian Heroism," 47.

5. Passion Play

1. Friedman, *Oberammergau*, 51.

2. John 1:11.

3. Pelikan, *Jesus Through the Centuries*, 30. Pelikan says that "crucial" was apparently coined by Sir Francis Bacon.

4. Augustine, *The Confessions*, bk. 8, ch. 12, 178–79.

6. My Rabbi

1. For a fuller description of my encounter with Pope John XXIII and what it meant to me, see Carroll, *American Requiem*, 76–79.

2. Hedwig Wahle, "Pioneers," 4. Later in this book, we will see the negative impact on Jewish-Christian relations of the Dreyfus affair, at the end of the nineteenth century. Wahle notes, significantly, that Isaac, as a young man, was a passionate defender of Dreyfus. It is not too much to assume that Isaac's important work, with its positive outcome, is a result of the Dreyfus affair.

3. For a discussion of the importance of Jules Isaac's work and its influence on Pope John XXIII, see Gregory Baum's introduction to Ruether, *Faith and Fratricide*, 2–4.

4. *Nostra Aetate*, in Abbot, *Documents of Vatican II*, 666.

5. Ibid., 665–66.

6. Eight prayers were said for various groups on Good Friday, each one accompanied by a ritual genuflection, except for the prayer *Pro perfidis Judaeis*. The prayer for Jews was not to be dignified by kneeling. Another Good Friday tradition that can spawn contempt for Jews remains a part of Catholic liturgy, the Reproaches, which are a litany of charges made by Jesus against a group he calls "my people." ("My people, what have I done to you? How have I offended you? Answer me! I led you out of Egypt, from slav-

ery to freedom, but you led your Savior to the cross," and so on.) Many liturgists re-gard the Reproaches as inherently anti-Jewish, or at least likely to be taken that way. About 40 percent of Catholic parishes in the United States use them as part of Good Friday services, but they remain in the official Catholic prayer books in all parishes. See John L. Allen, "Good Friday's Can of Worms," *National Catholic Reporter*, March 17, 2000.

7. John 19:6–7, 15.

8. John 1:11.

9. Romans 11:28.

10. In the nineteenth century, Jesus was commonly believed to be free of the taint of Jew-ish blood first because the Virgin Birth protected him from Joseph's Jewishness. Then the doctrine of Immaculate Conception (1854), which declared that Mary was con-ceived without sin, inoculated him against the Jewish blood of his maternal grandpar-ents.

11. Quoted by Neudecker, "Catholic Church and the Jewish People," 284.

12. Shapley, *Promise and Power,* 354.

13. Rabbi Marvin Hier of the Simon Wiesenthal Center would reflect this point of view in 1999, calling Pius XII "the Pope of the Holocaust" and declaring that the pope prayed in 1941 for a German victory over the Soviet Union. See "Rabbi's Condemnation of Pope Pius XII Criticized," *Catholic News Service,* May 18, 1999.

14. Hochhuth, *The Deputy,* 200.

15. Ibid., 204–5. Krister Stendahl, former dean of the Harvard Divinity School and the re-tired Lutheran bishop of Stockholm, told me that when his predecessor, the Swedish bishop Erling Eidem, was asked during World War II to go public with what he knew about the death camps, he refused, saying that after the war Sweden would be needed as a mediator.

16. Ibid., 206.

17. Eugene J. Fisher, "The Church and Antisemitism: Rome Is Due to Pronounce," *Na-tional Catholic Register,* July 14, 1996.

18. Küng, *Judaism,* 256.

19. One way to account for Hitler's not having been excommunicated is that the Church takes such drastic action to combat "wrong thinking" more than "wrong acting." The theologian Bernard J. Lee, S.M., comments, "To some extent, it is a function of the western deep story that Arius, Martin Luther, George Tyrrell, and Leonard Feeney were excommunicated, and Hitler was not." But such a distinction assumes that Hit-ler's actions were not rooted in "wrong thinking," and the Church saw no such dichot-omy when it came to Communism. Lee, *Jesus and the Metaphors of God,* 69.

20. I heard Father Bryan Hehir of the Harvard Divinity School cite this line in the spring of 1999 when discussing the NATO intervention in Kosovo.

21. Arendt, *Men in Dark Times,* 63. See also Küng, *Judaism,* 258.

22. Zahn, *German Catholics,* 203.

23. A. J. Heschel, *Moral Grandeur,* 231.

24. The Berrigan brothers, like many Catholics who followed them into the peace move-ment, were motivated to oppose the Vietnam War partly in reaction to the Catholic failure to oppose Hitler. See Zahn, *German Catholics,* xii.

25. A. J. Heschel, *Moral Grandeur,* viii.

26. Ibid.

27. Ibid.
28. A. J. Heschel, *God in Search of Man*, 25, 29.
29. A. J. Heschel, *Moral Grandeur*, xxii.
30. Ibid.
31. A. J. Heschel, *God in Search of Man*, 33.
32. Krister Stendahl helped me to see that Paul's "universalism" was still exclusive. Paul thought that both Jews and Gentiles were included in the new dispensation, but that said nothing about the rest of humankind. The "new Israel" is still a minority, a sign lifted up to others, but with no mandate to universal conversion. Jews never thought that God's will required all people to become Jews: "For all the peoples walk each in the name of its god, but we will walk in the name of the Lord our God for ever and ever" (Micah 4:5).
33. Quoted by Zahn, *German Catholics*, xiv.
34. Douglass, *Non-Violent Cross*, 11.
35. Isaiah 45:3.
36. My source for this tradition is M. L. Kagan, "The Book of Intentions (Kavvanot)," unpublished manuscript, cited with permission.
37. Augustine, *The Confessions*, bk. 12, ch. 16, 297.
38. A. J. Heschel, *Man Is Not Alone*, 257.
39. *Who Killed Jesus?* is the title of a book by John Dominic Crossan.
40. "The cross became the symbol both of Roman violence and of the faith of those who dared resist its inevitability . . . For Paul, the cross was vitally important as a way to transform a familiar cultural icon into its antithesis." Horsley and Silberman, *The Message and the Kingdom*, 161.
41. Quoted by Cornwell, *Hitler's Pope*, 25. The dating of Easter, according to an imprecise calendar, led the Church into the business of astronomy, a first and permanent scientific endeavor that assured mathematics its central place in Western civilization. Ironically, the Christian "science of Easter," in J. L. Heilbron's phrase, began in this rejection of the authority of the rabbis to set the date of Passover. "Early Christian communities had to apply to the leaders of a rival church to learn when to celebrate their principal feast. The ignominy of this procedure, and the difficulty of a timely dissemination of the result as the church spread, forced the bishops into arithmetic." Heilbron, *Sun in the Church*, 27–28.
42. Ruether, *Faith and Fratricide*, 245.
43. Greenberg, "Relationship of Judaism and Christianity," 13.
44. William Sloane Coffin, quoted by Nardi Reeder Campion, *Valley News*, June 19, 1999.

7. Between Past and Future

1. I learned this from the theologian Mary Boys, quoted by O'Hare, *Enduring Covenant*, 7. Citing Boys, O'Hare summarizes "eight tenets that define supersessionism: (1) revelation in Jesus Christ supersedes the revelation to Israel; (2) the New Testament fulfills the Old Testament; (3) the church replaces the Jews as God's people; (4) Judaism is obsolete, its covenant abrogated; (5) post-exilic Judaism was legalistic; (6) the Jews did not heed the warning of the prophets; (7) the Jews did not understand the prophecies about Jesus; (8) the Jews were Christ killers."
2. Wilson, *Paul*, 46.

3. Pelikan, *Jesus Through the Centuries,* 96. Pelikan cites the complaint against Christians of Julian, who ruled briefly as emperor in the middle of the fourth century: "You adore the wood of the cross and draw its likeness on your foreheads and engrave it on your house fronts."

4. Romans 10:1–4.

5. Genesis 27:34–38.

6. "For the longstanding claim of the Church that it *supersedes* the Jews in large measure continues the old narrative pattern in which a late-born son dislodges his first-born brothers, with varying degrees of success. Nowhere does Christianity betray its indebtedness to Judaism more than in its supersessionism." Levenson, *Death and Resurrection,* x. Because of this pattern, some Jews are less than moved when Christians refer to them as brothers, as Pope John Paul II often does. For example, at the Rome synagogue in 1986, he said, "You are our dearly beloved brothers and, in a certain way, it could be said that you are our elder brothers." John Paul II, *Spiritual Pilgrimage,* 63.

7. Quoted by Robert P. Ericksen, "Assessing the Heritage, German Protestant Theologians, Nazis, and the 'Jewish Question,'" in Ericksen and S. Heschel, *Betrayal,* 33.

8. "Along with most historians, I'm skeptical about the so-called lessons of history. I'm especially skeptical about the sort of pithy lessons that fit on a bumper sticker. If there is, to use a pretentious word, any wisdom to be acquired from contemplating a historical event, I would think it would derive from confronting it in all its complexity and its contradictions . . . the past in all its messiness . . . The desire to find and teach lessons of the Holocaust has various sources — different sources for different people, one supposes. Probably one of its principal sources is the hope of extracting from the Holocaust something that is, if not redemptive, at least useful. I doubt it can be done." Novick, *Holocaust in American Life,* 261–63.

9. See Bartoszewski, *Convent at Auschwitz,* 21.

10. Alessandra Stanley, "At Yad Vashem, Pope Tries to Salve History's Scars," *New York Times,* March 24, 2000.

11. "In the Pope's Words: 'The Echo of the Heart-Rending Laments.'" *New York Times,* March 24, 2000.

12. Deborah Sontag and Alessandra Stanley, "Ending Pilgrimage, the Pope Asks God for Brotherhood," *New York Times,* March 27, 2000.

13. Karen Armstrong, "A Pilgrim, Not a Pawn," *New York Times,* March 25, 2000.

14. John Paul II, General Audience Discourse, September 1, 1999, in *L'Osservatore Romano,* English edition, September 8, 1999, cited in "Memory and Reconciliation," 4.2.

15. Arendt, *Between Past and Future,* 10.

16. Fredriksen, *Jesus of Nazareth,* 76.

17. Landes, *Wealth and Poverty of Nations,* 98.

18. Arendt, *Between Past and Future,* 9.

19. John Paul II, introductory letter, "We Remember: A Reflection on the Shoah."

8. My Great-Uncle

1. *Mortal Friends* (Boston: Little, Brown, 1978); *Supply of Heroes* (New York: Dutton, 1986). The anecdote related here about my great-uncle's tombstone I first told in the acknowledgments of *Supply of Heroes.*

2. Another example of Irish complexity in this period is found in Conor Cruise O'Brien, *Memoir: My Life and Themes* (New York: Cooper Square Press, 2000). One of O'Brien's uncles was an Irish rebel killed during the 1916 Rising, another was a British soldier killed at the Somme.

3. Crossan, *Who Killed Jesus?*, 211–15.

4. Sanders, *Judaism*, 5–7. For an example of a scholar who is more skeptical of Josephus, see McLaren, "Turbulent Times?," 312.

5. *Jewish Antiquities*, 18.63–64. Quoted by Crossan, *Birth of Christianity*, 12. Note that Josephus's report of activities in the time of Jesus involves a time lag roughly equivalent to that between the Easter Rising of 1916 and my first visit to Ireland in 1969.

6. Crossan, *Who Killed Jesus?*, 5.

7. Ibid., 152.

9. Jesus, a Jew?

1. S. Heschel, *Abraham Geiger*, 11.

2. S. Heschel, "When Jesus Was an Aryan: The Protestant Church and Antisemitic Propaganda," in Ericksen and S. Heschel, *Betrayal*, 77.

3. Ibid., 73. Demonstrating the end result of this Aryanizing of Jesus, Heschel cites a catechism published by a pro-Nazi Protestant institute: "Jesus of Nazareth in the Galilee demonstrates in his message and behavior a spirit which is opposed in every way to that of Judaism. The fight between him and the Jews became so bitter that it led to his crucifixion. So Jesus cannot have been a Jew. Until today, the Jews persecute Jesus and all who follow him with unreconcilable hatred. By contrast, Aryans in particular can find answers in him to their ultimate questions. So he became the savior of the Germans." The catechism was published in 1941.

4. Yasir Arafat, meeting with Pope John Paul II at the Vatican in February 2000, saluted him as the successor of St. Peter, "a Palestinian." Obviously, it would not suit Arafat's political agenda to think of Peter as what he was, a Jew. Not long after this meeting, on March 10, the Vatican published "Memory and Reconciliation: The Church and the Faults of the Past." A short section called "Christians and Jews" reiterated the Vatican's earlier declaration that "Jesus was a descendant of David; that the Virgin Mary and the Apostles belonged to the Jewish people." The Church obviously sees the need to emphasize this.

5. The attitude of the Irish Catholic culture in which I was reared is captured in James Joyce's *Ulysses*. "Mendelssohn was a jew," the badgered Bloom cries out at one point, "and Karl Marx and Mercadante and Spinoza. And the Savior was a Jew and his father was a Jew. Your God." A character identified as "the citizen" takes offense at once. "Whose God?" Whereupon Bloom cuts him with, ". . . Your God was a jew. Christ was a jew like me." The citizen responds to this slander with rage. "By Jesus, says he, I'll brain that bloody jewman for using the holy name. By Jesus, I'll crucify him so I will. Give us that biscuitbox here." *Ulysses* (New York: Random House, 1961), 342.

6. Cooke, *God's Beloved*, 23.

7. John 14:11. It is John's failure to provide a genealogy for Jesus that Fichte cites as evidence that he is not Jewish.

8. Fredriksen, *Jesus of Nazareth*, 108.

9. "The Father metaphor for the God Jesus faces takes on a larger and larger life in the

evolution of the gospels. In Mark's gospel, Jesus speaks of God as 'Father' or 'the Father' four times (and the retention of the Aramaic *Abba* makes Jesus' historical use of it highly probable). Matthew has Jesus speak of God in those terms 32 times. This language is in Jesus' mouth 173 times in John's gospel. We are surely witnessing evolution in the faith articulation of the early communities." Lee, *Jesus and the Metaphors of God*, 160.

10. Pawlikoski, *Christ in Christian-Jewish Dialogue*, 93.

11. Lee, *Jesus and the Metaphors of God*, 53.

12. Cooke, *God's Beloved*, 23.

13. S. Heschel, *Abraham Geiger*, 12.

14. For example, Walter Grundman, a Protestant New Testament scholar and firmly pro-Nazi German, had cited Jesus' use of the word "Abba" in addressing God to make the point that Jesus had rejected the Hebrew word for "God" (although most Jews then and now would not utter the word in any case). What to me was an expression of Jesus' intimacy with his Father was, in the interpretation of Grundman, a hammer to use against Jews. "With the proclamation of the Kingdom of God as present," he wrote, "a new experience of God and a new understanding of God were linked. Internally, it had nothing to do with Judaism, but meant the dissolution of the Jewish religious world. That should be recognizable from the fact alone that the Jews brought Jesus Christ to the cross." (Quoted by S. Heschel, "When Jesus Was an Aryan," in Ericksen and S. Heschel, *Betrayal*, 76.) It matters greatly that Grundman wrote these words as the literal and physical "dissolution" of the Jewish world was under way, but it is not incidental that that theology was attractive to me years later.

15. Gilman, *Faith, Sex, Mystery*, 243–44.

16. Segal, *Rebecca's Children*, 1–2.

17. Ibid.

18. The phrase "true Israel" was not used by those first-century groups. It apparently was first used by Justin Martyr in the second century. See Simon, *Verus Israel*.

19. *Jewish Antiquities*, 17.42; Sanders, *Judaism*, 13–14. See also Fredriksen, *Jesus of Nazareth*, 64.

20. Sanders, *Judaism*, 13.

21. Ibid., 78.

22. Ibid., 41.

23. The Qumran manuscripts, the first of which is said to have been found in 1947 by a goatherd in a cave above the Dead Sea, are a compilation of more than six hundred fragments and texts in Hebrew, Greek, and Aramaic, representing almost the entire Hebrew Scriptures as well as commentaries, lists of rules, hymns, prayers, and psalms. These documents date to the period between about 200 B.C.E. and 68 C.E., and they reveal a great deal about the life and beliefs of the Essenes. Other manuscripts were discovered around the Dead Sea in the 1950s and 1960s. Altogether, these finds demonstrate that Judaism at the time of Jesus was far more varied, and sectarian, than scholars previously believed. For the first time, the early Christians could be seen, in full context, as one of many Jewish sects. That the last Qumran documents date to 68 C.E. is significant, because the Essenes, unlike Christians and Pharisees, were wiped out by the Roman assault against Jews that commenced that year.

24. *Jewish Antiquities*, 18.21; Fredriksen, *Jesus of Nazareth*, 64; Sanders, *Judaism*, 14.

25. Wilson, *Paul*, 56.

26. Matthew 22:20.
27. Fredriksen, *Jesus of Nazareth*, 64.
28. Segal, *Rebecca's Children*, 59.
29. Wilson, *Paul*, 21.
30. Broshi, "Role of the Temple," 35.
31. Sanders, *Judaism*, 127. See also Fredriksen, *Jesus of Nazareth*, 64.
32. Horsley and Silberman, *The Message and the Kingdom*, 15.
33. Fredriksen rejects the term "occupation" for the Roman presence in Judea, pointing out that the legions were concentrated in Syria, not Palestine. From those outposts, soldiers could sweep into Judea when necessary. But one of the characteristics of a police state is the relative invisibility of police. Occupation consists more in the mental state of knowing that rigid rule is ruthlessly enforced than in the obvious presence of troops. See Fredriksen, *Jesus of Nazareth*, 169.
34. So, for example, from a later period: "The tendency to understand war in late antiquity from a Roman perspective is also a historiographical tradition, which has been compounded by a pervasive, almost unconscious, desire to share the Roman point of view. So the Battle of Adrianople of 378 is a catastrophe; and the sack of Rome by Alaric in 410 is a political disaster. Similarly, the defeat of Attila and his Huns on the Catalaunian Plains in 451 is a good thing." Brent D. Shaw, "War and Violence," in Bowersock et al., *Late Antiquity*, 134.
35. Acts 22:25–29. Note that Paul, in his own writings, never refers to his being a Roman citizen.
36. Wilson, *Paul*, 9. It is important to note, in understanding early Christian claims that Jesus was the "Son of God," that the Mediterranean world had already heard such a claim from Caesar Augustus himself.
37. In the Vatican document "Memory and Reconciliation," the Church warns against that "historicism that would relativize the weight of past wrongs and make history justify everything" (4.2). Commenting on this passage, Leon Wieseltier wrote, "Moral absolutists cannot have it both ways. If moral values are timeless, then what is wrong now was wrong then." Wieseltier, "Sorry," 6.
38. Wilson, *Paul*, 3.
39. In early 2000, a dispute broke out between Palestinian Christians and Palestinian Muslims over construction of a mosque near the Christian shrine at Nazareth. The construction permit had been issued by the state of Israel, prompting some Palestinians to decry a new version of the old strategy of divide and rule.
40. Sanders, *Judaism*, 4.
41. Ibid.
42. Owing to a later error in composing the calendar, the year of Jesus' birth was not 0 but 4 B.C.E. See Horsley and Silberman, *The Message and the Kingdom*, 16.
43. For this understanding of the politics of Israel at the time of Jesus' birth, I am particularly indebted to Horsley and Silberman; see *The Message and the Kingdom*, 9–23.
44. Ibid., 20.
45. *Jewish Antiquities*, 17.250–89, quoted by Horsley and Silberman, *The Message and the Kingdom*, 20. "Those who appeared to be the less turbulent individuals he imprisoned," Josephus wrote of the Roman general, "the most culpable, in number about two thousand, he crucified."
46. Sanders, *Judaism*, 72. In Jerusalem today, archaeologists speculate that an ancient

cemetery may abut the Western Wall, but Jewish authorities discourage investigation because if a cemetery were found, Orthodox Jews would no longer be permitted to pray there.

47. "There should be no question or mystery about the brutality of Roman crucifixion. Were we not so familiar with the stylized image of Jesus on the cross and were we not so thoroughly programmed from our earliest school days to admire the . . . Roman Empire . . . we might be able to see this oppressive, genocidal, imperial mode of torture for what it was." Horsley and Silberman, *The Message and the Kingdom*, 85.

48. Luke 2:1.

49. Matthew 27:24.

50. *Embassy to Gaius*, 302, quoted by Crossan, *Who Killed Jesus?*, 148. See also Wilson, *Paul*, 56.

51. Crossan, *Who Killed Jesus?*, 148.

52. Fredriksen, *Jesus of Nazareth*, 86.

53. Wilson, *Paul*, 56.

54. Matthew 27:25.

55. "And as the narratives of Jesus' Passion evolve, we see their increasing tendency to exculpate Pilate and inculpate Jewish authorities — a sensible allocation of hostility and blame since, by the time the evangelists write, Jerusalem's priestly authorities were no more, and the new movement had to find its place in a world ruled by Rome." Fredriksen, *Jesus of Nazareth*, 185.

56. Wilson, *Paul*, 1, 4, 10.

57. Ibid., 12.

58. Ibid., 11.

59. Ibid., 10.

60. Foster, *Modern Ireland*, 484.

61. O'Brien and O'Brien, *History of Ireland*, 141.

62. Taylor, *Michael Collins*, 152.

63. For more on this aspect of the Nazi method, see Langer, *Admitting the Holocaust*.

64. "The stories of Pilate washing his hands of the matter and the bloodthirsty screams of the rabble who chose Barabbas over Jesus are all the work of later Christian writers who — unlike Jesus — were desperately intimidated by the Romans and turned the blame on the Jews to divert accusations of disloyalty or rebellion away from themselves." Horsley and Silberman, *The Message and the Kingdom*, 84.

65. The written New Testament is based on oral traditions that included sayings attributed to Jesus, stories about him, and hymns and ritualized confessions of faith. A first written document, now lost, is hypothesized and referred to by scholars as Q, probably a compilation of the sayings of Jesus, composed during the 50s. The letters of Paul were written during the 50s and early 60s, before his death around the year 64. The first Gospel to be written was Mark, around 68. The Gospels of Matthew and Luke were composed around 80 or shortly thereafter. John was written around 100.

66. Crossan, *Birth of Christianity*, 524.

67. Ibid., 525.

10. The Threshold Stone

1. *Against Apion*, 2.234, quoted by Sanders, *Judaism*, 42.

2. Küng, *Judaism*, 125.

3. Jews who did not join in the rebellion, and were able to separate themselves from those who did, as in Sepphoris in Galilee, were apparently not attacked by the Romans. Josephus says that Titus, the Roman general and later the emperor who led the siege of Jerusalem in 70, refused to expel Jews from Antioch, showing that Jewish subservience, not racial elimination, was his purpose. On this point, see *Jewish War*, 7.110–11.

4. Gilbert, *Atlas of Jewish History*, 15.

5. Ibid.

6. Ibid.

7. Fredriksen, *Jesus of Nazareth*, 38.

8. Mark 1:23–26.

9. Mark 3:22–27.

10. Mark 3:31.

11. Mark 8:33.

12. Luke 22:52.

13. Barbara H. Geller Nathanson, "Toward a Multicultural Ecumenical History of Women in the First Century/ies c.e.," in Elisabeth Schüssler Fiorenza, *Searching the Scriptures*, vol. 1, *A Feminist Introduction* (New York: Crossroad, 1993), 274.

14. Pagels, *Origin of Satan*, 99.

15. John 8:44.

16. Pagels, *Origin of Satan*, 104–5.

17. For this summary of the "quest for the historical Jesus," I am indebted to Brown, *Introduction to the New Testament*, 817–30.

18. Koester, *Introduction to the New Testament*, vol. 2, 74.

19. Eliot, "The Waste Land," in *Collected Poems*, 67.

20. I wrote about this moment in my memoir, *An American Requiem*, 252.

21. Meier, *A Marginal Jew: Rethinking the Historical Jesus*.

22. Matthew 21:12–13.

23. John 2:17–18.

24. John 2:18–22.

25. Mark 13:1.

26. Quoted by Jeremias, *Jerusalem in the Time of Jesus*, 24–25.

27. Levenson, "The Temple and the World," 275–6.

28. See, for example, Amos 2:4–5: "Thus says the Lord: 'For three transgressions of Judah, and for four, I will not revoke the punishment; because they have rejected the law of the Lord, and have not kept his statutes, but their lies have led them astray, after which their fathers walked. So I will send a fire upon Judah, and it shall devour the strongholds of Jerusalem.'" Or Amos 5:21–6:1: "I hate and despise your [Israel's] feasts, I take no delight in your solemn assemblies . . . Woe to those who are at ease in Zion."

29. Matthew 23:37–39.

11. Destroy This Temple

1. Avishai, *A New Israel*, 3.

2. Tracy, *Dialogue with the Other*, 4.

3. See, for example, Brown, *Introduction to the New Testament*, 819. The first quest would

have been the nineteenth-century effort discussed earlier, and the second would have come after World War II. The distinguishing note of the third quest, in the words of Tom Holmén, "is precisely its laying a clear emphasis and stress on the Jewishness of Jesus." From an unpublished paper, "The Jewishness of Jesus in 'The Third Quest.'"

4. Horsley and Silberman, *The Message and the Kingdom;* E. Schüssler Fiorenza, *Jesus;* Borg, *Jesus, A New Vision;* Fredriksen, *Jesus of Nazareth.*

5. Brown, *Introduction to the New Testament,* 829. Critics of Crossan, and the Jesus Seminar generally, complain of a perpetuation of the "criterion of dissimilarity," as if the "real" teachings of Jesus are only those that are dissimilar from Jewish teachings of his era and from second-century Christian teachings. This criterion leads to the conclusion that almost nothing reported in the Gospels actually originated with Jesus. But a philosophical assumption about human identity underlies this approach — namely, that we have our identity by virtue of the ways in which we differ from those around us. A contrasting view assumes that we have our identity in community, sharing it with others. Thus when Jesus cites the so-called golden rule in Matthew 7:12, the fact that it appears earlier in Ecclesiasticus 31:15 and Tobit 4:15 does not mean, ipso facto, he did not say it. Indeed, as a Jew familiar with Jewish Scriptures, why would he not have?

6. "Many academicians and clergy feel that, when it comes to the study of the New Testament, most laypersons are simply lacking in the skills, training, and interest requisite for their assimilating in depth what for academicians, clergy, and seminarians are, after all, areas of expertise and full-time commitment. The scientific study of the New Testament and the quest for the historical Jesus are held to be properly the domains of experts only . . . Many Christian clergy have learned in their own seminaries that those New Testament traditions most responsible for spawning ill-will between Christians and Jews do not genuinely go back to the historical Jesus. Yet they do not see how they can communicate . . . the idea that only *some* of the gospels' teaching go back to Jesus." Michael J. Cook, "Turning the Corner in Dialogue: A Jewish Approach to Early Christian Writings," in Fisher, *Interwoven Destinies,* 23.

7. Commenting on this painting, Jaroslav Pelikan asks "if there would have been an Auschwitz if every Christian church and every Christian home had focused its devotion . . . on icons of Christ not only as Pantocrator, but as Rabbi Jeshua-bar-Joseph, Rabbi Jesus of Nazareth, the Son of David, in the context of the history of a suffering Israel and a suffering humanity." Pelikan, *Jesus Through the Centuries,* 20. Significantly, Fredriksen, whose book *Jesus of Nazareth King of the Jews* is subtitled *A Jewish Life and the Emergence of Christianity,* used this painting on its cover.

8. Fredriksen points out (*Jesus of Nazareth,* 109), in fact, that when a sick person is described in Mark (6:56) as grasping at the "fringe" of the garment of Jesus, the Hebrew that stands behind the Greek original would have referred to the *tzitzit* that are still worn by devout Jews.

9. An example of how deeply ingrained in Christian thinking this "demonstrate a difference" impulse is can be found even in the Vatican's repentance declaration "Memory and Reconciliation," issued in March 2000. "Love of neighbor, absolutely central in the teaching of Jesus, becomes the 'new commandment' in the Gospel of John; the disciples should love as he has loved . . . that is, perfectly, 'to the end' (John 13:1). The Christian is called to love and to forgive to a degree that transcends every human standard of justice" (2:2).

10. John 1:11.

11. Rosemary Radford Ruether, "Christology and Jewish-Christian Relations," in Peck, *Jews and Christians*, 25.

12. Eugene J. Fisher, "The Church and Anti-Semitism: Rome Is Due to Pronounce," *National Catholic Register*, July 14, 1996. See also Fisher, *Interwoven Destinies*, 6.

13. Rahner, *Theological Investigations*, vol. 1, 155. He goes on: "The clearest formulations, the most sanctified formulas, the classic condensations of the centuries — long work of the Church in prayer, reflection and struggle concerning God's mysteries: all these derive their life from the fact that they are not an end but a beginning, not a goal but a means, truths which open the way to the — ever greater — Truth . . . every formula transcends itself (not because it is false but precisely because it is true) . . . This holds good for the Chalcedonian formulation of the mystery of Jesus too. For this formula is — a formula" (149–50). I gratefully acknowledge Padraic O'Hare for drawing my attention to this thought of Rahner's.

14. Ruether, *Faith and Fratricide*, 259.

15. Van Buren, *Theology of the Jewish-Christian Reality*, pt. 3, 30–33.

16. Quoted by Peters, *Jerusalem*, 80.

17. Ruether, *Faith and Fratricide*, 256.

18. Schillebeeckx, *Christ: The Sacrament of the Encounter with God*.

19. Quoted by Levenson, "The Temple and the World," 283.

20. Ibid., 284.

21. For diverse Jewish attitudes toward the Temple, see Sanders, *Judaism*, 52–54.

22. Bahat, *Atlas of Jerusalem*, 85.

23. Sanders, *Judaism*, 63.

24. Genesis 22:1–19.

25. Bahat, *Atlas of Jerusalem*, 83.

26. Ibid., 85. Today, Jews are not allowed to pray on the Temple Mount, a proscription enforced partly by rabbis, partly by Islamic authorities. I heard an Islamic official declare in Jerusalem in early 2000 that if the conflict between Israel and the Palestinian Authority were to be resolved, then, on the Islamic side, the ruling might be changed. Nothing intrinsic to Islam prevents Jews from praying on the site of the Temple. See James Carroll, "A Sharing of Faiths in Jerusalem," *Boston Globe*, February 23, 2000.

27. 1 Kings 8:27.

28. A. J. Heschel, *The Sabbath*, 1; Levenson, "The Temple and the World," 298.

29. See Neusner, *Method and Meaning*, 152. See also Ezrahi, *Booking Passage*, 9–10: "But what is 'remembered' is of course also imagined, as mimesis takes on the authority and license of memory and memory becomes an article of faith . . . This is an imaginative license that has no geographical coordinates: it is an affirmation and reconfiguration of the Jewish word as nomadic exercise and Jewish exile as a kind of literary privilege." The Jewish "homeland" has thus become the Jewish "text."

30. Levenson, "The Temple and the World," 297.

31. For example, Crossan sees the act in the Temple, whatever it was, as "what led immediately to Jesus' arrest and execution." (*Who Killed Jesus?*, 64.) But Fredriksen doubts that the "Temple tantrum" of Jesus would have drawn much notice from the Roman overseers. Rather, she locates the cause of Roman hostility to Jesus, in the enthusiastic way the crowds responded to him as he entered Jerusalem. She suggests that while Je-

sus did not himself have a political mission, the crowds thought he did, which made him dangerous to Rome. *Jesus of Nazareth,* 225–34.

32. Mark 15:38.

33. Wilson, *Paul,* 51.

34. Acts 7:55–60.

35. Koester, *Introduction to the New Testament,* vol. 1, 350.

36. In February 2000, I participated in a three-way discussion in Jerusalem among Muslims, Jews, and Christians about sacred space, with emphasis on the "risks and opportunities" of the shared Jewish-Muslim devotion to the Temple Mount. The Jews and Muslims at the conference began the painful but necessary process of "creating a new reality," as one put it, out of the old attitudes toward this most disputed acreage. See Carroll, "A Sharing of Faiths in Jerusalem."

37. Wilson, *Paul,* 45.

38. This does not mean that the *religious* dispute over the holy place of Jerusalem is to be resolved using only "political sovereignty" categories of nineteenth-century nationalism. But even secular Jews for whom "the Land" has no religious meaning as a sign of a covenant with the God of Israel share the attachment to place that originates in this faith.

39. John 2:21–22.

40. Segal, *Rebecca's Children,* 179. The title refers to words spoken by God to Rebecca, mother of the twin sons Jacob and Esau: "Two nations are in your womb, and two peoples, born of you, shall be divided; the one shall be stronger than the other, the elder shall serve the younger." (Genesis 25:23.) This background is one reason why, when contemporary Catholic spokespersons, with only good intentions, seek to honor Jews as "our elder brothers," as both "We Remember" and "Memory and Reconciliation" put it — and as John Paul II did, as we saw — Jews might wonder what is really being said.

41. Ezrahi, *Booking Passage,* 15.

42. For example, the Vatican's insistence on "international guarantees" for Jerusalem and its readiness to treat the Palestinian Authority as having some kind of sovereignty over sites in East Jerusalem in advance of a final peace settlement between Israel and the Palestinians.

43. John 11:45–53; Crossan, *Who Killed Jesus?,* 61.

44. See, for example, Matthew 23:13–29.

45. One would expect by now that the upper echelons of the Catholic Church would have assimilated the lessons of New Testament scholarship and begun to move away from an uncritical repetition of anti-Jewish denigration that salts the Christian Scriptures. Yet even "Memory and Reconciliation" continues the negative stereotype of "Scribes and Pharisees": "Isn't it a bit too easy to judge people of the past by the conscience of today (as the Scribes and Pharisees do according to Mt 23:29–32), almost as if moral conscience were not situated in time?" (1.4). In the cited passage, Jesus is portrayed as vilifying, "Woe to you Scribes and Pharisees, hypocrites!"

46. As noted, Fredriksen places the cause for Jesus' execution not in the Temple, but in his arrival in Jerusalem at the beginning of the festival week. One result of deemphasizing the Temple crime is to lessen the importance of Jesus' opposition to the central Jewish institution, which protects his Jewishness. If Fredriksen's reading of the history is cor-

rect, the question remains: Why did the evangelists put such emphasis on the Temple crime? The answer is tied to its polemical and symbolic significance, in light of the Temple's having recently been destroyed, as three of the four were writing. And, as we have seen, the evangelists had reasons to emphasize Jesus' opposition to a Jewish establishment.

47. Cooke, *God's Beloved*, 48.
48. Sanders, *Judaism*, 91.
49. Schillebeeckx, *Jesus*, 268.
50. Fredriksen, *Jesus of Nazareth*, 232.
51. Crossan, *Who Killed Jesus?*, 52.
52. Ibid., 64.
53. Isaiah 1:11.
54. Horsley and Silberman, *The Message and the Kingdom*, 76. "He [Jesus] arrived in the city as a traditional prophet of Israel who came to pronounce God's judgment against the ornate, Roman-style Temple."
55. Sanders, *Judaism*, 336–40.
56. Ibid.
57. Ibid., 338–39.
58. Mark 12:31; Leviticus 19:18.
59. Fredriksen says that the "ethical instruction in the New Testament texts," which embodies Jesus' message of love, largely "trace[s] back to the very earliest movement." *Jesus of Nazareth*, 103.
60. Horsley and Silberman, *The Message and the Kingdom*, 55.
61. Koester, *Introduction to the New Testament*, vol. 2, 82. For an elaboration of the antisectarian, unifying effect of Jesus' ministry, see Horsley and Silberman, *The Message and the Kingdom*, 55–57.
62. Matthew 5:45.
63. A typical example is this passage from the eminent mid-twentieth-century Roman Catholic theologian Hans Urs von Balthasar, who writes of "two images of God, the self-emptying Son stands opposed, for a moment, to God the Father who is still (Philippians 2) in some way depicted in the colours of the Old Testament palette . . . What is at stake . . . is an altogether decisive turn-about in the way of seeing God. God is not, in the first place, 'absolute power,' but 'absolute love.'" *Mysterium Paschale*, 28. More surprising, perhaps, is the reiteration of this notion of love as the "new commandment" in the Vatican declaration "Memory and Reconciliation," cited above.
64. Isaiah, in the words of Karen Armstrong, wanted Israelites to "discover the inner meaning of their religion. Yahweh wanted compassion rather than sacrifice." In this context, the Old Testament does indeed show God sternly rebuking his people, even displaying his revulsion at their sacrifices, but God's displeasure, in Isaiah, is manifested in the name of compassionate love. Armstrong makes the point that such regard for compassion toward the neighbor became "the hallmark of all the major religions formed" between 800 and 200 B.C.E. *History of God*, 44.
65. Horsley and Silberman, *The Message and the Kingdom*, 96–97.
66. Understanding the central meaning of Jesus' message as this apocalyptic proclamation of the imminence of God's Kingdom, Fredriksen concludes that what Jesus performed in the Temple was a symbolic act of prophecy: "The current Temple was soon

to be destroyed (understood: not by Jesus, nor by invading armies, but by God), to cede place to the eschatological Temple (understood: not built by the hand of man) at the close of the age." *Jesus of Nazareth*, 210.

67. Jeremiah 31:31–34. For a discussion of the *one* covenant, see Lohfink, *Covenant Never Revoked.*

68. Paul uses the phrase "new covenant," as in Galatians 4:24. In 1 Corinthians 2:14–15, Paul equates the "old covenant" with Moses, but this is the only time the phrase appears in the New Testament, and here it is not set in contrast to the new covenant. If Paul saw "two covenants," he certainly did not see them as discontinuous, in the manner of supersessionism.

69. Sanders, *Judaism,* 277.

70. S. Heschel, *Abraham Geiger,* 21.

71. Horsley and Silberman, *The Message and the Kingdom,* 62.

72. Koester, *Introduction to the New Testament,* vol. 2, 89. See also Horsley and Silberman, *The Message and the Kingdom,* 161.

73. 1 Corinthians 11:25; Hebrews 13:20; I Corinthians 5:7.

74. Deuteronomy 21:22–23.

75. For a discussion of this verse, see Crossan, *Who Killed Jesus?,* 163–68.

76. Quoted by Sanders, *Judaism,* 42.

77. John 10:10.

12. The Healing Circle

1. Luke 24:13–16.

2. Eliot, *Collected Poems,* 74–75.

3. Kübler-Ross, *On Death and Dying.*

4. Luke 24:18–21.

5. I first saw the connection between the elements of normal "grief work" and the narrative-constructing work of the first Christians while listening to a lecture by Helmut Koester, at Harvard in 1997.

6. Fredriksen, *Jesus of Nazareth,* 262.

7. The film *The Big Chill* captured this phenomenon. The dead man whose funeral gathers a collection of friends never appears in the movie except as a corpse, but his presence animates everything the grievers feel. (A then unknown actor named Kevin Costner played the corpse.)

8. I acknowledge my debt for this understanding to Professor Koester. Evidence exists for gatherings like what I am calling a healing circle. Here is Fredriksen's summary: "Within just five years of Jesus' death, evidence abounds of this new movement's wide and rapid dissemination. *Ekklēsiai,* small gatherings of its members, appear in the villages of Samaria and Judea as well as in the Galilee . . . Jerusalem, meanwhile, had become home to many of the original disciples (Gal 1:18, 2:1). According to Luke, the core community had been there continuously since the final pilgrimage of Jesus for Passover (Lk 24:53 . . . and passim)." *Jesus of Nazareth,* 236.

9. Luke 24:25–27.

10. Crossan, *Who Killed Jesus?,* 10.

11. See Brown, *The Death of the Messiah: From Gethsemane to the Grave. A Commentary on the Passion Narratives in the Four Gospels.*

12. Crossan, *Who Killed Jesus?*, 1.
13. Mark 15:34; Matthew 27:46.
14. Luke 23:46. The fact that the "last words" of Jesus vary in the Gospels reflects the differing theological concerns of the writers, not that Jesus said first one thing and then another.
15. Amos 8:9: "'And on that day,' says the Lord God, 'I will make the sun go down at noon, and darken the earth in broad daylight.'"
16. Matthew 27:51.
17. See note *w*, *The Jerusalem Bible* (New York: Doubleday, 1966), 63.
18. Zechariah 9:9.
19. Isaiah 53:2–5.
20. John 19:23–25.
21. Matthew 27:46; Mark 15:34. Krister Stendahl points out that, in rendering Jesus' cry in Hebrew — "*Eli, Eli, lama sabachthani?*" — the two Gospel accounts actually mix in the Aramaic word *sabachthani*, a violation of linguistic consistency that suggests Jesus actually did utter the verse. "He was so broken," Stendahl said to me, "that he couldn't keep the language straight."
22. John 19:28.
23. Psalm 22:16–18.
24. Luke 24:30–32.
25. Crossan, *Who Killed Jesus?*, 1. For a discussion of this dispute between Crossan and Brown, see Horsley and Silberman, *The Message and the Kingdom*, 69–70.
26. Matthew 27:54; Mark 15:39.
27. Luke 23:47.
28. Koester, *Introduction to the New Testament*, vol. 2, 166.
29. Dunn, *The Partings of the Ways*, 18.
30. Neusner, *Telling Tales*, 49. Fredriksen is another example of a scholar summing up the Judaism of the period: "Jews everywhere — I generalize, but safely — expressed a broad consensus on what was religiously important: the people, the Land of Israel, Jerusalem, the Temple, and Torah. Behind these concepts and subsuming them stood their unique commitment to the imageless worship of the one God of the universe." *Jesus of Nazareth*, 62. (One should note, perhaps, that Fredriksen is a Jew.)
31. Matthew 23:37.
32. Flannery, *The Anguish of the Jews*, 32.
33. Brown, *Introduction to the New Testament*, 82.
34. 2 Corinthians 11:24.
35. Flannery, *The Anguish of the Jews*, 36.
36. Matthew 5:17–48.
37. Matthew 5:20.
38. Aristotle, *The Poetics*, 11.2. As we saw, the Holocaust is the catastrophe (or *shoah*), in the sense of "moment of recognition," of this entire story.
39. James Joyce, cited by Janet Burroway, *Writing Fiction*, 11.
40. The phrase gives Marcel Simon the title of his book, *Verus Israel*.
41. Isaac, *Jesus and Israel*.
42. Elie Wiesel reports his unease when Cardinal Jean-Marie Lustiger, the Catholic archbishop of Paris and a convert from Judaism, describes himself as "a fulfilled Jew": "Does that mean he is a better Jew than those who have remained Jews?" Wiesel raises

the question with the cardinal, who takes the point, and "no longer uses the formula 'fulfilled Jew.'" Wiesel, *Sea Is Never Full*, 167–71.
43. For an elaboration of Christian demonization of Jews, see Pagels, *Origin of Satan*.

13. Paul, the Martyr of Shalom

1. Wilson, *Paul*, 29.
2. 1 Corinthians 13.
3. Wilson, *Paul*, 173.
4. Ibid., 51–55.
5. Acts 13:7–9. I am grateful to Krister Stendahl for helping me grasp this point about the names of Paul.
6. Sanders, *Paul and Palestinian Judaism*, 549.
7. Isaiah 2:3.
8. Fredriksen, *Jesus of Nazareth*, 135.
9. Ibid.
10. Galatians 2:15–16, 3:3.
11. Stendahl, "On Sacred Violence," 261. See also Stendahl, *Final Account: Paul's Letter to the Romans* (Minneapolis: Fortress Press, 1995).
12. 1 Thessalonians 2:16.
13. Stendahl, "On Sacred Violence," 262.
14. Romans 11:25–27.
15. Romans 11:28–29.
16. Koester, "Historic Mistakes Haunt the Relationship of Christianity and Judaism," 26–27.
17. Stendahl, "On Sacred Violence," 261.
18. Levenson, *The Death and Resurrection of the Beloved Son*, 230.
19. In Galatians 1:13 he writes, "For you have heard of my former life in Judaism, how I persecuted the Church." This has been read as if "Judaism" stands in contrast to "Christianity," but Paul could have had no such frame of reference. Instead, he can be understood simply as referring to what, formerly, he thought being a devout Jew required.
20. Acts 21:27–31.
21. Wilson, *Paul*, 208. See also Koester, *Introduction to the New Testament*, vol. 2, 323.
22. Gager, "The Parting of the Ways: A View from the Perspective of Early Christianity: 'A Christian Perspective,'" in Fisher, *Interwoven Destinies*, 65.

14. Parting of the Ways

1. I am indebted here to Christine Lehmann for her summaries of interviews with Helmut Koester.
2. Lee, *Jesus and the Metaphors of God*, 147.
3. It was called Septuagint because legend had it that seventy elders worked on the translation.
4. Koester, Lehmann interviews.
5. Maguire, "The Good Life," in Bowersock et al., *Late Antiquity*, 251.
6. Goodenough, *Jewish Symbols*, vol. 12, 191.

7. Marcus, *The Jew in the Medieval World*, 103.

8. Wilken, *John Chrysostom and the Jews*, 67.

9. Koester, "Historic Mistakes Haunt the Relationship of Christianity and Judaism," 27.

10. "Blessed be the ashes of that humane theologian," Moses Mendelssohn wrote of Augustine, "who was the first to declare that God was preserving us as a visible proof of the Nazarene religion. But for this lovely brainwave, we would have been exterminated long ago." Quoted by Saperstein, *Moments of Crisis*, 11.

11. Koester, "Historic Mistakes Haunt the Relationship of Christianity and Judaism," 26. Paul van Buren comments on this point: "A Christology for the Jewish-Christian reality needs to emphasize at this point that the context of the things concerning Jesus of Nazareth is *Israel's* Scriptures, not the Church's 'Old Testament.' The Church's 'Old Testament' differs from Israel's Scriptures even when (as in some branches of the Church) the text is a reasonably accurate translation of them. The difference lies in the Fact that the 'Old Testament' is bound together with a 'New Testament' for which it is thought to be a preparation and anticipation. The 'Old Testament' points ahead to Christ as the fulfillment of all the hopes and promises contained in it and so as its total completion. . . . The 'Old Testament' is certainly the context of the anti-Judaic Jesus of the anti-Judaic Church." Van Buren, *Theology of the Jewish-Christian Reality*, pt. 3, 31–32.

12. Koester, "Historic Mistakes," 26.

13. Thoma, *Christian Theology of Judaism*, 89.

14. Koester, "Historic Mistakes," 26–27. The colleague referred to is Dieter Georgi. Koester concludes, "If both the New Testament and the Mishnah were a tragic mistake, the Christians should be the first to acknowledge that the prophecy of Jesus and the vision of Paul of a renewal of Israel has not been fulfilled. If Paul's acceptance of Jesus implied that God had declared himself to be on the side of the victims of violence, on which side is God now? This question is no longer open for debate."

15. Matthew 5:17.

16. "Such a benevolent typology would rejoice and marvel in the analogous shape of Passover and Easter, of Aqidah and Golgotha, of Sinai and the Sermon on the Mount. But the supersessionist drive forced typological interpretation into adversarial patterns where the younger had to trump and trounce the older." Krister Stendahl, "Qumran and Supersessionism — and the Road Not Taken," in *Princeton Seminary Bulletin* 19, no. 2 (new ser., 1998), 136.

17. Parkes, *Conflict of Church and Synagogue*, 81.

18. Matthew 3:7.

15. The Lachrymose Tradition: A Cautionary Note

1. Quoted by Cynthia Ozick, introduction to *Rescuers*, xi. The story recalls another I heard from Krister Stendahl. Rabbi Marc Tannenbaum, a founder of Jewish-Christian dialogue, was asked, "Rabbi, tell me what makes you glad instead of what hurts you." To which he replied, "What makes us glad is if you don't persecute us anymore."

2. Quoted by Cohen, *Under Crescent and Cross*, 3.

3. Norman Roth, "The Jews in Spain at the Time of Maimonides," in Ormsby, *Moses Maimonides and His Time*, 17.

4. Goodenough, *Jewish Symbols*, vol. 12, 198.

5. Silberman, *Heavenly Powers,* 219–28.
6. Gilbert, Atlas of Jewish History, i.

16. The Heart of This Story Is a Place

1. Averil Cameron, "Remaking the Past," in Bowersock et al., *Late Antiquity,* 8.
2. The difference in postwar Soviet and American attitudes toward Germany was also partly a matter of the difference in wartime casualties, the Soviets having suffered something like 20 million dead, compared with about 300,000 Americans.
3. Schnell, *Maria Laach Abbey,* 3.
4. Drijvers, *Helena Augusta,* 23.

17. The Story of Constantine

1. Keith Hopkins, "Population," in Bowersock et al., *Late Antiquity,* 646.
2. Neusner, *Judaism and Christianity,* 15.
3. Richard P. McBrien, "Catholic Church," in *Encyclopedia of Catholicism,* 244.
4. Cameron, *Later Roman Empire,* 10.
5. Ibid., 43.
6. Béatrice Caseau, "Sacred Landscapes," in Bowersock et al., *Late Antiquity,* 26.
7. Gilbert, *Atlas of Jewish History,* 17.
8. For a discussion of the organizational impact of text canonization, see Halbertal, *People of the Book,* 19. "But the sealing of the text engenders both the bestowal and the removal of authority . . . The moment the text was sealed, authority was removed from the writers of the text and transferred to its interpreters; denied to the prophets and awarded to the Sages. 'Henceforth you must incline your ear to the works of the learned.'"
9. Shaye J. Cohen, "Judaism," in Bowersock et al., *Late Antiquity,* 528.
10. The Roman-imposed name "Palestine" (*Philistina*) evokes the ancient enemy of Israel and gives us the English word "philistine," a hint of the shadow that falls over the area today. See Cohn, *This Immortal People,* 67.
11. Ibid., 59.
12. Matthew 28:19.
13. Segal, *Rebecca's Children,* 176.
14. This summary is not a historical account but rather the story as it is usually told. My sources are Barnes, *From Eusebius to Augustine,* 371–91; Barnes, *Constantine and Eusebius,* 261–71; Frend, *Rise of Christianity,* 474–85.

18. The Cross and the Religious Imagination

1. Eusebius Pamphilus, "Life of Constantine," bk. 1, ch. 12, 485.
2. Frend, *Rise of Christianity,* 477.
3. Cameron, *Later Roman Empire,* 48.
4. Brown, *Augustine of Hippo,* 49.
5. Romans 6:6.
6. Romans 6:3; Galatians 3:27.

7. John 20:34.

8. *Dialogue with Trypho,* ch. 111, cited by Hershman, *Rivalry of Genius,* 61.

9. Zoeckler, *Cross of Christ,* x.

10. Vogelstein, *Rome,* 39.

11. Eusebius Pamphilus, "Life of Constantine," bk. 1, ch. 28, 490.

12. Ibid., ch. 30, 490.

13. Ibid., ch. 31, 491.

14. The death of Jesus would grip the imagination of the Latin West more than the Byzantine East, where, for example, the same Holy Sepulcher is referred to as the Church of the Resurrection. The cross would take second place to the iconic face of Christ, but when iconoclastic rejection of images sweeps the Byzantine world, the one image excepted was the cross. But in the West the emphasis would be absolute: "It was through the cross, not images, that the human race was redeemed." See Pelikan, *Christian Tradition,* vol. 3, 132.

15. Vogelstein, *Rome,* 102.

16. Neusner, *Judaism and Christianity,* 15.

17. Augustine, *The Confessions,* bk. 12, ch. 16, 293. Jerusalem as mother would take root in the Jewish imagination, but as a mother to be mourned: "the Holy City as a female figure of desolation and ruin; the dominant image. . . is that of Jerusalem as mother." Ezrahi, *Booking Passage,* 34.

18. Neusner, *Judaism and Christianity,* 58.

19. Ibid., 144.

20. Smallwood, *Jews under Roman Rule,* 543.

21. Brown, *Augustine of Hippo,* 125.

22. Pelikan, *Christian Tradition,* vol. 1, 71.

19. The Vision of Constantine

1. Eusebius Pamphilus, "Life of Constantine," bk. 1, ch. 19, 487–88.

2. Frend, *Rise of Christianity,* 476.

3. Cameron, *Later Roman Empire,* 171.

4. Eusebius Pamphilus, "Life of Constantine," bk. 1, ch. 43, 494.

5. Ibid., bk. 3, ch. 10, 522.

6. Cited by Frend, *Rise of Christianity,* 476.

7. Cameron, *Later Roman Empire,* 49.

8. Kelly, *Early Christian Doctrines,* 13.

9. Ibid., 83.

10. Frend, *Rise of Christianity,* 476.

11. Cameron, *Later Roman Empire,* 31.

12. Cited by Barnes, *From Eusebius to Augustine,* 376.

13. Frend, *Rise of Christianity,* 481.

14. Cameron, *Later Roman Empire,* 50.

15. Ibid., 56.

16. Ibid., 50.

17. Ibid., 57.

18. Cited by Frend, *Rise of Christianity,* 483.

19. Ibid.

20. Chadwick, *The Early Church*, 128.

21. For a discussion of Teutonic "tree piety," see Schama, *Landscape and Memory*, 216–18.

22. Chadwick, *The Early Church*, 10.

23. Goodenough, *Jewish Symbols*, 191.

24. Chadwick, *The Early Church*, 11. Moshe Halbertal calls attention to the fact that, while the canon of Scripture was more or less established during the Second Temple period, some diversity among various Jewish groups even on this central question may have continued after the Temple's destruction. Halbertal, *People of the Book*, 16.

25. Goodenough, *Jewish Symbols*, 197.

26. Cited by Drijvers, *Helena Augusta*, 55.

27. Smallwood, *Jews under Roman Rule*, 543.

28. Frend, *Rise of Christianity*, 484.

29. Ibid., 482.

30. Ibid., 484.

31. Cited by Barnes, *From Eusebius to Augustine*, 390. Barnes notes that some scholars dispute the historicity of the "Speech to the Assembly of the Saints," although he accepts it.

32. Frend, *Rise of Christianity*, 523.

33. Eusebius Pamphilus, "Life of Constantine," bk. 3, ch. 57, 535.

34. Cameron, *Later Roman Empire*, 59.

35. Tracy, *Analogical Imagination*. See also Lynch, *Christ and Apollo*.

36. Cameron, *Later Roman Empire*, 69.

37. I Corinthians 12.

38. Drijvers, *Helena Augusta*, 55.

39. Cited by Halbertal, *People of the Book*, 6. Halbertal says that this proverb was cited by Spinoza "as he describes the widespread sectarianism of the seventeenth century."

40. "Constantine Summons the Council of Nicaea," in Stevenson, *A New Eusebius*, 338.

41. Barnes, *Constantine and Eusebius*, 269–70. See also Drijvers, *Helena Augusta*, 56; Cameron, *Later Roman Empire*, 59.

42. Here is Eusebius's summary of what happened at the council: "On this faith being publicly put forth by us, no room for contradiction appeared; but our most pious emperor, before any one else, testified that it was most orthodox. He confessed, moreover, that such were his own sentiments; and he advised all present to agree to it, and to subscribe its articles and to assent to them, with the insertion of the single word Consubstantial which, moreover, he interpreted himself saying that the Son subsisted from the Father neither according to division, nor severance: for the immaterial and intellectual, and incorporeal nature could not be the subject of any bodily affection, but that it became us to conceive of such things in a divine and ineffable manner. And our most wise and most religious emperor reasoned in this way; but they, because of the addition of Consubstantial, drew up the following formulary." Stevenson, *A New Eusebius*, 345.

43. Frend, *Rise of Christianity*, 527.

44. Kelly, *Early Christian Doctrines*, 232. Kelly's translation of the creed differs slightly from the translation used in Catholic liturgy.

45. This translation is offered by Pelikan, *Christian Tradition*, vol. 1, 201.

46. Ruether, *Faith and Fratricide,* 172.
47. Frend, *Rise of Christianity,* 522.
48. For my understanding of this development I am especially indebted to Jaroslav Pelikan; see, especially, *Christian Tradition,* vol. 3, 133–34.
49. Cited by Ruether, *Faith and Fratricide,* 177.
50. Eusebius Pamphilus, "Life of Constantine," bk. 3, ch. 7, cited by Cameron, *Later Roman Empire,* 60.
51. Cited by Barnes, *From Eusebius to Augustine,* 383.
52. Eusebius Pamphilus, "Life of Constantine," bk. 1, ch. 30, 490.
53. The Vatican observance of the arrival of the third millennium was called *Jubilaeum A.D. 2000.* Its symbol was a cross in rainbow colors superimposed on a sky-blue globe; interlocking doves represented the continents.
54. Pelikan, *Christian Tradition,* vol. 3, 132.
55. Eusebius Pamphilus, "Life of Constantine," bk. 3, ch. 30, 528.

20. The True Cross

1. Drijvers, *Helena Augusta,* 5.
2. Eusebius Pamphilus, "Life of Constantine," bk. 3, ch. 44, 531.
3. Drijvers, *Helena Augusta,* 65.
4. Ibid., 67.
5. Ibid., 64.
6. Ibid., 85.
7. Cited by Drijvers, *Helena Augusta,* 82.
8. Ibid., 85.
9. Ibid., 87.
10. Ibid., 64f.
11. O'Mikle, *Pope Pius XII,* 55.
12. Drijvers, *Helena Augusta,* 90–93.
13. Augustine, *The Confessions,* bk. 6, ch. 3, 107.
14. See Stock, *Augustine the Reader,* 61–62.
15. Cited by Brown, *Augustine of Hippo,* 84.
16. Brown, *Augustine of Hippo,* 86. For another view of the relationship between Ambrose and Augustine, see Wills, *Saint Augustine,* 40–47.
17. Ambrose, "Funeral Oration on the Death of Emperor Theodosius," in Deferrari, *Fathers of the Church,* vol. 22, 326.
18. Ibid., 329.
19. Drijvers, *Helena Augusta,* 144.
20. For a reproduction of this painting, see Bairati, *Piero Della Francesca,* 48.
21. Drijvers, *Helena Augusta,* 144.
22. Isaac, *Anti-Semitism,* 57. For another example of this usage, see John Paul II, "From Historical Trust to Mutual Recognition," in *Spiritual Pilgrimage,* xvii.
23. Drijvers, *Helena Augusta,* 60.
24. Ibid., 61.
25. Barnes, *Constantine and Eusebius,* 262.
26. Cameron, *Later Roman Empire,* 85.

27. Barnes, *Constantine and Eusebius*, 263.

28. Ibid.

29. Luke 21:5–6.

30. To some Jews, "the emperor's action forecast the coming of the Messiah." See Neusner, *Judaism and Christianity*, 21.

31. Barnes, *Constantine and Eusebius*, 263.

32. Neusner, *Judaism and Christianity*, 21–22.

33. Cameron, *Later Roman Empire*, 97.

34. Neusner, *Judaism and Christianity*, 22. The ruins of the Temple would be a theologically based feature of the Jerusalem landscape until 638 C.E., when the Muslim caliph Omar ibn al-Khattab took the city. The Christian patriarch demanded that the new Islamic rulers continue the Christian prohibition of a Jewish presence in the Holy City, but Omar readmitted Jews, and out of respect for the Temple site, he ordered it cleaned up. When the Dome of the Rock was built, he permitted Jews to tend it. One of the ironies of political conflict in Jerusalem today is that the Temple Mount is a flashpoint between Jews and Muslims because both groups revere it. Christians do not, because Jesus is the "new Temple" and, beginning with Constantine, the Temple was superseded by the Holy Sepulcher.

35. Trevor-Roper, *Rise of Christian Europe*, 36.

36. Cited by Ruether, *Faith and Fratricide*, 193. See also Dudden, *St. Ambrose*, 371–81.

37. Ruether, *Faith and Fratricide*, 193–94.

21. Augustine Trembling

1. Brown, *Augustine of Hippo*, 124.

2. Wills, *Saint Augustine*, xii.

3. Garry Wills prefers the title *The Testimony*, which is a more accurate translation of the word *confessiones*, and does not suggest a preoccupation with sin and guilt, a misunderstanding of Augustine's emphasis. Ibid., xv.

4. Ibid., 44.

5. Augustine, *The Confessions*, bk. 5, ch. 8, 100.

6. Brown, *Augustine of Hippo*, 103.

7. Atkinson, "'Your Servant, My Mother,'" 141.

8. Augustine, *The Confessions*, bk. 9, ch. 10, 196–97.

9. Wills, *Saint Augustine*, 57.

10. Augustine, *The Confessions*, bk. 9, ch. 12, 200.

11. Ibid., bk. 5, ch. 9, 102.

12. Ibid., bk. 5, ch. 2, 92.

13. Augustine, *The Trinity*, 65.

14. Quoted by Harpur, *Revelations*, 8.

15. Augustine, "The Correction of the Donatists," in Schaff, *Nicene and Post-Nicene Fathers*, vol. 6, 641.

16. Cited by Brown, *Religion and Society*, 278.

17. Brown, *Augustine of Hippo*, 336.

18. Ruether, *Faith and Fratricide*, 173.

19. Cited by Ruether, *Faith and Fratricide*, 178.

20. Ibid., 179.
21. Ibid., 180.
22. Flannery, *The Anguish of the Jews*, 59–60.
23. Halbertal, *People of the Book*, 1–2.
24. Ezrahi, *Booking Passage*, 14, 11.
25. Fredriksen, "Paul," 622.
26. Augustine, *Adversus Judaeos*, in Deferrari, *The Fathers of the Church*, vol. 2, 408.
27. Augustine, "Tractates on the Gospel According to John," in Schaff, *Nicene and Post-Nicene Fathers*, vol. 7, 205.
28. Ruether, *Faith and Fratricide*, 173–74.
29. Augustine, *City of God*, bk. 4, ch. 34, 177.
30. Ibid., bk. 18, ch. 46, 827–28.
31. Fredriksen, "Paul," 622.
32. Ibid., 624.
33. Neusner, *Judaism and Christianity*, 146.
34. Fredriksen, "Paul," 624.
35. Quoted by Saperstein, *Moments of Crisis*, 11.
36. Augustine, *City of God*, bk. 19, ch. 21, 861–62.
37. Augustine, *The Confessions*, bk. 4, ch. 1, 71.

22. The Seamless Robe

1. Psalm 22:16–18.
2. John 19:24.
3. Crossan, *Who Killed Jesus?*, 1.
4. John 19:24–25.
5. "Trier: Colour City Guide with Map" (Pulheim: Rahmel-Verlag), 17.
6. Augustine, *The Confessions*, trans. Rex Warner (New York: New American Library, 1963), bk. 7, ch. 20, 157.
7. Augustine, *The Confessions*, trans. Pine-Coffin, bk. 5, ch. 8, 102.
8. Ibid., bk. 3, ch. 12, 101.
9. Ibid., bk. 5, ch. 8, 100–101.
10. Acts 1:26.
11. The century's third showing of the Robe was in 1996, a year when the reunification of Germany was central to the celebration.

23. The Danger of Ambivalence

1. News Brief, *National Catholic Reporter*, May 7, 1999.
2. The Catholic primate of Poland, Cardinal Jozef Glemp, denounced what he called "irresponsible groups" for erecting the new crosses, which, he said, diminished "the meaning of the cross symbol." He also said the conflict was being caused not by radical Catholics but by "continuous and increasing harassment by the Jewish side." The local prelate, Bishop Tadeusz Rakoczy, responded to the raising of the new crosses by siding with those who erected them, in defense of the papal cross. The Polish bishops' Permanent Council called for an end to "arbitrary stationing of crosses" at Auschwitz

and defended the continued presence of the papal cross, giving the Catholic protesters what they wanted in the first place.

3. U.S. State Department, "The Fate of the Wartime Ustasha Treasury," 2.

4. Robin Harris, "On Trial Again," *Catholic World Report*, August–September 1998, 41.

5. Morley, *Vatican Diplomacy*, 151, 159–60.

6. Craughwell, "Pius XII and the Holocaust," 52.

7. The State Department's report "The Fate of the Wartime Ustasha Treasury" puts the figure of Jews living in Croatia at between 35,000 and 45,000; Raul Hilberg says 6,000 survived. Hilberg, *Destruction of the European Jews*, vol. 2, 708–18.

8. Harris, "On Trial Again," 42.

9. The historian István Deák called the Rat Line "one of the most shameful episodes in the history of the Vatican." In addition to Pavelič, it enabled Josef Mengele, Adolf Eichmann, and Franz Stangle, the commandant of Treblinka, and "hundreds of [other] mass murderers to escape." Deák argues that Pius XII knew of and approved this activity. Deák, "The Pope, the Nazis, and the Jews, " 49.

10. U.S. State Department, "Fate of the Wartime Ustasha Treasury," 2.

11. Gordon, "Saint Edith?," 20.

12. Chazan, *European Jewry and the First Crusade*, 28–29.

24. The War of the Cross

1. *The Hebrew First-Crusade Chronicles: S*, cited by Chazan, *European Jewry*, 225. Chazan acknowledges the problem of the reliability of the originals of the two Hebrew chronicles of the Crusades because "each is replete with erasure, omissions, and blatant errors" (223). Despite such flaws, Chazan argues for their ultimate reliability (40–49).

2. "The Chronicle of Solomon bar Simson," in Eidelberg, *The Jews and the Crusaders*, 21.

3. Fulcher of Chartres, cited by Oldenbourg, *The Crusades*, 86. Oldenbourg also cites Ekkehard's figure of 300,000 and Raymond of Aguilers's of 100,000; she herself puts the number at 6,000 to 7,000 knights and 60,000 foot soldiers.

4. John France, "Patronage and the Appeal of the First Crusade," in Phillips, *The First Crusade*, 6.

5. "An equivalent movement nowadays would involve participation in the order of 1,320,000 persons." Ibid.

6. Oldenbourg, *The Crusades*, 593.

7. Ibid., 87.

8. Blake and Morris, "A Hermit Goes to War," 101.

9. Pelikan, *Christian Tradition*, 211.

10. In May 1999, Pope John Paul II made the first visit by a pope to a predominantly Orthodox country since 1054, traveling to Bucharest to meet with the Romanian patriarch Teoctist. The two old men prayed for an end to the Kosovo war, which, though mainly a conflict between Orthodox Serbs and nonreligious Muslim Albanians, reflected the wider Balkan conflict that, among other things, recapitulated the original East-West schism.

11. Augustine, *City of God*, bk. 19, ch. 7, 861. The full paragraph reads, "I shall be told that the Imperial City has been at pains to impose on conquered people not only her yoke, but her language also, as a bond of peace and fellowship, so that there should be no lack of interpreters but even a profusion of them. True; but think of the cost of this

achievement! Consider the scale of those wars, with all that slaughter of human beings, all the human blood that was shed!"

12. See Geremek, "Marginal Man," 347–74.

13. Parkes, *The Jew in the Medieval Community,* 103.

14. H. Liebershütz, "The Crusading Movement and Its Bearing on the Christian Attitude
Towards Jewry," in Cohen, *Essential Papers,* 271.

15. The seventeenth Council of Toledo, in 694. See Baron, *History of the Jews,* vol. 9, 136.

16. The emergence of money-based economies required of the Church mental and theological acrobatics. Here is Thomas Aquinas's rationale for the simultaneous condemnation and acceptance of the sin of usury: "The civil law leaves certain sins unpun-
ished to accommodate imperfect men who would be severely disadvantaged if all sins
were strictly prohibited by suitable sanctions. Human law, therefore, allows the taking
of interest, not because it deems this to be just but because to do otherwise would hin-
der the 'utilities' of a great many people." *Summa Theologiae,* 2.2.78, cited by Le Goff,
Your Money or Your Life, 49.

17. See Shatzmiller, *Shylock Reconsidered.*

18. Oldenbourg, *The Crusades,* 561.

25. The Incident in Trier

1. Oldenbourg, *The Crusades,* 87.

2. *The Hebrew First-Crusade Chronicles: L,* cited by Chazan, *European Jewry,* 287–88.

3. Ibid., 289–91.

4. Cited by Flannery, *The Anguish of the Jews,* 73.

5. Cited by Agus, "Rabbinic Scholarship in Northern Europe," 189.

6. Ibid., 196. Elie Wiesel reports telling a version of the same legend to Cardinal Jean-
Marie Lustiger, the Jewish-born archbishop of Paris, whose mother died at Auschwitz.
To Wiesel, the legend's relevance seems to lie in the possibility that Lustiger himself
could be elected pope. Wiesel, *Sea Is Never Full,* 173.

7. "The Crusades," *The Jewish Encyclopedia: A Descriptive Record of the History, Religion,
Literature, and Customs of the Jewish People from the Earliest Times to the Present Day,*
vol. 4 (New York: Funk and Wagnalls, 1903), 379.

8. Blake and Morris, "A Hermit Goes to War," 82.

9. Ibid., 84.

10. Colin Morris, "Peter the Hermit and the Chroniclers," in Phillips, *The First Crusade,*
32.

11. Flannery, *The Anguish of the Jews,* 92.

12. "The Crusades," *Jewish Encyclopedia,* 379.

13. The reference to "the place of execution" recalls that, as a sign of contempt, Christian
criminals were often put to death in Jewish cemeteries. Near the tablet bearing the
"Jewish Privilege" a visitor can still see a small sculpture of the "Jew's sow," an
antisemitic slur carved into a thirteenth-century choir stall.

14. "Cologne Cathedral and City Guide" (Pulheim: Rahmel-Verlag), 25.

15. Blake and Morris, "A Hermit Goes to War," 86.

16. Bahat, *Atlas of Jerusalem,* 86, 87.

17. Blake and Morris, "A Hermit Goes to War," 85.

18. Ibid., 87.

19. Quoted by Flannery, *The Anguish of the Jews*, 92.

20. The "A.D." notation was first introduced in the sixth century by a Scythian monk, Dionysius Exiguus. Even if he had not passed on the miscalculation of the birth of Jesus by four years, his calendar would not have matched ours because the Roman numerals he worked with had no zero. Bede's innovation was to extend the counting back "before Christ," using minus numbers, but he too had to calculate without the zero. See Man, *Atlas of the Year 1000*, 11.

21. *Merchant of Venice*, act 3, scene 1.

22. McDougall, *Promised Land, Crusader State: The American Encounter with the World Since 1776*.

23. Blake and Morris, "A Hermit Goes to War," 9.

24. Revelation 20:1–10.

25. Fasching, *Coming of the Millennium*, 13. According to Joseph Dan, a scholar at the Hebrew University in Jerusalem, it was Talmudic sources that had first divided "the six thousand year history of the universe into three parts: the age of *tohu* (chaos), the age of Torah, and the age of the messiah. These millennia will be followed by a thousand years of destruction, after which 'the next world' . . . will be created." Dan, *The Christian Kabbalah*, 69.

26. I am indebted to Harold M. Stahmer, emeritus professor of religion and philosophy at the University of Florida, for drawing my attention to the Nazi exploitation of this millennial mythology. The deeper point is that mythic impulses — Talmudic, medieval, and Nazi — divide time into three phases, with the millennium having special symbolic significance.

27. Romans 11:25.

28. Cited by Fasching, *Coming of the Millennium*, 20.

26. Mainz Anonymous

1. "The Crusades," *The Jewish Encyclopedia: A Descriptive Record of the History, Religion, Literature, and Customs of the Jewish People from the Earliest Times to the Present Day*, vol. 4 (New York: Funk and Wagnalls, 1903), 378.

2. Saperstein, *Moments of Crisis*, 18.

3. Flannery, *The Anguish of the Jews*, 93.

4. Ibid., 91. Léon Poliakov calls it "a thunderbolt out of a blue sky." *History of Anti-Semitism*, 46.

5. Cited by Hastings, *Victory in Europe*, 187.

6. Johnson, *Modern Times*, 403.

7. Howard Zinn, *A People's History of the United States* (New York: Harper and Row, 1980), 412.

8. Ibid.

9. Hastings, *Victory in Europe*, 149.

10. Manchester, *The Glory and the Dream*, 334.

11. Ibid., 333.

12. Hastings, *Victory in Europe*, 132.

13. "Chronicle of Solomon bar Simson," in Eidelberg, *The Jews and the Crusaders*, 23–24.

14. Ibid., 24, 28.

15. Chazan, *European Jewry,* 93.

16. Ibid.

17. "The Chronicle of Solomon bar Simson," in Eidelberg, *The Jews and the Crusaders,* 30.

18. Ibid., 25.

19. Ibid., 30–31.

20. Cited by Langer, *Admitting the Holocaust,* 37.

21. "The Chronicle of Solomon bar Simson," in Eidelberg, *The Jews and the Crusaders,* 32–33.

22. On this point, Jon Levenson comments, "Indeed the boldness with which Paul projects Jesus (and the Church) into the story of Abraham is a midrashic tour de force that has affected Jewish-Christian relations ever since." Levenson, *Death and Resurrection of the Beloved Son,* 210.

23. Galatians 3:13–16.

24. Levenson, *Death and Resurrection of the Beloved Son,* 125–30.

25. Chazan, *European Jewry,* 193.

26. John 2:19.

27. "The Chronicle of Solomon bar Simson," in Eidelberg, *The Jews and the Crusaders,* 32.

28. Poliakov, *History of Anti-Semitism,* 46.

29. Ibid., 86–87.

30. Ibid., 87. Poliakov concludes, "Thus appears that famous Jewish ambivalence: money is overvalued because without it death or expulsion threatens; and precisely because it is overvalued, it becomes the object of contempt, while other facets of life become more highly regarded."

31. The word "Kabbalah" means "tradition." "The beginnings of this movement are usually set in the last decade or two of the twelfth century C.E." Dan, *The Early Kabbalah,* 1. Harold Bloom says that the use of the word "Kabbalah" as applied to esoteric Jewish teachings about God dates to "about the year 1200." Bloom, *Kabbalah and Criticism,* 15.

32. Idel, *Kabbalah,* 198.

27. The Blood Libel

1. "Sefer Zekhirah," or "The Book of Remembrance of Rabbi Ephraim of Bonn," in Eidelberg, *The Jews and the Crusaders,* 128.

2. Solomon Grayzel, "The Papal Bull *Sicut Judaeis,*" in Cohen, *Essential Papers,* 232.

3. *Vita Prima,* 3.6, cited by E. Rozanne Elder, "St. Bernard of Clairvaux," in *Dictionary of the Middle Ages,* vol. 2, 190.

4. "Sefer Zekhirah," in Eidelberg, *The Jews and the Crusaders,* 122.

5. Ibid.

6. Cited by Saperstein, *Moments of Crisis,* 19.

7. Chazan, *In the Year 1096,* 144.

8. Cited by Modras, *The Catholic Church and Antisemitism,* 346–47.

9. Ibid. See also Küng, *Judaism,* 268.

10. Carroll, "The Silence," 61.

11. See, for example, Monsignor George C. Higgins, "Catholics and the Holocaust," *Tidings,* April 18, 1997.

12. Poliakov, *History of Anti-Semitism,* 58.
13. Richards, *Sex, Dissidence, and Damnation,* 105.
14. Ibid.
15. Saperstein, *Moments of Crisis,* 21.
16. "Same idea those jews they said killed the Christian boy. Every man has his price." James Joyce, *Ulysses,* (New York: Random House, 1961), 108.
17. Cited by Saperstein, *Moments of Crisis,* 20.
18. Ibid., 21.
19. In response, Rabbi James Rudin of the American Jewish Committee said, "It's really throwing a verbal hand grenade into both Catholic-Jewish relations and Israel relations. I think it's a real setback to Vatican-Israel relations. I'm particularly upset with the phrase 'blood libel.' He [the spokesman] knows that people were murdered because of a blood libel." *Jewish Week,* July 23, 1999, 14.
20. Cited by Richards, *Sex, Dissidence, and Damnation,* 105.
21. Quoted by Chazan, *In the Year 1096,* 145.
22. Ibid., 143.
23. Frank Rich, *New York Times,* October 13, 1998.
24. Poliakov, *History of Anti-Semitism,* 51. See also Cohn-Sherbok, *Crucified Jew,* 41.
25. Richards, *Sex, Dissidence, and Damnation,* 99–104.

28. Anselm: Why God Became Man

1. Küng, *Christianity,* 393.
2. Ibid., 393–94. Küng says that the *Decretum Gratian,* a compendium of existing Church law, was published around 1140, and that "in time three official (and one unofficial) collections of decretals were made, which together with the *Decretium Gratiani* formed the *Corpus Iuris Canonici.* The *Codex Iuris Canonici,* which is still in force today, worked out under curial direction, published in 1917/18 and then only lightly revised after the Second Vatican Council and republished in 1983, is based on it."
3. Pope Gelasius I in 495 had called himself *Vicarius Christi,* but with Innocent it became a common title for popes. It gave Rolf Hochhuth the title of his 1963 play, *The Deputy,* a stark indictment of Pius XII that is not unrelated to Innocent III.
4. Innocent III, "Sermon on the Consecration of a Pope," quoted by Brian Tierney, *The Crisis of Church and State, 1050–1300* (Englewood Cliffs, N.J.: Prentice-Hall, 1980), 132.
5. Fourth Lateran Council, Constitutions 3: "On Heretics," in Tanner, *Decrees of the Ecumenical Councils,* 234.
6. Bunson, *The Pope Encyclopedia,* 179.
7. Beckwith, *Early Medieval Art,* 11.
8. See *The New Catholic Encylopedia,* vol. 8, 407–8.
9. Cohen, *The Friars and the Jews,* 248–49.
10. Fourth Lateran Council, Constitutions 1: "On the Catholic Faith," in Tanner, *Decrees of the Ecumenical Councils,* 230.
11. Fourth Lateran Council, Constitutions 68: "That Jews Should Be Distinguished from Christians in Their Dress," in Tanner, *Decrees of the Ecumenical Councils,* 266.
12. Küng, *Judaism,* 164.
13. Carroll, "The Silence," 67.
14. Küng, *Christianity,* 415.

15. Ibid., 414.
16. It was in Anselm's spirit that Pope John Paul II issued his 1998 encyclical *Fides et Ratio* ("Faith and Reason"), a defense of the idea that faith and reason, while not the same, are not in conflict either. Reason is required for a proper grasp of revelation, and revelation is necessary for a full appreciation of truth.
17. Evans, *Anselm*, 22.
18. Anselm, *Cur Deus Homo*, preface, 31.
19. Cecil Roth, "The Medieval Conception of the Jew: A New Interpretation," in Cohen, *Essential Papers*, 300.
20. Anselm, *Cur Deus Homo*, bk. 1, ch. 20, 98.
21. Ibid., bk. 2, ch. 6, 120.
22. Ibid.
23. Pelikan, *Christian Tradition*, vol. 3, 118. I acknowledge my debt here to Pelikan's explanation of Anselm's doctrine of salvation, its significance, and its relation to what follows from it.
24. Anselm, *Cur Deus Homo*, bk. 1, ch. 11, 63.
25. Ibid., bk. 2, ch. 18, 165–66.
26. Küng, *Judaism*, 386.
27. Anselm, *Cur Deus Homo*, bk. 2, ch. 20, 174.
28. Quoted by Küng, *Judaism*, 386.

29. Abelard and Héloïse

1. McCallum, *Abelard's Christian Theology*, 31.
2. Thomas Gilby, O.P., "Abelard," *Encyclopedia of Philosophy*, vol. 1, 4.
3. Quoted by John F. Benton, "Peter Abelard," in *Dictionary of the Middle Ages*, vol. 1, 18.
4. McCallum, *Abelard's Christian Theology*, 32.
5. Quoted by Pelikan, *Christian Tradition*, vol. 3, 107. See also Eligii M. Buytaert, O.F.M., ed., *Petri Abaelardi Opera Theologica*, vol. 1, *Commentaria in Epistolam Pauli ad Romanos* (Turnholti, Belgium: Typographi Brepols Editores Pontificii, 1969), 117.
6. Romans 3:9, 25.
7. Quoted by Evans, *St. Bernard*, 155. See also Buytaert, *Petri Abaelardi Opera Theologica*, vol. 1, 117–18. For another view of the idea of Christ as example, see Irenaeus's *Against Heresies*.
8. Adams, *Mont St. Michel and Chartres*, 287.
9. Abelard, *Abelard's Adversities*, 25. Here is another translation of the same line: "She had a rather lovely face, and was unrivaled in her breadth of literary culture." Gilson, *Héloïse and Abelard*, 5.
10. Abelard, *Abelard's Adversities*, 26.
11. Ibid., 35.
12. Quoted by Gilson, *Héloïse and Abelard*, 83.
13. "Probs of Héloïse," 13, *Patrologia Latina*, Paris 1878–90, PL 178, 696. Quoted by Pelikan, *Christian Tradition*, vol. 3, 255.
14. Pelikan, *Jesus Through the Centuries*, 106.
15. McCallum, *Abelard's Christian Theology*, 20.
16. Pelikan, *Christian Tradition*, vol. 3, 255. It was the Anglican theologian John Macquarrie who drew my attention to the relevance to this question of the parable of the

Prodigal Son: "Lest we be tempted to construct too elaborate a theory of atonement, or to suppose that some particularly complex historical happening was necessary for God to be able to accept men, we should call to mind Christ's own parable of the prodigal who finds the father willing to receive him (Luke 15:11–32), though there is no special machinery to make possible a reconciliation . . . It is necessary indeed that some particular historical event should bring to light in a signal way 'the mystery hidden for ages and generations' (Col. 1:26), but no historical event changes God's attitude, or makes him from a wrathful God into a gracious God, or allows his reconciling work to get started — such thoughts are utterly to be rejected." Macquarrie, *Christian Theology*, 283.

17. Anselm, *Cur Deus Homo*, bk. 2, ch. 20, 174.
18. McCallum, *Abelard's Christian Theology*, 101.
19. That would come with the Fourth Lateran Council in 1215 and then — "Outside this Church there is no salvation" — with *Unam Sanctam*, the papal bull issued by Boniface VIII in 1302.
20. Pelikan, *Christian Tradition*, vol. 3, 255.
21. Armstrong, *History of God*, 203.
22. McCallum, *Abelard's Christian Theology*, 20. He quotes J. G. Sikes, who says, "Abelard alone believed that through the operation of their reason, men, before the Incarnation, accepted the Christian doctrine of the Trinity and so were numbered among the blessed." The word "alone" may overstate it, since "Hebrew saints" were seen as in some way blessed by figures like Augustine and Justin Martyr.
23. Abelard, "Dialogue Between a Philosopher, a Jew, and a Christian," *Patrologia Latina* 178, 1617–18. Quoted by Flannery, *The Anguish of the Jews*, 143.
24. Evans, *St. Bernard*, 158.
25. "Epistle 191.1," quoted by Armstrong, *History of God*, 203.
26. Letter 239, to Pope Innocent, *The Letters of St. Bernard of Clairvaux*, trans. Bruno Scott James (Stroud, U.K.: Sutton Publishing, 1998), 318.
27. Letter 241, to Cardinal Ivo, *Letters of St. Bernard*, 321.
28. Gilson, *Héloïse and Abelard*, 88.
29. Armstrong, *History of God*, 203.
30. Ibid.
31. Letter 239, to Pope Innocent, *Letters of St. Bernard*, 318.
32. Gilson, *Héloïse and Abelard*, 106.
33. Quoted by Gilson, *Héloïse and Abelard*, 106–8. Here is Abelard's creed:
    I believe in the Father, the Son, and the Holy Ghost, God in one nature, the true God in whom the Trinity of Persons in no way affects the unity of substance. I believe that the Son is the equal of the Father in all things, in eternity, in power, in will, in operation. I do not hold with Arius who with a perverse spirit, or rather seduced by a diabolical spirit, introduces grades into the Trinity, maintaining that the Father is greater, the Son less great though forgetting the precept of faith: "Thou shalt not mount by degrees to my altar" (Exod. 20:26). For to place a before and after in the Trinity is to mount the altar of God by degrees. I attest that the Holy Ghost is equal and consubstantial in all things with the Father and the Son, for it is He whom I often call in my books by the name of Goodness. I condemn Sabellius who held that the Person of the Father is the same as that of the Son, and believed that the Father suffered the Passion, whence the name Patripassians. I believe also that the Son of

God became the Son of Man in such a way that the one only person *consists* and subsists in two natures; that the same Son of God satisfied all the exigencies of the human condition which He assumed, even death itself, and that He revived and ascended into Heaven whence He shall come to judge the living and the dead. I affirm, finally, that all sins are remitted by baptism; that we need grace to begin good and to accomplish it; and that those who have fallen are restored by penance. Need I speak of the resurrection of the flesh? I shall call myself a Christian in vain if I did not believe that I should one day rise again.

This is the faith in which I live and from which my hope derives its strength. In this refuge I do not fear the noise of Scylla; I laugh at the whirlpool of Charybdis; nor do I fear the mortal chant of the Sirens. Let the tempest come; it will not shake me! The winds may blow, but I shall not be moved. The rock of my foundation is sure.

34. Letter 241, to Cardinal Ivo, *Letters of St. Bernard*, 321.
35. Benton, "Peter Abelard," 19.
36. Abelard, "Letters," 5, *Patrologia Latina*, PL 178, col. 212 AC, quoted by Gilson, *Héloïse and Abelard*, 85.
37. Abelard, *Abelard's Adversities*, 35. After they had castrated him, Abelard writes, "They immediately fled but two of them were caught and had their eyes put out and were castrated."
38. Heloise, "Letters," 2, *Patrologia Latina*, PL 178, 186–87, in Gilson, *Héloïse and Abelard*, 92.
39. Evans, *St. Bernard*, 167.
40. Quoted by Gilson, *Héloïse and Abelard*, 85.
41. Küng, *Christianity*, 396.
42. Ibid., 398.
43. David Berger, quoted by Chazan, *In the Year 1096*, 142.
44. Synan, *The Popes and the Jews*, 74.
45. Küng, *Christianity*, 394. The "two-sword" theory of church-state power is usually said to have originated with Pope Gelasius I (493–496).
46. Bernard of Clairvaux, *Five Books on Consideration*, bk. 4, ch. 7, 118.

30. Thomas Aquinas: Reason Against the Jews

1. Gilbert, *Atlas of Jewish History*, 34.
2. I learned of this distinction from Weaver, "Rooted Hearts/Playful Minds," 67.
3. Küng, *Great Christian Thinkers*, 113.
4. For further discussion of this legacy, see Saperstein, *Moments of Crisis*, 24.
5. David Berger, "The Jewish-Christian Debate in the High Middle Ages," in Cohen, *Essential Papers*, 491.
6. Bernard, "Sermo," 60, *Patrologia Latina*, PL 183, 1068, cited by Synan, *The Popes and the Jews*, 77.
7. O'Meara, *Thomas Aquinas*, 22.
8. *Summa Contra Gentiles*, 1.2, quoted by Küng, *Great Christian Thinkers*, 112.
9. O'Meara, *Thomas Aquinas*, 3.
10. Küng, *Great Christian Thinkers*, 120.
11. Küng, *Christianity*, 416.

12. Cohen, *The Friars and the Jews*, 125.
13. Chazan, *Daggers of Faith*, 38.
14. Richards, *Sex, Dissidence, and Damnation*, 97.
15. For a criticism of Christian ignorance of a living Judaism, see Van Buren, *Theology of the Jewish-Christian Reality*, pt. 2.
16. Küng, *Christianity*, 407.
17. Richards, *Sex, Dissidence, and Damnation*, 95.
18. Quoted by M. Cohen, *Under Crescent and Cross*, 39. See also J. Cohen, *The Friars and the Jews*, 66; Synan, *The Popes and the Jews*, 108.
19. J. Cohen, *The Friars and the Jews*, 74.
20. Quoted by Synan, *The Popes and the Jews*, 112. See also J. Cohen, *The Friars and the Jews*, 67.
21. O'Meara, *Thomas Aquinas*, 29.
22. J. Cohen, *The Friars and the Jews*, 63. See also M. Cohen, *Under Crescent and Cross*, 39. The first known ordered destruction of Jewish "books," recorded in 1 Maccabees 1:56, dates to the second century B.C.E., when the Syrian king sought to stamp out Jewish religion. "Any books of the Law that came to light were torn up and burned. Whenever anyone was discovered possessing a copy of the covenant or practicing the Law, the king's decrees sentenced him to death." The Nazis targeted Jewish books almost as ruthlessly as they did Jews. Assessing the destruction of nearly five hundred mainly Jewish libraries in Nazi-controlled Europe, one historian concluded that five million or more Jewish books were destroyed. This does not include books in the households of the six million Jews who were murdered. Friedman, "Fate of the Jewish Book," 82.
23. Saperstein, *Moments of Crisis*, 22.
24. J. Cohen, *The Friars and the Jews*, 63.
25. Saperstein, *Moments of Crisis*, 22.
26. Quoted by Cohn, *This Immortal People*, 75.

31. One Road

1. *USA Today*, September 29, 1997.
2. *Newsweek*, October 6, 1997, 64.
3. Conversation with Thomas Stransky, C.S.P., November 1996. Father Stransky is the rector emeritus of the Tantur Ecumenical Institute in Jerusalem and a veteran of the Catholic-Jewish dialogue.
4. When a Jewish organization recognized the cardinal archbishop of Paris, Jean-Marie Lustiger (né Aron Lustiger), for contributing to Catholic-Jewish understanding, the American head of the Anti-Defamation League denounced honoring him "because he converted out." We referred to Lustiger earlier in connection with Elie Wiesel's uneasiness about "fulfilled Jew." Lustiger had become a Catholic as a boy hiding with a French family during World War II. His mother died in Auschwitz. Lustiger had offered crucial support to the Jewish position on the convent at Auschwitz, and he had led the French bishops to confess their silence during the Holocaust as a *faute*, a sin. Yet such are the wounds opened in Jews by conversion that he is still regarded by many simply as an apostate.
5. John 14:5–6.

6. Alessandra Stanley, "Uneasy Relations: The Cross and the Crescent," *New York Times,* March 19, 2000.

7. On January 2, 1997, the Sri Lankan theologian Tissa Balasuriya was excommunicated for heresy, an event to which we will return. His condemned views primarily concerned adaptations of Christian doctrine to an Asian context and his experience of dialogue with Asian religions. More than a year later, the excommunication was lifted. Another example was the French Jesuit Jacques Dupuis, who fell under suspicion of heresy because of his book *Toward a Christian Theology of Religious Pluralism.* In September 2000 the Vatican published its latest assault on religious pluralism, *Dominus Iesus.*

8. Boniface VIII, *Unam Sanctam,* in *Medieval Sourcebook,* www.fordham.edu/halsal/source/b8-unam.html.

9. *Contra Errores Graecorum,* 2.36, cited by Küng, *Christianity,* 427.

10. Boniface VIII, *Unam Sanctam.*

11. O'Meara, *Thomas Aquinas,* 21.

12. Küng, *Christianity,* 427.

13. In rejecting Feeney's interpretation of Boniface VIII's dictum, the Church had a problem: how *not* to repudiate the pope's teaching even while moving away from it. The Vatican accomplished this, as Richard McBrien explains, by "distinguishing between those who 'really' (in Latin, *in re*) belong to the Church by explicit faith and Baptism, and those who belong to the Church 'by desire' (*in voto*)." This latter group includes those who would join the Church if only they knew the truth of its claims. Richard P. McBrien, *HarperCollins Encyclopedia of Catholicism,* 522.

14. Bunson, *The Pope Encyclopedia,* 52.

15. Cohen, *The Friars and the Jews,* 255.

16. Perhaps "roundly denounced" overstates the matter. In "Memory and Reconciliation," the Vatican background statement to the papal act of repentance in March 2000, the Church, implicitly referring to the Inquisition, expressed sorrow for "the use of force in the service of the truth." But at the actual ceremony of repentance in St. Peter's Basilica, Cardinal Ratzinger, whose Congregation for the Doctrine of the Faith had replaced the Inquisition, confessed only to the use of "methods not in keeping with the Gospel in the solemn duty of defending the truth." In both cases, the nature of the "truth" defended by regrettable means seems not to have been examined.

32. My Inquisition

1. *Ad Tuendam Fidem,* in *National Catholic Reporter,* July 17, 1998.

2. "Doctrinal Commentary on the Concluding Formula of the *Professio Fidei,*" *National Catholic Reporter,* July 17, 1998.

3. *The Tablet,* September 19, 1998.

4. *New York Times,* February 7, 1998.

33. Convivencia *to* Reconquista

1. Thomas F. Glick, "An Introductory Note," in Mann et al., *Convivencia,* 1.

2. Barrucand and Bednorz, *Moorish Architecture,* 39.

3. Ibid., 63.

4. Roth, "Jews in Spain," 14.

5. Ibid., 2.

6. Glick, "An Introductory Note," in Mann et al., *Convivencia,* 6. There is one problem with the way *convivencia* is recalled as a golden age for Jews. It was surely that for certain classes of Jews, the intellectuals and courtiers as well as a prospering middle class made up of practitioners of trades and crafts. But for a large number of less well off Jews, the pressures of the age were anything but golden. In that, they were perhaps not unlike the forever downtrodden peasantry.

7. Gilbert, *Atlas of Jewish History,* 10.

8. Roth, "Jews in Spain," 16. Roth notes that the extremity with which the Almohad invasion is often rendered constitutes an example of the "lachrymose tradition" of Jewish history. He emphasizes, instead, that "careful analysis of actual sources concerning the Almohad period reveals that most of the communities which were supposedly 'destroyed' in Spain were hardly affected at all" (17).

9. Kamen, *Inquistion and Society in Spain,* 2.

10. Roth, "Jews in Spain," 10.

11. Ibid.

12. Kamen, *Inquisition and Society in Spain,* 1–2.

13. Burns, *Emperor of Culture,* 3.

14. Kamen, *Inquisition and Society in Spain,* 2.

15. "Toledo," *Encyclopedia Judaica,* vol. 15 (Jerusalem: Keter, 1972), 1199.

16. Omer, *Synagogue of Samuel Halevy,* 188, 183.

17. Riera Vidal, *Jews in Toledo and Their Synagogues,* 7.

18. Omer, *Synagogue of Samuel Halevy,* 183.

19. Fletcher, *Moorish Spain,* 162.

20. Burns, *Emperor of Culture,* 60.

21. Baer, *Jews in Christian Spain,* vol. 1, 120.

22. *Encyclopedia Judaica,* vol. 15, 1202.

23. Baer, *Jews in Christian Spain,* vol. 1, 130.

24. Bloom, *Kabbalah and Criticism,* 24. Bloom dates the *Zohar*'s composition to the years between 1280 and 1286 and accepts Moses de Leon as its author, although the work may be more accurately defined as a compilation of numerous diverse sources going back many years before Moses de Leon. See Silberman, *Heavenly Powers,* 90.

25. Gershom Scholem, *Kabbalah,* 213. Harold Bloom says the *Zohar* is sometimes called the "Bible of Kabbalah." Bloom, *Kabbalah and Criticism,* 24–25.

26. Dan, *Early Kabbalah,* 36.

27. Silberman, *Heavenly Powers,* 90.

28. Bloom, *Kabbalah and Criticism,* 24.

29. Silberman, *Heavenly Powers,* 91.

30. Ibid., 92.

31. Ibid., 98.

32. Ibid.

34. Convert-Making: The Failure of Success

1. Quoted by J. Cohen, *The Friars and the Jews,* 66.

2. Ibid., 97.

3. Ibid. When Cohen's book was published in 1982, some scholars faulted the extremity of some of its claims, perhaps including this one. Yet as a statement of the ultimate purpose of the conversionist movement, it rings true to me. For another view, see Chazen, *Daggers of Faith.*

4. Romans 11:8.

5. Thomas Aquinas, *Summa Theologiae* (3a.47.5), 69.

6. I am indebted here to an unpublished paper by Adam Gregerman, "The Barcelona Disputation and Late Medieval Europe: An Analysis of Political and Social Change."

7. Cited by J. Cohen, *The Friars and the Jews,* 111.

8. Chazan, *Daggers of Faith,* 89–90.

9. Ibid., 100.

10. Quoted by Gregerman, "Barcelona Disputation," 7.

11. Ibid., 25.

12. J. Cohen, *The Friars and the Jews,* 109. The decrees also "demanded that blasphemous passages be expurgated from Jewish books" and "established a censorship commission to achieve that purpose."

13. Quoted by Synan, *The Popes and the Jews,* 117.

14. Quoted by Silberman, *Heavenly Powers,* 95.

15. Quoted by Synan, *The Popes and the Jews,* 119.

16. Chazan, *Daggers of Faith,* 181.

17. J. Cohen, *The Friars and the Jews,* 245.

18. Quoted by J. Cohen, *The Friars and the Jews,* 239.

19. Ibid.

20. Quoted by Poliakov, *History of Anti-Semitism,* 107–8.

21. Marcus, *The Jew in the Medieval World,* 43.

22. Harpur, *Revelations,* 60.

23. Bunson, *The Pope Encyclopedia,* 86.

24. Cited by Tuchman, *Distant Mirror,* 105. This order of dissection by a fourteenth-century pope, involving the mutilation of corpses, regarded by the Church as sacred ("temples of the Holy Ghost"), was at least as radical as it would be today for a pope, concerned about world population or the spread of AIDS, to lift the Catholic ban on "artificial contraception."

25. Marcus, *The Jew in the Medieval World,* 43.

26. Synan, *The Popes and the Jews,* 134.

27. Tuchman, *Distant Mirror,* 116. Tuchman cites reports of the number of Jewish deaths in Mainz on one day, August 24, 1349, as six thousand.

28. Poliakov, *History of Anti-Semitism,* 110.

29. Cited by Marcus, *The Jew in the Medieval World,* 46.

30. Quoted by Synan, *The Popes and the Jews,* 133. See also Tuchman, *Distant Mirror,* 112–16.

31. Synan, *The Popes and the Jews,* 134.

32. Poliakov, *History of Anti-Semitism,* 111.

33. Quoted by Marcus, *The Jew in the Medieval World,* 47.

34. Ruether, *Faith and Fratricide,* 206.

35. Ullmann, "The Mystery of 1492," 331.

36. Kamen, *Inquisition and Society in Spain*, 8. See also Benjamin R. Gampel, "Jews, Christians, and Muslims in Medieval Iberia: *Convivencia* Through the Eyes of Sephardic Jews," in Mann et al., *Convivencia*, 28.

37. Gampel, "Jews, Christians, and Muslims in Medieval Iberia," 28.

38. Baer, *Jews in Christian Spain*, vol. 2, 145.

39. Gampel, "Jews, Christians, and Muslims in Medieval Iberia," 29.

35. Expulsion in 1492

1. 2 Maccabees 7, translation from *The Jerusalem Bible* (Garden City, N.Y.: Doubleday, 1966).

2. Cited by M. Cohen, *Under Crescent and Cross*, 174.

3. Ibid. Cohen's exploration of the responses of Jews and Christians to persecution is especially informative (see ch. 10, "Persecution and Collective Memory").

4. Maimonides, *Letters of Maimonides*, 64.

5. Ibid.

6. Ibid., 65.

7. Ibid., 64.

8. MacKay, "Popular Movements and Pogroms," 52.

9. Stow, *Jews in Rome*, xi.

10. Quoted by Synan, *The Popes and the Jews*, 136.

11. Quoted by Kamen, *Inquisition and Society in Spain*, 25.

12. Bunson, *The Pope Encyclopedia*, 247.

13. Quoted by Saperstein, *Moments of Crisis*, 28.

14. *Cantate Domino*, in Tanner, *Decrees of the Ecumenical Councils*, 578.

15. Nicolaus of Cusa, *Toward a New Council of Florence*, 273.

16. I depend here on notes I took while listening to David Tracy lecture on Nicolaus of Cusa at the Harvard Divinity School, fall 1997.

17. Pelikan, *Christian Tradition*, vol. 4, 68.

18. *The American Heritage Dictionary of the English Language* (Boston: Houghton Mifflin, 1992), 86.

19. Nicolaus of Cusa, *Toward a New Council of Florence*, 231.

20. Ibid., 232–33.

21. Ibid., 266–67.

22. Baron, *History of the Jews*, vol. 13, 174. See also Flannery, *The Anguish of the Jews*, 124; Roth, *History of the Jews of Italy*, 206.

23. Gershom Scholem, "The Beginnings of the Christian Kabbalah," in Dan, *The Christian Kabbalah*, 17.

24. Quoted by Baron, *History of the Jews*, vol. 13, 175.

25. Paul J. W. Miller, in Pico Della Mirandola, *On the Dignity of Man*, xxx.

26. See Klaus Reichert, "Christian Kabbalah in the Seventeenth Century," in Dan, *The Christian Kabbalah*.

27. Synan, *The Popes and the Jews*, 146.

28. Benjamin R. Gampel, "Jews, Christians, and Muslims in Medieval Iberia," in Mann et al., *Convivencia*, 31.

29. Synan, *The Popes and the Jews*, 138.

30. Kamen, *Inquisition and Society in Spain*, 29.

31. Gampel, "Jews, Christians, and Muslims in Medieval Iberia," 31–32.

32. MacKay, "Popular Movements and Pogroms," 64.

33. Kamen, *Inquisition and Society in Spain,* 161.

34. Ibid., 175.

35. Ibid., 176.

36. J. Cohen, *The Friars and the Jews,* 50.

37. Kamen, *Inquisition and Society in Spain,* 188.

38. Ibid., 41.

39. Quoted by Kamen, *Inquisition and Society in Spain,* 191.

40. Bloom, *Kabbalah and Criticism,* 47.

41. Brenan, *St. John of the Cross,* 23.

42. Saint Teresa described a vision in which she was pierced by an angel's flaming golden arrow: "The pain was so great that I screamed aloud; but at the same time I felt such infinite sweetness that I wished the pain to last forever. It was not physical but psychic pain, although it affected the body as well to some degree. It was the sweetest caressing of the soul by God." Quoted by Janson, *History of Art,* 513.

43. Brenan, *St. John of the Cross,* 91–94.

44. Ibid., 95.

45. Judith Hershcopf Banki, "Some Reflections on Edith Stein," in Cargas, *The Unnecessary Problem of Edith Stein,* 46.

46. Gampel, "Jews, Christians, and Muslims in Medieval Iberia," 32.

47. Ibid., 32. See also Kamen, *Inquisition and Society in Spain,* 15. Franco's name is ironic, given that the cloud of fearful ignorance that fell on Spain in this period did not lift until the death of another Franco, nearly five hundred years later.

48. Harpur, *Revelations,* 22–23.

49. At a meeting with Jewish and Catholic scholars in Chicago in 1999, I heard Cardinal Edward Cassidy, head of the Vatican's Congregation for Religious Relations with the Jews, describe how his intervention had prevented the Congregation for the Causes of the Saints from proceeding with the canonization of Isabella. Cassidy said that his appeal was based on the damage such an act would do to Jewish-Catholic relations. The context of this discussion was the "cause" of the canonization of Pius XII, about which Cardinal Cassidy was noncommittal.

50. Gilbert, *Atlas of Jewish History,* 46–47.

51. Quoted by Cohn-Sherbok, *Crucified Jew,* 88.

52. Kamen, *Inquisition and Society in Spain,* 135.

53. Gampel, "Jews, Christians, and Muslims in Medieval Iberia," 32.

54. Kamen, *Inquisition and Society in Spain,* 17.

55. Baer, *Jews in Christian Spain,* vol. 2, 438.

56. Bernaldez, "Chron. de los Reyes Cathol. Colmentares, Hist. de Segovia," in Ackerman, *Out of Our People's Past,* 6.

57. Kamen, *Inquisition and Society in Spain,* 16.

58. Gilbert, *Atlas of Jewish History,* 46.

59. Ibid.

36. The Roman Ghetto

1. *National Catholic Reporter,* September 18, 1998.

2. Bunson, *The Pope Encyclopedia*, 13–15.

3. Renata Segre, "Sephardic Settlements in Sixteenth-Century Italy: A Historical and Geographical Survey," in Ginio, *Jews, Christians, and Muslims,* 117.

4. Roth, *History of the Jews of Italy,* 179.

5. Quoted by Roth, *History of the Jews of Italy,* 179.

6. Ibid.

7. Stow, *Catholic Thought,* xxxvii.

8. Ibid., xxxii.

9. Quoted by Synan, *The Popes and the Jews,* 146.

10. Stow, *Catholic Thought,* xix f.

11. Goldhagen, *Hitler's Willing Executioners,* 79.

12. Baron, *History of the Jews,* vol. 13, 217.

13. Goldhagen, *Hitler's Willing Executioners,* 55.

14. Quoted by Baron, *History of the Jews,* vol. 13, 217.

15. Ibid., 218.

16. Quoted by Marius, *Martin Luther,* 378.

17. Saperstein, *Moments of Crisis,* 29.

18. Quoted by Alice L. Eckardt, "The Reformation and the Jews," in Fisher, *Interwoven Destinies,* 112.

19. Baron, *History of the Jews,* vol. 13, 269.

20. Ibid., 222.

21. Oberman, *Roots of Anti-Semitism,* 46.

22. Quoted by Baron, *History of the Jews,* vol. 13, 227. In 1994, the Evangelical Lutheran Church in America issued a declaration to the Jewish community acknowledging and repenting "Luther's anti-Judaic diatribes and the violent recommendations of his later writings against the Jews." See http:// jcrelations.com/stmnts/elca.htm.

23. "John Calvin and his colleagues developed a branch of Christianity that had a deep appreciation of Hebrew scripture and biblical law/'Teaching' (heretofore only regarded as 'Jewish legalism,' a 'dead letter,' or an instrument of condemnation). This positive attitude toward Torah and toward Israel would develop in the latter part of the sixteenth century among Dutch and English millenarians and English puritans into a genuine interest in Jews as persons (though still with conversion as a goal)." Eckardt, "The Reformation and the Jews," 127.

24. Quoted by Baron, *History of the Jews,* vol. 13, 277.

25. Ibid., 278–79.

26. Kamen, *Inquisition and Society in Spain,* 22.

27. Quoted by Kamen, *Inquisition and Society in Spain,* 120.

28. Bunson, *The Pope Encyclopedia,* 6–7.

29. See R. Emmet McLaughlin, "Trent, Council of," *HarperCollins Encyclopedia of Catholicism,* 1267.

30. Quoted by Baron, *History of the Jews,* vol. 14, 24.

31. Bunson, *The Pope Encyclopedia,* 262.

32. Baron, *History of the Jews,* vol. 14, 27.

33. Quoted by Bunson, *The Pope Encyclopedia,* 264.

34. Baron, *History of the Jews,* vol. 14, 29. See also Flannery, *The Anguish of the Jews,* 155. Flannery says that, as Pope Paul IV, Caraffa allowed sixty converted Jews to be burned.

35. Francisco de Torres, *De Sola Lectione,* quoted by Kenneth R. Stow, "The Burning of

the Talmud in 1553, in Light of Sixteenth-Century Catholic Attitudes toward the Talmud," in Cohen, *Essential Papers,* 405.

36. Frances Yates explains: "The intense religious feeling which had inspired Pico to welcome Magia and Cabala as aids to religious insight persists very strongly in Bruno, who pursues his philosophical religion, or his religious philosophy, or his philosophical-religious magic, with the deepest earnestness and believes that it can become the instrument of a universal religious reform . . . He thus retains the word 'cabala' to describe his position." Yates, *Giordano Bruno,* 262.

37. Bruno, *The Expulsion of the Triumphant Beast,* 4.

38. "There was in me," he wrote, in what his translator, Arthur Imerti, called a kind of epitaph, "whatever I was able to do, which no future century will deny to be mine, that which a victor could have for his own: Not to have feared to die, not to have yielded to any equal in firmness of nature, and to have preferred a courageous death to a noncombatant life." Ibid., 64.

39. Alessandra Stanley, "Italian Atheists Rally Round Philosopher Burned at Stake," *International Herald Tribune,* February 19–20, 2000.

40. Kamen, *Inquisition and Society in Spain,* 118.

41. Ibid., 120.

42. *Cum Nimis Absurdum,* quoted by Vogelstein, *Rome,* 267.

43. Hay, *Roots of Christian Anti-Semitism,* 164.

44. Quoted by Eugene J. Fisher in *National Catholic Register,* October 27, 1998. I heard Cardinal Cassidy repeat this statement, that the "Church-ordered ghetto was the antechamber to the Nazi death camps," at the Jewish-Catholic meeting on March 30, 1999, in Chicago.

45. Rudavsky, *Emancipation and Adjustment,* 28.

46. Vogelstein, *Rome,* 269.

47. Isaiah 65:2.

48. Stow, "The Burning of the Talmud," 406.

49. Stow, *Catholic Thought,* 10.

50. Oberman, *Roots of Anti-Semitism,* 14.

51. Stow, *Catholic Thought,* 267.

52. Letter to Bernardino Ochino, cited in Stow, *Catholic Thought,* 270.

53. Romans 11:15, in *The Jerusalem Bible.*

54. Stow, *Catholic Thought,* 277.

55. Vogelstein, *Rome,* 276–77.

56. Stow, *Catholic Thought,* xviii.

57. Ellen Knickmeyer, "John Paul Beatifies Scorned, Beloved Popes," *Boston Globe,* September 4, 2000. In ceremonies in St. Peter's Square, John Paul II said of the beatification of Pius IX, "Beatifying a son of the Church does not celebrate particular historic choices that he has made, but rather points him out for imitation and for veneration for his virtue."

58. Quoted by Baron, *History of the Jews,* vol. 14, 68–69.

59. Saperstein, *Moments of Crisis,* 27. Eugene Fisher, a consistent advocate of the Church, while defending the New Testament from charges of antisemitism, clearly identifies the *limpieza* as the origin of racial antisemitism: "Racial antisemitism, as we know it today, does not seem to have made an appearance until the infamous 'purity of blood' laws of Spain in the fifteenth and sixteenth centuries." Fisher, *Seminary Education,* 37.

60. "We Remember: A Reflection on the Shoah," 3.4, 5.
61. Ruether, *Faith and Fratricide*, 203.
62. Padberg et al., *First Thirty Jesuit Congregations*, 204.
63. Ibid., 232.
64. Ibid., 534.
65. Ibid., 625. The sentence continues: ". . . or his lack of Catholic education." For a discussion of the Jesuit blood purity regulations, see Arendt, *Origins of Totalitarianism*, 102.
66. Bunson, *The Pope Encyclopedia*, 352–53. For a dramatic rendition of the Galileo tragedy, see Goodwin, *Hinge of the World*.
67. Carroll, "The Silence," 58.
68. Vogelstein, *Rome*, 294–95. For more on the Catholic taking of children from Jews, see Kertzer, *Kidnapping of Edgardo Mortara*.

37. The Religious Response of the Jews

1. Stow, *Jews in Rome*, lvi.
2. Kenneth R. Stow, "Sanctity and the Construction of Space: The Roman Ghetto as Sacred Space," in Mor, *Jewish Assimilation*, 54.
3. Ibid., 64. On the use of coffee, Stow comments, "First, one stimulated his body with this miraculous new beverage, and then he stimulated his soul by ritual devotion."
4. Ibid., 65.
5. Scholem, *Kabbalah*, 74.
6. For a general introduction to Luria, see Armstrong, *History of God*, 266–71.
7. Silberman, *Heavenly Powers*, 137, 140.
8. Ibid., 169.
9. Bloom, *Kabbalah and Criticism*, 41.
10. Silberman, *Heavenly Powers*, 173.
11. Bloom, *Kabbalah and Criticism*, 42–43.
12. Armstrong, *History of God*, 270.
13. Ibid., 272.
14. Ibid., 271.
15. Silberman, *Heavenly Powers*, 128.
16. Ibid., 211–12. Hasidism is a unique religious phenomenon, but it bears comparison to other seventeenth- and eighteenth-century movements, like Pietism in Germany, Jansenism in Ireland, Methodism in England, and the Great Awakening in the United States. All of these were reassertions of orthodoxy, as I heard Krister Stendahl put it once, "but with heat."
17. Leon Wieseltier, *New Republic*, March 2, 1998, 5.
18. Ruether, *Faith and Fratricide*, 203.
19. Arendt, *Origins of Totalitarianism*, 10.

38. Shema Yisrael!

1. Deuteronomy 6:4, In the traditional translation, offered by Elie Wiesel. Wiesel described his first return to Birkenau this way: "Time is suspended. We remain silent, each with his or her own thoughts. And then, softly at first, then louder and louder, I recite the prayer of the Jewish martyrs; the others join in. '*Shema Israel . . .*' Hear, O Is-

rael, the Lord is our God, the Lord is One. Once, five times . . . Why? Because back then, the victims, knowing the end was near, had recited that prayer. We needed to show our solidarity with those we loved and still love. And then because, on the threshold of death, all words become prayers, and all prayers become one." Wiesel, *Sea Is Never Full,* 193.

2. Deuteronomy 11:22.
3. Quoted by Carroll, "The Silence," 67.
4. Edward H. Flannery, preface to Hay, *Roots of Christian Anti-Semitism,* xxii.
5. John Paul II, General Audience Discourse, September 1, 1999, in *L'Osservatore Romano,* English edition, September 8, 1999, cited in "Memory and Reconciliation," 4.2.
6. A. J. Heschel, *Moral Grandeur,* 8–10.
7. George Steiner, the Tillich Lecture, Harvard University, April 8, 1999. I rely on notes I took at the lecture.
8. See Dewart, *Future of Belief.*
9. Denby, *Great Books,* 182–3.
10. In his homily at Auschwitz, June 7, 1979, John Paul II said, "I have come and I kneel on this Golgotha of the modern world, on these tombs." See John Paul II, *Spiritual Pilgrimage,* 7.
11. Psalm 104:29.
12. Allison P. Coudert, "Leibnitz, Locke, Newton, and the Kabbalah," in Dan, *The Christian Kabbalah,* 163.

39. Karl Marx, Second Son of Trier

1. Psalm 22:18.
2. Blumenberg, *Portrait of Marx,* 5.
3. Ibid., 7–8.
4. Lamentations 1:1–2.
5. For a discussion of the meaning of the Shema, see A. J. Heschel, *Man Is Not Alone,* 114–16.
6. For a discussion of the marginalization of the Jew, see Sachar, *Modern Jewish History,* 3–16.
7. Karl Marx, "The Eighteenth Brumaire of Louis Bonaparte," in *The Marx-Engels Reader,* 595.

40. Spinoza: From Rabbis to Revolution

1. Spinoza, Marx, and, eventually, Sigmund Freud would be lumped together as the Jews who did most to create modern consciousness, yet their relationships both to Judaism and to antisemitism would be inadequately understood. "The bulk of the Jewish community, and certainly the representatives of the Jewish religion, opposed all three of these heretics, but these names continue to be cited as a kind of litany of great 'Jewish contributions to Western culture' by people who do not know much about either Judaism or Jewish history — but there is nonetheless some truth in the proposition that these thinkers arose in part out of the Jewish situation in the pre-modern world. All three were reacting to the persistence of Jew-hatred, and each was trying to find a cure

to this disease of Western culture." Arthur Hertzberg, "The Enlightenment and Western Religion," in Fisher, *Interwoven Destinies*, 138.

2. Gullan-Whur, *Life of Spinoza*, 5.

3. Ibid., 7.

4. O'Malley, *Trent and All That*, 40. Some see the Counter-Reformation as having lasted
until the French Revolution (52), or even until Vatican II (50).

5. Ibid., 52–53.

6. Scruton, *Spinoza*, 4.

7. Nadler, *Spinoza*, 6.

8. Ibid., 114.

9. Scruton, *Spinoza*, 50–53.

10. His dictum is, "It is the nature of reason to perceive things under a certain aspect of
eternity (*sub quadam aeternitatis specie*)." Quoted by Scruton, *Spinoza*, 70.

11. Quoted by Nadler, *Spinoza*, 280.

12. Ibid., 341.

13. Quoted by Gullan-Whur, *Life of Spinoza*, 91.

14. Ibid., 70.

15. In 1706, the German lexicographer Johann Georg Wachter wrote a treatise comparing
Spinoza's philosophical framework to the ideational system of Kabbalah, a work to
which Leibniz had reference. See Dan, *The Christian Kabbalah*, 224.

16. Quoted by Gullan-Whur, *Life of Spinoza*, 71.

17. Ibid., 305.

18. Scruton, *Spinoza*, 52. Scruton associates the phrase with Goethe.

19. Quoted by Gullan-Whur, *Life of Spinoza*, 304–5.

20. It was Goethe, finally, who honored "as the first of Spinoza's achievements," in
Scruton's words, "the attack on superstition in the name of God." Scruton, *Spinoza*,
112.

21. Quoted by Scruton, *Spinoza*, 12.

22. Quoted by Gullan-Whur, *Life of Spinoza*, 306–7.

41. Voltaire and the False Promise of Emancipation

1. The full paragraph reads, "Men are born and remain free and equal in rights. Social
distinctions can be based only on public utility." See "Declaration of the Rights of
Man and Citizen," in Ravitch and Thernstrom, *Democracy Reader*, 55.

2. For a discussion of the Enlightenment idea of virtue, see MacIntyre, *After Virtue*,
49–59.

3. Count Clermont-Tonnerre, quoted by Rudavsky, *Emancipation and Adjustment*, 81.
Clermont-Tonnerre added that Jews who refused to surrender the things that kept
them apart should be shipped off to Palestine. Hertzberg, "The Enlightenment and
Western Religion," in Fisher, *Interwoven Destinies*, 139.

4. Quoted in Michael Burns, *Dreyfus*, 11.

5. See A. J. Heschel, *Man Is Not Alone*, 229–51.

6. Vogelstein, *Rome*, 332.

7. Ibid., 332, 349.

8. Ibid., 349.

9. Kenneth R. Stow, "Sanctity and the Construction of Space: The Roman Ghetto as Sacred Space," in Mor, *Jewish Assimilation,* 71.

10. Quoted by Padover, "Baptism of Karl Marx's Family," 37.

11. Ibid. See also Stepelevich, "Marx and the Jews," 152.

12. Berlin, *Karl Marx,* 19. Other scholars, like Padover, give the name as Herschel.

13. "Jewish Quarter," *Encyclopedia Judaica,* vol. 10 (Jerusalem: Keter, 1972), 84.

14. Vogelstein, *Rome,* 342.

15. Stepelevich, "Marx and the Jews," 151.

16. Padover, "Baptism of Karl Marx's Family," 39. Herschel Marx may not have hesitated to be baptized in the face of new Prussian restrictions, but he did protest their injustice. Padover comments, "Herschel Marx, unlike his son Karl, was not ashamed of his Jewish origins. The record, indeed, shows the contrary" (37). His ambition trumped his attachment to those origins, however.

17. Ibid., 37.

18. Stepelevich, "Marx and the Jews," 153.

19. Marx, "The Eighteenth Brumaire of Louis Bonaparte," in *The Marx-Engels Reader,* 595.

20. Berlin, *Karl Marx,* 21.

21. Ibid., 22.

22. Marx and Engels, *The Marx-Engels Reader,* 500.

23. McKay et al., *History of Western Society,* 699.

24. Quoted by McKay et al., *History of Western Society,* 603.

25. Hertzberg, *The French Enlightenment and the Jews,* 280. "Voltaire complained of the Inquisition all his life," Hertzberg writes. "He denounced the persecutions of the Jews many times as evidence of the unworthiness of the Church." Of course, Voltaire also said that Jews brought their sufferings on themselves.

26. Quoted in McKay et al., *History of Western Society,* 620. Echoing Voltaire, and returning us to the cross, is Diderot, who, in an article on the Crusades, described a "horde of priests, peasants and school children . . . [that] fell particularly on the Jews. They massacred them whenever they could find them; these brutish and impious people believed that they could properly avenge the death of Jesus by slitting the throats of the little children of those who had crucified him." Quoted by Hertzberg, *The French Enlightenment and the Jews,* 281.

27. Quoted by McKay et al., *History of Western Society,* 621.

28. Hertzberg, *The French Enlightenment and the Jews,* 305.

29. Quoted by Hertzberg, *The French Enlightenment and the Jews,* 305.

30. Ibid., 300.

31. Ibid.

32. Ibid., 313.

33. Hay, *Roots of Christian Anti-Semitism,* iv.

34. See "We Remember: A Reflection on the Shoah," 4.3: "The Shoah was the work of a thoroughly modern neopagan regime. Its antisemitism had its roots outside of Christianity."

35. Arendt, *Origins of Totalitarianism,* 8.

36. This Aristotelian structure of narrative is sometimes criticized as being culturally conditioned, but there are reasons to suggest that it derives from something basic to hu-

man experience. The chemist John C. Polanyi, for example, says, "*Scientia* is knowledge. It is only in the popular mind that it is equated with facts. That is flattering, since facts are incontrovertible. But it is also demeaning, since facts are meaningless; they contain no narrative. Science, by contrast, is storytelling. That is evident in the functioning of our primary instrument, the eye. The eye searches for shapes. It searches for a beginning, a middle, and an end. We sense this from personal experience. But we know it also from experiments in which light beams are reflected from the human eye. The eye, viewing a person's profile, does not scan it in a mechanical fashion: it pays attention to those features it judges significant. It does not simply point, as does a camera; it paints. Since painting is a skill, so too is seeing." Polanyi, "The Responsibility of the Scientist," 39.

37. E. M. Forster, quoted by Burroway, *Writing Fiction*, 14.

42. Jew as Revolutionary, Jew as Financier

1. Padover, "Baptism of Karl Marx's Family," 36.
2. Ibid., 40.
3. W. H. Auden, "September 1, 1939," in *Immortal Poems of the English Language: British and American Poetry from Chaucer's Time to the Present Day*, ed. Oscar Williams (New York: Washington Square Press, 1961), 584.
4. Marius, *Martin Luther*, 482.
5. The face remained central in the Eastern Church, but in the first millennium, "Christ's head was a continent-wide symbol of Christianity." Man, *Atlas of the Year 1000*, 37.
6. Alice L. Eckardt, "The Reformation and the Jews," in Fisher, *Interwoven Destinies*, 118.
7. Marius, *Martin Luther*, 377–78.
8. Ibid., 482–83.
9. Ibid., 380.
10. Ibid., 486.
11. Quoted by Goldhagen, *Hitler's Willing Executioners*, 111.
12. Quoted by Stepelevich, "Marx and the Jews," 152.
13. Ibid., 154.
14. Karl Marx, "On the Jewish Question," in *The Marx-Engels Reader*, 50.
15. Ibid., 48.
16. References to Marx's thought here are drawn from the article on Marx and Marxism in *Encyclopaedia Britannica*, 15th ed., vol. 23, 531–43.
17. Quoted by Avishai, *Tragedy of Zionism*, 35.
18. Padover, "Baptism of Karl Marx's Family," 43.
19. Marx, "On the Jewish Question," in *The Marx-Engels Reader*, 51.
20. See Sachar, *Modern Jewish History*, 21, 29. Sachar cites writers, like Werner Sombart and Baron d'Holbach, who promoted such views. Sombart's *The Jews and Modern Capitalism* (1911) saw in Judaism "the close relationship between religion and business, the arithmetical concept of sin, and above all the rationalization of life."
21. Magnus, *Jewish Emancipation*, 125.
22. See ibid., especially ch. 5, "The Business of Equality: Rhenish Liberals, Jewish Bankers, and Jewish Rights in Cologne, 1835–50." Magnus illustrates the interlocking network of these families with a joke that the Oppenheims told "about the signatures the re-

spective bank heads left on hotel register manifests when they traveled: 'R. de Frankfurt,' 'O. de Cologne'" (111).

23. Sachar, *Modern Jewish History*, 128–29.

24. Stepelevich, *Marx and the Jews*, 157.

25. Sachar, *Modern Jewish History*, 335.

26. Ibid., 336–37.

27. "Anti-Semites in the Duma," *Boston Globe*, December 21, 1998.

28. Quoted by Berlin, *Karl Marx*, 186.

29. *A Contribution to the Critique of Political Economy* (1859).

30. Marx, "The Civil War in France," in *The Marx-Engels Reader*, 652.

31. Berlin, *Karl Marx*, 187.

32. The Catholic Church's rejection of revolution as such would be given its clearest expression by Pope Leo XIII: "And if at any time it happens that the power of the state is
rashly and tyrannically wielded by Princes, the teaching of the Catholic Church does
not allow an insurrection on private authority against them, lest public order be only
the more disturbed, and lest society take greater hurt therefrom. And when affairs
come to such a pass that there is no other hope of safety, she teaches that relief may be
hastened by the merits of Christian patience and by earnest prayers to God." Encyclical *Quod Apostolici Muneris* (1878), quoted by Lewy, *The Catholic Church and Nazi
Germany*, 333.

33. Archbishop Konrad Gröber's "Handbook" for Catholics, widely circulated in Germany in the 1930s, defined Marxism as "the materialistic socialism founded primarily
by the Jew Karl Marx." Bolshevism was "an Asiatic state despotism . . . in the service of
a group of terrorists led by Jews." Ibid., 277.

34. *National Catholic Reporter*, December 11, 1998. Father Gumpel was cited earlier in this
book for resuscitating the old charge that "the Jews" killed Christ, a statement he
made the week after John Paul II's historic act of repentance in March 2000.

35. Küng, *Judaism*, 256. A condemnation of Communism was issued by the Holy Office,
successor to the Inquisition, on July 1, 1949. See "Pius XII, Pope," *New Catholic Encyclopedia*, vol. 11, 418.

36. Charles Coughlin, quoted by Brinkley, *Voices of Protest*, 266, 270–71.

37. Ibid., 266.

43. Revolution in Rome: The Pope's Jews

1. Quoted by John T. Ford, "Infallibility," *HarperCollins Encyclopedia of Catholicism*,
664.

2. Küng, *Infallible?*, 77.

3. Burns, *Dreyfus*, 50.

4. *Pastor Aeternus*, in Henry Edward, Archbishop of Westminster, *The Vatican Decrees in
Their Bearing on Civil Allegiance* (New York: Harper and Brothers, 1875), 154–55. See
also Küng, *Infallible?*, 77.

5. Hans Kühner, *Encyclopedia of the Papacy*, 229.

6. Ford, "Infallibility," 664.

7. Quoted by Hill, "'I Am the Tradition,'" 9.

8. *Pastor Aeternus*, in Edward, *Vatican Decrees*, 167.

9. Ibid., 159–60.
10. Gregory XVI, quoted in *National Catholic Reporter,* December 11, 1998.
11. Wolfe, "Liberalism and Catholicism," 16.
12. Vogelstein, *Rome,* 340.
13. Hill, "'I Am the Tradition,'" 9.
14. Vogelstein, *Rome,* 341.
15. Hill, "'I Am the Tradition,'" 9.
16. Quoted by Marvin R. O'Connell, "Oath Against Modernism," *HarperCollins Encyclopedia of Catholicism,* 926.
17. "de Maistre, Joseph," *HarperCollins Encyclopedia of Catholicism,* 406.
18. Quoted by Küng, *Infallible?,* 104–5.
19. Ibid.
20. Ibid., 106.
21. For a discussion of Honorius and other problems with papal infallibility, see Wills, *Papal Sin,* 270–72.
22. Hill, "'I Am the Tradition,'" 9.
23. Wolfe, "Liberalism and Catholicism," 20.
24. Bunson, *The Pope Encyclopedia,* 285.
25. Hill, "'I Am the Tradition,'" 9.
26. Bunson, *The Pope Encyclopedia,* 229, 271.
27. Kornberg, "Döllinger's *Die Juden,*" 235–36.
28. J. Cohen, *Essential Papers,* 232.
29. Vogelstein, *Rome,* 359.
30. See Kertzer, *Kidnapping of Edgardo Mortara.*
31. Rudavsky, *Emancipation and Adjustment,* 303. Marr "was said to be of Jewish extraction" himself.
32. Kornberg, "Döllinger's *Die Juden,*" 244.
33. Vogelstein, *Rome,* 345–47.
34. Ibid., 358.

44. Alfred Dreyfus and La Croix

1. Burns, *Dreyfus,* 3–4. I acknowledge my debt to Michael Burns's work for my understanding of Dreyfus's background and upbringing and the broad significance of his family story.
2. Ibid., 31–35.
3. Ibid., 51.
4. Quoted by Burns, *Dreyfus,* 86.
5. Ibid.
6. Hertzberg, *The French Enlightenment and the Jews,* 138.
7. Rudavsky, *Emancipation and Adjustment,* 276.
8. Burns, *Dreyfus,* 90.
9. Hoffman, *More Than a Trial,* 69.
10. Quoted by Burns, *Dreyfus,* 96.
11. See, for example, Hoffman, *More Than a Trial,* 17–35. Entries in both the *New Catholic Encyclopedia* (vol. 4, 1061) and the *Encyclopedia Judaica* (vol. 6, 224) begin by defining

Dreyfus as a figure in a famous treason case. However, the Catholic entry concludes with a paragraph beginning, "The Catholic Church was the first to suffer the consequences," while the Jewish conclusion was that the case proved "that hatred of the Jews" had survived.

12. Quoted by Burns, *Dreyfus*, 123.

13. Émile Zola, quoted in "Quand Zola S'Engageait pour le Capitaine Dreyfus," *La Croix,* January 12, 1998, 12.

14. Émile Zola, "I Accuse," quoted by Francq and Pankiw, *Dreyfus Affair*, 147.

15. See *La Croix,* January 11–12, 1998.

16. "Herzl, Theodor," *Encyclopedia Judaica,* vol. 8, 408.

17. Burns, *Dreyfus*, 436.

18. *New York Times,* February 9, 1994.

19. Burns, *Dreyfus*, 254.

20. See Wilson, *Ideology and Experience,* 514–15.

21. Bloy, *Pilgrim of the Absolute,* 247.

22. Wilson, *Ideology and Experience,* 541.

23. Quoted by Burns, *Dreyfus*, 237.

24. Wilson, *Ideology and Experience,* 522.

25. Quoted by Lewy, *The Catholic Church and Nazi Germany,* 327–28.

26. Wolfe, "Liberalism and Catholicism," 17.

27. Wilson, *Ideology and Experience,* 522.

28. Quoted by Wilson, *Ideology and Experience,* 522.

29. Bloy, *Pilgrim of the Absolute,* 247.

30. Wilson, *Ideology and Experience,* 520.

31. Abbé Brugerette, quoted by Wilson, *Ideology and Experience,* 520.

32. Quoted by Wilson, *Ideology and Experience,* 520.

33. Quoted by Hoffman, *More Than a Trial,* 68–69.

34. Burns, *Dreyfus*, 91–92.

35. Quoted by Burns, *Dreyfus*, 92–93.

36. Wilson, *Ideology and Experience,* 522.

37. *La Croix,* January 18, 1898. I gratefully acknowledge the research assistance of Christine Lehmann, who helped me obtain copies of original editions of the newspaper, and the translation assistance of Priscilla C. Deck.

38. Hoffman, *More Than a Trial,* 217.

39. *La Croix,* January 19, 1898.

40. *La Croix,* January 28, 1898.

41. Quoted by Wilson, *Ideology and Experience,* 555.

42. Ibid., 542.

43. Ibid., 533.

44. Ibid., 554.

45. Arendt, *Origins of Totalitarianism,* 116.

46. Wilson, *Ideology and Experience,* 519.

47. Hoffman, *More Than a Trial,* 82.

48. Quoted by Wilson, *Ideology and Experience,* 528.

49. Ibid., 531.

50. Burns, *Dreyfus*, 134, 245.

51. Quoted by Burns, *Dreyfus*, 152.
52. Quoted by Wilson, *Ideology and Experience*, 531.
53. Michael Marrus and Robert Paxton say that *La Croix* and "its affiliated publications reached half a million readers during the time of the Dreyfus Affair." *Vichy France and the Jews*, 30.
54. Wilson, *Ideology and Experience*, 559–60.
55. Ibid., 560.
56. Marrus and Paxton say of *La Croix*, "That venomous journal could step back from the brink, and seemed to be moderating at the end" of the affair. *Vichy France and the Jews*, 31.
57. Quoted by Wilson, *Ideology and Experience*, 523.
58. Hoffman, *More Than a Trial*, 195.
59. *La Croix*, January 12, 1998.

45. The Uses of Antisemitism

1. Arendt, *Origins of Totalitarianism*, 10, 93.
2. Ibid., 93.
3. See Goldhagen, *Hitler's Willing Executioners*.
4. The Dreyfus affair stirred sufficiently long-lasting passions that, as late as 1931, the premiere of a play on the subject was disrupted by "right-wing toughs." Marrus and Paxton, *Vichy France and the Jews*, 32.
5. Hoffman, *More Than a Trial*, 198.
6. Quoted by Arendt, *Origins of Totalitarianism*, 93.

46. Lucie and Madeleine

1. John Paul II, *Spiritual Pilgrimage*, 7.
2. Burns, *Dreyfus*, 162f.
3. Ibid., 163.
4. Quoted by Burns, *Dreyfus*, 163, 169.
5. Ibid., 208.
6. Ibid., 209.
7. Arendt, *Origins of Totalitarianism*, 109.
8. Quoted by Burns, *Dreyfus*, 183.
9. Arendt, *Origins of Totalitarianism*, 117.
10. Hoffman, *More Than a Trial*, 167.
11. Quoted by Burns, *Dreyfus*, 243.
12. Ibid., 467.
13. Ibid.
14. Ibid., 474.
15. Ibid., 481.
16. Roger Cohen, "French Church Issues Apology to Jews on War," *New York Times*, October 1, 1997.
17. Quoted by Marrus and Paxton, *Vichy France and the Jews*, 198.
18. Ibid., 201.
19. A few French bishops protested the internment and deportation of Jews, but, as

Marrus and Paxton put it, "the voices of opposition were neither loud nor clear" (*Vichy France and the Jews,* 199). They cite Pierrard's charge: "In the face of the 'Jewish problem' almost all Catholic France was as if anesthetized" (197).

20. Burns, *Dreyfus,* 483.
21. Ibid., 485–86.
22. Ibid., 487.

47. From Christian Anti-Judaism to Eliminationist Antisemitism

1. Conquest, *Harvest of Sorrow.*
2. Dadrian, *History of the Armenian Genocide.*
3. Germany employed its first concentration camp (a term coined by the Spaniards in Cuba) against the Hereros, the indigenous people of Germany's colony of South West Africa, today's Namibia. At the beginning of the twentieth century, the Hereros were driven into the desert, where tens of thousands died of thirst. See Lindqvist, *Origins of European Genocide,* 149–50.
4. See *Cantate Domino,* the bull issued at the Council of Florence in 1442 by Pope Eugene IV (1431–1447): "The holy Roman church firmly believes, professes and preaches that all those who are outside the Catholic church, not only pagans but also Jews or heretics and schismatics, cannot share in eternal life and will go into the everlasting fire which was prepared for the devil and his angels." Tanner, *Decrees of the Ecumenical Councils,* 520. By the late nineteenth century, a cliché of white colonial functionaries defined Africans as devils, as in, "A file of poor devils, chained by the neck, carried my trunks and boxes toward the dock." Quoted by Hochschild, *King Leopold's Ghost,* 119.
5. Quoted by Lindqvist, *Origins of European Genocide,* 107.
6. Ibid., 141.
7. Ibid., 147.
8. Dietrich, *Catholic Citizens in the Third Reich,* 36.
9. Lindqvist, *Origins of European Genocide,* 141.

48. Setting a Standard: The Church Against Bismarck

1. Karl Marx, "The Eighteenth Brumaire of Louis Bonaparte," in *The Marx-Engels Reader,* 595.
2. Ibid.
3. Marx, "Contributions to the Critique of Hegel's *Philosophy of Right:* Introduction," in *The Marx-Engels Reader,* 54.
4. Blackbourn, *Marpingen,* 44.
5. *HarperCollins Encyclopedia of Catholicism,* 795–96.
6. Blackbourn, *Marpingen,* 52.
7. *HarperCollins Encyclopedia of Catholicism,* 796.
8. "Church Recognizes 1987 Healing at Lourdes Shrine," *National Catholic Reporter,* February 26, 1999. The man cured reported of his experience, "It is as if God winked at me."
9. Blackbourn, *Marpingen,* 19.
10. Ibid., 18–19.
11. Bernstein and Politi, *His Holiness,* 295.

12. On May 13, 2000, after John Paul II traveled to Fátima to observe the twofold anniversary of his wounding and the apparition, the Vatican unveiled the "Third Secret of Fátima," a prophecy given by the Virgin to the children in 1917 of a "bishop clothed in white" who "falls to the ground, apparently dead, under a burst of gunfire." The Vatican asserted that the secret vision anticipated the 1981 assassination attempt. Alessandra Stanley, "Vatican Discloses the 'Third Secret' of Fátima," *New York Times,* May 14, 2000.

13. Blackbourn, *Marpingen,* 42.

14. Ibid., 53.

15. Ibid., 54.

16. H.W.L. Freudenthal, "Kulturkampf," *New Catholic Encyclopedia,* vol. 8, 267.

17. Döllinger, "The Jews in Europe," 211.

18. Kornberg, "Döllinger's *Die Juden,*" 244.

19. "Döllinger, Johann J. I. von," *HarperCollins Encyclopedia of Catholicism,* 427.

20. Kornberg, "Döllinger's *Die Juden,*" 244.

21. Ibid., 245.

22. Döllinger, "The Jews in Europe," 211.

23. Ibid., 242.

24. Ibid., 211.

25. Blackbourn, *Marpingen,* 84.

26. Ibid., 84.

27. Quoted by Blackbourn, *Marpingen,* 106.

28. Ibid., 106–7.

29. Quoted by Evans, *German Center Party,* 71.

30. Quoted by Blackbourn, *Marpingen,* 270.

31. Evans, *German Center Party,* 71.

32. Quoted by Blackbourn, *Marpingen,* 270.

33. Ibid., 107.

34. Ibid., 116.

35. Ibid., 117.

36. Ibid.

37. Ibid., 2.

38. Ibid., 272.

39. Ibid., 94.

40. Ibid., 352.

41. Ibid., 113.

42. Evans, *German Center Party,* 71.

43. Flannery, *The Anguish of the Jews,* 179.

44. Gilbert, *Atlas of Jewish History,* 64.

45. Flannery, *The Anguish of the Jews,* 180.

46. Blackbourn, *Populists and Patricians,* 172.

47. Evans, *German Center Party,* 404.

48. Quoted by Blackbourn, *Populists and Patricians,* 171. This passage can seem a prophetic antecedent to the famous Nazi-era statement by Martin Niemöller: "First they came for the Communists, but I was not a Communist — so I said nothing. Then they came for the Social Democrats, but I was not a Social Democrat — so I did nothing. Then came the trade unionists, but I was not a trade unionist. And then they came for

the Jews, but I was not a Jew — so I did little. Then when they came for me, there was no one left who could stand up for me." Peter Novick points out that this passage has often been tampered with to reflect various post-Holocaust agendas; for example, with the Jews being moved to first place in the litany of victims, the Communists being left off the list, and Catholics regularly added to it — as at the Holocaust memorial in Boston. See Novick, *The Holocaust in American Life,* 221.

49. Quoted by Evans, *German Center Party,* 73–74.
50. "Nobody ever outmaneuvered Bismarck in a fluid diplomacy." Kissinger, *Diplomacy,* 118.
51. Blackbourn, *Marpingen,* 350–51.
52. Ibid., 405.
53. Ibid., 54, 56. The unprecedented fervor for the Seamless Robe had, no doubt, been stimulated in part by the frustrated enthusiasm so many Catholics had shown for the apparitions at Marpingen. Bishop Korum had expressly discouraged belief in the competing cultic center, and it was in 1889 that one of the three girls, now twenty-one years old and working as a maid in a convent, confessed: "I am one of the three children who, nearly thirteen years ago in Marpingen, spread the rumour of having seen the Blessed Virgin and must to my regret make the deeply humiliating admission that everything without exception was one great lie." Quoted by Blackbourn, *Marpingen,* 352.

49. Eugenio Pacelli and the Surrender of German Catholicism

1. "Americanism" was identified with Isaac Hecker, the founder of the Paulist Fathers, the order to which I belonged. Defenders of Hecker insisted he was misunderstood by Rome, but his emphasis on the Holy Spirit as working through each Christian, instead of through the hierarchy, was a theological application of the core idea of American democracy. The American Catholic Church would, in fact, lead the rest of the Church to appreciate the importance of freedom of conscience and religious tolerance. Hecker's ideas would be vindicated by Vatican II.
2. Quoted by Cornwell, *Hitler's Pope,* 43. Cornwell's book was controversial, faulted especially for the sensationalism of its title and its subtitle, *The Secret History of Pius XII.* Critics like István Deák pointed out that Pius XII was not "Hitler's pope," since the two men hated each other, and that there was little that could be called "secret" in what Cornwell reported (Deák, "The Pope, the Nazis, and the Jews," 46). Ronald Rychlak offers an extensive rebuttal of Cornwell in *Hitler, the War, and the Pope,* but he, like other critics of Cornwell, failed to dismantle the overwhelmingly negative record Cornwell assembled, especially regarding Pacelli's diplomacy in Germany during the early 1930s. My review of *Hitler's Pope* was favorable. See Carroll, "The Holocaust and the Catholic Church," 107–12.
3. Cornwell, *Hitler's Pope,* 82.
4. Evans, *German Center Party,* 404.
5. Cornwell, *Hitler's Pope,* 83–84.
6. Blackbourn, *Populists and Patricians,* 179.
7. Ibid., 181.
8. Ibid., 169.
9. Cornwell, *Hitler's Pope,* 84.

10. Quoted by Cornwell, *Hitler's Pope,* 137

11. The bishops, meeting at Fulda from August 17 to 19, 1932, declared: "All the bishoprics have forbidden membership of the Party because parts of its official programme contain false teachings . . . Considerable numbers of people join the Party solely because of their support for the Party in the secular sphere, for its economic policies and political aims. But this cannot be justified. Support for the Party necessarily involves, whether one wants this or not, furthering its aims as a whole." Matheson, *Third Reich and the Christian Churches,* 6–7.

12. "Without therefore departing from the condemnation of certain religious and moral errors voiced in our earlier measures, the episcopate believes it has ground for confidence that the general prohibitions and admonitions mentioned above need no longer be regarded as necessary." Ibid., 10.

13. The statement goes on to admonish Catholics about their responsibility to obey the new government: "For Catholic Christians, to whom the voice of the church is sacred, it is not necessary at the present moment to make special admonition to be loyal to the lawful government and to fulfill conscientiously the duties of citizenship, rejecting on principle all illegal or subversive behavior." Quoted by Helmreich, *German Churches under Hitler,* 239.

14. Cornwell, *Hitler's Pope,* 86.

15. Ibid., 146.

16. Ibid., 86–87.

17. Dietrich, *Catholic Citizens in the Third Reich,* 102. See also Lewy, *The Catholic Church and Nazi Germany,* 331.

18. Evans, *German Center Party,* 393.

19. Cornwell, *Hitler's Pope,* 152. István Deák points out that Brüning was "quickly shunted aside without much, if any, protest by other German Catholics," and therefore downplays, against Cornwell, the significance of the concordat and the loss of the Center Party. Deák, "The Pope, the Nazis, and the Jews," 47.

20. Dietrich, *Catholic Citizens in the Third Reich,* 106.

21. Quoted by Cornwell, *Hitler's Pope,* 156.

22. Ibid., 158.

50. The Seamless Robe in 1933

1. The screenplay of *The Robe* was written by Philip Dunne, from the novel by Lloyd C. Douglas.

2. Psalm 22:18.

3. Dietrich, *Catholic Citizens in the Third Reich,* 98.

4. Wighton, *Adenauer,* 20.

5. Stehlin, *Weimar and the Vatican,* 180.

6. Blackbourn, *Populists and Patricians,* 178.

7. Blackbourn, *Marpingen,* 376–77. See also Dietrich, *Catholic Citizens in the Third Reich,* 101.

8. Helmreich, *German Churches under Hitler,* 245–46.

9. Schrader, *Church and State in Germany,* 8.

10. Quoted by Lewy, *The Catholic Church and Nazi Germany,* 104. See also Blackbourn, *Marpingen,* 377.

11. *Völkischer Beobachter*, quoted by Schrader, *Church and State in Germany*, 8.
12. "Denkschrift der Deutschen Bischöfe an Hitler," in Hans Muller, ed., *Katholische Kirche und Nationalsozialismus: Dokumente, 1930–1935* (Munich: Nymphenburger Verlagshandlung, 1963), 377. I gratefully acknowledge the Reverend Milton McC. Gatch for translation assistance. For a reference to the "handshake of trust," see Gordon Zahn, "Catholic Resistance? A Yes and a No," in Littell and Locke, *German Church Struggle*, 210. The bishops' message to Hitler ended, "We pray to Almighty God that he take under his protection the life of our Führer and Reich Chancellor, and that he grant his blessing to your great statesmanly goals." Less than a month later, the Nuremberg Laws were decreed, the severest attack yet on Jews. The bishops said nothing. Helmreich, *German Churches under Hitler*, 275–76.
13. Quoted by Lewy, *The Catholic Church and Nazi Germany*, 90.
14. The phrase is used by Helmreich, *German Churches under Hitler*, 249. The same phrase is commonly used to refer to the rooms in which Anne Frank and her family hid.
15. Quoted by Helmreich, *German Churches under Hitler*, 249.
16. Ibid.
17. Dietrich, *Catholic Citizens in the Third Reich*, 102.
18. Ibid., 105.
19. Zahn, "Catholic Resistance?," in Littell and Locke, *German Church Struggle*, 210.
20. Dietrich, *Catholic Citizens in the Third Reich*, 137.
21. Ibid.
22. Quoted by Dietrich, *Catholic Citizens in the Third Reich*, 137.
23. Dietrich, *Catholic Citizens in the Third Reich*, 195. The Vatican declaration "We Remember: A Reflection on the Shoah" praised "the well-known Advent sermons of Cardinal Faulhaber in 1933, the very year in which National Socialism came to power, at which not just Catholics but also Protestants and Jews were present, [and which] clearly expressed rejection of the Nazi anti-Semitic propaganda" (3.10). But is that so? Dietrich says that Faulhaber's sermons were "not condemnations of antisemitism." At the meeting I attended in Chicago in March 1999, Cardinal Cassidy, the principal author of "We Remember," was challenged on the point. An elderly rabbi who identified himself as having been sixteen years old and living in Munich at the time of Faulhaber's sermons remembered that the prelate had declared "that with the coming of Christ, Jews and Judaism have lost their place in the world." Historians present at the meeting recalled that the Nazi propaganda Faulhaber was rebutting referred to denigrations of the Old Testament, "Jewish Scriptures." Cardinal Faulhaber was careful to say that he was not defending Jewish people alive in his time. He was addressing, he said, only "Israel of biblical antiquity." His sermons, he insisted, "will discuss only pre-Christian Judaism." A year later, in a clarifying letter, his secretary insisted that the cardinal "had not taken a position with regard to the Jewish question of today." (Quoted by Lewy, "Pius XII, the Jews, and the German Catholic Church," in Ericksen and Heschel, *Betrayal*, 131.) In Chicago, the rabbi then asked how the Vatican today could single out such "resistance" for praise in a document that claimed to be concerned with the fate of Jewish persons? Cardinal Cassidy seemed embarrassed by the question, and answered, according to my notes, "These quotations were put into the document by historians . . . I did not have them in the original document." For further discussion of Cardinal Faulhaber's Advent sermons, see Hamerow, *On the Road to the Wolf's Lair*, 140–45.

24. Dietrich, *Catholic Citizens in the Third Reich,* 269.

25. Ibid., 283. István Deák says that "scores of priests" were jailed by the Nazis, "charged with sexual crimes or currency speculation." Deák, "The Pope, the Nazis, and the Jews," 47.

26. Helmreich, *German Churches under Hitler,* 358. Perhaps as many as 20 percent of Polish priests were murdered by the Nazis. Pius XII, who is so widely faulted for saying too little about the murders of Jews, said nothing about this atrocity against his own clergy, a silence that, Deák says, "remains more incomprehensible than his extreme lateness in objecting to the persecution of the Jews." Deák, "The Pope, the Nazis, and the Jews," 47.

27. Blackbourn, *Marpingen,* 376.

28. Ibid., 370–71. Blackbourn cites a 1935 source that between ten and fifteen thousand pilgrims were visiting annually, but this is lower than the number of people who came every day at the height of Marpingen enthusiasm in the 1870s.

29. *Mit Brennender Sorge* notably defends the Old Testament against Nazi assaults on it as Jewish: "God has given his commandments in sovereign form." But the papal defense, repeating the promise-fulfillment pattern that we noted as a foundational problem, extends only to the Scripture and its Christian significance: "The culmination of Revelation in the Gospel of Jesus Christ is final, binding forever." The encyclical condemns Nazi racism — "the so-called myth of blood and race" — but does not refer to antisemitism. The point of that distinction would become clearer as the Church consistently defended those Jews who had become Christians (victims of Nazi "racism," which did not recognize religious conversion) while saying nothing of Jews as such (victims of mere antisemitism). (*Mit Brennender Sorge,* in Matheson, *Third Reich and the Christian Churches,* 69–70.) In contrast to such indirection, another encyclical, *Divini Redemptoris,* appeared only days later. It was an uneuphemistic broadside against "bolshevistic and atheistic Communism . . . a barbarism . . . the satanic scourge . . . [the] terrorism that reigns today in Russia, where former comrades in revolution are exterminating each other." In Carlen, *Papal Encyclicals,* 537, 538, 542.

30. Cardinal Adolf Bertram, in Matheson, *Third Reich and the Christian Churches,* 11. The cardinal concluded his statement, "One might mention in passing that the Press, which is overwhelmingly in Jewish hands, has remained consistently silent about the persecution of Catholics."

31. Hoffmann, *History of the German Resistance,* 12.

32. Ibid., 15.

33. Ibid.

34. Quoted by Matheson, *Third Reich and the Christian Churches,* 36.

35. Quoted by Helmreich, *German Churches under Hitler,* 254.

51. Maria Laach and Reichstheologie

1. Joseph Lortz, quoted by Michael B. Lukens, "Joseph Lortz and a Catholic Accommodation with National Socialism," in Ericksen and S. Heschel, *Betrayal,* 159.

2. Ibid., 164–65.

3. Quoted by Harold M. Stahmer, "*Kristallnacht* and Political Catholicism: Maria Laach, Martin Buber, and Father Caesarius Lauer, O.S.B.," unpublished lecture delivered be-

fore the Jesuit Student Philosophical Union, Kraków, Poland, November 12, 1997, 16. I am indebted to Professor Stahmer, who lived at Maria Laach as a student in the early 1950s, for my understanding of Maria Laach's place in this story."

4. Ibid.
5. Zahn, *German Catholics*, 21–23.
6. I acknowledge this despite my own role as a celebrant of numerous folk Masses when I was a priest. I even took up the guitar for a time.
7. Konrad Adenauer, *Briefe 1945–1947* (selected correspondence), hrsg. von Rudolf Morsey und Hans-Peter Schwarz (Berlin 1983), S 172. Quoted by Scholder, *Requiem for Hitler*, 139.
8. Quoted by Hughes, *The Monk's Tale*, 68.
9. Robert P. Ericksen, "Assessing the Heritage: German Protestant Theologians, Nazis, and the 'Jewish Question,'" in Ericksen and S. Heschel, *Betrayal*, 23.
10. Quoted by Dietrich, *Catholic Citizens in the Third Reich*, 116.
11. Lukens, "Joseph Lortz," 155.
12. Lewy, *The Catholic Church and Nazi Germany*, 107.
13. Quoted by Lukens, "Joseph Lortz," 159.
14. Stahmer, "*Kristallnacht* and Political Catholicism," 15.
15. Lewy, *The Catholic Church and Nazi Germany*, 46.
16. Quoted by Lewy, *The Catholic Church and Nazi Germany*, 46.
17. Ibid., 86.
18. Quoted by Schrader, *Church and State in Germany*, 4.
19. Lewy, *The Catholic Church and Nazi Germany*, 86.
20. Schrader, *Church and State in Germany*, 5.
21. Quoted by Lewy, *The Catholic Church and Nazi Germany*, 86.
22. Hughes, *The Monk's Tale*, 66.
23. Quoted by Stahmer, "*Kristallnacht* and Political Catholicism," 15.
24. Hughes, *The Monk's Tale*, 66. When the Church launched a canonical investigation into the wartime activities of Angelo Roncalli, later Pope John XXIII, as part of the process of moving his "cause" toward beatification (he was beatified on September 3, 2000, together with Pius IX), it was learned that the money Roncalli, then apostolic nuncio to Turkey, used to purchase freedom for Jewish refugees "had come from Hitler's ambassador to Turkey, Franz von Papen, a Catholic who did not want the Nazis to win the war." Desmond O'Grady, "Almost a Saint: Pope John XXIII," *St. Anthony Messenger*, November 1996.
25. Lewy, *The Catholic Church and Nazi Germany*, 321.
26. Wighton, *Adenauer*, 57–61.
27. Ibid.
28. Ibid., 61.
29. Here is Stahmer's translation of a passage from *Adenauer: Eine Politische Biographie* by Henning Köhler: "A ghostly scene: applause and confidence shown to a conservative-Catholic policy and its representative von Papen, and hence also the applause for collaboration with Hitler; and during all this Adenauer, who had been removed from his political office, sat in a cell not far from the conference room."
30. See James Carroll, "Shoah in the News," Discussion Paper 27, Joan Shorenstein Center for Press, Politics, and Public Policy, John F. Kennedy School of Government, Harvard

University, October 1997. "Chamberlain Plans to Ask Roosevelt to Join in Movement to Rescue Jews" was a *New York Times* headline on November 15, 1938. "Nobody knows yet," the news story read, "where the emigrants can settle permanently, although the United States can take 30,000 annually under the quota system." David Wyman points out that a total of 21,000 Jews were admitted to America while it was at war, which was only 10 percent of the legal quota. Wyman, *Abandonment of the Jews*, 136.

52. Pius XII: Last Days of the Roman Ghetto

1. John Paul II, *Spiritual Pilgrimage*, 62.
2. See Passelecq and Suchecky, *Hidden Encyclical*. Because the unpublished encyclical, while condemning antisemitism in clear language, was also rife with traditional expressions of religious contempt for Judaism, many scholars regard its cancellation as a good thing. Others argue that even such a flawed encyclical could have helped some Jews survive.
3. See Marrus, *The Holocaust in History*. In the autumn of 1941, certain Catholic prelates in France denounced the Vichy regime's anti-Jewish legislation. Pétain's government sought an opinion from Rome. Marrus writes that "the French ambassador to the Holy See, Léon Bérard, sent an extensive report to Vichy on the Vatican's views. According to this diplomat the Holy See was not interested in the French antisemitic laws . . . So far as the French were concerned, the Vatican essentially gave them a green light to legislate as they chose against Jews" (180).
4. The message deplores the fact "that hundreds of thousands of people, through no fault of their own and solely because of their nation or race, have been condemned to death or progressive extinction." Robert Wistrich dismisses this as a "protest that lasted for the duration of a breath." "The Pope, the Church, and the Jews," 27.
5. Hochhuth, *The Deputy*, 146.
6. Zuccotti, *The Italians and the Holocaust*, 101, 104.
7. Ibid., 123. The Auschwitz registration numbers do not jibe with the totals given, so perhaps the log was not that meticulous. Morley, *Vatican Diplomacy and the Jews*, puts the number arrested at 1,259, the number sent to Auschwitz at 1,007 (180).
8. In late 1999, a joint Jewish-Catholic commission was established to study those archive documents to determine what Pius XII did and could have done about the Holocaust. The Jewish commission members were Michael Marrus, Robert Wistrich, and Bernard Suchecky. The Catholics were Eva Fleischner, Gerald Fogarty, and John Morley. In October 2000 the commission released a "preliminary report," saying its "investigation of the eleven volumes has generated many significant questions." Until further archives are opened, those questions remain unanswered. See http://www.bnaibrith.org/cpp/randa/vatican.html.
9. John Paul II, *Spiritual Pilgrimage*, 62.
10. "We Remember," n. 16.
11. The Vatican official Father Peter Gumpel, S.J., quotes the Jewish diplomat and historian Pinchas Lapide as writing, "Pius XII, the Holy See, the Vatican nuncios and the whole Catholic Church saved between 700,000 and 850,000 Jews from certain death" ("Justice for Pius XII," *Inside the Vatican*, June 1997, 22). See Pinchas Lapide, *Three Popes and the Jews* (New York: Hawthorne Books, 1967). István Deák, citing p. 214 of

Lapide's book, renders the quote as "the Catholic Church, under the Pontificate of Pius XII, was instrumental in saving at least 700,000, but probably as many as 860,000, Jews." Deák comments, "Ever since the publication of Lapide's book, his figure of 860,000 has been used by practically every defender of Pius XII . . . Lapide did not give any factual basis for his estimates" ("The Pope, the Nazis, and the Jews," 48; see also Flannery, *The Anguish of the Jews*, 226). The 1998 Vatican document "We Remember: A Reflection on the Shoah" leaps from Lapide's crediting the "whole Catholic Church" to crediting the pope. Here is Robert Wistrich's assessment of that "unconvincing and inflated" claim: "In no instance did the Pope's intervention result in much more than a temporary respite in the killing. On even the most favorable reading of the historical record, his actions over the course of the Shoah were prudent to a fault. We may never know exactly how many Jewish lives he was responsible for saving, but the number is almost certainly far smaller than that implied by the Vatican." Wistrich, "The Pope, the Church, and the Jews," 26.

12. Giacomo Saban, "Address," in John Paul II, *Spiritual Pilgrimage*, 72.
13. Eugene J. Fisher, in Foxman and Fisher, "Should the Vatican Beatify Its World War II Pope?," 49. Like Fisher, Margherita Marchione portrays this event in a light most favorable to Pius XII, describing it as "an official, personal protest through the papal Secretary of State." Marchione, *Memoirs of Jews and Catholics*, 16.
14. Richard Freiherr von Weizsäcker served as his father's defense attorney at Nuremberg, but in 1985, as president, he delivered a speech to the German parliament in which he confessed that Hitler, in accomplishing his act of genocide, "made the entire nation the tool of this hatred." See Donald W. Shriver, Jr., *An Ethic for Enemies: Forgiveness in Politics* (New York: Oxford University Press, 1995), 110.
15. Quoted by Morley, *Vatican Diplomacy and the Jews*, 181.
16. John Morley, "Pope Pius XII in Historical Context," unpublished paper presented at "Building on 'We Remember': A Consultation on the Vatican's Reflection on the Shoah," Catholic Theological Union, Chicago, March 30, 1999, 20.
17. Cornwell, *Hitler's Pope*, 314.
18. Morley, *Vatican Diplomacy and the Jews*, 184.
19. Fisher, in Foxman and Fisher, "Should the Vatican Beatify Its World War II Pope?," 49.
20. Morley, *Vatican Diplomacy and the Jews*, 186.
21. Cornwell, *Hitler's Pope*, 310.
22. Deák, "The Pope, the Nazis, and the Jews," 48. The pope "did nothing. He sent no warning messages to the Jewish community, messages which, unlike messages from German diplomats, would surely have been believed; nor did he try to address the SS command."
23. Morley, *Vatican Diplomacy and the Jews*, 209.
24. Graham Greene, "The Pope Who Remains a Priest," *Life*, September 24, 1951.
25. "We Remember" points out, for example, that Golda Meir sent a message of condolence: "When fearful martyrdom came to our people, the voice of the Pope was raised for its victims." In 1958, the world had barely begun to confront the history and meaning of the Holocaust. The play based on Anne Frank's diary, the beginning of that process, was only recently on Broadway. The Eichmann trial had yet to occur. The word "Holocaust" hadn't entered the discussion (it first appears in the *New York Times* index in 1980).

26. O'Mikle, *Pope Pius XII.*
27. Ibid., 25–26.
28. Ibid., 42.
29. Ibid., 59.
30. Deák, "The Pope, the Nazis, and the Jews," 49.
31. Peter Gumpel with Antonio Gaspari, "Justice for Pius XII," in *Inside the Vatican,* June 1997.
32. Peter Gumpel, "Pius XII as He Really Was," *The Tablet,* February 13, 1999. Quoted by Morley, "Pope Pius XII in Historical Context," 11.
33. Lewy, *The Catholic Church and Nazi Germany,* 309.
34. Zuccotti, *Under His Very Windows.*
35. John Paul II, *Spiritual Pilgrimage,* 72.
36. Kornberg, "Döllinger's *Die Juden,*" 239.
37. Goldhagen, *Hitler's Willing Executioners,* 110.
38. Lewy, *The Catholic Church and Nazi Germany,* 282.
39. Goldhagen, *Hitler's Willing Executioners,* 164.
40. Cornwell, *Hitler's Pope,* 243.
41. Ibid., 297.
42. Quoted by Kornberg, "Döllinger's *Die Juden,*" 239.
43. Flannery, *The Anguish of the Jews,* 226.
44. Lewy, *The Catholic Church and Nazi Germany,* 303.
45. Wills, *Papal Sin,* 33.
46. Lewy, *The Catholic Church and Nazi Germany,* 304.
47. Flannery, *The Anguish of the Jews,* 225.
48. Quoted by Lewy, *The Catholic Church and Nazi Germany,* 304.

53. Edith Stein and Catholic Memory

1. Fabrégues, *Edith Stein,* 11.
2. Sawicki, *Body, Text, and Science,* 188.
3. Ibid., 90.
4. Fabrégues, *Edith Stein,* 52.
5. *L'Osservatore Romano,* October 14, 1998.
6. See, for example, "The Convenient Saint," *The Guardian,* September 26, 1998; "A Martyr — But Whose?," *Time,* October 19, 1998; "Disharmony Swirls Around Future Saint," *Boston Globe,* October 10, 1998; Gordon, "Saint Edith?," 17–20.
7. "Vatican Official Criticizes Jews," *National Catholic Reporter,* December 11, 1998.
8. John M. Oesterreicher, *Walls Are Crumbling: Seven Jewish Philosophers Discover Christ* (London: Hollis and Carter, 1953).
9. See O'Hare, *Enduring Covenant,* 7–32.
10. *L'Osservatore Romano,* October 14, 1998.
11. Wills, *Papal Sin,* 52–53.
12. See Morley, *Vatican Diplomacy and the Jews,* 147–65.
13. I interviewed the two doctors responsible for the ill child's treatment and the Church official in charge of the investigation (see Carroll, "The Saint and the Holocaust," 52; see also Wills, *Papal Sin,* 59). Wills calls the Church's manipulation of its own canonization procedures in this case one of the Vatican's "historical dishonesties." He ob-

serves that the Church's determination to push this canonization through served a larger purpose: "Stein is very useful for maintaining the argument of *We Remember* . . . , that the church was more with the persecuted than with the persecutors during the Holocaust" (54).

14. Brenan, *St. John of the Cross,* 91–94.
15. See Kertzer, *Kidnapping of Edgardo Mortara.* Kertzer reports that Pius IX fumed at a delegation of Roman Jews who complained of his having taken the child: "Take care, for I could have done you harm, a great deal of harm. I could have made you go back into your hole" (159). This is surely a reference to his assumption that the Roman ghetto was his to establish or disestablish.
16. Knickmeyer, "John Paul Beatifies Scorned, Beloved Popes," *Boston Globe,* September 4, 2000.
17. Herbstrith, *Edith Stein,* 64. See also Baseheart, *Person in the World,* 25–26.
18. Baseheart, *Person in the World,* 26; Herbstrith, *Edith Stein,* 65; Sawicki, *Body, Text, and Science,* 197.
19. Author interview with Susannah Heschel.
20. Sawicki, *Body, Text, and Science,* 195.
21. Herbstrith, *Edith Stein,* 65.
22. Rachel Feldhay Brenner, "Ethical Convergence in Religious Conversion," in Cargas, *Unnecessary Problem of Edith Stein,* 79.
23. Baseheart, *Person in the World,* 25–26; Herbstrith, *Edith Stein,* 64–65.
24. Quoted by Baseheart, *Person in the World,* 26.
25. Herbstrith, *Edith Stein,* 101–3; Sawicki, *Body, Text, and Science,* 198. Marchione says that Pius XII intended to denounce the Nazi roundup of Jews after the Dutch bishops' letter, but he changed his mind. Of his statement, he was reported by his assistant to have said, "But if the Nazis find these sheets which are stronger than the bishops' letter, what will happen to the Catholics and the Jews under German control?" He is reported to have then burned the pages (*Yours Is a Precious Witness,* 153). For an explanation of why this account of the pope's action is implausible, to say the least, see Wills, *Papal Sin,* 67–68. István Deák states, "Apparently, the Pope believed that 40,000 Catholic Jews were killed as a consequence of the Archbishop's pastoral letter. But there were not 40,000 converts in the Netherlands: rather it seems that only about one or two hundred Catholic Jews were arrested." Deák, "The Pope, the Nazis, and the Jews," 48.
26. Quoted by Herbstrith, *Edith Stein,* 108.
27. Ibid., 106.
28. An example of the prevailing attitude is the report from Vichy's Vatican ambassador, Léon Bérard, referred to above. Bérard had sounded out Church officials on the subject of France's *Statut des Juifs,* the anti-Jewish legislation that paved the way for the deportations. Bérard summarized the Church position: "A Jew who has been properly baptized ceases to be Jewish and merges with the 'flock of Christ.'" This amounted, he said, to "the sole point on which the law of 2 June 1941 [the second *Statut de Juifs*] is in opposition to a principle espoused by the Roman Church." Marrus and Paxton, *Vichy France and the Jews,* 201.
29. See Stein, *Self-Portrait in Letters,* 238, 148, 163. See also Brenner, "Ethical Convergence in Religious Conversion," 99.
30. Quoted by Sawicki, *Body, Text, and Science,* 197.

31. Gordon, "Saint Edith?," 20.

32. Quoted by Sawicki, *Body, Text, and Science,* 214.

33. On July 12, 1999, John Paul II, at a papal Mass in Warsaw, beatified 108 Polish Catholics, mostly priests and nuns who had died as martyrs during World War II, mostly in the death camps, including 15 who had been killed at Auschwitz.

34. Quoted by Herbstrith, *Edith Stein,* 107.

54. The Broad Relevance of Catholic Reform

1. T. S. Eliot, "Little Gidding," *Collected Poems,* 208.

2. I wrote about this encounter in *An American Requiem,* 76–79.

3. "The often so misanthropic and bureaucratic Church must die," Hans Küng wrote, "and the philanthropic Church of Jesus must again and again resurrect in our hearts." Küng, *Reforming the Church Today,* 163.

4. Quoted by Peter Hebblethwaite, "John XXIII," *HarperCollins Encyclopedia of Catholicism,* 709.

5. "I am not infallible," he said. "The pope is infallible only when he speaks *ex cathedra.* But I will never speak *ex cathedra.*" Quoted by Küng, *Reforming the Church Today,* 69.

6. Hebblethwaite, "John XXIII," 710.

7. "Since women are becoming ever more conscious of their human dignity," he wrote, "they will not tolerate being treated as mere material instruments, but demand rights befitting a human person both in domestic and in public life." John XXIII, *Pacem in Terris,* in O'Brien and Shannon, *Catholic Documents,* 134.

8. Quoted by Hebblethwaite, "John XXIII," 709.

9. Küng, *Reforming the Church Today,* 66–67.

10. Reinhard Neudecker, S.J., "The Catholic Church and the Jewish People," in Latourelle, *Vatican II,* 283. When John XXIII was beatified in 2000, it was reported — as if to mitigate the negative publicity attached to Pius IX, with whom he'd been twinned — that John had "complained of a 'convoy of Jews' heading to Palestine and its holy sites, as if such a remark, however problematic, compared with the anti-Jewish record of Pius IX. Knickmeyer, "John Paul Beatifies Scorned, Beloved Popes," *Boston Globe,* September 4, 2000.

11. Arendt, *Men in Dark Times,* 63.

12. Neudecker, "The Catholic Church and the Jewish People," in Latourelle, *Vatican II,* 283.

13. Ibid.

14. Küng, *Reforming the Church Today,* 65.

15. For a pointed analysis of the "structure of deceit" tied to the Church's position on birth control, see Wills, *Papal Sin,* 78–9. The contemporary rejection of Church authority on this and other issues has been a definitive turn in the Catholic story. For example, here are the percentages by which American Catholics dissent from Church teaching: on birth control, 93%; divorce, 85%; abortion, 69%; homosexuality, 51%; women's ordination, 60%. See Wolfe, "Liberalism and Catholicism," 20.

16. "And all the people answered, 'His blood be on us and on our children!'" Matthew 27: 26.

17. Quoted by Neudecker, "The Catholic Church and the Jewish People," in Latourelle, *Vatican II,* 288.

18. Ibid., 286.

19. Ibid., 282–83.

20. Quoted by O'Malley, *Trent and All That,* 18.

21. Küng, *The Council, Reform, and Reunion,* 9–10.

22. Quoted by Küng, *The Council, Reform, and Reunion,* 162.

23. In this context, Hans Küng recalls Voltaire, but also Dante, who placed three popes in hell (Ibid., 46). Küng is the greatest contemporary advocate of Catholic reform, but he remains a fiercely committed Roman Catholic. The Vatican, under John Paul II, tried to silence him in 1979, as we saw, particularly because of his questions about papal infallibility, but Küng has refused to be silent. He has refused to leave the Church. His work remains an inspiration for me, which is why it is cited so often in this book. His case has special poignancy for Catholics for two reasons: First, his 1961 book *The Council, Reform, and Reunion,* cited here, gave expression to an entire generation's hope for Vatican II. He has suffered the consequences of the Church's failure to fulfill that hope. Second, his first conflict with the Catholic hierarchy came in the mid-1960s, when he dared to assert that the Roman Catholic Church was "co-responsible" with the Nazis for the Holocaust. See Carroll, "The Silence," 61.

24. That the dream of a Vatican III, in the spirit of John XXIII, inspires my kind is indicated by the fact that while I was editing this manuscript, I read the galleys of a memoir by John Dominic Crossan, who had so profoundly influenced my understanding of the historic Jesus and who had sparked reflections on my own Irish heritage. In his new book he writes, "I imagine something like this. There is a Third Vatican Council . . . [The Bishops] all implore God to take back the gift of infallibility and grant them instead the gift of accuracy." *A Long Way from Tipperary,* 98.

55. Agenda for a New Reformation

1. Küng, *Reforming the Church Today,* 160. A step toward such a lifting of the anathema was taken in the 1999 Joint Declaration on the Doctrine of Justification issued by the Lutheran World Federation and the Vatican. This statement represented a mutual acknowledgment by the former antagonists that each side had its point.

2. Küng, *The Council, Reform, and Reunion,* 74.

3. John 4:22.

56. Agenda Item 1: Anti-Judaism in the New Testament

1. Joyce Carol Oates, "The Calendar's New Clothes," *New York Times,* December 30, 1999.

2. Luke 24:25.

3. John 1:11.

4. John 8:23, 40–44.

5. See Levine, "Teaching Troubling Texts," 1.

6. The phrase is Christopher Leighton's, quoted by O'Hare, *Enduring Covenent,* 9.

7. See, for example, Fisher, *Seminary Education;* Cunningham, *Education for Shalom.*

8. Stendahl, *Paul among Jews and Gentiles.* See also Stendahl, *Final Account,* 1–7, 35–40.

9. Romans 11:1.

10. Luke 22:20.

11. Jeremiah 31:31–34. What the Revised Standard Version translates as "new covenant" carries the sense, in Hebrew, of "renewed."

12. Lohfink, *Covenant Never Revoked,* 83. Paul van Buren, a Christian leader in the Jewish-Christian dialogue, approached the problem this way: "As for ourselves, the Gentile Church, I believe that we are the fruit of one of the many renewals of the one covenant. It turned out strangely, but then so have many other creative renewals of that covenant. This particular renewal led to a new entity called the Church, consisting of Gentiles mostly, who found in one Jew an opening to the knowledge and love of the God of the covenant, and a calling to serve that God in a Gentile way. It is a tragedy of major proportions that we failed for so long to see that this was the universal God's particular calling for us, alongside Israel's particular calling. If we are beginning to see that now, it is because Christians have begun in the last couple of decades finally to meet Jews and so discover a living covenant." Van Buren, "When Christians Meet Jews," in Fisher, *Visions of the Other,* 65.

13. Tracy, *Analogical Imagination,* 426.

14. Baum, introduction to Ruether, *Faith and Fratricide,* 17–18.

15. Some scholars already routinely refer to "Hebrew Scriptures" and "Christian Scriptures" as a way of avoiding the Old Testament–New Testament dichotomy, but this division suggests that the Hebrew Scriptures are not part of what Christians revere. Another formulation, "First Testament" and "Second Testament," seems off too. "Apostolic Writings" is also used to define the specifically Christian texts.

16. In a session devoted to "troubling texts" at a meeting of the American Association of Religion in Boston, November 1999, I heard Professor Robert Goldenberg say, "Troubling texts are only truly troubling if the tradition is *not* troubled by them . . . An ethical act of reading requires a reading as if you are the Jew, the woman, the Canaanite. Then the glory of the texts is their troubling character."

17. Tracy, *On Naming the Present,* 14.

18. David Hartman, "Judaism Encounters Christianity Anew," in Fisher, *Visions of the Other,* 76–77, 79.

57. Agenda Item 2: The Church and Power

1. Quoted by Pelikan, *Jesus Through the Centuries,* 108.

2. John Paul II, "Universal Prayer: Confession of Sins and Asking for Forgiveness," March 12, 2000, http://jcrelations.com/stmnts/vatican3-00.htm.

3. Schüssler Fiorenza and Tracy, "The Holocaust as Interruption," 86.

4. Schüssler Fiorenza, *In Memory of Her,* xiv.

5. See Wills, *Papal Sin,* 2.

6. Quoted by Eugene Kennedy, "A Dissenting Voice," 28.

7. Quoted by Küng, *Reforming the Church Today,* 157.

8. Ibid., 156.

9. Ruether, *Faith and Fratricide,* 245.

10. Tracy, *On Naming the Present,* 14–15.

11. Hans Küng made this point in conversation with me. See Carroll, "The Silence," 60.

58. Agenda Item 3: A New Christology

1. Abraham Joshua Heschel, *The Insecurity of Freedom* (New York: Farrar, Straus and Giroux), 119.

2. Ruether, *Faith and Fratricide,* 246.

3. Tracy, *Dialogue with the Other,* 98.

4. Genesis 1:27.

5. Elizabeth A. Johnson, "Jesus and Salvation," *CTSA Proceedings* 49 (1994), 5.

6. John 6:63.

7. Rahner, *Theological Investigations,* vol. 5, 120.

8. Cardinal Joseph Ratzinger, "Universal Prayer: Confession of Sins and Asking for Forgiveness," March 12, 2000, http://jcrelations.com/stmnts/vatican3-00.htm.

9. Thomas F. O'Meara, in *Encyclopedia of Catholicism,* 1077.

10. Rahner, *Theological Investigations,* vol. 5, 116–17.

11. Numerous theologians have developed versions of this "anonymous Christianity," all seeking to protect the universalist claims for Jesus Christ. Raimon Panikkar, for example, speaks of "the Unknown Christ of Hinduism." For a discussion of the possibilities and limits of these approaches, see Dupuis, *Toward a Christian Theology of Religious Pluralism.*

12. Van Buren, *Theology of the Jewish Christian Reality,* pt. 3, 164–65.

13. Rahner, *Theological Investigations,* vol. 5, 116. I am indebted to Padraic O'Hare, who helped me appreciate Rahner's "enormous positive influence" on this question, despite — or perhaps because of — his commitment to the Catholic tradition. O'Hare, equally Catholic himself, has written: "Here in this radical Christocentrism, in a classic doctrinal understanding of salvation as victory, in the tradition of universalist Christian claims; here is religion as a source of brutality. It has been so in the past; it is so to an extent in the present. It could be so in the future. Universalist absolutism thrives on the diminishment of the other, on ignorance of the other." *Enduring Covenant,* 36.

14. Quoted by John L. Allen, Jr., "Doubts about Dialogue: Encounter with Other Religions Runs Up Against the Vatican's Hard Doctrinal Realities," *National Catholic Reporter,* August 27, 1999.

15. After a storm of protest greeted the Vatican's action, particularly from Balasuriya's fellow theologians, he was reinstated as a member of the Church, though he refused to recant his theological positions.

16. http://www.vatican.va/roman_curia/congreg...cfaith_doc_20000806_dominus-iesus_en.html.

17. Matthew 5:45.

18. Rahner, *Theological Investigations,* vol. 5, 171–72.

19. Rahner, *The Rahner Reader,* 20.

20. Macquarrie, *Christian Theology,* 183.

59. Agenda Item 4: The Holiness of Democracy

1. Curiously enough, the wall was breached on November 9, the anniversary of Kristallnacht. Because of the overwhelming significance of the dismantling of the wall, that anniversary trumped the earlier one in the German, and European, memory. This is a prime example of supersessionism.

2. "Playwright-Dissident Václav Havel Assumes the Presidency of Czechoslovakia," in *Lend Me Your Ears: Great Speeches in History,* selected and introduced by William Safire (New York: Norton, 1992), 629, 631.

3. Monsignor Lorenzo Baldisseri presented his diplomatic credentials as papal nuncio to the junta in Port-au-Prince on March 30, 1992, six months after the overthrow of Aristide. No other nation followed suit, and eventually, after an American invasion in 1994, Aristide was restored to the presidency.

4. Kwitny, *Man of the Century,* 467.

5. John Paul II, homily, St. Peter's Basilica, March 12, 2000.

6. John 18:37–38.

7. Lynch, *Christ and Apollo,* 118.

8. David Tracy, quoted by Kennedy, "A Dissenting Voice," 28.

9. Bednar, *Faith as Imagination,* 16f.

10. Tracy, *Analogical Imagination,* 362.

11. Lynch, *Christ and Apollo,* 136.

12. Tracy, *Analogical Imagination,* 363.

13. Ibid., 252.

14. Quoted by O'Brien, *Renewal of American Catholicism,* 106–7.

15. 1 Corinthians 13:12.

16. Ibid., 13:9.

17. 1 John 4:7–12.

18. Ibid., 3:12–13.

19. Spinoza, too, needs criticism. For an example of the offense Jews can take at his denigration of the Bible, see Heschel, *God in Search of Man,* 322.

20. David Tracy, "Religious Values after the Holocaust: A Catholic View," in Peck, *Jews and Christians,* 92.

60. Agenda Item 5: Repentance

1. James Joyce, *A Portrait of the Artist as a Young Man,* 8.

2. Quoted by Sarah Hall, "Past as Prologue: Blair Faults Britain in Irish Potato Blight," *New York Times,* June 3, 1997.

3. "Memory and Reconciliation," 4.1.

4. Ian Buruma, "War Guilt and the Difference Between Germany and Japan," *New York Times,* December 29, 1998. Buruma is the author of *The Wages of Guilt: Memories of War in Germany and Japan* (New York: Farrar, Straus and Giroux, 1994). In December 1999, the president of Germany, Johannes Rau, said, "I pay tribute to all those who were subjected to slave and forced labor under German rule and, in the name of the German people, beg forgiveness." But this was said at a private observance. A month later, at ceremonies dedicating the site for a Holocaust memorial near the Brandenburg Gate, Elie Wiesel urged the German parliament to "do it publicly. Ask the Jewish people to forgive Germany for what the Third Reich had done in Germany's name. Do it, and the significance of this day will acquire a higher level. Do it, for we desperately want to have hope for this new century." Quoted by Roger Cohen, "Wiesel Urges Germany to Ask Forgiveness," *New York Times,* January 28, 2000.

5. Quoted by Ben Lynfield, "For Israelis, Papal Visit Struck a Deep Chord," *National Catholic Reporter,* April 7, 2000.

6. Blumenthal, "Repentance and Forgiveness," 76.

7. Ibid., 81.

8. Quoted by John T. Pawlikowski, O.S.M., "Christian Theological Concerns after the Holocaust," in Fisher, *Visions of the Other*, 32.

9. As noted before, I attribute this observation to the columnist George Will, *Boston Globe*, May 8, 1998.

10. Boys, "The Cross," 22–23.

11. Van Buren, *Theology of the Jewish-Christian Reality*, pt. 3, 165.

12. *Mystici Corporis Christi*, in Carlen, *Papal Encyclicals*, 42.

13. Quoted by Cohn-Sherbok, *Crucified Jew*, 233.

14. Rahner, *Theological Investigations*, vol. 5, 15–16. Rahner goes on to say, "It would be silly self-deceit and clerical pride, group-egoism and cult of personality as found in totalitarian systems — which does not become the Church as the congregation of Jesus, the meek and humble of Heart — if it were to deny all this, or tried to hush it up or to minimize it, or made out that this burden was merely the burden of the Church of previous ages which has now been taken from her."

Epilogue: The Faith of a Catholic

1. James Carroll, "Germany at the Edge," *Boston Globe Magazine*, September 21, 1980, 72.

2. In October 1999, the bunker was unearthed again, by construction workers. They were ordered to cover it, as workers had done in 1994. The German government has refused to allow any marker at the site, and it is now being built upon, to be covered by a street. In 1998, workers discovered the bunker used by Joseph Goebbels. It will not be marked either, but it is on the site set aside for the Holocaust memorial, which will be built above it. See William Drozdiak, "As Hitler Bunker is Unearthed, Berlin Hastens to Bury It Again," *Boston Globe*, October 16, 1999.

3. Arendt, *The Human Condition*, 192.

4. Janson, *History of Art*, 454.

5. Arendt, *The Human Condition*, 236–37.

6. Quoted by Tina Chanter, "Neither Materialism Nor Idealism: Levinas's Third Way," in Milchman and Rosenberg, *Postmodernism and the Holocaust*, 143.

7. Arendt, *The Human Condition*, 237.

8. Rahner, *Theological Investigations*, vol. 5, 17.

9. Arendt, *The Human Condition*, 237.

10. John 18:27.

11. John 21:15–17.

12. John 6:68. Karl Rahner long ago drew me to this affirmation of faith as fundamental. *Theological Investigations*, vol. 5, 5.

BIBLIOGRAPHY

Abbot, Walter M., S.J., gen. ed. *The Documents of Vatican II.* Translations directed by Joseph Gallagher. New York: Herder and Herder/Association Press, 1966.

Abelard, Peter. *The Story of Abelard's Adversities (Historia Calamitatum).* Translated by J. T. Muckle. Toronto: Pontifical Institute of Medieval Studies, 1954.

Ackerman, Walter, ed. *Out of Our People's Past: Sources for the Study of Jewish History.* New York: United Synagogue Commission on Jewish Education, 1977.

Adams, Henry. *Mont St. Michel and Chartres.* Boston: Houghton Mifflin, 1905.

Adorno, Theodor W. "Education After Auschwitz." In *Never Again! The Holocaust's Challenge for Educators,* edited by Helmut Schreier and Mattias Heyl. Hamburg: Krämer, 1997.

Agus, I. A. "Rabbinic Scholarship in Northern Europe." In *The World History of the Jewish People,* 2d ser. Vol. 2, *Jews in Christian Europe, 711–1096. Medieval Period: The Dark Ages,* edited by Cecil Roth. Tel Aviv: Jewish History Publications, 1961, 189–209.

Allen, William Sheridan. "Objective and Subjective Inhibitants in the German Resistance to Hitler." In *The German Church Struggle and the Holocaust,* edited by Franklin H. Littell and Hubert G. Locke. Detroit: Wayne State University Press, 1974.

Ambrose, Saint. "Funeral Oration on the Death of Emperor Theodosius." In *The Fathers of the Church.* Vol. 22, *Funeral Orations by St. Gregory Nazianzen and St. Ambrose,* edited and translated by Roy Joseph Deferrari. New York: Fathers of the Church, Inc., 1953, 304–22.

Anselm, Saint. *Cur Deus Homo: Why God Became Man.* Translated by Edward S. Prout. London: Religious Tract Society.

Aquinas, Thomas. *Summa Theologiae.* Translated by Richard T. A. Murphy, O.P. New York: McGraw-Hill, 1964.

Arendt, Hannah. *Between Past and Future: Six Exercises in Political Thought.* New York: Viking, 1961.

———. *The Human Condition.* Chicago: University of Chicago Press, 1958.

———. *Men in Dark Times.* New York: Harcourt, Brace and World, 1968.

———. *The Origins of Totalitarianism.* Part 1, Antisemitism. New York: Harcourt, Brace and World, 1968.

Aristotle. *The Poetics.* Translated by S. H. Butcher. New York: Hill and Wang, 1991.

Armstrong, Karen. *A History of God: The 4,000-Year Quest of Judaism, Christianity, and Islam.* New York: Ballantine, 1994.

———. *Jerusalem: One City, Three Faiths*. New York: Ballantine, 1997.

———. *Visions of God: Four Medieval Mystics and Their Writings*. New York: Bantam, 1994.

Assmann, Jan. *Moses the Egyptian: The Memory of Egypt in Western Monotheism*. Cambridge: Harvard University Press, 1997.

Ateek, Naim S., Marc H. Ellis, and Rosemary Radford Ruether, eds. *Faith and the Intifada: Palestinian Christian Voices*. Maryknoll, N.Y.: Orbis Books, 1992.

Athanasius. "On the Incarnation of the Word" and "Prolegomena." In *Nicene and Post-Nicene Fathers*, 2d ser. Vol. 4, *Athanasius: Select Works and Letters*, edited by Philip Schaff and Henry Wace. Peabody, Mass.: Hendrickson, 1994.

Atkinson, Clarissa W. "'Your Servant, My Mother': The Figure of Saint Monica in the Ideology of Christian Motherhood." In *Immaculate and Powerful: The Female in Sacred Image and Social Reality*, edited by Clarissa W. Atkinson, Constance H. Buchanan, and Margaret R. Miles. Boston: Beacon Press, 1985, 139–72.

Augustine, Saint. *The City of God*. Translated by Henry Bettenson. London: Penguin, 1972.

———. *The Confessions*. Translated by R. S. Pine-Coffin. New York: Penguin, 1961.

———. *The Trinity*. Translated by Edmund Hill, O.P. Brooklyn, N.Y.: New City Press, 1991.

———. *Adversus Judaeos*. In *The Fathers of the Church*. Vol. 27, *Treatises on Marriage and Other Subjects*. Edited by Roy J. Deferrari. Translated by Sister Marie Liguori, I.H.M. New York: Fathers of the Church, 1955, 385–414.

Avishai, Bernard. *A New Israel: Democracy in Crisis, 1973–1988*. New York: Ticknor & Fields, 1990.

———. *The Tragedy of Zionism: Revolution and Democracy in the Land of Israel*. New York: Farrar, Straus and Giroux, 1985.

Baer, Yitzhak. *A History of the Jews in Christian Spain*. Vol. 1, *From the Age of Reconquest to the Fourteenth Century*. Vol. 2, *From the Fourteenth Century to the Expulsion*. Translated by Louis Schoffman. Philadelphia: Jewish Publication Society, 1961.

Bahat, Dan, with Chaim T. Rubinstein. *The Illustrated Atlas of Jerusalem*. Jerusalem: Carta, 1996.

Bainton, Roland H. *Erasmus of Christendom*. New York: Scribner, 1969.

Bairati, Eleonora. *Piero Della Francesca*. New York: Crescent, 1991.

Barnes, Timothy D. *Constantine and Eusebius*. Cambridge: Harvard University Press, 1981.

———. *From Eusebius to Augustine: Selected Papers, 1982–1993*. Aldershot, U.K.: Variorum, 1994.

Baron, Salo Wittmayer. *A Social and Religious History of the Jews: Late Middle Ages and the Era of European Expansion, 1200–1650*. Vol. 9, *Under Church and Empire*. Vol. 13, *Inquisition, Renaissance, and Reformation*. Vol. 14, *Catholic Restoration and Wars of Religion*. New York: Columbia University Press/Jewish Publication Society, 1965, 1969.

Barrucand, Marianne, and Achim Bednorz. *Moorish Architecture in Andalusia*. Köln: Taschen, 1992.

Bartoszewski, Wladyslaw T. *The Convent at Auschwitz*. New York: George Braziller, 1991.

———. *The Warsaw Ghetto: A Christian's Testimony*. Translated by Stephen G. Cappellari. Boston: Beacon Press, 1987.

Baseheart, Mary Catharine, S.C.N. *Person in the World: Introduction to the Philosophy of Edith Stein*. Dordrecht, Netherlands: Kluwer Academic Publishers, 1997.

Baum, Gregory. *The Social Imperative*. New York: Paulist Press, 1979.

Beckwith, John. *Early Medieval Art: Carolingian, Ottonian, Romanesque.* London: Thames and Hudson, 1969.

Bednar, Gerald J. *Faith as Imagination: The Contribution of William F. Lynch, S.J.* Kansas City: Sheed and Ward, 1996.

Bellow, Saul. *To Jerusalem and Back: A Personal Account.* New York: Viking, 1976.

Berlin, Isaiah. *Karl Marx: His Life and Environment.* London: Fontana Press, 1995.

Bernard of Clairvaux. *Five Books on Consideration: Advice to a Pope.* Translated by John D. Anderson and Elizabeth T. Kennan. Kalamazoo, Mich.: Cistercian Publications, 1976.

———. *The Letters of St. Bernard of Clairvaux.* Translated by Bruno Scott James. Stroud, U.K.: Sutton Publishing, 1998.

Bernstein, Carl, and Marco Politi. *His Holiness: John Paul II and the Hidden History of Our Time.* New York: Doubleday, 1996.

Blackbourn, David. *Marpingen: Apparitions of the Virgin Mary in Bismarckian Germany.* Oxford: Oxford University Press, 1993.

———. *Populists and Patricians: Essays in Modern German History.* London: Allen and Unwin, 1987.

Blackmann, Ann. *Seasons of Her Life: A Biography of Madeleine Korbel Albright.* New York: Scribner, 1998.

Blake, E. O., and C. Morris. "A Hermit Goes to War: Peter and the Origins of the First Crusade." In *Monks, Hermits, and the Ascetic Tradition: Papers Read at the 1984 Summer Meeting and the 1985 Winter Meeting of the Ecclesiastical History Society.* Edited by W. J. Sheils. London: Basil Blackwell, 1985, 79–108.

Blet, Pierre. *Pius XII and the Second World War: According to the Archives of the Vatican.* Translated by Lawrence J. Johnson. New York: Paulist Press, 1997.

Bloom, Harold. *Kabbalah and Criticism.* New York: Continuum, 1983.

Bloomberg, Marty, and Buckley Barry Barrett. *The Jewish Holocaust: An Annotated Guide to Books in English.* San Bernardino, Calif.: Borgo Press, 1995.

Bloy, Léon. *Pilgrim of the Absolute.* Edited by Raissa Maritain. Translated by John Coleman and Harry Lorin Binsse. London: Eyre and Spottiswoode, 1947.

Blumenberg, Werner. *Portrait of Marx: An Illustrated Biography.* Translated by Douglas Scott. New York: Herder and Herder, 1972.

Blumenthal, David R. "Repentance and Forgiveness." *Cross Currents* 48 (spring 1998): 75–82.

Boff, Leonardo, and Clodobis Boff. *Introducing Liberation Theology.* Translated by Paul Burns. Maryknoll, N.Y.: Orbis Books, 1990.

Bonfil, Robert. "Change in the Cultural Patterns of a Jewish Society in Crisis: Italian Jewry at the Close of the Sixteenth Century." *Jewish History* 3, no. 2 (fall 1998): 11–30.

Bonhoeffer, Dietrich. *A Testament to Freedom: The Essential Writings of Dietrich Bonhoeffer.* Edited by Geoffrey B. Kelly and F. Burton Nelson. San Francisco: HarperSanFrancisco, 1990.

Borg, Marcus J. *Jesus, a New Vision: Spirit, Culture, and the Life of Discipleship.* San Francisco: HarperSanFrancisco, 1987.

Borowitz, Eugene B. *Contemporary Christologies: A Jewish Response.* New York: Paulist Press, 1980.

———. "The Dialectic of Jewish Particularity." *Journal of Ecumenical Studies* 8, no. 3 (summer 1971): 560–74.

Borowski, Tadeusz. *This Way for the Gas, Ladies and Gentlemen.* Translated by Michael Kandel. New York: Penguin, 1976.

Bowersock, G. W., Peter Brown, and Oleg Grabar, eds. *Late Antiquity: A Guide to the Postclassical World.* Cambridge: Belknap Press, 1999.

Boys, Mary C. "The Cross: Should a Symbol Betrayed Be Reclaimed?" *Cross Currents* 44, no. 1 (spring 1994), 5–27.

———. *Has God Only One Blessing? Judaism as a Source of Christian Self-Understanding.* New York: Paulist Press, 2000.

Brenan, Gerald. *St. John of the Cross: His Life and Poetry.* London: Cambridge University Press, 1973.

Brett, Mark G., ed. *Ethnicity and the Bible.* Leiden, Netherlands: E. J. Brill, 1966.

Brinkley, Alan. *Voices of Protest: Huey Long, Father Coughlin, and the Great Depression.* New York: Vintage, 1983.

Bron, Michal, Jr., ed. *Jews and Christians: Who Is Your Neighbour after the Holocaust?* Acta Sueco-Polonica, Bokserie, 2. Uppsala, Sweden: Uppsala Universitet, 1997.

Broshi, Magen. "The Role of the Temple in the Herodian Economy." *Journal of Jewish Studies* 38, no. 1 (spring 1987), 31–37.

Brown, Peter. *Augustine of Hippo.* Berkeley: University of California Press, 1969.

———. *Religion and Society in the Age of Saint Augustine.* London: Faber and Faber, 1972.

Brown, Raymond E., S.S. *The Death of the Messiah: From Gethsemane to the Grave. A Commentary on the Passion Narratives in the Four Gospels.* 2 vols. New York: Doubleday, 1994.

———. *An Introduction to the New Testament.* New York: Doubleday, 1997.

Bruno, Giordano. *The Expulsion of the Triumphant Beast.* Translated and edited by Arthur D Imerti. New Brunswick, N.J.: Rutgers University Press, 1964.

Bunson, Matthew. *The Pope Encyclopedia: An A to Z of the Holy See.* New York: Crown, 1995.

Burns, Michael. *Dreyfus: A Family Affair. From the French Revolution to the Holocaust.* New York: HarperPerennial, 1992.

Burns, Robert I., S.J., ed. *Emperor of Culture: Alfonso X the Learned of Castile and His Thirteenth-Century Renaissance.* Philadelphia: University of Pennsylvania Press, 1990.

Burrell, David, and Yehezkel Landau, eds. *Voices from Jerusalem: Jews and Christians Reflect on the Holy Land.* New York: Paulist Press, 1992.

Burroway, Janet. *Writing Fiction: A Guide to Narrative Craft.* Boston: Little, Brown, 1987.

Buytaert, Eligii M., O.F.M., ed. *Petri Abaelardi Opera Theologica.* Vol. 1, *Commentaria in Epistolam Pauli ad Romanos.* Turnholt, Belgium: Typographi Brepols Editores Pontificii, 1969.

Cameron, Averil. *The Later Roman Empire: A.D. 284–430.* Cambridge: Harvard University Press, 1993.

Cargas, Harry James. *Shadows of Auschwitz: A Christian Response to the Holocaust.* New York: Crossroad, 1990.

———, ed. *The Unnecessary Problem of Edith Stein.* Lanham, Md.: University Press of America, 1994.

Carlebach, Julius. "The Problem of Moses Hess's Influence on the Young Marx." In *Publications of the Leo Baeck Institute, Year Book 17.* London: Secker and Warburg, 1973.

Carlen, Claudia, I.H.M., ed. *The Papal Encyclicals, 1939–1958.* Raleigh, N.C.: McGrath Publishing, 1981.

Carroll, James. *An American Requiem: God, My Father, and the War That Came Between Us.* Boston: Houghton Mifflin, 1996.

———. "The Holocaust and the Catholic Church." *Atlantic Monthly* 284, no. 4 (October 1999), 107–12.

———. "The Saint and the Holocaust." *The New Yorker,* June 7, 1999, 52–57.

———. "The Silence." *The New Yorker,* April 7, 1997, 52–68.

Chadwick, Henry. *The Early Church.* London: Penguin, 1993.

Chazan, Robert. *Daggers of Faith: Thirteenth-Century Christian Missionizing and Jewish Response.* Berkeley: University of California Press, 1989.

———. *European Jewry and the First Crusade.* Berkeley: University of California Press, 1987.

———. *In the Year 1096: The First Crusade and the Jews.* Philadelphia: Jewish Publication Society, 1996.

Coakley, Sarah. *Christ Without Absolutes: A Study of the Christology of Ernst Troeltsch.* Oxford: Clarendon Press, 1988.

Cohen, Jeremy. *The Friars and the Jews: The Evolution of Medieval Anti-Judaism.* Ithaca, N.Y.: Cornell University Press, 1982.

———, ed. *Essential Papers on Judaism and Christianity in Conflict: From Late Antiquity to the Reformation.* New York: New York University Press, 1991.

Cohen, Marc R. *Under Crescent and Cross: The Jews in the Middle Ages.* Princeton: Princeton University Press, 1994.

Cohen, Martin A., and Helga Croner, eds. *Christian Mission — Jewish Mission.* New York: Paulist Press, 1982.

Cohen, Shaye J. D. *From the Maccabees to the Mishnah.* Philadelphia: Westminster Press, 1987.

Cohn, Emil Bernhard, *This Immortal People: A Short History of the Jewish People.* Translated by Hayim Gorem Perelmuter. New York: Paulist Press, 1985.

Cohn-Sherbok, Dan. *The Crucified Jew: Twenty Centuries of Christian Anti-Semitism.* Grand Rapids, Mich.: Eerdmans Publishing/American Interfaith Institute and the World Alliance of Interfaith Organizations, 1997.

Conquest, Robert. *The Harvest of Sorrow: Soviet Collectivization and the Terror-Famine.* New York: Oxford University Press, 1986.

Constantine. "Constantine Summons the Council of Nicaea." In *A New Eusebius: Documents Illustrating the History of the Church to* A.D. *337,* edited and translated by James Stevenson. Cambridge, U.K.: SPCK, 1987, 338.

Cooke, Bernard J. *God's Beloved: Jesus' Experience of the Transcendent.* Philadelphia: Trinity Press International, 1992.

Cornwell, John. *Hitler's Pope: The Secret History of Pius XII.* New York: Viking, 1999.

Cott, Jeremy. "The Biblical Problem of Election." *Journal of Ecumenical Studies* 21, no. 2 (spring 1984), 199–228.

Cotter, James Finn. *Inscape: The Christology and Poetry of Gerard Manley Hopkins.* Pittsburgh: University of Pittsburgh Press, 1972.

Craughwell, Thomas. "Pius XII and the Holocaust," *Sursum Corda,* spring 1998.

Croke, Brian, and Jill Harries. *Religious Conflict in Fourth-Century Rome.* Sydney: Sydney University Press, 1982.

Crossan, John Dominic. *The Birth of Christianity: Discovering What Happened in the Years Immediately after the Execution of Jesus*. San Francisco: HarperSanFrancisco, 1998.

———. *The Historical Jesus: The Life of a Mediterranean Jewish Peasant*. San Francisco: HarperSanFrancisco, 1991.

———. *Jesus: A Revolutionary Biography*. San Francisco: HarperSanFrancisco, 1994.

———. *A Long Way from Tipperary: What a Former Irish Monk Discovered in His Search for the Truth*. San Francisco: HarperSanFrancisco, 2000.

———. *Who Killed Jesus? Exposing the Roots of Anti-Semitism in the Gospel Story of the Death of Jesus*. San Francisco: HarperSanFrancisco, 1995.

Cunningham, Phillip A. *Education for Shalom: Religion Textbooks and the Enhancement of the Catholic and Jewish Relationship*. Collegeville, Minn.: Liturgical Press, 1995.

Dadrian, Vahakn N. *The History of the Armenian Genocide: Ethnic Conflict from the Balkans to Anatolia to the Caucasus*. Providence: Berghahn Books, 1995.

Dan, Joseph, ed. *The Christian Kabbalah: Jewish Mystical Books and Their Christian Interpreters*. Cambridge: Harvard University Press, 1997.

———. *The Early Kabbalah*. Translated by Ronald C. Kiener. New York, Paulist Press, 1986.

Dawidowicz, Lucy S. *The War Against the Jews, 1935–1945*. New York: Bantam, 1975.

Dawson, Christopher. *The Making of Europe: An Introduction to the History of European Unity*. New York: Sheed and Ward, 1952.

Deák, István. "The Pope, the Nazis, and the Jews." *New York Review of Books* 47, no. 5 (March 23, 2000), 44–49.

Deferrari, Roy J., ed. *The Fathers of the Church*, vols. 22, 27. New York: Fathers of the Church, Inc., 1953, 1955.

Denby, David. *Great Books: My Adventures with Homer, Rousseau, Woolf, and Other Indestructible Writers of the Western World*. New York: Simon and Schuster, 1996.

Dershowitz, Alan M. *The Vanishing American Jew: In Search of Jewish Identity for the Next Century*. New York: Little, Brown, 1997.

Dewart, Leslie. *The Future of Belief: Theism in a World Come of Age*. New York: Herder and Herder, 1966.

Dietrich, Donald J. *Catholic Citizens in the Third Reich: Psycho-Social Principles and Moral Reasoning*. New Brunswick, N.J.: Transaction Books, 1988.

Dimsdale, Joel E. *Survivors, Victims, and Perpetrators: Essays on the Nazi Holocaust*. New York: Hemisphere Publishing, 1980.

Döllinger, Johann Ignaz von. "The Jews in Europe." In *Studies in European History: Being Academical Addresses Delivered by John Ignatius von Döllinger*. Translated by Margaret Warre. London: John Murray, 1890.

Douglass, James W. *The Non-Violent Cross: A Theology of Revolution and Peace*. New York: Macmillan, 1968.

Drijvers, Jan Willem. *Helena Augusta: The Mother of Constantine the Great and the Legend of Her Finding of the True Cross*. Leiden, Netherlands: E. J. Brill, 1992.

Dudden, F. H. *The Life and Times of Saint Ambrose*. Oxford: Clarendon Press, 1935.

Dunn, James D. G. *The Partings of the Ways: Between Christianity and Judaism and their Significance for the Character of Christianity*. Philadelphia: Trinity Press International, 1991.

———. *Unity and Diversity in the New Testament: An Inquiry into the Character of Earliest Christianity*. Valley Forge, Pa.: Trinity Press International, 1990.

———, ed. *Jews and Christians: The Parting of the Ways, A.D. 70 to 135.* Tübingen: J.C.B. Mohr (Paul Siebeck), 1992.

Dupuis, Jacques. *Toward a Christian Theology of Religious Pluralism.* Maryknoll, N.Y.: Orbis Books, 1997.

Edwards, John. *The Jews in Christian Europe, 1400–1700.* London: Routledge, 1988.

Eidelberg, Shlomo. *The Jews and the Crusaders: The Hebrew Chronicles of the First and Second Crusades.* Madison: University of Wisconsin Press, 1977.

Eisenhower, Dwight D. *Crusade in Europe.* New York: Doubleday, 1948.

Elie, Paul. "John Paul's Jewish Dilemma." *New York Times Magazine,* April 26, 1998.

Eliot, T. S. *Collected Poems, 1909–1962.* San Diego: Harcourt Brace Jovanovich, 1988.

Engel, David. *Facing a Holocaust: The Polish Government-in-Exile and the Jews, 1943–1945.* Chapel Hill: University of North Carolina Press, 1993.

Ericksen, Robert P. *Theologians under Hitler: Gerhard Kittel, Paul Althaus, and Emanuel Hirsch.* New Haven: Yale University Press, 1985.

Ericksen, Robert P., and Susannah Heschel, eds. *Betrayal: German Churches and the Holocaust.* Minneapolis: Fortress Press, 1999.

Eusebius Pamphilus. "The Life of the Blessed Emperor Constantine." In *Nicene and Post-Nicene Fathers,* 2d ser. Vol. 1, *Eusebius: Church History, Life of Constantine the Great, and Oration in Praise of Constantine,* edited by Philip Schaff and Henry Wace. Peabody, Mass.: Hendrickson, 1994.

Evans, Ellen Lovell. *The German Center Party, 1870–1933: A Study in Political Catholicism.* Carbondale: Southern Illinois University Press, 1981.

Evans, G. R. *Anselm.* Wilton, Conn.: Morehouse-Barlow, 1989.

———. *The Mind of St. Bernard of Clairvaux.* Oxford: Clarendon Press, 1983.

Ezrahi, Sidra DeKoven. *Booking Passage: Exile and Homecoming in the Modern Jewish Imagination.* Berkeley: University of California Press, 2000.

Fabrégues, Jean de. *Edith Stein.* Translated by Donald M. Antoine. Staten Island, N.Y.: Alba House, 1965.

Fackenheim, Emil. *To Mend the World.* New York: Schocken, 1982.

Falconi, Carlo. *The Silence of Pius XII.* Boston: Little, Brown, 1965.

Farmer, William R., and Roch Kereszty. *Peter and Paul in the Church of Rome: The Ecumenical Potential of a Forgotten Perspective.* New York: Paulist Press, 1990.

Fasching, Darrell J. *The Coming of the Millennium: Good News for the Whole Human Race.* Valley Forge, Pa.: Trinity Press International, 1996.

Fein, Helen. *Accounting for Genocide: National Responses and Jewish Victimization During the Holocaust.* New York: Free Press, 1979.

Feldman, Louis H. *Jew and Gentile in the Ancient World: Attitudes and Interactions from Alexander to Justinian.* Princeton: Princeton University Press, 1993.

Ficino, Marsilio. *The Book of Life.* Translated by Charles Boer. Irving, Tex.: Spring Publications, 1980.

Finkelstein, Norman G., and Ruth Bettina Birn. *A Nation on Trial: The Goldhagen Thesis and Historical Truth.* New York: Henry Holt, 1998.

Fishbane, Michael. *The Exegetical Imagination: On Jewish Thought and Theology.* Cambridge: Harvard University Press, 1998.

Fisher, Eugene J. *Seminary Education and Christian-Jewish Relations: A Curriculum and Resource Handbook.* Washington, D.C.: National Catholic Educational Association in cooperation with the American Jewish Committee and the Secretariat for Catholic-Jewish Relations, National Conference of Catholic Bishops, 1988.

——, ed. *Interwoven Destinies: Jews and Christians Through the Ages.* New York: Paulist Press, 1993.

——, ed. *Visions of the Other: Jewish and Christian Theologians Assess the Dialogue.* New York: Paulist Press, 1994.

Fisher, Eugene J., James A. Rudin, and Marc H. Tanenbaum, eds. *Twenty Years of Jewish-Catholic Relations.* New York: Paulist Press, 1986.

Flannery, Edward H. *The Anguish of the Jews: Twenty-three Centuries of Antisemitism.* New York: Paulist Press, 1985.

Fleischner, Eva, ed. *Auschwitz: Beginning of a New Era?* New York: Ktav, 1977.

Fletcher, Richard. *Moorish Spain.* Berkeley: University of California Press, 1993.

Foley, George Cadwalader. *Anselm's Theory of the Atonement.* New York: Longmans, Green, 1909.

Fornberg, Tord. *Jewish-Christian Dialogue and Biblical Exegesis.* Uppsala, Sweden: Studia Missionalia Upsaliensia, 1988.

Foster, R. F. *Modern Ireland, 1600–1972.* London: Allen Lane/ Penguin, 1988.

Foxman, Abraham H., and Eugene J. Fisher. "Should the Vatican Beatify Its World War II Pope?" *Moment,* February 1999, 46.

Francq, Henri, and Mary (Hrenchuk) Pankiw. *The Dreyfus Affair: The Clique of Saint-Dominique Street.* Sherbrooke, Quebec: Naaman, 1986.

Fredriksen, Paula. *Jesus of Nazareth King of the Jews: A Jewish Life and the Emergence of Christianity.* New York: Knopf, 1999.

——. "Paul." In *Augustine Through the Ages: An Encyclopedia,* Allan D. Fitzgerald, O.S.A., gen. ed. Grand Rapids, Mich.: Eerdmans, 1999.

Frend, W.H.C. *The Rise of Christianity.* London: Darton, Longman and Todd, 1984.

Freud, Sigmund. *Moses and Monotheism.* Translated by Katherine Jones. New York: Vintage, 1967.

Friedman, Philip. "The Fate of the Jewish Book During the Nazi Era." In *Jewish Book Annual: The American Year Book of Jewish Literary Creativity.* New York: Jewish Book Council, 1997.

Friedman, Saul S. *The Oberammergau Passion Play: A Lance Against Civilization.* Carbondale: Southern Illinois University Press, 1984.

Fritzsche, Peter. *Germans into Nazis.* Cambridge: Harvard University Press, 1998.

Gager, John G. *The Origins of Anti-Semitism: Attitudes Toward Judaism in Pagan and Christian Antiquity.* New York: Oxford University Press, 1985.

——. *Reinventing Paul.* New York: Oxford University Press, 2000.

Gaillardetz, Richard R. *Witnesses to the Faith: Community, Infallibility, and the Ordinary Magisterium of Bishops.* New York: Paulist Press, 1992.

Geremek, Bronislaw. "The Marginal Man." In *The Medieval World,* edited by Jacques Le Goff, translated by Lydia G. Cochrane. London: Parkgate Books, 1997, 347–71.

Gilbert, Martin. *The Atlas of Jewish History.* New York: William Morrow, 1993.

Gilman, Richard. *Faith, Sex, Mystery: A Memoir.* New York: Simon and Schuster, 1986.

Gilson, Étienne. *Héloïse and Abelard.* Ann Arbor: University of Michigan Press, 1992.

Ginio, Alisa Meyuhas, ed. *Jews, Christians, and Muslims in the Mediterranean World after 1492.* London: Frank Cass, 1992.

Goldberg, Michael. *Jews and Christianity: Getting Our Stories Straight.* Philadelphia: Trinity Press International, 1991.

——. *Why Should Jews Survive? Looking Past the Holocaust Toward a Jewish Future.* New York: Oxford University Press, 1995.

Goldhagen, Daniel Jonah. *Hitler's Willing Executioners: Ordinary Germans and the Holocaust.* New York: Knopf, 1996.

Goodenough, Erwin R. *Jewish Symbols in the Greco-Roman Period.* Vol. 12, *Summary and Conclusions.* New York: Pantheon, 1965.

Goodich, Michael, Sophia Menache, and Sylvia Schein, eds. *Cross-Cultural Convergences in the Crusader Period: Essays Presented to Aryeh Grabois on His Sixty-fifth Birthday.* New York: Peter Lang, 1995.

Goodwin, Richard. *The Hinge of the World.* New York: Farrar, Straus and Giroux, 1998.

Gordon, Cyrus H., and Gary A. Rendsburg. *The Bible and the Ancient Near East.* New York: Norton, 1997.

Gordon, Mary. "Saint Edith?" *Tikkun* 14, no. 2 (March–April 1999), 17–20.

Grant, Michael. *Saint Peter: A Biography.* New York: Scribner, 1995.

Green, Garrett. *Imaging God: Theology and the Religious Imagination.* San Francisco: Harper and Row, 1987.

Greenberg, Irving. "The Relationship of Judaism and Christianity: Toward a New Organic Model." *Quarterly Review* 4, no. 4 (winter 1984), 4–22.

Greene, Graham. "The Pope Who Remains a Priest." *Life,* September 24, 1951.

Gregory, Brad S. *Salvation at Stake: Christian Martyrdom in Early Modern Europe.* Cambridge: Harvard University Press, 1999.

Gullan-Whur, Margaret. *Within Reason: A Life of Spinoza.* London: Jonathan Cape, 1998.

Haas, Christopher. *Alexandria in Late Antiquity: Topography and Social Conflict.* Baltimore: Johns Hopkins University Press, 1997.

Halbertal, Moshe. *People of the Book: Canon, Meaning, and Authority.* Cambridge: Harvard University Press, 1997.

Halbertal, Moshe, and Avishai Margalit. *Idolatry.* Translated by Naomi Goldblum. Cambridge: Harvard University Press, 1992.

Hallamish, Moshe. *An Introduction to the Kabbalah.* Translated by Ruth Bar-Ilan and Ora Wiskind-Elper. Albany: State University of New York Press, 1999.

Hamerow, Theodore S. *On the Road to the Wolf's Lair.* Cambridge: Harvard University Press, 1997.

Hamerton-Kelly, Robert G. *Sacred Violence: Paul's Hermeneutic of the Cross.* Minneapolis: Fortress Press, 1992.

Haran, Menahem. *Temples and Temple-Service in Ancient Israel: An Inquiry into Biblical Cult Phenomena and the Historical Setting of the Priestly School.* Winona Lake, Ind.: Eisenbrauns, 1985.

Harpur, James. *Revelations: The Medieval World.* New York: Henry Holt, 1995.

Hartman, David. *A Heart of Many Rooms: Celebrating the Many Voices Within Judaism.* Woodstock, Vt.: Jewish Lights, 1999.

——. "Judaism Encounters Christianity Anew." In *Visions of the Other: Jewish and Christian Theologians Assess the Dialogue,* edited by Eugene J. Fisher. New York: Paulist Press, 1994.

——. *A Living Covenant: The Innovative Spirit in Traditional Judaism.* Woodstock, Vt.: Jewish Lights, 1997.

Hastings, Max. *Victory in Europe: D-Day to V-E Day.* Boston: Little, Brown, 1985.

Hay, Malcolm. *The Roots of Christian Anti-Semitism.* New York: Freedom Library Press, 1981.

Heaney, Seamus. *The Government of the Tongue: Selected Prose, 1978–1987.* New York: Farrar, Straus and Giroux, 1989.

Hebblethwaite, Peter. *Paul VI: The First Modern Pope.* New York: Paulist Press, 1993.

———. *In the Vatican: How the Church Is Run — Its Personalities, Traditions, and Conflicts.* Bethesda, Md.: Adler and Adler, 1986.

Heilbron, J. L. *The Sun in the Church: Cathedrals as Solar Observatories.* Cambridge: Harvard University Press, 1999.

Heller, Celia S. *On the Edge of Destruction: Jews of Poland Between the Two World Wars.* New York: Schocken, 1980.

Helmreich, Ernst Christian. *The German Churches under Hitler: Background, Struggle, and Epilogue.* Detroit: Wayne State University Press, 1979.

Herbstrith, Waltraud. *Edith Stein: A Biography.* Translated by Father Bernard Bonowitz, O.C.S.O. San Francisco: Harper and Row, 1985.

Hertzberg, Arthur. *The French Enlightenment and the Jews.* New York: Columbia University Press/Jewish Publication Society, 1968.

Heschel, Abraham Joshua. *God in Search of Man: A Philosophy of Judaism.* New York: Noonday, 1997.

———. *Man Is Not Alone: A Philosophy of Religion.* New York: Noonday, 1997.

———. *Moral Grandeur and Spiritual Audacity.* Edited by Susannah Heschel. New York: Noonday, 1997.

———. *A Passion for Truth.* New York: Farrar, Straus and Giroux, 1973.

———. *The Sabbath: Its Meaning for Modern Man.* New York: Noonday, 1997.

Heschel, Susannah. *Abraham Geiger and the Jewish Jesus.* Chicago: University of Chicago Press, 1998.

Hilberg, Raul. *The Destruction of the European Jews.* 3 vols. New York: Holmes and Meier, 1985.

———. *Perpetrators, Victims, Bystanders: The Jewish Catastrophe, 1933–1945.* New York: HarperCollins, 1992.

Hill, Roland. "'I Am the Tradition': How the Pope Became Infallible." *Times Literary Supplement,* no. 5009 (April 2, 1999), 9.

Hillesum, Etty. *An Interrupted Life: The Diaries of Etty Hillesum, 1941–1943.* New York: Washington Square Press, 1985.

Hirshman, Marc. *A Rivalry of Genius: Jewish and Christian Biblical Interpretation in Late Antiquity.* Translated by Batya Stein. Albany: State University of New York Press, 1996.

Hochhuth, Rolf. *The Deputy.* Translated by Richard Winston and Clara Winston. New York: Grove Press, 1964.

Hochschild, Adam. *King Leopold's Ghost: A Story of Greed, Terror, and Heroism in Colonial Africa.* Boston: Houghton Mifflin, 1998.

Hoffman, Eva. *Shtetl: The Life and Death of a Small Town and the World of Polish Jews.* Boston: Houghton Mifflin, 1997.

Hoffman, Peter. *The History of the German Resistance, 1933–1945.* Translated by Richard Barry. Cambridge: MIT Press, 1997.

Hoffman, Robert L. *More Than a Trial: The Struggle over Captain Dreyfus.* New York: Free Press, 1980.

Holy Bible. Revised Standard Version. New York: Nelson, 1952.

Horsley, Richard A., and Neil Asher Silberman. *The Message and the Kingdom: How Jesus and Paul Ignited a Revolution and Transformed the Ancient World.* New York: Grosset/Putnam, 1997.

Hughes, H. Stuart. *Prisoners of Hope: The Silver Age of the Italian Jews, 1924–1974.* Cambridge: Harvard University Press, 1983.

Hughes, Kathleen, R.S.C.J. *The Monk's Tale: A Biography of Godfrey Diekmann, O.S.B.* Collegeville, Minn.: Liturgical Press, 1991.

Idel, Moshe. *Kabbalah: New Perspectives.* New Haven: Yale University Press, 1988.

———. *Studies in Ecstatic Kabbalah.* Albany: State University of New York Press, 1988.

Isaac, Jules. *Has Anti-Semitism Roots in Christianity?* Translated by Dorothy Parkes and James Parkes. New York: National Conference of Christians and Jews, 1961.

———. *Jesus and Israel.* Translated by Sally Gran. New York: Holt, Rinehart and Winston, 1971.

Janson, H. W. *History of Art.* New York: Abrams, 1986.

Jeremias, Joachim. *Jerusalem in the Time of Jesus: An Investigation into Economic and Social Conditions During the New Testament Period.* Translated by F. H. Cave and C. H. Cave. Philadelphia: Fortress Press, 1969.

John Paul II. *Spiritual Pilgrimage: Texts on Jews and Judaism, 1979–1995.* Edited by Eugene J. Fisher and Leon Klenicki. New York: Crossroad/Anti-Defamation League, 1995.

Johnson, Paul. *Modern Times: The World from the Twenties to the Eighties.* New York: Harper and Row, 1980.

Josephus, Flavius. *The Jewish War,* books 1–7. Translated by H. St. J. Thackeray. Cambridge: Harvard University Press, 1997.

Joyce, James. *A Portrait of the Artist as a Young Man.* New York: Viking, 1960.

———. *Ulysses.* New York: Random House, 1961.

Kamen, Henry. *Inquisition and Society in Spain: In the Sixteenth and Seventeenth Centuries.* Bloomington: Indiana University Press, 1985.

Kaplan, Edward K. *Holiness in Words: Abraham Joshua Heschel's Poetics of Piety.* Albany: State University of New York Press, 1996.

———, and Samuel H. Dresner. *Abraham Joshua Heschel: Prophetic Witness.* New Haven: Yale University Press, 1998.

Katz, Jacob. *Exclusiveness and Tolerance: Studies in Jewish-Gentile Relations in Medieval and Modern Times.* London: Oxford University Press, 1961.

Katz, Steven. *Post-Holocaust Dialogues: Critical Studies in Modern Jewish Thought.* New York: New York University Press, 1983.

Kaufman, Gordon D. *God, Mystery, Diversity: Christian Theology in a Pluralistic World.* Minneapolis: Augsburg Fortress, 1996.

Keegan, John. *The Battle for History: Re-Fighting World War II.* New York: Vintage, 1996.

Kelly, J.N.D. *Early Christian Doctrines.* San Francisco: Harper and Row, 1978.

Kennedy, Eugene. "A Dissenting Voice: Catholic Theologian David Tracy." *New York Times Magazine,* November 9, 1986.

Kenny, Anthony. *Catholics, Jews, and the State of Israel.* New York: Paulist Press, 1993.

Kersting, Hans. *Rundewege Mainz.* Bamberg, Germany: Bayerische Verlagsanstalt Bamberg, 1993.

Kertzer, David I. *The Kidnapping of Edgardo Mortara.* New York: Knopf, 1997.

———. *Sacrificed for Honor: Italian Infant Abandonment and the Politics of Reproductive Control.* Boston: Beacon Press, 1993.

Kimelman, Reuven. "Birkat Ha-Minim and the Lack of Evidence for an Anti-Christian Jewish Prayer in Late Antiquity." In *Jewish and Christian Self-Definition,* vol. 2, edited by E. P. Sanders. Philadelphia: Fortress Press, 1980.

Kissinger, Henry. *Diplomacy.* New York: Simon and Schuster, 1994.

———. "The White Revolutionary: Reflections on Bismarck." In *Philosophers and Kings: Studies in Leadership,* edited by Dankwart A. Rustow. New York: George Braziller, 1970.

Klenicki, Leon, ed. *Toward a Theological Encounter: Jewish Understandings of Christianity.* New York: Paulist Press, 1991.

———, and Geoffrey Wigoder, eds. *A Dictionary of the Jewish-Christian Dialogue.* New York: Paulist Press, 1995.

Koester, Helmut. *Introduction to the New Testament.* Vol. 1, *History, Culture, and Religion of the Hellenistic Age.* Vol. 2, *History and Literature of Early Christianity.* Philadelphia: Fortress Press; Berlin and New York: De Gruyter, 1982.

———. "Explaining Jesus' Crucifixion." *Bible Review* 11, no. 3 (June 1995), 16.

———. "Historic Mistakes Haunt the Relationship of Christianity and Judaism." *Biblical Archeology Review* 21, no. 2 (March–April 1995), 26–27.

———. "The Passion Narratives and the Roots of Anti-Judaism." *Bible Review* 9, no. 1 (February 1993), 5.

Kornberg, Jacques. "Ignaz von Döllinger's *Die Juden in Europa:* A Catholic Polemic Against Antisemitism." *Journal for the History of Modern Theology* 6, no. 2 (1999), 223–45.

Kraabel, A. T. "Unity and Diversity among Diaspora Synagogues." In *The Synagogue in Late Antiquity,* edited by Lee I. Levine. Philadelphia: American Schools of Oriental Research, 1987, 49–60.

Kraemer, Ross S. "Jewish Tuna and Christian Fish: Identifying Religious Affiliation in Epigraphic Sources." *Harvard Theological Review* 84, no. 2 (April 1991), 141–62.

Kristeller, Paul Oskar. *Renaissance Thought and Its Sources.* New York: Cambridge University Press, 1979.

Kübler-Ross, Elisabeth. *On Death and Dying.* New York: Macmillan, 1969.

Kugel, James L. *The Bible as It Was.* Cambridge: Belknap Press, 1997.

Kühner, Hans. *Encyclopedia of the Papacy.* Translated by Kenneth J. Northcott. New York: Philosophical Library, 1958.

Küng, Hans. *On Being a Christian.* Translated by Edward Quinn. New York: Doubleday, 1976.

———. *Christianity: Essence, History, and Future.* Translated by John Bowden. New York: Continuum, 1995.

———. *The Council, Reform, and Reunion.* Translated by Cecily Hastings. New York: Sheed and Ward, 1961.

———. *Great Christian Thinkers.* Translated by John Bowden. New York: Continuum, 1994.

———. *Infallible? An Unresolved Enquiry.* Translated by John Bowden. New York: Continuum, 1994.

———. *Judaism: Between Yesterday and Tomorrow.* Translated by John Bowden. New York: Crossroad, 1992.

———. *Reforming the Church Today: Keeping Hope Alive.* Translated by Peter Heinegg et al. Edinburgh: T. & T. Clark, 1992.

Kwitny, Jonathan. *Man of the Century: The Life and Times of Pope John Paul II.* New York: Henry Holt, 1997.

La Farge, John, S.J. *The Manner Is Ordinary.* New York: Harcourt, Brace and Company, 1954.

Landes, David S. *The Wealth and Poverty of Nations: Why Some Are So Rich and Some So Poor.* New York: Norton, 1998.

Langer, Lawrence L. *Admitting the Holocaust: Collected Essays.* New York: Oxford University Press, 1995.

———. *Holocaust Testimonies: The Ruins of Memory.* New Haven: Yale University Press, 1991.

Lanzman, Claude. *Shoah: An Oral History of the Holocaust. The Complete Text of the Film.* New York: Pantheon, 1985.

Latourelle, René, ed. *Vatican II: Assessment and Perspectives, Twenty-five Years After (1962–1987),* vol. 3. New York: Paulist Press, 1989.

Lee, Bernard J., S.M. *Jesus and the Metaphors of God: The Christs of the New Testament.* New York: Paulist Press, 1993.

Le Goff, Jacques. *Your Money or Your Life: Economy and Religion in the Middle Ages.* New York: Zone Books, 1988.

———, ed. *The Medieval World.* Translated by Lydia G. Cochrane. London: Parkgate Books, 1990.

Lemkin, Raphael. *Axis Rule in Occupied Europe.* Washington, D.C.: Carnegie Endowment for International Peace, 1944.

Lerner, Michael. *Jewish Renewal: A Path to Healing and Transformation.* New York: Putnam, 1994.

Levenson, Jon D. *The Death and Resurrection of the Beloved Son: The Transformation of Child Sacrifice in Judaism and Christianity.* New Haven: Yale University Press, 1993.

———. "The Temple and the World." *Journal of Religion* 64, no. 3 (July 1984), 275–98.

———. "The Universal Horizon of Biblical Particularism." In *Ethnicity and the Bible,* edited by Mark G. Brett. Leiden, Netherlands: Brill, 1996.

Levi, Primo. *If Not Now, When?* Translated by William Weaver. New York: Penguin, 1986.

———. *The Reawakening.* Translated by Stuart Woolf. New York: Simon and Schuster, 1995.

———. *Survival in Auschwitz: The Nazi Assault on Humanity.* Translated by Stuart Woolf. New York: Simon and Schuster, 1996.

Levinas, Emmanuel. *Totality and Infinity: An Essay on Exteriority.* Translated by Alphonso Lingis. Pittsburgh: Duquesne University Press, 1969.

Levine, Nancy, ed. "Teaching Troubling Texts." *Textual Reasoning: The Journal of the Postmodern Jewish Philosophy Network* 8, no. 2 (November 1999).

Lewy, Guenter. *The Catholic Church and Nazi Germany.* New York: McGraw-Hill, 1964.

Lindqvist, Sven. *"Exterminate All the Brutes": One Man's Odyssey into the Heart of Dark-

ness and the Origins of European Genocide. Translated by Joan Tate. New York: New Press, 1996.

Lipstadt, Deborah E. "Aryan Nation." *New York Times Book Review,* April 26, 1998.

Littell, Franklin H., and Hubert G. Locke, eds. *The German Church Struggle and the Holocaust.* Detroit: Wayne State University Press, 1974.

Lodahl, Michael E. *Shekhinah/Spirit: Divine Presence in Jewish and Christian Religion.* New York: Paulist Press, 1992.

Lohfink, Norbert, S.J. *The Covenant Never Revoked: Biblical Reflections on Christian-Jewish Dialogue.* Translated by John J. Scullion. New York: Paulist Press, 1991.

Lynch, William F., S.J. *Christ and Apollo: The Dimensions of the Literary Imagination.* New York: New American Library, 1963.

Lyotard, Jean-François. *Heidegger and "the jews."* Translated by Andreas Michel and Mark S. Roberts. Minneapolis: University of Minnesota Press, 1990.

MacIntyre, Alisdair. *After Virtue: A Study in Moral Theory.* Notre Dame: University of Notre Dame Press, 1981.

MacKay, Angus. "Popular Movements and Pogroms in Fifteenth-Century Castile." *Past and Present* 55 (May 1972), 33–67.

Macquarrie, John. *Jesus Christ in Modern Thought.* Philadelphia: Trinity Press International, 1991.

———. *Principles of Christian Theology.* New York: Scribner, 1966.

Magnus, Shulamit S. *Jewish Emancipation in a German City: Cologne, 1798–1871.* Stanford: Stanford University Press, 1997.

Maimonides, Moses. *Letters of Maimonides.* Edited and translated by Leon D. Stitskin. New York: Yeshiva University Press, 1977.

Man, John. *Atlas of the Year 1000.* Cambridge: Harvard University Press, 1999.

Manchester, William. *The Glory and the Dream: A Narrative History of America, 1932–1972.* Boston: Little, Brown, 1973.

Mandell, Sara. "Who Paid the Temple Tax When the Jews Were under Roman Rule?" *Harvard Theological Review* 77, no. 2 (April 1984), 223–32.

Mann, Vivian B., Thomas F. Glick, and Jerrilynn D. Dodds, eds. *Convivencia: Jews, Muslims, and Christians in Medieval Spain.* New York: George Braziller/Jewish Museum, 1992.

Marchione, Margherita. *Yours Is a Precious Witness: Memoirs of Jews and Catholics in Wartime Italy.* New York: Paulist Press, 1997.

Marcus, Jacob R. *The Jew in the Medieval World: A Source Book, 315–1791.* Cincinnati: Sinai Press, 1938.

Marius, Richard. *Martin Luther: The Christian Between God and Death.* Cambridge: Belknap Press, 1999.

Marks, Jane. *The Hidden Children: The Secret Survivors of the Holocaust.* New York: Fawcett Columbine, 1993.

Marrus, Michael R. *The Holocaust in History.* New York: New American Library, 1987.

———, and Robert O. Paxton. *Vichy France and the Jews.* New York: Schocken, 1983.

Marx, Karl, and Friedrich Engels. *Collected Works.* Vol. 1, *Karl Marx, 1835–1843.* New York: International Publishers, 1976.

———. *The Marx-Engels Reader.* Edited by Robert C. Tucker. New York: Norton, 1978.

Matheson, Peter, ed. *The Third Reich and the Christian Churches: A Documentary Account of Christian Resistance and Complicity During the Nazi Era.* Edinburgh: T. & T. Clark, 1981.

Maybaum, Ignaz. *The Face of God after Auschwitz.* Amsterdam: Polak and Van Gennep, 1965.

McBrien, Richard P., gen. ed. *The HarperCollins Encyclopedia of Catholicism.* San Francisco: HarperSanFrancisco, 1995.

McCallum, J. Ramsey. *Abelard's Christian Theology.* Merrick, N.Y.: Richwood, 1976.

McDougall, Walter A. *Promised Land, Crusader State: The American Encounter with the World Since 1776.* Boston: Houghton Mifflin, 1997.

McGuckin, John A. *St. Cyril of Alexandria: The Christological Controversy — Its History, Theology, and Texts.* Leiden, Netherlands: E. J. Brill, 1994.

McIntyre, John. *St. Anselm and His Critics: A Re-Interpretation of the* Cur Deus Homo. Edinburgh: Oliver and Boyd, 1954.

McKay, John P., Bennett D. Hill, and John A. Buckler. *A History of Western Society.* Boston: Houghton Mifflin, 1995.

McLaren, James S. "Turbulent Times? Josephus and Scholarship on Judaea in the First Century c.e." *Journal for the Study of the Pseudepigrapha,* suppl. ser. 29. Sheffield, U.K.: Sheffield Academic Press, 1998.

Meier, John P. *A Marginal Jew: Rethinking the Historical Jesus.* New York: Doubleday, 1991.

"Memory and Reconciliation: The Church and the Faults of the Past." http://jcrelations. com/stmnts/vatican12-99.htm.

Mickelm, Nathaniel. *National Socialism and the Roman Catholic Church.* London: Oxford University Press, 1939.

Milchman, Alan, and Alan Rosenberg, eds. *Postmodernism and the Holocaust.* Amsterdam: Rodopi, 1998.

Miles, Margaret R. "Santa Maria Maggiore's Fifth-Century Mosaics: Triumphal Christianity and the Jews." *Harvard Theological Review* 86, no. 2 (April 1993), 155–75.

Miles, Siân, ed. *Simone Weil: An Anthology.* New York: Weidenfeld and Nicolson, 1986.

Modras, Ronald. *The Catholic Church and Antisemitism: Poland, 1933–1939.* Chur, Switzerland: Harwood Academic Publishers, 1994.

Möltmann, Jurgen. *The Crucified God: The Cross of Christ as the Foundation and Criticism of Christian Theology.* Translated by R. A. Wilson and John Bowden. New York: Harper and Row, 1974.

Mor, Menachem, ed. *Jewish Assimilation, Acculturation, and Accommodation: Past Traditions, Current Issues, and Future Prospects.* Lanham, Md.: University Press of America, 1992.

Morley, John F. *Vatican Diplomacy and the Jews During the Holocaust, 1939–1943.* New York: Ktav, 1980.

Murphy-O'Connor, Jerome, O.P. *Paul: A Critical Life.* Oxford: Oxford University Press, 1996.

Nadler, Steven. *Spinoza: A Life.* New York: Cambridge University Press, 1999.

Neudecker, Reinhard, S.J. "The Catholic Church and the Jewish People." In *Vatican II: Assessment and Perspectives: Twenty-five Years After (1962–1978),* vol. 3, edited by René Latourelle. New York: Paulist Press, 1989.

Neusner, Jacob. *The Jewish War Against the Jews.* New York: Ktav, 1984.

———. *Judaism and Christianity in the Age of Constantine: History, Messiah, Israel, and the Initial Confrontation.* Chicago: University of Chicago Press, 1987.

------. *Method and Meaning in Ancient Judaism*. Missoula: Scholars Press, 1979.

------. *Telling Tales: Making Sense of Christian and Judaic Nonsense: The Urgency and Basis for Judeo-Christian Dialogue*. Louisville: Westminster/John Knox Press, 1993.

------, and Ernest S. Frerichs, eds. *"To See Ourselves as Others See Us": Christians, Jews, "Others" in Late Antiquity*. Chico, Calif.: Scholars Press, 1985.

Nicholas, Lynn H. *The Rape of Europa: The Fate of Europe's Treasures in the Third Reich and the Second World War*. New York: Vintage, 1995.

Nicolaus of Cusa. *Toward a New Council of Florence: "On the Peace of Faith" and Other Works by Nicolaus of Cusa*. Translated by William F. Wertz, Jr. Washington, D.C.: Schiller Institute, 1993.

Nolte, Ernst. *Three Faces of Fascism: Action Française, Italian Fascism, National Socialism*. Translated by Leila Vennewitz. New York: New American Library, 1969.

Novick, Peter. *The Holocaust in American Life*. Boston: Houghton Mifflin, 1999.

Oberman, Heiko A. *The Roots of Anti-Semitism in the Age of Renaissance and Reformation*. Translated by James I. Porter. Philadelphia: Fortress Press, 1984.

O'Brien, Conor Cruise. *Memoir: My Life and Themes*. New York: Cooper Square Press, 2000.

------. *The Siege: The Saga of Israel and Zionism*. New York: Simon and Schuster, 1986.

O'Brien, David J. *The Renewal of American Catholicism*. New York: Paulist Press, 1972.

O'Brien, David J., and Thomas A. Shannon, eds. *Renewing the Earth: Catholic Documents on Peace, Justice, and Liberation*. Garden City, N.Y.: Image Books, 1977.

O'Brien, Máire, and O'Brien, Conor Cruise. *A Concise History of Ireland*. London: Thames and Hudson, 1972.

O'Carroll, Michael. *Pius XII: Greatness Dishonored*. Dublin: Laetare Press, 1980.

Ochs, Peter, ed. *The Return to Scripture in Judaism and Christianity: Essays in Post-Biblical Scriptural Interpretation*. New York: Paulist Press, 1993.

O'Donnell, Christopher, O.Carm. *Ecclesia: A Theological Encyclopedia of the Church*. Collegeville, Minn.: Liturgical Press, 1996.

O'Hare, Padraic. *The Enduring Covenant: The Education of Christians and the End of Antisemitism*. Valley Forge, Pa.: Trinity Press International, 1997.

Oldenbourg, Zoé. *The Crusades*. Translated by Ann Carter. New York: Pantheon, 1966.

O'Malley, John W. *The First Jesuits*. Cambridge: Harvard University Press, 1993.

------. *Trent and All That: Renaming Catholicism in the Early Modern Era*. Cambridge: Harvard University Press, 2000.

O'Meara, Thomas Franklin, O.P. *Thomas Aquinas: Theologian*. Notre Dame: University of Notre Dame Press, 1997.

Omer, Mordechai, ed. *The Synagogue of Samuel Halevy ("El Transito"), Toledo, Spain*. Tel Aviv: Genia Schreiber University Gallery, Tel Aviv University, 1992.

O'Mikle, Stephen, ed. *Pope Pius XII: His Voice and Life*. New York: Wilson, 1958.

Ormsby, Eric L., ed. *Moses Maimonides and His Time*. Washington, D.C.: Catholic University of America Press, 1989.

Ozick, Cynthia. "Of Christian Heroism." *Partisan Review* 59, no. 1 (1992), 47.

------. Introduction to *Rescuers: Portraits of Moral Courage in the Holocaust*, by Gay Block and Malka Drucker. New York: Holmes and Meier, 1992.

Padberg, John W., S.J., et al., trans. *For Matters of Greater Moment: The First Thirty Jesuit General Congregations. A Brief History and a Translation of the Decrees*. St. Louis: Institute of Jesuit Sources, 1994.

Padover, Saul K. "The Baptism of Karl Marx's Family." *Midstream* 24, no. 6 (June–July 1978), 36–44.

Pagels, Elaine. *The Origin of Satan.* New York: Vintage, 1996.

Parkes, James. *The Conflict of the Church and the Synagogue: A Study in the Origins of Antisemitism.* New York: Atheneum, 1981.

———. *The Jew in the Medieval Community: A Study of His Political and Economic Situation.* New York: Hermon Press, 1976.

Passelecq, Georges, and Bernard Suchecky. *The Hidden Encyclical of Pope Pius XI.* Translated by Steven Rendall. New York: Harcourt Brace, 1997.

Patterson, David. *Along the Edge of Annihilation: The Collapse and Recovery of Life in the Holocaust Diary.* Seattle: University of Washington Press, 1999.

Pawlikowski, John T. *Christ in the Light of the Christian-Jewish Dialogue.* New York: Paulist Press, 1982.

———. "The Vatican and the Holocaust: Putting 'We Remember' in Context." *Dimensions* 12, no. 2 (winter 1999), 11–16.

Peck, Abraham J., ed. *Jews and Christians after the Holocaust.* Philadelphia: Fortress Press, 1982.

Pelikan, Jaroslav. *The Christian Tradition: A History of the Development of Doctrine.* Vol. 1, *The Emergence of the Catholic Tradition, 100–600.* Vol. 3, *The Growth of Medieval Theology, 600–1300.* Vol. 4, *Reformation of Church and Dogma, 1300–1700.* Chicago: University of Chicago Press, 1971, 1978, 1984.

———. *The Excellent Empire: The Fall of Rome and the Triumph of the Church.* San Francisco: Harper and Row, 1987.

———. *Jesus Through the Centuries: His Place in the History of Culture.* New Haven: Yale University Press, 1985.

Perelmuter, Hayim Goren. *Harvest of a Dialogue: Reflections of a Rabbi/Scholar on a Catholic Faculty.* Edited by Dianne Bergent, C.S.A., and John T. Pawlikowski, O.S.M. New York: Ktav, 1997.

———. *Siblings: Rabbinic Judaism and Early Christianity at Their Beginnings.* New York: Paulist Press, 1989.

Peters, F. E. *Jerusalem: The Holy City in the Eyes of Chroniclers, Visitors, Pilgrims, and Prophets from the Days of Abraham to the Beginnings of Modern Times.* Princeton: Princeton University Press, 1985.

Pettersen, Alvyn. *Athanasius.* London: Geoffrey Chapman, 1995.

Phillips, Jonathan, ed. *The First Crusade: Origins and Impact.* Manchester, U.K.: Manchester University Press, 1997.

Pico della Mirandola, Giovanni Francesco. *On the Dignity of Man, On Being and the One, Heptaplus.* Translated by Charles Glenn Wallis, Paul J. W. Miller, and Douglas Carmichael. Indianapolis: Hackett, 1998.

Poliakov, Léon. *The History of Anti-Semitism.* Vol. 1, *From the Time of Christ to the Court Jews.* Translated by Richard Howard. New York: Vanguard, 1965.

Polyani, John C. "The Responsibility of the Scientist." *Bulletin of the American Academy of Arts and Sciences,* May–June 1999.

Prinz, Arthur. "New Perspectives on Marx as a Jew." In *Year Book 15.* New York: Leo Baeck Institute, 1970.

Rahner, Karl, S.J. *The Rahner Reader.* Edited by Gerald McCool. New York: Seabury, 1975.

————. *Theological Investigations.* Vol. 1, *God, Christ, Mary, and Grace.* Translated by Cornelius Ernst, O.P. Baltimore: Helicon Press, 1965. Vol. 5, *Later Writings.* Translated by Karl-H. Kruger. London: Darton, Longman and Todd, 1975.

Ramsey, Paul. "The Just War According to St. Augustine." In *Just War Theory,* edited by Jean Bethke Elshtain. New York: New York University Press, 1992.

Ratzinger, Joseph, with Vittorio Messori. *The Ratzinger Report: An Exclusive Interview on the State of the Church.* Translated by Salvator Attannasio and Graham Harrison. San Francisco: Ignatius Press, 1985.

Ravitch, Diane, and Abigail Thernstrom. *The Democracy Reader.* New York: Harper-Collins, 1992.

Richards, Jeffrey. *Sex, Dissidence, and Damnation: Minority Groups in the Middle Ages.* London: Routledge, 1990.

Riegner, Gerhart. *A Warning to the World.* Cincinnati: Hebrew Union College/Jewish Institute of Religion, 1983.

Riera Vidal, Pedro. *The Jews in Toledo and Their Synagogues.* Translated by J. MacNab. Toledo, Spain: G. Menor, 1958.

Rosenberg, David. *Dreams of Being Eaten Alive: The Literary Core of the Kabbalah.* New York: Harmony, 2000.

Rosenzweig, Franz. *The Star of Redemption.* Translated by William Hallow. Notre Dame: University of Notre Dame Press, 1985.

————. *Understanding the Sick and the Healthy: A View of World, Man, and God.* Cambridge: Harvard University Press, 1999.

Roskies, David G., ed. *The Literature of Destruction: Jewish Responses to Catastrophe.* Philadelphia: Jewish Publication Society, 1989.

Roth, Cecil. *The History of the Jews of Italy.* Philadelphia: Jewish Publication Society, 1946.

————, ed. *The Dark Ages: Jews in Christian Europe, 711–1096.* New Brunswick, N.J.: Rutgers University Press, 1966.

Roth, Norman. "The Jews in Spain at the Time of Maimonides." In *Moses Maimonides and His Time,* edited by Eric L. Ormsby. Washington, D.C.: Catholic University of America Press, 1989.

Rousmaniere, John. *A Bridge to Dialogue: The Story of Jewish-Christian Relations.* New York: Paulist Press, 1999.

Rubenstein, Richard L. *After Auschwitz: Radical Theology and Contemporary Judaism.* Indianapolis: Bobbs-Merrill, 1966.

————. *The Cunning of History: The Holocaust and the American Future.* New York: Harper and Row, 1975.

————. *The Religious Imagination: A Study in Psychoanalysis and Jewish Theology.* New York: Bobbs-Merrill, 1969.

Rudavsky, David. *Emancipation and Adjustment: Contemporary Jewish Religious Movements, Their History and Thought.* New York: Diplomatic Press, 1967.

————. *Modern Jewish Religious Movements: A History of Emancipation and Adjustment.* New York: Behrman House, 1979.

Ruderman, David B., ed. *Preachers of the Italian Ghetto.* Berkeley: University of California Press, 1992.

Rudin, A. James. "Reflections on the Vatican's 'Reflection on the Shoah.'" *Cross Currents* 48, no. 4 (winter 1998–99), 518–29.

Ruether, Rosemary Radford. *Faith and Fratricide: The Theological Roots of Anti-Semitism.* New York: Seabury, 1974.

Rychlak, Ronald J. *Hitler, the War, and the Pope.* Columbus, Miss.: Genesis Press, 2000.

Sachar, Howard M. *The Course of Modern Jewish History.* New York: Vintage, 1990.

——. *Farewell España: The World of the Sephardim Remembered.* New York: Knopf, 1994.

Safranski, Rüdiger. *Martin Heidegger: Between Good and Evil.* Cambridge: Harvard University Press, 1998.

Sanders, E. P. *Jesus and Judaism.* Philadelphia: Fortress Press, 1985.

——. *Judaism: Practice and Belief, 63 B.C.E.–66 C.E.* Philadelphia: Trinity Press International, 1992.

——. *Paul and Palestinian Judaism: A Comparison of Patterns of Religion.* Philadelphia: Fortress Press, 1977.

——, ed., with A. I. Baumgarten and Alan Mendelson. *Jewish and Christian Self-Definition.* Vol. 2, *Aspects of Judaism in the Greco-Roman Period.* Philadelphia: Fortress Press, 1980.

Sandmel, Samuel. *Anti-Semitism in the New Testament?* Philadelphia: Fortress Press, 1978.

——. *We Jews and Jesus.* New York: Oxford University Press, 1965.

Saperstein, Marc. *Moments of Crisis in Jewish-Christian Relations.* Philadelphia: Trinity Press International, 1989.

Sardel, Rochelle G. *The Outraged Conscience.* Albany: State University of New York Press, 1984.

Sartre, Jean Paul. *Anti-Semite and Jew.* Translated by George J. Becker. New York: Grove Press, 1962.

Sawicki, Marianne. *Body, Text, and Science: The Literacy of Investigative Practices and the Phenomenology of Edith Stein.* Dordrecht, Netherlands: Kluwer Academic Publishers, 1997.

Schaff, Philip, ed. *Nicene and Post-Nicene Fathers,* 1st ser. Vol. 4, *Augustin: The Writings Against the Manichaeans, and Against the Donatists.* Vol. 7, *Augustin: Homilies on the Gospel of John, Homilies on the First Epistle of John, Soliloquies.* Peabody, Mass.: Hendrickson, 1994.

——, and Henry Wace, eds. *Nicene and Post-Nicene Fathers,* 2d ser. Vol. 1, *Eusebius: Church History, Life of Constantine the Great, and Oration in Praise of Constantine.* Peabody, Mass.: Hendrickson, 1994.

Schama, Simon. *Landscape and Memory.* New York: Vintage, 1995.

Schiffman, Lawrence H. *From Text to Tradition: A History of Second Temple and Rabbinic Judaism.* Hoboken, N.J.: Ktav, 1991.

Schillebeeckx, Edward. *Christ: The Sacrament of the Encounter with God.* Translated by Paul Barrett. New York: Sheed and Ward, 1963.

——. *Jesus: An Experiment in Christology.* Translated by Hubert Hoskins. New York: Seabury, 1979.

Schnell, E. *Maria Laach Abbey.* Regensburg: Schnell and Steiner, 1997.

Scholder, Klaus. *A Requiem for Hitler and Other New Perspectives on the German Church Struggle.* Philadelphia: Trinity Press International, 1989.

Scholem, Gershom. *Kabbalah.* New York: Quadrangle/New York Times, 1974.

——. *Major Trends in Jewish Mysticism.* New York: Schocken, 1941.

———. *Origins of the Kabbalah.* Edited by R. J. Zwi Werblowsky. Translated by Allan Arkush. Princeton: Jewish Publication Society/Princeton University Press, 1987.

Schrader, Frederick Franklin. *Church and State in Germany: The Concordat of 1933 Between the Holy See and the German State.* New York: Friends of Germany, 1933.

Schreier, Helmut, and Mattias Heyl, eds. *Never Again! The Holocaust's Challenge for Educators.* Hamburg: Krämer, 1997.

Schüssler Fiorenza, Elisabeth. *Jesus: Miriam's Child and Sophia's Prophet. Critical Issues in Feminist Christology.* New York: Continuum, 1994.

———. *In Memory of Her: A Feminist Theological Reconstruction of Christian Origins.* New York: Crossroad, 1989.

———, ed. *Searching the Scriptures.* Vol. 1, *A Feminist Introduction.* New York: Crossroad, 1993.

———, and David Tracy. "The Holocaust as Interruption and the Christian Return to History." *Concilium,* October 1984.

Schwartz, Regina M. *The Curse of Cain: The Violent Legacy of Monotheism.* Chicago: University of Chicago Press, 1997.

Scruton, Roger. *Spinoza.* Oxford: Oxford University Press, 1986.

Segal, Alan F. *Rebecca's Children: Judaism and Christianity in the Roman World.* Cambridge: Harvard University Press, 1986.

Shannon, Thomas A. *The Ethical Theory of John Duns Scotus: A Dialogue with Medieval and Modern Thought.* Quincy, Ill.: Franciscan Press, 1995.

Shapley, Deborah. *Promise and Power: The Life and Times of Robert McNamara.* Boston: Little, Brown, 1993.

Shatzmiller, Joseph. *Shylock Reconsidered: Jews, Moneylending, and Medieval Society.* Berkeley: University of California Press, 1990.

Sheehan, Thomas. *The First Coming: How the Kingdom of God Became Christianity.* New York: Random House, 1986.

Sheils, W. J., ed. *Monks, Hermits, and the Ascetic Tradition: Papers Read at the 1984 Summer Meeting and the 1985 Winter Meeting of the Ecclesiastical History Society.* London: Basil Blackwell, 1985.

Shriver, Donald W., Jr. *An Ethic for Enemies: Forgiveness in Politics.* New York: Oxford University Press, 1995.

Shulvass, Moses A. *The Jews in the World of the Renaissance.* Translated by Elvin I. Kose. Leiden, Netherlands: E. J. Brill, 1973.

Silberman, Neil Asher. *Heavenly Powers: Unraveling the Secret History of the Kabbalah.* New York: Grosset/Putnam, 1998.

Silberstein, Laurence J., and Robert L. Cohn, eds. *The Other in Jewish Thought and History: Constructions of Jewish Culture and Identity.* New York: New York University Press, 1994.

Simon, Marcel. *Verus Israel: A Study in Relations Between Christians and Jews in the Roman Empire (A.D. 135–425).* London: Littman Library of Jewish Civilization, 1996.

Smallwood, E. Mary. *The Jews under Roman Rule: From Pompey to Diocletian.* Leiden, Netherlands: E. J. Brill, 1976.

Smiga, George M. *Pain and Polemic: Anti-Judaism in the Gospels.* New York: Paulist Press, 1992.

Sperling, Harry, and Maurice Simon, trans. *The Zohar.* London: Soncino Press, 1984.

Stehlin, Stewart A. *Weimar and the Vatican, 1919–1933: German-Vatican Diplomatic Relations in the Interwar Years.* Princeton: Princeton University Press, 1983.

Stein, Edith. *Edith Stein: Life in a Jewish Family, 1891–1916.* Translated by Josephine Koeppel, O.C.D. Washington, D.C.: ICS Publications, 1986.

———. *Edith Stein: Self-Portrait in Letters, 1916–1942.* Translated by Josephine Koeppel, O.C.D. Washington, D.C.: ICS Publications, 1993.

Steinlauf, Michael C. *Bondage to the Dead: Poland and the Memory of the Holocaust.* Syracuse, N.Y.: Syracuse University Press, 1997.

Steinsaltz, Adin. *The Essential Talmud.* Translated by Chaya Galai. New York: Basic Books, 1976.

Stendahl, Krister. *Energy for Life. Reflections on a Theme: "Come Holy Spirit — Renew the Whole Creation."* Brewster, Mass.: Paraclete Press, 1999.

———. *Final Account: Paul's Letter to the Romans.* Minneapolis: Fortress Press, 1995.

———. *Holy Week Preaching.* Philadelphia: Fortress Press, 1974.

———. *Paul among Jews and Gentiles, and Other Essays.* Philadelphia: Fortress Press, 1976.

———. "Can Christianity Shed Its Anti-Judaism?" *Brandeis Review,* spring 1992, 24–27.

———. "From God's Perspective We Are All Minorities." *Journal of Religious Pluralism* 2 (1993), 1–13.

———. Qumran and Supersessionism — and the Road Not Taken." *Princeton Seminary Bulletin* 19, no. 2 (1998), 134–42.

———. "On Sacred Violence: How to Unmask It and How Not To." *Dialog* 32 (Fall 1993), 261–64.

Stepelevich, Lawrence S. "Marx and the Jews." *Judaism* 23 (spring 1974), 150–60.

Stern, J. P. *Hitler: The Führer and the People.* Berkeley: University of California Press, 1975.

Stevenson, J., ed. *A New Eusebius: Documents Illustrating the History of the Church to* A.D. *337.* London: SPCK, 1987.

Stock, Brian. *Augustine the Reader: Meditation, Self-Knowledge, and the Ethics of Interpretation.* Cambridge: Belknap Press, 1996.

Stow, Kenneth R. *Catholic Thought and Papal Jewry Policy, 1555–1593.* New York: Jewish Theological Seminary, 1977.

———. *The Jews in Rome.* Vol. 1, *1536–1551.* Leiden, Netherlands: E. J. Brill, 1995.

———. *Taxation, Community, and State: The Jews and the Fiscal Foundations of the Early Modern Papal State.* Stuttgart: Anton Hiersemann, 1982.

Stowers, Stanley K. *A Rereading of Romans: Justice, Jews, and Gentiles.* New Haven: Yale University Press, 1994.

Stravinskas, Peter, and Klenicki, Leon. *A Catholic-Jewish Encounter.* Huntington, Ind.: Our Sunday Visitor, 1994.

Sumruld, William A. *Augustine and the Arians: The Bishop of Hippo's Encounters with Ulfilan Arianism.* Selinsgrove, Pa.: Susquehanna University Press, 1994.

Synan, Edward A. *The Popes and the Jews in the Middle Ages.* New York: Macmillan, 1965.

Szulc, Tad. *Pope John Paul II: The Biography.* New York: Scribner, 1995.

Talmage, Frank Ephraim, ed. *Disputation and Dialogue: Readings in the Jewish-Christian Encounter.* New York: Ktav/Anti-Defamation League, 1975.

Tanner, Norman P., S.J., ed. *Decrees of the Ecumenical Councils.* Vol. 1, *Nicaea I to Lateran V.* Washington, D.C.: Georgetown University Press, 1990.

Taylor, Rex. *Michael Collins*. London: New English Library, 1970.

Thoma, Clemens. *A Christian Theology of Judaism*. Translated by Helga Croner. New York: Paulist Press, 1980.

———, and Michael Wyschogrod, eds. *Understanding Scripture: Explorations of Jewish and Christian Traditions of Interpretation*. New York: Paulist Press, 1987.

Trachtenberg, Joshua. *The Devil and the Jews*. New York: Harper and Row, 1966.

Tracy, David. *The Analogical Imagination: Christian Theology and the Culture of Pluralism*. New York: Crossroad, 1981.

———. *Blessed Rage for Order: The New Pluralism in Theology*. Chicago: University of Chicago Press, 1996.

———. *Dialogue with the Other: The Inter-Religious Dialogue*. Grand Rapids, Mich.: Eerdmans, 1991.

———. *On Naming the Present: God, Hermeneutics, and Church*. Maryknoll, N.Y.: Orbis Books, 1994.

Trevor-Roper, Hugh. *The Rise of Christian Europe*. New York: Harcourt Brace Jovanovich, 1975.

Troyer, Johannes. *The Cross as Symbol and Ornament*. Philadelphia: Westminster Press, 1961.

Tuchman, Barbara W. *A Distant Mirror: The Calamitous Fourteenth Century*. New York: Knopf, 1978.

Ucko, Hans. *Common Roots, New Horizons: Learning about Christian Faith from Dialogue with Jews*. Geneva, Switzerland: WCC Publications, 1994.

Ullmann, Thilo. "From Tolerance to Persecution." *The World & I*, April 1996, 290–95.

———. "The Mystery of 1492." *The World & I*, August 1993, 328–32.

U.S. State Department Report, "The Fate of the Wartime Ustasha Treasury." In "U.S. and Allied Wartime and Postwar Relations and Negotiations with Argentina, Portugal, Spain, Sweden, and Turkey on Looted Gold and German External Assets and U.S. Concerns about the Fate of the Wartime Ustasha Treasury: June 1998 Supplement to Preliminary Study on U.S. and Allied Efforts to Recover and Restore Gold and Other Assets Stolen or Hidden by Germany During World War II." www.state.gov/www/regions/eur/rpt_9806_ng_links.html.

"Universal Prayer: Confession of Sins and Asking for Forgiveness." http://jcrelations.com/stmnts/vatican3-00.htm.

Van Buren, Paul M. *A Theology of the Jewish-Christian Reality*. Part 1, *Discerning the Way*. Part 2, *A Christian Theology of the People Israel*. Part 3, *Christ in Context*. Lanham, Md.: University Press of America, 1995.

Visotzky, Burton L. *Fathers of the World: Essays in Rabbinic and Patristic Literatures*. Tübingen: J.C.B. Mohr (Paul Siebeck), 1995.

Vogelstein, Hermann. *Rome*. Translated by Moses Hadas. Philadelphia: Jewish Publication Society, 1941.

Von Balthasar, Hans Urs. *Mysterium Paschale: The Mystery of Easter*. Translated by Aidan Nichols, O. P. Grand Rapids: William B. Eerdmans Publishing Company, 1990.

Wahle, Hedwig. "Pioneers in Christian-Jewish Dialogue: Some Known and Unknown Pioneers of Continental Europe." *SIDIC* (*Service International de Documentation Judeo-Chrétienne*, English ed.) 30, no. 2 (1997), 2–9.

Walzer, Michael. *On Toleration*. New Haven: Yale University Press, 1997.

Weaver, Mary Jo. "Rooted Hearts/Playful Minds: Catholic Intellectual Life at Its Best." *Cross Currents* 48, no. 1 (spring 1998), 61–74.

Weil, Simone. *The Need for Roots: Prelude to a Declaration of Duties Towards Mankind.* Translated by A. F. Wills. London: Ark, 1987.

———. *Waiting for God.* Translated by Emma Craufurd. New York: Harper and Row, 1973.

"We Remember: A Reflection on the Shoah." http://jcrelations.com/stmnts/vatican3-98.htm.

Wiesel, Elie. *All Rivers Run to the Sea: Memoirs.* New York: Knopf, 1995.

———. *And the Sea Is Never Full: Memoirs, 1969–.* Translated by Marion Wiesel. New York: Knopf, 1999.

———. *The Gates of the Forest.* New York: Bard, 1966.

———. *The Trial of God.* New York: Schocken, 1979.

Wieseltier, Leon. "Correspondence." *New Republic,* March 2, 1998, 5.

———. "Sorry." *New Republic,* March 27, 2000, 6.

Wiesenthal, Simon. *The Sunflower: On the Possibilities and Limits of Forgiveness.* New York: Schocken, 1997.

Wighton, Charles. *Adenauer — Democratic Dictator: A Critical Biography.* London: Frederick Muller, 1963.

Wilken, Robert L. *John Chrysostom and the Jews: Rhetoric and Reality in the Late Fourth Century.* Berkeley: University of California Press, 1983.

Wills, Garry. *Papal Sin: Structures of Deceit.* New York: Doubleday, 2000.

———. *Saint Augustine.* New York: Viking, 1999.

Wilson, A. N. *Paul: The Mind of the Apostle.* New York: Norton, 1997.

Wilson, Marvin R. *Our Father Abraham: Jewish Roots of the Christian Faith.* Grand Rapids, Mich.: Eerdmans, 1989.

Wilson, Stephen. *Ideology and Experience: Antisemitism in France at the Time of the Dreyfus Affair.* Rutherford, N.J.: Fairleigh Dickinson University Press, 1982.

Winiewicz, J. M. *Have We Allies Inside Germany?* Free Europe Pamphlet No. 11. London: Free Europe, 1944.

Wistrich, Robert S. "The Pope, the Church, and the Jews." *Commentary* 107, no. 4 (April 1999), 22–28.

Wolfe, Alan. "Liberalism and Catholicism." *American Prospect,* January 31, 2000, 16–21.

Wolfe, Gregory, ed. *The New Religious Humanists: A Reader.* New York: Free Press, 1997.

Wolter, Allan B., O. F. M. "John Duns Scotus on the Primacy and Personality of Christ." In *Franciscan Christology: Selected Texts, Translations, and Introductory Essays,* edited by Damian McElrath. St. Bonaventure, N.Y.: Franciscan Institute Publications, 1980.

Wolter, Allan B., O.F.M., and Blane O'Neill, O.F.M. *John Duns Scotus: Mary's Architect.* Quincy, Ill.: Franciscan Press, 1993.

Wood, E. Thomas, and Stanislaw M. Jankowski. *Karski: How One Man Tried to Stop the Holocaust.* New York: Wiley, 1994.

Wyman, David S. *The Abandonment of the Jews: America and the Holocaust, 1941–1945.* New York: Pantheon, 1984.

Yates, Frances A. *Giordano Bruno and the Hermetic Tradition.* London: Routledge and Kegan Paul, 1978.

Yerushalmi, Yosef Hayim. *Zakhor: Jewish History and Jewish Memory.* Seattle: University of Washington Press, 1982.

Young, James E. *The Texture of Memory: Holocaust Memorials and Meaning.* New Haven: Yale University Press, 1993.

Young-Bruehl, Elisabeth. *Hannah Arendt: For Love of the World.* New Haven: Yale University Press, 1984.

Zahn, Gordon C. *German Catholics and Hitler's Wars: A Study in Social Control.* Notre Dame: University of Notre Dame Press, 1989.

Zoeckler, Otto. *The Cross of Christ: Studies in the History of Religion and the Inner Life of the Church.* Translated by Rev. Maurice J. Evans. London: Hodder and Stoughton, 1877.

Zuccotti, Susan. *The Italians and the Holocaust: Persecution, Rescue, and Survival.* Lincoln: University of Nebraska Press, 1987.

——. *Under His Very Windows: The Vatican and the Holocaust in Italy.* New Haven: Yale University Press, 2001.

INDEX